The **Rough**

Jordan

written and researched by

Matthew Teller

ROUGH GUIDES

Contents

Jordan's people
colour section following
p.184

Petra unpackaged
colour section following
p.312

◀◀ Wadi Rum on horseback ◀ Columns, Temple of Artemis, Jerash

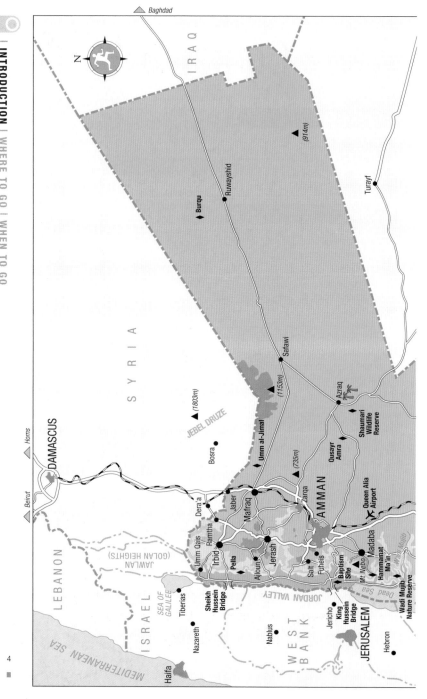

Metres

1500
1000
500
200
100
0
below sea level

0   50 km

Bahrain

Sakakah

SAUDI   ARABIA

Tabuk

Jeddah

Bayir
(1113m)

(1008m)

Jafr

Qasr Tuba

Qatraneh
(1035m)

Jurf ad-Darawish

DESERT HIGHWAY

HEJAZ RAILWAY (DISUSED)

Ma'an

Mudawwara

KING'S HIGHWAY

Karak

Safi

Tafileh

Dana
(1641m)

Dana Nature
Reserve

Shobak

Petra
(1727m)

(1488m)

Rum

WADI RUM

Jebel Umm
ad-Daami
(1834m)

ISRAEL

WADI   ARABA

S. ARABA

Wadi Araba
Crossing

Eilat

Aqaba

GULF OF
AQABA

Nuweiba

Introduction to
Jordan

Western travellers have been exploring the Middle East for well over a century, but Jordan is a relative newcomer to tourism, welcoming only a fraction of the numbers who visit neighbouring Egypt and Israel. The country's popular image abroad encompasses not much more than camels, deserts and bedouin, and there's little awareness of Jordan's mountains and beaches, its castles and ancient churches, the urbanity of its people and richness of its culture.

Jordan is largely **desert**, but this one bland word covers a multitude of scenes, from the dramatic red sands and towering cliffs of the far south to the vast stony plains of volcanic basalt in the east. The northern hills, rich with olive trees, teeter over the rift of the **Jordan Valley**, which in turn runs down to the **Dead Sea**, lowest point on earth. The centre of the country is carpeted with tranquil fields of wheat, cut through by expansive canyons and bordered by arid, craggy mountains. At the southernmost tip of the country, beaches fringe the warm waters of the **Red Sea**, which harbours some of the most spectacular coral reefs in the world.

Jordan is part of the land bridge linking Europe, Africa and Asia, and has seen countless armies come and go. Greeks, Romans, Muslims, Christian Crusaders and more have left evidence of their conquests, and there are literally thousands of **ruins** and **archeological sites** from all periods in every corner of the country. In addition, Israel and Palestine,

Fact file

• The **Hashemite Kingdom of Jordan** (in Arabic, al-Mamlakeh al-Urduniyyeh al-Hashmiyyeh, or **al-Urdun**) covers an area of around 92,000 square kilometres – a little more than Portugal and a little less than Indiana. About 85 percent is desert. The highest and lowest points are Jebel Umm ad-Daami (1834m) and the Dead Sea shore (408m below sea level).

• Well over 90 percent of the **population** of around 6.2 million are **Muslim Arabs**, with small minorities of Muslim **Circassians** and **Chechens**, as well as **Christian Arabs**. Almost 38 percent of the population is below the age of 15.

• Jordan is a **constitutional monarchy**, with universal suffrage over the age of 20. The king appoints the Prime Minister and together they appoint the cabinet. In the bicameral **National Assembly**, the forty-member Senate is appointed by the king and the eighty-member House of Representatives voted in by proportional representation. The single biggest sector in the **economy** – traditionally dependent on phosphates and potash production – is now **tourism**, which generates thirteen percent of GDP.

• The average **annual wage** in Jordan is around JD5000 (US$7100).

Jordan's neighbours to the west, have no monopoly on **biblical history**: it was in Jordan that Lot sought refuge from the fire and brimstone of the Lord; Moses, Aaron and John the Baptist all died in Jordan; and Jesus was almost certainly baptized here. Even the Prophet Muhammad passed through.

And yet the country is far from being stuck in the past. Amman is a thoroughly modern capital, and Jordan's respectable rate of economic growth means that grinding poverty is the rare exception rather than the rule. Kids may sell you gum or offer to shine your shoes, but you'll see more desperate begging in the streets of any European or North American city than anywhere in Jordan. Government is

▼ Nut seller, Madaba

stable, with leanings towards democracy under a constitutional monarchy, and manages to be simultaneously pro-Western, pro-Arab, founded on a bedrock of Muslim authority and dedicated to ongoing peace with Israel. **Women** are better integrated into positions of power in government and business than almost anywhere else in the Middle East, military conscription has been abolished, and Jordanians are exceptionally highly educated: just over 2.5 percent of the total population is enrolled at university, a proportion comparable to the UK. Traditions of **hospitality** are ingrained, and taking up some of the many invitations you'll get to tea or a meal will expose you to an outlook among local people that is often as cosmopolitan and world-aware as anything at home. Though surrounded by instability, Jordan is the **safest** country in the Middle East

▲ Family fun at the Dead Sea

by quite a long way, and domestic extremism is virtually non-existent.

Most people take great pride in their ancestry, whether they're present or former desert-dwellers (**bedouin**) or from a settled farming tradition (**fellahin**). Across the desert areas, people still live and work on their **tribal** lands,

Jordan's flag

Jordan's flag is a source of national pride. It is adapted from the revolutionary banner of the Great Arab Revolt of 1916–17, when Arab armies led by the Hashemites – a noble dynasty, now led by King Abdullah II of Jordan, which traces its origins back to the Prophet Muhammad – overthrew the rule of the Ottoman Empire in the Middle East.

The flag has three equal horizontal bands. At the top is **black**, representing the **Abbasid Caliphate** that ruled from Baghdad in the eighth and ninth centuries; in the middle is **white**, representing the **Umayyad Caliphate** that ruled from Damascus in the seventh and eighth centuries; and at the bottom is **green**, representing the **Fatimid Caliphate** that ruled from Cairo in the tenth and eleventh centuries. On the hoist side is a **red triangle** representing the **Great Arab Revolt** of 1916–17. Within the triangle is a seven-pointed **white star** which symbolizes the seven verses of the opening sura (verse) of the Quran; the points represent faith in one God, humanity, national spirit, humility, social justice, virtue and hope.

whether together in villages or apart in individual family units; many town-dwellers, including substantial numbers of Ammanis, claim tribal identity. Belonging to a tribe (an honour conferred by birth) means respecting the authority of a communal leader, or sheikh, and living in a culture of shared history, values and principles that often crosses national boundaries. Notions of honour and mutual defence are strong. Tribes also wield a great deal of institutional power: most members of Jordan's lower house of parliament are elected for their tribal, rather than political, affiliation. The **king**, as sheikh of sheikhs, commands heartfelt loyalty among many people and deep respect among most of the rest.

> **Your most abiding memories are likely to be of Jordan's natural environment**

National identity is a thorny issue in Jordan, which has taken in huge numbers of **Palestinian** refugees since the foundation of the State of Israel in 1948. Many people from tribes resident east of the River Jordan before 1948 resent this overbalancing of the country's demography, and the fact that incoming Palestinians, having

9

developed an urbanized, entrepreneurial culture, dominate private-sector business. For their part, Jordanians of Palestinian origin – estimated to make up as much as sixty percent of the population – often resent the "East Bank" Jordanians' grip on power in government and the public sector. All are Jordanian citizens, but citizenship tends to mean less to many of Palestinian origin than their national identity, and less to many East Bankers than their tribal affiliation. Large numbers of long-stay guest workers from Egypt muddy the issue still further. "Where are you from?" – a simple enough question in most countries – is in Jordan the cue for a life story.

Where to go

Jordan's prime attraction is **Petra**, an unforgettably dramatic 2000-year-old city carved from sandstone cliffs in the south of the country. Its extraordinary architecture and powerful atmosphere imprint themselves indelibly on most visitors' imaginations.

There is a wealth of other **historical sites**, outstanding among them the well-preserved Roman city of **Jerash**, but also including **Umm Qais**, set on a dramatic promontory overlooking the Sea of Galilee, and **Pella**, where Jerusalem's Christians fled Roman persecution in the first century AD. **Madaba**, which became an important Christian town and regional

► Highway in the eastern desert

The search for water

Jordan is among the ten most **water-poor** countries in the world. Annual consumption per capita (calculated as renewable water resources withdrawn) is about 170 cubic metres, compared with 630 as the world average, 800 across the Middle East/North Africa region – and 1,650 in North America. Almost a third of the water used in Jordan comes from non-sustainable or non-renewable sources. Three decades of pumping from the once-abundant **Azraq** oasis (see p.209) has brought it to the point of collapse. A major tributary of the River Jordan, the **Yarmouk**, sports a large dam shared by Jordan and Syria, and all the major valleys leading down to the **Dead Sea** are now dammed in an effort to stop water draining into the salty lake (which has contributed to its rapid shrinking; see p.131). Every winter the local newspapers publish reports tabulating levels of water storage in the country's reservoirs, while Jordanians anxiously wait for rain. Water rationing is in place in Amman over the summer. it is hoped that schemes to pipe water from desert aquifers and to construct shared desalination plants on the Red Sea will alleviate the problem. Time will tell.

centre for mosaic art during the Byzantine period, houses the oldest known map of the Middle East, in the form of a large mosaic laid on the floor of a church. After the Muslim conquest, the Umayyad dynasty built a series of retreats in the Jordanian desert, now dubbed the "**Desert Castles**", including the bath-house of **Qusayr Amra**, adorned with naturalistic and erotic frescoes, and **Qasr Harraneh**, perhaps the most atmospheric ancient building in the country. Centuries later, the Crusaders established a heavy presence in southern Jordan, most impressively with the huge castles at **Karak** and **Shobak**. The Arab resistance to the Crusader invasion left behind a no less impressive castle at **Ajloun** in the north.

Jordan also counts as part of the "Holy Land" for its **religious sites**, most importantly the **Baptism Site** of Jesus on the banks of the River Jordan, and **Mount Nebo**, from where Moses looked over the Promised Land. John the Baptist met his death at Herod's hilltop palace at **Mukawir** after Salome danced her seductive dance. Nearby are

Bab adh-Dhraa, one of the leading contenders for the site of biblical Sodom, and **Lot's Cave**, where Abraham's nephew sought refuge from the destruction of Sodom and Gomorrah. Most of these, and other sites such as the **tomb of Aaron** at Petra, are holy to Muslims, Jews and Christians alike, while there are also plenty of specifically Muslim sites, including a holy tree in the desert at **Biqya'wiyya**, said to have sheltered the Prophet Muhammad himself, and literally dozens of shrines and tombs in every corner of the country.

Your most abiding memories of a visit are likely to be of Jordan's varied and beautiful natural **environment**. With its sheer cliffs and red sands, austere **Wadi Rum** – where David Lean filmed *Lawrence of Arabia* – presents the classic desert picture of Jordan, and is the starting point for camel treks of anything from an hour to a week. Less well-known are the gentle northern hills around the **Ajloun forests**, hosting walks through flower-strewn meadows and cool, shady woodland. In the south, the tranquil **Dana Nature Reserve** encompasses a swathe of territory from verdant highland orchards down to the sandy desert floor, and offers

Transliterating Arabic

Many sounds in **Arabic** have no equivalent in English, and any attempt to render them in English script is bound to be imprecise. Place names are the biggest sources of confusion, varying from map to map and often from sign to sign – you'll see roadsigns to Wadi Seer, Wadi El Sseir, Wadi Alsear and Wadi as-Sir, all referring to the same place. In this book we've tried to stick to a phonetically helpful, common-sense system, while also staying close to existing English renderings. The definite article "al" and its variations have been removed from all place names other than compound ones: Al-Aqaba, Ar-Ramtha and As-Salt have all been shortened (Aqaba, Ramtha, Salt), but Umm al-Jimal and Shuneh al-Janubiyyeh stay as they are. For more on the intricacies of Arabic, see p.407.

extensive opportunities for bird- and wildlife-spotting. The protected **Wadi Mujib** is a giant canyon, 4km wide at the top, that narrows to a high, rocky gorge carrying a fast-flowing river down to the salty **Dead Sea**, an inland lake too buoyant for swimming but perfect for floating, your body supported by the density of the salty water. Last but not least, Jordan has some of the world's best diving and snorkelling in the coral-fringed Red Sea off **Aqaba**.

When to go

Despite the small size of the country, you'll find wide variations in **climate** whenever you arrive, often because of the topography: Amman, Petra and Wadi Rum all lie well over 800m above sea level, Dana and Ajloun are even higher (up to 1500m), whereas the Dead Sea lies 400m below sea level. The same January day could have you throwing snowballs in Ajloun or topping up your tan on the Red Sea beaches at Aqaba.

The best time to visit is **spring** (March–May), when temperatures are toasty but not scorching, wildflowers are out everywhere (even the desert is carpeted), and the hills and valleys running down the centre of the country

▶ Red Sea snorkelling at sunset, Aqaba

▼ Desert patrol, Petra

are lush and gorgeously colourful. The worst of the rain is over by March, though it doesn't entirely peter out in Amman and the hills until late April. Humidity is pleasant everywhere, and low, clear sunlight draws a spectacular kaleidoscope of colour and texture from the desert rocks. There's only one drawback – a desert wind, loaded with dust and grit, which blows regularly each spring or early summer out of the Arabian interior. It's known across the Middle East as the *khamseen* ("fifty"), after the

> Jordan is the safest country in the Middle East by a long way

fifty days it traditionally persists (although in Jordan it rarely lasts longer than a few days), and can darken the sky and raise the temperature by 10°C, coating everyone and everything in a layer of sand.

In **summer** (roughly June–Sept), Amman can sizzle – up to 40°C in the city centre – and you'll find little respite in the rest of the country, although the hills around Ajloun catch some cooler breezes. Temperatures at the Dead Sea and Aqaba have been known to top 50°C, with Aqaba in particular suffering from an intolerable hot wind that makes you feel like you're basting in a fan-assisted oven. High, hazy light flattens the brown landscape and bleaches any beauty out of the desert, and you'll find it's too uncomfortably hot countrywide to do any walking or sightseeing between noon and 4pm.

14

Typical **autumn** weather (mid-Sept to mid-Nov) mostly passes Jordan by, with only a few weeks marking the shift out of high summer – if you catch it, this can be a lovely time to visit. The first rains fall in early or mid-October, making the parched countryside bloom again and the torrid temperatures drop to more manageable levels.

In **winter** (roughly Dec–Feb), Amman can be desperately chilly, with biting winds sweeping through the valleys, rain showers and even snowfall, although the sun is still never far away. With short days and freezing nights, Petra winters can be taxing; exceptional lows of -8°C have been recorded. Rum is more temperate, but Aqaba is the only retreat, with sunshine and warmth even in the depths of January (average Red Sea and Dead Sea water temperatures vary little either side of a balmy 24°C all year).

Elevation, average minimum and maximum temperatures and average rainfall.

	Jan	Apr	July	Oct
Amman (800m)				
Average temperatures (°C)	3–12	9–23	18–32	14–27
Average rainfall (mm)	64	15	0	7
Aqaba (sea level)				
Average temperatures (°C)	9–21	17–31	25–39	20–33
Average rainfall (mm)	5	4	0	1
Dead Sea (400m below sea level)				
Average temperatures (°C)	11–21	19–31	27–40	22–33
Average rainfall (mm)	13	7	0	1
Irbid (600m)				
Average temperatures (°C)	5–13	10–22	19–31	15–27
Average rainfall (mm)	111	51	0	14
Petra (1100m)				
Average temperatures (°C)	4–12	11–22	18–36	14–24
Average rainfall (mm)	43	14	0	2
Rum (950m)				
Average temperatures (°C)	4–15	12–25	19–36	13–29
Average rainfall (mm)	19	7	0	2

things not to miss

It's not possible to see everything that Jordan has to offer in one trip – and we don't suggest you try. What follows is a selective and subjective taste of the country's highlights: outstanding natural landscapes, ancient ruins, outdoor activities and the spectacular site of Petra. They're arranged in five colour-coded categories to help you find the very best things to see, do and experience. All entries have a page reference to take you straight into the Guide, where you can find out more.

01 Petra Page **259** • Magnificent ancient city hidden away in the craggy mountains of the south – Jordan's (and one of the world's) most famous must-see attractions.

03 Jordanian cuisine Page 44
• Sample some of the Middle East's finest restaurants, dotted throughout the streets of upmarket West Amman – or just go for a delicious bowl of authentically prepared hummus with fresh bread.

02 Mount Nebo Page 231
• On this summit above the Dead Sea (named in Deuteronomy), where Moses looked out over the Promised Land, stands a monastery church richly decorated with mosaics.

04 Wadi Mujib Page 238
• Jordan's "Grand Canyon", now protected as a nature reserve, with gorge-walking and canyoning amid the rugged valleys.

05 **Hospitality** Page **57** • The hospitality of Jordanians is legendary: whether you're passing through a city or travelling across the desert, you're bound to be invited in for tea.

06 **Ajloun** Page **167** • Set amidst the northern hills is a magnificent Crusader-period castle, within easy reach of a tranquil nature reserve offering walks and exploration among highland forests.

07 **Walking** Page **50** • There are plenty of opportunities to get off the beaten track in Jordan's back country for a day or a week, whether alone or with an adventure tour company.

08 Dana Page **250** • Jordan's flagship nature reserve, covering a sweep of territory from highland cliffs to the sandy desert floor. Whether you come for the hiking, the natural environment or the silence, you won't want to leave.

10 The Baptism Site Page **137** • A pilgrimage spot alongside the River Jordan at the place where Jesus was baptized, commemorated by dozens of ancient churches and hermitages.

09 Camel-riding Page **51** • Don't miss the chance to saddle up and shuffle off into the sands on the "ship of the desert".

11 **Jerash** Page **154** • A spectacularly well-preserved Roman city located in the hills north of Amman, complete with paved and colonnaded streets, grand temples, intimate marketplaces and mosaic-floored churches.

13 **The King's Highway** Page **217** • Meandering its way north and south along the lonely hilltops, this most picturesque of historic routes links the farming towns of southern Jordan.

12 **Karak castle** Page **248** • Stoutest and starkest remnant of the Crusaders' occupation of the country.

14 **Umm Qais** Page **176** • Atmospheric Roman and Ottoman site in the far north of Jordan, offering spectacular views over the Sea of Galilee – and relatively few tourists.

15 **Ancient Amman** Page **101** • Roman columns and ruins of an Islamic-era palace tower over Amman city centre, atop Jebel al-Qal'a (Citadel Hill).

17 **Modern Amman** Page **105** • Take time out from ruin-hunting to explore the Jordanian capital's buzzing cafés, art galleries and restaurants – a side of the city few visitors experience.

16 **Red Sea diving & snorkelling** Page **348** • You don't have to be a diver to come nose-to-nose with a turtle: coral reefs and multicoloured fish await just beneath the surface of this warmest and clearest of seas.

18 **The "Desert Castles"** Page **195** • A string of early-Islamic forts, palaces, hunting lodges and caravanserais amid the stony desert plains east of Amman. The picture shows Qasr Harraneh, one of the best of the bunch.

20 **The Dead Sea** Page **129** • Enjoy spectacular sunsets at the lowest point on earth, as you float easily on this inland lake supported only by the density of the salty water.

19 **Azraq Wetlands** Page **208** • Boardwalks lead through reed-beds amid the Azraq oasis, in the deserts east of Amman – perfect for nature walks and bird-watching excursions.

21 **Madaba** Page **221** • Historic market town near Amman that was a centre for mosaic art in the Byzantine period. Pictured is the oldest known map of the Middle East, laid in mosaic form on the floor of a church.

22 **Wadi Rum** Page **321** • Experience the atmosphere of the open desert in the stunning company of sheer mountain giants, red dunes and vast, silent panoramas.

Basics

Basics

Getting there

Jordan is served by daily nonstop flights from London and easy one-stop connections from around the UK, as well as nonstop routings from major European, North American and Southeast Asian hubs.

Queen Alia International Airport in **Amman (AMM)** handles almost all incoming flights to Jordan. Some charter flights come into **Aqaba (AQJ)**, which is linked to Amman by daily short-hop shuttles on the national carrier **Royal Jordanian**.

When to travel

The **best times to visit** Jordan, weather-wise, are spring (March–May) and autumn (Sept & Oct), but this is also when air fares and package deals are at their most expensive. Winter, when fares are lower, can be too chilly for comfortable sightseeing – and in summer you face the disadvantages of extreme heat and the peak season for tourism from the Gulf countries (as well as the holy month of fasting, Ramadan, which falls in July and/or Aug each year until 2015).

Air fares also peak in the periods surrounding major **Islamic holidays** such as Eid al-Fitr and Eid al-Adha (see p.396), when thousands – or, in the case of the hajj pilgrimage to Mecca, millions – of people are on the move. For weeks before the hajj (which takes place in Nov until 2011, then Oct in 2012–14), whole planes get block-booked for pilgrims on many routes into the Middle East – not just flights into Saudi Arabia, but also connections via Jordan and neighbouring countries. For two weeks after the pilgrimage, few planes out of the region have spare capacity. It pays to check when Islamic holidays are due to fall (see p.70); book well ahead if you want to fly at or near those times.

One thing to watch when planning an itinerary is your scheduled **arrival time**: many flights from London, for instance, are afternoon departures, landing in Amman in the late evening – which means your head may not actually hit the pillow until midnight or later. In addition, many return flights to London take off from Amman at breakfast

time, necessitating a pre-dawn wake-up call. This means that UK visitors can "lose" a day at either end of their holiday.

Flights from the UK and Ireland

Flying to Amman from London Heathrow there is a choice of daily nonstop services on bmi and Royal Jordanian. Low-season return fares on bmi are around £400–450 (RJ are slightly pricier) – though frequent offers and seat sales can knock £100 off. In high season add £50–100. Flight time is 5 hours.

Bmi is also a good choice if you're starting **from elsewhere in the UK**: it has shuttle flights into Heathrow from Manchester, Glasgow, Belfast and elsewhere. Turkish Airlines has competitive fares from Stansted and Manchester to Amman via Istanbul; Cyprus Airways flies cheaply from Heathrow and Stansted via Larnaca; or check out Malev from Gatwick via Budapest. Air France flies from airports around the UK to Amman via Paris, but at a premium.

Charter flights – generally Gatwick **to Aqaba** – can be a bargain: you could get a return flight plus seven nights' accommodation for £500–600, often much less if you book last-minute. Such packages are advertised widely in newspaper travel sections.

From **Dublin**, bmi has good fares via Heathrow – around €500 return in low season (add €150 or so in high season),

> As this book went to press there was talk of boosting flight links between the UK and Jordan. By the time you come to research your trip, you may find a greater choice of airlines and routes than is shown here – along with, perhaps, lower fares. Check online or contact the Jordan Tourism Board (see p.71) for the latest info.

matched by Malev via Budapest. Air France via Paris, Turkish via Istanbul and Lufthansa via Frankfurt are other, often pricier options.

Airlines in the UK and Ireland

Air France UK ☎0871 66 33 777, Republic of Ireland ☎01/605 0383; ⓦwww.airfrance.co.uk.
bmi UK ☎0870 60 70 555, Republic of Ireland ☎01/283 0700; ⓦwww.flybmi.com.
Cyprus Airways UK ☎020 8359 1333, ⓦwww.cyprusairways.com.
Lufthansa UK ☎0871 945 9747, Republic of Ireland ☎01/844 5544; ⓦwww.lufthansa.co.uk.
Malev UK ☎0870 909 0577, Republic of Ireland ☎0818 555 577; ⓦwww.malev.com.
Royal Jordanian UK ☎08719 112 112, ⓦwww.rj.com.
Turkish Airlines UK ☎0844 800 6666, Republic of Ireland ☎01 844 7920; ⓦwww.thy.com.

Travel agents in the UK and Ireland

UK

ebookers ⓦwww.ebookers.com.

Expedia ⓦwww.expedia.co.uk.
Lastminute.com ⓦwww.lastminute.com.
North South Travel ☎01245/608 291, ⓦwww.northsouthtravel.co.uk.
STA Travel ☎0871 230 0040, ⓦwww.statravel.co.uk.
Trailfinders ☎0845 058 5858, ⓦwww.trailfinders.com.
Travelocity ⓦwww.travelocity.co.uk.

Republic of Ireland

ebookers ☎01/431 1311, ⓦwww.ebookers.ie.
Joe Walsh Tours ☎01/241 0800, ⓦwww.joewalshtours.ie.
Trailfinders ☎01/677 7888, ⓦwww.trailfinders.ie.
USIT ☎01/602 1906, ⓦwww.usit.ie.

Flights from the US and Canada

From North America Royal Jordanian flies nonstop to Amman from New York JFK, Chicago and Montréal, plus one-stop direct from Detroit. RJ's codesharing deals offer good connections from a range of other cities.

Six steps to a better kind of travel

At Rough Guides we are passionately committed to travel. We feel strongly that only through travelling do we truly come to understand the world we live in and the people we share it with – plus tourism has brought a great deal of **benefit** to developing economies around the world over the last few decades. But the extraordinary growth in tourism has also damaged some places irreparably, and of course **climate change** is exacerbated by most forms of transport, especially flying. This means that now more than ever it's important to **travel thoughtfully** and **responsibly**, with respect for the cultures you're visiting – not only to derive the most benefit from your trip but also to preserve the best bits of the planet for everyone to enjoy. At Rough Guides we feel there are six main areas in which you can make a difference:

• Consider what you're contributing to the **local economy**, and how much the services you use do the same, whether it's through employing local workers and guides or sourcing locally grown produce and local services.

• Consider the **environment** on holiday as well as at home. Water is scarce in many developing destinations, and the biodiversity of local flora and fauna can be adversely affected by tourism. Try to patronize businesses that take account of this.

• Travel with a purpose, not just to tick off experiences. Consider **spending longer** in a place, and getting to know it and its people.

• Give thought to how often you **fly**. Try to avoid short hops by air and more harmful night flights.

• Consider **alternatives to flying**, travelling instead by bus, train, boat and even by bike or on foot where possible.

• Make your trips "**climate neutral**" via a reputable carbon offset scheme. All Rough Guide flights are offset, and every year we donate money to a variety of charities devoted to combating the effects of climate change.

London to Amman daily.

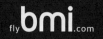

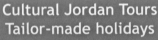

Delta also flies direct to Amman from JFK (either nonstop or via Paris), with numerous options from around the US. United offer good connections with European airlines such as bmi (at London) and Lufthansa (at Frankfurt), while British Airways, Air Canada and others can also fly you from major cities with a change of plane (sometimes codesharing with other airlines). Turkish Airlines flies Chicago or New York nonstop to Istanbul, with a shuttle on to Amman; EgyptAir does the same from JFK via Cairo.

Expect a round-trip fare in high season of around US$1000–1400 from the east and Midwest, US$1600–2000 from the west, and C$1100–1800 out of Canada. All these drop slightly in low season. Flight time is eleven hours from the East Coast or fifteen hours from the West Coast, not including stops on the ground.

Airlines in North America

Air Canada ☎ 1-888/247-2262, ⓦ www .aircanada.com.
British Airways ☎ 1-800/247-9297, ⓦ www .ba.com.
Delta ☎ 1-800/241-4141, ⓦ www.delta.com.
EgyptAir ☎ 212/581-5600, ⓦ www.egyptair.com.
Lufthansa ☎ 1-800/399-5838, ⓦ www .lufthansa.com.
Royal Jordanian US ☎ 1-800/223-0470 or 212/949-0050, Canada ☎ 1-800/363-0711; ⓦ www.rj.com.
Turkish ☎ 1-800/874-8875, ⓦ www.thy.com.
United ☎ 1-800/538-2929, ⓦ www.united.com.

Travel agents in North America

Cheapflights ⓦ www.cheapflights.com.
Expedia ⓦ www.expedia.com.
Hotwire ⓦ www.hotwire.com.
Priceline ⓦ www.priceline.com.
STA Travel ☎ 1-800/781-4040, ⓦ www.statravel .com.
Travel Cuts US ☎ 1-800/592-CUTS, Canada ☎ 1-866/246-9762, ⓦ www.travelcuts.com.
Travelocity ⓦ www.travelocity.com.

Flights from Australia and New Zealand

There are no direct flights to Jordan **from Australasia** – though, thanks to code-sharing, it's relatively easy to put together a one-stop routing: Qantas or Thai to Bangkok, for instance, then direct to Amman with Royal Jordanian. Pricier alternatives include Emirates via Dubai or Etihad via Abu Dhabi.

Return fares from **Australia** are likely to start around A$2000; add A$500 or more in high season. From **New Zealand**, reckon on NZ$3000–3500.

Airlines in Australia and NZ

Emirates Australia ☎ 1300 303 777, New Zealand ☎ 0508 364 728; ⓦ www.emirates.com.
Etihad Australia ☎ 1800 998 995, ⓦ www.etihad.com.
Qantas Australia ☎ 13 1313, New Zealand ☎ 09/357 8900; ⓦ www.qantas.com.
Royal Jordanian Australia ☎ 02/9244 2701, New Zealand ☎ 03/365 3910; ⓦ www.rj.com.
Thai Australia ☎ 1300 651 960, New Zealand ☎ 09/377 3886; ⓦ www.thaiair.com.

Travel agents in Australia and NZ

Cheapflights ⓦ www.cheapflights.com.au.
Flight Centre ⓦ www.flightcentre.com.au.
Harvey World ⓦ www.harveyworld.co.nz.
Lastminute ⓦ www.lastminute.com.au.
STA Travel Australia ☎ 13 4782, New Zealand ☎ 0800/474 400; ⓦ www.statravel.com.au.
Trailfinders Australia ☎ 1300/780 212, ⓦ www.trailfinders.com.au.

Organized tours

Many **organized tours** follow a fairly similar pattern – a week or so in Jordan, comprising stays in Amman, Petra, Aqaba and/or the Dead Sea, with sightseeing on the way and excursions to sites like Jerash and Wadi Rum. The advantage of these packages is that they get you a good-value flight-plus-accommodation deal; by booking a tour in advance you can end up staying in posh hotels for bargain prices. The disadvantage, of course, becomes clear if you fancy an extra day or two on your own to explore Petra once you get there.

Where fixing up an organized tour really comes into its own is if you have a particular kind of holiday in mind. If you want to know all about Jordan's archeological sites, learn how to scuba-dive, or if you have your heart set on seeing a Sinai rosefinch (Jordan's national bird), specialist tour operators can sell you ready-made packages or tailor-make a tour to suit your requirements.

Adventure companies can often throw in activities such as camel-trekking, desert camping or snorkelling, and many operators specialize in pilgrimage tours to sites of biblical interest. You can also arrange tours directly with specialist tour companies in Jordan.

Tour operators in the UK

General cultural/historical

Abercrombie & Kent ☎ 0845 618 2200, ⓦ www.abercrombiekent.co.uk. Upmarket tours and tailor-made trips.
Ancient World Tours ☎ 020/7917 9494, ⓦ www.ancient.co.uk. Archeological, historical and cultural itineraries.
Andante Travels ☎ 01722/713800, ⓦ www.andantetravels.co.uk. Small-scale, personalized, expert-led archeological/historical tours.
Audley Travel ☎ 01993/838400, ⓦ www.audleytravel.com. High-quality tailor-made trips both on and off the beaten track, with a special focus on the nature reserves.
Bales Worldwide ☎ 0845 057 1819, ⓦ www.balesworldwide.com. One of the biggest operators to Jordan – a family-owned company offering a wide range of escorted tours as well as tailor-made itineraries.
Cox & Kings ☎ 020/7873 5000, ⓦ www.coxandkings.co.uk. Highly respected and long-established company offering gilt-edged cultural and historical tours to Jordan.
Dragoman ☎ 01728/861133, ⓦ www.dragoman.com. Extended overland journeys in purpose-built expedition vehicles; several itineraries pass through Jordan.
Elite Vacations ☎ 01707/371000, ⓦ www.elitevacations.com. Cultural historical tours.
Far Frontiers ☎ 0844 800 9029, ⓦ www.farfrontiers.co.uk. Classic historical tours of Jordan in conjunction with the Royal Geographical Society.
Intrepid ☎ 020/3147 7777, ⓦ www.intrepidtravel.com. Cultural trips for independent-minded travellers.
Kumuka Worldwide ☎ 0800 389 2328, ⓦ www.kumuka.com. "Soft" adventure trips and overland expeditions around the Middle East that include Jordan.
Kuoni ☎ 01306/747002, ⓦ www.kuoni.co.uk. Large holiday operator, with a range of trips to Jordan.
Longwood Holidays ☎ 020/8418 2500, ⓦ www.longwoodholidays.co.uk. Good range of cultural tours, flying into Amman, Aqaba or Ovda (near Eilat, Israel).

Martin Randall Travel ☏ 020/8742 3355, ⓦ www.martinrandall.com. Small-group cultural tours, led by experts on art and archeology.

Noble Caledonia ☏ 020/7752 0000, ⓦ www.noble-caledonia.co.uk. Cultural tours of Jordan linked into cruises around the eastern Med.

On The Go Tours ☏ 020/7371 1113, ⓦ www.onthegotours.com. Highly respected firm offering lively, expertly guided group tours, as well as tailor-made trips and unusual, insider angles on exploring Petra.

Original Travel ☏ 020/7978 7333, ⓦ www.originaltravel.co.uk. Short breaks, including a packed five days in Jordan.

Peltours ☏ 0844 225 0120, ⓦ www.peltours.com. Holiday operator with a range of packages to Jordan.

Scott Dunn ☏ 020/8682 5075, ⓦ www.scottdunn.com. Luxury tailor-made tours, staying in some out-of-the-way corners.

Silk Road and Beyond ☏ 020/7371 3131, ⓦ www.silkroadandbeyond.co.uk. Good range of cultural trips around Jordan.

Somak Holidays ☏ 020/8423 3000, ⓦ www.somak.co.uk. Historical and cultural tours.

Steppes Travel ☏ 01285/885333, ⓦ www.steppestravel.co.uk. Expertly prepared tailor-made trips.

The Traveller ☏ 020/7436 9343, ⓦ www.the-traveller.co.uk. Historical, archeological and cultural tours led by expert lecturers.

Titan HiTours ☏ 0800 988 5823, ⓦ www.titanhitours.co.uk. Classic escorted tours of major historical sites.

Travelsphere Holidays ☏ 0870/240 2426, ⓦ www.travelsphere.co.uk. Well-designed holidays to Jordan's major sites.

Voyages Jules Verne ☏ 0845 166 7003, ⓦ www.vjv.com. Major Jordan operator with years of experience, offering a range of innovative, well-thought-out (and keenly priced) holiday options all round the country, covering Jordan alone or in combination with other countries.

Adventure/outdoors specialists

Adventure Company ☏ 01420/541007, ⓦ www.adventurecompany.co.uk. Guided "soft" adventure trips for individuals and families.

ATG Oxford ☏ 01865/315678, ⓦ www.atg-oxford.co.uk. High-quality outdoor itineraries, concentrating on Dana and Petra and including excellent long walks with some of Jordan's best walking guides.

Exodus ☏ 0845 863 9600, ⓦ www.exodus.co.uk. Small-group adventure tour operators, with specialist programmes including walking, trekking, scrambling and cycling.

Explore ☏ 0845 013 1539, ⓦ www.explore.co.uk. A wide range of small-group tours, treks, expeditions and safaris, staying mostly in small hotels or bedouin tents.

Families Worldwide ☏ 0845 051 4567, ⓦ www.familiesworldwide.co.uk. Specialists in adventure holidays for families.

Headwater ☏ 01606/720199, ⓦ www.headwater.com. Guided walking tours to remote corners of Jordan.

High Places ☏ 0114/275 7500, ⓦ www.highplaces.co.uk. Great-value trekking and climbing in Wadi Rum and Petra.

Imaginative Traveller ☏ 0845 077 8802, ⓦ www.imaginative-traveller.com. Well-respected adventure operator with a good range of tours.

KE Adventure ☏ 017687/73966, ⓦ www.keadventure.com. Treks and adventure tours, including the Dana–Petra trek.

Naturetrek ☏ 01962/733051, ⓦ www.naturetrek.co.uk. Small-group birdwatching and botanical tours of Jordan with expert guidance.

Nomadic Thoughts ☏ 020/7604 4408, ⓦ www.nomadicthoughts.com. Tailor-made trips to Jordan.

NOMADS ☏ 01457/873231, ⓦ www.nomadstravel.co.uk. Small operation run by Tony Howard and Di Taylor, the British climbing duo who opened up Rum to international tourism in the 1980s. They provide detailed, knowledgeable advice on all aspects of independent exploration of Jordan's wilder corners.

Peregrine Adventures ☏ 0844 736 0170, ⓦ www.peregrineadventures.com. Broad range of Jordan tours that reach some lesser-known highlights.

Ramblers ☏ 01707/331133, ⓦ www.ramblersholidays.co.uk. Good choice of Jordan tours, including some unusual walks and side-trips.

Ride World Wide ☏ 01837/82544, ⓦ www.rideworldwide.co.uk. High-quality horseriding holidays in Wadi Rum.

Tribes Travel ☏ 01728/685971, ⓦ www.tribes.co.uk. Tailor-made trips that explore Jordan's natural environment, working with the Royal Society for the Conservation of Nature.

Walks Worldwide ☏ 01524/242000, ⓦ www.walksworldwide.com. Leading walking and outdoors operator to Jordan, with a broad range of tours to suit all levels of capability, including family trips and the epic Dana–Petra trek. Highly recommended.

Wild Frontiers ☏ 020/7736 3968, ⓦ www.wildfrontiers.co.uk. Adventure trips into and around Petra.

Wildlife & Wilderness ☏ 01625/838225, ⓦ www.wildlifewilderness.com. High-quality tailor-made trips focusing on culture, walking and nature.

Diving specialists

Aquatours ☎020/8398 0505, ⓦwww.aquatours
.com. Jordan diving specialist, combining underwater
trips with cultural itineraries.
Planet Dive ☎0870 749 1959, ⓦwww
.planetdive.co.uk. Good range of dive options at
Aqaba, plus side-trips to Rum and Petra.

Horseriding specialists

Equine Adventures ☎0845 130 6981, ⓦwww
.equineadventures.co.uk. Well-provisioned trips
including extended horserides through Wadi Rum.
Equitour ☎0800 043 7942, ⓦwww.equitour
.co.uk. Tours on horseback around Petra or Wadi
Rum.
In The Saddle ☎01299/272997, ⓦwww
.inthesaddle.co.uk. High-quality tours around Petra
and Wadi Rum on horseback.
Unicorn Trails ☎01767/600606, ⓦwww
.unicorntrails.com. Horseriding holidays in the Wadi
Rum desert.

Pilgrimage tours

Guiding Star ⓦwww.guidingstar2.com. A leading
pilgrimage operator with offices in Jerusalem and
Amman, founded in 1961. Combining Christian sites
with adventure excursions and cultural exploration,
they are exceptionally well connected, and can design
a unique itinerary on request.
Maranatha Tours ☎01753/689568, ⓦwww
.maranatha.co.uk. Specialist in biblical pilgrimage
tours to Jordan and around the Middle East.
McCabe Pilgrimages ☎0800 107 3107, ⓦwww
.mccabe-travel.co.uk. Pilgrim tours to Jordan, often
in conjunction with Egypt.
Pilgrim Travel ☎01304/215572, ⓦwww
.pilgrimtraveluk.ltd.uk. Leading operator of church
tours to Jordan and other Middle East destinations.
Sam Smith Travel ☎01446/774018, ⓦwww
.samsmithtravel.com. Small firm specializing in
pilgrimages and trips to Petra.
Worldwide Christian Travel ☎0845 458 8308,
ⓦwww.christian-travel.com. Biblical and pilgrimage
tours to Jordan and Israel.

Tour operators in North America

Abercrombie & Kent ☎1-800/554-7016,
ⓦwww.abercrombiekent.com. Fully escorted luxury
tours to Jordan and its neighbours.
Absolute Travel ☎1-800/736-8187, ⓦwww
.absolutetravel.com. Customized tours with all the
trimmings.
Adventure Center ☎1-800/228-8747, ⓦwww
.adventurecenter.com. Hiking and "soft adventure"

specialists, with a wide range of options including
cultural tours, walking, cycling and more.
Adventures Abroad ☎1-800/665-3998, ⓦwww
.adventures-abroad.com. Small-group adventure
specialists, with a range of offerings including Jordan
and its neighbours.
AER World Tours ☎1-800/492-0254, ⓦwww
.aertours.com. Custom-designed travel, in small
groups with private guides.
Ancient Adventures ☎1-800/353-4978,
ⓦwww.ancientadventures.com. A range of
tours all round the Middle East, some historical/
cultural, others incorporating diving or "soft"
adventure.
Bestway Tours ☎1-800/663-0844, ⓦwww
.bestway.com. A range of cultural tours.
Caravan-Serai Tours ☎1-800/451-8097,
ⓦwww.caravan-serai.com. Leading specialists to
the Middle East, with a range of excellent, culturally
aware tours to Jordan and all across the region.
Owned and run by the award-winning, Jordanian-born
businesswoman Rita Zawaideh.
Cox and Kings ☎1-800/999-1758, ⓦwww
.coxandkingsusa.com. Long-established top-of-
the-range tour operator, with several Middle Eastern
offerings.
Destinations & Adventures International
☎1-800/659-4599, ⓦwww.daitravel.com. Broad
range of Middle Eastern cultural trips, including
Jordan.
Distant Horizons ☎1-800/333-1240, ⓦwww
.distant-horizons.com. Specialist in unusual,
culturally minded angles on Middle East destinations,
including Jordan.
Elderhostel ☎1-800/454-5768, ⓦwww
.elderhostel.org. Specialists in educational and
activity programmes for senior travellers, including
journeys around Jordan.
Far Horizons ☎1-800/552-4575, ⓦwww
.farhorizons.com. Expert-led archeological and
historical tours of Jordan.
FreeGate Tourism ☎1-888/373-3428, ⓦwww
.freegatetours.com. Cultural tours around Jordan,
alone or in combination with its neighbours.
Hiking World ☎916/443-5731, ⓦwww
.hikingworld.org. High-quality hiking trips in some
far-flung corners of Jordan.
HLO Tours ☎1-800/736-4456, ⓦwww.hlotours
.com. Specialists in tailor-made trips, with many years
of experience in the Middle East.
IsramWorld ☎1-800/223-7460, ⓦwww.isram
.com. Long-established tour operator with a diverse
selection of Middle Eastern offerings.
Key Tours ☎1-800/576-1784, ⓦwww.keytours
.com. Package deals to Amman, Petra and the
Dead Sea.

Maranatha Tours ☎1-800/545-5533, ⊛www
.maranathatours.com. Specialist in biblical
pilgrimage tours.

Sita Tours ☎1-800/421-5643, ⊛www.sitatours
.com. Historical trips around Jordan.

Spiekermann Travel ☎1-800/645-3233,
⊛www.mideasttrvl.com. Experts on Middle Eastern
travel, with hosted tours around Jordan.

TCS Expeditions ☎1-800/727-7477, ⊛www
.tcs-expeditions.com. Opulent tours by private jet to
destinations worldwide, including stops in Jordan for
Petra and Wadi Rum.

Travcoa ☎1-866/591-0070, ⊛www.travcoa
.com. Luxury escorted tours through Syria and
Jordan.

Travel In Style ☎415/440-1124, ⊛www
.travelinstyle.com. Specialists in the eastern
Mediterranean, with a good range of tours to Jordan
alongside options to Egypt, Syria and Israel.

Trek Holidays ☎1-888/456-3522, ⊛www
.trekholidays.com. Offers details of dozens of
small-group adventure trips to Jordan run by various
different agents – well worth a browse.

Wilderness Travel ☎1-800/368-2794, ⊛www
.wildernesstravel.com. Cultural exploration around
Jordan and beyond.

Ya'lla Tours ☎1-800/644-1595, ⊛www
.yallatours.com. Middle East specialist, with a wide
range of trips and packages covering Jordan.

Tour operators in Australia and NZ

Abercrombie & Kent Australia ☎1300/851 800,
New Zealand ☎0800/441 638; ⊛www
.abercrombiekent.com.au. Classy operator with a
strong reputation – upmarket luxury tours.

Adventure World Australia ☎1300/363 055, New
Zealand ☎0800/238 368, ⊛www.adventureworld
.com.au. Agents for a wide array of international
adventure companies – well worth a browse.

Kumuka Worldwide Australia ☎1300/667 277,
New Zealand ☎0800/440 499; ⊛www.kumuka
.com. "Soft" adventure trips and overland expeditions.

Martin Randall Travel Australia ☎1300/559 595,
⊛www.martinrandall.com. British company running
small-group cultural tours, led by expert lecturers.

Passport Travel Australia ☎03/9500 0444,
⊛www.travelcentre.com.au. Tour options on the
Red Sea and around the Middle East.

Peregrine Adventures Australia ☎03/8601 4444,
⊛www.peregrineadventures.com. Broad range of
Jordan tours that reach some lesser-known highlights.

Sun Island Tours Australia ☎1300/665 673,
⊛www.sunislandtours.com.au. Package holidays
and full travel arrangements for the Middle East.

World Expeditions Australia ☎1300/720 000, New
Zealand ☎0800/350 354; ⊛www.worldexpeditions
.com.au. Australian-owned adventure company,
with a broad programme of trekking and adventure
expeditions, including Jordan and Syria.

Travel from neighbouring countries

Many independent travellers arrive in Jordan on an overland odyssey between
Istanbul and Cairo. Border crossings are straightforward, and most nationalities
can get a Jordanian visa on arrival (except at the King Hussein/Allenby Bridge
between Jerusalem and Amman).

From Damascus

The easiest way to get to Amman from the
Syrian capital **Damascus**, barely 100km
north of the Jordanian frontier, is by
serveece, or shared taxi. They depart day
and night from the Sumriyeh (Somaria)
garage in western Damascus, for S£700
(JD11) per seat. It's common for individuals
to buy two seats (or couples to buy three) to
give a roomier ride – or you can charter the
whole car (usually four or five seats). There
are 24-hour banks at the border. The usual
terminus in Amman is Abdali, but for a little
bit extra the driver will drop you off anywhere
you want. Journey time is about three hours.

Comfortable Karnak and JETT **buses** to
Amman leave from Kadem station in
Damascus (☎011 441 0531) daily at 7am and

The Israeli stamps problem

If you intend to visit Israel, the West Bank or Gaza as part of a longer journey in the region, you need to bear in mind that it is the official policy of almost all Middle Eastern and North African countries (except, principally, Egypt, Jordan and Morocco) to refuse entry to people who have **evidence of a visit to Israel** in their passports. "Evidence" includes not only Israeli stamps, but also Jordanian entry or exit stamps from the border-posts at the Sheikh Hussein/Jordan River Bridge, the King Hussein/Allenby Bridge and the Wadi Araba/Yitzhak Rabin crossing (Aqaba–Eilat), as well as Egyptian stamps from the border-posts at Taba (near Eilat) and Rafah in northern Sinai. Visas issued in Israel for travel to any country and flight itineraries that specify Tel Aviv (or TLV) will also bar you, as will anything in Hebrew discovered in your belongings.

That said, we've had reports of travellers holding Israeli stamps getting into certain countries (Tunisia, Oman and the UAE, among others) without any difficulty, but this can't be relied upon. Syrian and Lebanese officials are the least flexible in this regard.

The best advice is to construct your itinerary so that you **visit Israel last**, after Syria and the rest. Alternatively, you can apply in your home country, well in advance, for a **second passport**: many countries issue these to people travelling around the Middle East as a matter of routine, but it's then up to you to ensure that your tally of entry and exit stamps in each passport adds up, and that you don't hand the wrong passport over to the wrong border official.

If you hold only one passport, there is no foolproof method of avoiding a giveaway stamp. If you're feeling lucky, and you've entered Jordan by air, sea or across the land borders from Syria, Iraq or Saudi Arabia, then you could try using *only* the King Hussein (Allenby) Bridge to cross from Jordan to the West Bank and back (while making sure that your Jordanian visa does not expire in the meantime). At this bridge Israeli and Jordanian immigration officials will usually stamp you both in and out on a **piece of paper** if you ask, thus avoiding any permanent evidence of having been "on the other side" (as many travellers refer to Israel, to avoid detection by eavesdropping officials). However, the success of this depends on not running into an official who decides to stamp your passport regardless.

It's a well-known ploy of travellers who have unwittingly acquired evidence of an Israeli visit to **lose their passports** deliberately in Egypt or Jordan and apply for new ones from their embassies. However, an unused passport issued in Cairo or Amman is as much evidence to Syrian consular officials of a visit to "Occupied Palestine" (as Syrian visa application forms put it) as a border stamp. Even if the loss of your old passport was genuine, you may still find yourself refused entry to Syria on this suspicion.

3pm. The fare is around US$11 or JD8 or S£600. Reckon on a journey time of four hours, since everyone must clear customs and immigration before the bus can carry on (which is one reason to go by serveece instead). Buses terminate next to the JETT External Lines office, in the Abdali district. It's wise to book seats one day ahead. Extra buses are laid on in the peak summer season.

At the time of writing, there was no passenger service between Damascus and Amman on the historic Hejaz **railway** line. **Flying** takes longer than driving.

From Jerusalem

No public transport runs directly between **Jerusalem** and Amman: the only way to go is with a combination of bus, taxi and/or serveece. All traffic is funnelled towards the single border crossing open to the public (Sun–Thurs 8am–4.30pm, Fri & Sat 8am–3pm; ℡02 548 2600), known to the Palestinians and Israelis as the **Allenby Bridge** (Jissr Allenby in Arabic; Gesher Allenby in Hebrew), but to the Jordanians as the **King Hussein Bridge** (Jissr al-Malek Hussein). On a good day, the journey can take as little as two

Details of fees, regulations and transport for crossing into Jordan via the King Hussein/Allenby Bridge, the Sheikh Hussein/Jordan River Bridge and the Rabin/Wadi Araba border are given at the Israel Airports Authority site ⍵ www.iaa.gov.il.

hours; on a bad day, it can be more than five. This crossing-point is also notoriously subject to the ebb and flow of Middle Eastern politics, and can close at short notice.

Although you must have a **visa** to enter Jordan, they are not issued at this bridge – which, thanks to a complex piece of official doublethink, is not viewed by Jordan as an international border (no Jordanian flags fly over it). If you try to cross without already holding a Jordanian visa, you'll be turned back by Israeli passport control.

Israeli buses from West Jerusalem don't go to the bridge. Instead, use the serveeces (shared taxis) departing frequently from **East Jerusalem** for around NIS35 per person, run by Abdo travel agency opposite Damascus Gate (☎02 628 3281). Set out early in the morning, or book your ride in advance: by about midday, when serveeces stop running, your only certain option is a taxi for around NIS180. Buses also run to the bridge from Jericho and other West Bank cities.

Within the bridge terminal, you must pay an Israeli **departure tax**, currently NIS157 (around US$42). If you intend using your passport for overland travel beyond Jordan, be sure to tell the Israeli officials to stamp the loose immigration forms only – not your passport. A bus (JD4) makes the short trip across the bridge to the Jordanian arrivals terminal. Serveeces do the one-hour journey direct to Tabarbour station in Amman (JD6 per person) or you could take a taxi (about JD30).

From Tel Aviv and Nazareth

Buses of Trust International Transport run regularly from the Israeli cities of **Tel Aviv** and **Nazareth** direct to Irbid and Amman. From Tel Aviv, buses depart from the Central Bus Station (Sun–Fri 2pm; NIS180; ☎050 553 8762). From Lower Nazareth, departures are from the Trust office (daily 3.30pm; NIS160;

☎04 646 6660). These two buses – which avoid passing through the West Bank – meet at a bridge over the River Jordan about 6km east of Bet She'an (Beisan in Arabic), known to the Israelis as the **Jordan River crossing** (Sun–Thurs 6.30am–9pm, Fri & Sat 8am–8pm; ☎04 609 3400), and to the Jordanians as the **Sheikh Hussein Bridge** or simply the Northern Crossing. You pay an Israeli departure tax, currently NIS90 (about US$23), plus around NIS5 for a bus across the bridge. On the Jordanian side, after buying a visa (JD10), all passengers board a waiting bus which sets off for Irbid (dropping off at the Trust office near Safeway) and on to Amman, terminating at the Trust office near 7th Circle. Reckon on 5 hours end to end – and always book one day in advance.

You can also cross independently, with a taxi from Bet She'an to the bridge (around NIS25) and another taxi to Irbid (around JD25) or Amman (around JD50). Alternatively book with an Israeli travel agency: Mazada Tours (☎03 544 4454, ⍵ www.mazadatours .com) operates daily trips on request from Tel Aviv to Amman via this bridge, for around US$150 including border taxes and visa.

Flying from Tel Aviv to Amman – at the time of writing only possible on Royal Jordanian (☎03 516 5566, ⍵ www.rj.com), at around US$240 one-way – offers the lure of spectacular scenery over desert hills and the Dead Sea. Flight time is about thirty minutes.

From Eilat

Another crossing-point from Israel is in the south, between the neighbouring Red Sea resort cities of **Eilat** (Israel) and Aqaba (Jordan), known to the Israelis as the **Yitzhak Rabin** or **Arava crossing** (Sun–Thurs 6.30am–8pm, Fri & Sat 8am–8pm; ☎08 630 0555), and to the Jordanians as the **Wadi Araba** or Southern crossing. From Eilat bus station, it's reached most easily by taking a taxi (around NIS40) or by simply walking 2km to the border. There's an Israeli departure tax, currently NIS90 (about US$23). Once you're through the formalities (note the tip on p.65 regarding free Jordanian visas at this crossing), a serveece into central Aqaba (5km) costs about JD3 per person, a taxi about JD12.

From Cairo and the Sinai

Buses do run from **Cairo** to Amman, though it's an uncomfortable journey of at least 20 hours. Jordanian JETT and Egyptian SuperJet buses run twice weekly from the Almaza terminal in Heliopolis (☎02 2290 9013). The East Delta bus company runs four weekly services from the Sinai terminal in Abbassiya. The fare on either is around US$90–110 including the Nuweiba–Aqaba ferry, payable in dollars only. Royal Jordanian and EgyptAir **fly** from Cairo to Amman (around US$240; flight time 1hr 30min). RJ also flies from Sharm el-Sheikh (around US$200).

There are two **ferry** services from the Sinai coast to Aqaba. **Arab Bridge Maritime** (Cairo ☎02 2262 0036, Nuweiba ☎069 352 0472; ⊛www.abmaritime.com.jo) runs boats from **Nuweiba** – though their timetable is notoriously unreliable and can change from month to month. Expect lengthy delays: six hours is not uncommon. At the time of writing, a **catamaran** departs daily at 1pm (economy US$70; first class US$90; 1hr), and a slow **ferry** departs daily at midnight (US$65; 3hr). There's a tax of E£50. Arrive at the port, 8km south of Nuweiba, at least 2 hours early to buy tickets (with US dollars only). On boarding, you'll have to hand over your passport, which will be returned to you at Aqaba passport control (see p.65 for info about Aqaba visas). A serveece into central Aqaba (9km) is JD1.50 per person, a taxi JD6. Check for details of extra departures in peak season (during summer, at the end of Ramadan, and around the hajj and Eid al-Adha).

An alternative ferry runs from the marina at **Taba Heights**, 70km north of Nuweiba. It is designed as a cruise for people staying at Taba's luxury hotels, but qualifies as passenger transport. There are departures daily at around 7.30am and 8.30am to Tala Bay, 15km south of Aqaba (a taxi into the city is about JD9), as well as a boat most days at noon or 1pm which docks at the giant flagpole in central Aqaba. Passports are checked on arrival (see p.65 for info about Aqaba visas). The one-way fare is around US$70, which includes taxes and marina fees for non-hotel guests; the trip takes 30 minutes. It is operated by the Jordanian company **Sindbad**: for details, contact their Egyptian agent **Pro Tours** (Cairo ☎02 3303 8487, Taba ☎069 358 0076; ⊛www .protourstravel.com), or any of the Taba Heights hotels. You must book at least one day in advance.

It's cheaper and often easier to go **overland** through the Israeli resort of Eilat. **Taba**, on the Egyptian-Israeli border, is well served by transport from Nuweiba, Dahab and Cairo. The crossing is open 24 hours daily, but it's difficult to find transport inside Israel during the Jewish *shabbat*, so avoid making the trip between 2pm Friday and 8pm Saturday. There's a small Egyptian departure tax (around E£50), and most nationalities are routinely issued with a free Israeli visa on arrival. Once in Israel, a combination of city buses and walking will get you to the Jordanian border (*hagvul ha-yardeni* in Hebrew), but it's easier to take a taxi (around NIS80–100). For details about crossing into Jordan, see "From Eilat" above. Total journey time is about two or three hours – though the passport stamps you pick up will disqualify you from subsequently entering Syria and many other Middle Eastern countries.

Getting around

Jordan's public transport is a hotchpotch. Bus routes cover what's necessary for the locals, and there is little or no provision for independent travellers. With some highly visitable places inaccessible by public transport, the best way to see the whole of Jordan is to rent a car for at least part of your stay.

Buses and serveeces

The most common way of getting between cities is by **bus**, most of which are fifteen- or eighteen-seater minibuses. Some larger buses and air-conditioned coaches also serve as public transport. Throughout this book, we've used "bus" as a catch-all term, though in most cases minibuses are the only transport option available. Few timetables are in operation: buses tend to depart only when they're full. This means that, on less-travelled routes especially, you should factor in sometimes quite considerable waiting time for the bus to fill up. Once you get going journeys are rarely arduous: roads are good, and the longest single journey in the country, from Amman to Aqaba, is unlikely to take more than four hours. All buses and minibuses have their point of origin and **destination** painted in Arabic script just above either brake-light on the rear of the vehicle.

Bus **fares** are very low. As a guide, a half-hour hop between towns costs JD0.30–0.40 one-way. Slightly longer journeys, such as Amman to Jerash, or Karak to Tafileh, are in the order of JD0.80–1. Rip-offs are rare: if you ask the fare, you'll invariably be told the truth. Expect inflated fares on routes serving major tourist sites: Petra to Wadi Rum is JD5. There is no competition between minibus operators.

A few companies operate large, air-con **buses** in competition with the minibuses on some long-distance runs. Jordan Express Tourist Transport, or JETT, has daily timetabled services Amman–Aqaba and Amman–Petra; Trust International Transport operates Amman–Aqaba and Irbid–Aqaba; Hijazi operates Amman–Irbid, mainly for Yarmouk University students; and there are a few others. These all offer the advantages of comfort and speed over the minibuses, and most allow you to book in advance (in person only, at the company's office).

On most inter-city routes, shared taxis (universally known as **serveeces**) tout for business alongside the buses. These are white cars, often seating seven or eight people, which offer, at a slightly higher price, the single advantage of speed over the same journey by bus – though being squashed into the back seat on a long journey can counter in discomfort what might be gained in time. Serveeces also operate the system of departing when full, but because there are fewer seats they leave more frequently. If you're carrying bulky or heavy luggage, you may find that serveece, and some minibus, drivers will charge you a small supplement per bag.

For getting around **within cities**, most places have their own systems of short-hop buses and serveeces.

Bus and serveece **etiquette** says that men should sit next to men and women next to women (except for married partners or siblings), and you should stick to this rule when you can. No one will be mortally offended if circumstances force you to sit next to a Jordanian of the opposite sex, but you may find that other passengers shuffle themselves around before departure to avoid this happening.

Hitchhiking

Hitching a ride on well-travelled routes such as Amman to Petra will likely take you hours (or days), since drivers won't have a clue why you can't just get the bus like everyone

An explanation of Jordan's money is on p.69.

else. However, in areas where buses may be sporadic or nonexistent – the eastern desert, the southern portions of the King's Highway, the link road from the Desert Highway into Wadi Rum, or just from one village to the next on quiet country roads – local drivers stick to a well-established countryside protocol about picking people up if they have space. The way to show you're hitching is to hold out your arm and loosely flap your index finger.

The first rule – apart from foreign women never hitching alone – is that you should always be prepared to **pay something**, even if your money is refused when offered. Trying to freebie your way around the country will inspire contempt rather than camaraderie. Travellers who decide to hitch should do so always in pairs. The risk of unpleasantness is minuscule but nonetheless does exist; women should never sit next to men, and spontaneous offers of hospitality should be accepted only with extreme caution. **Water** and a **hat** are vital accoutrements: dehydration is probably the greatest threat.

Driving

Compared with Egypt or Syria, **driving** in Jordan is a breeze; compared with the West, it's a challenge. Apart from driving on the right and always obeying a policeman, **rules of the road** tend to have individual interpretations. Most roads aren't marked out in lanes, so overtaking on both sides is normal – always accompanied by a blast or two on the horn – as is pulling out into fast-moving traffic without looking. There is no universally accepted pattern of **right of way**. It's wise to follow the locals and sound your **horn** before many types of manoeuvre; out in the sticks, look out for kids playing on the hard shoulder and give a warning honk from a long way back. **Traffic lights** are always respected – cameras record red-light runners – as are most **one-ways**. Right of way on roundabouts goes to whoever's moving fastest.

Road surfaces are generally good, although there are lots of **unmarked speed bumps** and rumble strips in unexpected places (including main highways), as well as killer potholes. Look out for drifting sand in the desert: if you're going too fast when you hit a patch of sand, you can be spun off the road before you know it. **Speed limits** – posted regularly – are generally 100kph on highways and 90kph on main roads, dropping to 60kph or 40kph in built-up areas. Mobile police radar traps catch speeders, with spot fines around JD25.

On major roads, **directional signs** are plentiful and informative; most have English as well as Arabic. Large brown signs around the country direct tourists to major sites, superseding older blue signs. On unsigned back roads, the only fail-safe method of finding the right direction is to keep asking the locals.

Night driving is considerably more scary. Lighting is often poor, so speed bumps, uneven road surfaces, children or animals (or objects) in the road and potholes all become invisible. Slow-moving trucks and farm vehicles often chug along in the dark without lights or reflectors. It's common – if inexplicable – practice on dark country roads to flip to main beam when you see somebody coming, dazzling them blind. Many people flash their headlights to say "get out of the way", but some do it to say "OK go ahead", others merely to say hello: you must make up your own mind at the time which it is.

Although a normal **driving licence** from home is sufficient, an International Driving Permit can be useful, since it has an Arabic translation; these are available very inexpensively from motoring organizations in your home country.

Renting a self-drive car

For reaching all corners of the country at your own pace, a **rental car** is a worthwhile – sometimes essential – investment, best arranged before you arrive. The rental market is huge, but most local firms cater more to Jordanians' friends and family than to Westerners – although you can get unearth some great deals on the fly, many of these tiny outfits are no more than a guy with a phone renting out old cars on the cheap with no insurance, no papers and no service.

Amman has roughly 120 car rental firms, all of which can match or undercut the international agencies' rates – but few of which maintain equivalent levels of quality and service. The best-value and most conscientious outfit is **Reliable**, located in Abdoun, not far from 5th Circle (☎06 592 9676, ⓦwww.rentareliablecar.com). They charge about JD30 a day for a new or one-year-old car (manual or automatic) with air conditioning, comfortable for four people, including unlimited mileage and full insurance. Prices drop for longer rental periods. They'll bring the car to you, and you can drop it off for free, at the airport or anywhere in Amman, 24 hours a day – and their customer service is excellent. Collision damage waiver (CDW) costs a few dinars more, but is worth it. Options such as theft protection (TP) are unnecessary.

Cheaper deals are available elsewhere (as low as JD15–20/day) – but this will buy you an older vehicle, dodgier paperwork and less reliable backup when you're out on the road.

The global names have broader coverage (and higher prices). **Hertz** (☎06 553 8958, ⓦwww.hertz.com) is good for one-way rentals, letting you drop the car off for free at any of their Amman offices, the airport, the Dead Sea, Petra or Aqaba. **Avis** (☎06 569 9420, ⓦwww.avis.com.jo) and **Europcar** (☎06 565 5581, ⓦwww.europcar.jo) – both with offices in Amman, the airport, the King Hussein/Allenby Bridge and Aqaba – are similar. A listing of other firms is at ⓦwww.visitjordan.com.

A few agencies rent out **four-wheel-drive** vehicles (called "four-by-fours") from about JD50 a day upwards. These are essential for getting to out-of-the-way archeological sites and touring the desert, but you need familiarity with 4x4 driving – and a local guide with you – before you head off-road. For all but the most dedicated adventurers, a normal car is fine. It's a good idea to keep a few litres of bottled water in the car, in case you get stranded in some remote spot.

If you're in an **accident**, to claim costs back from the insurance company you'll need a full written report from the police, and from the first doctor on the scene who treated any injuries.

Fuel

Almost all **petrol** stations have attendants to do the pumping for you: either hand over, say, JD10 or JD20 before he starts, or just ask for "full". All petrol sold in Jordan is unleaded – standard 90 octane (*tisaeen*) or

pricier 95 octane (*khamsa wa-tisaeen*). Diesel (*deezel*) is available rarely. Most stations accept **cash only**.

Accidents

Despite the Jordanian driving style, **accidents** are infrequent, and rarely amount to more than a prang. However, under Jordanian law any accident involving a car and a **pedestrian** is automatically deemed to be the fault of the driver: if you hit anybody, cause any sort of injury, or even if someone falls out of a window onto your stationary vehicle, you will be held responsible. Goats, sheep, donkeys and camels roam more or less freely beside roads, but if you **hit an animal**, you will have to pay the owner compensation. With a goat costing, say, 100JD, and a camel ten times as much, you'd do well to keep your eyes peeled.

If you're in any sort of accident while behind the wheel of a **rental car**, call the rental company first, since – if they're trustworthy – they will call the police on your behalf and then send someone out to pick you up. Otherwise, call the police yourself on ☎191.

Taxis and chauffeur-driven cars

Apart from a fleet of silver radio-cabs in Amman which can be hired by phone – at a premium – all **taxis** are yellow with green panels in Arabic on both front doors, and they'll go anywhere if the price is right. Inexpensive and quite often essential within Amman, their good value declines the further afield you want to go; renting a taxi to cover the transport-thin eastern desert, for instance, will cost you almost twice as much as if you drove there yourself in a rental car (but, obviously, with less of the stress). As far as **fares** go, other than within Amman city limits, where taxis are metered, you'll have to negotiate with the driver before setting off. Ballpark figures for particular routes are given in the guide, but where you're inventing your own itinerary, you'd do well to ask the advice of a disinterested party (such as a hotel receptionist) beforehand. Jordanian **women** would never get in the front seat next to a male driver (there are very few female taxi-drivers), and, wherever possible, foreign women should follow suit and sit in the back.

Most rent-a-car agencies can provide a **driver** for the day for about JD25 on top of the price of the rental; on a longer trip, JD45 a day should cover his food and accommodation costs.

Trains

At the time of writing, no scheduled passenger **trains** were operating in Jordan. The historic, narrow-gauge Hejaz Railway (see p.110), running from the Syrian border to Amman and south into the desert, was hosting only freight trains and occasional specials chartered by foreign tour operators and steam enthusiasts. A proposal to launch tourist services on the line from Aqaba to Wadi Rum – otherwise reserved for trains carrying phosphates to port from desert mines – has so far come to nothing.

Planes

Royal Jordanian (☎06 510 0000, ⓦwww .rj.com) operates the only domestic **air** route, between Amman (Queen Alia) and Aqaba. Flights run once or twice daily and take a little over half an hour. At JD48 one-way, this isn't prohibitively expensive, and means you can travel from city centre to city centre in around ninety minutes (including check-in and ground transfers), compared with more than four hours overland. In addition, the airborne views over the desert, the Dead Sea and the Petra mountains are exceptional; sit on the right-hand side heading south.

Bicycles

Cycling around the country is a very pleasant way to travel, although barely a handful of locals cycle (mostly in the flat Jordan Valley) and you're likely to be regarded as mad if you try. Apart from the heat and steep hills, the only dangers are oblivious drivers and – very occasionally – groups of stone-throwing kids in remote villages. Although it may seem counter-intuitive you should try to dress conservatively if you're planning a solo ride in the hinterlands: rural villagers simply aren't used to lurid skin-tight Lycra.

There are no bike rental firms in Jordan. Check ⓦwww.cycling-jordan.com for details of like-minded locals, weekend bike trips and spare-parts outlets. The adventure tour operator Terhaal (ⓦwww.terhaal.com) runs regular mountain-bike excursions around Madaba, Mukawir and the Dead Sea.

Accommodation

Accommodation in Jordan runs the gamut from the cheapest fleapit dives all the way up to international-standard luxury five-star hotels. Amman, Petra and Aqaba have a wide choice covering all price brackets and Jordan's Dead Sea hotels are known as some of the best spa resort complexes in the world.

The **Jordan Hotels Association** (ⓦwww .johotels.org) grades all hotels from one to five stars, with "unclassified" hotels off the bottom end of the scale. Bear in mind, though, that their system isn't wholly reliable: in this book we review a prominent two-star establishment that, in Europe, would be judged three-star, while at least one of Amman's five-star hotels in truth merits only four.

Room rates vary according to the season. The high season for tourism from non-Arab countries is spring (March–May) and autumn (Sept–Nov). This is when hotels are at their busiest, and when it is **essential to book**

An explanation of Jordan's money is on p.69.

Hotel price codes

Throughout this book, hotels have been categorized according to the price codes given below, which indicate the normal price for the **least expensive double room** in an establishment during the **high season** (excluding the 8 percent tax and 10 percent service charge levied in all hotels priced ❸ and above). **Single rooms** can cost anything between seventy and a hundred percent of the double-room rates. Where a hotel also offers beds in **shared rooms**, a price *per person* to share has been given.

❶ JD20 and under	❹ JD41–50	❼ JD76–95
❷ JD21–30	❺ JD51–60	❽ JD96–120
❸ JD31–40	❻ JD61–75	❾ JD121 and over

well in advance. In April and October, especially, it can be difficult to find a room at any budget in Petra and Aqaba. Summer (June–Aug) is when Arab tourism from the Gulf states is at its peak, but these visitors tend to prefer to stay in self-catering apartment suites, so some hotel bargains can be had. Hotels in Aqaba stay busy all winter long (Oct–April), when the luxury hotels on the Dead Sea are also often completely full – block-booked either by conference delegates or by tour groups, or packed with wealthy Ammanis on weekend breaks.

All hotels above ❸ in our price-coding system tack eight percent **government sales tax** onto their quoted prices and generally accept payment by credit card; some also add another ten percent **service charge**. These two surcharges are often indicated by "++" (or "plus-plus"). Wherever you go you'll find healthy competition. Out of high season, a little gentle bargaining can often bring a discounted rate.

Standards vary widely within each price bracket and sometimes within each hotel: if the room you're shown isn't good enough, ask to see others. Things to look out for are **air conditioning** (or at the very least a ceiling fan) in summer and **heating** in winter; both are essential almost everywhere. South- or west-facing rooms that receive direct sunshine are liable to become ovens on summer afternoons and so stay uncomfortably hot during the night; you'd do well in Aqaba to reject a sea view in favour of a cooler, north-facing balcony. Cheaper hotels may not have 24-hour hot water: ask in advance at what times hot water is available.

On a **backpacker budget**, there's a network of traveller-style hotels in all the major towns, and you'll easily get onto the grapevine for bargain excursions. In the **mid-range**, you can take advantage of some excellent-value small hotels – almost all family-run – dotted on and off the beaten track, as well as comfortable lodges and cabins within several of Jordan's nature reserves. At the **top end**, Jordan's finest hotels can compete on equal terms with the best in the world.

Budget hotels

Jordan's **cheapest hotels** – to be found in all town centres – aren't hotels at all. They're essentially dosshouses, catering to guest labourers and/or long-distance truckers. Universally filthy, they're best avoided by even the most frugal travellers: washing facilities are likely to be spartan or nonexistent, and there might be only one squat toilet to share.

Slightly up from these – though still well inside the ❶ bracket – are **budget** hotels aimed either exclusively at Western tourists, or at both locals and tourists; often the latter will have some means of separation, like reserving one whole floor for locals only and another for tourists only. You'll often find a choice of shared or private rooms, housing two, three or four beds, perhaps with some en-suite rooms as well. It's perfectly acceptable to check things out before agreeing to pay: see if the sheets are clean (it's common practice in these places to leave the sheets at least two weeks between changes; insist on clean bedding before taking the room), the bed is stable, the flyscreens on the windows are intact, the ceiling fan works, the water in the bathroom is hot (or at least lukewarm), the toilets don't smell too much, and so on. It's a good rule to keep your **passport** with you at all times: with the risk of pickpocketing at virtually zero, the hotel "safe" (often just an unlocked drawer) is rarely safer than your own pocket.

Women travelling alone or together on a rock-bottom budget will have to play things by ear. In general – although not always – hotels with price code ❶ that are geared towards Western backpackers will be safe and welcoming for women, whereas those that are mainly geared up for locals should be avoided. Paying slightly more to stay in hotels with better security and privacy is wise.

Breakfast is never included in hotels in the ❶ price range, and – counting as an optional extra – provides some scope for bargaining in hotels priced ❷ and above.

Mid-range hotels

Mid-range hotels – in the ❹, ❺ and ❻ brackets – are all often decent, family-run establishments that take a pride in offering good service. Other than at Petra, they're just as likely to be targeting visiting Arab families as foreign tourists and thus can't afford to get a reputation for slovenliness. Lobbies are often done up in grandiose style, featuring gilt, fake marble and lots of glitter: don't be too dazzled, though, since a fancy lobby can sometimes prelude distinctly drab or gloomy rooms.

If you're after colonial character, you'll be disappointed: being a bedouin backwater, Jordan missed out on the grand age of hotel-building – and Amman's venerable *Philadelphia Hotel*, built soon after the 1921 foundation of the emirate, was rather short-sightedly bulldozed in the 1980s. Instead, look for character in the modest but comfortable lodges and cabins within several of Jordan's nature reserves, notably Dana, Ajloun and Azraq.

Luxury hotels

The **luxury** end of the market can offer remarkable value for money. An over-concentration of hotels priced ❼, ❽

and ❾ means that, with prudent advance booking (which can bring you bed and breakfast for less than the room-only walk-up rate), you could bring the cost of a five-star splurge down to a half or even a third of what you might pay in Europe for equivalent facilities. There are very few independently owned luxury hotels left in Jordan: almost all belong to one or other of the big global hotel groups – InterContinental (which includes Crowne Plaza and Holiday Inn), Mövenpick, Marriott, Kempinski and the like. All five-star hotels can cater for **non-smoking** guests on request, generally with non-smoking floors.

Camping

Jordan has barely any facilities for **camping**. Just a handful of independently run sites exist, often in beautiful locations but with a minimum of amenities. Some hotels, notably at Petra, allow you to camp in their grounds. Several of the RSCN's nature reserves have excellent campsites, including Dana and Ajloun, but you have to pay for the tents that are provided: pitching your own tent is prohibited.

At Wadi Rum, all the local desert guides (and most of the outside companies that take tourists to Rum) have campsites for their own customers, comprising traditional bedouin black goat-hair tents pitched in some beauty spot, often with a decent toilet block, kitchen and even makeshift showers: all bedding and amenities are supplied. If you prefer to visit (and camp) alone, a tent is not normally necessary outside the winter months, but Rum can be chilly at night year-round, and tents do keep away scorpions – as well as the winter and spring rains. It's always preferable, of course, to sleep under the stars.

Elsewhere you should be judicious: the authorities disapprove of rough camping on the grounds of safety – though if you camp far away from habitation and tourist hot spots, no one will bother you. Always avoid lighting fires: wood is a very scarce commodity. Ideally, use a multi-fuel stove or camping gas.

Food and drink

Bedouin tradition values home cooking over eating out. As a consequence, most of Jordan's restaurants are simple places serving straightforward fare. Excellent restaurants do exist, but must be sought out. Unadventurous travellers can easily find themselves stuck in a rut of low-quality falafel and kebabs, departing the country never having tasted the best of what's on offer.

Unless you stick to a diet of familiar "international" cuisine and take every meal in upmarket hotels or restaurants, you're likely to be **eating with your fingers** at least some of the time – especially if you sample Arab styles of cooking, whether at low-budget hummus parlours or gourmet Lebanese restaurants. In budget diners, the only **cutlery** on the table will be a spoon, used to eat rice and soupy stews. More upmarket restaurants will provide cutlery, but even here, flaps or pockets of flat bread (similar to the pitta bread seen in the West) count as knife, fork and spoon – torn into pieces for scooping up dips, mopping up sauces, tearing meat off the bone and constructing personal one-bite sandwiches. Since the **left hand** is traditionally used for toilet purposes, Jordanians instinctively always eat only with the **right**. In restaurant situations no one will be mortally offended if you use your left hand for a tricky shovelling or tearing manoeuvre, but using your left hand while eating from a communal platter in someone's house would be considered unhygienic; see p.58 for more on this kind of etiquette.

Nowhere in the country can you avoid **cigarette smoke**, least of all in cafés and restaurants.

When to eat

Most people have **breakfast** relatively early, before 8am. Lunch is eaten between 1 and 3pm, and many people take a break around 6pm for coffee and sweet pastries. The main meal of the day is eaten late, rarely before 8pm; in Amman and Aqaba, restaurants may not start to fill up until 9.30 or 10pm. However, in keeping with the bedouin tradition of relying on home cooking, you'll find that even quite large towns in the bedouin heartland of southern Jordan, such as Madaba or Karak, have a bare handful of small, plain restaurants that do a roaring trade in early-evening takeaways and close up by 9pm.

Breakfast

The traditional Jordanian **breakfast** is a bowl of hot **fuul** (boiled fava beans mashed with lemon juice, olive oil and chopped chillis), always served with a long-handled ladle from a distinctive bulbous cooking jar and mopped up with fresh-baked *khubez* (flat bread) – guaranteed to keep you going for hours. **Hummus**, a cold dip of boiled chickpeas blended with lemon juice, garlic, sesame and olive oil, is lighter. Both *fuul* and hummus can be ordered to takeaway (*barra*) in plastic pots. Bakeries that have an open oven (*firin*) offer a selection of savoury pastries, including *khubez bayd* (a kind of small egg pizza) and bite-sized pastry triangles (*ftayer*) filled with cheese (*jibneh*), spinach (*sabanekh*), potato (*batata*) or meat (*lahmeh*). Larger bakeries also have chunky breadsticks, sesame-seed bread rings (*kaak*), thick slabs of crunchy toast (*garshella*) and rough brown bread (*khubez baladi*). Along with some olives (*zaytoon*) and yoghurt – either runny (*laban*) or creamy (*labneh*) – it's easy to put together a picnic breakfast.

Prices are nominal. A bowl of *fuul* or hummus costs around JD0.70; small baked nibbles JD0.20–0.40. Bread is sold by weight, with a kilo of large *khubez* (about five pieces) or small *khubez* (about eleven pieces) roughly JD0.50.

For a list of useful culinary terms in Arabic, see p.412.

An explanation of Jordan's money is on p.69.

Hotel breakfasts vary wildly. At budget establishments, expect pretty poor fare (thin bread, margarine, processed cheese, marmalade, and so on). Larger hotels, though, pride themselves on offering absurdly lavish breakfast buffets, encompassing hummus and other dips, dozens of choices of fresh fruit, fresh-baked bread of all kinds, pancakes with syrup, an omelette chef on hand and a variety of cooked options from hash browns, baked beans and fried mushrooms to "beef bacon" (a substitute for real bacon, which, being forbidden under Islam, is not available at most hotel buffets). Some offer Japanese specialities such as miso soup and sushi.

Street snacks

The staple **street snack** in the Middle East is **falafel**, small balls of a spiced chickpea paste deep-fried and served stuffed into *khubez* along with some salad, a blob of *tahini* (sesame-seed paste) and optional hot sauce (*harr*). Up and down the country you'll also find **shawerma** stands, with a huge vertical spit outside to tempt in customers. *Shawerma* meat is almost always lamb (only occasionally chicken), slabs of it compressed into a distinctive inverted cone shape and topped with chunks of fat and tomatoes to percolate juices down through the meat as it cooks – similar to a Turkish-style doner kebab. When you order a *shawerma*, the cook will dip a *khubez* into the fat underneath the spit and hold it against the flame until it crackles, then fill it with thin shavings of the meat and a little salad and hot sauce.

Depending on size, a falafel sandwich costs about JD0.50, a *shawerma* sandwich about JD1.

Restaurant meals

The cheapest budget **diners** will generally only have one or two main dishes on view – roast chicken or *fuul* or stew with rice – but you can almost always get hummus and salad to fill out the meal. In better-quality **Arabic restaurants**, the usual way to eat is

to order a variety of small starters (*mezze*), followed by either a selection of main courses to be shared by everyone, or a single, large dish for sharing.

Good Arabic restaurants might have thirty different choices of **mezze**, from simple bowls of hummus or *labneh* up to more elaborate mini-mains of fried chicken liver (*kibdet djaj*) or wings (*jawaneh*). Universal favourites are *tabbouleh* (parsley salad), *fattoush* (salad garnished with squares of crunchy fried bread), *warag aynab* (vine leaves stuffed with rice, minced vegetables, and often meat as well) and spiced olives. *Kibbeh* – the national dish of Syria and Lebanon and widely available at better Jordanian restaurants – is a mixture of cracked wheat, grated onion and minced lamb pounded to a paste; it's usually shaped into oval torpedoes and deep-fried, though occasionally you can find it raw (*kibbeh nayeh*), a highly prized delicacy. Portions are small enough that two people could share five or six *mezze* as a sizeable starter or, depending on your appetite, a complete meal. Bread and a few pickles are always free.

Mezze are the best dishes for **vegetarians** to concentrate on, with enough grains, pulses and vegetables to make substantial and interesting meat-free meals that cost considerably less than standard meat dishes. Filling dishes such as *mujeddrah* (lentils with rice and onions) and *mahshi* (cooked vegetables stuffed with rice) also fit the bill.

Main courses are almost entirely meat-based. Any inexpensive diner can do half a chicken (*nuss farooj*) with rice and salad. Kebabs are also ubiquitous (the chicken version is called *shish tawook*). Lots of places also do lunchtime meaty stews with rice; the most common is with beans (*fasooliyeh*), although others feature potatoes or a spinach-like green called *mulukhayyeh*.

Jordan's national speciality is the traditional bedouin feast-dish of *mensaf* – chunks of

Hidden costs and tipping

See p.64 for details of hidden service charges, and p.71 for guidance on tipping.

boiled lamb or mutton served on a bed of fatty rice, with pine nuts sprinkled on top and a tart, yoghurt-based sauce on the side to pour over. You'll also find some delicious Palestinian dishes, including *musakhan* (chicken steamed with onions and a sour-flavoured red berry called sumac) and *magloobeh* (essentially chicken with rice). A few places, mainly in Amman and the north, do a high-quality Syrian *fatteh* (meat or chicken cooked in an earthenware pot together with bread, rice, pine nuts, yoghurt, herbs and hummus, with myriad variations).

Good **fish** (*samak*) is rare in Jordan; Amman and Aqaba's fish restaurants can't match the succulent St Peter's fish served fresh at the *Resthouse* in Pella. **Pork** is forbidden under Islam and only appears at expensive Asian restaurants.

Simple meals of chicken, stew or kebabs won't **cost** more than about JD4 for a stomach-filling, if not gourmet, experience. Plenty of Arabic and foreign restaurants dish up varied, high-quality meals for JD8–10. It's possible to dine sumptuously on *mezze* at even the most expensive Arabic restaurants in the country for less than JD15 or JD20 per head, although meaty main courses and wine at these places can rapidly torpedo a bill into the JD40s per head without too much effort.

Sweets

A Western-bred, naughty-but-nice guilt-ridden attitude to confectionery can only quail in the face of the unabashedly sugar-happy, no-holds-barred Levantine sweet tooth: most **Arabic sweets** (*halawiyyat*) are packed with enough sugar, syrup, butter and honey to give a nutritionist the screaming horrors.

The traditional Jordanian way to round off a meal is with fresh fruit. Restaurants may offer a small choice of desserts, including some of the items described below, but inexpensive eateries frequently have nothing sweet. However, all large towns have plenty of **patisseries** for *halawiyyat*: it's common to take a quarter- or half-kilo away in a box to munch at a nearby coffee house.

There are three broad categories of *halawiyyat*: large round trays of hot, fresh-made confections, often **grain-based**, which are

sliced into squares and drenched in hot syrup; piles of pre-prepared, bite-sized honey-dripping **pastries** and cakes; and stacks of dry sesame-seed or date-filled **biscuits**. The best of the hot sweets made in trays is *k'naffy* (or *kunafeh* or *kanafa*), a heavenly Palestinian speciality of buttery shredded filo pastry layered over melted goat's cheese. *Baglawa* – layered flaky pastry filled with pistachios or other nuts – is available in any number of different varieties. Juice-stands often lay out tempting trays of *hareeseh*, a syrupy semolina almond-cake, sliced into individual portions. Of the biscuits, you'd have to go a long way to beat *maamoul*, buttery, crumbly rose-scented things with a date or nut filling. Everything is sold **by weight**, and you can pick and choose a mixture: a quarter-kilo (*wagiyyeh*) – rarely more than JD2 – is plenty for two.

Large restaurants and some patisseries also have **milk-based** sweets, often flavoured deliciously with rosewater. King of these is *muhallabiyyeh*, a semi-set almond cream pudding served in individual bowls, but the Egyptian speciality *Umm Ali* – not dissimilar to bread pudding, served hot, sprinkled with nuts and cinnamon – runs a close second.

Curiously elastic, super-sweet **ice cream** (*boozeh*) is a summer standard. During Ramadan bakeries and patisseries make fresh *gatayyif* – traditional **pancakes** – often on hotplates set up on the street. Locals buy stacks of them for stuffing at home with nuts and syrup.

Fresh fruit and picnic food

Street markets groan with **fresh fruit**, including apples from Shobak and oranges, mandarins and bananas from Gaza and the Jordan Valley. Local bananas (or the common Somali ones) are smaller, blacker and sweeter than the bland, oversized clones imported from Latin America. In the late spring, Fuheis produces boxes of luscious peaches; local grapes come from the Balqa and Palestine. Exquisite dates, chiefly Iraqi, Saudi and Omani, are available packed year-round and also fresh in late autumn, when you'll also see stalls selling small, yellow-orange fruit often still on the

Eating during Ramadan

Throughout the month of **Ramadan** (see p.395) Muslims are forbidden by both religious and civil law from **smoking** and from **eating or drinking** anything – including water and, in the strictest interpretations, even their own saliva – during the hours of daylight. Throughout Ramadan, almost all cafés and restaurants nationwide (apart from those in big hotels) stay closed until sunset, whereupon most do a roaring trade into the early hours. Markets, groceries and supermarkets are open during the day for purchases, with slightly truncated hours.

All shops close for an hour or two around dusk to allow staff to break the fast with family or friends – and this is a great time to join in. Restaurants of all kinds, including those within hotels, make the sunset "breakfast" meal – known as **iftar** – a real occasion, with special decorations, themed folkloric events or music and general merriment. Even the cheapest diners will rig up party lights and lay out tables and chairs on the street to accommodate crowds of people, all sitting down together to share the experience of breaking the day's fast. Many people have two or three light dinners as the evening goes on, moving from one group of friends or relatives to the next.

For **foreigners**, nothing serious will happen if you inadvertently light up a cigarette in public during the day, but the locals will not thank you for walking down the street munching a sandwich: if you do, expect lots of shouting and perhaps some unpleasantness. All four- and five-star hotels serve both food and soft drinks to foreigners during daylight, although they will only do so in places out of view of the street. If you're travelling on a tight budget and are buying picnic food for both breakfast and lunch, you'll need to exercise a good deal of tact during the day in eating either behind closed doors or well out of sight in the countryside.

It is illegal for supermarkets and the majority of restaurants (that is, all those below a certain star rating) to sell **alcohol** for the entire month. At the time of writing, it was possible for non-Jordanians to buy and consume alcohol during Ramadan in five-star hotels and a handful of independent restaurants (mostly in Amman), but you may find the rules have changed when you visit.

branch; these are *balah*, sweet, crunchy unripe dates that seldom make it to the West. Look out for pomegranates around the same time, while spring and summer are the season for local melon and watermelon.

For **picnic** supplements, most towns have a good range of stalls or mobile vendors selling **dried fruit** and roasted **nuts and seeds**. Raisins, sultanas, dried figs and dried apricots can all be found cheaply everywhere. The most popular kind of seeds are *bizr* (dry-roasted melon, watermelon or sunflower seeds), the cracking of which in order to get at the minuscule kernel is an acquired skill. Local almonds (*luz*) are delectable. Pistachios and roasted chickpeas are locally produced; peanuts, hazelnuts and cashews are imported. It's often possible to buy individual **hard-boiled eggs** from neighbourhood groceries, and varieties of the local salty white **cheese** (*jibneh*) are available everywhere.

Tea, coffee and other drinks

The main focus of every Jordanian village, town and city neighbourhood is a **coffee house**, where friends and neighbours meet, gossip does the rounds and a quiet moment can be had away from the family. The musicians, poets and storytellers of previous generations have been replaced everywhere by TV music or sport, although a genial, sociable ambience survives. However, traditional coffee houses (unlike the Starbucks-style espresso bars which predominate in West Amman and elsewhere) are exclusively male domains and bastions of social tradition; foreign women will always be served without hesitation, but sometimes might feel uncomfortably watched.

The national drink, lubricating every social occasion, is **tea** (*shy*), a strong, dark brew served scalding-hot and milkless in small glasses. The traditional method of tea-making is to boil up loose leaves in a pot together with several spoons of sugar to allow maximum flavour infusion. In deference to foreign taste buds, you may find the sugar being left to your discretion, but the tannins in steeped tea are so lip-curlingly bitter that you'll probably prefer the Jordanian way.

Coffee (*gahweh*), another national institution, has two broad varieties. **Turkish coffee** is what you'll come across most often. Made by boiling up cardamom-flavoured grounds in a distinctive long-handled pot, then letting it cool, then reboiling it several times (traditionally seven, though in practice two suffices), it's served in small cups along with a glass of water as chaser. Sugar is added beforehand, so you should request your coffee unsweetened (*saada*), medium-sweet (*wasat*) or syrupy (*helweh*). Let the grounds settle before sipping, and leave the last mouthful, which is mud, behind. **Arabic coffee**, also known as bedouin coffee, is an entirely different, almost greenish liquid, unsweetened and pleasantly bitter, traditionally made in a long-spouted brass pot set in hot embers. Public coffee houses don't have it, and you'll only be served it – often, rather prosaically, from a thermos flask – in a social situation by bedouin themselves (for example, if you're meeting with a police officer or government official, or if you're invited to a family tent in Wadi Rum).

Coffee houses also serve soft drinks and a wide range of seasonal **herbal teas**, including mint, fennel, fenugreek, thyme, sage and camomile. In colder seasons at coffee houses and street-stands, you'll come across the winter-warmer **sahleb**, a thick milky drink made from a ground-up orchid tuber and served very hot sprinkled with nuts, cinnamon and coconut.

A coffee house is also the place to try a tobacco-filled water pipe, known by different names around the Arab world but most familiarly in Jordan as a "**hubbly-bubbly**" or *argileh*. Many upscale restaurants offer an *argileh* as a postprandial digestive. It is utterly unlike smoking a cigarette: the tobacco is nearly always flavoured sweetly with apple or honey, and this, coupled with the smoke cooling as it bubbles through the water chamber before you inhale, makes the whole experience pleasant and soothing.

Water

Although Jordanians drink **water** freely from the tap, you might prefer not to: it is chlorinated strongly enough not to do you any harm (it just tastes bad), but the pipes it runs through add a quantity of rust and filth you could do without. All hotels above three stars have water filtration systems in place, which help. Bottles of **mineral water**, both local and imported, are available inexpensively in all corners of the country. A standard 1.5-litre size costs roughly JD0.35 if you buy it individually, less if you buy a six-pack from a supermarket or grocery. Expect to pay more in out-of-the-way places – JD1 or more inside Petra. Check that the seal is unbroken before you buy. Inexpensive diners always have jugs of tap water (*my aadi*) on the table, but in restaurants waiters will quite often bring an overpriced bottle of mineral water to your table with the menu – which you're quite entitled to reject. Recycling facilities for plastics are few and far between. If you can, crush the bottles that you buy and take them out of the country with you when you leave.

Fresh juice and squash

Most Jordanian towns have at least one stand-up **juice-bar**; these are great places for supplementing a meagre breakfast or replenishing your vitamin C. Any fruit in view can be juiced or puréed. Sugar (*sukkr*) and ice (*talj*) are automatically added to almost everything; however, considering ice blocks are often wheeled in filthy trolleys along the roadside and broken up with a screwdriver, you might like to give it a miss – if so, request your juice *bidoon talj* ("without sugar" is *bidoon sukkr*). Most freshly squeezed juices, and mixed juice cocktails, cost JD0.35–0.40 for a "small" glass (actually quite big), double that for a pint. Mango, strawberry and other exotic fruit cost a little more.

More popular, and thus easier to find, are much cheaper ready-made **fruit squashes**. Dark-brown *tamarhindi* (tamarind, tartly refreshing) and *kharroub* (carob, sweet-but-sour), or watery *limoon* (lemon squash) are the best bets; other, less common, choices include *soos* (made from liquorice root, also dark brown and horribly bitter) and *luz* (sickly sweet white almond-milk). All are around JD0.10 a glass.

Alcohol

Drinking **alcohol** is forbidden under Islam. That said, Jordan is not Saudi Arabia, and alcohol is widely available – but you have to look for it: the market streets and ordinary eateries of most towns show no evidence of the stuff at all.

Apart from in big hotels, the only **restaurants** to offer alcohol are upscale independently owned establishments and tourist resthouses at some archeological sites. Most big supermarkets and some smaller convenience stores sell alcohol. Amman has a lot of **bars**, not all of them inside hotels. Places such as Aqaba and Petra that serve tourists (or Madaba, with a prominent Christian population) also have some bars. Expect to find little or no alcohol elsewhere.

Drinking alcohol in public, or showing signs of drunkenness in public – which includes on the street, in cafés or coffee houses, in most hotel lobbies, on the beach or even in the seemingly empty desert or countryside – is utterly taboo and will cause great offence to local people.

The predominant local **beer** is Amstel, brewed under licence and very palatable. It's available in cans and bottles, and also on draught in some bars: a large glass costs around JD5.

There's a good range of Jordanian **wines**. The "Grands Vins de Jordanie" brand of Zumot (𝕎www.zumotgroup.com) includes fruity Cabernet and Merlot (labelled St George) and fresh, very drinkable Chardonnay/Sauvignon Blanc (labelled Machaerus). Haddad, trading as Eagle (𝕎www.eagledis .com), are best known for their bright Mount Nebo whites, alongside the Jordan River range which includes a Cabernet Sauvignon, a rich, plummy Shiraz and a light, spicy Chardonnay. These – along with widely available Palestinian "Holy Land" wines – are around JD6–10 a bottle, much less than imported wines. The top local **spirit** is anise-flavoured *araq* (similar to Turkish *raki*), drunk during a meal over ice, diluted with water. A bottle of premium *araq* – whether from Zumot, Eagle or more prestigious Lebanese distilleries – will set you back JD15 or so.

The media

With the widespread use of English in public life, you'll have relatively good access to news while in Jordan. International newspapers and magazines are on sale, the local English-language press is burgeoning and satellite TV is widespread.

Arabic press

Among the region's conservative and often state-owned **Arabic press**, Jordan's newspapers, all of which are independently owned, have a reputation for relatively well-informed debate, although strict press laws – and the slow process of media liberalization – cause much controversy. The two biggest dailies, *ad-Dustour* ("Constitution") and *al-Ra'i* ("Opinion"), are both centrist regurgitators of government opinion; *al-Ghad* ("Tomorrow") has a fresher outlook. There's a host of other dailies and weeklies, ranging from the sober to the sensational.

English-language press

International newspapers are widely available from the news kiosks in all big hotels and also from some bookshops. The *International Herald Tribune* and most British dailies and Sundays are generally one or two days late (JD2 and upwards). Look out for excellent regional papers such as *The National* (@www.thenational.ae), published daily in Abu Dhabi and available same day in Amman, and Cairo's *Al-Ahram Weekly* (@weekly.ahram.org.eg).

For **local newspapers** in English, the *Jordan Times* (@www.jordantimes.com) is published daily except Saturdays, featuring national news, agency reports and pro-government comment, as well as useful what's-on information. The weekly *Star* (@www.star.com.jo) tends to be more independent-minded, but it's a thin read.

There's a lively market for Jordanian **magazines**, with a range of English-language monthlies including glossy *Living Well* (@www.livingwell-magazine.com), upmarket lads' mag *Nox* (@www.nox-mag.com) and sober *Jordan Business* (@www.jordan-business.net). Plenty of international magazines are available, from *Cosmopolitan* to *The Economist*.

TV and radio

Jordanian TV (@www.jrtv.jo) isn't up to much. Almost all hotels have **satellite TV**, featuring CNN, BBC World News, Al Jazeera English, plus a few movies and sitcoms in English, alongside dozens of Arabic, European and Asian channels.

As well as stations devoted to Arabic pop and old-time classics, Amman has several English-language music **radio** stations playing Western rock and dance. Radio Jordan's English station (on 96.3FM in Amman and 855kHz AM nationwide) – mostly chart hits – has some news bulletins. **BBC World Service** (@www.bbcworldservice.com) broadcasts on 1323kHz AM (medium wave) but can be difficult to pick up.

Adventure tours and trekking

Taking an organized tour once you arrive in Jordan can turn out to be the most rewarding way to get to some of the more isolated attractions in the hinterland.

There are hundreds of Jordanian **tour operators** dealing with incoming tourism, but only a handful can take you off the beaten track: the principal outfits are listed below. To get a good idea of the terrain, as well as some route descriptions and advice, have a look at general Jordan-enthusiast websites, such as the well-informed @www.jordanjubilee.com and @www.nomadstravel.co.uk. See p.327 for a list of recommended desert guides at Wadi Rum.

Adventure tour operators and specialist independent guides in Jordan

Bait Ali ☎ 079 554 8133, @www.baitali.com. Small operation on the outskirts of Wadi Rum, run by Tahseen and Susan Shinaco. Their connections with the Swalhiyeen tribe, who occupy the lands north of Rum, give access to terrain that other guides in the area do not cover. As well as camels, jeeps and hiking, they offer adventure sports such as quad bikes and horseback safaris.

Cycling Jordan @www.cycling-jordan.com. Amman-based club of bike enthusiasts who organize regular group rides into the countryside and the desert, chiefly for locals (though all are welcome). Bikes, helmets and gear are provided.

Desert Guides ☎ 03 203 3508, @www.desertguides.com. Aside from trekking and climbing in the southern desert, this respected outfit run by qualified mountain guide and old Jordan hand Wilfried Colonna can arrange guided multi-day wilderness treks on pure-bred Arabian horses.

Desert Guides Company ☎ 06 552 7230, @www.desertguidescompany.com. Experts in horseriding tours in and around Wadi Rum (including a six-day ride from Petra to Rum), led by renowned adventure guide Hanna Jahshan. Also with a full deck of adventure options nationwide.

Camel rides

Many visitors from the West come to Jordan never having laid eyes on a **camel**, yet almost all arrive full of all kinds of ideas about the creatures; myths about the simplicity of desert life, the nobility of the bedouin and the Lawrence-of-Arabia-style romance of desert culture all seem to be inextricably bound up in Western minds with the camel. In truth, the bedouin long since gave up using camels either as a means of transport or as beasts of burden: Japanese pick-ups are faster, sturdier, longer-lived and less bad-tempered than your average dromedary. However, some tribes still keep a few camels, mostly for nostalgic reasons and the milk, though some breed and sell them. The bedouin that live in or close to touristed areas such as Petra and Rum have small herds of them to rent out for walks and desert excursions. There are no wild camels left in Jordan: any you see, in however remote a location, belong to someone.

If you're in any doubt about whether to take the plunge and have a **camel ride**, then rest assured that it's a wonderful experience. There's absolutely nothing to compare with the gentle, hypnotic swaying and soft shuffle of riding camel-back in the open desert. The Wadi Rum area is the best place in Jordan to try it out, with short and long routes branching out from Rum and Diseh all over the southern desert. Take as long as you like, but anything less than a couple of hours' riding isn't really worth it.

As a beginner's tip, the key to not falling off a camel is to hang onto the pommel between your legs; the animal gets up from sitting with a bronco-style triple jerk that flings you backwards, then forwards, then back again. If you're not holding on as soon as your bottom hits the saddle you're liable to end up in the dust. Once up and moving, you have a choice of riding your mount like a stirrupless horse, or copying the locals and cocking one leg around the pommel.

Discovery ☎ 06 569 7998, ⊛ www.discovery1 .com. An environmentally aware approach to sustainable tourism, coupled with an encyclopedic knowledge of natural and historical attractions in all corners of the country. Specializing in incentive travel for companies, but with a vast range of all kinds of trips and adventure tours on offer.

Jordan Beauty ☎ 079 558 1644, ⊛ www .jordanbeauty.com. Specialists in hiking and trekking, specifically in the Petra area, with excellent local knowledge. Also able to construct innovative, keenly priced tours around the country.

Jordan Inspiration ☎ 077 609 7581, ⊛ www .jitours.com. Small, flexible company based in Wadi Musa, with a wide range of tour options in Petra and around the country.

Jordan Tracks ☎ 079 648 2801, ⊛ www .jordantracks.com. Specialized team based in Wadi Rum, focusing on desert services but also able to put together modest trips around Jordan.

La Beduina ☎ 03 215 7099, ⊛ www .labeduinatours.com. Specialists in fully supported adventure trips and treks in and around Petra, but also offering a broad range of itineraries nationwide including diving, mountain-biking and horseriding. Flexible enough to put together any sort of itinerary at short notice.

Petra Moon ☎ 03 215 6665, ⊛ www.petramoon .com. One of Jordan's leading adventure tour operators, and unique in offering low-impact jeep trips into the remote countryside around Petra. Very well connected, they can set you up with good local guides for hikes and long-distance horse or camel rides, and give you full backup support all the way.

Terhaal ☎ 05 325 1005, ⊛ www.terhaal.com. Outstanding eco-aware adventure tour company based in Madaba that has been instrumental in opening up new hiking and mountain-biking routes off the King's Highway around Mukawir. Specialists in canyoning in the Dead Sea gorges, with many unique routes and combinations. Also with scuba and other options, including Petra hikes and scrambling in Rum – alongside a full programme of regular group trips that are open to all.

Wild Jordan (RSCN) ☎ 06 463 3589 or 461 6523, ⊕ tourism@rscn.org.jo, ⊛ www.rscn.org.jo. Wild Jordan is the ecotourism arm of Jordan's dynamic Royal Society for the Conservation of Nature (RSCN), which creates and protects all of Jordan's nature reserves as part of a national programme emphasizing nature conservation (including wildlife reintroductions) and environmental issues. They have exclusive responsibility for developing sustainable tourism in the reserves: no other operator runs trekking and camping inside the Dana reserve, canyoning and gorge-walking within Wadi Mujib, forest walks at Ajloun or Dibbeen, or birdwatching at the Azraq Wetlands (all of which are protected areas). Their eco credentials are impeccable, and they work closely with local people, developing socioeconomic projects to support communities living in and near the reserves. The eco-friendly lodges and cabins they design to accommodate visitors are staffed by locals. Prices are concomitantly higher than elsewhere – but your money could barely go to a better cause.

Yamaan Safady ☎ 079 564 1911, ⓦ www .adventurejordan.com. One of Jordan's most prominent and experienced adventure tour guides (with certification in mountain search and rescue and first aid), Yamaan organizes regular adventure trips for locals and tourists to canyons and mountain sites all round Jordan, publicized via his email list. You generally have to bring your own gear (change of clothes or shoes, sleeping bag if on an overnight trek, etc) as well as food and water.

Trekking

The opportunities for getting out into Jordan's varied landscapes are limited only by your own preparation and fitness. It's easy for anyone of moderate ability to embark on half- or full-day **walks** from most towns. What you can't expect is any kind of trail support: no signposts, no refreshment facilities and often no trail markers; there are also virtually no maps useful for walkers available. In recompense, you'll generally be walking alone in pristine countryside. For greater insight, and a full range of detailed route descriptions, your best bet is to get hold of almost the only book on the subject – *Jordan: Walks, Treks, Caves, Climbs and Canyons* by Di Taylor and Tony Howard (2008 edition; see p.404).

Trekking in Jordan is in its infancy, other than in the unique mountains and deserts of Wadi Rum, where it plays an important role in the local economy: as at Petra, trekking services at Rum are offered by **local people** who still proudly consider themselves bedouin. Plenty of the best routes in and around Rum – as well as ancient caravan trails around Petra – are known only to the locals.

Elsewhere, only a handful of individuals and the **RSCN** (Royal Society for the Conservation of Nature) understand the theory and practice of trekking. Through its "Wild Jordan" office, the RSCN offers carefully controlled access to the country's **nature reserves** – environmentally fragile, protected landscapes that are largely off-limits to visitors: the RSCN allows trekking only on **designated trails** with qualified RSCN nature guides. On no account should you enter the reserves without permission, or stray off-trail.

Outside these places, in the rugged mountains near Aqaba or the green hills of the far north, for example, there are no marked trails and no guides. Indeed, it is highly unlikely that while walking you'll come across anyone other than locals, some of whom may be happy to guide you – and all of whom will welcome you with the full warmth of Jordanian hospitality. Offers of tea and refreshment are likely to flow thick and fast as you pass through rural villages.

See p.43 for guidance on camping.

Terrain

Jordan's **terrain** is spectacularly varied. Anyone expecting a desert country will be astonished by the alpine-style meadows of **north Jordan**, which are carpeted in flowers in springtime, warm breezes carrying the aromas of herbs and pine. The hills of Ajloun in April are simply captivating – a gentle terrain, with no real hazards other than the lack of water. The RSCN's forest reserves at Ajloun and Dibbeen offer access into the area.

The **Dead Sea hills**, also dubbed the "Mountains of Moab", offer a more savage prospect, gashed by wild canyons which flash-flood after rains. They require respectful treatment. Their northern reaches fall within the boundaries of the RSCN's **Mujib** reserve, where you can tackle the spectacular descent of the Mujib gorge, though independent adventure guides also offer access to similar exploration of neighbouring canyons outside the reserve such as Wadi Zarqa Ma'in or Wadi Mukheiris.

The southern part of the Moab hills around **Karak**, with excellent trekking and canyoning, is also outside the Mujib reserve. Hiking here, alongside water in the midst of harsh desert terrain, is always a pleasure. This part of the country is still very much off the beaten track, but you may be able to find

Aerial adventures

Jordan's **Royal Aero Sports Club** (☎03 205 8050, ⓦwww.royalaeroclub.com), based at Aqaba airport, runs **sightseeing flights** in microlights or ultralights, from JD30 for a short overfly of the beach to JD80 for an excursion around the bay. **Skydiving** from 10,000 feet, done while hooked to an instructor, costs JD240. At least three passengers can take a serene one-hour journey at dawn by **hot-air balloon** over the deserts of Wadi Rum, for JD130 per person. All these must be booked in advance.

On Fridays the **Royal Jordanian Gliding Club** (☎06 487 4587, ⓦwww .rjglidingclub.com), based at Marka airport in Amman, can take you up for a uniquely silent view of the capital for about JD15.

a company or a specialist guide organizing trips to the beautiful and varied canyon of Wadi ibn Hammad.

Further south is the RSCN reserve at **Dana**, its ancient village perched like an eyrie above the wild Wadi Dana. This is, understandably, the pride of the RSCN, who organize some excellent treks past oases and ancient copper mines down to their wilderness lodge in Wadi Faynan, as well as other routes in far-flung parts of these hills, including around their remote Rummana campsite.

The fabulous city of **Petra** is concealed beyond the next range of hills to the south. While you could spend days hiking around this remarkable site, most walkers will feel the urge to explore further. Navigating paths through this craggy range of mountains is, however, extremely complex, and waterholes are few: until you gain confidence in the area, you should take a local guide. Independent guides offer a superb four-night wilderness trek from Faynan (on the edge of the Dana reserve) all the way to Petra, and local companies in Wadi Musa can set up excellent week-long camel- or horseriding treks from Petra to Rum.

At **Wadi Rum**, don't let the multitudes of tour buses deter you. Out in the desert, away from the very few, well-travelled, one-hour safari routes taken by day-trippers, all is solitude. The rock climbing in Rum is world-famous, but for the walker there is also much to offer, both dramatic canyon scrambles and delightful desert valleys. Again, be sure of your abilities if you go without a guide: bedouin camps are rare and only those intimate with Rum will find water. Far better is to get to know the local bedouin

and hire a guide: a real desert experience is just as much about the people as the place. The rigorous ascent of the mighty Jebel Rum by a bedouin hunting route – well known to qualified guides – or the relatively easy scramble to the summit of Jebel Umm ad-Daami, Jordan's highest mountain, is a world-class experience open to any fit and confident person.

Clothing, equipment and preparation

You should take a minimalist approach to **clothing** and **equipment**. Heavy boots aren't necessary; good, supportive trainers or very lightweight boots are adequate. Quality socks are important and should be washed or changed frequently to keep the sand out and minimize blisters. Clothing, too, should be lightweight and cotton or similar: long trousers and long-sleeved tops will limit dehydration and are essential on grounds of modesty when passing through villages or visiting bedouin camps. A sunhat, proper protective sunglasses and high-factor sunblock are also essential, as are a light windproof top and fleece. Basic **trip preparation** also includes carrying a mobile phone (bear in mind that coverage can be patchy, particularly on mountains and in canyons), a watch, a medical kit and a compass, and knowing how to use them all. You should carry a minimum of three litres of water per day for an easy walk, perhaps six or eight litres per day for exertive treks or multi-day trips. On **toilet procedures**, if you're caught short in the wilds, make sure that you squat far away from trails and water supplies, and bury the result deeply. Toilet paper is both unsightly and unhygienic (goats will eat anything!); the best way to clean yourself is with water, but if you must use paper, either burn it or store it in a plastic bag and dispose of it correctly when you get back to a town.

Part of your preparation for trekking in Jordan must involve familiarizing yourself with the dangers of **flash floods**, most pertinently if you intend walking in narrow valleys and canyons, even in the desert: deluges are life-threatening. You should carry 10m of **rope** for emergency use.

There are no official search and rescue organizations, so, however straightforward your hike may seem, you must **always tell someone** responsible (such as a reliable friend or the tourist police) where you are going. You must then follow or stick close to your stated route, and check in when you return or reach your destination.

Hiring trekking/adventure guides

Fees for **trekking guides** vary throughout Jordan. The **RSCN** sets its own rates within each of the reserves – at the time of writing, for instance, in Dana a group of up to 18 people pays JD15–20 for one hour or JD35–40 for six hours, whereas in Mujib each person pays around JD10 to be guided along an easy trail (2–3hr) or up to JD45 for guiding on a full-day trek. As visitor numbers to the reserves are limited, you should always book well in advance.

In **Rum**, you should reckon on roughly JD50–60 per person for a high-quality full-day jeep tour in a vehicle seating four to six people with a knowledgeable English-speaking guide, including dinner, overnight desert camping with everything provided, and breakfast. (Cheaper deals are widely available – but you get what you pay for.) Guiding on scrambles and climbs that require ropes for safety costs considerably more, in the order of JD150–200 per day – and rightly so; it's a responsible job. Whatever you're planning, it's always best to book ahead.

Rates are similar in the Petra area, where adventure/trekking guides are only bookable through local tour companies. To be guided on a private one-day adventure trek – for instance through a gorge such as Wadi bin Hammad near Karak, Wadi Ghweir near Dana or one of the canyons above the Dead Sea – expect to pay in the order of JD80–120 per person, less if it's on easier terrain (and less if you join a scheduled group trip, such as through one of the operators listed on p.50).

If you've enjoyed your trip, **tipping your guide** is entirely appropriate. Ten percent would be fine, but you may want to give more – or perhaps a gift of a useful item of clothing or equipment. RSCN guides working in the reserves are not allowed to accept tips.

Culture and etiquette

Your experience of Jordanian people is likely to be that they are, almost without exception, decent, honest, respectful and friendly. It seems only right that you should return some of that respect by showing a grasp of some basic aspects of Jordanian, Arab and Muslim culture.

If it's possible to generalize, the three things that annoy local people most about foreign tourists in Jordan are **immodest dress**, **public displays of affection** and **lack of social respect**. In this section we try to explain why, and how to avoid causing upset.

Nonetheless, as you travel through the country you will doubtless see dozens of tourists breaking these taboos (and others),

Words of welcome

Ahlan wa sahlan is the phrase you'll hear most often in Jordan. It's most commonly rendered as "welcome", but translates directly as "family and ease", and so might come out better in English along the lines of "Relax and make yourself at home [in my house/shop/city/country]". With hospitality a fundamental part of Arab culture, there's no warmer or more open-hearted phrase in the language. Everybody uses it, in all situations of meeting and greeting, often repeated like a mantra in long strings.

As a visitor, you needn't ever say *ahlan wa sahlan* yourself, but you'll have to field torrents of them from the locals. The proper response – even if you're walking past without stopping – is *ahlan beek* (*beeki* if you're talking to a woman). Alternatively you can acknowledge the welcome with a smile and *shukran* ("thank you") or an informal *ahlayn!* ("double *ahlan* back to you!").

The catch-all word used to invite someone – whether welcoming an old friend into your home or inviting a stranger to share your lunch (surprisingly common) – is **itfuddal**, often said together with *ahlan wa sahlan*. Translations of *itfuddal* (*itfuddalee* to a woman, *itfuddaloo* to more than one person) can vary, depending on circumstance, from "Come in" to "Go ahead" to "Can I help you?" to "Here you are", and many more. A respectful response, whether or not you want to take up the offer, is to smile and say *shukran* ("thank you").

sometimes unwittingly, sometimes deliberately. Nothing bad happens to them. Jordan is a relatively liberal society and there are no Saudi-style religious police marching around to throw offenders in jail. Jordanians would never be so rude as to tell visitors to their country that they are being crass and insensitive; instead, they'll smile and say, "Welcome to Jordan!" – but still, the damage has been done. You might prefer to be different.

Incidentally, you may also see Jordanians acting and dressing less conservatively than we recommend here. That is, of course, their prerogative – to shape, influence or challenge their own culture from within, in whatever ways they choose. It goes without saying that tourists do not share the same rights over Jordanian culture. The onus is on visitors to fit in.

Dress codes

Outward appearance is the one facet of interaction between locals and Western tourists most open to misunderstandings on both sides. A lot of tourists, male and female, consistently flout simple **dress codes**, unaware of just how much it widens the cultural divide and demeans them in the eyes of local people. Clothes that are unremarkable at home can come across in Jordan as being embarrassing, disrespectful or offensive.

Jordanians and Palestinians place a much greater emphasis on personal grooming and style of dress than people tend to in the West: for them, consciously "dressing down" in torn or holey clothes is unthinkable. In addition, for reasons of **modesty**, many people expose as little skin as possible, with long sleeves and high necklines for both sexes.

Male dress codes

Visiting tourists who wear **shorts** on the street give roughly the same impression that they would wandering around Bournemouth or Baltimore in their underpants. **Long trousers** are essential in the city, the country and the desert, whatever the weather – clean and respectable light cotton, denim or canvas ones in plain colours (not flimsy, brightly patterned beach-style trousers). If you must wear shorts, go for the loose-fitting knee-length variety rather than brief, shape-hugging athlete's shorts. Any top that doesn't cover your shoulders and upper arms counts as underwear. Wear a T-shirt if you like, but a **buttoned shirt** broadcasts a sounder message about the kind of value you place on cultural sensitivity. Jordanian men never, in any situation, walk around topless.

From a woman's perspective – some sample experiences

"It's easy for women to travel alone in Jordan. You'll be pleasantly surprised, as I was, by people's reactions – the best preparation is just to head out with self-confidence, curiosity and a sense of humour. People are extremely willing to help, and almost everyone invited me for tea – a boy selling tablecloths, taxi-drivers, even the guardian in the museum.

Travelling for a time with a male friend felt a little unreal. Suddenly, people stopped talking to me and paid attention only to him. This was probably due more to respect for me than condescension, but I couldn't help feeling a little upset – though it put me in a great position to just observe events.

It is vital to be able to take things lightly. For instance, I was followed by a bunch of teenage boys for at least an hour through the whole of Salt. They had a great time, running around and making jokes. My mistake was to try and get away. I should have stayed and talked to them, lived up to my role and – best of all – taken a picture. They'd have loved that."

Anna Hohler, journalist

"One day in Karak, I was doing some exercises in my hotel room. The door was locked, the shades were down. I happened to glance up. Above the closet there was a small set of windows (hadn't noticed them before), with a man's face, quickly disappearing.

The following morning, when I saw Mr Peeper in the lobby, he stared right at me without an ounce of shame. Being spied on is no surprise in any culture, but his lack of shame was a cultural lesson for me – not about relations between men and women in Jordan (because I think Jordanian women command a great deal of respect), but rather because I was assumed not to question his rights over my body.

Female dress codes

To interact as a Western woman in Jordanian society with some degree of mutual respect, you'll probably have to go to even greater lengths than men to adjust your normal style of dress, although it is possible to do so without compromising your freedom and individuality too much. **Loose-fitting, opaque clothes** that cover your legs, arms and chest are a major help in allowing you to relate normally with local men. On women, **shorts** appear flagrantly provocative and sexual, as do Lycra leggings. **T-shirts** are also best avoided. The **nape of the neck** is considered particularly erotic and so is best covered, either by a high collar or a thin cotton scarf.

Hair is another area where conservatism helps deter unwanted attention. Jordanian women who don't wear a headscarf rarely let long hair hang below their shoulders; you might like to follow suit and clip long hair up. To some people, women with **wet hair** are advertising sexual availability, so you may prefer to dry your hair before going out. If your hair is **blonde**, you must unfortunately resign yourself to a bit more inquisitive attention – at least when walking in more conservative areas.

Social interactions

Social interaction in Jordan is replete with all kinds of seemingly impenetrable verbal and behavioural rituals, most of which can remain unaddressed by foreigners with impunity. A few things are worth knowing, however.

The energy which Jordanians put into social relationships can bring shame to Westerners used to keeping a distance. Total strangers greet each other like chums and chat happily about nothing special, passers-by ask each other's advice or exchange opinions without a second thought, and old friends embark on five-minute volleys of salutations and cheek-kisses, joyful arm-squeezing or back-slapping, and earnest enquiries after health, family, business and news. Foreigners more used to avoiding

You can regulate the respect you receive according to the way you dress. Complying with the standards of the place you're visiting relieves you from harassment. It also signals your intention to understand. The assumptions about Western women are so image-based that changing your image will change your reception. It's as simple as that."

Karinne Keithley, dancer

"Living and working in Jordan was rewarding and very comfortable. Modifying my dress and behaviour to match social norms helped immensely. Just wearing loose clothes and long-sleeved shirts made me feel more confident and relaxed, especially in more traditional areas, and allowed local people to take me seriously. Being friendly with men I didn't know inevitably got me in trouble, since they interpreted it as flirting: I tried never to smile at men on the street and to keep my interactions with waiters and shopkeepers on a reserved and businesslike footing. This doesn't mean I didn't get stared at – I did. But I came to accept that in some places, as a foreigner, I was an exotic sight to be seen, as much as Jordanian people are exotic to visitors.

The flipside of avoiding men's stares was that I could smile and look freely at women. Since most women adopt a serious, frozen expression on the street it was a great surprise, smiling tentatively at a woman passer-by or exchanging a few words of greeting, to see her face light up with a broad smile in response. I had an immediate, spontaneous connection which surpassed words and cultural differences."

Michelle Woodward, photographer

strangers and doing business in shops quickly and impersonally can come across as cold, uninterested and even snooty. Smiling, learning one or two of the standard forms of **greeting** (see p.408), acknowledging those who are welcoming you and taking the time to exchange pleasantries will bring you closer to people more quickly than anything else.

People **shake hands** in Jordan much more than in the West, and even the merest contact with a stranger is normally punctuated by at least one or two handshakes to indicate fraternity.

Personal space

Personal space is treated rather differently in Arab cultures from in the West: for all intents and purposes, it doesn't exist. **Queuing** is a foreign notion, and in many situations hanging back deferentially is an invitation for other people to move in front. Jordanians also relate to the **natural environment** rather differently from Westerners. Sitting alone or with a friend in

the most perfectly tranquil spot, you may well find someone coming up to you blocking the sunset and eager for a chat. It can be difficult, if not impossible, to convey your desire to be alone.

Invitations

It's almost inevitable that during your time in Jordan you'll be **invited** to drink tea with someone, either in their shop or their home, and it's quite likely too that at some point you'll be invited for a full meal at someone's house. Jordanians take hospitality very much to heart, and are honestly interested in talking to you and making you feel comfortable. However, offers tend to flow so thick and fast that it would be difficult to agree to every one, yet people are often so eager it can also be difficult – and potentially rude – to refuse outright.

First and foremost, whether you're interested or not, is to take the time to chat civilly; nothing is more offensive than walking on without a word or making an impatient gesture, even if they're the twentieth person

Gestures and body language

There's a whole range of **gestures** used in Arab culture which will either be new to you or which carry different meanings from the same gesture in your home country. Rather than nodding, **yes** is indicated by inclining your head forwards and closing your eyes. **No** is raising your eyebrows and tilting your head up and back, often accompanied by a little "tsk" noise (which *doesn't* indicate impatience or displeasure). Shaking your head from side to side means **I don't understand**. A very useful gesture, which can be used a hundred times a day in all kinds of situations, is **putting your right hand over your heart**: this indicates genuineness or sincerity, and can soften a "no thanks" to a street-seller or a "sorry" to a beggar, or reinforce a "thank you very much" to someone who's helped you. Many people in the south of Jordan will instinctively touch their right hand to their heart after shaking hands.

One hand held out with the palm upturned and all five fingertips pressed means **wait**. A side-to-side wrist-pivot of one hand at chest level, palm up with the fingers curled, means **what do you want?** If someone holds their flat palm out to you and draws a line across it with the index finger of the other hand, they're asking you for whatever **document** seems relevant at the time – usually a passport. You can make the same gesture to ask for the bill (check) in a restaurant.

Pointing at someone or something directly with your index finger, as you might do at home, in Jordan casts the evil eye; instead you should gesture imprecisely with two fingers, or just flap your whole hand in the direction you mean. **Beckoning** with your palm up has cutesy and overtly sexual connotations; instead you should beckon with your palm facing the ground and all four fingers together making broom-sweeping motions towards yourself.

In all Arab cultures, knowingly showing the **soles of your feet or shoes** to someone is a direct insult. Foreigners have some leeway to err, but you should be aware of it when crossing your legs while sitting: crossing ankle-on-knee means your sole is showing to the person sitting next to you. Copying the Jordanian style of sitting on a chair – always keeping both feet on the floor – is safest. Sitting on the floor requires some foot-tucking to ensure no one is in your line of fire. Putting your feet up on chairs or tables is not done.

Another major no-no is **picking your teeth** with your fingers; you'd break fewer social taboos if you were to snort, spit into a plastic bag, jiggle a finger in your ear and pick your nose in public. Most diners and restaurants offer toothpicks, which should be used surreptitiously behind your palm.

that day to stop you. If you're invited and you don't want to accept, a broad smile with your head lowered, your right hand over your heart and "*shukran shukran*" ("thank you, thank you") is a clear, but socially acceptable, no. You may have to do this several times – it's all part of the social ritual of polite insistence. Adding "*marra okhra, insha'allah*" ("another time, if God wills it") softens the "no" still further, indicating that you won't forget their kind offer.

The advice below applies if you have personally been invited to a private gathering. If you are attending, for example, a "bedouin dinner" as part of a tour-group itinerary, the event is commercial: you are paying for the experience, so the same social norms and

values don't apply. In this situation, your bedouin hosts will be tourism professionals, probably with good English.

Before the meal

If you're invited to eat with someone **at home** and you choose to accept, the first thing to consider is how to **repay your host's hospitality**. Attempting to offer money would be deeply offensive – what is appropriate is to bring some token of your appreciation. A kilo or two of sweet pastries handed to your host as you arrive will be immediately ferreted away out of sight and never referred to again; the gesture, however, will have been appreciated. Otherwise, presenting gifts directly will generally cause embarrassment, since complex social etiquette demands that such a gift be refused several times before acceptance. Instead, you can acknowledge your appreciation by giving gifts to the small children: pens, small toys, notebooks, even picture-postcards of your home country will endear you to your hosts much more than might appear from the monetary value of such things.

It's worth pointing out that you should be much more sparing and – above all – generalized in praising your host's home and decor than is common in the West, since if you show noticeable interest in a particular piece, big or small, your host is obliged to give it to you. Minefields of complex verbal jockeyings to maintain dignity and family honour then open up if you refuse to accept the item in question. Many local people keep their reception rooms relatively bare for this reason.

If you're a **vegetarian**, you would be quite within social etiquette to make your dietary preferences clear before you accept an invitation. Especially in touristy areas, vegetarianism is accepted as a Western foible and there'll be no embarrassment on either side. Elsewhere, it can help to clarify what seems an extraordinary and unfamiliar practice by claiming it to be a religious or medical obligation. All their best efforts notwithstanding, though, veggies should prepare themselves to have to sit down in front of a steaming dish of fatty meat stew and tuck in heartily, while still looking like they're enjoying it.

During and after the meal

This section outlines some of the things which may happen once you **sit down to eat** with a family. It may all seem too daunting for words to try and remember everything here. The bottom line is, you don't: you'd have to act truly outrageously to offend anyone deeply. Your host would never be so inhospitable as to make a big deal about some social blunder anyway.

Once you arrive for a meal, you may be handed a thimbleful of bitter **Arabic coffee** as a welcoming gesture; down it rapidly, since everyone present must drink before

sociabilities can continue. Hand the cup back while jiggling your wrist: this indicates you don't want any more (if you just hand it straight back, you'll get a refill). The meal – often a *mensaf* (see p.45) – may well be served **on the floor** if you're in a tent, generally with the head of the household, his adult sons and any male friends squatting on one knee or sitting cross-legged around a large communal platter; Western women count as males for social purposes and will be included in the circle. As guest of honour, you may be invited to sit beside the head of the household. Even if wives and daughters are present, they almost certainly won't eat with you, and you may find that they all stay out of sight in another part of the tent or house for the duration of your visit. If they do, it would be grossly impertinent to enquire after them.

Once the food appears (generally served by the women), and the host has wished you "*sahtayn!*" ("[May you eat] with two appetites!"), you should confine yourself to eating – strictly with your right hand only – from that part of the platter directly in front of you. Your host may toss over into your sector choice bits of meat – probably just ordinary bits, but perhaps the tongue, brains or, as an outside possibility, the eyes – which, if they land in front of you, it would be inexplicable to refuse. It's possible that everyone present will share a single **glass of water**, so if the only glass visible is put in front of you, it's not a cue for you to down it.

While eating, locals will be careful not to **lick their fingers**, instead rolling their rice and meat into a little ball one-handed and popping it in from a short distance; however, it takes ages to learn how to do this without throwing food all over yourself, and you'll have enough social leeway to subtly cram in a fistful as best you can. It's no embarrassment – in fact, it's almost obligatory – to make a horrible greasy mess of your hands and face. People do not linger over eating, and rarely pause to chat: you may find that everyone chomps away more or less in silence.

Stop eating (or slow down) **before you're full**, partly because as soon as you stop you'll be tossed more food, and partly because no one will continue eating after you – the guest of honour – have stopped (so if you sit back too soon you'll be cutting the meal short). Never finish all the food in front of you, since not only does this tag you as greedy, it's also an insult to your host, who is obliged to keep your plate well stocked. Bear in mind, too, that dinner for the women and children is whatever the men (and you) leave behind.

When you've **finished**, your right hand over your heart and the words "*al-hamdu-lillah*" ("thank God") make clear your satisfaction.

Everyone will get up and walk away to wash hands and face with soap, before adjourning to lounge on cushions, perhaps around the fire. **Coffee** will be served in tiny handleless cups; take two or three before returning the cup with a jiggle of your wrist. Then there'll be endless glasses of sweet, black **tea**, along with bonhomie, conversation and possibly an *argileh*. It's your host's unspoken duty to keep the tea flowing whatever happens, so after you've had enough – one or two glasses at least – stem the tide by saying "*da'iman*" ("may it always be thus") and then simply ignore your full glass.

Couples: displaying affection

Couples travelling together need to be aware of Jordanian social norms. Put simply, **public displays of affection** between men and women are not acceptable. Even if you're married, walking arm-around-waist or arm-over-shoulder, touching each other's face or body or kissing each other are likely to be viewed as deeply distasteful – as if you were bringing the intimacy of the bedroom into the public sphere. It is possible occasionally in Amman to see husbands and wives walking hand-in-hand, but it's rare.

Answering questions

People will be genuinely (and innocently) interested in you as visitors, and their **questions** may flow thick and fast. Aside from "What's your name?" and "Where are you from?", you're likely to be asked about how many **children** you've got, what their names are, why you don't have more, and so on. If you have none, *lissa* ("later") or

masha'allah ("according to God's will") are two respectful, comprehensible ways to say so. Other useful phrases are given on p.410. Having a few photos to pass around (even if they're digital images on a phone or camera) of children, parents, brothers, sisters, nephews and nieces can break the ice, should any ice need breaking. However, note that men never enquire after another man's **wife** – not even her name: the conversation should stay strictly on work and kids.

If you're travelling as an **unmarried couple**, saying "We're just good friends" means little and merely highlights the cultural divide. Being able to show a wedding/engagement ring (a cheap fake will do), even if you have no nuptials planned, makes things instantly clear and understandable. See p.410 for how to say "We're getting married next year" in Arabic, along with other handy phrases. For a woman travelling alone, a ring – indicating an absent husband – is a powerful signifier of respectability.

Gay and lesbian travellers

Homosexual acts are illegal in Jordan. Amman has a small underground **gay** scene, for the most part invisible to outsiders. Social disapproval of an overtly gay lifestyle is strong: dalliances between young, unmarried men are sometimes understood as "letting off steam", but they are accepted – if at all – only as a precursor to the standard social model of marriage and plenty of kids. Although women form strong bonds of friendship with each other to the exclusion of men, public perception of **lesbianism** is almost nonexistent, although again Amman has a small, word-of-mouth scene.

A by-product of the social divisions between men and women, though, is that visiting gay or lesbian couples can feel much freer about limited **public displays of affection** than straight couples: cheek-kissing, eye-gazing and hand-holding between same-sex friends in public is normal and completely socially acceptable.

Sexual harassment

Sexual harassment of **women travellers** in Jordan is extremely rare. As outlined above, the single most effective way to stop it happening at all is to understand the Jordanian concept of **modesty** and to dress accordingly.

Most harassment never goes beyond the verbal – perhaps including hissing or making kissy noises – and unless you're sufficiently well versed in Arabic swear-words to respond in kind (worth it for the startled looks), it's ignorable.

A tiny fraction of incidents involve groping. If you take the fight to your harasser, by pointing at him directly, shouting angrily and slapping away his hand, you're likely to **shame** him to his roots in front of his neighbours. Accusing him of bringing himself and his country into public disrepute – *aayib!* is Arabic for "shame!" – is about the most effective dissuasive action you could take.

Onlookers are likely to be embarrassed and apologetic for your having suffered harassment. Unmarried or unrelated men and women do not touch each other in public (apart from possibly to shake hands in a formal setting), and any man who touches you, even on the elbow to guide you, has overstepped the mark and knows it.

More serious harassment – blocking your path or refusing to leave you alone – is even less likely, and assault is virtually unknown. In Jordan strangers are much more likely to help a foreigner in distress than might be the case at home, and in an emergency you shouldn't hesitate to appeal directly for help to shopkeepers or passers-by, or to bang on the nearest front door.

Shopping for crafts

Unlike Syria, Palestine and Egypt, the trading history of Jordan mostly revolves around goods passing through rather than being produced; no city within the boundaries of modern Jordan has ever come close to matching the craftsmanship on display in the workshops and bazaars of Aleppo, Damascus, Jerusalem and Cairo.

Traditionally, people in Jordan have simply made whatever they needed for themselves – carpets, jugs, jewellery – without their skills being noticed or valued by outside buyers. Today, although a handful of outlets around the country sell local (and some imported) **crafts**, Jordan has no Damascus-style craft bazaars. You may come across items of aesthetic value here and there, but your chances of picking up bargain antiques are very small, and any that you might come across almost certainly originate from outside Jordan. For the record, Jordanian law forbids the purchase of any item dating from before 1700.

There are only three rules of **bargaining**: first, never to start the process unless you want to buy; second, never, even in jest, to let a price pass your lips that you're not prepared to pay; and third, never to lose your temper. However, the lack of a tradition of bazaar-style haggling results in a reluctance among Jordanian merchants even to embark on the process. In most everyday situations, you'll rapidly be brought up short against an unbudgeable last price – which, unlike in the Cairo or Damascus bazaars, really is the last price, take it or leave it.

Embroidery and weaving

The field where Transjordanian people have the strongest tradition is in **hand-embroidered textiles**, although up to a few decades ago such fabrics tended to stay within the confines of the town producing them and generally never came onto the open market. Embroidered jackets, dresses and cushion covers are now available everywhere, in both traditional and modern styles, but relatively few are high-quality, handmade items.

Sheep's wool and goat's hair have been used since time immemorial to **weave** tents, carpets, rugs, cushions, even food-storage containers, for family use; the two fibres woven together form a waterproof barrier. Rarer camel hair went to make rugs. Up until the 1920s, natural dyes were always used: indigo (planted in the Jordan Valley), pomegranate, onion peel and mulberries were all common, as was the sumac berry (red), kermes insect dye (crimson), cochineal (pink), and even yellowish soil. Salt, vinegar or soda were added in order to make the colours fast.

Since the 1980s, local and international development projects – Save The Children among them – have been involved in nurturing traditional **bedouin weaving**. By doing so, and by establishing retail outlets in Amman and elsewhere for the sale of woven items, they have managed to rejuvenate a dying craft, and simultaneously create extra sources of income for the weavers, who are almost without exception rural women. The quality of **carpets**, **rugs** and **home furnishings** produced under these various projects is first-rate, although prices are concomitantly high.

The older, more traditional colours – deep reds, navy blues, greens, oranges and blacks – as well as the traditional styles of stripes and diamonds, are being augmented these days by brighter, chemically dyed colours and more modern patterns, to appeal to a new, Western-inspired clientele, but there is usually a good range of traditional and modern pieces on offer. In Madaba, Jerash and Irbid you may see carpet shops featuring upright treadle looms; these are operated only by men, and almost exclusively in the cities, to produce mainly derivative items for sale. These have their own appeal, but the majority of traditionally designed woven pieces are made by women, who use only a ground loom, which they set up either in front of their home tent in springtime or at village workshops.

A more affordable woven craft is **weaving with straw**, a skill of northern Jordanian women, to produce large multicoloured trays, mats, storage containers or wall-hangings. Baskets made of local **bamboo**, woven by men in Himmeh (aka Mukhaybeh) on the River Yarmouk, often find their way to Amman for sale in crafts centres.

Jewellery

Many Jordanians have inherited their parents' and grandparents' preference – stemming partly from previous generations' nomadic existence, and partly from a rural mistrust of urban institutions – for investing their money in **jewellery** rather than in banks. Until recently, bedouin brides wore their personal wealth in silver jewellery, and retained the right throughout their married lives to do with it what they wanted, husbands' wishes notwithstanding. Owning jewellery was – and still is – something of a safety net for women against the possibility of abandonment, divorce or widowhood.

Traditionally, the bedouin much preferred **silver** to gold; indeed, it's just about impossible to find genuine old gold in Jordan. The **Gold Souk** – a collection of tiny modern jewellery shops huddled together in Downtown Amman – has excellent prices, but almost everything is of generic modern design.

If you're after more distinctive jewellery, you should be aware that, although there are a few Jordanian designers producing new, hand-made items, practically all the new jewellery you'll see in craft shops has been imported from Turkey, India or Italy. Chunky **bedouin jewellery** that looks old generally turns out to have been made seventy or eighty years ago, and much old "silver" is in fact a mix of eighty percent silver and twenty percent copper. Practically all the "old" necklaces you might see will have been strung recently on nylon thread using stones and silver beads from long-dispersed older originals.

However, none of this detracts from the fact that beautiful and unique items are available; especially striking are necklaces that combine silver beads with beads of coloured glass, **amber** or semiprecious stones. Different stones have different significances: blue stones protect the wearer from the evil eye, white stones stimulate lactation during breast-feeding, and so on. You might also find rare Circassian **enamelwork**, dramatically adding to a silver bracelet or necklace's charm. However, note that all **precious stones** in Jordan are imported, mostly from Turkey.

Metalwork, wood and glass

In Amman, **copper** and **brass** items, such as distinctive long-spouted *dalleh* coffee-pots, candlesticks, embossed or inlaid platters and the like, are generally mass-produced Indian and Pakistani pieces. You might find original Yemeni or Iraqi curved silver **daggers** on sale, in amongst the reproductions.

Wood is a scarce resource in Jordan, and although you may find some Jordanian-carved pieces (simple cooking implements,

mostly, of local oak and pistachio) practically all the elegant wooden furniture you'll come across – wardrobes, chairs, beautiful inlaid chests and the like – originates (and is much cheaper) in Syria. You might spot some original hand-carved wooden implements used in the bedouin coffee-making process, such as a *mihbash*, or grinder, and a *mabradeh*, an ornamented tray for cooling the coffee beans after roasting. Prices in Amman for **olive-wood** or **mother-of-pearl** pieces from Bethlehem or the famous **blown glass** of Hebron (now also made in Na'ur, just outside Amman) can be half what you might pay in Jerusalem.

Travelling with children

Children are universally loved in Jordan, and travelling with your family is likely to provoke spontaneous acts of kindness and hospitality from the locals.

Children are central to Jordanian society – many couples have four or five, and double figures isn't uncommon. Middle-class extended families tend to take pleasure in spoiling kids rotten, allowing them to stay up late and play endlessly, but as a counterpoint, kids from low-income families can be seen out on the streets at all hours selling cigarettes. The streets are quite **safe** and even very young children walk to school unaccompanied.

Only the cheapest hotels will bar children; most will positively welcome them (with deals on extra beds or adjoining rooms), as will all restaurants, although discounts may have to be negotiated. There are a few **precautions** to bear in mind. Foremost is the **heat**: kids' sensitive skin should be protected from the sun as much as possible, both in terms of clothing (brimmed hats and long sleeves are essential) and gallons of sunblock. Heatstroke and dehydration can work much faster on children than on adults. Sunglasses with full UV protection are vital to protect sensitive eyes. Kids are also more

vulnerable than adults to **stomach upsets**: you should definitely carry rehydration salts in case of diarrhoea. Other things to watch out for include the crazy traffic (especially for British kids, who'll be used to cars driving on the other side of the road), stray animals that may be disease carriers, and jellyfish and poisonous corals off Aqaba's beaches.

Children will love riding camels in Wadi Rum, and even Petra's threadbare donkeys may hold an appeal. Most of the archeological sites will probably be too rarefied to be of more than passing interest (aside, possibly, from exploring towers and underground passages at Karak, Shobak or Ajloun castles); spotting vultures, ibex and blue lizards at Dana or Mujib may be a better bet, and the glass-bottomed boats at Aqaba are perennial favourites. Children born and brought up in urban environments will probably never have experienced anything like the vastness and silence of the open desert, and you may find they're transfixed by the emptinesses of Wadi Rum or the eastern Badia.

Travel essentials

Addresses

Notwithstanding the efforts of cartographers and government officials, Jordan doesn't use **street addresses**: nameplates you see on street corners are largely ignored by locals, who navigate either in relation to prominent landmarks or by asking passers-by. Mail is delivered only to PO boxes at post offices. If you have an appointment, it's a good idea to phone in advance to get detailed directions.

Costs

By Western standards, Jordan is a good-value destination. It's possible to see the sights, eat adequately, sleep in basic comfort and get around on public transport for roughly £40/US$60 a day. If you like things more comfortable – staying in good mid-range hotels, eating well, perhaps renting a car to see some out-of-the-way places – reckon on nearer £75/US$115 a day per person. To travel independently while hiring drivers and guides, staying in five-star hotels and generally living the high life, aim for £150/US$225 a day per person.

Jordan has a **government sales tax**, which applies at different rates, depending on the goods/services involved, up to about 14 percent: bear in mind that, in many situations, the price you see (or are told) doesn't include this tax, which is only added on when you come to pay. In Aqaba, sales tax is lower than the rest of Jordan. In addition, hotels and restaurants above a certain quality threshold automatically add a **ten percent service charge** to all bills. They are legally obliged to state these charges somewhere, although it can be as surreptitious as a tiny line on the bottom of a menu, or just a simple "++" attached to a hotel price-list, as in "Double Room JD60++". If you try to bargain, you'll often find the "plus-plus" suddenly disappearing from view.

Crime and personal safety

The sense of honour and hospitality to guests embedded deep within Arab culture, coupled with a respect for others, means that you're extremely unlikely to become a victim of crime while in Jordan. Along with the ordinary police, Jordan maintains a force of English-speaking **tourist police**, identifiable by their armbands with English lettering. Posted at all tourist sites nationwide, they can deal with requests, complaints or problems of harassment. Any representation by a foreigner, whether to the tourist police or the ordinary local police, will generally have you ushered into the presence of senior officers, sat down and plied with coffee, with your complaint taken in the utmost seriousness. The nationwide police **emergency number** is ☎191.

Terrorism and **civil disorder** in Jordan are extremely rare. The political and religious make-up of Jordanian society – as well as the invisible grip of the security services – makes domestic terrorism exceptionally unlikely. All big hotels have barriers keeping vehicles clear of the entrance, and airport-style security for everyone entering the building (including compulsory baggage X-ray and body search). Armed police patrol all major tourist sites. Regardless of the impression you might get from the nightly news, you'd be in no more danger travelling round Jordan than you would be in your home country.

Customs and duty-free

You're permitted to buy 200 **cigarettes**, one litre of spirits and two litres of wine **duty-free** on arrival in the country. All borders and airports have duty-free shops open long hours, but if you forget to buy your allowance of alcohol, cigarettes, perfume and/or electronic goods when you arrive, you can go to the Duty-Free Shop on Tunis Street near 5th Circle in Amman (☎06 567 8147) within 14 days, where the whole range is available. Bring your passport.

The area around Aqaba is a **Special Economic Zone**, with lower taxes and its own customs rules: on all roads into the city, you'll have to pass through a customs station. On departing the zone, there are Red and Green Channels, as in an airport. Personal items, up to 200 cigarettes and one litre of alcohol that you bought in the zone are exempt from duty.

Electricity

The supply in Jordan is 220V AC, 50Hz – the same as in Europe. Most new buildings and big hotels have British-style square three-pin **sockets**. Older buildings tend to have two-pin sockets for European-style thick-pronged, round plugs.

Entry requirements

All visitors to Jordan must hold passports valid for at least **six months** beyond the proposed date of entry to the country. On arrival at all airports, as well as at all land and sea borders – apart from the King Hussein/Allenby Bridge – most nationalities are routinely issued with a **single-entry visa**. If you arrive at Aqaba, it's free (see below); if you arrive anywhere else, it costs JD10.

(Note that citizens of certain developing countries cannot obtain a visa on arrival and must instead apply at the nearest Jordanian embassy at least three months prior to travel. A full list of these is at ⓦ www.visitjordan.com.)

If you plan to enter Jordan for the first time via the King Hussein/Allenby Bridge, you must already hold a visa. If, however, you left Jordan via this bridge and are returning the same way, you don't need to buy another visa as long as your current one is still valid.

For **groups** of five or more people, whose journey has been arranged by a travel agent and who intend to stay in Jordan for at least two nights, visa fees are waived. A **multiple-entry visa** costs roughly twice the price of a single-entry – the equivalent of £21/US$31 – but is available only from Jordanian embassies and consulates.

Both single- and multiple-entry visas are valid for a stay of **thirty days**. If you're planning to stay longer than that, you must **register with the police** in the last couple of days before the thirty-day period is up – a simple, free, five-minute procedure which grants a three-month extension.

Always carry your **passport** on your person: you'll need it to check into hotels and to ease your way through any checkpoints.

Visas at Aqaba

If you enter Jordan at Aqaba – which stands at the centre of the **Aqaba Special Economic Zone** (**ASEZ**) – you are granted a **free** 30-day visa on arrival at Aqaba's airport, seaport or the land crossings from Israel (Eilat) or Saudi Arabia (Durra). You are then free to travel around Jordan as you like. Staying more than a month involves

Embassies and consulates

Full lists are at ⓦ www.mfa.gov.jo.

Jordanian embassies abroad
Australia ☎ 02/6295 9951, ⓦ www.jordanembassy.org.au.
Canada ☎ 613/238-8090, ⓦ www.embassyofjordan.ca.
UK ☎ 020/7937 3685, ⓦ www.jordanembassyuk.org.
USA ☎ 202/966-2664, ⓦ www.jordanembassyus.org.

Embassies and consulates in Amman
Australian ☎ 06 580 7000, ⓦ www.jordan.embassy.gov.au.
Canadian ☎ 06 520 3300, ⓦ www.international.gc.ca.
Irish ☎ 06 551 6807, ⓦ www.foreignaffairs.gov.ie.
New Zealand ☎ 06 463 6720, ⓦ www.nzembassy.com.
UK ☎ 06 590 9200, ⓦ www.britain.org.jo.
US ☎ 06 590 6000, ⓦ jordan.usembassy.gov.

extending an ASEZ visa, which can be done only at the offices of **ASEZA** (Aqaba Special Economic Zone Authority) in Aqaba itself. If you arrive in Jordan elsewhere – other than the King Hussein/Allenby Bridge – and you let the passport officials know that you intend to go directly to Aqaba, you are entitled to get a free ASEZ visa rather than a standard JD10 visa. In these cases, though, you must **register** at the ASEZA offices in Aqaba within 48 hours of your arrival in Jordan: if you miss this deadline, you become liable for the cost of the visa plus a fine.

Health

No immunizations or vaccinations are required before you can enter Jordan. However, before you travel, it's strongly recommended that you make sure you're up to date with **immunizations** against hepatitis A, polio, tetanus (lockjaw), tuberculosis and typhoid fever. You should consult a doctor at least two months in advance of your departure date, as there are some immunizations that can't be given at the same time, and several take a while to become effective.

Travel clinics

Australia & NZ TMVC ☏1300 658844, ⊛www .tmvc.com.au.
Canada CSIH ☏613/241-5785, ⊛www.csih.org.
Ireland TMB ☏1850 487674, ⊛www.tmb.ie.
UK MASTA ☏0870 606 2782, ⊛www.masta.org.
US CDC ☏1-800/232-4636, ⊛www.cdc .gov/travel.

Dehydration

Top of the list of Jordan's maladies, well ahead of the worst creepy-crawlies, is **dehydration**, which can work insidiously over days to weaken you to the point of exhaustion without your ever showing any signs of illness. Equally – and just as dangerously – if you're sweating profusely during activity (such as hiking), even experienced walkers can go from alert and vigorous to dizzy and apathetic in as little as half an hour, due solely to loss of body fluids. It is essential to carry *lots* of water with you on these walks: one bottle is not enough.

An adult should normally drink two litres of water a day; from day one in the Middle East, you should be drinking at least three litres – and, if you're exerting yourself in hot conditions, more than double that. It's a matter of pride among the desert bedouin not to drink water in front of foreigners, but if you copy them you're likely to make yourself ill. Drinking to quench your thirst just isn't enough in a hot climate, since the combination of the sun's evaporation and your own sweating can pull water out of your system far quicker than your body can deliver thirst messages to your brain: you must drink well beyond thirst-quenching if you're to head off the lethargy and splitting headaches – and potentially serious physical and mental incapacity – caused by dehydration. **Alcohol** and **caffeine** exacerbate the effects of dehydration.

Travellers' diarrhoea

If you arrive in Jordan directly from the West (or Israel), give your stomach a chance to acclimatize: avoid street food for a few days and spend a little extra to eat in posher, but cleaner, restaurants. Every eating place, from the diviest diner upwards, will have a sink with soap for washing your hands. Nonetheless, few travellers seem to avoid **diarrhoea** altogether. Instant recourse to **drugs** such as Imodium or Lomotil that plug you up (in fact, what they do is paralyse your gut) is not advisable; you should only use them if you absolutely must travel (eg if you're flying). The best thing to do is to wait, eat nothing for at least 24 hours and let it run its course, while constantly replacing the fluids and salts that you're flushing away. Maintaining fluid intake (even if it all rushes out again) is vitally important. **Oral rehydration solutions** such as Dioralyte or Electrosol are widely available worldwide, sold in sachets for dissolving in a glassful of clean water. They're marketed as being for babies, but will make you feel better and stronger than any other treatment. If you can't get the sachets, make up your own solution with one heaped teaspoon of salt and twelve level teaspoons of sugar added to a standard-sized (1.5-litre) bottle of mineral water. You need to keep downing the stuff, whether or not the diarrhoea is continuing – at least a litre of the solution per day interspersed with three litres of fresh water. Bouts of diarrhoea rarely last longer than 24–48 hours.

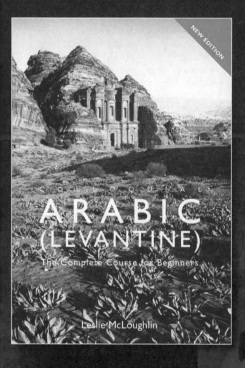

If it goes on for longer than four days, seek medical advice. Nasty but easily treatable diseases such as giardiasis and amoebiasis must be tested for by a stool examination. If there is blood in your diarrhoea, you've most likely got dysentery and must see a doctor.

Heat exhaustion and sunstroke

The Jordanian sun can be scorchingly intense, and – obvious though it sounds – you should do all you can to **avoid sun exposure**, especially if you're travelling in high summer (May–Sept). Head protection is essential. Lightweight 100 percent cotton clothes – such as long-sleeved shirts, and long trousers or ankle-length skirts – will allow air to circulate close to your skin to keep you cool and limit both sunburn and dehydration. If you feel very hot, dizzy and faint but aren't sweating, you may have **sunstroke**: get out of direct sun immediately, and into air conditioning and/or cold water as soon as possible. Call a doctor.

Bites and stings

Malaria is not present in Jordan – though **mosquitoes** and **sandflies** are. **Snakes** are frightened of humans; if you walk slowly and noisily, any snakes present will slither away. To avoid tangling with **scorpions** and **spiders** never walk barefoot, and if you're camping always shake out your shoes and clothes before wearing them.

Treatment in Jordan

Every town has a **pharmacy** (saydaliyyeh), generally staffed by fluent English-speaking professionals trained to Western standards. Unless you're obviously a hospital case, these are where you should head first, since a pharmacist charges nothing for a "consultation", and can either prescribe a remedy on the spot or refer you to a local doctor. If you're given a medicine, find out explicitly from the pharmacist what the dosage is, since printed English information on the box might be sketchy.

If you need a **doctor** (doktoor), ask your embassy to recommend one or check first with a pharmacist. All doctors are trained in English, many in hospitals in the UK or US. If you're in real trouble, aim for the emergency room of a **hospital** (moostashfa) – and call the emergency helpline of your embassy (see p.65) to ask for advice. Consultation fees and medical costs are much lower than back home, but you should still get signed **receipts** for everything in order to claim money back from your insurance company when you return.

Insurance

It's essential to take out a good **travel insurance** policy to cover against theft, loss of property and illness or injury. Before paying for a new policy, however, it's worth checking whether you are already covered: home insurance may cover your possessions when overseas, many private medical schemes include cover when abroad and premium bank accounts and/or credit cards often have travel insurance included. After exhausting these possibilities, contact a specialist travel insurance firm. Rough Guides offers tailor-made travel insurance through Columbus Direct, including a low-cost backpacker option, a short break option, a typical holiday option, and others. Sports and activities, such as trekking or diving, can usually be included. See ⓦwww .roughguides.com/shop – or call UK ☎0870 033 9988, Australia ☎1300 669 999, NZ ☎0800 559 911, or worldwide ☎+44 870 890 2843.

Mail

Airmail **letters and postcards** can take a week or two to Western Europe, up to a month to North America or Australasia. Asking someone to write the destination country in Arabic can help avoid things going astray. It's safest to ignore the street postboxes and instead send your mail from larger post offices, all of which have a box for airmail (barid jowwy). Stamps (tawabe'a) cost well under JD1, but parcels are expensive (JD10–15 for 1kg). International **courier** firms are well represented in Amman and Aqaba.

Maps

For all general purposes, the **maps** in this book should be adequate. Many international map publishers cover Jordan, but few offer close detail and most omit newer roads and/or mark villages or archeological sites inaccurately. The *GeoProjects* 1:730,000 map (third edition or later) leaves out some detail but is probably the best available outside Jordan. Other maps, including city maps and plans for Petra and other sites, are available in Jordan, many produced by the Royal Jordanian Geographic Centre (Ⓦwww.rjgc.gov.jo).

Money

The Jordanian unit of currency is the **dinar**, abbreviated to JD. Most people refer to the dinar as a "*jaydee*" or a "*lira*". There are two subdivisions: one dinar comprises either 1000 **fils** or 100 **piastres** (*qirsh*). Locals always think in piastres; they only refer to fils when talking to foreigners. A hotel, restaurant or shop bill will show either "14.65" or "14.650", both of which mean 14 dinars and 65 piastres (that is, 650 fils). In this book, we are sticking to two decimal places only.

Banknotes are JD50, JD20, JD10, JD5 and JD1, all with Arabic on one side and English on the other. For coins, there's a gold, seven-sided **half-dinar** coin inset with a circular silver bit in the middle; a smaller **quarter-dinar** coin, also gold and seven-sided but without the silver inset; and silver coins of **ten piastres** and **five piastres**. Coppers of one piastre are virtually worthless. Note that ten-piastre coins are the same size, weight and value as older **100 fils** coins which are still in circulation. Similarly, five-piastre coins have an identical twin, marked as **50 fils**. All coins state their value on them somewhere in tiny English lettering.

In verbal exchanges, you'll find that people quite often leave the denomination off the end of prices. If they say something costs "*ashreen*" (twenty), it's up to you to decide whether they mean 20 fils (a throwaway amount), 20 piastres (ie 200 fils; the price of a street snack or a short bus ride), or 20 JDs (the cost of a double room in a small hotel). Nicknames also pop up: 10 piastres is a *barizeh* and 5 piastres is a *shilin*.

Changing and carrying money

Few banks in the West keep Jordanian dinars on hand, but you should be able to **order** them with a few days' notice. It's a good idea to bring JD50 or so with you in cash, to cover visa and transport costs on arrival.

Most hotels and shops above the cheapest level accept plastic, but Jordan is a cash society: just about everywhere the preferred method of payment is local currency. **Security**-wise, Jordan is safer than anywhere in the West: you can carry wads of cash around in your pocket on a crowded rush-hour bus or at 2am in a dark alley without concern. You're more likely to be invited for tea than mugged.

There's no black market in **currency exchange**. For changing cash or traveller's cheques (in all major currencies), every town has a welter of banks, with identical exchange rates, and there are also plenty of independent change offices. **Cash machines (ATMs)** are widespread, always with an English option.

Opening hours and public holidays

Normal **office** hours are Sunday to Thursday 8.30am to 3.30pm. Jordan's **weekend** is Friday and Saturday; this is when public sector offices (such as government departments) are closed. However, private sector businesses may run a six-day week, closing only on Fridays. If somebody tells you a particular attraction is open "every day", quite often they mean every day except Friday.

Although Muslims pray together in the mosque on a Friday, the concept of a "sabbath" or "day of rest" does not translate: downtown **shops** and **markets** are generally open seven days a week, roughly 8 or 9am to 8 or 9pm, though some more upmarket shops might close for two or three hours in the middle of the afternoon, and almost everywhere shuts for an hour or two around Friday midday prayers. All **transport services** operate seven days a week.

During **Ramadan**, the Muslim holy month of fasting, everything changes. Shops and offices open from 9am to 2 or 3pm (closed Fri), while street markets operate every day until about an hour before sunset. Banks and government departments may only be open for two or three hours in the morning. Some shops might re-open for a couple of hours after dark.

Fixed public holidays

Jordan's **secular national holidays** tend to be low-key affairs, involving limited celebrations and/or military parades; government offices are closed, but shops and businesses often open as normal. The exception is the king's birthday, which can involve a three- or four-day break in the last week of January.

Jordan's **Christians** are mostly Orthodox and follow the Julian calendar, which varies from the Gregorian calendar used in the West by a couple of weeks. Nevertheless, everyone has agreed to celebrate Christmas Day together on December 25, and since 1994 that date has been marked as a national holiday (although Muslim shops and businesses are open as normal).

Jan 1 New Year's Day
Jan 30 King Abdullah's Birthday
May 1 Labour Day
May 25 Independence Day
June 9–10 Accession Day & Army Day
Nov 14 King Hussein Remembrance Day
Dec 25 Christmas Day

Islamic holidays and Ramadan

Islamic religious holidays, based on the Hijra calendar, are marked by widespread public observance. All shops and offices are closed and non-essential services are liable to be suspended. See p.396 for more info. The following dates are approximate, since each holiday is announced only when the moon has been seen clearly by an authorized cleric from Jordan's Ministry of Islamic Affairs. Quoted dates could vary by a couple of days. The start of the holy month of **Ramadan** is also included here; Ramadan is not a holiday, but since it comprises 30 days of restricted business hours, its first day is a useful date to know.

Mowlid an-Nabawi (Prophet Muhammad's birthday) – 26 Feb 2010; 15 Feb 2011; 4 Feb 2012; 24 Jan 2013.

Eid al-Isra wal-Miraj (Night Journey to Heaven) – 8 July 2010; 28 June 2011; 16 June 2012; 5 June 2013.

Ramadan – begins 22 Aug 2009; 11 Aug 2010; 1 Aug 2011; 20 July 2012.

Eid al-Fitr (3 days) – begins 20 Sept 2009; 10 Sept 2010; 30 Aug 2011; 19 Aug 2012.

Eid al-Adha (4 days) – begins 27 Nov 2009; 16 Nov 2010; 6 Nov 2011; 26 Oct 2012.

1st of Muharram (Islamic New Year) – 18 Dec 2009; 7 Dec 2010; 26 Nov 2011; 15 Nov 2012.

Phones

Landline numbers are seven digits prefixed by a two-digit **area code**: 02 covers northern Jordan, 03 southern Jordan, 05 the Jordan Valley and central and eastern districts, and 06 the Amman area.

Mobile phone numbers are ten digits long (07 plus eight digits). For info on Jordan's networks and coverage maps, look under Technology/Roaming at ⓦwww.gsmworld.com. You can walk into any phone or electronics shop (there are dozens in every town), buy a SIM card, plug it into your handset and be up and running with a Jordanian number in minutes, for JD10 or

Useful numbers

Emergencies
Traffic accidents ☏190
Police ☏191
Ambulance ☏199

Phoning home
To the UK ☏0044
To the Republic of Ireland ☏00353
To the US or Canada ☏001
To Australia ☏0061
To New Zealand ☏0064

Calling Jordan from abroad
First dial your **international access code** (00 from the UK, Ireland and New Zealand; 011 from the US and Canada; 0011 from Australia), followed by **962** for Jordan, then the Jordanian number excluding the initial zero.

Jordan Jubilee

Of the array of personal websites devoted to Jordan, one stands out. ⓦ**www
.jordanjubilee.com** is a fascinating, encyclopedic and vastly knowledgeable
collection of information for travellers of all stripes – backpackers, cultural
explorers, trekkers and armchair enthusiasts alike. Written and maintained (ad-free
and not-for-profit) by the engaging Ruth Caswell, who was born in Wales, lives in
Paris and Petra, and is often to be found exploring the wilder corners of Rum,
"Jordan Jubilee" is a true labour of love – and an invaluable resource.

less. Topping up with scratch-cards (buyable everywhere) is straightforward. Calling and texting is very inexpensive – much cheaper than relying on roaming with your home network. Basic handsets can be had for perhaps JD20–30.

Smoking

Smoking is banned in public places, including airports, museums and on public transport. However, enforcement is minimal and in effect it's impossible to escape cigarette smoke anywhere in the country.

Time

Jordan is usually two hours ahead of London, seven hours ahead of New York and eight hours behind Sydney. **Daylight Saving Time** operates from the last Friday in March to the last Friday in October. For full details, check ⓦwww.timeanddate.com.

Tipping

In a good restaurant, even when a service charge is included, it's customary to round the bill up slightly as well. Low-budget local diners don't expect **tips** and will never press you for anything. In most everyday situations a quarter-dinar tip (ie JD0.25) is a perfectly satisfactory indication of your appreciation for a service, such as a hotel porter loading your bags onto a bus or taxi. Taxi-drivers deserve ten percent of the meter charge; if a driver has spent half a day shuttling you from place to place, JD5 is in order. An appropriate tip for a bellboy in a four- or five-star hotel who brings your bags up to your room would be half a dinar (JD0.50) – or JD1 if you're feeling generous. See p.54 for guidance on tipping specialist guides.

Tourist information

The **Jordan Tourism Board** (JTB), part affiliated to the Ministry of Tourism and part private, publicizes the country's tourist assets abroad. In most countries, the account for handling promotion of Jordan is awarded to a local PR company, so contact details (see below) can, and do, change.

Jordan Tourism Board

ⓦ www.visitjordan.com
Jordan ☏06 567 8444.
UK ☏020/7371 6496.
US & Canada ☏1-877/SEE-JORDAN or 703/243-7404.

Useful websites

ⓦ**www.visitjordan.com** Jordan's official tourism portal.
ⓦ**www.kingabdullah.jo** Detailed features on history, the royal family, politics and tourism.
ⓦ**www.jordantimes.com** Leading English-language newspaper.
ⓦ**www.petrapark.com** Official website for Petra Archeological Park.
ⓦ**www.rscn.org.jo** Excellent information on Jordan's nature reserves.
ⓦ**www.jordanjubilee.com** Knowledgeable and entertaining travel site.
ⓦ**www.nomadstravel.co.uk** For climbing and trekking enthusiasts.
ⓦ**www.andrewsi.freeserve.co.uk** Informative birdwatching site.
ⓦ**www.jmd.gov.jo** Weather forecasts and climate data.

Travellers with disabilities

Jordan makes few provisions for its own citizens who have limited mobility, and this is reflected in the negligible facilities for tourists.

The best option is to plump for an **organized tour** – sightseeing is liable to be complicated enough that leaving the practical details to the professionals will take a weight off your mind. Throughout the country pavements are either narrow and broken or missing altogether, kerbs are high, stairs are ubiquitous and wheelchair access to hotels, restaurants and public buildings is pretty much nonexistent. Hotel staff and tourism officials, although universally helpful, are generally poorly informed about the needs and capabilities of tourists with limited mobility. Travelling with an able-bodied helper and being able to pay for things like a

rental car (or a car plus driver) and good hotels will make things easier.

All Jordan's ancient sites are accessible only by crossing rough and stony ground. Scrambling around at Jerash or Karak is hard enough for those with full mobility; for those without, a visit represents a major effort of energy and organization. Petra has better access: with advance planning, you could arrange to rent a horse-drawn cart to take you from the ticket gate into the ancient city, from where – with written permission obtained ahead of time from the tourist police – you could be picked up in a car and driven back to your hotel.

Guide

Guide

Amman

CHAPTER 1 # Highlights

* **Roman Theatre** Impressive ancient arena at the heart of the capital. See p.97

* **The Downtown souks** Immerse yourself in the bustle of Amman's market streets. See p.99

* **Jordan Museum** The most comprehensive overview of Jordan's archeological heritage. See p.101

* **Umayyad Palace** Restored eighth-century governor's residence that dominates Amman's hilltop citadel. See p.102

* **Rainbow Street** Explore the quirky shops and cafés of this attractive old neighbourhood. See p.104

* **Contemporary art** Get a new angle on Amman at the city's thriving art galleries. See p.107

* **Arabic cuisine** Dine in style at sophisticated, elegant restaurants such as Fakhr el-Din or Tannoureen. See p.112

* **Shopping** Whether browsing in dusty bazaars or at glitzy malls, shopping puts you at the heart of what makes Amman tick. See p.117

▲ Shopping for vegetables, Downtown Amman

Amman عمّان

Consistently overlooked and underrated by travellers to the Middle East, the Jordanian capital **AMMAN** stands in marked contrast to its raucous neighbours, with none of the grand history of Damascus, not a whiff of Jerusalem's tension and just a tiny fraction of Cairo's monuments. It's a civilized, genial city with unexpected charm, that is bathed in a new spirit of dynamism: investment is pouring in, new buildings are going up, neighbourhoods are being rejuvenated and the city is humming with cafés, galleries and commerce. If you're dreaming of medieval mosques, gloomy spice bazaars and fading romance, go elsewhere; if you want a handle on how a young, buzzy Arab capital is making its way in the world, Amman is for you.

Amman is a thoroughly twentieth-century invention: it was no more than an unregarded, muddy farming village when Emir Abdullah chose it to be his **new capital** in 1921. The sense of Amman being a village-made-good is highlighted when you spend some time on the busy Downtown streets. Here the weight of history that is a constant presence in the heart of many Middle Eastern cities is manifestly lacking, replaced instead by a quick-witted self-reliance. This energy stems in large part from displacement, with most Ammanis identifying themselves as originating somewhere else: Circassians, Iraqis and above all Palestinians have arrived in the city in large numbers, voluntarily or forcibly exiled from their homelands. The distinctive cultures they have brought are still jostling for living space with the culture of the native bedouin. Indeed, scratching beneath Amman's amiable surface reveals a whole cluster of multiple personalities jockeying for supremacy: Western-educated entrepreneurs make their fortunes cheek-by-jowl with poverty-stricken refugees, Christians live next door to Muslims, conservative Islamists and radical secularists tut at each other's doings, Jordanians of Palestinian origin assert their identity in the face of nationalistic tendencies among "true" Jordanians, and so on. What it is to be Ammani is an ongoing dispute that shows no signs of resolution.

For the time-pressed ruin-hunter, then, there's little more than an afternoon's sightseeing to be done; however, if you're on a long, slow journey of familiarity you could easily spend days exploring the slopes of Amman's towering hills, getting under the city's skin while seeing nothing in particular. The capital's impressive **Roman Theatre** and eighth-century **Umayyad Palace** are the only significant monumental attractions, augmented by the **national museum**, but of equal, if not greater, interest is contemporary Amman's burgeoning arts scene. The arts centre of **Darat al-Funun**, the **National Gallery** and regular music events can add a surprising perspective to your experience of the city's life.

Day-trips from Amman

Distances in Jordan are small, and it's easy to base yourself in Amman and make a series of day-trips out to a number of nearby attractions. The main draw is floating your day away at the unmissable **Dead Sea** (p.129); you could combine this with a visit to the nearby **Baptism Site** of Jesus (p.137). Alternatively, the amiable old town of **Madaba** (see p.221) is within easy reach – and, with your own transport, you could construct a gentle, circular day-trip from Amman to Madaba, then the Mount Nebo mosaics, then the Dead Sea (with or without the Baptism Site), and back to Amman. If you start early, and maintain a reasonable pace, this circuit is also possible by bus.

A pleasant day-trip into the hilly countryside **west of Amman** could take in the Hellenistic palace of **Qasr al-Abd** (p.149) and the adjacent caves and crafts workshops of **Iraq al-Amir**, the beautiful old Ottoman capital of **Salt** (p.145) and a meal or a stroll in the lanes of old **Fuheis** (p.148).

North of Amman, the Roman ruins at **Jerash** (p.154) make for a great half-day excursion, set in some lovely rolling countryside. Combine Jerash with a visit to **Ajloun** castle (p.167) to make a day of it.

East of Amman, a circuit of roads takes in the fascinating so-called "**Desert Castles**" (p.195) – this is easy to do by taxi or your own vehicle, but impossible on public transport.

Some history

The first known settlement near Amman dates from over nine thousand years ago, a Neolithic farming town near the **Ain Ghazal** spring in the hills to the northeast of the modern city. This was one of the largest such towns discovered in the region, three times bigger than contemporary Jericho. Artisans from among its two thousand inhabitants produced strikingly beautiful human busts and figurines in limestone and plaster, some of the earliest statuettes ever discovered (now on display in the Amman museum).

Around 1800 BC, during the Bronze Age, the hill now known as **Jebel al-Qal'a**, which overlooks the central valley of Amman, was fortified for the first time. According to Genesis, the area was inhabited by giants before the thirteenth-century BC arrival of the **Ammonites**, mythical descendants (along with the Moabites) of the drunken seduction of Lot by his own two daughters. By 1200 BC, the citadel on Jebel al-Qal'a had been renamed **Rabbath Ammon** (Great City of the Ammonites) and was capital of an amply defended area which extended from the Zarqa to the Mujib rivers. Rabbath – or Rabbah – is mentioned many times in the Old Testament; the earliest reference, in Deuteronomy, reports that, following a victory in battle, the city had seized as booty the great iron bed of King Og, last of the giants. Later, the book of Samuel relates that, around 1000 BC, the Israelite **King David** sent messengers to Rabbah with condolences for the death of the Ammonite king. Unfortunately, the Ammonites suspected the messengers were spies: they shaved off half their beards, shredded their garments and sent them home in ignominy. In response to such a profound insult, David sent his entire army against Rabbah, although he himself stayed behind in Jerusalem to develop his ongoing friendship with **Bathsheba**, who soon became pregnant. On David's orders, her husband **Uriah** was placed in the front line of battle against Rabbah and killed. David then travelled to Rabbah to aid the conquest, threw the surviving Ammonites into slavery and returned home to marry the handily widowed Bathsheba. Their first child died, but their second, Solomon, lived to become king of Israel.

The feud simmered for centuries, with Israel and Judea coveting the wealth gathered from lucrative trade routes by Ammon and its southern neighbours, Moab and Edom. In the absence of military or economic might, Israel resorted to the power of prophecy. "The days are coming," warned **Jeremiah** in the sixth century BC, "that a trumpet blast of war will be heard against Rabbah of Ammon." The city was to become "a desolate heap" with fire "destroying the palaces". In a spitting rage at the Ammonites' celebration of the Babylonian conquest of Jerusalem in 587 BC, **Ezekiel** went one better, prophesying that Rabbah was to be occupied by bedouin and to become "a stable for camels".

After Alexander the Great conquered the region in 332 BC, his successor Ptolemy II Philadelphus rebuilt Rabbah and named it **Philadelphia**, the "city of brotherly love". Turmoil reigned following the Seleucid takeover in 218 BC until the Romans restored order by creating the province of Syria in 63 BC. Philadelphia was at its zenith as the southernmost of the great Decapolis cities (see p.156), and benefited greatly from improved trade and communications along the **Via Nova Traiana**, completed in 114 AD by Emperor Trajan to link the provincial capital Bosra with the Red Sea. The **Romans** completely replanned Philadelphia and constructed grand public buildings, among them two theatres, a nymphaeum, a temple to Hercules and a huge forum, all of which survive.

In Byzantine times, Philadelphia was the seat of a bishopric and was still a regional centre when the Arabs conquered it in 635; the city's name reverted to Amman under the Damascus-based **Umayyad** dynasty. Amman became a regional capital and, around 720, its Umayyad governor expanded the Roman buildings surviving on Jebel al-Qal'a into an elaborate palatial complex, which promptly collapsed in the great earthquake of 749. Following the **Abbasid** takeover shortly afterwards, power shifted east to Baghdad and Amman's influence began to wane, although it continued to serve as a stop for pilgrims on the way south to Mecca. Over the next centuries, travellers mention an increasingly desolate town; by the time **Circassian** refugees were settled here by the Ottomans in the 1870s, Amman's hills served only as pastureland for the local bedouin – Ezekiel's furious prophecy come true. The Circassians, however,

Amman's annual festivals

Amman's biggest annual event is the **Jordan Festival**; see p.157 for details. The **Amman Summer Festival** is held from mid-July to mid-August in the King Hussein Park, featuring DJs, dance troupes, music shows and a kids' zone with puppetry, face-painting and more. As part of the summer festival, "**Amman Stairs**" comprises informal evenings of music and art staged on some of the staircases that climb the hills of Amman's older neighbourhoods, including Jebel al-Lweibdeh and Jebel al-Qal'a.

The **Amman International Theatre Festival** (ⓦ www.alfawanees.com) in March stages experimental drama from around the world in Arabic and English; the **Franco-Arab Film Festival** (ⓦ www.lecentre-jo.org) in July hosts screenings of French/Arab films alongside music and cultural events; late August sees the **European Street Art Festival**, featuring urban art and street theatre around the city; while in November, the **European Film Festival** (ⓦ www.eufilmfestivaljordan.com) screens art-house cinema and the **Jordan Short Film Festival** (ⓦ www.jordanfilmfestival.com) focuses on short films from around the world. December's **Amman Stand-Up Comedy Festival** (ⓦ www.ammancity.gov.jo) showcases local and international talent, with some events in English.

For all these, ask around near the time for information, or check notices in the *Jordan Times* newspaper.

revived the city's fortunes, and when the **Emirate of Transjordan** was established in 1921, Emir Abdullah chose Amman to be its capital.

Modern Amman

Up to 1948, Amman comprised only a village of closely huddled houses in the valleys below Jebel al-Qal'a, with a handful of buildings on the lower slopes of the surrounding hills. But in that year **Palestinians**, escaping or ejected from the newly established State of Israel, doubled the city's population in just two weeks. Makeshift camps to house the refugees were set up on the outskirts, and, following another huge influx of Palestinian refugees from the West Bank, occupied by Israel in 1967, creeping development began to merge the camps with the city's sprawling new suburbs.

A fundamental shift in Amman's fortunes came with the outbreak of the **Lebanese civil war** in 1975. Before then, Beirut had been the financial, cultural and intellectual capital of the Middle East, but when hostilities broke out, many financial institutions relocated their regional headquarters to the security of Amman. Most subsequently departed to the less parochial Gulf, but they nonetheless brought with them money, and with the money came Western influence: today there are parts of West Amman indistinguishable from upscale neighbourhoods of American or European cities, with broad leafy avenues lined with mansions, and fast multi-lane freeways swishing past strip malls and glass office buildings. A third influx of Palestinians – this time expelled from Kuwait following the 1991 **Gulf War** – again bulged the city at its seams, squeezing ever more urban sprawl along the roads out to the northwest and southwest.

When King Hussein signed a **peace treaty** with Israel in 1994, ending a state of war that had persisted since 1948, many Ammanis hoped for the opening of a new chapter in the city's life; Amman's intimate links with Palestinian markets and its generally Western-oriented business culture led many to believe wealth and commerce – not to mention Western aid – would start to flow. Building development burgeoned across the city, but for several years many of the new hotels and office buildings were white elephants, with Amman seeing little economic comeback from political rapprochement with Israel.

Since the early years of this century that situation has changed. Substantial quantities of **US aid** are starting to have an effect. Jordan's political and economic institutions are strengthening. With the government's increasing **liberalization** of the economy, confidence in Amman as a city on the up is growing. Private sector investment has rocketed, much of it coming instead from Arab countries. With a carefully nurtured international image as the moderate and hospitable face of the modern Arab world – an image that rings true for visitors – Amman today can be said to enjoy a greater influence in the region and the world than at any time since the Romans.

Orientation

Amman is a city of hills, and any map of the place can only give half the story. Although distances may look small on paper, the reality is that traffic and people are funnelled along streets often laid on valley-beds or clinging to the side of steep hills: to reach any destinations above Downtown you'll generally have to zigzag up sharp gradients.

The area known in English as **Downtown**, in Arabic as *il-balad* (literally "the city"), is the historical core of Amman; Roman Philadelphia lies beneath its streets and as late as the 1940s this small area comprised virtually the whole of

Street names

Street names in Amman are a relatively recent innovation. For decades, the city survived without them: people simply named streets after local landmarks. Under a recent mayoral initiative, every street has now been given a name, which appears in Arabic and English on prominent signs. Yet the new system will take a few years to bed in, and some anomalies remain. Probably the most confusing thing for visitors is that the sequence of major traffic intersections along Zahran Street on Jebel Amman – known to everyone as 1st Circle, 2nd Circle, and so on – are labelled instead with the names of royals and politicians. Our list below decodes them, and a few others. *Sharia* is "street" and always precedes the name. Both *duwaar* (circle) and *maydan* (square) are used to mean "traffic intersection". Many streets are named after royals: *al-malek* is "King" and *al-malka* or *al-malekah* is "Queen". Similarly, *al-amir* or *al-ameer* is "Prince" and *al-ameera* "Princess" – so "Prince Muhammad Street" translates as *Sharia al-Amir Muhammad*.

Official name	Common name
Downtown	
Quraysh Street	Saqf Sayl
Jebel Amman	
King Abdullah I Square	1st Circle (*duwaar al-awwal*)
Wasfi at-Tall Square	2nd Circle (*duwaar al-thaani*)
King Talal Square	3rd Circle (*duwaar al-thaalith*)
Prince Ghazi bin Muhammad Square	4th Circle (*duwaar al-raabe*)
Prince Faisal bin al-Hussein Square	5th Circle (*duwaar al-khaamis*)
Prince Rashid bin el-Hassan Square	6th Circle (*duwaar al-saadis*)
Prince Talal bin Muhammad Square	7th Circle (*duwaar al-saabe*)
King Abdullah II Square	8th Circle (*duwaar al-thaamin*)
Shmeisani and beyond	
Jamal Abdul-Nasser Intersection	Interior Circle (*duwaar al-dakhliyyeh*)
Square de Paris	Lweibdeh Circle
Arar Street & Sharif Nasser bin Jameel Street	Wadi Saqra
Wasfi at-Tall Street	Gardens Street
Yubil Circle (jct Gardens/Medina St)	Waha Circle (*duwaar al-waha*)
Queen Rania al-Abdullah Street	University Street
King Abdullah II Street	Medical City Street

the city. Downtown forms a slender T-shape nestling in the valleys between six hills. At the joint of the T, and the heart of the city, is the imposing **Husseini Mosque**, which faces along **King Faysal Street**, the commercial centre of Downtown and home to most of its budget hotels. The other main thoroughfare of Downtown – Hashmi Street and King Talal Street, together forming the cross-piece of the T – runs in front of the mosque, passing to the west most of Amman's street markets, and to the east the huge **Roman Theatre**. Towering over Downtown are several hills, including **Jebel al-Qal'a** ("Citadel Hill"), site of a partly restored **Umayyad Palace**.

Amman's wealth is concentrated in upmarket **West Amman**; other districts to the north, south and east are poorer and more populous. The various neighbourhoods of **Jebel Amman** form the heart of the city's rich western quarter. Running along the crest of the ridge is **Zahran Street**, the main east–west traffic artery, punctuated by numbered intersections known as "**circles**" (not all of them are roundabouts, and most feature overpasses and/or multi-level,

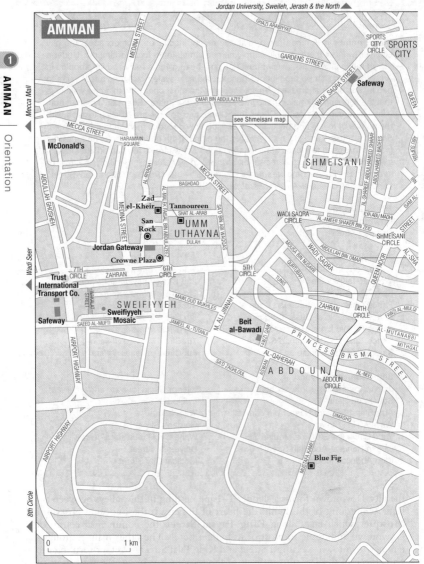

Jordan University, Sweileh, Jerash & the North ▲

AMMAN

Mecca Mall ◄

Wadi Seer ◄

8th Circle ◄

see Shmeisani map

SHMEISANI

McDonald's

Zad
el-Kheir
Tannoureen
San
Rock
Jordan Gateway
Crowne Plaza
Trust
International
Transport Co.
Safeway

UMM
UTHAYNA

SWEIFIYYEH
Sweifiyyeh
Mosaic

Beit
al-Bawadi

ABDOUN

Blue Fig

Safeway

SPORTS
CITY
CIRCLE
SPORTS
CITY

0   1 km

▼ Queen Alia Airport, Dead Sea, Madaba & the South

crisscrossing tunnels that keep the traffic moving). Closest to Downtown, **1st Circle** marks a quiet district with some elegant old stone buildings, focused on the cafés and galleries of cobblestoned Rainbow Street. The area around **2nd Circle** has backstreets comprising close-knit neighbourhoods with rows of shops and diners. Ministries, offices and big hotels cluster around busy **3rd Circle**, behind which are quiet and pleasant upscale residential districts with some fine restaurants. The slopes around **4th** and **5th Circles** are where the Prime Minister's Office and many embassies are located (as well as more big

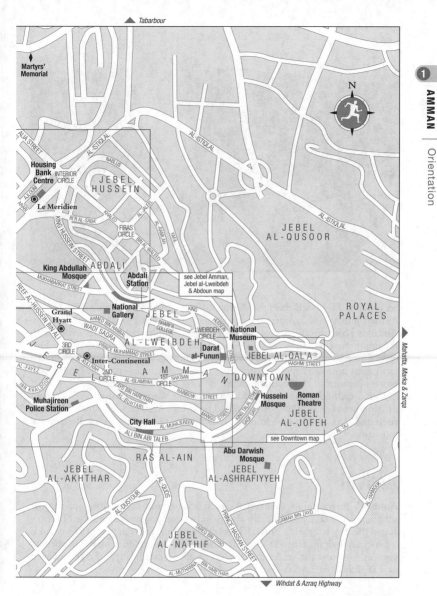

Tabarbour

Martyrs'
Memorial

N

ALIA STREET

AL-ISTIQLAL

AL-ISTIQLAL

**Housing
Bank
Centre** INTERIOR
CIRCLE

NABLUS

**JEBEL
HUSSEIN**

AL-ISTIQLAL

Le Meridien

AL-QUM

KING HUSSEIN STREET

KHALED

BUR AL-SABA'

**FIRAS
CIRCLE**

BIN AL-WALEED

AL-JALEEL

AL-RAMI AN

YAFA

**JEBEL
AL-QUSOOR**

**King Abdullah
Mosque**

ABDALI

MUKHABARRAT STREET

**Abdali
Station**

KING

HUSSEIN

see Jebel Amman,
Jebel al-Lweibdeh
& Abdoun map

**ROYAL
PALACES**

REEF AL-HUSSEIN BIN ALI

**Grand
Hyatt**

WADI SAQRA

**National
Gallery**

AHMED BIN HANBAL

SHARIFA
COLLEGE

JEBEL

LWEIBDEH
CIRCLE

**National
Museum**

J
E
B
E
L

3RD
CIRCLE

AL-FAYEZ

PRINCE MUHAMMAD STREET

AL-KULLIYA

2ND
CIRCLE

Inter-Continental

AL-LWEIBDEH

**Darat
al-Funun**

A M M A N

AL-ISLAMIYAH

1ST
CIRCLE

SHA'BAN

STREET

JEBEL AL-QAL'A

HASHMI STREET

DOWNTOWN

IBN KHALDOUN

ZAYD BIN HARETHAH

AL-BUHTARI

RAINBOW

STREET

**Muhajireen
Police Station**

AL-MUHAJIREEN

City Hall

ALI BIN ABI TALEB

MANGO STREET

KING TALAL STREET

SHOE SOUK

**Husseini
Mosque**

**Roman
Theatre**

**JEBEL
AL-JOFEH**

AL-TAJ

see Downtown map

RAS AL-AIN

**Abu Darwish
Mosque**

**JEBEL
AL-AKHTHAR**

AL-DUSTOUR

AL-QUDS

**JEBEL
AL-ASHRAFIYYEH**

USAMAH BIN ZAYD

AL-YARMOUK

**JEBEL
AL-NATHIF**

TARIQ BIN ZIYAD

PRINCE HASSAN STREET

BIN HARETHAH

AL-MUTHANNA

▼ *Wihdat & Azraq Highway*

Mahatta, Marka & Zarqa

hotels); **6th Circle** – overlooked by the twin towers of the Jordan Gateway development – lies near the cafés and boutiques of Sweifiyyeh and Umm Uthayna; **7th Circle** marks the start of the Airport Road/Desert Highway heading south, and features supermarkets, petrol stations and drive-through fast-food outlets; and busy **8th Circle** hosts hard-working neighbourhoods at the western limits of the city proper.

The next hill over from Jebel Amman is **Jebel al-Lweibdeh**, a monied residential neighbourhood which is home to the **National Gallery** and several

▲ Taking in the views, Jebel al-Qal'a

art galleries. Lweibdeh abuts the district known as **Abdali**, currently being transformed into a new business district centred on a cluster of skyscrapers. Above
Abdali lies **Shmeisani**, one of the city's liveliest commercial areas, sprinkled with
restaurants and pavement cafés. Beyond here, the northwestern suburbs dribble
on for miles out to **Jordan University**. South of Shmeisani, **Sweifiyyeh**, the
city's most upscale shopping district, lies below 6th Circle – fittingly close to the
lavish mansions of **Abdoun**, residence of most of Jordan's millionaires.

Within spitting distance of Abdoun's villas, the **Wadi Abdoun** valley marks a
division between rich West Amman and poor East Amman – of which **Muhajireen** and **Ras al-Ain** are closest to Downtown, the latter hosting the national
museum.

Arrival

Amman's many points of **arrival** are far-flung, and unless you opt for the
simplicity of a taxi you'll nearly always have a rather involved onward journey
across the city to reach a hotel. However, one thing you can always count on is
a generally helpful attitude from bystanders. The worst that might happen to
you on your first day in Amman would be an overabundance of offers of help
or a slightly inflated taxi fare.

By air

Amman has two airports, but all intercontinental traffic comes into the main
Queen Alia International Airport – see the box opposite for full information.

Marka Airport (otherwise known as Amman Civil Airport; code ADJ),
a small airfield 5km east of Downtown, is served only by regional charters.

For full details on **renting a car**, turn to p.39.

Queen Alia International Airport

Amman's main **Queen Alia International Airport** – code **AMM**, abbreviated locally to QAIA – is located on the edge of the desert, 35km south of Amman and about 18km east of Madaba. It is signposted off Jordan's main north–south highway, which is known in the south as the Desert Highway and around Amman as the Airport Road.

Between 2009 and 2012, the airport is undergoing major changes. A vast new terminal, designed by British architect Norman Foster, is being built alongside the existing buildings, which will be demolished following the handover to the new terminal in late 2011. Until then, expect a certain amount of disruption.

Before the new airport is open

The current airport has two terminals, occupying opposite halves of a single, H-shaped building. **Terminal 1** (the South Terminal) is used mainly by Royal Jordanian, and **Terminal 2** (the North Terminal) is used mainly by other carriers. To get from one to the other, simply cross the road – or, if you are already "air-side" (that is, upstairs), make your way through the Duty-Free Shop, which occupies the cross-piece of the H. There are no **left-luggage** facilities.

Arrival

Almost all nationalities are routinely issued with a **visa** on arrival (details on p.65). At the visa desk, one official will take your passport and fee (10JD, in cash dinars only) and his colleague will stamp you in. Bank counters for changing money are alongside. You then proceed downstairs to ground level for baggage reclaim. Porter service is officially free, but if you ask for help, a tip of 1JD is fine, 2JD generous. Beside the reclaim carousels is a small **duty-free shop**. Your suitcases must be X-rayed and then you come through to the arrivals hall.

Airport **taxis** wait outside, and drivers will approach you. Fares to all destinations are fixed: they are posted beside one of the exit doors. From the airport to Amman costs JD20–22 (depending on the district), to the Dead Sea JD34, to Petra JD77, to Aqaba JD111. Prices include baggage.

You can ignore claims that there are no buses: **Airport Express buses** leave from marked points outside both arrival halls to Tabarbour station, dropping off first in Shmeisani (daily hourly 7am–11pm, then every 2hr overnight; takes 45min; driver's mobile ☏077 731 6000). The fare is JD3, including baggage.

Departure

A **taxi** from anywhere in Amman should cost around JD18–20; **driving time** is about 45 minutes. **Airport Express buses** (info ☏06 489 1073) leave from Tabarbour station (daily hourly 6am–10pm, then every 2hr overnight; JD3 including baggage), picking up also from marked stops at Interior Circle in Shmeisani and 7th Circle. Ask your hotel to confirm the schedule.

If you're flying with **Royal Jordanian**, avoid the airport queues by using RJ's **City Terminal** at 7th Circle (daily 7.30am–9.30pm; ☏06 585 6855). Here, you can check your bags in and receive a boarding card, anywhere **between 24 hours and 3 hours in advance** of your departure; using this facility gives you an **extra baggage allowance** of 10kg above the usual limit. You can then go back into the city or, if your flight is imminent, take RJ's private bus direct to the airport (every 30min; JD3). You're led through a fast-track gate direct to passport control.

Airport hotel

The only **hotel** at the airport is the four-star *Golden Tulip*, previously known as the *Alia* (☏06 445 1000, ⊛www.goldentulip.com; ➐), located about 1km along the link road between the airport and the highway. Facilities are adequate but it's rather soulless: most of its business comes from transit passengers.

Some domestic shuttles to and from Aqaba formerly operated from here and may do so again in future. A **taxi** to Downtown costs about JD2.

By bus or serveece

Amman has numerous termini scattered all over the city for local and international arrivals by bus or serveece (shared taxi). Where you end up depends partly on where you're coming from, and partly on what form of transport you're using.

Serveeces from Damascus arrive alongside a large parking area in the **Abdali** district (pronounced *AB-d'lee*) – formerly a major bus station, now under redevelopment.

Scheduled JETT (and partner) buses from Aqaba, Damascus, Cairo and other cities terminate alongside the **JETT offices**, about 1km uphill from Abdali. Grab any taxi or serveece heading downhill to reach the Downtown hotels.

Tabarbour station (aka North station, *mujemma ash-shamal*), 5km north of Abdali, is the terminus for buses and serveeces from towns north of Amman – including Jerash, Ajloun, Irbid and Salt – as well as some from Madaba. Airport Express buses from Queen Alia airport, and serveeces from the King Hussein/Allenby Bridge (for Jerusalem) also terminate here. Reckon on a taxi fare of about 3JD to reach the city-centre hotels.

Wihdat station (aka South station, *mujemma al-janoob*), 5km south of Downtown Amman near Middle East Circle, is where buses and serveeces from the south of Jordan arrive – chiefly Aqaba, Petra, Ma'an, Karak and some from Madaba – as well as a handful of international buses. It lies a 3–4JD taxi ride from any hotels. Serveeces run frequently between Wihdat and Tabarbour, and Wihdat and Raghadan, for less than JD0.50.

Muhajireen station, 2km southwest of Downtown, directly beneath the hill of 3rd Circle, is the arrival point for minibuses from west of Amman, including the Dead Sea, Wadi Seer, Shuneh al-Janubiyyeh and some from Madaba.

Raghadan station, in the heart of Downtown, at the time of writing hosted only serveeces serving neighbourhoods within Amman: the buses from here to nearby destinations such as Zarqa, Salt and Madaba had been shifted 2km east to the **Mahatta station**, pending an overhaul of transport services in the area.

Buses run by **Trust International Transport** from Aqaba, as well as from Tel Aviv and Nazareth, terminate outside the company's office at the corner of Saleh al-Smadi and Ibn al-Fata streets near the big Safeway supermarket by 7th Circle. A taxi ride to Downtown is about JD4.

By train

At the time of writing, no scheduled passenger **trains** were operating in Jordan: service on the historic Hejaz Railway line from Damascus had been suspended, reportedly permanently.

Information

Amman has no **tourist information** office. The Greater Amman Municipality (GAM) has an English website at ⓦ www.ammancity.gov.jo – but it's pretty thin. For printed brochures, contact the Jordan Tourism Board (JTB) in your home country before you depart; p.71 gives contacts and a list of websites offering specialist information. Bookshops within five-star hotels stock good **maps** – invariably better than the free JTB handouts. For details about Jordan's nature reserves, and to book overnight stays, walks or meal-stops at any of them, drop into the Wild Jordan centre (see p.105).

City transport

Due to its geography and the unplanned nature of its expansion, Amman doesn't have an integrated **transport system**: buses and serveeces compete on set routes around the city (you'll never have to wait long beside a main road to flag one or other of them down), but none runs to a timetable. Few people pay heed to the roadside bus-stop pillars that appeared in some districts recently: most buses and all serveeces will stop anywhere. The fares quoted below are approximate.

Expect major changes over the next few years. A light railway is under construction between Amman and Zarqa, which may be extended to encompass a city-centre network. The mayor's office is also grappling with bringing order to the current, chaotic system of buses and serveeces: this may include transport maps, marked stops, published fares, and so on. Time will tell. In the meantime, make use of the **Amman City Tour** buses (see below): 10JD for their 24-hour pass is pretty good value.

Serveeces

Serveeces (shared taxis) are essential for getting quickly and easily up the hills surrounding Downtown, and for crossing between districts. They operate like small buses, with between four and six passengers cramming in and everyone paying a flat fare. You can get in or out wherever you like on the set route. All Amman's city serveeces are **white** cars, with black stencilled panels in Arabic on both front doors stating the general district they're going to. The cars tend to form long nose-to-tail lines at the bottom of the Downtown hills; the first passengers in the queue pile into the last car in line, which then pulls out and grinds its way past all the others up the hill and away. All the rest then roll backwards one place and the same thing happens again.

No official information or route maps exist: the only sure-fire way to find out which serveece goes where is to ask passers-by or local shopkeepers. If you want

Heavy traffic

Traffic in Amman – especially West Amman – can be horrendous. There's an estimated one car for every seven residents; with the population approaching two million, that makes for one almighty traffic jam. Add to that an influx during the summer of tens of thousands of visitors from Saudi Arabia and the Gulf, almost all of whom drive their own cars, and the problem reaches crisis levels. All this isn't helped by the local driving style: lane discipline is nonexistent, cars are frequently parked (or double-parked) to block the flow of traffic, roundabouts are a free-for-all, poor traffic-light phasing often leads to gridlock, and so on. Many pinchpoints around the city experience all-day congestion (streets in the complex Downtown one-way system, and in and around Shmeisani, are often nose-to-tail), and you should allow up to an hour to cross the city during the day. Thursday afternoons – the start of the weekend getaway – are notoriously bad. Respite comes overnight, and on Fridays.

to pick up a serveece partway along its route, a bunch of people forming themselves into a queue on the kerbside is a sure sign of a stop. When you want to **get out**, saying *"allah yaatik al-afyeh"* ("God give you strength") will have the driver veering over to the kerb for you.

Fares are in the order of JD0.20–0.30 per person, except on long crosstown routes, which can be JD0.50 or more. Serveeces run frequently from 7am to about 7pm, after which time they tend to operate as unmetered taxis.

Taxis

Roughly a quarter of all cars in Amman are yellow **taxis**; the metered fares are relatively cheap and they can whisk you to places that might take hours to get to by any other means. Unless you're starting from a remote neighbourhood or are planning a journey in the middle of the night, you'll rarely have to wait long to be able to hail one. You should insist on the **meter** being switched on before you start moving, though practically all drivers will do it anyway as a matter of course. The meters *always* work; if a driver claims it's broken and tries to negotiate a fixed fare with you, simply say *"ma'alesh"* ("forget it") and wait for another taxi to come along. Although fares don't rise at night, the proportion of "broken" meters does.

At the time of writing, the flagfall starting rate was JD0.25, with JD0.10 added for every 58m of travel. A ten-minute ride should cost something like JD1.50–1.80, with a crosstown journey JD4 or more. Don't misplace the decimal point: we've had reports of first-time visitors seeing "1600" on the meter, and handing over JD16 instead of JD1.60. Not every driver will point out the mistake.

Although most drivers know their way around pretty well, no Ammani relates to street names. Unless you're going somewhere obvious, like Wihdat station or the Roman Theatre, first give the name of the neighbourhood you're heading for, then, as you get closer, tell the driver which building you want, or maybe a nearby landmark: if he's not familiar with it, he'll quite likely just drive around asking passers-by for directions.

Walking in Amman

Walking in Amman is a mixed bag. It's absolutely the only way to get around Downtown, but once you venture further out, distances between sights lengthen and the uptown hills feel like mountain peaks.

You can walk from one end of **Downtown** to the other in about twenty or thirty minutes, staying on the flat the whole way. **Jebel al-Lweibdeh** and the lower reaches of **Jebel Amman** (below 3rd Circle) are residential and can be explored on foot, but elsewhere, if you try to walk, you'll generally find yourself slogging along streams of traffic in neighbourhoods designed for driving.

However, one of the most delightful discoveries of old Amman – largely ignored by visitors and locals alike – are the **flights of steps** which trace direct paths up and down the steep Downtown hills, dating from the days in the 1930s and 1940s when hillside residences were otherwise inaccessible. Countless flights – many weed-ridden and crumbling – crisscross the area below 1st Circle on Jebel Amman, the nose of Jebel al-Lweibdeh, the flanks of Jebel al-Qal'a and the hills above the Roman Theatre, passing now and then through private backyards, beneath washing lines or past deserted, once-grand villas. If you're decently dressed and sensitive to the fact that you're tramping through people's gardens – as well as to the possibility that the steps you happen to have chosen might not go anywhere – you're basically free to explore.

A new fleet of silver-coloured **luxury taxis** was launched in 2009, with higher fares (flagfall around JD0.60), trained drivers and a central radio dispatch system. They are – uniquely – bookable by phone and online (☎ 06 579 9999, ⓦ www.taxi-jo.com).

Buses

City buses compete with serveeces on popular routes around the city – but, with Arabic-only destination boards and no route maps, they are unlikely to be of much use to short-stay visitors.

More useful are the large air-conditioned coaches of the hop-on/hop-off **Amman City Tour** (ⓦ www.ammancitytour.com), which make a regular circuit daily between 10am and 8pm (6pm in winter), stopping at 45 marked points from the Roman Theatre and Jebel al-Qal'a right out to Shmeisani, the King Hussein Park, Mecca Mall, Sweifiyyeh, Abdoun, Rainbow Street and back to Downtown: the website has a detailed map. A full circuit takes about two hours, with the gap between buses about 40 minutes. A tourist pass, valid for unlimited rides in 24 hours, is JD10 – buyable on board and from some hotels.

Accommodation

Amman has **accommodation** to suit all budgets. Hoteliers city-wide are tuned into the needs and expectations of Western tourists, but outside the luxury end of the market, you'll find that their margins are tight: standards are sometimes make-do, although the welcome extended to guests is invariably warm. **Inexpensive** options are in Downtown. The best **mid-range** hotels are a bit further out, on Jebel Amman, while **luxury** hotels are spread throughout the city's upscale districts.

With Amman's unusual appeal – focused much more on atmosphere and gentle exploration rather than on a specific set of must-see attractions – there's an odd division to staying here. All the antiquities are in Downtown, but all the decent hotels (above budget levels) are several kilometres away in West Amman. It takes a shift in attitude to appreciate the value of this: the cafés and streetlife outside your hotel in, say, Shmeisani are just as much an Amman "attraction" as the Roman antiquities far away in Downtown.

In the high season (March–Oct), many places across all price brackets fill up quickly, and you'd be well advised to **book ahead**, even for the cheapest of the cheap. There are no **campsites** in or near Amman.

Inexpensive hotels

At first glance, Downtown Amman seems crammed with **inexpensive hotels**, lining all the main streets, but most of them should be avoided: they are either grimly unappealing dives – tape holding the windows together, unchanged beds, thick dust and ancient bathrooms – or simply labourers' dosshouses. Female travellers may not feel safe at many of these places. Hostel-booking websites don't help, falsely publicizing many distinctly shabby establishments as backpacker-friendly.

Despite this, there are some good-value inexpensive hotels out there. Key attributes aside from cleanliness are some form of air cooling in summer – whether a ceiling fan or air conditioning (a table fan won't do) – and heating in winter. Rooms on higher floors tend to be less prone to dust and traffic noise.

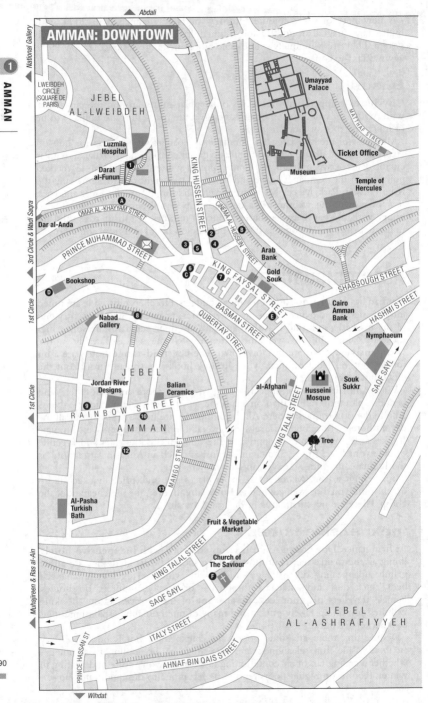

AMMAN: DOWNTOWN

Abdali

National Gallery

LWEIBDEH CIRCLE (SQUARE DE PARIS)

JEBEL AL-LWEIBDEH

Umayyad Palace

MATTHAF STREET

Luzmila Hospital

Darat al-Funun ❶

Ticket Office

Museum

Temple of Hercules

ⓐ

OMAR AL-KHAYYAM STREET

Dar al-Anda

KING HUSSEIN STREET

CINEMA AL-HUSSEIN STREET

3rd Circle & Wadi Saqra

PRINCE MUHAMMAD STREET

❸ ❺ ❹

❷ ⓑ

Arab Bank

Gold Souk

SHABSOUGH STREET

1st Circle

Bookshop

ⓓ

❻ ⓒ

KING FAYSAL STREET

❼

Cairo Amman Bank

HASHMI STREET

BASMAN STREET

ⓔ

Nabad Gallery

❽

QUBERTAY STREET

Nymphaeum

1st Circle

JEBEL

SAQF SAYL

Jordan River Designs

Balian Ceramics

al-Afghani

KING TALAL STREET

Husseini Mosque

Souk Sukkr

❾

RAINBOW STREET

❿

AMMAN

⓫ Tree

⓬

MANGO STREET

⓭

Al-Pasha Turkish Bath

Fruit & Vegetable Market

Muhajireen & Ras al-Ain

KING TALAL STREET

Church of The Saviour

ⓕ

JEBEL AL-ASHRAFIYYEH

SAQF SAYL

PRINCE HASSAN ST

ITALY STREET

AHNAF BIN QAIS STREET

Wihdat

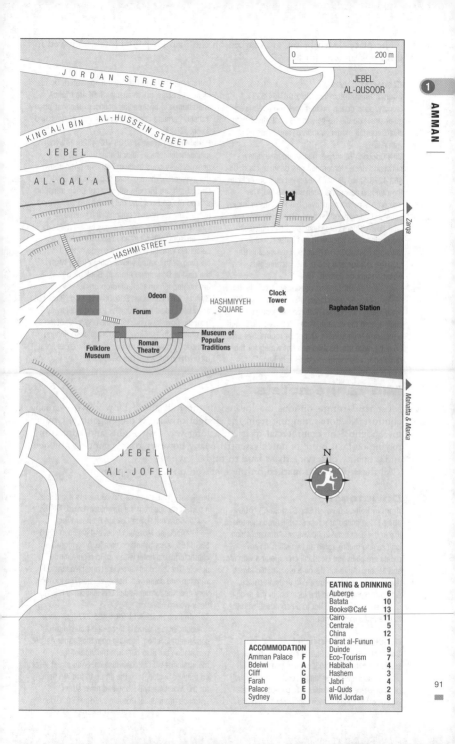

JORDAN STREET

KING ALI BIN AL-HUSSEIN STREET

JEBEL

AL-QAL'A

JEBEL
AL-QUSOOR

0   200 m

Zarqa

HASHMI STREET

Odeon

Forum

Roman
Theatre

Folklore
Museum

Museum of
Popular
Traditions

HASHMIYYEH
SQUARE

Clock
Tower

Raghadan Station

Mahatta & Marka

JEBEL

AL-JOFEH

N

ACCOMMODATION

Amman Palace	F
Bdeiwi	A
Cliff	C
Farah	B
Palace	E
Sydney	D

EATING & DRINKING

Auberge	6
Batata	10
Books@Café	13
Cairo	11
Centrale	5
China	12
Darat al-Funun	1
Duinde	9
Eco-Tourism	7
Habibah	4
Hashem	3
Jabri	4
al-Quds	2
Wild Jordan	8

The places listed below are marked on the map on p.90. Hotels reviewed in this book are safe for all.

Downtown

Bdeiwi Omar al-Khayyam St ☏ 06 464 3394. A friendly, good-quality budget hotel, on a relatively quiet street up the hill behind the post office, with clean, spartan rooms (with fans) and reliable hot water. ❶

Cliff Opposite *Hashem*'s restaurant in an alley between Prince Muhammad and Basman sts ☏ 06 462 4273. Once Jordan's leading backpacker hotel, the *Cliff* has nowadays been superseded. The welcome is as warm as ever, but tired decor, lumpy beds and noise from the next-door restaurant can let it down. Rooms are clean, but have only cold-water sinks and fans (with no heaters). Hot showers cost JD0.50. Other features include free luggage storage and use of the kitchen, plus transport around Jordan. ❶

🏃 **Farah** Off Cinema al-Hussein St ☏ 06 465 1443, ⓦ www.farahhotel.com.jo. Dynamic, ambitiously run budget hotel on six floors, up an alley behind the cinema, with a lift, nice decor and a pleasant front garden. Out of 24 rooms, five are en suite, with a/c, heating and hot water; for the remainder, every three rooms share two

bathrooms (with time-restricted hot water). Dorms, of various sizes, are available. Staff are friendly and attuned to backpacker needs: expect cut-price transport around Jordan, deals on airport runs, and so on. ❶–❷

Palace King Faysal St ☏ 06 462 4326, ⓦ www .palacehotel.com.jo. Take the lift up to an unexpectedly good backpacker-style hotel above the main drag, more or less opposite the Gold Souk. Staff are friendly, offering cut-price transport around the country, and the rooms are well turned out, including cheaper options with shared bathrooms. The top-floor rooms stand out: for its a/c, en-suite bathroom and two connecting balconies wrapping around the side of the building, with rooftop views, room 404 (a twin) is the best in Downtown Amman. Book for a discounted airport pick-up/drop-off. ❶–❷

Sydney 9th of Shaaban St ☏ 06 464 1122. Basic but adequate budget hotel, located a short walk away from the Downtown bustle, at the beginning of the hill climbing to 1st Circle. Rooms are clean enough and comfortable, even though the public areas are a bit tired and hot water can be sporadic. ❶

Mid-range hotels

Most **mid-range** options are located in the hills above Downtown – small, comfortable hotels, ranging from the straightforward to the elegant, but often in residential or commercial districts, a long way from sights and attractions: relying on taxis is pretty much essential. Many, however, offer a gentle ambience and a quality of service that's hard to find elsewhere.

All these places are marked on the maps on p.90, p.93 or p.95.

Downtown

Amman Palace Quraysh St ("Saqf Sayl") ☏ 06 464 6172. Pitched at a respectable Arab clientele, this is the best hotel in Downtown Amman (which isn't saying much), rated as two stars. Its seventy rooms are plain and clean, all en suite and with a/c and heating. Although it's on a main traffic street, upper-floor rooms are quiet. An unusual choice, with atmosphere – and the location, in the middle of the souk, is unique. Not to be confused with the *Palace Hotel* (see above). ❸

Abdali & around

Canary Opposite Terra Sancta College, Jebel al-Lweibdeh ☏ 06 463 8353, ⓔ canary_h@hotmail .com. Peaceful two-star family hotel that gets much of its business from Western tour groups, where 21 clean, comfortable doubles come with TV, fan and

breakfast – and prices for individuals are negotiable. A perfect escape from the Downtown crush. ❷–❸

🏃 **Caravan** Police College Rd near King Abdullah Mosque, Jebel al-Lweibdeh ☏ 06 566 1195, ⓔ caravan@go.com.jo. A comfortable, characterful old hotel with a solid reputation to uphold. The 27 rooms are clean and pleasant, all with fan and some with balcony – and the location, very near the former Abdali bus station, is handy. Book well in advance. ❷–❸

Toledo King Hussein St ☏ 06 465 7777, ⓦ www .toledohotel.jo. Tolerable three-star hotel in a convenient location, backing onto the former Abdali bus station but also built into the side of the mountainous hill of Jebel Hussein. From street level on the Abdali side, take the lift up to the 7th floor for the Moorish-style lobby and main street entrance (from Jebel Hussein's Al-Razi St). Older

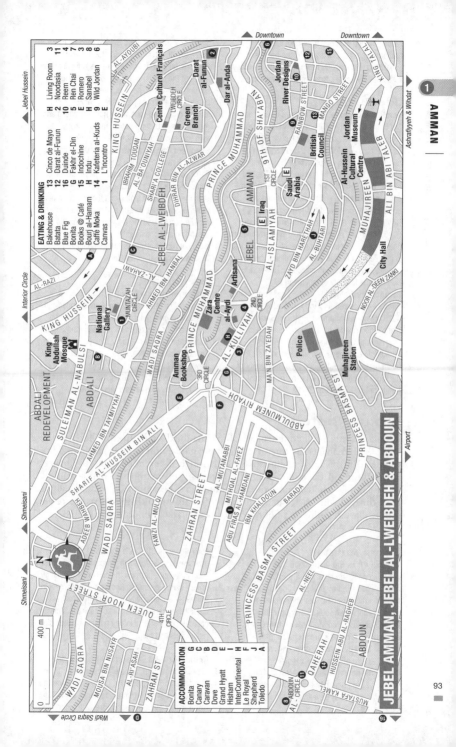

JEBEL AMMAN, JEBEL AL-LWEIBDEH & ABDOUN

EATING & DRINKING

Bakehouse	13
Batata	12
Blue Fig	16
Bonita	G
Books @ Café	15
Caffè Moka	H
Canvas	14

Cinco de Mayo	11
Darat al-Funun	12
Duinde	10
Fakhr el-Din	G
Indochine	H
Indu	H
Kafeteria al-Kuds	14
L'Incontro	1

Living Room	H
Noodasia	2
Reem	11
Ren Chai	5
Romero	E
Sanabel	H
Wild Jordan	9
	E

ACCOMMODATION

Bonita	G
Canary	C
Caravan	B
Dove	D
Grand Hyatt	E
Hisham	I
InterContinental	H
Le Royal	F
Shepherd	J
Toledo	A

rooms, though decently furnished, are a bit tired, and bathrooms decidedly poky; the hotel is expanding, though, and new rooms may be ready by the time you visit. Non-smoking available. ❸

Jebel Amman

Bonita Inn Opposite *InterContinental* hotel, near 3rd Circle ☎ 06 461 5061, Ⓦ www.bonitaamman .com. More like a cheerful guesthouse than a hotel: its six rooms, located above a good Spanish restaurant and tapas bar, are often booked up weeks ahead. Staff are friendly and approachable; the rooms, though modest in size and rather 80s in decor, are decent, comfortable, clean and cosy, with en-suite bathrooms and a/c. A great choice. ❹
Dove Qurtubah St, between 4th and 5th Circles ☎ 06 569 7601. A small, ex-Best Western two-star hotel located in a far-flung residential district, with cool breezes and nice views. Unremarkable rooms are spacious, some with balconies; prices will halve with a little encouragement. ❸
Hisham Off Mithqal al-Fayez St near the French Embassy, between 3rd and 4th Circles ☎ 06 464 4028, Ⓦ www.hishamhotel.com.jo. Small, long-established residential hotel in the embassy quarter with an excellent reputation and unfailingly courteous and efficient staff. A peaceful terrace, pub, good food and plenty of personal touches make this one of the best family hotels in Jordan. ❺–❻

San Rock International Behind *Crowne Plaza Hotel*, off 6th Circle ☎ 06 551 3800, Ⓦ www .sanrock-hotel.com. A fine mid-range tourist hotel – one of the best in the city – with spacious, comfortable rooms, good facilities (a/c, spotless bathrooms) and prompt, efficient service. It's located on a quiet backstreet near the shops and restaurants of Umm Uthayna and Sweifiyyeh, a long way out of the centre. ❻
Shepherd Zaid bin al-Harith St, a backstreet midway between 1st and 2nd Circles ☎ 06 463 9197, Ⓦ www.shepherd-hotel.com. An excellent choice with a touch of class, comfortably close to both the Downtown sights and the uptown restaurants. Rooms are pleasant and quiet (with a/c), service is calm and the breakfast is good. Its reputation and consistently good standards bring in plenty of repeat business from tourists and businesspeople alike. ❹–❺

Shmeisani

Al-Qasr Metropole Arroub St ☎ 06 568 9671, Ⓦ www.alqasrmetropole.com. Quality upper-mid-range hotel on a quiet residential street behind Shmeisani. Cosy rooms are very light and bright, with all the facilities – go for those on the upper floors, which have balconies and spectacular city views. One of the top choices for business people bored with five-star isolation. Also with an excellent penthouse bar and restaurants. ❻–❼

Luxury hotels

Amman boasts a full complement of international-grade **luxury** hotels, almost all of them managed by one or other of the global hotel groups. Booking direct online nabs the most competitive rates, though if you're prepared to chance it and walk in off the street without a booking, you might find that a gentle bit of bargaining could secure you a discounted corporate rate at substantially less than the walk-in "rack rate". All these offer **no-smoking rooms** on request – most have no-smoking floors – and all are marked on the maps on p.82, p.93 or p.95.

Jebel Amman

Crowne Plaza 6th Circle ☎ 06 551 0001, Ⓦ www.cpamman.com. Not a pretty building, and now dwarfed by the giant Jordan Gate twin towers directly behind, but nonetheless an excellent five-star hotel, newly upgraded in 2009. Rooms are comfortable and service is outstanding. This is a great choice for a first night in the city if you're driving in from the airport – turn off the Airport Highway at 7th Circle, just nearby – and the hotel stands within walking distance of the shops and restaurants of both Swayfiyyeh and Umm Uthaina. ❾

Four Seasons 5th Circle ☎ 06 550 5555, Ⓦ www .fourseasons.com/amman. Probably the grandest hotel in the city, perhaps the country – a palatial, fifteen-storey landmark. Rooms are the largest in Amman – exceptionally well appointed, with every detail taken care of. The public areas are stunningly opulent, and there's a large spa and a clutch of top restaurants and bars. You could want for nothing more. ❾
Grand Hyatt 3rd Circle ☎ 06 465 1234, Ⓦ www .amman.hyatt.com. Superbly designed hotel on the main road between 3rd Circle and Shmeisani, replete with every international business facility along with a giant fitness centre with indoor and

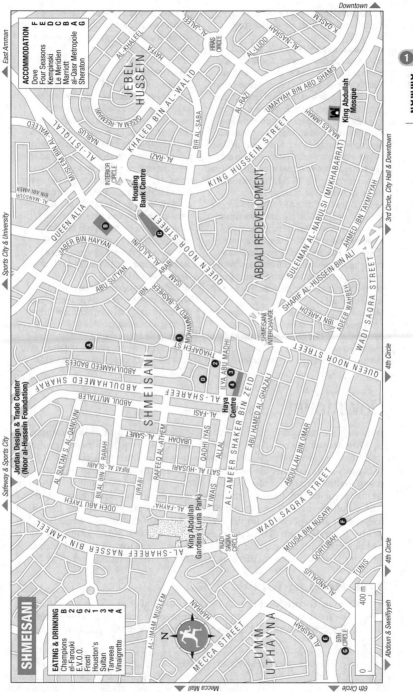

SHMEISANI

ACCOMMODATION
Dove	F
Four Seasons	E
Kempinski	D
Le Meridien	C
Marriott	B
al-Qasr Metropole	A
Sheraton	G

EATING & DRINKING
Champions	B
el-Farouki	2
E.V.O.O.	G
Frosti	2
Houston's	1
Sultan	3
Tarweea	4
Vinaigrette	A

Downtown ▲

East Amman ◄

Sports City & University ◄

Safeway & Sports City ◄

JEBEL HUSSEIN

FIRAS CIRCLE

AL-KHALEEL
HAYFA
AL-JALEEL
K. QASEM
AL-NASRAH
AL-LUDD

KHALED BIN AL-WALID
QASEM AL-REMAWI
NABLUS
AL-ISTIQLAL
MUSLEM BIN AL-WALEED
AL-RAZI
BIR AL-SABA

King Abdullah Mosque

UMAYYAH BIN ABD SHAMS
MAJLES UMMAH
MALES UMMAH
AL-RAZI

KING HUSSEIN STREET

INTERIOR CIRCLE
AL-MANSUR BIN ABI AMER

Housing Bank Centre

QUEEN ALIA
JABER BIN HAYYAN
ABU SUTYAN
BDIY
ISAM
(BDIY) AL-ALUNI
QUEEN NOOR STREET

ABDALI REDEVELOPMENT

SULEIMAN AL-NABULSI (MUKHABARRAT)
AHMED IBN TAYMIYYAH

3rd Circle, City Hall & Downtown ►

SHMEISANI INTERCHANGE

SHARIF AL-HUSSEIN BIN ALI
IBN FARED
ADEEB WAHBEH
WADI SAQRA STREET

THAQAFEH ST
ILYA ABU MADHI
AL-SHAREEF
Haya Centre
AL-FASI

SHMEISANI

Jordan Design & Trade Center (Noor al-Hussein Foundation)

ABDULHAMEED SHARAF
ABDULHAMEED BADEES
ABDUL MUTTALEB
AL-SAMET
UBADAH
QADHI IYAS
SATTI AL-HUSARI
ALLAL
AL-AMEER SHAKER BIN ZEID

AL-SULTAN S. AL-QANOUN
RABAH
RIFAT AL-SLAIBI
RAFEEG AL-ATHEM
URABI
YIWAIS
BILAL BIN
AL-FAYHA
AL-IMAM MUSLEM

ODEH ABU TAYEH
AL-SHAREEF NASSER BIN JAMEL

ABU HAMED AL-GHAZALI
ABDULLAH BIN OMAR

WADI SAQRA STREET

QUEEN NOOR STREET

4th Circle ►

King Abdullah Gardens (Luna Park)
WADI SAQRA CIRCLE

MOUSA BIN NUSAYR
QORTUBAH
TUNIS
AL-ANDALUS

4th Circle ►

MECCA STREET
HARRAN
AL-BASHA
5TH CIRCLE
AL-BASHA

UMM UTHAYNA

N

0 ——— 400 m

Mecca Mall ◄

6th Circle ►

Abdoun & Sweilfiyeh ►

5th Circle ►

outdoor pools, several excellent restaurants, nightclub and supremely comfortable guest rooms. ⑨

InterContinental 2nd Circle ☎06 464 1361, ⓦwww.interconti.com/amman. One of the city's landmarks, and the standard choice for visiting journalists, diplomats and CEOs; taxi-drivers often call it by its old name of *Funduq al-Urdun* (*Jordan Hotel*), harking back to the days when it was the only luxury hotel in the country. Now completely renovated and extended, it has modern, spacious, well-appointed rooms and is packed with all kinds of diversions, from a crafts gallery to live music. Star features include the cafés in the lobby and on the rear terrace, one of the city's best bookshops and an excellent Indian restaurant. ⑨

Le Royal 3rd Circle ☎06 460 3000, ⓦwww .leroyalamman.com. Part of a small international chain, and located within the huge cylindrical tower overlooking 3rd Circle. Guest rooms are spacious and luxurious, with formal, traditional styling; many have spectacular city views. Within the same building is a three-storey shopping mall, taking in boutiques, cafés, restaurants and a multi-screen cinema. ⑨

Sheraton 5th Circle ☎06 593 4111, ⓦwww .sheratonamman.com. Occupying an odd, rather ugly turreted monolith facing onto 5th Circle, this is nonetheless one of Amman's top five-star hotels. Guest rooms are spacious, airy and bright, styled

pleasantly with light colours and fabrics and soft, luxurious textures. Public areas, and the acclaimed restaurants, are glitteringly lavish, but designed with some character. ⑨

Shmeisani

Kempinski Abdul Hamid Shoman St ☎06 520 0200, ⓦwww.kempinski-amman.com. Recent addition to Amman's five-star pack, perfectly placed in the heart of Shmeisani's commercial district, with shops, cafés and restaurants on the doorstep. The styling is fresh and ultramodern throughout – no stuffy opulence, wood panelling or swirly carpets here. Instead, think cool, spacious rooms, chic public areas and sharp, genial service. A sophisticated, design-conscious choice. ⑨

Le Meridien Queen Noor St ☎06 569 6511, ⓦwww.lemeridienamman.com. Lavish and luxurious, with a touch of style to its fittings. A good range of rooms – all superbly appointed – gives some flexibility in pricing, and there's a swathe of restaurants, bars and fitness facilities. Very near Interior Circle. ⑨

Marriott Issam al-Ajlouni St ☎06 560 7607, ⓦwww.ammanmarriott.com. A popular and long-standing city landmark, rising high above Shmeisani. Weighing value against quality, this is one of the best options for its unfussy comfort, swift, intelligent service and excellent facilities. A great choice if you prefer five-star character to mere opulence. ⑨

Downtown وسط البلد

Although you shouldn't leave Amman without having spent at least some time in **Downtown**, the cramped valleys between towering hills shelter comparatively few obvious sights. Rather, Downtown is the spiritual and physical heart of the city and is unmissable for its streetlife. This is the district that most strongly resembles the stereotype of a Middle Eastern city – loud with traffic and voices, Arabic music blaring from shopfronts, people selling clothes, coffee, cigarettes or trinkets on the street. The handful of Roman ruins that survive here have been irreverently incorporated into the everyday bustle of the city: the banked seating of the huge **Roman Theatre** is always dotted with small groups of locals seeking refuge from the traffic noise, and the adjacent **forum** is filled with trees and cafés, a public meeting place today as it was two millennia ago.

The Roman forum

The **Roman forum**, dominating the heart of Downtown, is the best place to begin. The massive theatre was the centrepiece of Roman Philadelphia, and also the initial focus for Amman's modern settlement late in the nineteenth century.

There is a **map** of Downtown Amman on p.90.

Renovating Downtown

The government and municipality have settled on a new **master plan** for Amman (Ⓦ www.ammanplan.gov.jo), including a revamp of the Downtown area. The Ras al-Ain district, at the western end of Talal Street, has been transformed by the construction of a new City Hall, the Al-Hussein Cultural Centre and the Jordan Museum. Next in line is what has been dubbed "Wadi Amman" – principally the area around the Roman Theatre. This is set to host one (possibly two) new hotels, shops, a public library and new transport links – including, potentially, a funicular railway running up to the citadel. By the time you visit, you may find renovations in full swing.

As you approach from the main Hashmi Street, winding your way through the trees, an impressively long Corinthian colonnade and some original Roman paving are the only physical remains of Philadelphia's **forum**, the marketplace which filled the gap between the theatre and the street. What also survives, however, is the spirit of the place: this whole area is still Downtown's main hangout, as Ammanis crowd the little cafés, promenade up and down in the dappled sunshine, guzzle ice cream and sweets, meet friends and snooze on the grass.

Several nineteenth-century travellers to Amman reported seeing the remains of a large **propylaeum**, or ornamental gateway, on the edge of the forum; this still stood in 1911 but has since disappeared. If you stop in front of the Theatre and look back towards the street, high on the summit of Jebel al-Qal'a opposite you'll spot the columns of the Temple of Hercules; originally, the propylaeum stood here at what was the foot of a tremendous monumental staircase leading down from the temple, linking the religious and social quarters of the city.

The Roman Theatre

Cut into a depression in the hillside, the **Roman Theatre** (Sat–Thurs roughly 8am–sunset, Fri 10am–4pm; JD1) is impressively huge, and the view, as well as the ability to eavesdrop on conversations between ant-like people on the stage below, definitely repays the steep climb to the top. The structure was built between 169 and 177 AD, during the reign of Emperor Marcus Aurelius, for an audience of almost six thousand, and is still occasionally filled today for concerts. Above the seating is a small, empty **shrine** with niches; the dedication isn't known, although part of a statue of Athena was discovered during clearance work. Standing on the stage or in the orchestra – the semicircle in front of the stage – you can get a sense of the ingenuity of the theatre's design: the south-facing stage is flooded with sun throughout the day, while virtually every spectator remains undazzled and in cool shadow. To discover the incredible acoustics, stand in the middle of the orchestra and declaim at the seating, and your normal speaking voice will suddenly gain a penetrating echo; step off that spot and there's no echo. Furthermore, two people crouching down at opposite ends of the orchestra can mutter into the semicircular stone wall below the first row of seats and easily hear each other.

To the sides of the stage are two small museums, housed in vaults beneath the auditorium. On the right as you walk in, the **Folklore Museum** (same hours & ticket) displays mannequins engaged in traditional crafts and a moderately interesting reconstruction of an old-fashioned living-room. More worthwhile is the **Jordanian Museum of Popular Traditions**, opposite (same hours & ticket), which enlivens the well-worn theme of traditional clothing, jewellery and customs by rooting it firmly in the present-day life of ordinary people. The

▲ Roman theatre, Downtown Amman

vaulted rooms are full of examples of national dress, with detailed notes and occasional photographs to set them in context. Other exhibits include pieces of antique bedouin jewellery and a fascinating range of stones used in healing, as well as mosaics downstairs gathered from Madaba and Jerash (and viewable up close).

The Odeon

Facing onto the forum area outside the theatre is the Roman **Odeon** (closes 1hr earlier; same ticket). This renovated freestanding theatre, seating about five hundred, dates from slightly earlier than its bigger neighbour and was probably the venue for either parliamentary-style council meetings or small-scale drama. In antiquity, the whole building would probably have been roofed. Amman's grand old *Philadelphia Hotel*, the country's first (and, for many decades, only) hotel, was built in the 1920s beside the Odeon on the banks of the Sayl Amman, which was then a stream flowing through the city centre; sadly, the hotel was demolished in the 1980s to make way for Downtown redevelopment – which then never really took off.

The Husseini Mosque and around

From the Roman Theatre, lively **Hashmi Street** storms west past *shawerma* stands, juice bars, patisseries and cafés towards the commercial hub of Downtown and the focal, pink-and-white-striped **Husseini Mosque**. Like everything else in Amman, this is a relatively recent construction, although a mosque has stood here since 640 (and, before that, a Byzantine cathedral). However, any remnant of the original building was erased when Emir Abdullah ordered the site cleared for construction of the current mosque in 1932. It remains one of Amman's most important places of worship, and is often also the focus for political demonstrations. You're free to wander inside, as long as you are dressed suitably decently.

The building on the corner opposite the mosque formerly held Amman's best-loved coffee house, the grand old **Arab League Café** – a stalwart here for over fifty years, with its fine balcony overlooking the bustle below. In 2002, after a wrangle between the building's owners (one wanted to keep it as it was; the other wanted to rebuild), the café was closed by court order and – to the horror of seemingly everyone in the city bar the owners themselves – gutted. In a city which already lacks history, a piece of the past has been lost.

The area around the mosque remains the heart of Amman's **bazaars**. To the east lies a bustling warren of alleys known as the **Souk Sukkr** (Sugar Market), where stalls sell everything from dates and spices to soap and mops. To the west of the mosque, the main street funnelling traffic out of Downtown is **King Talal Street**, lined with stores selling ordinary household goods, fabric and bric-a-brac; a little way down on the left, hidden behind a row of shopfronts, is the city's main fruit and vegetable market.

The main street parallel to King Talal Street follows exactly the course of the Roman *decumanus maximus*, which was formed by paving over the free-flowing stream beneath. The street – officially Quraysh Street – is still popularly known as the **Saqf Sayl** (Roof of the Stream), but these days the *sayl* is dry, having been tapped much further upstream to provide drinking water. This is the busiest and liveliest area of the city, with cobblers, CD stalls and hawkers of soap and tooth-brushes competing for space under the pavement colonnades with a dirt-cheap secondhand clothes market. There's also a small bus station here serving villages near Amman.

The Nymphaeum

On the Saqf Sayl behind the Husseini Mosque, excavation and restoration work on the Roman **Nymphaeum** has been going on for years, seemingly without end. It's very similar in design to the huge nymphaeum at Jerash, which has been dated to 191 AD; at that time, Philadelphia too was at its zenith. The site is fenced and is usually off-limits, though the guardian may not object to you exploring. However, apart from the immensity of the building (and its newer reconstruction), there's not an awful lot to admire. Nymphaea – public fountains dedicated to water nymphs – were sited near rivers running through major cities throughout the Greco-Roman world. This one, facing onto an open plaza at the junction of the two principal city streets, the east–west *decumanus* and the north–south *cardo*, was originally two storeys high and must have been quite a sight, dominating the area. Colonnades of Corinthian columns would have drawn even more attention towards the concave building, which was lavishly faced in marble, with statues of gods, emperors or city notables filling the niches all around.

King Faysal Street ساحة الملك فيصل

The Husseini Mosque faces up **King Faysal Street** (also known as Faysal Square), modern Amman's oldest thoroughfare, occupying the valley between Jebel Amman to the south and Jebel al-Qal'a to the north. Although it follows exactly the course of the Roman *cardo*, any trace of the ancient past has been built over: the oldest buildings, with elegant arched windows and decorated stone balconies, date only from the 1920s. One of the nicest, at no. 12 (beside the Arab Bank), is open to visitors – known as the "**Duke's Diwan**" (Sat–Thurs roughly 8am–sunset; free). This building, which dates from 1924, formerly served as the main post office, an annexe of the Ministry of Finance and, from the 1950s, as the *Haifa Hotel* (whose sign still lies in one of the rooms). In the last few years it has been renovated as a labour of love by a prominent Jordanian businessman, Mamdouh Bisharat, who owns land in the village of Mukhaybeh (see p.179) and is known as the "Duke of Mukhaybeh" – hence "Duke's Diwan"

The Circassians

The first people to settle in Amman in modern times were Muslim refugees from Christian persecution in Russia. The **Circassians**, who began arriving in the 1870s, trace their origins back to mountain villages above the eastern Black Sea, in the region of the **Caucasus** around present-day Georgia and Chechnya.

In the 1860s, Russian military offensives in the Caucasus forced 1.5 million people out of their homes into exile in Ottoman Turkish territory. Some headed west towards the fertile lands of the Balkans (establishing Muslim communities in and around Bosnia), while others drifted south into the Ottoman province of Syria. Stories began to filter back to those left behind of life in a Muslim land, and many Circassian and Chechen villages went en masse into voluntary exile. European governments lent their weight to the Ottoman policy of dumping the refugees on ships bound for distant Syria.

Meanwhile, Amman had been uninhabited for virtually a thousand years. In 1877, Selah Merrill, a visiting American archeologist, "spent part of one night in the great theatre... The sense of desolation was oppressive. Kings, princes, wealth and beauty once came here to be entertained, where now I see only piles of stones, owls and bats, wretched *fellahin* [peasants] and donkeys, goats and filth." The first Circassian refugees arrived the following year, setting up home in the galleries of the theatre; others founded new villages in the fertile valley of Wadi Seer to the west and among the deserted ruins of Jerash to the north. The presence of settlers caused some conflict with local tribes, but the Circassians held their own in skirmishes with the bedu, and soon a mutual respect and a formal pact of friendship emerged between them. After 1900, Circassian labour was central to the building of the Hejaz railway line, and Circassian farmers became famed for their industry. One of their great innovations was the reintroduction of the wheel: with no roads to speak of, wheeled transport hadn't been used in Transjordan for centuries.

When, in the 1920s, Emir Abdullah established a new state and chose Amman to be its capital, he bound the Circassian community into his new administration: loyal and well-educated families were the mainstay of both the officer corps and the civil service. Over the years, however, overt expressions of Circassian culture faded: Arabic became the lingua franca, the use of national dress died out and, with the rise in land prices following the influx of Palestinian refugees in 1948, many Circassians sold their inherited farmlands around Amman for the building of new suburbs. However, their internal identity remained strong, and Circassians today form an integrated minority of around 25,000.

(a *diwan* is a place for meetings and gatherings). The entrance gives onto a long flight of steps. At the top is an atmospheric suite of seven rooms around a central hallway, decorated with old photos of Amman, paintings and cabinets of bric-a-brac. Students, artists and Ammani old-timers often gather here, to compare notes and chew the fat. Roam around as you like; you'll inevitably be invited by the caretaker to drink tea on the balcony. The *diwan* also hosts occasional informal concerts and artistic events.

Opposite, another fine old building known as Al-Rasheed Courts has been converted into the **Eco-Tourism Café** – a bizarre, misleading name for a perfectly ordinary locals' coffee house: indulging in a tea and an *argileh* on their balcony, hanging over the street, is a great way to absorb the Downtown atmosphere.

Alongside the *diwan* – aside from the wonderful pastry shop **Habiba**, renowned for its delicious *kunafeh* (see p.46) – is the **Gold Souk**, a series of tiny jewellery shops clustered together in a little network of alleys; see p.119 for more about buying gold. Nearby is Shabsough Street, named after the

Shabsough tribe of Circassians who first settled here (see box), from which stairs rise up to Jebel al-Qal'a.

Faysal Street is another area slated for renovation: when you visit, you may find billboards removed, old buildings restored, new cafés installed, and so on. The most far-reaching proposal for change – redirecting traffic and pedestrianizing the street – was unfortunately scotched early on in the planning process, but there is little doubt, nonetheless, that the street could do with a wash-and-brush-up.

The Jordan Museum   متحف الاردن

Southwest of the Husseini Mosque, King Talal Street and the Saqf Sayl meet at a large traffic intersection. To the south rises the hill of Ashrafiyyeh (see p.109), while dead ahead (west), in the valley of the Sayl Amman, is an area known as **Ras al-Ain** (Source of the Spring). Here, just past a delightful open colonnaded plaza featuring a **fountain** at its centre, stands the large, new **Jordan Museum**, opened in late 2009. This sleek building houses the national archeological collection, as well as exhibits on Jordan's history and the story of the Hashemite royal family; the exact layout, though, had not been finalized as this book went to press. Expect halls to be designed thematically, with interactive displays and a strong educational angle. Partnerships established with institutions including the Louvre, the Smithsonian and museums in London, Switzerland and elsewhere are likely to ensure world-class temporary shows. Check the website ⓦwww .jordanmuseum.jo for the latest details, including opening hours and prices.

Just nearby to the west stands the **Al-Hussein Cultural Centre** and Amman's **City Hall**. Both were co-designed by one of the Arab world's leading architects, Jafar Touqan, and both are light, airy and dynamic, often hosting exhibitions of contemporary art and free concerts, bringing affluent West Ammanis into a Downtown neighbourhood they might otherwise never visit. This regeneration of what was formerly a traffic island of dusty wasteground in a low-income neighbourhood is one of Amman's recent success stories – and it looks set to continue, with proposals to convert the site of an old cigarette factory near City Hall into the "Darat King Abdullah II", a theatre and concert venue to serve as a home for the Amman Symphony Orchestra. Discussions are continuing.

Jebel al-Qal'a   جبل القلعة

Jebel al-Qal'a (Citadel Hill) has been a focus for human settlement since the Paleolithic Age, more than 18,000 years ago. Unfortunately, when the Romans moved in to occupy the area, they cleared away whatever they found, including the remains of the Ammonite city of Rabbath Ammon, and chucked it over the side of the hill: Bronze Age, Iron Age and Hellenistic pottery shards have been found mixed up with Roman remains on the slopes below. Of the remains surviving today, the most impressive by far is a huge **Umayyad palace** complex on the upper terrace of the Citadel, dating from the first half of the eighth century. On the middle terrace below and to the south lies the Roman **Temple of Hercules**, its massive columns dramatically silhouetted against the sky. East of the temple, Roman fortifications protect the grassy lower terrace, which has no visible antiquities.

The easiest way to reach the summit is by **taxi** (JD1 from Downtown). For the ambitious who prefer to **walk**, the twenty-minute ascent is extremely steep. About 150m along Shabsough Street as you head east, and just past the second turning on the left, a side-street has a wide flight of steps leading left up the hillside. Turn right at the top, and head up any way you can from here: there are crumbling steps most of the way, often leading through private backyards. You'll eventually arrive at the wall below the Temple of Hercules. If you're **driving**, head east out of Downtown towards Zarqa, come off, pass under the highway, and rejoin it heading west. Look hard to spot the brown sign for the Jebel al-Qal'a antiquities pointing right; exit here, and at the traffic lights bear left steeply up the hill, along King Ali bin al-Hussein Street. Three-quarters of the way up is a hairpin left turn, which brings you to the ticket office.

Admission to the whole hilltop site (Sat–Thurs 8am–7pm, winter closes 4pm, Fri 10am–4pm) was formerly JD2, but you may find that has changed when you visit: the museum here, which formerly held the national archeological collection, changed status in 2009.

The Temple of Hercules

The **Temple of Hercules**, with its towering columns that are visible from Downtown, was built in the same period as the Roman Theatre below. The temple stands on a platform at the head of the monumental staircase which formerly led up from the lower city: the blocks on the cliff edge mark the position of the staircase, and afford a tremendous panoramic view over the city centre that is particularly striking at **sunset**, when – in addition to the visual dramatics – the dozens of mosques in the city all around start broadcasting the call to prayer almost simultaneously.

There is work under way here to consolidate the hillside, and the master plan for redevelopment of Amman city centre (see p.97) involves re-establishing the ancient link between the hilltop and valley floor – by means of stairways or, possibly, a funicular railway. This may mean works are ongoing.

The columns, which were re-erected in 1993, formed part of a colonnaded entrance to the **cella**, or inner sanctum. Within the *cella* – these days often the scene of hard-fought football games among the local kids – a patch of bare rock is exposed, which, it's thought, may have been the sacred rock that formed the centrepiece of the ninth-century BC Ammonite Temple of Milcom on this spot. The Roman dedication to Hercules is not entirely certain but, given the quantity of coins bearing his likeness found in the city below, pretty likely.

The Umayyad Palace

Climbing the path to the upper terrace from the Temple of Hercules, you'll pass a small ruined **Byzantine church** on the right, dating from the fifth or sixth centuries, which reused many of the columns from the nearby temple. The church formed part of a Byzantine town which probably covered much of the hill and which is still being excavated. About 20m further north are a huge round cistern and the remains of an olive-pressing works.

The huge **Umayyad Palace** complex stretches over the northern part of the hill. Part of the palace was built over pre-existing Roman structures, and an entire

---

A new museum?

Opposite the Temple of Hercules stands what was formerly the National Archeological Museum. In 2009 the national collection was moved to the Jordan Museum at Ras al-Ain (see p.101), making way for what was proposed, at the time of writing, to be a new museum devoted to the history of Amman. No details were available as this book went to press.

colonnaded Roman street was incorporated into it. Built after 720, when Amman was a provincial capital, the complex probably combined the residential quarters of the governor of Amman with administrative offices. It was still in use during the Islamic Abbasid (750–969) and Fatimid (969–1179) periods, although much of the brand-new palace was never rebuilt following a devastating earthquake in 749.

The first building you come to, and the most impressive, is the domed **entrance hall**, reached by crossing the first of four plazas. Built over an earlier Byzantine building (which is why it's in the shape of a cross), the hall is decorated with stucco colonnettes and Persian-style geometric patterns, set off by foliage rosettes and a houndstooth zigzag. Much renovation has been carried out here in recent years, not all of it subtly – the new stucco around the interior walls deliberately clashes with the original work, and in 1998 a new dome was hastily constructed above the building, riding roughshod over considerable archeological controversy about whether there ever was a dome here in antiquity. Between the entrance hall and the cistern is a small **baths**, although only a changing area and the "cold room" survive.

Beyond the entrance hall is the second large plaza, from which the **colonnaded street** leads ahead. This was the heart of the administrative quarter, surrounded by nine separate office or residential buildings (of which only four have been excavated), each in the typical Umayyad style of a self-contained *bayt* – small rooms looking onto a central courtyard. The *bayts* were constructed within the pre-existing Roman enclosure, possibly a temple, whose exterior walls are still visible in places. To the west of the courtyard is "Building F", which may have been the site of official audiences, since it was of elegant design and situated close to the entrance hall; two large *iwans* – audience rooms open on one side – with triple arcades give onto a central courtyard, from where a staircase led to an upper storey.

At the far end of the colonnaded street, a decorated doorway takes you through the Roman wall into the third plaza and the private **residential quarters** of the ruler of Amman. Rooms open from three sides, but the plaza is dominated by a huge *iwan*, which presages a domed, cruciform **throne room**, or *diwan*. According to Umayyad protocol, the ruler always stayed hidden behind a curtain during audiences – the tiny passageway between the *iwan* and the *diwan* could have served this purpose. To either side lie the largely unexcavated residential *bayts* for the ruling household. At the back of the *diwan*, a doorway leads through to the fourth and final plaza – a private affair, looking north over the massive Roman retaining wall to the hills opposite.

West Amman

Of the other quarters of the city, you're most likely to visit sprawling, relatively wealthy **West Amman**, home to practically all of the city's upmarket hotels, as well as restaurants and nightlife. Key areas to explore include **Jebel al-Lweibdeh**, an attractive residential neighbourhood that is home to the **National Gallery**, and the lower reaches of **Jebel Amman**, particularly around **1st Circle**, where the cafés and quirky shops of **Rainbow Street** make for some of the city's most pleasant strolling.

Jebel Amman: around 1st Circle   جبل عمان

In general, West Amman is too large to attempt aimless exploratory rambling, though if you have a spare afternoon to fill, you might like to take a wander

There is a **map** of Jebel Amman on p.93.

through the leafy streets **around 1st Circle** on Jebel Amman. When Amman was a small town occupying the Downtown valley-floors, this gentle neighbourhood was the preserve of the elite, including royalty, families wealthy through business or commerce, politicians and ambassadors, British commanders of the army, and so on. The quiet streets either side of **Rainbow Street** are still lined with many fine old villas dating from the 1920s and 1930s, remnants of this time, most of them freestanding one- or two-storey buildings surrounded by walled gardens.

Along Rainbow Street   شارع راينبو

As you head east from 1st Circle, Rainbow Street – named after the Rainbow Cinema on the right – is lined with shops, cafés and boutiques preceding the walled and gated **British Council**. Beyond here, the street dips sharply; partway along on the left is a **mosque** with a fine old minaret, while an anonymous-looking town house on a minor street to the right, with a dark shade of plaster and curved Art Deco-style balcony railings, was where King Talal lived for a time before his accession, and where both the late King Hussein and his brother Prince Hassan were born.

Two of the most attractive villas in the area, both well signposted, are beside each other just off Rainbow Street about 250m east of the British Council. On the corner is an elegant symmetrical villa set back from the street and faced in local stone, with a stepped portico and tall, slender windows, that's now used as showrooms for the crafts of **Jordan River Designs** and **Bani Hamida** (see p.119). Alongside it is a one-storey villa – once home to Major Alec Kirkbride, the first British Ambassador to Jordan – with a beautiful portico of pointed arches, wrought-iron window-bars, and a lovely garden centred on a star-shaped fountain. Both these houses were built in the late 1920s by Salim al-Odat, an architect originally from Karak. Just round the corner with Asfour Street is a pair of houses built for Egyptian businessman and adviser to Emir Abdullah **Ismail Bilbaysi**, a smaller one dating from the 1930s with a semicircular balcony featuring a lavishly painted ceiling visible from the street, and beside it a much larger villa designed in the 1940s in a consciously medieval Mamluke style, with bands of alternating pink and white stone and pointed arches.

Amman's hammam

Hammams (Turkish baths) are common in Cairo, Damascus and many other Middle Eastern and North African cities, elegant and civilized places to steam the city dust out of your pores – but Amman is an exception: its short recent history means that it doesn't share the centuries-old urban traditions of its neighbours. There is, for all intents and purposes, only one *hammam* in the city, the modern **Al-Pasha Turkish Bath** (daily 10am–midnight; ☎06 463 3002, ⊛www.pashaturkishbath.com), located on Mahmoud Taha Street, opposite the Ahlia girls' school; coming from 1st Circle along Rainbow Street, it's the fifth street on the right. It is beautifully designed in traditional style and offers two hours of soaking, scrubbing, lathering and olive-oil massaging with professional male or female therapists for JD25. There are men-only hours, women-only hours and you can book ahead as a mixed group or a couple; call for details. Afterwards, don't miss out on herbal tea and/or a light meal of *mezze* in the beautiful garden courtyard – there are few more pleasant retreats in the city centre.

▲ Books@Café, Jebel Amman

Continuing past more cafés and crafts outlets down Rainbow Street, you come to the distinctively modernistic **Mango House** on the right, at the corner with Omar bin al-Khattab Street (aka Mango St). In smooth, reddish stone with curving, pillared balconies, it was built in the late 1940s by Kamal and Ali Mango, members of one of Amman's most prominent business dynasties. On the other side of Rainbow Street is a long, low house, the whole facade of which is sheltered beneath an elegant Circassian-style porticoed balcony; its most famous resident was Said al-Mufti, a Circassian who was prime minister in the 1950s and also mayor of Amman. Following Mango Street to the right brings you past more cafés and another fine villa, now home to the **Royal Film Commission**, before – on the right – the widely known **Books@Café**, an attractive bookshop and café-bar shoehorned into another historic old house. A few doors further is the print gallery **Jacaranda**, past which the road climbs to a mini-roundabout; to the right is the Al-Pasha *hammam* (see box opposite), while straight on leads past shops towards the *Shepherd Hotel* (see p.94) and 2nd Circle.

Wild Jordan and around

Just below the Mango House, at a T-junction where Rainbow Street ends at a set of steep stairs clattering down the hill into Downtown, if you walk left (slightly uphill) on Othman bin Affan Street you'll come to the striking **Wild Jordan** centre, designed by architect Ammar Khammash for the Royal Society for the Conservation of Nature (RSCN). It is also reachable from 1st Circle by taking the fourth turning on the left and following the street round.

Inside, as well as information about how to visit Jordan's nature reserves, you'll find a 🏃 **nature shop** (daily 9am–5pm) selling all kinds of pieces designed in traditional style by Jordanian craftworkers – often rural women – ranging from jewellery to painted ostrich eggs and handwoven bags. Also on sale are organic herbs, dried fruits and spices, produced on the reserves. There are often free **exhibitions** of photographs or art inspired by Jordan's natural environment. The cool, shaded balcony of the excellent **café** here (see p.116) – which serves organic food, drinks and smoothies – offers one of Amman's

Souk Jara

In the summer months, don't miss **Souk Jara**, a popular, easy-going flea market of antiques, crafts, T-shirts and other streetwear, art and food. Established by JARA (the Jebel Amman Residents' Association; ⓦ www.jara-jordan.com), it is held on Fawzi Malouf Street, just off Rainbow Street, every Friday between mid-May and early September, from 10am to 10pm, and often includes impromptu concerts, film screenings and other activities. The website has more details.

most spectacular **views**, looking over the valleys of Downtown and across to Jebel al-Qal'a. Opposite, between the hills, rises a gigantic flagpole with – if the wind is low – an enormous Jordanian flag fluttering lazily. The pole stands a shade under 127m high, and the flag itself is 30m by 60m – an impressive visual monument, but not a world record. A few doors along from Wild Jordan is the beautiful **Nabad** art gallery, housed in a particularly fine old villa with a secluded rear terrace.

The other direction at the T-junction – downhill – leads into Kherfan Street: a stroll along from the corner stands **Beit Shocair**, an old three-storey villa in the Syrian style, with rooms opening off a central courtyard with a fountain. It's worth stopping here: the house is full of atmosphere, the terrace has another wonderful view and several artists rent space here to sell crafts, jewellery and lanterns. A café is also planned.

Jebel al-Lweibdeh   جبل اللويبدة

Amman has a dynamic contemporary arts scene, and some of the best galleries are within walking distance of each other in the neat, respectable neighbourhood of **Jebel al-Lweibdeh**, overlooking the hubbub of Downtown. The area has a relatively high proportion of Christian residents, and you'll find a tangibly different atmosphere from other parts of the city: many women are unveiled, there is less of a laid-back streetlife, and you may well hear the unfamiliar sound of church bells.

Darat al-Funun   دارة الفنون

A few minutes' walk above Downtown stands an idyllic refuge from the noise and bustle. Head for Omar al-Khayyam Street, which leads steeply up behind the Downtown post office; turning right at the first hairpin, you'll soon come in sight of a high stone wall. With gates to left and right, this wall defines the grounds of **Darat al-Funun** (Sat–Thurs 10am–7pm; ☏06 464 3251, ⓦ www.daratalfunun .org; free), a lush haven of tranquillity housing a centre for contemporary Arab art. The "little house of the arts", as its name translates, comprises a set of three 1920s villas in a beautiful, shaded hillside garden, within which lie the remains of the small sixth-century Byzantine **Church of St George**. The "Blue House", at the top of the steeply terraced complex, houses changing exhibitions, and its wooden porch – a common feature of Circassian architecture, added to the building as an acknowledgment of the Circassian presence in the city – serves as a tiny **café**, Amman's most beautiful and peaceful. On the same level is the former home of Emir Abdullah's court poet, now a private studio for visiting artists. Below is the main building, the former official residence of Lieutenant-Colonel Frederick

There is a **map** of Jebel al-Lweibdeh on p.93.

Peake, or "Peake Pasha", British Commander of the Arab Legion in the 1920s and 1930s. It sports a wonderful semicircular portico and has been superbly renovated by Jordanian architect Ammar Khammash to house well-lit **galleries**, studios and an excellent **art library**. Legend has it that, on his stay in late 1921 as a guest of Peake, T.E. Lawrence wrote much of *Seven Pillars of Wisdom* in this building.

Exhibitions at Darat al-Funun vary from grand overviews of contemporary Arab art to small shows from local artists, with everything publicized on the gallery website. There are also plenty of **lectures and performances**, often staged atmospherically in the ruined church, and all events are free to the public. Even if art isn't your strong point, dropping in gives a sense of a flourishing side of Jordanian culture that's barely touched upon by most visitors.

Makan and Dar al-Anda

If you turn left out of the top gate of Darat al-Funun, a short walk straight ahead and then behind the al-Saadi mosque will bring you to another of Jebel al-Lweibdeh's arts centres, **Makan** (☎06 463 1969, ⊛ www.makanhouse.net). It's a small, alternatively minded place started up by the enthusiastic Ola Khalidi that stages exhibitions and events, and also serves as a venue for informal concerts and film-screenings – links with the Amman Filmmakers' Cooperative (⊛ www.alif.com) are strong. Its balcony has another spectacular view out over the city.

Further along the same street, ochre adobe walls announce **Dar al-Anda** (☎06 462 9599, ⊛ www.daralanda.com), a gallery and cultural centre staging concerts, workshops and arts events. The original building, which was built in 1939, has been beautifully restored, and – along with newer buildings around the courtyard – now houses a library for children, a studio, a guest apartment for resident artists, and so on. Opening hours for both vary (and often include a break in mid-afternoon), but it's worth popping by on the off-chance to see what's happening.

National Gallery   المتحف الوطني

Leaving from the top gate of Darat al-Funun, it's a stiff five-minute climb north past the Luzmila Hospital to the roundabout known as Lweibdeh Circle on top of the hill; the little park on the roundabout has been prettified thanks to the

---

Art in Amman

Aside from the National Gallery and the three galleries mentioned in this section (Darat al-Funun, Makan and Dar al-Anda), there are many other ways to access Amman's art scene: below are just a few. Current shows are publicized in the *Jordan Times*. **Nabad** (⊛ www.nabadartgallery.com) stands just off Rainbow Street, showcasing changing exhibitions in an atmospheric, traditional villa setting. Umm Uthayna hosts the **Orfali Gallery** (⊛ www.orfali.net), which also hosts concerts and other events, and the **Foresight32 Gallery** (⊛ www.foresightartgallery.com), also an exhibition venue and cultural centre. Nearby in Sweifiyyeh the **Broadway Gallery** (⊛ www.broadway-gallery.com) stages local shows. **The Gallery**, at the *InterContinental Hotel*, is a long-standing favourite, displaying paintings and photographs. As well as bank buildings and hotels, cafés such as *Canvas, Blue Fig, Duinde* and others (see p.112) host shows by local artists, as does the Al-Hussein Cultural Centre in Ras al-Ain. Just out of town in Fuheis (see p.148), **Rowaq al-Balqa** (⊛ www.rowaq.net) showcases contemporary Jordanian art in a rural village setting. It's also worth looking online at the work of **Ammar Khammash** (⊛ www.khammash.com), an artist, designer and architect who has worked on several high-profile projects in the capital and nationwide.

French Embassy and renamed "Square de Paris". Ten minutes or so from here on the flat along quiet, shady Shari'a College Street, past the Terra Sancta religious academy, will bring you to Muntazah Circle, an oval expanse of green lined with elegant town houses. One of these, on the right, is the **Jordan National Gallery of Fine Arts** (daily 9am–7pm; closed Tues & Fri; JD3; Ⓦ www.nationalgallery .org), also reached on a short, signposted walk from Abdali. This is the country's premier establishment showcase for contemporary art, with artists from Jordan, the Arab world and the wider Islamic world all represented in a changing programme of shows drawing on the 2000-work permanent collection. Exhibitions are split between the main building and an annexe in a town house opposite; take time to stroll in the pleasant garden between the two, which (at one end) also houses the chic *Canvas* art lounge and café (see p.112).

Further afield

Aside from exploring the excellent shopping possibilities (for more on which, see p.117), there are few specific sights to head for in the busy, sprawling neighbourhoods of West Amman.

Hidden among the fashion boutiques of Sweifiyyeh is a Byzantine **mosaic**, discovered by chance in the garden of a private house in 1969. The mosaic, of which only the left-hand portion survives, originally formed the floor of a late sixth-century church and is in a good state of preservation. Bordered with foliage, it depicts a red-tongued lion, a laden donkey and more, along with white-bearded faces in each corner, personifications of the seasons. It lies on the main Hamra Street, protected under a roofed shelter, but was locked and unattended at the time of writing (previously open Mon–Thurs & Sat 8am–2pm; free).

On the northern edge of the Sports City stadium in Shmeisani is the **Martyrs' Memorial** (*Sarh ash-Shaheed;* Sat–Thurs 9am–4pm; free), Jordan's national military museum, housing a display of military memorabilia from the Great Arab Revolt of 1916–17 to the present day. It's a moving, worthwhile visit.

Royal Automobile Museum and Children's Museum

Following King Hussein's death in 1999, King Abdullah II established in his father's memory the **Royal Automobile Museum** (Mon & Wed–Sun 10am–7pm; JD3; Ⓦ www.royalautomuseum.jo). This fine building, designed by star Jordanian architect Jafar Touqan, blends in with its natural surroundings by being partly sunk into the earth and clad in untreated stone. The interior is wonderfully airy and spacious. From the entrance hall, you wander through the exhibition areas, adorned with vehicles with a royal connection, ranging from a 1916 Cadillac through some elegant Rolls-Royces (and even a 1952 Triumph Thunderbird motorbike) to a Porsche 911 turbo. Images, dioramas and noticeboards give background information to the various vehicles so beloved of King Hussein and his predecessors.

The museum is set within the **Al-Hussein National Park**, a large tract of hilly land on the western outskirts of the city, off King Abdullah II Street. This is Amman's favourite green space, and many people come out here – especially on a Friday – to stroll, picnic or play games. At the highest point of the park is a monument to King Hussein, while alongside the Automobile Museum is the wonderful **Children's Museum Jordan** (Sat–Thurs 9am–6pm, Fri 10am–7pm; closed Tues; JD3; Ⓦ www.cmj.jo), another superbly designed building – by Jordanian architects Faris & Faris – that is packed with toys, games, hands-on exhibits, art equipment and all kinds of fun for kids, from toddlers to teens, including a gift shop and on-site restaurant.

East Amman

Wealthy West Amman is the most accessible part of the city outside Downtown, and you're unlikely to have much reason to visit the city's other, chiefly low-income neighbourhoods, often collectively dubbed **East Amman**, even though they spread to north, east and south. The deepening gap of culture and affluence between the two "halves" of the city leads local wags to claim that you need a passport these days to cross from West to East Amman; that's an exaggeration, but if you venture out to the handful of landmarks in the east – the **Hejaz Railway Museum**, for instance, or the **Cave of the Seven Sleepers** pilgrimage site – you'll certainly feel as if you've left the ritzy shops and hotels of West Amman far behind.

Hejaz Railway Museum   متحف الخط الحجازي

The Mahatta district, about 2km east of Downtown, is home to the **Hejaz Railway Museum** (Sun–Thurs 8am–2pm; JD1; ☏06 489 5413), occupying one of the century-old red-roofed stone buildings that comprise Amman's old railway station on the Hejaz line that originally ran between Damascus and Medina (see box overleaf). It stands on King Abdullah I Street, at the foot of the hill that climbs towards Marka. The museum itself is a modest affair, comprising models, railway memorabilia, maps, bits of old equipment and so on – though a revamp was announced in 2009, so things may have moved on by the time you visit. Just as exciting is the chance to roam the yards and train sheds – still home to many fine old locomotives – chat with the engineers and explore the restored Pullman carriages. You can normally turn up unannounced, though it's always best to phone ahead.

Abu Darwish Mosque   مسجد أبو درويش

Perched over Downtown to the south is **Jebel al-Ashrafiyyeh**, the highest and steepest hill in the city, topped by the peculiar black-and-white-striped **Abu Darwish Mosque**, built in 1961 by a Circassian immigrant. On the inside it's unremarkable, but outside, it's an Alice-in-Wonderland palace, complete with a row of black-and-white chess pawns atop its walls and multicoloured fairy lights after dark. It is visible from points around the city – including, memorably, from the terrace at *Books@Café* on Jebel Amman (see p.105). The only other reason to come up here is for the panoramic **view**, yet there are no clear sightlines from street level; you'll have to – subtly – get onto the roof of one of the apartment buildings just down from the mosque. Any effort will be amply rewarded, though, especially early in the morning or after sunset: from this high up, the entire city is laid out like a relief map at your feet.

Cave of the Seven Sleepers   اهل الكهف

In the southeastern outskirts, tucked away in the run-down suburb of Abu Alanda, the **Cave of the Seven Sleepers** (daily 8am–5pm; free) – known in Arabic as Ahl al-Kahf – is a pilgrimage site associated with a story recorded in the Quran about seven young Christian men who escaped Roman religious persecution by hiding in a cave. God put them to sleep for hundreds of years, and when they awoke, their attempts to buy food with ancient coins aroused incredulity. The youths were taken to the governor – by that time a Christian – who realized that a miracle had occurred, and ordered celebrations. Their work of enlightenment done, the men returned to the cave, where God put them to sleep for good.

The Hejaz railway

The plan to build a **railway** to facilitate the Muslim pilgrimage, long touted in the Ottoman capital, Istanbul, was finally approved by the sultan in the 1890s. At that time, a camel caravan travelling the 1300km from **Damascus** to the holy cities of **Medina** and **Mecca**, in the Hejaz region of western Arabia, took the best part of two months – a difficult journey through harsh country that left the pilgrims vulnerable to exhaustion, disease and bandits. The train, it was proposed, would cut this to a mere three days. The route chosen for the line (and the adjacent **Desert Highway** that came later) followed almost exactly the pilgrimage route in use since the sixteenth century. By 1908, with goodwill funds pouring in from all over the Islamic world, modern, comfortable carriages, a luxury Pullman car and even a rolling mosque (with two-metre minaret) were running three times a week along the full length of the line from Damascus to Medina, bringing new wealth and sophistication to villages such as Amman and Ma'an along the route.

During World War I, Faysal and Abdullah, the sons of Sherif Hussein of Mecca, and the British colonel T.E. Lawrence ("of Arabia"), organized the **Arab Revolt** in the Hejaz (more information on p.371). They moved north up the rail line, harassing the Turkish supply lines, blowing up trains and eventually taking Damascus. After the war and the collapse of the Ottoman Empire, money could be found to rebuild the line only as far as Ma'an. With its holy *raison d'être* negated, the railway lay semi-dormant for decades, and the only passenger services – between Damascus and Amman – came and went, subject to fluctuations in diplomatic relations.

In 1992, a British advertising company hit on the idea of filming an ad for extra-strong mints on the old Hejaz steam locomotives, paying the railway handsomely for the privilege. More enquiries came in, following which profits from passenger service paled into insignificance beside the requests for **special charters** from diplomats and train buffs wanting nostalgic rides into the desert, and from film crews and tour operators capitalizing on the legend of Lawrence. Many five-star package tours to Jordan now include an afternoon of champagne and caviar on a steam-drawn Pullman, with the added "surprise" of a mid-desert Lawrence-style raid on the train by mounted bedouin warriors.

However, these charters all head south from Amman into the desert: as this book went to press, service on the line northwards to Damascus – used far more for freight than passengers – has been suspended, with part of the route subsumed into the new Amman–Zarqa light railway. Jordan's transport ministry is also starting to put plans in place for a new national rail network that may, it is hoped, link up with the high-speed railways currently being built around Mecca and Medina in Saudi Arabia. The Hejaz railway itself may have finally reached the end of the line – but the dream that inspired it is back on track.

The atmospheric cave, one of many Byzantine rock-cut tombs nearby, is set into the hillside next to a modern mosque, built to service the tide of people who come to pay their respects. In antiquity, a small church was built literally on top of the cave: the *mihrab* of its later conversion into a mosque is directly overhead. The decorated entrance, shaded by an ancient olive tree, is topped by five medallions, one of which is a cross. Inside are alcoves with four sarcophagi, one of which has a much-worn hole through which you can peek at an eerie jumble of bones. The walls show remains of painted decoration, with a curious eight-pointed star recurring many times – a Byzantine Christian symbol.

To reach the site, head 4km south from Downtown, over Jebel al-Ashrafi-yyeh and through the low-income neighbourhood of Wihdat to the major traffic intersection of **Middle East Circle** (*duwaar ash-sharq al-awsat*). Keep going south for another 2.4km to a signposted turn to Abu Alanda, which will bring you up the hill to a little roundabout in the middle of the neighbourhood. Turn right onto Ahl al-Kahf Street, and the cave is 1300m further on. By **taxi** from Downtown, expect to pay JD8–10 for the return trip, with waiting time included.

Eating and drinking

Amman has some fine options for **eating out**. There are numerous first-rate Arabic **restaurants**, but also places offering affordable and surprisingly good Indian, Chinese, European and international cuisine. On a tighter budget, you'll find dozens of inexpensive **local diners**, many in Downtown. Ammanis also have an incorrigible sweet tooth, which they are constantly placating with visits to the city's many **patisseries**, for honey-dripping pastries and cakes, or its **coffee houses** and **cafés**, for syrupy-sweet tea and coffee (and soft drinks by the crateful). There are **bars** scattered across the city, ranging from Western-style lounges to covert liquor dens in Downtown back alleys.

Cafés and snacks

Coffee houses are tucked away in just about every alley in Downtown. These traditional places are often shunned by hip young locals, however, who prefer to kill their hours in newer, Western-style pavement **cafés** in Abdoun, Shmeisani and other uptown neighbourhoods (including within all the big shopping malls), where people-watching is easier and where women can feel more comfortable. If you fancy refreshment on the hoof, stop in at one of the **juice bars** dotted around Downtown and other districts, some doling out tamarind, carob and fruit squashes, others serving fresh-squeezed juices of all kinds; p.48 has more info.

All the places listed below are marked on the maps on p.82, p.90, p.93 or p.95.

Downtown

Auberge Alley off Prince Muhammad St (unmarked entrance). Small café one floor below the *Cliff Hotel* and uncompromisingly male. However, the coffee is good and the tiny balcony a great place to watch the street go by.

Centrale King Hussein St, at the corner with King Faysal St. Traditional coffee house above the street that soaks up the morning sun.

Eco-Tourism Café (aka *Al-Rasheed Courts*) In an alley off King Faysal St, opposite the Arab Bank. Downtown's most relaxed and foreigner-friendly coffee house, with a younger, hipper crowd than most. The balcony – Downtown's best – is a pleasant place to hang out and chat with local 20-somethings, many of whom migrate here from uptown West Amman for an after-dark *argileh* in the kind of traditional surroundings Abdoun cannot muster.

Habibah King Hussein St, near the corner with King Faysal St (Arabic sign only, but it's unmissably big, symmetrical blue-on-white). The best patisserie in the city, if not the country, piled high with every conceivable kind of sweetmeat, pastry and biscuit, all very affordable. There's a mixed-company café upstairs for eat-ins. Smaller pop-in branches are dotted around the city, including very nearby – just off King Faysal St next to the "Duke's Diwan".

Jabri King Hussein St, close to *Habibah*. Another patisserie institution, with much the same stock as *Habibah*, plus OK ice cream. Also with a mixed upstairs restaurant for coffee and sweets or a full meal. Branches in Shmeisani and elsewhere.

Turn to p.412 for a list of useful culinary terms in Arabic.

Jebel Amman

Bakehouse Just off Rainbow St, below 1st Circle. Small, one-room coffee shop tucked away in the shopping streets behind the British Council – bagels, muffins and (so many expats claim) the best cup of coffee in Amman. Closes around 6pm.

Batata Rainbow St, below 1st Circle. Jordan's only local-style "chippy" for takeaway French fries, freshly prepared with a choice of sauces – good, cheap and piping hot.

Books@Café Mango St, just off Rainbow St, below 1st Circle ⊛ www.booksatcafe .com. A funky, urban atmosphere unlike anywhere else in Jordan, with a bookshop downstairs and great coffee, smoothies and light meals upstairs. Wonderful terrace views and a friendly clientele are pluses. Well worth a visit.

Duinde Rainbow St, below 1st Circle ⊛ www .salam-kanaan.com. Beautiful, atmospheric little corner café in this strollable neighbourhood, with an eclectic array of shabby-chic furniture, works by local artist Salam Kanaan and found objects creating a seductively laid-back ambience.

Reem 2nd Circle. A hole-in-the-wall pavement stand, serving Amman's most flavourful and succulent *shawerma*, bar none. At lunchtime, early evening and around midnight, this little place is single-handedly responsible for slowing the traffic around 2nd Circle – cars, limos and taxis triple-park as drivers head over from around the city to collect family-sized orders.

Wild Jordan Othman bin Affan St, just off Rainbow St. Wonderful organic café with the best view in Amman. See p.105.

Jebel al-Lweibdeh

Canvas Opposite National Gallery ☎ 06 463 2211. Chic, elegantly designed café-restaurant set amid a quiet garden directly midway between the two buildings of the National Gallery. A cool, arty retreat, with sofas for chilling out and exhibitions by local artists on the walls. A popular spot for relaxed weekend brunches: think quesadillas, salads and wraps (JD6–12 or so). Book ahead on Fridays.

Darat al-Funun Opposite Luzmila Hospital. This gallery complex and arts centre (see p.106) has the quietest, most attractive little open-air café in Amman, hidden among shady gardens. Open until 6pm. Closed Fri.

Shmeisani

el-Farouki Central Shmeisani. The most congenial of Shmeisani's coffee houses, with good, fresh-roasted coffee (Arabic-style or filter) and a relaxed backroom where women can puff in peace.

Frosti Beside *el-Farouki*. Amman's finest ice cream and frozen yoghurt, bar none, with takeaway or outdoor seating.

Sultan An-Nahda Street. Huge, popular pavement-side café (one of several on this main drag), with a big terrace to watch the people and traffic stream by.

Abdoun

Caffè Moka Al-Qaherah St, Abdoun Circle. Rather pretentious little Italian-style café-cum-patisserie with a clientele of rich kids and ladies who lunch. Nonetheless, the food – salads, light meals and pastries – is good and the coffee is worth paying for.

Sanabel Abdoun Circle. Chic patisserie in the heart of Abdoun, with an attractive glass-fronted eating area looking out over the bustle.

Tché Tché Abdoun Circle. Relaxed postmodern-style café that attracts flocks of hip young Ammanis, male and female, who hang out, gossip and smoke top-quality hubbly-bubbly. Branches around West Amman.

Restaurants

Amman's **restaurants** cover a broad spectrum, from backstreet canteens ladling meat stew to air-conditioned palaces serving international delicacies. There is also plenty of opportunity for cheap and tasty snacking: falafel sandwiches and bowls of *fuul* or hummus are unbeatable, and street *shawerma* stands are everywhere (Amman's **best shawerma**, however, is from *Reem* on 2nd Circle; see above). All the better restaurants, and virtually all the non-Arabic places, are located in uptown districts.

In addition to the places listed here, you could copy some Ammanis and drive down to the big hotels on the **Dead Sea** for a special dinner: each hotel (see p.132) has several restaurants covering diverse cuisines, and the high quality of food and service – combined with the romantic setting – makes for a memorable evening out. The journey (45min there, an hour coming back) takes only a bit longer than crossing Amman through heavy traffic.

Many upmarket restaurants provide **valet parking** for diners. A reasonable tip, presuming that you're not left standing around waiting, is 1JD.

All the restaurants listed below are marked on the maps on p.82, p.90, p.93 or p.95.

Arabic

Budget

Cairo Down a side-street behind the Husseini Mosque, Downtown. The most convivial of a trio of celebrated Downtown diners (the others are *al-Quds* and *Hashem*), serving basic fare such as roast chicken and stew. You'd have to stuff yourself to part with more than JD2.50; expect to share a table. Daily 8am–11pm.

🏃 **Hashem** In an alley opposite *Cliff Hotel*, Downtown. A fast-paced outdoor diner that is an Amman institution, founded by restaurateur Hashem al-Turk in the 1920s. Tables are set out all down the shaded alley, as well as in a couple of internal rooms, and there are just two dishes to choose from – *fuul* (hot beans) or hummus. Ask for *fuul* and you'll get the standard Jordanian version (see p.44), but there are plenty of variations; for instance, *fuul masri* is Egyptian-style, without the chilli but with a dollop of *tahini*, while *qudsiyyeh* is Jerusalem-style – *fuul* with a blob of hummus in it. All are freshly made, tasty and cost pennies. Flat bread, chopped onion and a sprig of mint are free (the restaurant gets through a staggering 50kg of onions a day). The stand opposite sells bags of cheap falafel balls as a side-dish, and tea-waiters periodically stride around shouting "*shy, shebab?*" (tea anyone?) – grab a glass off the tray. You can eat well for JD1.50. Almost all the waiters are Egyptian, earning a shade above the minimum wage; tips are optional. Daily 24hr.

Kafeteria al-Kuds (Jerusalem) On Rainbow St, below 1st Circle, Jebel Amman. Not to be confused with the Downtown *al-Quds* restaurant (see below). This is a tiny hole-in-the-wall joint, near the British Council, that serves what many claim to be the best falafel in Amman. Catch them when the falafel is fresh-fried and crispy hot, and you'll never look back. Daily about noon–9pm or later.

al-Quds King Hussein St, next to *Habibah* patisserie, Downtown. The best restaurant in Downtown (which isn't saying much), serving a range of rather overcooked Arabic specialities, including the celebrated bedouin speciality *mensaf* (lamb with rice). Prices are reasonable – a full meal needn't set you back more than JD3 or so – but the menu is in Arabic only and the waiters won't stop to chat. Daily 7am–11pm.

Tarweea Part of the Haya Cultural Centre, roughly opposite *KFC* in Shmeisani. The classiest low-cost Arabic restaurant in the city (*tarweea* is Lebanese dialect for "brunch"), an intimate and spotlessly clean place that is a quality alternative to Shmeisani's junk-food fixation, and streets ahead of anything Downtown. Music from the Egyptian diva Umm Kalthoum plays at a comfortable decibel level and the uniquely friendly waiters will talk you through the menu. Highlights include an excellent Lebanese *fatteh*, tasty giant-sized stuffed falafel balls and plenty of varieties of *fuul* and hummus, not to mention kebabs and a free platter of pickles, olives, mint and rocket leaves that's almost a dish in itself. Don't miss their fresh-baked *manaqeesh zaatar* bread. A meal here is unlikely to set you back more than JD4. Daily 24hr.

Mid-range and expensive

Bourj al-Hamam At *InterContinental Hotel*, 2nd Circle, Jebel Amman ☎ 06 464 1361. Exquisite

---

Secondhand smoke

It's very difficult to avoid **secondhand smoke** wherever you go: cigarette smoke and more fragrant postprandial *argileh* smoke are both very common, with acrid cigar smoke an occasional hazard in the five-star hotel restaurants. To avoid it, try eating earlier than is usual – booking for lunch at 12.30pm, say, or for dinner at 7pm – and thereby leaving before the place fills up. Nonetheless you may still find people around you lighting up before, during and after the meal, oblivious to diners at neighbouring tables. When reserving, mention clearly that you'd like to be seated in a no-smoking area (which, if it exists, is almost always hidden away in the back somewhere) – but, depending on the restaurant's facilities and how busy it is, you should still be prepared to have to put up with fumes: smoke-free areas are simply not in high demand.

Lebanese cuisine in this elegant hotel restaurant, serving all the classic *mezze* dishes with style and pinpoint authenticity. Generally packed nightly: this is a classy dining spot for business people and the city's elite. Expect JD20 a head. Daily 12.30–3.30pm & 7.30–11.30pm.

Fakhr el-Din 40 Taha Hussein St, behind Iraqi Embassy, between 1st and 2nd Circles, Jebel Amman ☎06 465 2399, ⊛www .fakhreldin.com. One of Jordan's best restaurants, catering to the royal and diplomatic upper crust and housed in a tasteful 1920s villa, renovated by top architect Ammar Khammash and retaining its old-world atmosphere of understated charm. The food – formal Lebanese cuisine with a Syrian twist – is as impeccable as the service, yet judicious choices can keep the bill around JD15 – not, however, if you indulge in the highly acclaimed, but expensive, raw meat platter, which includes fine *kibbeh nayeh*. Unusually for an Arabic restaurant, leave space for dessert: both the *osmaliyyeh* (crispy shredded pastry over fresh cream, doused in syrup) and *muhallabiyyeh* (rose-scented almond cream pudding) are exquisite. Reservations essential, especially in summer for dining on the patio amid the lemon trees. Daily 1–4pm & 7–11pm.

Haret Jdoudna Excellent Arabic restaurant, worth the trip to nearby Madaba. See p.230.

Houwara On King Abdullah II St (aka Medical City St), north of 8th Circle towards Sweileh ☎06 535 4210. Attractive mid-priced Lebanese restaurant set back from the ring road on the city's western edge. Decor, with wooden lattice screens and art on the walls, is attractive, and the food is very good: there's a hefty range of *mezze* including a spot-on *muhammara* (a delicately spiced nut-based dip), quality *shanklish*, plus *tabbouleh* and *samakeh harra* as good as you'd expect (the latter a speciality of the Lebanese port of Tripoli, fish with onions, nuts and spiced *tahini*). The *shish tawook* is good, and the kebabs and mixed grills especially tender. In the tradition of upscale Arabic restaurants, though, the service can be over-formal, with a horde of waiters hovering to spoon out your *tabbouleh* and constantly fill your glass. Daily noon–midnight.

Reem al-Bawadi Just off Duwaar al-Waha (the junction of Medina St and Gardens St), Tla'a al-Ali, suburban West Amman ☎06 551 5419. Delightfully over-the-top kitsch-laden affair devoted to showy power-dining (Colonel Gaddafi has been known to drop by), complete with tent, fake castle, fountains, palm trees and neon lights. The menu is in Arabic only, but the waiters are

happy to talk you through the options; few restaurants offer such untrammelled good service – formal but not stiff, warm yet discreet. The food is excellent, but you'd come as much for the atmosphere, and to take a leisurely three or four hours over lunch or dinner in a comfortable, unhurried setting. Families welcome. No alcohol. Daily noon–midnight.

Sahtain At Kan Zaman tourist village ☎06 412 8391. A classy out-of-town restaurant seating four hundred diners in subtly lit vaults – it's an atmospheric place to eat a good (though overpriced) buffet, with Arabic music and dance nightly. See p.119 for details of how to reach Kan Zaman. Daily 7pm–midnight, also Fri 1–4pm.

Tannoureen Shatt al-Arab St, Souk Umm Uthayna ☎06 551 5987. On balance, this is probably the best Arabic restaurant in Jordan – award-winning Lebanese cuisine of the highest quality in an elegant, expensive setting. Hardened restaurant critics, with an eye for a fake, declare the *mezze* here to be "out of this world" – the only difficulty is choosing from the long list of options, both hot and cold. You'll have trouble leaving space for a main course, but try: the *shish tawook* is exquisite, and the kebabs and mixed grill perfectly tender and flavour-rich. Desserts are spectacular, but not many diners make it that far. The courteous service is unusually warm and understated, as is the decor, which includes many paintings of old Jordanian and Palestinian villages. All in all, quite an experience. JD20 per head and upwards. Booking essential. Daily 1–4pm & 7–11pm.

Zad el-Khair 45 Faisal bin Abdul-Azeez St, Umm Uthayna ☎06 554 0057, ⊛www.zadelkhair.com. Outstanding Iraqi restaurant, acclaimed by Amman's many Iraqi expats as serving the best food this side of the Tigris. Alongside a welter of Lebanese *mezze* and kebabs, the signature dish is *masqoof*, Baghdadi river fish (usually carp) dried in the sun, baked in clay, split and then barbecued whole in a distinctive clasp. It arrives at the table steaming and fragrant, with the flesh sweet and buttery, scooped out by hand with pieces of torn flat bread. Served alongside is *amba*, a Baghdadi sauce of mango and turmeric displaying Indian influence. A memorable experience in a sophisticated setting, aided by courteous service and Iraqi music. Booking essential. Daily 1–4pm & 7–11pm.

Zuwwadeh Excellent Arabic restaurant in nearby Fuheis. See p.148.

Asian

China Just off Rainbow St, below 1st Circle, Jebel Amman ☎06 463 8968. Low-key place (also known as "Abu Khalil", after the owner) that's been around for years, with a dedicated East Asian expat clientele. The food is good, and with careful selections it's easy to keep the outlay around JD10. Daily noon–3.30pm & 7pm–midnight.

Indochine At *Grand Hyatt Hotel*, 3rd Circle ☎06 465 1234. Outstanding Vietnamese restaurant, furnished with louvred doors, rattan and wooden ceiling fans to evoke the colonial-era 1930s. Excellent food ranges from starters like Thai beef salad, deep-fried spring rolls and shrimp fritters to mains such as prawns and straw mushrooms in spicy lemongrass soup, ginger chicken simmered in caramel, and shrimp satay in peanut sauce. From around JD20 per head. Booking essential. Daily 6.30pm–midnight.

Indu At *InterContinental Hotel*, 2nd Circle, Jebel Amman ☎06 464 1361. Expensive but spectacularly good Indian food, served in a subtle, sophisticated dining area away from the bustle of the hotel's lobby cafés and restaurants. Tandoori is a speciality and there's plenty for vegetarians. Look out for the changing menus of regional Indian dishes. Daily 12.30–3.30pm & 7.30–11.30pm.

Noodasia Abdoun Circle ☎06 593 6999. Great, lively Asian restaurant. Decor is chic and contemporary (think dark wood and polished chrome), and the food delicious: the spring rolls are perhaps the best in Amman, *pad Thai* or Szechuan beef are popular staples and the sushi is outstanding. Presentation is immaculate, service efficient. Daily 12.30–3.30pm & 7–11.30pm.

Ren Chai Off 4th Circle ☎06 462 5777, ⓦwww .renchai.com. Amman's leading Chinese restaurant, offering a swanky, super-cool dining experience, whether on the open terrace or in the sleek designer interior. Dim sum, soups and sizzling mains are all authentically prepared, while delicacies including abalone and lobster fill out a long, varied menu. Daily noon–3pm & 7–11.30pm.

European

Blue Fig Amir Hashem St, Abdoun ☎06 592 8800, ⓦwww.bluefig.com. A casual café/bar, designed by one of Jordan's top architects, that draws in a sleek, chic crowd. The ambience is cool and sophisticated, with world music and fusion beats booming out loud. The walls display works by local artists, and there are regular live music sessions. Daily 8.30am–1am. Booking essential on Thursday nights and Fridays (especially for breakfast/brunch). Branches around town.

Bonita Opposite *InterContinental Hotel*, off 3rd Circle ☎06 461 5061, ⓦwww.bonitaamman.com. The best Spanish restaurant in town, known for its

paella (one of which is vegetarian) at JD25 for two, and also serving "international" cuisine: go for a juicy steak (around JD12). Alongside is a tapas bar with Mexican beer, dozens of cheap nibbles and some live bands. Restaurant daily noon–midnight, bar daily 7.30pm–midnight.

Casereccio Off Abdoun Circle ☎06 593 4772. Casual Italian restaurant that gets jammed solid on Fridays (when the quality of food and service can suffer); on other days, you'll find the wood-fired pizzas, fresh pastas and crêpes excellent, with a meal easily affordable at JD8 or so per head. No alcohol. Daily noon–3pm & 7–11pm.

E.V.O.O. At *Sheraton Hotel*, 5th Circle ☎06 593 4111. Classy, spacious Italian restaurant (the name stands for *Extra Virgin Olive Oil*). Ignore the pretension: the food is very good, with a broad selection of antipasti prepared immaculately and a long, enticing menu of main courses. The decor is elegant but not stuffy, the service calm and efficient. Expect around JD20 per head. No smoking. Daily 12.30–3.30pm & 7.30–11.30pm.

L'Incontro At *Grand Hyatt Hotel*, 3rd Circle ☎06 465 1234. A truly elegant place to dine, with sophisticated Milanese-chic decor and an attractive outside patio. The Italian food is superb, with a frequently changing menu, and the service outstanding. Bank on JD20 per head. Daily 12.30–3.30pm & 7.30–11.30pm.

Living Room Opposite *InterContinental Hotel*, off 3rd Circle ☎06 464 4227, ⓦwww.romero-jordan .com. Cosy haven above *Romero* restaurant (see below): climb the stairs to enter a classy, wood-panelled bar, lounge and dining area, where you can relax with a beer or tuck into familiar favourites including steak, ribs, sandwiches and even sushi. Daily 1pm–1am.

Pizza Reef Medina St, 200m north of Duwaar al-Waha (the junction of Medina St and Gardens St), Tla'a al-Ali, suburban West Amman ☎06 568 7087. The best pizza in the city – thin-crust, wood-fired fresh to order and not expensive (around JD4 for two people). They can make up anything you fancy, with or without meat or cheese – their unique *labneh*-and-rocket offering with extra rosemary is delectable. Nearby sister outlet *Pizza Rimini* (turn right off Gardens at the Best supermarket before Duwaar al-Waha and go 100m, ☎06 568 6324) does all the same stuff including takeaways. You'll probably need a taxi and/or a detailed map to find either. Both open daily: *Reef* 4pm–midnight (closed Mon); *Rimini* noon–11pm (closed Tues).

Romero Opposite *InterContinental Hotel*, off 3rd Circle ☎06 464 4227, ⓦwww.romero-jordan.com. Splendid Italian restaurant – an Amman institution that has been around since the 1970s, updated with style and elegance. The pastas, risottos and meaty mains are spot on, and there's a long wine list to accompany. Service is uniquely calm and friendly, and the food outstanding, but you could get away with as little as JD15 per person. Daily 1–4pm & 7–11pm.

Wild Jordan Othman bin Affan St, off Rainbow St, below 1st Circle ☏06 463 3542, ⊛www .wildjordancafe.com. Wonderful café/restaurant attached to the Royal Society for the Conservation of Nature's Wild Jordan building (see p.105), with a stunning view over Downtown Amman from the balcony. Prices are high, but the food is mostly organic, with many ingredients grown locally on the RSCN nature reserves around Jordan. Examples include spinach and mushroom salad with hazelnut and lime dressing, smoked salmon on wild rocket, lean steak sandwich, wholewheat spaghetti with light pesto, and so on (all these JD5–10). Their smoothies are sensational – and don't miss the thirst-quenching frozen lemonade

with fresh mint. Daily 11am–midnight. Booking advisable on Fridays.

North American

Champions At *Marriott Hotel*, Shmeisani ☏06 560 7607. A roomy, lively American diner-cum-sports-bar, crammed with TVs. Food includes nachos, burgers and fajitas, in enormous portions; wash it all down with a pitcher of beer. JD12 sees you stuffed. English football is shown live, as is every other conceivable sporting occasion. Alcohol also served during Ramadan. Daily noon–1am.

Cinco de Mayo At *InterContinental Hotel*, 2nd Circle ☏06 464 1361. Tacos, burritos and fajitas, plus succulent steaks – pricey but well prepared, with lots for vegetarians as well. Squeeze your way past the expense-account journos at the bar. Daily 12.30–3.30pm & 7.30–11.30pm.

Houston's 11th of Ab St, Shmeisani ☏06 562 0610. Casual Tex-Mex joint, crammed on weekend nights. Huge salads, draught beer and the best nachos around. Daily noon–midnight.

Bars

Amman has a wide range of **bars**, from swish upmarket hotel pubs to dingy dives in back alleys. All those in Downtown Amman – of which the *Jordan Bar*, behind the *Cliff Hotel*, is typical – are seedy hangouts devoted to sedentary drinking, with no attraction whatsoever other than the alcohol. Uptown neighbourhoods in West Amman offer a classier ambience along with ear-blasting sound systems and small dancefloors (Thurs is the big night out). Modesty in **dress** for both men and women goes out the window in these places: T-shirts, short skirts and the like are common. Beers are roughly JD4 a bottle for foreign imports, the same for a half-litre of draught Amstel.

Blue Fig Amir Hashem St, south of Abdoun Circle ☏06 592 8800, ⊛www.bluefig.com. A cool fixture on West Amman's burgeoning in-scene, whose decor and young, wealthy clientele wouldn't look out of place in Soho or San Francisco. The architect-designed interior is chic and classy, taking in a couple of bars, two spacious floors of tables, plus couches dotted around and a terrace out back for summer lounging. The food – mostly light bites – is great if a little pricey, using local and imported ingredients imaginatively. Live music weekly. Daily 8.30am–1am. Booking essential for Thursday nights.

Books@Café Mango St, just off Rainbow St, below 1st Circle ⊛www.booksatcafe.com. This much-loved bookstore-cum-café in a beautiful part of town is a great place to hang out. The decor is colourful and funky, the staff and clientele are about as hip as each other and there's always a buzz. Sit out on the front terrace, looking across the city lights, or lounge inside or on the rear

terrace (where there's often a big screen showing sports or the latest Arabic music videos). Light meals and good coffee complete the effect. Daily 10am–1am.

Irish Pub At *Dove Hotel*, between 4th and 5th Circles. Stalwart of Amman's pub scene – a small, appealingly gloomy basement that owes little to the Emerald Isle, but nonetheless does a good imitation of a British student bar, with lino underfoot, not enough places to sit and a cramped dancefloor. Gets packed out on hectic Thursday nights. Daily 6pm–2am or so.

JJ's At *Grand Hyatt Hotel*, 3rd Circle. Super-cool nightclub – supposedly members-only, although you're unlikely to have any difficulty getting in – featuring Amman's wealthy uptown set dancing to up-to-date music by British DJs. Mon–Sat 10pm–3am.

Saluté Behind Iraqi Embassy, between 1st and 2nd Circles. Feisty, trendy bar that pulls in a young crowd for long nights of sociable drinking amid loud music. Twinkly views from its plate-glass windows over the valley are an added draw. Daily 7pm–1am.

Vinaigrette At *Al-Qasr Metropole Hotel*, Shmeisani ⓦ www.vinaigrette-jo.com. Compact little bar, also serving light bites. Overlook the service (peremptory) and the music (loud) for the location. It is perched on the 7th floor of the hotel, which itself stands on one of the highest points in Shmeisani: the views all round are stunning, even more so at night. The floor-to-ceiling windows can be rather disconcerting but it's worth booking for a window table nonetheless. Daily noon–11.30pm.

Shopping

Shopping is a great way to experience Jordanian culture – and it can bring you closer than almost any other activity to understanding what makes Amman tick. An excellent way to spend your first morning in the city would be to set yourself a modest shopping goal: a domed alarm clock that sounds the call to prayer, for instance, or a set of decorative Islamic prayer beads. Head out with a few dinars and roam the Downtown shopping streets till you have what you want: the item may be worth little, but the process of finding it and buying it will be a memorable experience.

King Talal Street, in Downtown, is lined with shops selling **household goods** where you could browse for interesting everyday items; good buys include a Turkish coffee service (a tiny pot for boiling the grounds plus six handleless cups on a tray) or an *argileh*, often steel but occasionally brass (check the joints carefully for leaks). There are many outlets near the Husseini Mosque where you could pick up a simple but attractive cotton-polyester *jellabiyyeh* (full-length robe) for less than JD10, or a *keffiyeh* (chequered or plain headcloth) for around JD2.50. And some **food** items can make great souvenirs, such as a kilo of fresh-roasted coffee ground with cardamom, or a box of succulent dates.

Other fascinating areas for window-shopping (and people-watching) include **Sweifiyyeh**, the grid of streets to the southwest of 6th Circle – packed with all kinds of shops from designer boutiques and jewellery shops to groceries and cafés (and the chic Al-Baraka Mall): one innovation here is **Wakalat Street**, Amman's first pedestrianized zone, with upscale fashion and pavement cafés. The **Shmeisani** district, around Abdul Hameed Shoman Street, is more humdrum, while the shopping area around Firas Circle in **Jebel Hussein** has a different feel, with office workers and ordinary families browsing around.

Shopping malls

Amman's **shopping malls** can be great to explore – less glitzy than Dubai's, not as bland as those in Europe, and often buzzing with people browsing or hanging out. Two of the biggest at the time of writing are **Mecca Mall** (ⓦ www.meccamall.jo), located near the western end of Mecca Street, and **City Mall**, not far away on King Abdullah II Street (both Sat–Thurs 10am–10pm, Fri 2–10pm; food outlets open later). Spread over multiple floors, these behemoths – with abundant parking – take in literally hundreds of shops, dozens of cafés and restaurants, cinemas and other entertainment, kids' zones and more. Don't spurn the malls as some kind of foreign import: many ordinary Ammanis shop here, and they represent, in their own way, as much an authentic expression of modern Jordanian culture as the Downtown bazaars.

▲ Out and about, Downtown Amman

Souvenirs and local crafts

Compared to Cairo, Jerusalem, Damascus and Aleppo, which all have centuries-old souks and long traditions of craftsmanship, Amman is a modern lightweight, with no memorable **bazaars** to explore. Where the city scores is in its range of **bedouin crafts** from Jordan and Palestine at prices a fraction of Jerusalem's, and – most of all – in some amazingly inexpensive **gold**.

There's only a handful of genuine craft shops in Amman, most located around 1st and 2nd Circles, and they tend to be associated with projects to revive or nurture the skills of local craftspeople; prices are legitimately high and you're certain to be purchasing quality goods. **Souvenir shops** which are simply retail outlets for local or imported merchandise are more numerous: here prices can be high without necessarily implying a matching quality. There are many of the latter within walking distance of **Lweibdeh Circle**, which is a good place to get a sense of what's available.

al-Afghani Opposite the Husseini Mosque, Downtown. Also branches around town. Amman's most famous souvenir shops, originally founded in Palestine in 1862 by a merchant from Kabul and still in the same family. The Downtown shop is a wonderful little Aladdin's cave, crammed to the ceiling with everything from Bohemian glass to ornate Cairene Ramadan lamps; serious browsing is better undertaken at the branches on Jebel al-Lweibdeh.

Artisana (Jordan Arts and Crafts Centre) Krishan St, off 2nd Circle. Wide range of attractive handicrafts and home furnishings, well presented for a free-spending clientele.

al-Aydi (Jordan Craft Development Centre) Off 2nd Circle behind *InterContinental Hotel*. The best place to buy locally produced handmade crafts. Staff work as advisers and design consultants to about a hundred local craftspeople – mostly rural women – who share in the shop's profits. There's a huge variety of pieces, everything from olive-wood carving to mother-of-pearl, hand-blown glassware, textiles of all kinds (including hand- and machine-embroidered jackets and dresses), jewellery, ceramics, baskets and more, both old and new. It also stocks the biggest collection of carpets in the country – Jordanian, Iraqi and Kurdish, ranging from antique pieces to newly mades.

Badr ad-Duja 15 Abu Tammam St, off 2nd Circle Ⓦ www.badr-adduja.com.jo. Excellent range of crafts, including embroidery, rugs, jewellery, glassware, ceramics and home furnishings.

Balian Rainbow St, below 1st Circle Ⓦ www .armenianceramics.com. Wonderful little shop, on a corner at the downhill end of Rainbow St, serving as an outlet for the distinctive ceramics made by the Balian family of Jerusalem, with pieces ranging from individual tiles to complete room decorations.

Beit al-Bawadi Fawzi Qawuqji St, Abdoun Ⓦ www.beitalbawadi.com. High-quality ceramics,

carpets and bric-a-brac from JOHUD (the Jordanian Hashemite Fund for Human Development).

al-Burgan 12 Tal'at Harb St, behind *InterContinental Hotel*, 2nd Circle Ⓦ www.alburgan.com. Family-run business offering a good range of quality pieces at modest prices – see the excellent website for details.

The Gold Souk A network of alleys off King Faysal St, Downtown. Dozens of tiny shops all next to each other, selling modern gold jewellery at highly competitive prices (see box).

Jordan River Designs Rainbow St, below 1st Circle Ⓦ www.jordanriver.jo. A project originally set up by Save The Children, selling simple, bright and pricey handmade home furnishings from a lovely old 1920s-era villa. In the same courtyard is an outlet for superb carpets woven by women of the Bani Hamida tribe, where you can pick up a small wall-hanging for JD30, although reasonably sized rugs start from around JD70 and large carpets can be as much as JD500.

Kan Zaman Al-Yadoudeh village, 3km off the airport road at the Madaba exit (turn left, not right to Madaba), about 15km south of Amman. Kan Zaman ("Once Upon A Time") was formerly a farming estate, established in the nineteenth

Buying gold

Prices for gold jewellery in Amman are some of the cheapest in the world. Not only is there a constant, massive demand in Jordan for gold, used in marriage dowries, but workmanship on gold jewellery is charged by weight here – a scheme which turns out to be very economical by world standards. The upshot is that it's well-nigh impossible to find the same quality of work or purity of gold outside Jordan for less than three or four times the Amman price. In the Downtown Gold Souk, you can be paying a measly few dinars per gram for finished pieces in **21-carat gold** (which is very popular, partly because its orangey-yellow hue looks good against darker skin, and partly because its purity and investment value make it most desirable for dowries).

When buying, you have to know, at least sketchily, what you're looking at and what you want, and you have to be prepared to devote some hours to making a purchase. Browsing from shop to shop to get a sense of the market can be a pleasure: Jordan is mercifully free of the kind of tedious hard-sell haggling for which the Middle East is notorious. Be aware that there are no hallmarks; instead, look for a stamp indicating **gold purity** in parts per thousand: "875" indicates 21-carat, while "750" is 18-carat. When you buy, you will be given two receipts: one for the per-gram market value of the item, another for the cost of the workmanship. The honour system among gold merchants – both in the Downtown Gold Souk and elsewhere – is very strong, and means that it is very unlikely you'll be misled. Styles of jewellery vary – although everyone will happily make you up a necklace of a gold tag shaped with your name in Arabic – and, with prices as low as they are, commissioning a custom-made piece to your own design doesn't command the kind of absurd prices that the same thing in the West might do.

As a footnote, Jordan is a bad place to buy **jewels** or precious stones, since everything is imported. However, **silver** is sold in the same way as gold, although it is much less popular and you may have to search for it; prices, though, can be absurdly low.

century – it has undergone a makeover to become a tourist village, in Ottoman style. Prices in the lavish antiques shop are sky-high. Another shop nearby sells glassware, jewellery and ceramics made by ArtiZaman (you can visit their workshops downstairs), although it's easy to find items of the same quality and design for much less elsewhere.

Ola's Secret Garden 38 Kherfan St, off Rainbow St, below 1st Circle. Housed in the beautiful Beit Shocair (see p.106), this shop sells paintings, mosaics, jewellery, home furnishings and clothes created by designer Ola Mubaslat. Her designs feature natural and organic forms; browsing is a pleasure. In the same house, artist Omar Hajawi sells his superb handmade brass lanterns, and there are plans to open more craft outlets and a café.

Silsal Off 5th Circle ⓦ www.silsal.com. Workshop and retail outlet for superb handmade ceramics, made on-site in the pottery studio and sold nation-wide (including in the airport duty-free shop). Designs are modern, often incorporating traditional

elements such as Islamic calligraphy and motifs. Beautiful souvenir pieces, as well as everyday items such as mugs, bowls and vases.

Souk Ayyadi Mecca Mall ⓦ www.tamweelcom .org. Showroom for products created through Tamweelcom, the Jordan Micro-Credit Company, which was established by the charitable Noor al-Hussein Foundation to revive traditional crafts. It has created jobs for thousands of mostly rural women in a number of schemes around the country, producing a wide range of top-quality crafts, ceramics, embroidered home furnishings, handmade paper and more.

Wild Jordan Othman bin Affan Street, off Rainbow St, below 1st Circle ⓦ www.rscn.org.jo. Within this centre, run by the Royal Society for the Conserva-tion of Nature, is a "nature shop", which sells pieces designed in traditional style by Jordanian craftworkers – often rural women. These range from unusual contemporary jewellery to painted ostrich eggs and handwoven bags. Also on sale are organic herbs, dried fruits and spices, produced on the reserves.

Moving on from Amman

Amman is the centre of Jordan's **transport** network. Where your onward transport leaves from depends partly on what your destination is and partly on how you want to get there. There are four main bus and serveece stations: **Tabarbour**, **Wihdat**, **Muhajireen** and **Mahatta**. Along with the offices of bus companies including JETT and Trust, which also serve as termini, departure points are widely spaced across the city. Location details are given on p.86. Some inter-city buses do not run on Fridays.

To Jerash and the north

Tabarbour, also known as *mujemma ash-shamal* (North station), is the main departure point for buses and serveeces to destinations in the north of Jordan, including **Jerash**, **Irbid** and **Ajloun**. To get to Irbid, there are also large, air-con coaches run by Hijazi (every 15–20 mins) and JETT (hourly) from Tabarbour station. For Umm Qais and the far north, change in Irbid.

To Azraq and the east

The only direct public transport between Amman and points east are minibuses from Tabarbour to **Mafraq**, where you should change for Umm al-Jimal and the far desert; and minibuses from Tabarbour or Mahatta to **Zarqa**, from where minibuses depart to Hallabat and Azraq. There is no public transport along the Amman–Azraq highway apart from a minibus from Mahatta to **Muwaqqar**, making it impossible to reach Qasr Harraneh and Qusayr Amra without your

See p.78 for some ideas for **day-trips** out of Amman.

own transport; many travellers resort to hiring a taxi or joining a "tour" run by a hotel (see p.195).

To the Dead Sea and west of Amman

Early-morning minibuses (7–9am) from Muhajireen station run direct to the "Amman Beach" resort on the **Dead Sea**, but only if there's demand – likely on a Friday. Others stop short at the crossroads town of **Shuneh al-Janubi-yyeh**, about 15km north of the Dead Sea. From Shuneh, minibuses head to the village of **Sweimeh**, 3km northeast of the Dead Sea hotels; the driver might be willing to take you on to Amman Beach for a little extra.

Transport to towns **west of Amman** include minibuses from Tabarbour or Mahatta to **Salt**; from Tabarbour to **Fuheis**; and from Muhajireen to **Wadi Seer**. For the northern Jordan Valley take a bus from Tabarbour to **Dayr Alla**; change there for Pella.

To Petra and the south

Minibuses to **Wadi Musa/Petra** (3hr) leave from Wihdat station, also known as *mujemma al-janoob* (South station). Departures are more common in the morning (from 6.30am onwards) than the afternoon. Serveece-drivers tend to quote prices higher than normal to start with; some hopefuls to Petra start as high as JD10, although the real price is nearer JD5–6 (or JD4–5 on the bus).

Another way to Petra is a daily round-trip coach run by JETT from its Abdali office (☎06 566 4146, ⓦwww.jett.com.jo), departing at 6.30am. Should you

Petra scams

It's worth being aware of the **scams** used by some taxi-, serveece- and bus-drivers plying the heavily travelled tourist route from Amman to Petra. No public buses, minibuses or serveeces from Amman to Petra follow the scenic **King's Highway**, and any drivers who claim they do are trying to gouge you for an inflated fare. For comparison purposes, the true cost of hiring a private taxi to drive you from Amman along the King's Highway to Petra is around JD70–80.

Some of the budget hotels in Amman take advantage of this to offer cut-price **"tours"** to Petra along the King's Highway, stopping off at various places on the way. You'll get what you pay for on these: often a driver who speaks little English, a cramped, all-day drive, and whistle-stop photo breaks. They can, nonetheless, be an economical way to glimpse the countryside. Beware of drivers on the day claiming, for instance, that the section of the King's Highway through the Wadi Mujib canyon is closed so they have to go on the Desert Highway instead: this is invariably just a ploy to get out of a long drive. The most reliable of these King's Highway jaunts to Petra is run by the excellent *Mariam Hotel* in Madaba (see p.224).

Many Amman serveece- and taxi-drivers have deals running with certain hotels in Wadi Musa: they bring tourists directly to the hotel, and the hotel pays them **commission** for each one, passing that cost on to you in the form of a higher room rate. You may find that your taxi-driver offers to **phone ahead** to a hotel on your behalf while driving: if you're able to understand Arabic, you'll hear that, rather than asking if they have a room available, he's instead asking how much commission the hotel would pay him if he brought you to the door. If the hotel refuses to cough up, he'll turn to you and claim it's full before offering to try another. The best way to avoid all this is to insist that you get dropped off in the middle of Wadi Musa town so you can find a hotel independently. In any case, not all hotels in Wadi Musa are recommendable: if a place hasn't made it into our listings on p.271, there's a reason.

choose to make a day-trip of it, the same coach arrives back in Amman around 7.30pm; in between, you get about six hours in Petra – enough to see a few highlights. The fare is JD7 one-way, JD14 return.

Minibuses and serveeces to **Karak**, **Shobak**, **Tafileh** and **Ma'an**, and a few to **Qadisiyyeh** (for **Dana**), also leave from Wihdat. If there is no transport to Petra, take a bus or serveece to Ma'an, where you might catch a connecting bus (if not, a Ma'an–Petra taxi is JD10–12).

Minibuses to **Madaba** run on various routes from Tabarbour, Mahatta, Muhajireen and Wihdat stations, but bear in mind that there is no direct public transport from Amman to destinations south of Madaba along the picturesque **King's Highway**: all minibuses and serveeces from Amman use the Desert Highway. However, the *Mariam Hotel* runs its own bus from Madaba to Petra along the King's Highway; see p.224 for details.

To Aqaba

There are several options for reaching **Aqaba**. From Wihdat station, minibuses (5hr; about JD6.50) and serveeces (4hr; about JD7.50) depart regularly, the drivers touting for business by barking "Aqabaqabaqaba!" over their revving engines. JETT (Ⓦwww.jett.com.jo) has large air-con coaches departing daily to Aqaba (4hr 30min) from its three Amman offices: at Wihdat station (☎06 477 5663; 8am, 2.30pm, 6pm; JD6.50), Tabarbour station (☎06 506 5008; 8.30am, 1pm, 4.30pm; JD7) and in the Abdali district (☎06 566 4146; 6–8 daily: first 7am, last 7.30pm; JD7). Trust International Transport (☎06 581 3427) also runs large air-con coaches to Aqaba from its office near the Safeway supermarket by 7th Circle (4–6 daily: first 7.30am, last 7pm; JD7.50). It's worth calling ahead to confirm schedules and to book a seat.

Royal Jordanian (☎06 510 0000, Ⓦwww.rj.com) has two **flights** a day from Amman's Queen Alia airport to Aqaba (JD48).

To neighbouring countries

Amman is linked into overland and air networks around the Middle East. The two most travelled routes – to **Damascus** and **Jerusalem** – are described in detail below. Needless to say, your passport and **visas** must all be in order before you buy a ticket or set out on any of these journeys, and don't forget to factor in the JD5 **departure tax** levied at every land and sea border.

To Damascus

Going from Amman to **Damascus** (about 180km by road) is quick and easy, as long as your paperwork is in order. Before you travel – indeed, before you leave home – check the latest rules on visas for Syria. At the time of writing, UK passport-holders, for instance, cannot get a Syrian visa on the border and must buy one in advance (price in London: £32). Rules for other nationalities vary. If you need a visa in advance, you must get it from a Syrian Embassy in or near your home country; the embassy in Amman will issue a visa only if you hold Jordanian residency. Bear in mind, too, the difficulties surrounding Israeli stamps; see p.35.

The simplest method of reaching Damascus is by **serveece** from any of the private companies lining the road either side of the old bus station at Abdali. The sign of a part-filled serveece waiting for passengers is an open boot (trunk). As soon as you approach, the driver will start touting for business with "Sham, Sham, Sham!" (one of the Arabic names for Damascus). The fare is JD11 per person. It's common for individuals to buy two seats (or couples to buy three) to give a roomier ride – or you can charter the whole car (usually four or five

Amman–Jerusalem: the bureaucracy

The contradictory **bureaucracy** surrounding the journey from Amman to Jerusalem is grotesque. The **Jordanians** view the West Bank as being intimately linked with Jordan: if you have a single-entry Jordanian visa and cross the King Hussein/Allenby Bridge to spend time in the West Bank or Israel, then return *the same way* to Jordan, the Jordanians don't see you as ever having left the country and you don't need to buy a new Jordanian visa, as long as your current one is still within its validity (bear in mind, though, the unusually high Israeli departure tax – see p.36). You must buy a new Jordanian visa if you return to the country having used any other route out or in.

However, once you cross the King Hussein Bridge from Jordan into the West Bank, the **Israeli** authorities view you as arriving in Israel proper, and routinely issue free tourist visas on arrival, valid throughout Israeli- and **Palestinian**-administered West Bank territory and Israel itself (as yet, the Palestinians do not issue their own visas). As a foreigner, you'll be waved through any checkpoints on the "Green Line" between the West Bank and Israel proper, a border you'll find marked on Jordanian maps but not Israeli ones.

seats). Serveeces run 24 hours a day and – aside from the driver stashing some items to sell in Syria – they go fast and direct in around three hours. Cars terminate at the Sumriyeh (Somaria) garage in western Damascus, but may be able to drop off elsewhere.

Buses operated by JETT (☎06 569 6151, ⊛www.jett.com.jo) and their Syrian partner Karnak are cheaper than serveeces but slower, partly since they have to wait for everyone to clear passport control before continuing. Buses depart daily from the JETT office 1km uphill from Abdali – a luxury coach at 7am (JD8.50) and a regular coach at 3pm (JD7.50). There may be four or five extra buses a day in high summer. All terminate at Kadem station in Damascus. Other companies around Abdali run buses to Damascus, on various schedules: ask around for details.

At the time of writing, passenger **trains** on the historic Hejaz Railway line between Amman and Damascus had been suspended, reportedly permanently. **Flying** takes longer than driving.

To Jerusalem and the West Bank

As the crow flies, Amman and **Jerusalem** are only about 50km apart, but the Jordan Valley and a heavily fortified frontier bridge lie in the way. No buses or serveeces run directly between the two cities. The only way to go is with a combination of buses and taxis/serveeces, changing at a bridge known to the Jordanians as the **King Hussein Bridge**, or Jissr al-Malek Hussein, and to the Israelis and Palestinians as the **Allenby Bridge** – Gesher Allenby in Hebrew, Jissr Allenby in Arabic (Sun–Thurs 8am–4.30pm, Fri & Sat 8am–3pm). On a good day, the journey can take as little as two hours; on a bad day, it can be more than five. It is not unknown for the bridge to be closed at short notice during periods of tension.

From Tabarbour station in Amman, **serveeces** run direct to the bridge (1hr; about JD5); stay on until you reach the foreigners' – *not* the locals' – terminal. After the formalities, you have to sit and wait for anything up to two hours for a bus to fill up, which covers no-man's-land on either side of the bridge and drops you at the Israeli terminal (10min; JD3).

An easier option is to take the 7am daily **JETT bus** from JETT's Abdali office (☎06 566 4146; driver's mobile ☎079 580 0856); book one day ahead, or turn up no later than 6.30am to guarantee a seat. The JD7.50 fare (which doesn't include departure tax) takes you across to the Israeli terminal. Beware the bus-driver taking the passports of all the passengers to give en masse to the immigration officials for stamping; if you want yours to stay unsullied, take it in to them yourself.

At passport control at the **Israeli arrivals terminal**, you should be loud and clear in asking for your passport not to be stamped: many travellers have reported the Israeli immigration officials forgetting after being asked only once. For more on the Israeli stamps issue, see p.35. There's a **bank** to change money. A serveece (*sheroot* in Hebrew) will be waiting outside; the one-hour ride to **East Jerusalem**, dropping you at the Damascus Gate of the Old City, costs about 35 Israeli shekels (NIS). If you walk out of the bridge terminal and to your right, you'll find the exit area from the locals' building, where you can pick up buses to **West Bank** cities such as Jericho, Bethlehem and Ramallah.

To Tel Aviv and Nazareth

Buses run direct from Amman to the Israeli cities of **Nazareth** (Lower Nazareth; daily 8.30am; JD30) and **Tel Aviv** (Central Bus Station; Sun–Fri 8.30am; JD35). Trust International Transport (☎06 581 3427) is the Jordanian side of the operation. All buses leave from outside their office, which is at the corner of Saleh al-Smadi and Ibn al-Fata streets near Safeway supermarket by 7th Circle. They travel first to Irbid, then cross using the northern **Sheikh Hussein Bridge**; at no point do you pass through the West Bank. Arrive at least half an hour before departure for security checks. **Flying** from Amman's Queen Alia airport to Tel Aviv – at the time of writing only possible on Royal Jordanian (☎06 510 0000, ⊛www.rj.com), at around JD175 one-way – offers the lure of spectacular views over the Dead Sea. There are usually two flights a day; flight time is around thirty minutes.

To Cairo

Buses do run from Amman to **Cairo**, though it's an uncomfortable journey of at least 20 hours; you'd do better to break your journey in Aqaba and/or the Sinai along the way – see p.354 for details. To reach Cairo, you need a full Egyptian tourist visa (JD12), issued at airports and at land and sea borders, sometimes in US dollars only. JETT (☎06 569 6151, ⊛www.jett.com.jo) and their Egyptian partner SuperJet run buses twice weekly to the Almaza terminal at Heliopolis in Cairo; the fare (JD77) includes the Aqaba–Nuweiba ferry. It's advisable to book up to a week ahead. Other Abdali-based bus companies compete, all of them cheaper and even less comfortable. Royal Jordanian (☎06 510 0000, ⊛www.rj.com) and EgyptAir (☎06 463 6011, ⊛www.egyptair.com) **fly** several times daily to Cairo (1hr 30min; JD180 one-way).

Around the Middle East

JETT and other transport companies around Abdali run regular buses and serveeces direct to many other cities, including Homs, Hama and Aleppo; Beirut; Jeddah, Madina, Riyadh and Dammam; Kuwait; Baghdad; and points further afield in the Gulf, Turkey, Yemen and Libya. Middle Eastern **airlines** fly from Amman to their hub cities – including low-cost regional airlines Air Arabia (☎06 560 3666, ⊛www.airarabia.com), Fly Dubai (☎06 550 7660, ⊛www.Flydubai.com) and Jazeera (☎06 445 1576, ⊛www.jazeeraairways.com), which have cut-price flights from Amman to Dubai or Sharjah. Other low-cost carriers serve cities in Saudi Arabia and elsewhere.

Listings

Airport information ☏06 445 2700. See also p.85.

Banks and exchange See p.69.

Children's activities As well as the excellent Children's Museum (see p.108), aim for the Haya Centre (☏06 566 5195) in Shmeisani – it stages plays, puppet theatre, music and activities for children, and has a playground, café, kids' library and a small planetarium. English-speaking families are welcome (there's a small admission charge); call ahead for details and opening hours. Mecca Mall (ⓦwww.meccamall.jo), on Mecca St, has child-friendly diversions including adventure zones, karting and skating. Teenagers will love paintballing in the forests north of Amman (see ⓦwww.jordanadventure.com), while on the airport road, 12km south of 7th Circle, is the Amman Waves aqua park (ⓦwww.ammanwaves.com).

Embassies and consulates See p.65.

Emergencies Police ☏191; ambulance ☏193; fire ☏06 462 2090 or 461 7101.

Mail Most big hotels offer postal services at a small premium. The main Downtown post office (daily 7am–7pm, Fri until 1pm; shorter hours in winter) is on Prince Muhammad St. Others, with the same hours, are on 1st Circle (opposite Saudi consulate); at the *InterContinental Hotel*; near the Centre Culturel Français off Lweibdeh Circle; beneath the Housing Bank Centre in Shmeisani; and elsewhere. For sending valuables, you're better off using couriers such as Aramex (☏06 551 5111, ⓦwww.aramex.com), DHL (☏06 580 0800, ⓦwww.dhl.com.jo) or FedEx (☏06 551 1460, ⓦwww.fedex.com/jo).

Medical care The Khalidi Hospital (☏06 464 4281), near 4th Circle, is one of Jordan's best and has a 24hr emergency room. There are pharmacies nearby, or head to Jacob's Pharmacy on 3rd Circle (daily 8.30am–midnight).

Police and complaints The courteous and efficient English-speaking Tourist Police are on duty 24hr a day at the Jebel al-Qal'a ruins and the Roman Theatre; they will take any queries or complaints very seriously. Their administration (☏06 569 0384 or 569 0363, ⓔtourisim.dept@psd.gov.jo [sic]) comes under the Public Security Directorate, which is part of the Ministry of Interior. The main Downtown police station is halfway along King Faysal St, opposite the Arab Bank; there's also a police station opposite the *InterContinental Hotel*. In other areas, or if you're in real distress, tell any passer-by that you want the *buleece* (police), and someone is bound to help.

Visa extensions To extend your visa beyond the standard thirty days, you must register at any police station – a simple, free, five-minute procedure. For any queries, ask your hotel (or an Arabic-speaking friend) to call the Borders and Residence Department (☏06 550 5360, ⓦwww.rbd.psd.gov.jo), part of the Public Security Directorate, on your behalf.

Travel details

Buses and serveeces

JETT office, Abdali to: Aqaba (6–8 daily; 4hr); King Hussein Bridge (1 daily; 1hr); Petra (1 daily; 3hr).

Mahatta station to: Madaba (30min); Salt (40min); Wadi Seer (30min); Zarqa (New station; 25min).

Muhajireen station to: Dead Sea ("Amman Beach"; 1hr 30min); Madaba (30min); Shuneh al-Janubiyyeh (1hr); Wadi Seer (25min).

Tabarbour station to: Ajloun (1hr 30min); Aqaba (5hr); Dayr Alla (1hr); Fuheis (35min); Irbid (New Amman station; every 15min; 1hr 15min to 2hr); Jerash (1hr); King Hussein Bridge (1hr); Madaba (30min); Mafraq (Bedouin station; 1hr); Queen Alia Airport (every 30min; 45min); Salt (35min); Zarqa (New station; 35min).

Trust office, 7th Circle to: Aqaba (4–6 daily; 4hr).

Wihdat station to: Aqaba (4–5hr); Karak (2hr); Ma'an (2hr 30min); Madaba (30min); Shobak (2hr 45min); Tafileh (2hr 30min); Wadi Musa/Petra (3hr).

Domestic flights

Amman (Queen Alia airport) to: Aqaba (2 daily; 45min).

International buses and serveeces

Abdali (taxi offices) to: Beirut (8–12hr); Damascus (3–7hr).

JETT office, Abdali to: Cairo (2 weekly; 21hr); Damascus (2 daily; 3hr 30min).

Trust office, 7th Circle to: Nazareth (1 daily; 4hr); Tel Aviv (1 daily except Sat; 6hr).

Useful Arabic place names

| Amman | عمّان | Jordan | الاردن |

Within Amman

1st Circle	الدوار الاول	JETT station	مجمع جيت
2nd Circle	الدوار الثاني	Jordan University	جامعة الاردنية
3rd Circle	الدوار الثالث	Kan Zaman	كان زمان
4th Circle	الدوار الرابع	Mahatta station	مجمع المحطة
5th Circle	الدوار الخامس	Marka	ماركا
6th Circle	الدوار السادس	Middle East Circle	دوار الشرق الاوسط
7th Circle	الدوار السابع	Muhajireen station	مجمع المهاجرين
8th Circle	الدوار الثامن	Ras al-Ain	راس العين
Abdali	العبدلي	Sahab	سحاب
Abdoun	عبدون	Shmeisani	الشميساني
Ahl al-Kahf	اهل الكهف	Sport City	المدينة الرياضية
Downtown	وسط البلد	Sweifiyyeh	الصويفية
Hejaz train station	محطة السكة الحديد	Umm Uthayna	ام اذينة
Interior Circle	الدوار الداخلية	Tabarbour	طبربور
Jebel Amman	جبل عمّان	Tabarbour station	مجمع الشمال
Jebel al-Ashrafiyyeh	جبل الاشرفية	Tla'a al-Ali	تلاع العلي
Jebel Hussein	جبل الحسين	Trust office	مكتب شركة الثقة
Jebel al-Lweibdeh	جبل اللويبدة	Wihdat	الوحدات
Jebel al-Qal'a	جبل القلعة	Wihdat station	مجمع الجنوب

Near Amman

For destinations further afield in Jordan, see the end of each relevant chapter.

Baptism Site	المغطس	Queen Alia Airport	مطار الملكة علياء
Dead Sea	البحر الميّت	Sweileh	صويلح
King Hussein Bridge	جسر الملك حسين	Zarqa	الزرقاء

Outside Jordan

Beirut	بيروت	Jericho	اريحا
Cairo	القاهرة	Jerusalem	القدس
Damascus	دمشق	Nazareth	الناصرة
Dera'a	درعا	Tel Aviv	تل ابيب

The Dead Sea
and around

CHAPTER 2   # Highlights

* **The Dead Sea** Float your day away at the lowest point on earth. See p.129

* **Baptism Site** Widely accepted location of Jesus' baptism, on the banks of the River Jordan. See p.137

* **Salt** Elegant Ottoman-era hilltown of honey-stone villas and winding lanes. See p.145

* **Fuheis** Wander the peaceful alleys of this picturesque backwater town in the scenic Balqa hills. See p.148

* **Qasr al-Abd** A white palace, two millennia old, set amid beautiful countryside west of Amman. See p.149

▲ Floating on the Dead Sea

The Dead Sea and around

B arely a handful of kilometres west of Amman's city limits, the rugged highlands of central and northern Jordan drop away dramatically into the Dead Sea rift. This giant valley marks a geological dividing line as well as a political one, with the Arabian plate to the east shifting a few centimetres a year northwards, and the African plate to the west moving slowly southwards. Between the two is the River Jordan, defining Jordan's western border as it flows into the large, salty inland lake of the **Dead Sea**, famed as the lowest point on earth.

This whole area is within easy reach of the capital, and serves for many visitors as an alternative base – on the shore of the Dead Sea are ranged a number of world-class luxury hotels. It also works well as the source of some choice day-trips. Taking a dip in the Dead Sea and relaxing on its salty beaches should form an unmissable part of anyone's itinerary, and you'll also find, in the rolling hills of the Balqa region that rise towards Amman, some low-key, little-visited small towns and villages, such as the graceful old Ottoman capital **Salt** and its neighbour **Fuheis**, that bring a refreshing change from the hustle and bustle of the big city.

The area's main historical draw is the most authoritative and best-documented candidate for the **Baptism Site** of Jesus, located on the east bank of the River Jordan about 8km north of the Dead Sea shore. The combination of archeology, the extraordinary natural environment and the momentous associations of the place mean that this is one of the Middle East's most important religious destinations. Continuing the biblical theme, in the barren hills overlooking the southeastern part of the Dead Sea is **Lot's Cave**, where Abraham's nephew sought refuge from the destruction of Sodom and Gomorrah.

The Dead Sea البحر الميت

Forming what has been called the world's biggest open-air spa, the amazing **DEAD SEA** (*al-Bahr al-Mayit* in Arabic) is a major highlight of a visit to the Middle East. Swimming in it is a memorable experience, quite unlike anything else on the planet.

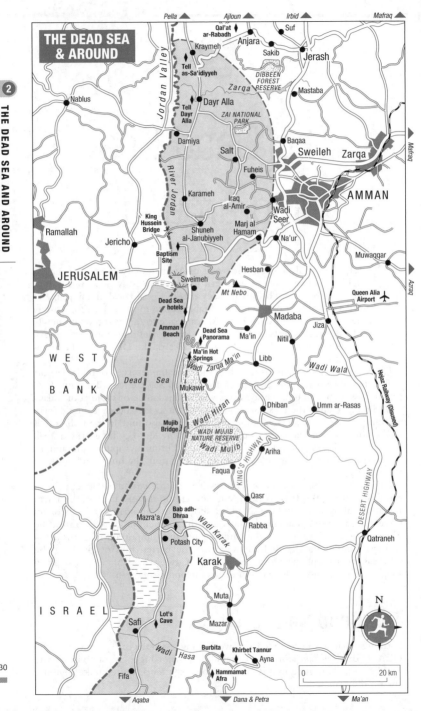

THE DEAD SEA & AROUND

The lake occupies the Great Rift Valley, a deep geological cleft which can be traced from Turkey all the way into East Africa. Its shoreline – at 400m below sea level – marks **the lowest point on Earth**, and is stiflingly hot for much of the year.

The Dead Sea got its name in antiquity due to its uniquely salty water, which kills off virtually all marine life: seawater is about three or four percent salt, but Dead Sea water is over thirty percent. It is fed mainly by the River Jordan, flowing south from Galilee, but due to the geological upheavals it has no outflow; instead, water evaporates off the surface at the rate of millions of litres a day, leading to continuous precipitation of salt onto the beach and a thick atmospheric haze overhead which dampens sound down to almost nothing – there's little to hear but lapping water anyway. The haze also filters out harmful UVB sunrays, handily allowing tanning but not burning.

The major reason for a visit, though, is that the lake's high salinity makes the water so **buoyant** that it's literally impossible to sink; Olympic swimmers and

The dying Dead Sea

The future of the Dead Sea is in doubt. In the 1950s, the lake's surface area was about a thousand square kilometres; today, it's less than seven hundred and still falling. The water level has already dropped by a startling 30m, and is continuing to fall by a metre a year. The problem is that greater and greater inroads have been made into the lake's **freshwater sources**: today, far more water evaporates from the lake than flows into it. There are several dams across the River Jordan (as well as across its tributary, the Yarmouk), and – as part of its national water-conservation programme – Jordan has dammed all the major rivers in its territory that formerly flowed directly into the Dead Sea, including the Zarqa Ma'in, the Mujib and the Hasa. In addition, both Israel and Jordan have developed major mineral and potash industries at the southern end of the lake which depend on large-scale evaporation for production.

Since the 1970s, **Lynch's Strait**, a channel of water which formerly connected the northern and southern parts of the lake, has dried out, turning the Lisan peninsula into a landbridge. Dangerous sinkholes are opening up in the soft ground on both shores. If things continue as they are, some estimates say the Dead Sea will dry up completely in fifty years.

In 2002, the Israeli and Jordanian governments called for concerted action to save the Dead Sea. They launched a plan – with the Palestinian Authority – to build the so-called **Red-Dead Canal**, to bring seawater 250km from the Red Sea at Aqaba to replenish the Dead Sea. The 400m drop in altitude would mean that large quantities of hydroelectric power could be generated, and there would also be shared desalination plants creating up to 850 million cubic metres a year of potable water by reverse osmosis, thus substantially easing the region's critical shortage of water. The brine residue left after desalination would then be pumped into the Dead Sea to restore its natural water level. A feasibility study on the canal project is due to report soon after this book goes to press.

However, not everyone is happy. **Friends of the Earth Middle East** (@www.foeme .org), a coalition of Israeli, Palestinian and Jordanian environmental groups, has voiced several concerns – not least that it would take ten years to implement the Red-Dead plan whereas the Dead Sea needs immediate action. In addition, as it currently stands, the Red-Dead scheme allows the unplanned exploitation of the Dead Sea's resources to continue, with no bar on the numbers of hotels being built, and no imperative for sustainable development. There have, as yet, also been no detailed environmental studies on how the addition of huge quantities of seawater might affect the Dead Sea's delicate ecological balance – or on the possible impact of a pipeline breach in the open desert. Time will tell whether the Red-Dead Canal is the answer.

hopeless paddlers alike become bobbing corks. As you walk in, you'll find your feet are forced up from under you – you couldn't touch the bottom if you tried and if you lie back you'll find the water supports you like a cradle. You ride too high in the water to swim, and should you attempt a few strokes you'll find you just splash ineffectually and are likely to get water in your eyes, which is a very unpleasant experience. The salt will also make you very aware of every little cut and open blemish on your skin. Nonetheless, the sensation of floating completely unaided and silent on a flat, hot sea surrounded by hazy mountains is worth the discomfort.

Other diversions include covering yourself in the hot, sulphurous black **mud** which collects in pools on the beach; letting it dry in the sun before washing it off will leave you with tingling muscles and baby-soft skin. However, scorching heat (well over 40°C in summer) and exceptionally low humidity make **dehydration** a real danger, and while you're out in the open you should be drinking twice or three times as much water as normal to compensate.

Many people come here for **therapeutic tourism**: both the waters and the mud have medically proven benefits, putting many severe skin diseases and joint problems into long-term remission. Calcium, magnesium, bromine, sulphur and bitumen – all with beneficial properties – are found in extremely high concentrations, and, in addition, the air is very highly oxygenated, due to the combination of high rates of evaporation, high temperatures, high atmospheric pressure and low humidity. Celebrated skin-care products from the Dead Sea can be bought all over the country, and internationally. All the big hotels have medical centres, which are often booked solid for months ahead.

The Dead Sea is a popular spot for a weekend outing: roads, hotels and facilities can get crowded on Fridays and holidays. Bikinis and regular swimwear are fine at the hotel beaches and Amman Beach, but elsewhere a T-shirt and long shorts are a minimum. One thing to bear in mind, if you're planning a dip but want to avoid the big hotels, is that you should make sure you have access to a **freshwater shower**: Dead Sea brine is thick and oily, and leaves an uncomfortable layer of salt on your skin that you'll want to wash off before dressing.

Dead Sea hotels and beaches

At the end of the main highway down from Amman is a T-junction: the highway bends left towards the Dead Sea hotels, while a minor road heads right to the Baptism Site (see p.137). The old road to Jerusalem formerly led straight on at this junction, but the King Abdullah Bridge which carried it over the river was bombed in the 1967 war and never rebuilt; it has now been superseded by the King Hussein Bridge 8km upstream.

About 8km south of the T-junction, past a big conference centre and the Al-Wadi Resort water park (ⓦwww.alwadiresort.com), is the **luxury hotel** zone, comprising a cluster of four- and five-star properties complete with pools, spas, showers, bathtubs, flushing toilets and a fairly extensive acreage of irrigated and hand-watered gardens, planted in what is naturally barren, salty soil. Almost all the fresh water for this hotel strip is piped from Wadi Mujib, which is severely depleted as a result. In such a desperately water-poor country, it's a moot point whether luxury development in this particularly arid spot is entirely a good thing. Nonetheless, more hotels and leisure complexes are planned: in addition to the properties listed below, expect – at least – a Holiday Inn, Crowne Plaza and Swiss-Belhotel (2010) and an InterContinental (2012).

This zone at the lake's northeastern corner includes almost the only developed **beaches** along Jordan's shoreline, the remainder of which is mostly lined with jagged, salt-encrusted rocks. Hotels usually allow beach access to non-guests – expect a fee over JD15 – but may turn you away if they're particularly busy: phone ahead wherever possible. There are no towns or villages within easy reach, meaning that if you stay overnight your only entertainment options lie within your hotel (or you could stroll to the next-door hotel instead). Amman is about an hour's drive away; sites such as the Dead Sea Panorama (see p.134), Mount Nebo (p.231) and the Baptism Site (p.137) are closer at hand.

Dead Sea Mövenpick ☎05 356 1111, ⓦwww .movenpick-deadsea.com. Outstanding choice with unusual taste and character. The lobby is supremely elegant – cooled by a flowing artificial stream and waterfall – while the bar features a stunning wooden ceiling, hand-carved in Damascene style. Below the main buildings, the guest rooms are housed in two-storey buildings of local stone and plaster, superbly designed to imitate and blend in with the lumpy Dead Sea landscape of low, rounded marl hills; they're arranged around a succession of quiet, village-style courtyards featuring tinkling fountains and set among exotic flower gardens, all with shaded balconies and full amenities. Further down the complex are a variety of restaurants – Italian, Asian, haute cuisine – plus a small amphitheatre for live music at sunset, a large open-air pool, and steps leading down to the beach. Off to one side is the ultra-chic spa (ⓦwww.zaraspa.com). ❾

Dead Sea Spa Hotel ☎05 356 1000, ⓦwww .jordandeadsea.com. Relatively modest four-star hotel that – compared with its ritzy neighbours – offers unusual value. It's especially good for day-trippers or weekenders looking to avoid splurging at the big hotels, and was completely refurbished in 2008. Guest rooms are large and comfortable, and the on-site medical centre was the pioneer for therapeutic tourism in Jordan. ❽

Jordan Valley Marriott ☎05 356 0400, ⓦwww.marriott.com/qmdjv. Excellent holiday hotel, built in a large U-shape around three swimming pools – including an infinity pool facing west across the Dead Sea. Its public areas are spacious, airy and well designed, while the guest rooms are exceptional. Twelve cafés, bars and restaurants occupy several levels within the main reception building and seafront locations across the site, including outlets for Italian, Arabic, Asian and French brasserie-style cuisine. There are also diversions such as beach volleyball, a tennis court and live music at sunset, as well as an on-site spa and, of course, a beach. ❾

Kempinski Ishtar Dead Sea ☎05 356 8888, ⓦwww.kempinski-deadsea.com. One of the Middle East's leading luxury hotels, breaking through the barrier of mere five stars. Set amid the gardens, lagoons and numerous palm-shaded pools are separate enclaves, including private villas and beach complexes, featuring cool designer interiors done up in a mock Babylonian style (Ishtar was the Babylonian goddess of love). The public areas are cool and airy, and many of the restaurants are recommendable, including the quirky, brightly colourful *Obelisk* designer eatery. The spa area is vast, including twenty treatment rooms alongside pools and steam rooms galore. ❾

Amman Beach

Some 2km south of the hotel zone is the **AMMAN BEACH** resort (daily 24hr; JD12). Don't be fooled by the name: Amman is about an hour away (and over 1200m up in the hills). At the time of writing, this is the Dead Sea's only **public beach**, and it's also the most easily accessible low-budget option for Dead Sea beach-bumming – not least because the main car park serves as the terminus for public buses from Amman and elsewhere. It's a well-run place with trees, plenty of shade and even patches of lawn; the entry ticket includes access to the beach and swimming pool. Spread around the site are facilities for children, including a play park and various beach games; an OK restaurant with buffet meals (around JD10); and good-quality beach facilities, including separate male and female changing areas, towel-rental and freshwater showers. You can also **pitch a tent** here (JD14).

Transport practicalities

The Dead Sea is easy to reach on a fast dual-lane road that branches off the Amman–Airport highway. With your own transport, it's easy to construct a circular day-trip route from either Amman or Madaba to take in the Baptism Site, the Dead Sea and Mount Nebo (see p.231).

Buses from Amman for the Dead Sea leave from Muhajireen station. Early-morning buses (7–9am) run direct to "Amman Beach", but only if there's demand – guaranteed on a Friday. Others may stop short at the crossroads town of **Shuneh al-Janubiyyeh** (see p.143), about 15km north in the Jordan Valley. You can also reach Shuneh by bus from Salt, Dayr Alla and Madaba (via Mount Nebo). From Shuneh, frequent minibuses head to the village of **Sweimeh**, 3km northeast of the hotel zone; the driver might be willing to take you on to Amman Beach for a little extra.

The **last bus** back to Amman departs from Amman Beach at around 5pm, the last from Shuneh around 6pm (both an hour or two earlier in winter). If you miss these, a **taxi** from Amman Beach to Amman is about JD35, or you could pay JD5 for a taxi to the Rameh junction (at the foot of the climb to Amman) and then hitch.

South of Amman Beach, the Dead Sea road runs along the shoreline, eventually reaching Aqaba 278km away. This is a good, fast **driving route** with spectacular scenery that shifts from the deep blue of the Dead Sea to the sandy deserts of the Wadi Araba (see p.355).

Dead Sea Panorama مجمع بانوراما البحر الميت

On the main road 5km south of Amman Beach is a marked turn-off climbing into the mountains: follow it up 9km of steep switchbacks to reach the **DEAD SEA PANORAMA** complex (daily 9am–5pm; winter closes 4pm; JD2; ⓦwww.rscn.org.jo). This sensitively designed building – managed by Jordan's Royal Society for the Conservation of Nature (RSCN) – perches on a cliff-edge with spectacular views over the Dead Sea; footpaths lead away from the parking area to viewpoints, and there's a short walking trail that covers a circular route around the site. Within the main building is the excellent **Dead Sea Museum**, covering four themes in fascinating detail: the geological origins of the Dead Sea, the ecology of the region, its archeology and history, and issues surrounding future conservation. The museum is spacious, modern and air-conditioned: the exhibits and accompanying videos make for an absorbing visit. Next door is an RSCN **nature shop**, selling handmade crafts and jewellery.

The complex also includes a good ✈ **restaurant** (daily noon–10.30pm; ⓣ05 349 1133 or 079 715 5584), a pleasant, upscale venue to sample high-quality Arabic food in the air-conditioned interior or out on the terrace. Reckon on around JD20–25 a head for a fine selection of hot and cold *mezze*, salads, kebabs and grills; alcohol is served. It's a popular spot for weekend dining: book ahead.

From a T-junction just above the Panorama, a turn-off heads 2km to the luxury *Six Senses* spa resort at Hammamat Ma'in (see p.235), while the main road continues to climb to the plateau, passing through Ma'in village and ending after about 30km at Madaba (p.221).

South along the Dead Sea road

From the Panorama turn-off, it's another 7km south to a series of thermal springs at **Zara**, lying downstream from the hot waterfalls of Hammamat Ma'in (see p.235). Zara is a very popular Friday outing spot, with cars lined up along the highway, and people alternating between dipping in the Dead Sea and washing the salt off in the warm spring water. Men can splash around freely but even in the secluded valleys women should only venture in fully clothed. A few hundred metres south of Zara are the remains of King Herod's baths and Dead Sea port at **Callirhoë**, although there's little left to see other than a handful of column drums and the remnants of a harbour wall.

Mujib Nature Reserve   محمية الموجب الطبيعية

The Dead Sea road continues to the **Mujib Bridge**, 27km south of Amman Beach, a graceful 140-metre construction crossing the outflow of the River Mujib; on the lake side of the bridge you can splash around in the refreshing river water. The valley system, which extends high into the mountains, is the centrepiece of the **MUJIB NATURE RESERVE** (for more, see p.241; Ⓦ www.rscn.org.jo). Below the bridge, on the cliff side of the road, is the **visitor centre** (daily 8am–4pm; ☏077 742 2125). Staff here have maps, brochures and light refreshments, and can advise on walking routes, though you should always **book in advance** directly or through the RSCN's "Wild Jordan" centre in Amman (see p.51). The easy – but memorably dramatic – **Siq Trail** (April–Oct only; JD1pp self-guided; JD12pp with guide; 2.5hr) heads into the Mujib gorge, leading you between towering sandstone cliffs to the base of a waterfall before returning; you may be wading or even swimming some sections. A tougher alternative is the **Ibex Trail** (year-round; JD20pp; guide compulsory; 4hr), which heads from the Mujib Bridge south to a steep access route up into the mountains, traversing a number of dry valleys on the way to a ranger station: you may spot ibex roaming wild here. The **Malaqi Trail** (April–Oct only; JD55pp; guide compulsory; 7–9hr) is a classic canyoning route, graded difficult, which initially follows the Ibex Trail before descending into the Mujib gorge and heading upstream to the confluence with the Wadi Hidan, then returning – via a 20m waterfall abseil – to the Mujib Bridge. These and other walks that start from the reserve's eastern highland entrance at Faqua (see p.241) are outlined on the website. All routes are closed during Ramadan.

On the Mujib river delta nearby stands a cluster of modest 🛏 **chalets** (☏079 720 3888, Ⓦ www.rscn.org.jo; ❻) that are compact and simple but still comfortable. Each is air-conditioned but not en suite – the communal shower and toilet block is separate – and comes with its own shaded terrace looking north over a quiet beach that is pleasant for a float (and has showers). They are open year-round, but even the staff admit that the air conditioning isn't enough to ease the blistering temperatures of high summer (June–Aug). Alongside is a pleasant restaurant block offering meals (JD6–15) and lunchboxes – though only with **advance booking**. Access isn't easy: until a sealed road has been laid, check in first at the Mujib Bridge visitor centre, from where staff will drive you over to the chalets in their 4x4.

Prices at Jordan's RSCN-run nature reserves are high. The RSCN makes no apologies for this: it says that the reason it exists is to protect Jordan's natural environment, and that it has built lodges and developed tourism as a tool for generating funds to help conservation and support rural communities. You may or may not agree with their pricing policy – but this kind of responsible tourism is virtually unknown in the Middle East, and the RSCN are pioneers. For now, until tourism schemes emerge that are truly community-owned, paying extra to visit the RSCN reserves is a good way to ensure that your money goes to benefit rural people and habitats.

Bab adh-Dhraa   باب الذراع

The road continues south alongside the Dead Sea, hugging the salt-spattered shore below rocky cliffs. Some 24km south of Mujib is **MAZRA'A**, a small town on the **Lisan Peninsula** – now a belt of dry land across the lake. Exploring the peninsula isn't encouraged by the Arab Potash Company, but it's still possible to turn off at the company's sign, drive out a little way and then venture into the soft white sand on foot. You might stumble upon one of the old **Byzantine monasteries** that lie ruined here, unexcavated, in an eerie landscape forever sultry and thick with haze.

About 1km south of Mazra'a is a turn-off leading up into the hills to Karak (see p.242). Take this road for about 1km and you'll come to the Bronze Age *tell* of **Bab adh-Dhraa**, rising on your left. It's a sparse site, offering a thick city wall and a handful of foundations: the attraction is in relating the place to a name. Bab adh-Dhraa is the site of a large town which flourished around 2600 BC – some graves in the huge **necropolis** across the road date from as early as the fourth millennium – and is the leading candidate for biblical **Sodom**, location of so much depravity that God felt compelled to raze the city and kill its inhabitants. Standing on the *tell* today, amid barren rocks on the hazy shores of a salt lake, you can only wonder what on earth the poor Sodomites must have been up to in these rooms to deserve such a fate.

Sodom and Gomorrah

The tale in Genesis of how God punished the depravity of the inhabitants of **Sodom and Gomorrah**, and how **Lot** and his wife escaped, is one of the best-known biblical stories. After arriving in Canaan (Palestine), Lot and his uncle Abraham began to bicker over grazing grounds. They separated, and Lot pitched his tents at the southeastern corner of the Dead Sea near Sodom, one of the five "cities of the plain" (the others were Gomorrah, Zoar, Admah and Zeboyim). "But," as Genesis warns, "the men of Sodom were wicked and sinners before the Lord exceedingly." One evening, Lot was visited by two angels, come to warn him of the city's impending divine destruction. Lot, his wife and two daughters fled and "the Lord rained upon Sodom and Gomorrah brimstone and fire." Every one of the five cities was destroyed, and every person killed. As they were fleeing, Lot's wife disobeyed a divine order not to look back at the destruction, and was turned into a pillar of salt.

Seemingly the last people left alive in the world, Lot and his daughters sought refuge in a cave in the mountains. Calculating that, with all potential mates vaporized, they were likely to die childless, the daughters hatched a plan to get their father so drunk he wouldn't be able to tell who they were, whereupon they would seduce him and thus preserve the family. Everything worked to plan and both daughters gave birth to sons; the elder named her child **Moab**, and the younger Ben-Ammi, or "father of **Ammon**".

The last of these bizarre biblical episodes has been commemorated for centuries, and possibly millennia, at a cave-and-church complex in the hills above Safi. Ruins within Safi itself, as well as at four other scanty Early Bronze Age sites nearby (Bab adh-Dhraa, Numayra, Fifa and Khanazir), show evidence of destruction by fire. At Numayra, archeologists also found the skeletons of three men whose bones were crushed by falling masonry. These five could possibly be the "cities of the plain". The only fly in the ointment is that they were razed around 2350 BC, several hundred years before the generally accepted era of Abraham and Lot, although archeologists are still debating the precise timescales involved.

Lot's Cave and Museum كهف النبي لوط

Some 22km south of the Karak turning on the Dead Sea road, a sign points left to **Lot's Cave** – a rich archeological site that has thrown up evidence of Early and Middle Bronze Age habitation, as well as Nabatean pottery, Byzantine mosaics and the earliest example of carved wood yet discovered intact in Jordan: a door that dates from the seventh century Umayyad period. The location – not to mention the notion of standing in Lot's sandalprints – is dramatic enough to warrant a visit.

About 1km along this turn-off you'll spot **Lot's Museum** – a grand, semicircular building designed to showcase the historical heritage of the Jordan Valley/Dead Sea area. It was due to open in 2009, soon after this book went to press.

From the museum, a track continues steeply up the hill to a parking area at the foot of steps leading up to the cave itself. The guardian will accompany you up to the site, which involves a tiring climb of almost **300 steps**. The Ministry of Tourism are in the process of constructing a shelter over the site; it may be complete by the time you visit.

The first area you come to is a **court**, part of which has slipped down the hill, but which originally served to support the floor of the **church** above. The main **apse** has seating for the bishop and is slightly raised. Five **mosaics** – one dated April 606, another May 691 – have been renovated, and will be uncovered for viewing once the site shelter is complete. The **narthex** was originally entered from the right, via a doorway from the court below; this ingenious piece of design enabled visiting Jewish and Muslim pilgrims to avoid stepping inside the church and instead head straight for the holy **cave**, the entrance to which is to the left of the apse. A beautifully carved **lintel** over the cave entrance, marked with crosses, presages an interior mosaic which mimics the round stones embedded in the roof. All around the church was spread a **monastery**, and the remains of six or seven isolated cells are dotted around the parched hillside. The views from the church over the Dead Sea and the nearby town of Safi are stunning.

Safi and beyond الصافي

SAFI, at the southern tip of the Dead Sea, is the phosphate capital of Jordan, although – under the name Zoar – it also has a history as one of the five biblical "cities of the plain", along with Sodom and Gomorrah. The southernmost portion of the Dead Sea has been corralled into huge evaporation pans for Jordan's phosphate and chemical industries and, with its neighbour, the lush farming village of **FIFA** a bit further south, Safi shares a natural hothouse that is one of the most intensively farmed areas of Jordan, with bananas, tomatoes and other fruits as staple irrigated crops.

Just beyond Fifa, a scenic turn-off climbs to Tafileh (see p.249), while continuing south brings you into the long **Wadi Araba**, with drifting sand and wandering camels all the way south to Aqaba. See p.355 for more on this route.

Bethany: the Baptism Site المغطس

One of the most important recent discoveries in Middle Eastern archeology has been the identification of a site on the east bank of the River Jordan, near the Dead Sea, as **Bethany-beyond-the-Jordan**, the place where John the Baptist lived, and where he most likely **baptized Jesus Christ**. Archeologists have uncovered a wealth of sites – 21 at the last count – along **Wadi Kharrar**, a small

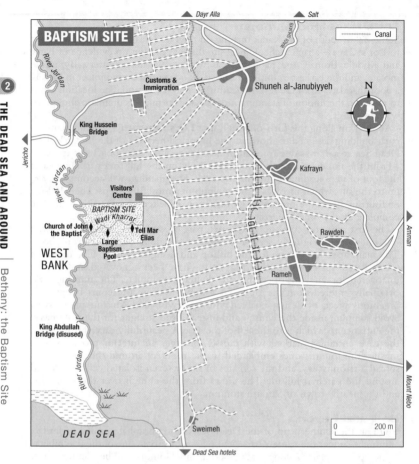

side-valley of reeds and flowing water that runs for 2km from its source down to the River Jordan. These discoveries – eleven Byzantine churches, five baptismal pools from the Roman and Byzantine periods, caves of monks and hermits, and lodges for pilgrims – plus a wealth of medieval accounts of pilgrims and travellers to the area, rapidly convinced both Jordanian and international opinion as to the veracity of the site.

This is almost the lowest point on earth, over 350m below sea level; the air is thick, hot and heavy. On the banks of the Wadi Kharrar, you're in the midst of the biblical Plains of Moab; views across the baked ground, punctuated by the occasional wizened tree, enable you to pick out individual buildings and cars in Jericho. Underfoot is a soft, chalky marl that seems to deaden sound; only when you get close to Wadi Kharrar itself can you hear the chirping of birds and the soughing of the dense beds of reeds and tamarisk that line the watercourse. Flanking the River Jordan itself is a jungle-like thicket, tropically hot and humid – more akin to Southeast than Southwest Asia.

Visiting outside winter (Nov–Feb) means that you'll have to cope with scorching temperatures, often topping 45°C in summer. The best advice is to arrive at 8am and explore in the relative cool of the morning. But don't let this put you off; for its historical resonance, natural austerity and religious power, this is an extraordinary place.

Some history

This stretch of desolate plain flanking the River Jordan has been a focus for spirituality since Old Testament times: Judaism, Christianity and Islam all recall momentous events which took place in this relatively small part of the southern Jordan Valley. First mention is in Genesis, when **Lot** separated from Abraham and "chose the plain of Jordan" to pitch his tents, after which **Jacob** wrestled with God a little way north at Penuel. A sizeable proportion of the Book of Numbers is set at the Israelites' camp, "pitched in the plains of Moab by Jordan opposite Jericho", following which **Moses** delivers a long summation in Deuteronomy before going up "from the plains of Moab unto the mountain of Nebo", where he died. **Joshua** led the tribes across the river, which miraculously halted its flow, an event mirrored centuries later in 2 Kings, when the prophets **Elijah** and **Elisha** again stopped the flow of the river, as a chariot and horses of fire took Elijah up to heaven – according to ancient tradition, from the rounded hillock alongside Wadi Kharrar now known as Tell Mar Elyas (Elijah's Hill).

It was because of the associations with the prophet Elijah that, a thousand years later, John, an ascetic holy man with a prophetic vision, took up residence near the same hillock, using the numerous small springs of sweet water to symbolically cleanse people of sin; locals soon flocked to this **John the Baptist**. Most biblical mentions describe the baptisms taking place "in Jordan", which probably referred loosely to this general area. The River Jordan, which often flooded to a width of 1km or more, would have been rapid (in Aramaic, *yardeen* – from which "Jordan" is derived – means "fast-flowing water") and deep, offering no easy access from the often steep bank. By contrast, the dozens of tiny side-springs, some of which rise within

▲ The Greek Orthodox Church of St John, Baptism Site

pools barely 100m from the river, are protected and more manageable as immersion points.

The Gospel of St John mentions "**Bethany–beyond–the–Jordan**, where John was baptizing"; the spot – unconnected with Bethany near Jerusalem – was also known as Bethabara or Beit-Abara, "the House of the Crossing-Point". A later account says that **Jesus** "returned again across the Jordan to the place where John had first started baptizing". There is no explicit mention of when or where John baptized Jesus, but the accumulated weight of tradition and historical evidence places it in or near Wadi Kharrar, within easy reach of plentiful supplies of spring water, alongside the Roman road between Jericho and Nebo (thereby within easy reach of potential converts), but far enough out of reach to mean that John could criticize King Herod with impunity.

As early as 333 AD, the anonymous **Pilgrim of Bordeaux** identified the site of Bethany-beyond-the-Jordan as lying five Roman miles (just under 7.5km) north of the Dead Sea, corresponding almost exactly to the point where the Wadi Kharrar enters the river: "here is a place by the river, a little hill on the far bank, where Elijah was caught up into heaven". From then on, many ancient texts mention several churches in the same area dedicated to John the Baptist and Elijah. The sixth-century pilgrim **Theodosius** described the riverside "Church of St John, which the emperor Anastasius built [in about 500 AD]; this church is very lofty, being built above chambers on account of the flooding of the Jordan" – a description which corresponds almost exactly with one of the churches uncovered recently. Other pilgrims at this time talked of the whole valley being "full of hermits". The place was important enough to merit inclusion on the **Madaba mosaic map** (see p.226).

The accounts continued through the Middle Ages, with Bethany-beyond-the-Jordan taking its place in a **pilgrimage route** linking Jerusalem, Jericho, Hesban and Mount Nebo. From the twelfth to the eighteenth century, Bethany was home to **Greek Orthodox monks**, who were reported still to be present as late as the turn of the twentieth century (the whole site is still in the custody of the Greek Orthodox Church), but most ruins lay undiscovered while knowledge of the whereabouts of Bethany-beyond-the-Jordan faded from collective memory.

Archeological investigations at Tell Mar Elias and along Wadi Kharrar had to be abandoned at the outbreak of **war** in 1948, and for many years the site lay in a militarized border zone. It was only after the 1994 **peace treaty** between Jordan and Israel that the area could be swept for landmines and again opened for study. The momentous discoveries that rapidly followed convinced the Jordanian authorities, and then the broad mass of specialist opinion worldwide, that the long-lost "Bethany-beyond-the-Jordan" had been rediscovered.

Practicalities

The site (daily 8am–6pm; winter closes 4pm; last entry 1hr before closing; JD7; Ⓦwww.baptismsite.com) is signposted from the T-junction at the end of the highway down from Amman. The highway bends left (south) to the Dead Sea hotels, while to the right (north) is a minor road to the Baptism Site. Note that if you're approaching from the Dead Sea hotels, you have to follow the highway round to the right and then make a U-turn in order to get onto the Baptism Site road.

From the junction, it's 5km to a gateway across the road, where you pay the admission fee and receive a free brochure (with a map). A little ahead is the parking area in front of the palm-shaded **Visitors' Centre**, which has toilets, souvenir shops and refreshment kiosks, and which is where the **official site guides** wait. If you're visiting independently in a car (or privately hired taxi),

A proliferation of churches

In recent years many **new churches** have been built at the Baptism Site, as the world's Christian denominations clamour to be represented at this hugely important site. The planning process is strict, and all the new buildings are modest and unintrusive – many rather beautiful. By the time you visit there will be – or are planned – Coptic, Armenian, Ethiopian, Syrian Orthodox, Roman Catholic, Greek Orthodox, Anglican, Lutheran and Baptist churches, along with other institutions and prayer centres, as well as monasteries and/or pilgrim hostels belonging to the Greek Orthodox, Latin and Russian Orthodox churches.

If you're here to affirm your Christian faith, you can request to be taken for a private religious ceremony at any of several baptism pools and centres around the site. Someone from your own party can officiate or you can ask for a local priest to conduct the ceremony. Contact ☏077 760 7036 or ✉promotionunit@baptismsite .com several weeks in advance.

an official site guide (free with entry ticket) can accompany you, in your own vehicle, for a tour around the site. Private vehicles without a site guide are banned within the site. Otherwise, you must wait at the Visitors' Centre for a free **shuttle bus** (every 15–20min), which makes a round trip to the three separate areas of the site. Allow a minimum visit of **one hour** – though an in-depth tour of the whole site could take up to three hours.

Tell Mar Elyas (Elijah's Hill) is alongside **Parking 1**; the Baptism Pools and pilgrims' station are by **Parking 2**; and John the Baptist's Church down by the River Jordan is a short walk from **Parking 3**. Fresh drinking water is provided at several points (but you should ideally carry your own), and there are toilets at Parking 3, as well as at the Visitors' Centre. You can also – with advance notice – elect to tackle the hot and tiring **walk** from the Visitors' Centre to Tell Mar Elyas and onwards on a marked trail along the south bank of the Wadi Kharrar to John's Church and the River Jordan. It's about 4km in total, but allow three hours one way.

Note that the pools and springs are mostly or completely dry from late May until late October.

Along Wadi Kharrar   وادي الخرار

The site comprises six square kilometres focused around the small **Wadi Kharrar**, which runs westwards for 2km on a meandering course from beside the rounded hillock of **Tell Mar Elyas** down to join the River Jordan amid fourteen small springs around the **Church of John the Baptist**. Midway along is a set of ancient **baptism pools**.

Tell Mar Elyas (Elijah's Hill)   تل مار الياس

At the head of the little Wadi Kharrar, alongside **Parking 1**, stands the low **Tell Mar Elyas**. A few metres south of the *tell*, a number of remains have been uncovered. The most prominent sight is a large freestanding arch, raised in 1999 from 63 stones (to commemorate the death at 63 of King Hussein) over the foundations of a rectangular church dating from the fourth or fifth century. Since March 21, 2000, when the then pope celebrated Mass beneath this arch and, in a gesture of reconciliation, faced west to bless Jerusalem then east to bless Mount Nebo, the site has been known as the **Church of John Paul II**. A few metres away are the foundations of a larger rectangular building, with some fragments of a mosaic floor remaining, that has been dubbed a **prayer hall**.

Around here is a complicated web of water channels, pool-beds, a pear-shaped well (once circular, but distorted by earth movements) and a large **cistern**, still with its plastered interior, that formerly was covered by a barrel vault of sandstone quarried 20km away at Sweimeh topped with a mosaic floor (remnants of which have been preserved). With the level of settlement in antiquity, and the numbers of baptisms performed here, a great deal of water was needed: pipes and aqueducts channelled water to the site from several kilometres away, but still the 100-cubic-metre cistern wasn't enough, and a second, smaller cistern was built nearby.

The small *tell* features a trinity of trinities – three churches, three caves and three baptism pools – encircled by a wooden catwalk. Proceeding clockwise, on the west side of the *tell* is a cave which forms the apse of a small Byzantine **church**, with small niches to the east and south and tiny fragments of its mosaic floor. An open chapel on the northwest side leads round to the large, late-Byzantine **northern church**, now sheltered from the elements, which incorporates a strange black stone into its apse to commemorate the fire which accompanied Elijah's rise to heaven. Its detailed mosaic floor includes an intriguing cross motif in diamonds and an inscription in Greek which dates it to "the time of **Rhotorius**" (early sixth century). Up a couple of steps on the northeastern side of the *tell* are two **pools** from the Roman period, one cut later with the addition of a fourteen-metre-deep well. Further round is a large rectangular pool, plastered, and with a line of four steps leading into it – for group baptisms, it's been suggested.

The Pilgrims' Station, Baptism Pool and caves

Paths lead down from the *tell* area to the footpath along the south side of Wadi Kharrar, which features several sites attesting to the faith of Byzantine pilgrims and ascetics. Around 500m west of the *tell* are the remains of a *lavra*, a complex of hermits' cells, while further west – near **Parking 2** – is a large **Baptism Pool**, designed to hold 300 people, built roughly on its lower courses but with well-dressed sandstone ashlars further up. Channels fed spring water to the pool; a fifth- or sixth-century building excavated on a small promontory directly above the pool, with views over the whole valley, may well have been a hostel for visiting pilgrims (it has now been dubbed the **Pilgrims' Station**).

Immediately to the west, the *ghor*, or broad valley floor, gives way to the *zor*, or narrow, deep-set flood-plain flanking the River Jordan itself. Cut into the loose marl of these cliffs, and now accessible by modern steps, are two **caves**, each featuring prayer niches; one of the caves has three interior apses. The seventh-century writer John Moschus records the pilgrimage to Sinai of a monk John, from Jerusalem; while recovering from a fever in the *lavra* of Safsafas, John the Baptist appeared to him and said, "This little cave is greater than Mount Sinai: our Lord Jesus Christ himself visited me here."

Church of John the Baptist

The Old Testament prophet Jeremiah spoke of the "**jungle of the Jordan**", and the contrast in the natural environment between Tell Mar Elyas and the churches on the banks of the Jordan itself couldn't be stronger. This narrow strip flanking the river is quite unlike anywhere else in the country: paths from the wild and knobbly lunar landscape of the desert-like *zor* around **Parking 3** plunge into a wall of woody tamarisk bushes so thick that, had a way not been cut, it would be impossible to force your way through. Inside the thicket of reeds and tamarisk, the air is steamy and tropical, full of the chirruping of birds and the hum of insects, and marked by a constant babble of water from the fourteen springs that flow all around (indeed, the name "Kharrar" is thought to be onomatopoeic).

A five- or ten-minute walk through the "jungle" – past a number of springs and rest areas – brings you to a clearing marked by a modern pool and the sheltered remains of the sixth- or seventh-century **Church of John the Baptist**, situated alongside two more churches, which were built more or less on top of one another; the floor of the lower one, tiled in triangular, square and octagonal flags of marble, has been exposed, and there are also marble Corinthian capitals from long-fallen columns lying nearby. Beneath a shelter is the altar and mosaic floor of the main church, which was formerly raised up above the level of the river on an arched vault to protect it from flooding – exactly as medieval pilgrims recorded. Pillars from this vault still lie where they fell in antiquity, on the north side of the church building. Byzantine stairs, three of them black marble or bitumen, interspersed with white marble from Asia Minor, lead from the apse to what is still known as the **Spring of John the Baptist**. A marble fragment commemoratively marked "IOY. BATT." (a Latin abbreviation of "John the Baptist") that was found in the church is on display in the Visitors' Centre.

The River Jordan نهر الاردن

About 200m west of the ancient church, via a laid path through the tamarisks, stands the modern Greek Orthodox **Church of St John**, alongside other churches (see box, p.141). Opposite, shaded steps lead down to a wooden platform on the **River Jordan** itself – not the grand, Amazon-like spectacle of imagination, but rather a low, muddy stream, these days barely a metre deep and less than 10m wide at this point. On the opposite bank, in Israeli-occupied territory, is a complex known as Qasr al-Yahud – a white stone terrace, complete with chapel, that lacks any historical or religious authenticity. (Alternative Israeli baptism sites further north are unashamedly commercial affairs, where "pilgrims" pay to be dipped in the river.)

Linger here awhile, if you can: despite its modest appearance these days, the Jordan is one of the world's great rivers, with huge religious and historical significance. There are very few other places along its course where you can get this close to the water – and none has such drama.

The walk back to Parking 3 leads you on a different route via two more river lookouts, perched high above the banks.

The southern Jordan Valley

North of the Baptism Site extends the long, hot **Jordan Valley**; for more, see p.181. The main settlement in these southern stretches, among the farming villages of the valley floor, is the crossroads market town of **SHUNEH AL-JANUBIYYEH** (South Shuneh), served by buses running south to the Dead Sea and into the hills to Mount Nebo and Madaba, north along the Jordan Valley road to Dayr Alla (see below), and east to Salt and Amman; taxis do the short run west to the King Hussein Bridge crossing-point.

North of Shuneh, the Jordan Valley road cuts a straight path through simple villages and past swathes of farmland. Points of interest are few and far between down here: the culture is all rural and agricultural and the archeological

King Hussein/Allenby Bridge

Turn to p.35 for information about arriving in Jordan via the **King Hussein/Allenby Bridge**, and p.123 for details of transport to the bridge from Amman.

sites – though plentiful – are strictly for scholars: barely one stone stands upon another in any of them.

A few kilometres beyond Shuneh lies the humdrum town of **Karameh**, site of a major dam; 16km north is an old road sign pointing west to the Palestinian city of Nablus, harking back to the days before 1967 when territory on both sides of the river was Jordanian (the turn-off leads to a bridge now reserved for agricultural traffic).

Dayr Alla and around   دير علا

Some 26km north of Karameh is the market town of **DAYR ALLA**, served by buses from Amman, Salt and valley destinations. Rising beside the road about 1km north of the town – whose name translates as "High Monastery" and has nothing to do with Allah or Islam – is the large **Tell Dayr Alla**. Some historians link this site with biblical Penuel, where Jacob wrestled with God; others associate it with Succoth, site of an ironworks that produced pieces used in the Temple of Solomon in Jerusalem. One excavation uncovered an inscription in red and black ink on plaster, dated around 800 BC, relating tales of prophecy by Balaam, a seer mentioned in the Bible (Numbers 22–24). Heading down the street that hugs the south flank of the *tell* brings you to an office; as well as providing information and impromptu refreshment, staff can unlock the small **museum** (daily except Fri 8am–1pm & 2–5pm; free), which houses a collection of interesting bits and bobs from sites throughout the valley as well as an explanation of the Balaam text. The *tell* itself, punctured by deep excavation trenches exposing anonymous walls and rooms, is barely worth the effort of the climb.

Around 9km north of Dayr Alla is the town of **Kraymeh**, served by buses from Ajloun as well as the valley villages north and south. Just before the town, opposite an isolated mosque with a stone minaret, a road branches west towards the huge mound of **Tell as–Sa'idiyyeh**, some 2km away, home to a large city in the Late Bronze Age, during the thirteenth and twelfth centuries BC. Halfway along the right-hand slope of the *tell*, a reconstructed Iron Age **stone staircase** leads up from a spring-fed pool to the summit; excavation trenches display remnants of an Egyptian-style public building (Sa'idiyyeh may have been a northern outpost of the Egyptian empire) and city wall. The *tell* gives stunning views along the length of the valley, though the River Jordan itself, only a few hundred metres away, is still invisible in its gorge.

North of here, buses follow the valley road for 20km or so to the town of Mshare'a, access point for the ancient site of Pella (see p.182).

Turn to p.181 for coverage of the northern part of the Jordan Valley.

The Balqa hills   البلقاء

The gentle hills which roll westward from Amman down to the Jordan Valley through the historic **Balqa** region – of which the graceful old town of **Salt** is capital – are laced with lush, beautiful valleys and dotted with pleasant towns such as **Wadi Seer** and **Fuheis**, the latter with an appealing little crafts quarter. Near Wadi Seer is one of the few examples of Hellenistic architecture surviving in the Middle East – the impressive white palace of **Qasr al-Abd**, set in open countryside near an ancient cave system known as **Iraq al-Amir**. All these places are easily accessible by bus from Amman, and could together form an unusual half- or full-day trip by car.

Salt السلط

For many centuries, **SALT** was the only settlement of any size in Trans-jordan. A regional capital under the Ottomans, the town – whose name derives from the ancient Greek *saltos*, meaning "thick forest" – came into its own in the late nineteenth century, when merchants from Nablus arrived to expand their trading base east of the river. Into what was then a peasant village of shacks boxed between precipitous hills, the merchants brought sophisticated architects and masons to work with the honey-coloured local limestone; buildings were put up in the ornate Nabulsi style to serve both as grand residences and as merchandise centres. With open trade to and from Palestine, Salt's boom continued into the 1920s; the new Emirate of Transjordan was formally proclaimed in 1921 in the town's main square, but by then the railway from Damascus had reached nearby Amman and Emir Abdullah chose the better-connected town to be his

▲ Street scene, Salt

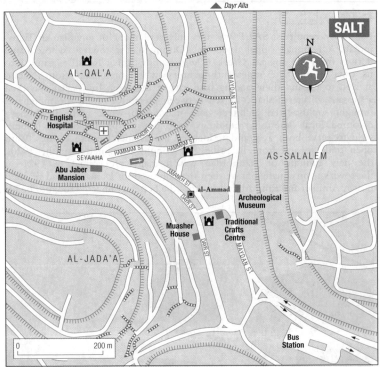

▲ Dayr Alla

SALT

N

AL-QAL'A

English
Hospital

KHADIR ST

MAYDAN ST

SEYAAHA

HAMMAM ST

HAMMAM ST

AS-SALALEM

Abu Jaber
Mansion

AMANEH ST

al-Ammad

Archeological
Museum

DAIR ST

Muasher
House

Traditional
Crafts
Centre

DAIR ST

AL-JADA'A

MAYDAN ST

Bus
Station

0   200 m

Amman & Shuneh al-Janubiyyeh ◢

capital. As quickly as Salt had flourished, it went into decline: superseded by Amman, it was cut off by war in 1948 from its traditional trade outlet to the Mediterranean at Haifa, then again in 1967 from its Palestinian twin, Nablus.

As a consequence, Salt has seen none of the headlong modernization that has afflicted the capital: much of the **Ottoman architecture** in the old quarter has survived, as has peace and quiet, perfect for aimless exploration. A city-wide renovation project has been running for several years, upgrading the old mansions and creating an infrastructure for tourism. You may find things have moved on by the time you visit.

The Town

Standing under the huge eucalyptus at the road junction a short walk up from the bus station, you are surrounded by three towering hills: to your right are the bare rocky slopes of **as-Salalem**, to the left rises the tree-adorned peak of **al-Jada'a**, and straight ahead is **al-Qal'a**, named for the Mamluke fortress on its summit which was demolished in 1840 and finally swept away recently for a white-domed mosque. Walking a little way along Maydan Street, you'll spot the arched and pillared facade of the modern **Salt Archeological Museum** (Sat–Thurs 8am–7pm, Fri 9am–4pm; winter closes earlier; JD2; ⊛jordan.nlembassy.org /culture), housing a fascinating collection that includes a working model of a Mamluke sugar mill and an impression of a Neolithic dolmen landscape. The Ottoman-era building is equally interesting, known as Beit Touqan, once the stately residence of the Touqan family (King Hussein's third wife, Queen Alia, was a

Touqan). A few café tables in the enchanting upper courtyard entice you to linger.

Turning left at the Arab Bank a few minutes further along Maydan Street leads you into narrow Hammam Street (the eponymous *hammam* was razed in the 1930s for lack of customers). This lane, known as **Souk al-Hammam**, is lined with buildings – including a wonderful old mosque – which date from Salt's golden age and hosts what is Jordan's oldest souk, an ordinary market of food and household goods that nonetheless is full of atmosphere.

Hammam Street emerges at the **Seyaaha**, Salt's main plaza, dominated on one side by the graceful arched facade of the **Abu Jaber mansion**, newly renovated home of the Historic Old Salt Museum – due to open after this book went to press, and billed as offering walking tours around the old quarter to view more rejuvenated town houses. Bending sharply to the right is tiny Khadir Street, with several flights of steps leading steeply up the hill. Partway up you'll see the colonnaded honey-stone **English Hospital**, its gates still bearing an "EH" monogram; the building is now the Middle East's first vocational training centre for people with disabilities. The view from the summit, bathed in sunshine, out over the town to the rolling Balqa hills beyond, is worth the hard climb.

Practicalities

Buses run to Salt from both Tabarbour and Mahatta stations in Amman, as well as from the flyover at Sweileh (the same pick-up point as for buses to Fuheis – see below). Meagre **information** about the town can be had from the Department of Antiquities office (☏05 355 5651) at the museum. For refreshment while wandering, there are a few **coffee houses** dotted around; one of the best spreads itself over Dayr Street next to the white-domed mosque close to the museum. **Restaurants** are exclusively in the spit-and-sawdust category, and king among them is *al-Ammad*, which has been churning out quality shish-kebabs to the Salti cognoscenti for a century or more. It's on Amaneh Street, nine doors up from the Cairo Amman Bank, with no sign in English or Arabic; spot it by the small plaque beside the door which outlines its history (in English).

If you're heading for the Jordan Valley, it's worth knowing that the road from Salt down to Shuneh al-Janubiyyeh follows the beautiful and dramatic **Wadi Shuayb**, a perpetually flowing stream lush with undergrowth all year and carpeted with wildflowers in spring; this is a much more impressive route down to the valley floor than the highway from Amman. North of Salt, on the Dayr Alla road, the **Zai National Park** is perfect picnic territory, thick forest with rough trails and plenty of wild nooks.

Pigeon-fancying

At sunset in towns all across Jordan, you'll see small, tight flocks of pigeons wheeling overhead. Pigeon-fancying is surprisingly popular, and has taken on something of a shady image, since the point of it is not to race the birds, but rather to kidnap prize specimens from other people's flocks. In every neighbourhood, as the sun goes down, people emerge onto the flat rooftops and open up their ramshackle pigeon coops, sometimes twirling a lure on a length of rope to keep the flock dipping and swooping, sometimes holding a female bird up so that the males will circle around. Neighbours will often deliberately exercise their flocks at the same time, to try and persuade each other's birds to defect; similarly, some well-trained flocks can be enticed to fly off to another part of town to bring back new individuals. Newspapers report that enthusiasts gain three or four new birds a week, yet lose roughly the same number. Many fanciers keep their identities secret, since – for obvious reasons – they're popularly seen as being not entirely trustworthy.

Fuheis الفحيص

Set among rolling hills near Salt – and just 15km northwest of Amman – **FUHEIS** (pronounced "f-hayce") is a prosperous but rarely visited small town with a delightful, partially restored old quarter of rooftop restaurants and sleepy craft shops. The town is 95 percent Christian and boasts at least five churches, three of which date back to the nineteenth century. Its easy-going atmosphere – and, in summer, the best peaches in Jordan – makes Fuheis a pleasant place to spend an afternoon.

The town has two distinct halves. The first, known as **al-Allali** (with a large calligraphic sculpture in the central Shakr roundabout), is newer and less attractive; make sure you carry on down the steep hill to the old part of town, known as **al-Balad**. Between the two lies a vast cement factory, Jordan's biggest and Fuheis's main claim to fame: over seventy percent of the town is employed at the plant, but local people have suffered for years from clouds of cement dust and soaring rates of asthma. There have long been calls to raise standards or relocate the fifty-year-old plant away from populated areas: it remains both a blessing for the town, and a curse.

Al-Balad comprises a district of quiet lanes and hundred-year-old stone cottages alongside the deep Wadi Rahwa. It had been slated for demolition when, in 1992, a local character opened an art gallery here; he then bought up the cottages one by one and converted them into a self-contained arts and crafts neighbourhood, known as **Rowaq al-Balqa** (shops open daily except Tues 4–10pm; ⓦwww.rowaq.net). This quarter makes for an interesting short wander, and the tiny rural lanes come into their own in the golden light of late afternoon. During August, Fuheis hosts a small-town **carnival** of music and dance, while a recent innovation is the **Fuheis Festival** (ⓦwww.fuheisfestival .com), with music and cultural events staged in the week before Christmas.

Practicalities

On the road north from Amman past Jordan University, just beyond the centre of **Sweileh**, a crossroads town on the northwestern fringes of Amman, take the clearly marked turn-off towards Salt. This minor road winds through pine forest, passing the Royal Stables at Hummar before entering Fuheis. The town is served by **buses** from Amman's Tabarbour station. If you're coming from Wadi Seer, Salt or Jerash, aim for Sweileh; dozens of buses stop at or near the large roundabout beneath Sweileh's trademark flyover, from where you can pick up the Amman–Fuheis buses (ask the locals where to stand). All Fuheis buses run through al-Allali down to their terminus beside a grandiose equestrian statue which dominates the tiny al-Balad roundabout. Note that the last bus back to Amman leaves at around 9pm in summer, 7pm in winter.

Tucked away in renovated old stone houses in the Rowaq lanes are a couple of good Arabic **restaurants**. Top choice is the excellent and reasonably priced 🏕 *Zuwwadeh* (daily 10am–midnight; ☎06 472 1528, ⓦwww.zuwwadeh.com), in an atmospheric house shaded by a giant eucalyptus tree. This is a favourite informal out-of-town dining spot for affluent Ammanis; the fact that Fuheis is Christian gives it an allure of decadence for urbanite Muslims seeking to let their hair down a little, and on weekend nights in particular the place is crowded with families and groups of friends. *Zuwwadeh*'s kebabs and *fatteh* are superb, but you could choose from their inventive list of *mezze* and dine lavishly for less than JD10. There is live music nightly from an accomplished *oud* player. One speciality of the house, which is likely to put an interesting spin on your journey back to Amman, is an alcoholic *argileh* – it looks the same as the ordinary version, but instead of water in the bubble chamber the management substitute *araq*. Book ahead, at weekends especially.

Wadi Seer وادي السير

Though barely 12km from central Amman, the town of **WADI SEER** ("Valley of Orchards") – small and peaceful, filled with trees and birdsong – has the atmosphere of the countryside. Add to the natural beauty a couple of small-scale archeological gems and the area merits an exploratory picnic, although, if you choose a Friday for your outing, you'll discover that most of Amman has had the same idea. **Buses** from Amman depart from Muhajireen station and drop off at Wadi Seer's bus station, perched above a roundabout in the town centre.

Originally settled by Circassian immigrants in the 1880s, Wadi Seer boasts many nineteenth- and early twentieth-century Ottoman stone buildings in the streets around the centre, including a red-roofed mosque of yellowish limestone with one of the most beautifully carved minarets in the country.

Wadi Seer is the staging-post for a journey out to the striking Hellenistic palace of **Qasr al-Abd**, located 10km west alongside the village of Iraq al-Amir. It's easy to charter a **taxi** in Wadi Seer to take you to the *qasr*, wait and bring you back (about JD6–8), or to take a **bus** (see below) to the *qasr* gates, but this is a lovely part of the country in which to dawdle, and the **walk** along the road from Wadi Seer to Iraq al-Amir slopes gently downhill all the way, hugging the side of a fertile valley and passing through a series of villages. The scenery is soft on the eye, the valley thick with fig, olive, cypress and pomegranate trees and watered by a perpetually flowing stream; springtime sees a riot of poppies and wild iris. However, banish thoughts of riverside footpaths and unspoilt nature: the walk is all on the tarmac road and this is Jordanian country life in the raw – litter, half-built houses, curious children and all.

Iraq al-Amir عراق الامير

A road leading from Wadi Seer town-centre roundabout is signed "Iraq al-Ameer Street". About 4km out, it reaches the valley floor and passes a **Roman aqueduct**; the spartan *al-Yannabeea* **café** (daily 7am–midnight) occupies a perfect spot on the grassy bank here – good if you fancy a cold drink, though the food isn't up to much. They have usable toilets.

Just before the café, a detour for the energetic leads steeply up to the left; after about 500m, a fork to the left gives access to rough paths up the hillside. A short scramble will bring you to two eerie caves known as **ad-Dayr** (meaning "the monastery"). They look rather like a medieval pigeon-fanciers' den: the interiors are lined with small triangular niches, and stone grilles are still in place over the cave windows.

Beyond the café, the road continues straight – apart from one left fork marked in English – for another 6km or so to **IRAQ AL-AMIR** (meaning "Caves of the Prince"). Just before you reach the village, you'll spot the smoke-blackened **caves** high up to the right of the road. However there's not much to get excited about: most are malodorous, and there's nothing to see but the view across the fields and a single ancient Hebrew inscription beside one of the cave entrances, referring to the family who built the white palace visible down in the valley. In the village itself, in an old stone cottage, is a **handicrafts project** (Sat–Thurs 8am–3pm) staffed by local women producing a variety of top-quality items, including handmade paper (the only such centre in Jordan), textiles, foods such as *zaatar* and olives, ceramics and more. Everything is on sale here and in craft shops around the country.

Qasr al-Abd قصر العبد

After passing through Iraq al-Amir village, the road ends about 1km further on at the gates of the **Qasr al-Abd**, a strikingly beautiful pre-Roman country villa set on a platform above the fields. The villa was begun in the years around 200 BC by Hyrcanus, a member of the powerful Tobiad family, as the centre-piece of a lavish, cultivated estate; its name, meaning "Palace of the Servant", derives from a fifth-century BC member of the clan, who is mentioned in the Old Testament as being a governor, or "servant", of Ammon. Hyrcanus died in 175 BC and the palace was never completed; indeed, for some reason the huge limestone building blocks – some up to 25 tonnes in weight – were originally laid precariously on their half-metre edges, and dutifully collapsed at the first earthquake, in 365 AD. Since then, the building has been only sporadically occupied, possibly during the Byzantine period by Christian monks. It was only in the 1980s that the palace could be partially reconstructed by industrial cranes; before then, the fallen masonry was too heavy to be reassembled.

When you arrive, the guardian will probably materialize to unlock the gates. Inside, only a few courses of the internal walls still stand, although picture windows still ring the building and stairs lead up to a now-collapsed second storey. The main attractions, though, are outside. Around the walls are elegant carvings of wild animals, appropriate for such a rural setting although it's unlikely such beasts roamed the area even in antiquity. At ground level on both sides of the building are dolomite leopards doubling as fountains, and around the top of the walls are eagles and lions. The best of all, high up on a back corner, is a lioness – complete with mane for some reason – suckling her cubs.

Off to one side of the villa is a small modern building housing a **museum** (open on request), housing photos of the site and some informative notes, including translations of a text by the first-century Roman historian Josephus describing the villa and its animal carvings in uncannily accurate detail. If the electricity is on, the guardian will play the excellent historical slide-show for you; even if it's off, he still deserves a tip (JD2–3).

Travel details

Buses and serveeces

Dayr Alla to: Amman (Tabarbour station; 1hr).
Dead Sea (Amman Beach) to: Amman (Muhajireen station; 1hr 30min); Shuneh al-Janubiyyeh (30min).
Fuheis to: Amman (Tabarbour station; 35min).
Salt to: Amman (Mahatta station; 40min); Amman (Tabarbour station; 35min); Dayr Alla (40min); Shuneh al-Janubiyyeh (30min).

Shuneh al-Janubiyyeh to: Amman (Muhajireen station; 1hr); Dayr Alla (40min); Dead Sea (Amman Beach; 30min); Madaba via Mount Nebo (1hr); Salt (30min).
Wadi Seer to: Amman (Mahatta station; 30min); Amman (Muhajireen station; 25min); Iraq al-Amir (20min).

Useful Arabic place names

Dead Sea	البحر الميت	Mazra'a	المزرعة
Fifa	فيفة	Shuneh al-Janubiyyeh	الشونة الجنوبية
Jordan Valley	غور الاردن	Sweileh	صويلح
Karameh	الكرامة	Sweimeh	سوعمة
Kraymeh	الكريمة	Wadi Mujib	وادي الموجب

Jerash and the north

CHAPTER 3 # Highlights

✳ **Jerash** Explore the Roman streets, then watch the spectacle of chariot racing in the restored hippodrome. See p.154

✳ **Ajloun** A half-ruined Saracen castle, lording it over the rolling countryside. See p.167

✳ **Walking in the hills** Jordan's lush northern hills are perfect hiking territory, notably the Ajloun forests. See p.169

✳ **Umm Qais** Roman ruins perched on a cliff edge with magnificent Galilee views. See p.176

✳ **The Yarmouk Gorge road** A great scenic drive, with spectacular views of the Golan Heights. See p.180

✳ **Pella** View the ruins over a glass of chilled white wine and stay for some countryside hospitality. See p.182

▲ The Oval Plaza, Jerash

3

Jerash and the north

The rolling hills of **northern Jordan** hold some of the loveliest countryside in the whole Middle East, acres of olive and fig trees, patches of ancient pine forest and fields of wheat, interspersed with fertile, cultivated valleys pointing the way west down to the deep Jordan Valley. This is the most densely populated part of the country, and every hill and wadi has its village. Many of the local people are Jordanian, but plenty of towns also have a significant population of Palestinians, who continue to farm the East Bank of the Jordan much as they did the West Bank and Galilee before having to flee in the wars of 1948 and 1967.

In biblical times, this was the greater part of the area known as the **Decapolis** (more information on p.156), and extensive ruins of important Roman cities survive, most notably at **Jerash**, north of Amman, and **Umm Qais**, in the far northwest. West of Jerash, the ruins of an Arab-built Crusader-period castle dominate the hills above **Ajloun**, which is also the location for the lovely **Ajloun Forest Reserve**, set amid isolated forests of evergreen oak.

To the west is the swelteringly subtropical **Jordan Valley**, more than 200m below sea level, carrying the trickling River Jordan south to the Dead Sea. Ongoing excavations here at the Decapolis city of **Pella** have revealed continuous habitation for at least five thousand years before the Romans arrived.

Buses link all towns and – with less regularity – just about every village. Jerash deserves at least half a day, preferably more, and you should clear a night in your

Ideas for exploring northern Jordan

Most tourists never venture further north than Jerash – such a pity, since this can be a rewarding area to visit, very different from the desert. Even if you're relying on public transport, it's easy to construct a **one-night tour**: start with a bus from Amman's Tabarbour station to **Ajloun** (p.167), for a morning exploring the castle, the town and the olive groves. Then move on to the Roman ruins at **Jerash** (p.154) before taking a late-afternoon bus to **Irbid** (p.173). Next day, return direct to Amman or extend the trip with a morning at **Umm Qais** (p.176).

Renting a car (see p.39) gets you easy access to the beautiful **Ajloun Forest nature reserve** (p.170) or rural walks such as the **Al-Ayoun Trail** (p.169). The tour outlined above works fine – best visit Jerash first, before Ajloun – or, if you're starting from the Dead Sea for instance, you could drive through the Jordan Valley to **Pella** (p.182), continue to Umm Qais for lunch, and head via Irbid to Ajloun for dinner and overnight in the reserve, with a half-day walk next morning and an easy drive on to Salt (p.145), Jerash or Amman.

schedule to stay (and walk) in the wonderful Ajloun Forest Reserve, which is hard to reach without a **car**.

Jerash جرش

One of the best-preserved and most explorable Roman cities in the eastern Mediterranean, set in the bowl of a well-watered valley about 50km north of Amman, **JERASH** is the principal focus of a trip into northern Jordan. With its monumental and sophisticated public buildings tempered by charmingly human touches, the ancient city is likely to inspire even if you are on the jaded final leg of a ruin-hopping tour of the region.

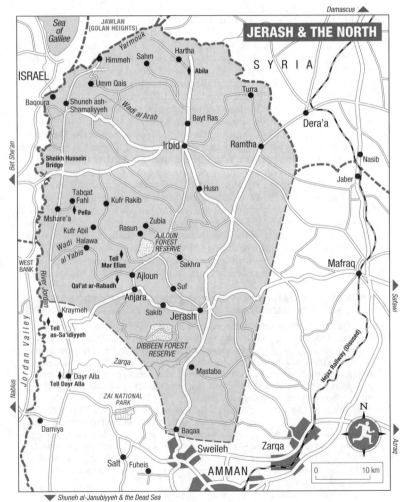

Jerash is a huge site, and easily merits a full day; if you have only a couple of hours, you could rapidly absorb the **Oval Plaza** – with its temple and theatre – the **Cardo**, the **Sacred Way** leading up to the **Temple of Artemis** and the **North Theatre**, but without really doing the place justice. Make sure you time your visit to coincide with one of the shows of Roman-style **chariot racing** (see box, p.161) that are staged daily in the **hippodrome**: they are quite a spectacle.

Some history

Set in the fertile hills of **Gilead**, which is mentioned frequently in the Old Testament as being a populated and cultivated region, the Jerash area has attracted settlement since prehistory: Paleolithic and Neolithic implements have been uncovered nearby, and archeological investigation around the South Gate of the city has revealed evidence of settlement going back to the Middle Bronze Age (around 1600 BC).

Gerasa (the ancient name for Jerash) was founded around 170 BC, the relatively small settlement of that time focused around the Temple of Zeus and the low hill opposite. Very little evidence of this Hellenistic period survives today.

It was around this time that the idea of the **Decapolis** first emerged (see box). Gerasa and its Decapolis neighbours were "liberated" by the Romans under Pompey in 63 BC and granted autonomy under the higher authority of the **Province of Syria**. The century which followed saw unprecedented growth and stability in Gerasa, and it was during the first century AD that the basic town plan as it survives today was laid down: a colonnaded north–south axis cut by two colonnaded side-streets, along with a temple to Zeus (built over the pre-existing temple) fronted by an oval plaza, expansion of the temple to Artemis and construction of the South Theatre.

In 106, when **Emperor Trajan** reorganized Roman authority in the region around his new Province of Arabia, Gerasa lost its autonomy and was governed from the provincial capital, Bosra. Gerasa gained a link by a branch road to Trajan's new highway running between Bosra and the Red Sea, while other main roads linked the city with Philadelphia and Pella. Suddenly, Gerasa found itself not only close to the provincial capital but also astride the highly lucrative trade routes that had been jealously guarded by the Nabateans for so long. In 129–130, Gerasa briefly became the centre of the Roman Empire, as Trajan's successor, **Hadrian**, wintered in the city; in his honour, the Gerasenes built a new monumental arch outside the southern walls, and embarked on major expansion works, including widening of the main street and renovation of temples and public buildings. Hadrian's visit ushered in a golden age for the city, and Gerasa's population may have touched 25,000 during the later second and early third centuries.

Civil disorder in Rome in the 190s heralded the end of the boom. Taxation increased to help cover greater military expenditure – which fuelled further resentment, as well as crippling inflation – and the Persian **Sassanians** began to whittle away at the eastern flanks of the empire. Trade was seriously affected, and in Gerasa the lavish programme of public works was cut back.

A sea change took place when, in 324, **Christianity** became the official religion of the eastern empire. Gerasa embraced the new religion shortly afterwards, and during the fifth and sixth centuries dozens of churches went up, though pre-existing buildings were ransacked for stones and columns, giving a botched, make-do feel to many of Gerasa's churches. By the late seventh century, the city was literally crumbling from shoddy workmanship and lack of

The Decapolis

From the time of Alexander the Great, a group of around ten important cities of the Middle East began to be associated together. Bastions of urban **Greek** culture in the midst of a **Semitic** rural population, these cities were founded or re-founded during or following Alexander's consolidation of power in the Levant in the late fourth century BC. **Decapolis** means "Ten Cities" in Greek, but classical authors disagreed on both the number and identity of the ten: one list, from the first century AD, comprises, in modern-day Jordan, Philadelphia (Amman), Gadara (Umm Qais), Gerasa (Jerash) and Pella; in modern Syria, Damascus, Raphana, Hippos, Dion and Canatha; and in Israel, Scythopolis (Bet She'an). Although it's tempting to imagine the Decapolis cities working together in a formal league of cooperation, no records survive of such a pact, and it seems instead that the term was used simply to refer to the geographical area of northern Transjordan and southern Syria: the Gospels of Matthew and Mark, for example, mention the Decapolis only as a region. All that can be said for sure is that the Decapolis cities shared a common history and culture.

After the **Roman** armies arrived in 63 BC, the area enjoyed a sizeable degree of both affluence and autonomy. The population within the cities – by this stage predominantly of Middle Eastern origin – spoke much more Greek than Latin (the latter was only used on formal occasions and in official documents), and were almost certainly also fluent in **Aramaic**, the language spoken in the countryside. Even in its heyday, Jerash, for instance, remained at core a Semitic society, its ancient local traditions overlaid with Greco-Roman ideas.

By the second century, the Decapolis appears to have expanded; a list from this period names eighteen cities, including, in Jordan, Abila (Qwaylbeh), Arbela (Irbid) and Capitolias (Bayt Ras, near Irbid). However, historical confusion subsequently reigns supreme, with some authors indicating the Decapolis to be a part of Syria, others seeming to show that Syria was a part of the Decapolis, and still more including cities that seem to have played no part in the common history and culture of the original ten. It was **Emperor Trajan** who effectively broke the cultural bonds in the Decapolis and sowed the seeds of this confusion. His Province of Arabia, created in 106 AD, included only some of the cities: Pella and Scythopolis, for instance, remained within the Province of Syria. Bosra became the new provincial capital, and although Decapolis centres such as Gerasa and Philadelphia subsequently experienced a golden age in culture and sophistication, Trajan's reorganization ensured that their horizons now encompassed more than merely their own region: they were bonded firmly into the greater Roman order. By the time of the division of empire into east and west under **Diocletian** at the end of the third century, the notion of a special, parochial link between the cities of the Decapolis was dead.

maintenance. **Persian** forces were able easily to occupy the once-grand metropolis for a dozen years or so from 614.

After the Muslim victory over the Byzantines in 636, it was long theorized that Gerasa – subsequently arabized to Jerash – had slipped into anonymous decline: a small, jerry-built **Umayyad** mosque and a handful of kilns were the only evidence from the Islamic period in the city. However, one of the most exciting recent digs has uncovered a large congregational **mosque** from the Umayyad period in the heart of the city centre, with what has been suggested is a governor's house attached. Work is ongoing, but it seems Jerash may have been stronger and more populous in the early Muslim period than was previously thought. Nonetheless, the cataclysmic earthquake of 749 seems to have brought the city to its knees, and for a thousand years Jerash lay deserted.

At the beginning of the nineteenth century, **European** explorers – including, on a four-hour visit, Burckhardt – were taken around the ruins by local bedouin, and news of the "discovery" of the ancient city of Gerasa spread rapidly. Throughout the nineteenth century, and up until the present day, archeological investigation at Jerash has been continuous and wide-ranging, although large areas remain untouched beneath the grass.

In modern times, a new lease of life for the ancient city came from an unexpected quarter. In 1879, in the same process of migration and resettlement that brought **Circassian** settlers to the deserted ruins of Amman, the Ottoman authorities directed refugee Circassians to settle in the ruins of Jerash. They occupied what is believed to have been the Roman residential quarters, on the east bank of the river, and the bustling town which has since grown up there, now capital of its own governorate, still has Circassians in the majority.

Practicalities

From the big intersection at Sweileh on Amman's northwestern outskirts – reachable from Shmeisani on Queen Rania/University Street or from 8th Circle on King Abdullah II/Medical City Street – the highway north plunges steeply down the slope into beautiful countryside, with hills on the horizon sometimes snowcapped as late as April. After passing **Baqaa**, the biggest of Jordan's UN-run Palestinian refugee camps – today a city of 100,000-plus – you'll spot a well-signed turning for "South Jerash" just after a bridge over the River Zarqa. This road follows the west bank of the Wadi Jerash, lush with eucalyptus and olive trees, for 6km into Jerash itself.

At a set of traffic lights overlooked by the giant Hadrian's Arch, a left turn leads to Ajloun, but if you go straight ahead for 50m you'll see a side-turning to the left just in front of the arch which heads down to a free **parking area** and a fake tourist **bazaar**, within which is the site **ticket office** (daily 7.30am–sunset; JD8). Steps lead up to Hadrian's Arch, from where it's a 400m walk beside the Hippodrome to reach the **Visitors' Centre** (daily 8am–7pm; winter closes 5pm), which houses an informative exhibition on the history and architecture of Jerash. Alongside the Visitors' Centre is the *Resthouse* restaurant, an office co-ordinating local guides and the mighty South Gate, main entrance to the ancient city.

Public **buses** and serveeces from Amman's Tabarbour station, Irbid, Ajloun and elsewhere arrive at the **bus station**, sited on the Ajloun road 800m west of Hadrian's Arch (try and persuade the driver to drop you at the arch instead, to save doubling back). Local serveeces and minibuses shuttle between the bus station and the town centre. Note that public transport out of Jerash ends by about 5.30pm; after that time, you'll have to either hitch or negotiate a taxi fare.

Hiring a **guide** to lead you around the ruins can bring a visit to life: these fluent professionals are generally very knowledgeable. Their standard rate is JD15 for a tour lasting an hour and a quarter.

The Jordan Festival

Jordan's major summer festival of music and the arts was founded in 1980 as the Jerash Festival, staged during July and early August amid the Roman ruins. In 2008 it metamorphosed into the **Jordan Festival**. Audiences of thousands pack Jerash's open-air theatres as well as venues in Amman and at the Dead Sea to see big-name Arab performers, as well as star-studded evenings of jazz, pop and opera, running alongside landmark exhibitions of contemporary art and photography. Check Ⓦ **www.visitjordan.com/jordanfestival** for more information.

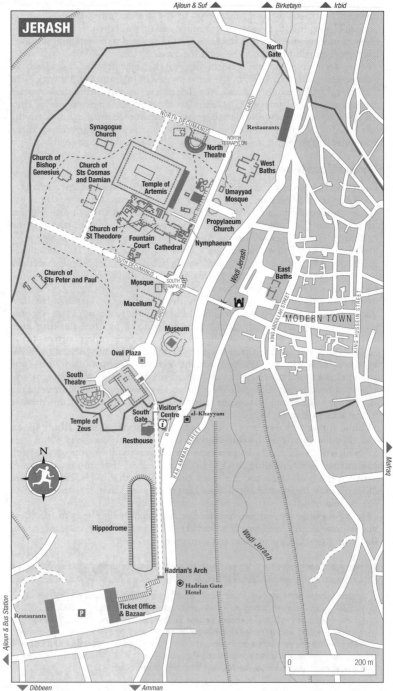

JERASH

Ajloun & Suf — Birketayn — Irbid

North Gate

NORTH DECUMANUS

Restaurants

Synagogue Church

NORTH TETRAPYLON

North Theatre

Church of Bishop Genesius

Church of Sts Cosmas and Damian

West Baths

Temple of Artemis

Umayyad Mosque

Church of St Theodore

Propylaeum Church

Fountain Court

Cathedral

Nymphaeum

SOUTH DECUMANUS

Wadi Jerash

East Baths

Church of Sts Peter and Paul

Mosque

SOUTH TETRAPYLON

MODERN TOWN

Macellum

CARDO

KING ABDULLAH STREET

KING HUSSEIN STREET

Museum

Oval Plaza

South Theatre

Temple of Zeus

South Gate

Visitor's Centre

al-Khayyam

RAB AMMAN STREET

Resthouse

Mafraq

N

Hippodrome

Wadi Jerash

Hadrian's Arch

Hadrian Gate Hotel

Ajloun & Bus Station

Restaurants

P

Ticket Office & Bazaar

0   200 m

Dibbeen — Amman

Accommodation and eating

The only **hotel** in Jerash is the ☘ *Hadrian Gate* (☎077 779 3907; ❸), on the main road beside Hadrian's Arch. Run by a cheerful Yemeni, it comprises five immaculate doubles and triples, most en suite: go for the private en-suite room 105 on the roof, with a panoramic terrace. It's slightly overpriced but pleasant – and in a great location.

Nicer still is the *Olive Branch* (☎02 634 0555, ⓦwww.olivebranch.com.jo; ❺), in the hills 8km northwest of Jerash. Buses to **Suf town** (not Suf refugee camp) can drop you close by. If you're driving, follow roadsigns to Suf until, 7.5km from Jerash, you'll spot a sign pointing left to Ajloun (this is where you should ask the bus to drop you). From the sign, a minor road winds 1.5km through olive groves to the hotel, which is set in a lovely, peaceful location offering an enormous panorama out over the hills. (Another route to the hotel comes off the Jerash–Ajloun road: take an Ajloun minibus, ask to be dropped at the hotel's sign, and walk 2km along the turn-off road.) A taxi fare from Jerash is about JD5. The hotel's airy rooms are all en suite, comfortable and clean; some have a balcony and a few boast two-person bathtubs in the room. You can camp in their grounds – which include a shaded swimming pool – for JD12 (less if you bring your own tent).

For **eating**, few visitors bother to explore beyond the JD10 lunchtime buffet at Jerash's *Resthouse* (☎02 635 1437) beside the Visitors' Centre, priced high for the location (and the a/c) rather than its distinctly average cuisine. An adjacent café section sells cold bottled beer. After years of mediocrity, the *Lebanese House* (☎02 635 1301, ⓦwww.lebanese-house.com), set amid fields off a country lane 750m south of Hadrian's Arch (signposted from the Ajloun road), is once again a fine choice for all kinds of *mezze* and grills; gastronomes are arguing about whether it has regained its status as the best restaurant in the area. Considerably down the scale, the *al-Khayyam*, virtually opposite the Visitors' Centre, has a standard range of kebabs and *mezze*, while at the Irbid junction in the northern part of town are a few more Arabic garden restaurants.

Hadrian's Arch and the Hippodrome

The first monument you see as you approach Jerash from Amman is the huge **Hadrian's Arch**, poised over a traffic junction. The eleven-metre-high triple-arched gateway, which originally stood to almost 22m and which has been restored and partially reconstructed, was built to honour the visit of the Roman Emperor Hadrian to Jerash in 129–130 AD. The huge arches, which probably had wooden doors, are flanked by engaged columns unusually decorated with capitals at the bottom rather than the top. Over 400m from the city walls, the positioning and structure of the arch point to a grandiose scheme for southward expansion of Gerasa. The municipal authorities seem to have been envisioning the arch as an enormous city gate, since its side walls were left untrimmed to enable tight bonding with new perimeter walls. The plan remained unrealized, however, and when it became clear, maybe a century or so later, that the city wasn't going to expand, two small side-pavilions, with niches mirroring the arch's side entrances, were added.

On the west side of Hadrian's Arch, an array of small arches belongs to the reconstructed south wall of the **Hippodrome**, which has undergone extensive renovation work. This was the scene of ancient Gerasa's sporting festivals and chariot races; 1500 years on, it is again (see box, p.161). At 244m long, and seating up to 15,000 spectators, it is impressively large for Jerash, but is nonetheless the smallest hippodrome so far discovered in the Roman Empire: by contrast, the Circus Maximus in Rome could accommodate over 157,000 people. Jerash's arena has garnered international attention, though,

▲ A school trip to Jerash

for the preservation of remnants of its original starting-gates as well as some areas of original seating.

Walking north towards the Visitors' Centre takes you past a series of shops built into the Hippodrome on the left, and the small, ruinous Byzantine **Church of Bishop Marianos** on the right, erected in 570 among Roman and Byzantine tombs on what was then the main Gerasa–Philadelphia road.

The southern part of the ancient city

Beyond the Visitors' Centre stands the reconstructed **South Gate**, the principal entry point into the ancient city. It seems from the wheel ruts on the thresholds that the west door was reserved for wheeled traffic, and that the central and east doors were used principally by pedestrians. Near the gate is a section of the three-metre-thick wall which originally ran for over 3.5km around the city, a fourth-century strengthening of the original, thinner first-century wall.

Beyond the gate, the split-level **South Street** runs between what is believed to be a Hellenistic settlement on the right, and the restored vaults supporting the lower terrace of the **Temple of Zeus** complex to the left. It gives onto what is one of the most impressive pieces of Roman urban design in the world, the **Oval Plaza**. The plaza comprises a large central paved area enclosed by two curving colonnades, both irregular bent ellipses and of different lengths, forming an elegant, smooth entry into the city proper while deftly linking the east–west axis of the Temple of Zeus with the north–south axis of the main street, the Cardo. Approaching from the south, the shorter western arm of the colonnade draws your eye (and your feet) towards the opening of the Cardo, which may originally have been marked by a prominent triple arch. Beautiful stone paving swirls around the plaza following the curve of the Ionic colonnades. Two slightly wider intercolumnar spaces on the west show where small side-streets led in from residential districts. The podium in the centre of the plaza may have supported a statue; in the seventh century, a water tank was built around it, and pipes are still visible set into the paving.

The South Theatre

From the plaza a track climbs west up to the **South Theatre**, the most magnificent of all Jerash's monuments and the largest of the city's three theatres. Now extensively restored, it was built in the 90s AD to seat over three thousand, the cost of construction partly offset by contributions from wealthy Geraseans.

Chariot racing

Jerash is the backdrop for a revival of the Roman sport of **chariot racing**, with choreographed contests and displays of Roman military prowess staged in the restored Hippodrome (see Ⓦ**www.jerashchariots.com**). The company RACE ("Roman Army and Chariots Experience") organizes the reconstructions, which have been based on extensive research by academics and enthusiasts – including such luminaries as the technical adviser for the Oscar-winning movie *Gladiator* and an Italian actor who drove chariots in the 1950s epic *Ben Hur*. After surveying Roman hippodromes around the world, experts settled on Jerash as being the most suitable, for its modest size, good state of preservation and well-visited setting.

From the earliest days of Classical Greece, around 650 BC, right through to the fall of Constantinople in 1453, chariot races followed a broadly similar format – four chariots competing around seven anticlockwise laps of the arena. The Jerash re-enactments follow the same guidelines. *Ben Hur* summons up images of gleaming, armour-plated war-chariots racing improbably quickly behind four horses, but in reality the Romans (unlike the Britons and the Celts) used chariots only for racing, not in battle, so they built less visually impressive, but much faster, fifty-kilogram wicker-work chariots, drawn by two horses. The new Jerash chariots fall somewhere between Hollywood romanticism and the flimsy, but historically accurate, truth.

The shows – with music, live English commentary and historical scene-setting – are impressive, featuring trumpeters, legionaries in authentic Roman battledress, gladiators armed with swords and tridents and, of course, charioteers, everything meticulously choreographed. All the costumes and equipment have been manufactured in Jordan, and everyone involved in the show is from Jerash – most are ex-army or police. RACE keeps around seventy locals in salaried employment as actors, technical crew and stable-hands: for this reason, if no other, the project deserves your support.

There are shows **all year round** (Sat–Thurs 11am & 2pm, Fri 11am; JD12), except in bad weather. In winter the Friday show is moved to 10am, and during Ramadan there are no shows on Tuesdays. Buy tickets on the spot.

Inscriptions record such generosity, and lower seats on the shadier western side of the auditorium are numbered (notable citizens could presumably reserve these prime spots). You enter the theatre into the orchestra, and there are plenty of acoustic games to play: talking while standing at the midpoint of the orchestra gives an effect as good as a PA system, and if two people at opposite ends stick their heads into the round indentations below the seats they can hear each other's mutterings quite clearly. The stage has been restored in stone – it was probably wood originally – and the *scaenae frons*, or backdrop, would have had another storey on top of the beautifully carved detail that exists today.

The Temple of Zeus

Adjacent to the theatre on the same hill, the **Temple of Zeus** in its heyday must have towered over the city, and, like its sister temple of Artemis in the city centre, was intended to be visible from all parts of Jerash. Originally surrounded by gigantic Corinthian columns 15m high (the three that are standing now were re-erected in 1982 in the wrong place), the temple was built in 162–163 AD on the foundations of a first-century predecessor, which itself replaced a temple from the second century BC. The inner sanctum is plain and simply decorated, and the massive front wall is 4.5m thick to accommodate stairs up to the roof. In front of the temple, huge dismembered columns have lain untouched since the day of some cataclysmic earthquake in antiquity; the slope they lie on, now covered with earth and overgrown, probably conceals a monumental staircase. From above, the layout of the *temenos*, or sacred terrace, below the temple is clear, with remains of an altar to the left; the far side of the *temenos* is supported on the restored vaults visible from South Street. What is also clear from here is the vast extent of ancient Gerasa: as well as the entire sweep of the ancient ruins, much of modern Jerash is visible. Behind a minaret in a distant space between buildings in the town, you can spot a surviving remnant of the eastern city wall.

The ancient city centre

The colonnaded **Cardo**, the main boulevard of Jerash, leads north from the Oval Plaza into the city centre. Some 800m long, the street was originally laid out with Ionic columns, but at some point during the remodelling of the city in the second century, it was widened as far as the Temple of Artemis and the columns updated to the grander Corinthian order. Along the Cardo the columns supported a continuous architrave, and a wide covered pavement on both sides gave access to shops behind. Because of the gentle gradient, each column stands a few centimetres higher, and is slightly shorter, than the last; where the column height would have been too small to maintain strict architectural proportion, the architrave was halted, bracketed into the side of the next column and begun again at a higher level. The diagonal street paving is marked by deep grooves worn by centuries of metal-wheeled traffic, while round drain covers give access to an underground sewerage system.

The four tallest columns in this section mark the entrance on the left to the **macellum**, the ancient food market, an octagonal courtyard built around a central fountain and surrounded by small shops. Originally there were massive tables in four corners of the courtyard; strikingly carved supports survive in the farthest corner. Opposite the *macellum*, steps lead up to the small site **museum** (daily 8.30am–5pm; Nov–March closes 4pm), the garden of which is dotted with carved sarcophagi and chunks of statuary. Inside are exhibits tracing the settlement of Jerash from Neolithic times, including a good explanation of ancient coinage.

The South Tetrapylon

A little way further, the Cardo meets the first of Jerash's two major cross-streets, the **South Decumanus**, at an intersection known as the **South Tetrapylon**. At the centre of this circular plaza are four freestanding podia, each of which was decorated with shell niches and held four columns topped by a square entablature. A statue probably stood between the four columns of each podium. This impressive structure was designed to turn a simple street junction into a grand meeting point flanked with shops, while not impeding traffic circulation from street to street. To the east, the South Decumanus crossed the river into what were probably Gerasa's residential neighbourhoods at the **South Bridge**. The bridge has been restored, but a modern fence bars access.

On the southwest corner of the junction, new excavations have revealed a large congregational **mosque** from the eighth-century Umayyad period, set crooked to the street so that its three *mihrabs* faced south towards Mecca. What has been suggested is a governor's house stands alongside to the southwest, indicating that this spot may have been the city's nexus of power at the time. Investigation is continuing, but this building is already providing a fascinating link between the pagan Gerasa of the ancient world and modern, Muslim Jerash.

The Nymphaeum

From the South Tetrapylon, the Cardo was expanded to its widest extent, and Byzantine raising of the pavement included the addition of small niches down at ankle level, either for small statues or, possibly, streetlights. The wheel-ruts from chariot traffic are particularly pronounced in this section. Eight tall columns on the left mark the entrance to the Cathedral (see p.165), while beyond, fronted by four even taller columns, is Gerasa's lavish **Nymphaeum**. Completed in 191 AD, and dedicated to dancing, singing water nymphs, the Nymphaeum was nothing more than a grandiose public fountain, but the sight and sound of water splashing in abundance from such a finely carved monument must have been delightful. Even today, dry, the carving which survives on the two-storey semicircular recess is impressive. Originally, the lower storey was faced in green marble, while painted plaster covered the upper storey; traces of the green and orange design survive in the topmost niche on the left. Concealing the holes in the lower niches, statues were probably designed to appear to be pouring water into the basin below, from which lion's-head fountains spat water into shallow basins at pavement level (one of Jerash's most endearing small details is the basin carved as four fish kissing, their eyes serving as drainage holes). The huge red granite laver in front is a Byzantine embellishment.

Beyond the Nymphaeum, thirteen ordinary-sized columns presage four gigantic ones marking the entrance to the Temple of Artemis.

The Temple of Artemis complex

The most important edifice in the ancient city, the **Temple of Artemis** was approached via a long east–west **Sacred Way** which originated somewhere in the residential eastern quarters and cut across the Cardo at the point marked by the four huge columns. The best way to discern the route is to pick a path to the east through the jumble of rubble opposite the four columns and stand on top of the apse of what is called the **Propylaeum Church**, ingeniously created from elements of the Roman street. In the sixth century, when the cult of Artemis had passed into historical memory, the Christian inhabitants of Gerasa sealed off the old Sacred Way with the apse and used the colonnades of the street as the divisions within the church between nave and aisles. Between here and the Cardo, a plaza – decorated with beautiful spiral-twisted columns topped with a delicately carved architrave that now lies in chunks nearby – became the atrium of the new church. Behind, down below the Propylaeum Church, a Roman bridge carrying the Sacred Way once spanned the river; one of the few monuments of Gerasa to survive in modern Jerash is the huge East Baths building, which you can see opposite.

Back on the west side of the Cardo, a portico leads you to the **Propylaeum** itself, a massive, ornately decorated gateway dedicated in 150 AD, which gives onto a monumental staircase of seven flights of seven steps. At the top – but still well below the temple proper – is a terrace with the foundations of a small **altar**; from here, another monumental staircase, originally over 120m wide, takes you up to the level of the sacred courtyard, or *temenos*, with a dramatic view of the temple.

The temple

The Temple of Artemis is set far back in a vast **courtyard** some 161m deep and 121m wide, which was originally lined on all four sides with a colonnade and is now cluttered with the ruins of Byzantine and Umayyad pottery kilns and workshops. The temple has clung onto its huge **portico**, whose clustered limestone columns have turned peachy bronze over the centuries. Inserting a long stick or a key between the drums of any of them (the fourth on the left is a favourite) demonstrates how these mammoth pillars were designed to sway gently, in order to absorb the effects of earth tremors and high winds – and have been doing so for almost two millennia without toppling.

The **cella**, or inner sanctum, is today exposed, but would originally have been surrounded by a peristyle of six columns across each short side, eleven on each longer side; the capitals of those that stand are still in place, but some elements of the entablature have never been found, pointing to the possibility that the temple was never completed. The inner walls of the *cella* would have been richly decorated with slabs of marble supported on hooks fitting into the holes all round the walls, which were pilfered during the Byzantine period to adorn churches. At the back is the single focus of all this wealth of extraordinary architecture along the Sacred Way: the niche which once housed the image of Artemis, daughter of Zeus and goddess of the forests, who cared for women and brought fertility to all creatures.

The northern part of the ancient city

From the Temple of Artemis courtyard, a track leads north to the back of the restored **North Theatre**. Much smaller than its southern twin, this was originally constructed in the 160s AD to be a small performance space or council chamber; many of the seats in the lower rows are marked with Greek names, referring to tribes which voted in the city council. On the two ends of the semicircular orchestra wall, lovely little stone reliefs show women and boys dancing and playing different musical instruments. Upper rows of seats were constructed early in the third century to give a total capacity of around 1600, but by the fifth century the building seems to have gone out of use as a theatre. Much reconstruction and renovation work has been done here, not least in the orchestra, with its beautiful marble flooring. The restored theatre saw its first public performance in more than 1500 years when, in 1997, the Palestinian poet Mahmoud Darwish gave a reading to a packed house.

In front of the theatre is a reconstructed **plaza**, with huge Corinthian columns on one side of the street faced by an equally huge colonnade on the other that is flanked by unusual double columns ingeniously knitted into the walls of the theatre itself. To the right of the plaza, the **North Decumanus** meets the main Cardo at a rebuilt junction-point known as the **North Tetrapylon**. Simpler than the South Tetrapylon, this dates from the late second-century remodelling of Gerasa and comprises arches on all four sides leading into a small, domed central space.

On the eastern side of the Cardo rise the huge arches of the **West Baths**, which includes a room fronted by two columns which has somehow clung onto its elegantly constructed domed brick roof. A fraction south, an area of ruins close to the Cardo is a small **Umayyad mosque**, with a reused Roman shell niche serving as a makeshift *mihrab*.

Beyond the tetrapylon, the northernmost section of the Cardo is the quietest part of the city. Ignored during the city's second-century facelift, this part of the street retains its original, plain Ionic colonnade, and is the same width as when initially laid out in the first century AD. The peaceful walk ends after some 200m at the **North Gate**, dating from 115 AD, from which a road led on to Pella. The gate is a cleverly designed wedge shape, in order to present a square facade both to the Cardo and to the Pella road. From here, you can either continue your northerly progress for 1.5km to visit Birketayn (see below), or retrace your steps partway down the Cardo to explore the Cathedral and surrounding ruined churches.

The Cathedral and the western churches

Fifteen Byzantine **churches** have so far been uncovered in Jerash, and wending a path through the largely unexcavated southwestern quarter of the ruins to visit nine of them, starting with the Cathedral and ending up near the South Theatre, brings you out of the main crush of the central sights.

The **Cathedral Gateway**, marked by eight large columns on the Cardo just south of the Nymphaeum, is a large, elaborate construction which originally presaged a now-vanished second-century temple, thought to have been dedicated to Dionysius. During the fourth century, the old temple was converted by the Christian Gerasenes into the large church which survives today, at the head of a monumental **staircase**. The walls flanking the stairs originally supported high enclosed and roofed colonnades on both sides, but earthquakes toppled the lot. The old pagan temple probably faced west – as does the Temple of Artemis – but the new church had to face east: the Byzantine architects seem to have been less concerned about aesthetic harmony than their Roman predecessors, and calmly plonked the apse of the new church plum across the head of the staircase. To provide some focus for the ascent, a small shell niche **Shrine to Mary** was placed on the blank exterior wall of the apse. Originally dedicated to "Michael, Holy Mary and Gabriel", it's still possible to read the Greek for Gabriel in red paint on the right of the band beneath the shell.

Left or right from the shrine, the narthex brings you round into the **Cathedral** itself, a shadow of its former self. Little is known about this building, and its dedication or even the supposition that it was Gerasa's cathedral remain unconfirmed. Colonnades, of which only bits and pieces remain scattered about, divided the nave and the aisles, and the high side walls were decorated with elaborate glass mosaics. Pale pink limestone flagstones survive in the aisles. To the south of the cathedral is a small **chapel**.

Immediately west of the cathedral, a portico beautifully paved in red and white octagons and diamonds leads into the atrium, known as the **Fountain Court** after the square fountain in its centre fed by water brought from the great reservoir at Birketayn (see below). Roman historians, including Pliny, hinted that Gerasa held festivals to Dionysius (the god of wine) at which water miraculously turned into wine, and the idea must have been a tenacious one: after the Dionysian temple here had been converted into a church, it duly became the venue for festivals celebrating Jesus' performance of the same feat at Cana. During these festivals, so the historian Epiphanius records, the square fountain in this court miraculously began to flow with wine.

To the side of the paved portico is a small room known as the **Glass Court**, named for the enormous quantity of glass fragments discovered there. The weeds and rubble carpeting its floor conceal beautiful mosaics, reburied for protection.

Left (west) of the Glass Court, a staircase leads up to the tiny **Sarapion Passage**, its octagonal flags running beneath precarious lintels out to the **Stepped Street**. Turning left up the street brings you past the maze of tiny rooms forming the Byzantine **Baths of Placcus**, which date from an unusually late 455 AD, evidence that luxurious Roman bathing habits died hard. Dominating the baths to the left are twin colonnades of the **Church of St Theodore**, dating from 496. Nothing remains of the main superstructure of the building, the marble paving of the nave and aisles or the glass mosaics which covered both the interior walls and the semi-dome over the apse; all that does remain is the huge apse itself, nosing out dramatically above the Fountain Court below.

The western churches

A path from St Theodore's leads west over scrubby hillocks, reaching after 150m a group of three interconnected churches built between 529 and 533. On the right, the **Church of Saints Cosmas and Damian** houses the best of Jerash's viewable mosaics, although the only way to see them is to lean over the high wall around the church; the church doors are locked. Cosmas and Damian were twin brothers born in Arabia in the late third century, who studied in Syria and became famous for always providing medical services for free. Their church is floored with a large mosaic open to the elements, which shows birds and animals in a geometric grid of diamonds and squares. Just below the chancel screen, the dedicatory inscription is flanked by portraits of the donors of the church; to the left is Theodore swinging a censer in his official robes as a kind of church trustee, and to the right his wife Georgia, her hands upraised.

From here, it's possible to work your way back easily to the *Resthouse* through the adjacent circular **Church of John the Baptist** and **Church of St George**, both with fragments of floor mosaics surviving. Alternatively, you could make your way up to the high ground north of Cosmas and Damian, where stands the ruined **Synagogue Church**, invisible from below. A Jewish synagogue originally stood here, oriented westwards towards Jerusalem, with a floor mosaic depicting the Flood and various Jewish ritual objects. On its conversion into a church in 530 or 531, during a period of Jewish persecution under Emperor Justinian, a new geometric mosaic was laid over the original, and the orientation of the building reversed, with an apse laid in what was formerly the synagogue's vestibule.

South of here lie the ruins of the **Church of Bishop Genesius**, built in 611 just three years before the Persian invasion and featuring a prominent benched apse. On a hill 300m south, tucked inside the southwestern city walls not too far from the South Theatre, the **Church of Saints Peter and Paul** and, close by, the **Mortuary Church** are slowly being reclaimed by Mother Nature.

Birketayn

Branching off the main route north to Irbid, two smaller roads pass in front of Gerasa's North Gate. The road on the left climbs towards Suf, but an easy walk along the other, leading directly away from the gate, brings you after 2km to **Birketayn** (Arabic for "two pools"). Set in a shaded valley in a crook of the road, this is a Roman double reservoir – restored in the 1960s – which fed water into Gerasa. Birketayn was the venue for the notorious Maiumas festivals, nautical celebrations of ancient origin which involved, among other things, the ritual submersion of naked women. By the time of Gerasa's heyday, the festivals seem to have become thinly veiled excuses for open-air orgies, and were duly banned by the city's early Christian rulers. In 396 AD the rule was relaxed, provided that the festival followed "chaste customs"; however, the pleasures of the flesh seem to have proved irresistible, since three years later the ban was reimposed. Some 130 years passed before the festival was again resurrected and incorporated by the Gerasenes into their Christian faith as a kind of harvest celebration, purged of eroticism.

Overlooking the reservoir stands the thousand-seat **Festival Theatre** and, beyond, a path leads through the trees to the ruined **Tomb of Germanus**, standing amid sown fields, some columns upright and others – along with the empty sarcophagus – entwined in thistles down the slope.

Around Jerash

Jerash is set amid verdant hills cut through by countless lush valleys, and even in the height of summer, when the hills are baked brown and dry, you'd miss a good deal of the beauty of Jordan if you neglected the chance for a trip into the countryside. Thick forests of pine, oak and pistachio covered these slopes until the early 1900s, when large areas were cleared to provide timber for the Hejaz Railway, both for track-building and for fuel. Enough forest has survived, though, around **Ajloun** and **Dibbeen** – both within half an hour's drive of Jerash – to give plenty of walking and picnicking possibilities in what is the most southerly area of complete pine forest in the world. Ajloun also has a magnificent Crusader-period **castle** perched among olive groves on a hilltop just outside the town.

Ajloun عجلون

A thriving market town, **AJLOUN** (pronounced "adge-loon"), 25km west of Jerash, has been a centre of population for a thousand years or more. Marking the centre of the town, 150m along the market street from the bus station, is a **mosque** that dates from probably the early fourteenth century. The square base of its minaret, as well as the simple prayer hall and carved Quranic inscriptions set into the walls, are original; ask the guardian if he will show you around inside.

Ajloun castle (Qal'at ar-Rabadh) قلعة الربض

The history of Ajloun is bound up in the story of the **castle** – in Arabic, the **Qal'at ar-Rabadh** – which towers over it from the west. A perfect location, with bird's-eye views over the surrounding countryside and over three major wadis leading to the Jordan Valley, the hill on which the castle sits, Jebel Auf, is said to have formerly been the site of an isolated Christian monastery, home to a monk named Ajloun. By 1184, in the midst of the Crusades, the monastery had fallen into ruin, and an Arab general and close relative of Salah ad-Din, **Azz ad-Din Usama**, took the opportunity to build a fortress on the ruins, partly to

▲ Ajloun castle

limit expansion of the Crusader kingdoms (Belvoir castle stands just across the River Jordan to the west and the Frankish stronghold of Karak is ominously close), partly to protect the iron mines of the nearby hills and partly to show a strong hand to the squabbling clans of the local **Bani Auf** tribe. Legend has it that, to demonstrate his authority, Usama invited the sheikhs of the Bani Auf to a banquet in the newly completed castle, entertained and fed them, then threw them all into the dungeons. The new castle also took its place in the chain of beacons which could transmit news by pigeon post from the Euphrates frontier to Cairo headquarters in twelve hours. From surviving records, it seems that Ajloun held out successfully against the Franks.

Expanded in 1214–15 by Azz ad-Din Aybak (who also worked on Qasr Azraq), Ajloun's castle was rebuilt by **Baybars** after being ransacked by invading **Mongols** in 1260. Ottoman troops were garrisoned here during the seventeenth and eighteenth centuries, but when the explorer Burckhardt came through in 1812, he found the castle occupied only by forty members of a single family. Earthquakes in 1837 and 1927 caused a great deal of damage, and consolidation work on the surviving structures is ongoing.

These days, the castle (daily 8am–6pm; Nov–March closes 4pm; JD1) is entered from a modern parking area below the walls. A **moat bridge** cuts through the east wall. A long, sloping passage leads up to an older, arched entrance, decorated with carvings of birds, and just ahead stands the original entrance to Usama's fortress. Although the warren of chambers and galleries beyond is perfect for scrambled exploration, with all the rebuilding over the centuries it's very difficult to form a coherent picture of the castle's architectural development; there's even – in this Muslim-built, wholly Muslim-occupied castle – one block carved with a cross, presumably part of the monk Ajloun's monastery. However, a climb to the top of any of the **towers** gives breathtaking views over the rolling landscape, and these more than make up for any historical confusion.

Off to the side of the castle road are acres of olive groves, carpeted in spring with wildflowers and perfect **walking** territory.

Outside the rainy (and occasionally snowy) winter months, the gentle terrain of north Jordan allows **walkers** to make their own explorations – preferably in the springtime, when the flowers are at their best. There are no marked trails, so you're free to wander at will over the verdant hills.

A fine **two-day trek** leads 36km from the fortress of **Ajloun** down to the ruins of **Pella**. Bring water, since places to replenish supplies are widely spaced. From the castle walls at Ajloun you can see the line of the route: west along the ridge, then down right into the thickly forested valley and up west to a saddle between rounded hills, on the far side of which is concealed the **Wadi al-Yabis** (also known as Wadi Rayyan). The walk down this long and varied valley is particularly beautiful, first passing through natural forests to reach a knoll on its right side, with Ottoman ruins; this makes for an idyllic campsite, with a view to the setting sun behind the Palestinian hills. The second day covers about 20km, with a pleasant morning walk down through olive groves. The path crosses and re-crosses the stream, until a larger stream enters from the right after a couple of hours. Cross the confluence and take a track north through well-tended orchards where birds dart between pomegranate blossoms in spring. The trail rises steeply to the hilltop village of **Kufr Abil**, from where various options down 6km of country lanes take you almost to the Jordan Valley, emerging above the village of **Tabqat Fahl** at the ruins of **Pella** (see p.182).

This and others walks in the area are described in detail in *Jordan: Walks, Treks, Caves, Climbs, Canyons* by Tony Howard (see p.404).

The Al-Ayoun Trail

In the first such cooperative tourism venture in Jordan, three villages north of Ajloun, on the edge of the RSCN reserve (see p.170), have clubbed together to develop a new walking path. This **Al-Ayoun Trail** (*ayoun* means springs) runs for 12km through some beautiful – and otherwise completely unvisited – countryside. It was opening to walkers as this book went to press in 2009: in years to come, expect innovations such as trail support, waymarking and a locally run guesthouse to open. Until then, it's perfectly possible to walk the route anyway; allow a full day and carry plenty of water. The trail begins in **Rasun** village, a short drive from the RSCN headquarters. Past Rasun, at the RSCN's Soap House, the trail forks right down into the Wadi Orjan, lush with figs, pomegranates, carob and cherries, before proceeding into **Orjan** village. The path climbs, offering views into Wadi al-Yabis/Wadi Rayyan, before dropping into Wadi Abu Kharoub, lined with carob trees, and up again past olive groves and a cemetery into **Baoun** village. After zigzagging through the village and beyond, the trail picks up a shepherd track which crosses the hills and climbs to a mosque at **Listib**, ending at the hilltop site of **Tell Mar Elyas** (see p.172).

An excellent full-colour brochure (with map) gives information on nearby sites such as Bronze Age dolmen fields and Byzantine hermitages, as well as the Aisha al-Baouniya Cultural Forum, established in Baoun to honour the sixteenth-century mystic and poet Aisha al-Baouniya, one of Islam's most renowned female Sufi theologians. The brochure is available locally, or is downloadable at ⓦwww .abrahampath.org (the Al-Ayoun Trail has been supported by the Abraham Path Initiative, an international project fostering the development of a long-distance walking route from Sanliurfa in Turkey to the Palestinian city of Hebron). Before you set out, contact Mahmoud Hawawreh, the English-speaking director of the Cultural Forum (☏077 707 2212) – or the Orjan municipality (☏02 647 5766) – for information, guidance and access to local hospitality. They can also give advice about arranging transport at either end of the route.

Practicalities

Buses run to **Ajloun** from Amman, Irbid, Jerash and Kraymeh (in the Jordan Valley), but the road from Jerash (23km) is the most beautiful way to approach, loping over the hills among stands of pine and olive trees, with the castle silhouetted on the horizon for half the way. If you're driving from Jerash, don't miss (after 18.5km) the turning right (north) to Ajloun in the town of Anjara. To reach the castle, a **bus** shuttles from Ajloun bus station, infrequently during the week but more often on Fridays and Saturdays; reckon on JD6 or so for a **taxi** to take you up, wait and bring you down again. If you fancy the stiff **walk** up (3km), start from the town-centre roundabout (topped with a kitsch model of the castle) and head up the road with the minaret on your left.

There are two **hotels** on this quiet castle road, both long past their best: service and facilities are very tired. The first is the *Qal'at al-Jabal* or *Jabal Castle* (☎02 642 0202; ❸), with a nice garden in front; all rooms are en suite and with balconies, and some have great castle views. A few hundred metres further up is the smaller *Ajloun Hotel* (☎02 642 0524; ❸), much the same. Despite their drabness, these are both popular with Jordanians for weekend getaways and may be full in July and August. **Eating** options are limited to simple restaurants in the town centre: picnicking on the castle slopes is a good alternative.

Around Ajloun

For drivers, the major route down to the **Jordan Valley** from Ajloun is via Anjara and Kufranjeh, but there is a more beautiful back way down between the hills. Turn off the castle road at the *Jabal Castle Hotel*, fork left after 4km and right 4km further. The rustic village of **Halawa** appears after another 7km, in the middle of which there's a steeply sloping fork; the road to the left (which runs past the post office) will eventually deliver you after 10km of lovely countryside around **Wadi al-Yabis** (also known as Wadi Rayyan) to the Jordan Valley highway, or you could follow signs direct to **Pella** (see p.182).

Ajloun Forest Reserve   محمية غابات عجلون

One of Jordan's most beautiful hideaways is the Royal Society for the Conservation of Nature's **AJLOUN FOREST RESERVE** (ⓦ www.rscn.org.jo), spread over remote hillsides about 9km north of Ajloun. This is lovely countryside, situated around 1200m above sea level – the coolness compared to Jerash is noticeable, and when it's sweltering a short drive away in the Jordan Valley it can be balmy and fresh up here.

The reserve comprises thirteen square kilometres of rolling Mediterranean woodland – mainly evergreen oak, with some pistachio, carob and wild strawberry trees along with olive groves. The **fauna** covers some very European names: wild boar, foxes and badgers are all common (alongside striped hyena, Asiatic jackals and wildcats), as are **birds** such as tits, finches and jays. **Roe deer** – previously extinct in the wild – have been successfully reintroduced to the reserve by the RSCN. Staying a night or two, or just dropping in for a meal and a walk, is strongly recommended.

Several **walking trails** head out from the reserve centre. Of the self-guided trails, the **Scenic Viewpoint Trail** (2km; 1hr) is a short circuit heading up through the forest to a nearby hilltop – especially beautiful in springtime when wildflowers carpet the ground. More rewarding is the **Soap Makers' Trail** (7km; 3–4hr; JD3pp), which leads through the woods and up to the stunning Eagle Viewpoint before continuing down into Rasun village to end at the Soap House, an RSCN-run community project that employs local women manufacturing speciality soaps by hand from olive oil and floral essences. (You can buy the soap, branded as Orjan, here and at every RSCN centre around Jordan.) A minibus will run you back to the centre.

Longer trails (all April–Oct only) must be done with an RSCN guide: a group of up to five people pays around JD150 for a day's guiding, which also includes a locally prepared lunch out in the countryside, often donkeys on hand to take some of the strain, and return transport by minibus. The **Village Orchards Tour** (12km; 6hr) extends the Soap Makers' Trail beyond Rasun to pass springs, copses and olive groves around Orjan village. The **Prophet's Trail** (8.5km; 4hr) heads off in the other direction, south past caves and across hillside meadows before climbing to Tell Mar Elyas (see below); an optional extension, graded as "difficult", continues for another 10km (5–6hr) to Ajloun Castle. Another route is the **Rockrose Trail** (8km; 3–4hr), a scenic countryside walk of moderate difficulty, crossing wooded valleys and ridges on a beautiful looping path.

Practicalities

There's no **public transport** anywhere near the reserve: you'll have to either **drive** yourself or go by **taxi** (JD6–8 from Ajloun). From Ajloun town centre, with the castle road to your left, head straight on (north) up the hill on the road towards Irbid. After 4.7km, turn left towards Ishtafeina (or Eshtafena) village. (If you're coming the other way, this junction lies 24.5km south of the Yarmouk University campus in Irbid city centre.) The reserve is clearly signposted down 4km of twisting country lanes.

The reserve is **open** all year round (admission 5JD), though note that freezing temperatures and snow are common in winter. Always **book in advance** directly (☏02 647 5673) or through the RSCN's "Wild Jordan" centre in Amman (see p.51), even if you're only dropping by for a stroll. With 48 hours' notice, staff can prepare a hearty meal (JD10) at the rooftop **restaurant**. Panoramic views from here extend to the West Bank and as far as the snowcapped Jebel ash-Sheikh peak in southern Lebanon.

Amid olive trees behind the office is the 🍴 **accommodation** (prices include breakfast). To one side are attractive, Scandinavian-style **cabins** (❻) with cement floors, raised wooden verandas and comfy beds and sofas; they all have en-suite bathrooms and heaters. Across the way is a cluster of wooden lodges, dubbed **tented bungalows** (❺). They have canvas walls, but are built above ground on stilts, with proper floors, and each has four single beds inside; a shower-and-toilet block is nearby. The silence up here is wonderful.

Anjara عنجرة

The small market town of **ANJARA** sits 3km south of Ajloun on the main road up from the Jordan Valley towards Jerash. Local legend has it that Jesus, Mary and the disciples once stopped overnight at a cave near the town, where Jesus gave a sermon. There's nothing in the Bible about this, but it is known that Jesus

Prices at Jordan's RSCN-run **nature reserves** are high. The RSCN makes no apologies for this: it says that the reason it exists is to protect Jordan's natural environment, and that it has built lodges and developed tourism as a tool for generating funds to help conservation and support rural communities. You may or may not agree with their pricing policy – but this kind of responsible tourism is virtually unknown in the Middle East, and the RSCN are pioneers. For now, until tourism schemes emerge that are truly community-owned, paying extra to visit the RSCN reserves is a good way to ensure that your money goes to benefit rural people and habitats.

crossed the Jordan many times, and Anjara then (as now) straddled a junction of roads. The exact location of the cave being unknown, in the 1920s an Italian Catholic priest, Father Foresto, decided a plot of land in the town would have to do for a commemorative church, and arranged for a 150-year-old life-size wooden statue of the Madonna to be brought over from Italy. The church went up in the 1950s, and then in 1971 Father Nimat – who is still the chief cleric in Anjara – built a shrine for the statue in the churchyard, known as **Sayyidat al-Jebel** (or **Our Lady of the Mountain**), and had its walls decorated with (rather kitsch) murals. Following the seal of approval from the Vatican that this is indeed a sanctified site, Christian pilgrims now flock to Anjara to visit the diminutive shrine in its rubbly artificial grotto. From Anjara's central junction, the square steeple of the Catholic church, with its distinctive red roof, is clearly visible just below the main road; if the gates aren't open, ask around locally, since Father Nimat lives nearby, and will be happy to unlock the shrine for you.

Tell Mar Elyas تل مار الياس (خربة الوهادنة)

Another holy site, this time sacred to Muslims as well as Christians, lies tucked away in the hills west of Ajloun – hard to reach without your own transport. **Tell Mar Elyas** (or Elias) is generally accepted as the birthplace of the prophet Elijah, who is named in 1 Kings as "Elijah the Tishbite" (Tishbe has long been associated with Listib, a region lying 8km west of Ajloun) and who is also proclaimed in the Quran as a "messenger". The visitable archeological remains are of a large church on a windswept hilltop; the **driving** route, along a beautiful, quiet country lane clinging to the contours of the forested slopes, is just as memorable. From Ajloun centre, head up the hill towards the castle, then turn off at the *Qal'at al-Jabal* hotel. At a crossroads after 1km, go steeply down to the left. After 4km, a junction is marked with a sign to Mar Elyas (and another to the village of **Wahadneh**, where there's a modern church dedicated to Elijah); head right at the sign for just under 2km, go left for 1km, then take an unsigned dirt track left uphill for 400m to the parking area at the foot of the *tell*. You could **walk** here on the half-day Prophet's Trail from the Ajloun nature reserve (see p.171).

The guardian will probably emerge to greet you as you make the short scramble up the rough stairs to the hilltop, where you'll find the ruins of a huge, cruciform **church**, roughly 33m by 32m. Only the foundations and a course or two of stones are left. One of the exposed floor **mosaics**, in white letters on a red background, has been dated to 622 AD – a time of upheaval in Jordan, with the Byzantine forces in full retreat in the face of the Islamic armies sweeping northwards. There has been, as yet, no satisfactory reason put forward as to why the authorities were building churches amid such political instability. Beside the apse is a **sacristy**, floored with a plain mosaic, and there are some beautiful mosaic designs surviving against the north wall, including multicoloured chevrons and an elaborate drinking vessel with grapes. At the western end of the church is a section on a slightly lower level, possibly a narthex, which incorporates a deep **well** beside an ancient oak. Many of the trees in the area are bedecked with strips of cloth, tied round the branches by devout pilgrims – both Christian and Muslim – as a mark of respect for the prophet; a good time to visit is on Elijah's commemoration day of July 21, when there are special celebrations.

Dibbeen Forest Reserve محمية غابات دبين

A large area of cool, fragrant, pine-forested hillside southwest of Jerash, the **Dibbeen Forest Reserve** (Ⓦ www.rscn.org.jo) – like its neighbour near Ajloun – is a beautiful, and remote, getaway. In 2004 the forest (about eight square kilometres) was declared a protected area under the RSCN, who have begun a scheme to promote environmental conservation and launch sustainable development with local people. International hotel developers have also got their eyes on this forest, and legal disputes about where – and how much – building work may be done are ongoing. For now you are free to visit for walks or picnics with a view amid the stands of Aleppo pine and evergreen oak, but there are no facilities. This is a popular spot for family outings: expect Fridays and Saturdays to be busy.

No public transport runs near the reserve. If you're **driving**, from the traffic lights at Hadrian's Arch in Jerash head towards Ajloun, then after 100m turn left and follow signs; this road continues through the Ghazza Palestinian refugee camp and down into the lush Wadi Haddada past the reforestation projects at Jamla. A **taxi** from Jerash is about JD6.

Irbid إربد

Although **IRBID** has been inhabited since Chalcolithic times and has also been identified as the Decapolis city of Arbela, almost nothing survives from its ancient past. This busy, crowded city – around 75km north of Amman – is genial enough, with rambling souks filling the downtown alleyways, but there's little to merit a diversion. It is most often visited as a staging-post for journeys into the far north of Jordan; if time is short, give it a miss.

The City

Rising above the bustle of the downtown markets is Irbid's *tell*, its steep streets now lined with offices. Behind the municipality building, the old Ottoman **Dar as-Saraya** (Governor's House), built in the mid-nineteenth century, has been restored to serve as a rather good **antiquities museum** (Sat–Thurs 8am–4pm, Fri 10am–4pm; Ⓦ www.dam.gov.jo). Admission is likely to be around JD2. Rooms around the courtyard exhibit fine pottery from Pella and other Jordan Valley sites, as well as Greco-Roman statues from Umm Qais and a splendid mosaics collection. Staff can provide information about Irbid and the local area, and will also direct you down the street to **Beit Arar** (Sat–Thurs 8am–3pm; free), an atmospheric Ottoman courtyard house – once home to the nationalist poet Mustafa Wahbi al-Tal (1897–1949), who wrote under the pseudonym "Arar". It's a pleasant place to relax and browse through the displays on the poet's life.

South of the city centre is the campus of Jordan's highly regarded **Yarmouk University**, around which has evolved a funky quarter of studenty restaurants, music stores and internet cafés centred on Arshaydat Street (known to all as University St). Yarmouk's modest **Museum of Jordanian Heritage** (Sat–Wed 10am–5pm; free) is worth a visit; from the main gate, continue straight ahead until the second roundabout, and the museum is the second building to the right, part of the Institute of Archeology and Anthropology. All periods of Jordan's history are explained clearly on informative panels, and illustrated with interesting artefacts, from 9000-year-old statues to antique farm tools. Upstairs, displays focus on traditional crafts.

Practicalities

Irbid has numerous **bus** stations, of which three serve destinations other than local villages. The **New Amman station** (*mujemma amman al-jdeed*), 200m or so east of the Sports City stadium, has buses serving Amman's Tabarbour station (including a/c Hijazi coaches), Ajloun, Jerash, Mafraq and elsewhere.

The **Valleys station** (*mujemma al-aghwar*), located off Palestine Street about 2km west of downtown, serves destinations including Mshare'a (for Pella) and the Sheikh Hussein Bridge. About 1.5km north of downtown on Fadl al-Dalgamouni Street is the **North station** (*mujemma ash-shomali*), for buses to Umm Qais. In addition, **Trust International Transport** runs comfortable, air-con buses from its office near the Safeway supermarket direct to Aqaba (daily 8.30am & 4pm; 6hr; JD11.50). Minibuses link all the bus stations (though they

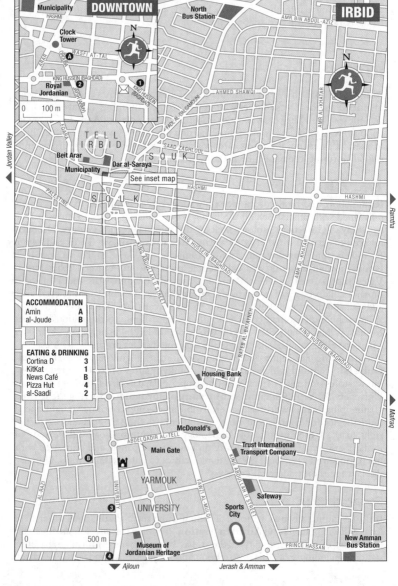

are marked in Arabic only – ask around for help). A taxi fare across the city shouldn't come to more than JD1.50.

Irbid's best **hotel** is the *Al-Joude* (☎02 727 5515; ❸), near the Yarmouk campus, hidden off University Street at the end of quiet Manama Street. It has clean and spacious en-suite rooms, friendly staff and the excellent *News Café* downstairs (who provide a room-service menu). The same owners are planning a new five-star hotel alongside. Otherwise, the best of an unimpressive bunch of rock-bottom cheap hotels in the market streets downtown is the *Amin*, on Orouba Street (☎02 724 2384; ❶), with cleanish rooms and dorms, plus hot showers.

Restaurants are basic. Downtown, falafel and *shawerma* stalls tempt, or you might try the gloomy *al-Saadi* restaurant on Baghdad Street for plain Arabic fare. The *KitKat* patisserie, along Baghdad Street, serves delicious *kunafeh* and other sweet treats. Virtually every establishment on University Street is an eating house of some kind, though many are pretty ordinary. Western-style fast food predominates. The buzzing *News Café* under the *al-Joude* hotel has decent pizzas, pasta, salads, sandwiches and the like, washed down with good coffee or a cold beer. Nearby, the Italian restaurant *Cortina D* isn't bad, though it's no better than *Pizza Hut* up the road. For picnic ingredients, the large **supermarket** Safeway (daily 24hr) isn't far away.

The far north

The land hard up against the Syrian border in the **far north** of Jordan is hilly farming country, especially beautiful in springtime when a riot of colour covers the fields between groves of olives and figs. The ancient trees around the picturesque village of **Umm Qais**, perched on the very edge of the Transjordanian plateau, are famed for producing some of the choicest olives in the region, although the village is best known for the atmospheric ruins of Gadara – where Jesus performed one of his most famous miracles – and for spectacular views out over the Sea of Galilee. Below coils the dramatic gorge of the **River Yarmouk**, which flows west to meet the River Jordan just south of the Sea of Galilee, and which now marks the border between Jordan and the Israeli-occupied Golan Heights (Jawlan in Arabic). Travel along the gorge is restricted. Nestled among palm trees and banana plantations below the heights is **Himmeh**, graced with a laid-back air that belies the Israeli watchtowers within shouting distance. Further east, tucked away in the peaceful Wadi Qwaylbeh north of Irbid, lie the part-excavated ruins of **Abila**, another of the Decapolis cities, featuring a hillside rock-cut cemetery decorated with Byzantine frescoes.

Umm Qais   ام قيس

Off the beaten track 30km northwest of Irbid, tucked into the angle of borders formed by Jordan, Israel and the Golan, the windswept village of **UMM QAIS** is well worth the effort of a long journey, whether you visit on a day-trip from Irbid or stay overnight to relish the still twilight and fresh, chilly morning. The main attraction is exploring the remote, widespread ruins of the Decapolis city of **Gadara**, some of which are jumbled together with the striking houses of black basalt and white limestone of an abandoned Ottoman village.

Since the foundation of the State of Israel in 1948, Palestinians who were expelled from or fled their homes have come here specifically to savour the spectacular **views** over their former homeland – the waterfront city of Tabari-yyeh (Arabic name for Tiberias), the choppy lake itself, and the villages and lush countryside of the Galilee. The tradition is continued today by many Palestinian Jordanians, who either refuse to travel into Israel on principle or who have been denied entry visas.

Umm Qais is a popular choice for Friday outings, when the parking area can be filled with family cars and youth-club buses, and the ruins swamped by teenagers more interested in having a raucous good time than absorbing the atmosphere. Umm Qais is unmissable, but do pick your moment to visit.

Some history

After the death of Alexander the Great in 323 BC, Gadara was founded by the **Ptolemies** as a frontier station on their border with the Seleucids to the north

▲ Umm Qais, with the Golan Heights and Sea of Galilee behind

Miracle of the Gadarene swine

Gadara's main claim to fame centres on a story recounted in the New Testament about **Jesus** crossing the Sea of Galilee. The following version is in Matthew 8:28–32:

And when he came to the other side, to the country of the Gadarenes, two demoniacs met him, coming out of the tombs, so fierce that no one could pass that way. They cried out, 'What have you to do with us, O Son of God? Have you come here to torment us before the time?' Now a herd of many swine was feeding at some distance from them. And the demons begged him, 'If you cast us out, send us away into the herd of swine.' And he said to them, 'Go.' So they came out and went into the swine; and the whole herd rushed down the steep bank into the sea, and perished in the waters.

(*gader* is a Semitic word meaning "boundary"). In 218 BC, the Seleucids took the city, but came under siege a century later from the Jewish Hasmoneans; when the Roman general **Pompey** imposed order throughout Syria in 63 BC, he personally oversaw the rebuilding of Gadara as a favour to one of his favourite freedmen, a Gadarene. The city won a degree of autonomy, and became a prominent city of the **Decapolis** (see box, p.156).

Roman rule – particularly following Trajan's annexation of the Nabatean kingdom in 106 AD – brought stability and prosperity. As at Jerash, Gadara saw large-scale public building works during a second-century **golden age**, including construction of the great baths at Himmeh. Literary sources describe Gadara at this time as a city of great cultural vitality, a centre for philosophy, poetry and the performing arts, where pleasure-seeking Romans came from all over the empire. As early as the third century BC, a native of the city, **Menippos** had risen to become renowned in Greece as a Cynic philosopher and satirist. By the second century AD, the city's Cynic streak was flourishing in the hands of **Oenomaos**, a nihilist and critic, although perhaps the city's best-known sons are **Philodemus**, a mid-first-century BC Epicurean philosopher, and **Meleager**, a highly regarded love poet. **Theodoros of Gadara** was a famous rhetorician of the first century BC, who taught the Emperor Tiberius. Later, two Gadarenes of the third century AD stand out: **Apsines** taught rhetoric in Athens; and the scientist **Philo** refined Archimedes' calculations of mathematical pi.

By 325 AD Gadara was the seat of a **bishopric**, but its proximity to the decisive battles at Pella and Yarmouk, when Muslim armies defeated the Christian Byzantines, led to the establishment of Muslim rule over the city well before the foundation of the Umayyad caliphate in Damascus in 661. However, a series of **earthquakes** not long afterwards destroyed much of Gadara's infrastructure, and the town went into rapid decline. At some point in the Middle Ages, its name changed to Umm Qais, possibly derived from the Arabic *mkes* (frontier station) or *maqass* (junction).

In 1806, the German traveller Ulrich Seetzen identified the ruins as those of Gadara. During the 1890s, a small **village** grew up on the Roman ruins, the inhabitants reusing the pre-cut stones to build their homes around graceful courtyards. A modern village soon developed nearby, but people continued to occupy the Ottoman cottages right through until 1986, when the 1500 inhabitants accepted payment from the Ministry of Tourism to leave their homes, in order to enable archeologists to clear the site for excavation.

However, since then not a single square of village land has been cleared. In the mid-1990s the ministry changed its tune, backing instead a project to convert

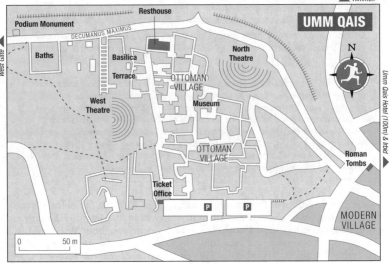

the Ottoman cottages into a **tourist village** and chalet-style hotel. A handful of houses were renovated – among them the buildings now housing the *Resthouse* and the museum – but work then stalled. Other schemes have come and gone, but for much of the year the abandoned Ottoman village and its once-grand Roman neighbour stand quiet, tour groups sweeping in and out, weeds growing higher and dust-devils infiltrating the long narrow streets.

The site

The **site** (daily 7am–sunset; JD3) occupies a hill on the west side of the modern village of Umm Qais, with the **ticket office** up some steps from the car park on the south side of the hill. On the way, in a hollow at the turn-off from the modern village, you'll pass two **Roman tombs**; the basalt doorways are beautiful, but, disappointingly, there's nothing to see inside.

Following the street along from the ticket office will bring you into the abandoned Ottoman village, where you can wander freely in and out of the weed-ridden courtyards and dusty alleys. The street leads to the evocative **West Theatre**. The theatre is built entirely of basalt, and its three thousand spectators – including VIPs in freestanding high-backed power chairs – had a fine view west over the city (now a grassy hill dotted with olive trees). North of the theatre is Gadara's most dramatic space, the **Basilica Terrace**, cut into the bedrock on one side and supported by vaulted **shops** below on the other. Its main feature, closest to the theatre, is a square Byzantine church dating from the fifth or sixth century. A small narthex opens into an outer circular passageway, still paved with coloured geometric tiles, which encloses a central octagon demarcated by basalt columns which probably supported a dome. Within the octagon, a small depression and apse housed the altar, behind which stands a thin, pink marble column carved with a cross. On the north side of the terrace, the white limestone paving and columns of the atrium stand in stark contrast to the black columns of the church. The atrium gives onto Gadara's main, paved street, the **Decumanus Maximus**, the clear line of which can be traced east and west.

Above the terrace to the east rise the restored arches of the *Resthouse*, but the rest of the city extends for a kilometre westward, largely unexcavated beneath the fields. About 100m west of the terrace is a ruined **podium monument** of unknown usage. Opposite stands a ruined **baths** complex. Some 250m further on is a colonnaded section of the street, and away to the left are the remains of more baths and a small forum. After another 100m you'll spot a circular structure, foundations of the tower of a gate across the street, within which steps lead down into a locked underground mausoleum. Gadara's **West Gate**, with an exposed section of basalt street, is 200m further on. Alongside the modern tarmac road (which formerly ran to Tiberias) are the remains of a **hippodrome**, culminating, 300m further on, in a partly reconstructed **monumental gateway** to the city, designed to impress visitors approaching from the Jordan Valley below. Looking back from here gives an idea of the enormous size of Gadara in its heyday, and the impossible task of excavating it all.

Back at the Basilica Terrace, following the Decumanus around the edge of the hill brings you to the grassy bowl of the **North Theatre**, its stones plundered to build the Ottoman cottages. Above, behind a grand gateway, is the site **museum** (daily 8am–6pm; Nov–March closes 4pm), occupying the former residence of the Ottoman governor, an elegant building on two storeys, with a portico and a lovely, peaceful internal courtyard. Highlights of the collection include a headless marble statue of Tyche found in the West Theatre, mosaics from around the city and carved sarcophagi.

Practicalities

Buses to and from Irbid's North station stop on Umm Qais's main street. The village's only **accommodation** is the basic *Umm Qais Hotel* on the main street (☎02 750 0080; ❶). Standard, shared bathrooms are on the reception floor, while more comfortable en-suite rooms are up above.

There are good *fuul*-and-falafel **diners** either side of the hotel (the *fuul* up here, prepared with sumac and other spices, makes an interesting change from Amman-style). However, you shouldn't leave Umm Qais without sitting awhile on the terrace of the ⚜ **Resthouse** (☎02 750 0555, ⓦwww.romero-jordan .com; daily 10am–sunset), a sensitively renovated Ottoman building in the midst of the ruins. This gives the single best **view** in the country, a breathtaking, wind-exposed 180-degree sweep taking in the Jordan Valley, the Sea of Galilee (with the Israeli city of Tiberias in plain view), the Yarmouk Gorge and, most impressive of all, the Golan Heights, pointing the way north towards snowcapped Jebel ash-Sheikh (Mount Hermon) on the Lebanese border. A meal here costs around JD10 and, since the place is under the same management as Amman's *Romero* restaurant, the food is very good.

Himmeh (Mukhaybeh)   الحمة (المخيبة)

In Roman times, Gadara's lavish baths complex, built around the seven hot springs at **HIMMEH**, was grand enough to bear comparison with the fabulous imperial baths at Baiae, near Naples. Modern Himmeh – also known as **Mukhaybeh** – is a shadow of its former self, and has been divided by modern boundary-drawing: most Roman remains are now in what the locals call "Syrian Himmeh", on the north bank of the Yarmouk in territory currently occupied by Israel, and there is little or no historical interest in what is signposted as "**Jordan Himmeh**": from Umm Qais head down the steep hill to a crossroads, from where the village is 4km straight on.

Hemmed in by the towering Golan Heights – with its easily visible Israeli jeep patrols – and lying some 200m below sea level, the village is crowded with palm trees and banana plants that thrive in the sweltering, subtropical conditions. However in 2007, following scandals over pollution and poor maintenance, Himmeh's spa complex was shut down and demolished. Related businesses, including hotels, have also gone under – and the future remains uncertain.

Mamdouh Bisharat, a leading Jordanian philanthropist and patron of the arts (see p.99 for details of his cultural salon in Amman) – widely known as the "Duke of Mukhaybeh" after a nickname bestowed on him by King Hussein – has a farm here employing many local people, and takes an active interest in the village's fortunes. He has very kindly offered Rough Guide readers the chance to stay – by prior arrangement only – at his private villa in the village, which has its own spring and Roman pool. Call Mr Bisharat for details (℡079 616 6000).

The Yarmouk Gorge road وادي اليرموك

Himmeh is as far east along the Yarmouk as you're allowed to venture, but with your own transport you can head west alongside a portion of the deep and dramatic **Yarmouk Gorge** (all buses go back up the hill to Umm Qais). The **views** on this tense frontier road are spectacular – even better looking east than they are looking west – gazing down into the Yarmouk, across to the Sea of Galilee and up to the Golan Heights. Drive slowly and remember you are under constant surveillance here from both the Jordanian army and the Israeli army; although you might be able to snatch a photo or two of the beautiful scenery, or of the **wrecked bridge**, bombed in the 1967 war and still hanging over the gorge, you may find the soldiers objecting. There are checkpoints every few hundred metres, for which you should always stop and show your **passport**. After 6km of this you come to a junction where the only option is to turn left, and this road delivers you after another 7.5km to the town of **Shuneh ash-Shamaliyyeh** (North Shuneh), at the head of the Jordan Valley, a pleasant enough little market town. The village of Tabqat Fahl – alongside the ancient site of **Pella** – is a short drive south (see p.184).

Baqoura الباقورة

Northwest of Shuneh lies **Baqoura**. This tiny sliver, less than a kilometre square, was occupied by Israel in 1967 and returned to Jordan under the 1994 peace treaty. It is a military zone: visiting isn't easy, but it's popular as a local beauty spot and retains an intriguing cross-border identity. From the Shuneh junction, head north for 3.4km to a checkpoint, where they might let you through to drive another 1.2km to the end of the road at an army base, where you must park your car. If you explain that you're interested in seeing Baqoura, an officer may find some transport and accompany you: they won't let you explore here alone. From the base a road heads down for about 1km and crosses the Yarmouk on a rickety bridge alongside a half-ruined hydroelectric station – the first in the Middle East, built in 1927 by Russian engineer Pinchas Rutenberg and damaged by Iraqi shelling in 1948. Up above is a hilltop parking area known as the **"Island of Peace"**, with a breathtaking view: from here you can see the confluence of the Yarmouk and the Jordan just below, with the cultivated fields of the Israeli kibbutz Ashdot Yaakov all around, the route of the old railway line from Haifa to Damascus visible and cars passing on the Israeli highway opposite. Israeli farmers are permitted to rent land here – in Jordan – until 2019: you may pass Israeli pick-ups on these roads. This car park, and the surrounding area, was formerly where Israeli and Jordanian day-trippers mixed freely, until 1997 when a Jordanian soldier, Ahmed Daqamseh, murdered seven Israeli schoolgirls here. He is serving life with hard labour, yet his name remains notorious, a blight on this beautiful place.

Abila   قويلبة

Lying virtually unknown in the cradle of the lush Wadi Qwaylbeh, 12km north of Irbid, the lonely ruins of the Decapolis city of **Abila** have only just begun to be excavated from the grassy fields. Its Roman-Byzantine **cemetery**, comprising dozens of tombs cut into a neighbouring hillside, makes for some remarkable exploration: many are still adorned with their original frescoes. The experience of stumbling across portraits of long-dead Abilenes gazing back into your torchlight from the rock-cut coffins that once held their bones is one to be remembered. Bear in mind that you're on your own here: there's no development of the site at all, and no facilities for visitors.

By **car**, follow signs from Irbid for Umm Qais until you reach a set of traffic lights about 7km north of the city, where the main Umm Qais road branches off left. Continue straight on here until you reach a quiet fork in the road, which divides in front of an isolated domed mosque close to Wadi Qwaylbeh (11km north of Irbid). **Buses** running from Irbid's North station towards **Hartha** bear left at this fork, which is a good place to get out, since the best way to approach Abila is to head right at the fork; walk or drive exactly 900m along this road, and then walk left straight across the fields. This will bring you to a dry-stone wall, teetering over the steep flank of the Wadi Qwaylbeh. Prominent against the sky on a hilltop opposite is a columned seventh-century church, while the slope below the wall shelters Abila's necropolis. Very near the wall are two of the beautifully painted **tomb caves**, while others are scattered across the slope; persistent exploration is required. The caves which hold frescoes are gated and locked, but it's likely that the guardian (a local shepherd) will arrive to lead you around. Some **frescoes** are in remarkably good condition, delightful portraits of men and women, flowers and fruits, and one a spectacular scene of dolphins covering the ceiling.

Working your way north (right) along the cave-dotted slope brings you, after about 2km, to a modern building which overlooks the Roman **bridge** across the stream, leading into the ancient city centre past the remains of a large Byzantine church. You can make out the bowl of a **theatre** next to a section of basalt-paved Byzantine **street**. Follow the track curling up to the hilltop **church**, with its alternating basalt and limestone columns. Olive groves conceal the Hartha road from the church; once on the road, you could hitch a ride back to Irbid, or wait for the (infrequent) buses.

The northern Jordan Valley

The deep cleft of the **Jordan Valley** carries the River Jordan south from the Sea of Galilee (some 200m below sea level) to the Dead Sea (400m below), a distance of only 104km as the crow flies, but the meandering river twists and writhes for more than three times that length. Set down in a deep gorge flanked by a desolate flood plain (the *zor*), the river is never visible from the main road, which runs through the *ghor*, or cultivable valley floor, well to the east. Flanked by 900-metre-high mountains on both sides and enjoying a swelteringly subtropical climate of low rainfall, high humidity and scorching temperatures, the valley with its fertile alluvial soil is perfect for **agriculture** on a large scale: this vast open-air green-house can produce crops up to two months ahead of elsewhere in the Middle East and can even stretch to three growing seasons annually. As early as five thousand years ago, foodstuffs from the valley were being exported to nearby states, and irrigation systems and urban development progressed hand-in-hand soon after.

The southern part of the Jordan Valley is covered on p.143.

Agriculture has remained at the heart of the valley economy, from the wheat, barley, olives, grapes and beans of the Bronze Age to an extensive sugar-cane industry under the Mamlukes. Since the late nineteenth century, rapid development – and, in particular, the building of the **King Abdullah Canal** in the 1960s to irrigate the eastern *ghor* – has led to a burgeoning agricultural industry that supplies most of Jordan's tomatoes, cucumbers, bananas, melons and citrus fruits, as well as producing a surplus for export.

In contrast to the prosaic vistas of concrete piping, plastic greenhouses and farm machinery that characterize the area today, well over two hundred **archeological** sites have been catalogued in the valley, although – with the notable exception of the Roman-Byzantine remains at **Pella** – almost all of them are Neolithic or Bronze Age settlements on the summits of *tell*s, with little to see other than stone foundations. South of Pella, a few kilometres from the river's outflow into the Dead Sea lies the **Baptism Site** of Jesus, covered on p.137.

Transport in the valley mostly comprises buses shuttling north and south along the highway between the main hubs of Shuneh ash-Shamaliyyeh, Kraymeh, Dayr Alla and Shuneh al-Janubiyyeh, stopping at all points in between. Bearing in mind the excessive heat – summer temperatures regularly top 45°C – and the lack of tourist facilities, the best way to see the valley is in your own vehicle. By bus, you could devote either a half- or a full-day to the trip, starting from Irbid and heading south to end in Amman, or vice versa. The only **accommodation** comprises a few rooms at Pella.

Pella and around طبقة فحل

For archeologists, **PELLA**, comprising a large *tell* overlooking a well-watered valley protected by hills, is quite thrilling, possibly the most significant site in all of Jordan; evidence has been found of human activity in the area for nearly a million years, with extensive remains from almost all periods from the Paleolithic through to the Mamluke. The *tell* itself has been occupied for the last six thousand years almost without interruption. However, though it's definitely worth the journey, Pella can appear rather underwhelming to non-archeologists, with – in effect – little more than three ruined Byzantine churches to divert attention from the beautiful hill-walking all around. Nonetheless, it's a beautiful spot, and makes a pleasant stop on a journey along the Jordan Valley.

Some history

The reasons for Pella's long history have much to do with its location on the junction of major trade routes: north–south between Arabia and Syria, and east–west between the Transjordanian interior and the Mediterranean coast. With its positioning almost exactly at sea level – the Jordan Valley yawns below – Pella has a comfortably warm climate and is watered both by the gushing springs in the bed of the Wadi Jirm and by a reasonable annual rainfall. In addition, it was surrounded in antiquity by thick oak forests, since felled, which at more than one point provided the backbone of the city's economy.

From artefacts discovered near Pella, it seems that **Stone Age** hunters roamed the area's forests and savannahs up to about a million years ago, bagging native game such as elephants, deer and lions. By five thousand years ago, a **Neolithic** farming village was spread out above the springs in the main Wadi Jirm, and remains have been uncovered of a larger, terraced **Chalcolithic** settlement just below Jebel Sartaba, southeast of the *tell*. By the early third millennium BC, during the **Bronze Age**, there was a thriving city at Pella, extensive evidence of which has been excavated from the *tell*: pieces dating from at least four main periods of occupation around the sixteenth and fifteenth centuries BC include luxury items imported from Egypt, Syria and Cyprus – indicating well-established trade links – such as bronze pins, stylized sculpture, gold thread, alabaster bottles, cuneiform clay tablets and beautiful inlaid ivory boxes. In the thirteenth century BC, Pella was the principal supplier to Pharaonic Egypt of wood for chariot spokes. **Iron Age** cities flourished on the *tell* up to the seventh century BC, but during the Persian period (539–332 BC) it seems that the area was abandoned.

The **Hellenistic** period is the first for which the name of Pella can be attested from historical records, and was a time of considerable affluence for the city. In 218 BC, the Seleucid king Antiochus captured Pella on a sweep through Palestine and Transjordan, and thereafter occupation of the site spread over the *tell*, the slopes of Tell Husn opposite, the so-called "Civic Complex" area on the valley floor and the peak of Jebel Sartaba.

In 83 BC, the Jewish **Hasmonean** leader Alexander Jannaeus crossed into Transjordan from Palestine and sacked pagan Pella and its neighbours Gadara, Gerasa and others. The arrival twenty years later of Pompey and the **Roman** army imposed order in Pella as elsewhere in the Decapolis region, and the city settled down to a period of stability, minting its own coins and embarking on a programme of building. However, one legacy of the city's location above a perpetually flowing spring is that, due to a rise in alluvium levels, it's been impossible to excavate in the valley bed. Consequently, virtually nothing of the Roman period apart from a small theatre survives, although coins found here depict a nymphaeum, various temples, probably a forum, a baths and lavish public buildings dotted throughout the city.

A massacre of twenty thousand Jews in a single hour at Caesarea in Palestine in 66 AD fuelled a widespread Jewish revolt against Roman rule, and amid the turmoil the nascent **Christian** community of Jerusalem fled en masse to the relative safety of Pella – though they returned by the time of the rebuilding of Jerusalem, around 130 AD. Pella reached its zenith during the **Byzantine** fifth and sixth centuries, with churches, houses and shops covering the slopes of the *tell* and Tell Husn, and pottery from North Africa and Asia Minor indicating significant international trade. However, by the seventh century, the city was again in decline; in 635, **Muslim** forces defeated the Byzantine army near Pella, and the city reverted to its pre-Hellenistic Semitic name of Fahl. The devastating earthquake of 749 destroyed most of Pella's standing structures, and the city lay abandoned for several centuries, small groups of farmers coming and going throughout the Abbasid and Mamluke periods.

The site

Although there may not be much romance left to Pella, it's certainly in a beautiful location. Sweet spring water cascades out of the ground on the floor of the **Wadi Jirm**; and the imposing bulk of the sheer **Tell Husn** to one side, the long, low *tell* on the other and **Jebel Abu al-Khas** between them (on which stands the modern, triple-arched *Resthouse*) enclose the little valley with high slopes of green, leaving only the vista westwards over the Jordan Valley. The abundant spring water, however, has proved irresistible to modern agriculture, and 100m beyond the antiquities stands a pumping station serving a lush area of irrigated farmland. Constantly chugging machinery and a reek of agrichemicals make for an annoying accompaniment to a visit.

Before you reach the main site, you'll see the remains of the **West Church** behind barbed wire on the edge of the modern village. The church was built in the late fifth or early sixth centuries, in Pella's prime, and is one of the largest Byzantine churches uncovered in the entire Middle East. The main valley is dominated by the standing columns of the **Civic Complex Church** on the edge of the bubbling spring. All the re-erected columns belong to the church's atrium; to the east, in front of a finely paved portico, are two exquisite columns of green swirling marble, one of which cracked in two as it fell in antiquity. The church itself, its columns collapsed like a house of cards, has three apses, and was originally decorated with glass windows, glass mosaic half-domes, stone mosaics on the walls and floor, and chancel screens of marble. The **monumental staircase** in front was added in the seventh century, when the valley floor was some two to three metres below its current level. To one side of the church is the bowl of a small Roman **theatre**, built in the first century AD to seat about four hundred; many of its stones were plundered to build the church staircase. Across the whole area of the modern springs, there may once have stretched a forum, with the stream channelled below through subterranean vaulting, some of which is still visible.

The **tell** itself – on the left as you face the *Resthouse* – is likely to excite only archeologists. Although several different excavations have revealed dozens of levels of occupation over millennia, all there is to see for the layperson are the crisscrossing foundations of coarser and finer walls at different levels and a couple of re-erected columns. Of most accessible interest is a small **Mamluke mosque** close to the modern dig-house, with a plaque commemorating the decisive Battle of Fahl of 635. Excavations alongside it have unearthed the massive stone blocks of a **Canaanite temple** dating to 1480 BC, the largest yet discovered from that period. You'd have to be very keen to scale the precipitous **Tell Husn** opposite in order to poke around the sixth-century Byzantine fortress on its summit.

The steep path between the Civic Complex ruins and the *Resthouse* coils up the hillside past the columns of the small, atmospheric **East Church**, built in the fifth century overlooking the lower city and originally accessed by a monumental staircase from below. The atrium has a small pool in the centre.

Behind the *Resthouse*, Jordanian architect Ammar Khammash has built the private **Pella Museum** (Ⓦwww.pellamuseum.org). It explores Jordan's history before archeology, showcasing fossils and exploring geological formations. Admission is by appointment only; the website has contact information, or ask at the *Resthouse*.

Practicalities

The ruins of Pella are situated close to the modern village of **TABQAT FAHL**, about 2km up a steep hill from the town of **Mshare'a** on the valley-floor highway. One or two **buses** run direct to Tabqat Fahl village from Irbid's Valleys station, but there are much more frequent departures from Irbid to Mshare'a, from where it's not difficult to hitch or even hike up the hill.

About 1km beyond the entrance gate to the site, on the hillside of Jebel Abu al-Khas, is the wonderfully cool and shady **Pella Resthouse** (Ⓣ079 557 4145, Ⓦwww.romero-jordan.com; daily 8am–sunset). This oasis of a place, designed by Ammar Khammash with a spectacular terrace perched high above the ruins,

Jordan's people

Although Jordan has a relatively homogeneous population, Jordanian society is nonetheless characterized by overlapping layers of identity: the country's 6.2 million people share much of the ethnic, religious and social mix of the wider Middle East, overlaid with a widespread, and often strong, tribal identity. Throughout the country you'll encounter articulate, worldly outlooks peppered with expressions of religious and social sensibility that sound refreshingly unfamiliar to Western ears.

Tea by the roadside ▲

St John's Roman Catholic cathedral, Madaba ▼

Friday prayers, Husseini Mosque, Amman ▼

Ethnicity

Almost Jordan's entire population is **Arab**. This is an ethnic term, but also marks a pan-national identity, largely because nation-states are a relatively recent arrival in the region: many people in Jordan feel a much stronger cultural affinity with Arabs from nearby countries than, say, Britons might feel with Belgians. The bedouin (see overleaf) add a deeper layer of meaning by often regarding themselves to be the only true, original Arabs. Jordan has tiny ethnic minorities of **Circassians** and **Chechens** (who are Muslim), **Armenians** (Christian) and **Kurds** (Muslim) – all of whom are closely bound into Jordanian society – as well as **Dom** gypsies (Muslim).

Religion

Roughly 92 percent of Jordanians are **Sunni Muslim**, and though the big cities – chiefly Amman and Aqaba – show a modestly secular influence in parts, the observance of Islam is a central part of daily life for most people across Jordan. The call to prayer sounds five times a day in every city, town and village.

Jordan's largest religious minority, totalling around six percent, are the various denominations of **Christians**, most of whom are Greek Orthodox, but also including Melkite Catholics, Roman Catholics, Syrian Orthodox, Armenian Orthodox, Coptic Orthodox, Maronites and some Protestants (Lutherans, Baptists, Episcopalians and others). There are also small communities of **Shia Muslims**, **Druze** and **Bahai**. Expats aside, there are no **Jews** in Jordan.

Nationality

There persists in some quarters a perceived difference between people whose origins lie in families long resident on the east bank of the River Jordan, and people whose families originate on the west bank of the river. All are **Jordanian** citizens, yet Jordanians of **Palestinian** origin are estimated to number between half and three-quarters of the total population. Roughly seven percent are expats, including guest workers – many of them **Egyptian**, **Sri Lankan** and **Filipino** – alongside a sizeable population of **Iraqi** refugees.

▲ In the market

▼ Wearing the traditional headcloth

Tribe

A **tribe** is an extended grouping of families who cultivate a distinctive tradition of history and folklore (mainly oral) and assert ownership of a particular territory.

Three of Jordan's many tribes are the **Rualla** in the east, the **Bani Sakhr** in the centre and the **Howeitat** in the south. Not all tribes are desert-dwelling – there are many whose background is rural – and tribal territories, which predate nation-states, often extend across international borders. Some tribes are made up of clans and branches which have taken on tribe-like status, others have banded together in larger, often pan-national, tribal confederations. All of these concepts are rather loose. For a lot of Jordanians, though, tribal identity is at least as strong as religious or national identity.

See p.397 for an article examining some issues of tribal culture.

Bedouin and fellahin

Within tribal identity, many people make a distinction in Jordan – as in other Middle Eastern countries – between two broad social traditions. The **bedouin** originate in families who are current or former desert-dwellers: they may once have been nomadic, but are almost all now settled. Some still live in tents in the desert or the desert margins, following traditional lifestyles, but many do not: a police officer in Amman or a marketing executive in Aqaba might be as bedouin as a camel-guide in Wadi Rum. By contrast the **fellahin** originate from a settled, rural, farming tradition, often in the north and west of Jordan. They frequently have strong historic links – often of family or tribe – to rural communities across the borders in Syria and Palestine.

Bedouin tea ▲

A weekend day-trip ▼

The next generation ▼

The next generation

Like many countries across the Middle East, Jordan has a **young population**: more than a third of Jordanians are under the age of 15. This is also one of the **best-educated** countries in the developing world. Almost everyone you come across will be able to hold some sort of conversation in English (and possibly in French, Spanish and German as well), and if you make a point of visiting, say, Jordan University in Amman or Yarmouk University in Irbid, you'll see students from all income groups and social backgrounds mixing freely. The traditional emphasis on engineering and the sciences is giving way to **new technology** and even filmmaking: Aqaba's Red Sea Institute of Cinematic Arts, backed by Steven Spielberg, is turning out directors and cinematographers of world-class standard. The heritage-style image of Jordan as a nation of simple tent-dwellers, scratching a living from the desert sands, is just part of the story.

is worth a visit on its own merits. Its fresh-squeezed juices and cold beers are an obvious attraction in a place as sultry as Pella, but the main draw is a plate of the best and freshest fish in Jordan, plucked daily from the river and served up with *mezze* for under JD10 (their grilled chicken is a succulent alternative). An accompanying bottle of chilled white wine might persuade you to leave ruin-hunting in the hot sun until next time.

The friendly, English-speaking *Resthouse* manager, Deeb Hussein – whose family have been in the area since 1885 – operates the only place to **stay**, the small but highly recommended ⚁ *Pella Countryside Hotel*, set among peaceful olive groves on the edge of Tabqat Fahl (☎079 557 4145 or 077 618 4337, ⓔdheebjawahreh575@hotmail.com; ❸ inc. half-board). Its modest en-suite rooms (with a/c) are simple but comfortable and very clean, with the appeal of genuine hospitality and an excellent dinner and breakfast.

Around Pella

Longer exploration of the area around Pella can take the form of a combination of ruin-hunting and adventure hiking – but you should definitely discuss your plans first with the *Resthouse* manager, who knows both the history and the topography of the area intimately. If you head past the East Church to curve up behind the *Resthouse*, you'll find rough trails leading across the hills for an hour or more out to the peak of **Jebel Sartaba**; here stands a Hellenistic fortress, rather less dramatic in itself than the remoteness of the location and the stunning views across the hills and valleys west into Israel and Palestine and east towards Ajloun.

Kahf il-Messih   كهف المسيح

Equally explorable is the route by car or on foot northwards into the hills to a little-explored site known as **Kahf il-Messih**, or the Jesus Cave. Access is straight along the approach road from the Jordan Valley (instead of taking the side-turn up to the *Resthouse*); the road is rocky and bad, but taken slowly is passable in an ordinary car.

Some 200m beyond the *Resthouse* junction is a fork; straight on, after 1.6km, you'll arrive at a highly photogenic **rock arch** through which flows the warm Wadi Hemmeh. Circle around to view it from the other side, where you'll also spot a small building which once housed the hot spring itself, now reduced to a stagnant pool. Back at the fork, the other road heads uphill for 2.4km; turn right here, then continue on, ignoring small roads which join from the side. After 7.3km, in the middle of the village of **Kufr Rakib**, take the right fork. As you leave the village, beneath the twin arches, take the right fork again, then a small road on the right after 1km, and left after another 1.3km into the locality of **Bayt Eidiss**. About 300m further is a spreading **oak tree**, marking the site of the Jesus Cave, with its arched entrance facing north. Local legend – thoroughly unsubstantiated – has it that Jesus stayed in the cave for some days before going to meet John for his baptism. It has Roman-style *loculi*, or alcoves for bodies, cut side-by-side into the bedrock. The oak tree is also the object of some veneration by the locals. Beside it is a flat rectangular area for treading grapes, complete with rock-cut channels and pools for collecting the juice.

The rolling hills all around are beautiful and quiet, many of them laced with extensive networks of caves and dotted with the odd archeological ruin (a small mosaic-floored church has been unearthed on one of the hills opposite). The village of **Kufr Abil**, a stop on the long walk between Ajloun and Pella (see p.169), is only a few kilometres south of here.

Sheikh Hussein Bridge (Jordan River Crossing)

Well signposted off the valley highway north of Pella is the **Sheikh Hussein Bridge** (or **Jordan River Crossing**), which heads into Israel; about 5km north of Mshare'a is the turn-off for cars and buses, which share a terminal (Sun–Thurs 6.30am–9pm, Fri & Sat 8am–8pm), while trucks use a separate terminal, signposted 4km further north. Buses from Amman and Irbid use the bridge on their way to and from Tel Aviv and Nazareth (see p.000), but it's also possible to cross independently (see p.000). A taxi from the bridge to Irbid is about JD25, to Amman about JD50.

Turn to p.143 for coverage of the southern part of the Jordan Valley.

Travel details

Buses and serveeces

Ajloun to: Amman (Tabarbour station; 1hr 30min); Irbid (New Amman station; 45min); Jerash (30min); Kraymeh (30min); Qal'at ar-Rabadh (10min).
Irbid (New Amman station) to: Ajloun (45min); Amman (Tabarbour station; every 15min; 1hr 15min–2hr); Jerash (35min); Mafraq (Fellahin station; 45min); Ramtha (20min).
Irbid (North station) to: Himmeh (1hr); Qwaylbeh (20min); Umm Qais (45min).
Irbid (Trust office) to: Aqaba (2 daily; 6hr).
Irbid (Valleys station) to: Mshare'a (45min); Sheikh Hussein Bridge (1hr); Shuneh ash-Shamaliyyeh (30min); Tabqat Fahl (1hr).

Jerash to: Ajloun (30min); Amman (Tabarbour station; 1hr); Irbid (New Amman station; 35min); Mafraq (Fellahin station; 40min).
Qwaylbeh to: Irbid (North station; 20min).
Shuneh ash-Shamaliyyeh to: Dayr Alla (50min); Irbid (Valleys station; 30min); Mshare'a (20min).
Tabqat Fahl to: Irbid (Valleys station; 1hr 15min); Mshare'a (15min).
Umm Qais to: Himmeh (15min); Irbid (North station; 45min).

International buses and serveeces

Irbid (New Amman station) to: Damascus (2hr).
Irbid (Trust office) to: Nazareth (1 daily; 3hr); Tel Aviv (6 weekly; 5hr).

Useful Arabic place names

Dibbeen	دبين	Kufr Rakib	كفر راكب
Halawa	حلاوة	Mshare'a	المشارع
Hartha	حرثا	Ramtha	الرمثا
Irbid	اربد	Shuneh ash-Shamaliyyeh	الشونة الشمالية
– New Amman station	مجمع عمّان الجديد	Suf town	بلد سوف
– North station	مجمع الشمالي	Sweileh	صويلح
– Trust office	مكتب شركة الثقة	Tabqat Fahl	طبقة فحل
– Valleys station	مجمع الاغوار	Wadi Qwaylbeh	وادي قويلبة
Jordan Valley	غور الاردن	Wadi al-Yabis	وادي اليابس
Kufr Abil	كفر ابيل	Yarmouk University	جامعة اليرموك

The eastern desert

CHAPTER 4

Highlights

* **The "Desert Castles" loop**
Take one or two days from
Amman to follow a circuit
around the eastern desert.
See p.195

* **Qasr Hallabat** Magnificently
restored "desert castle", with
fine mosaics and bags of
atmosphere. **See p.196**

* **Qasr Harraneh** Atmospheric
"desert castle", cool, dark
and musty. **See p.197**

* **Qusayr Amra** Bawdy eighth-
century frescoes adorning a
desert bath-house. **See p.199**

* **Azraq** Palm-fringed oasis
town, with a unique wetland
nature reserve and splendid
eco-lodge. **See p.202**

* **Burqu** Wander on the shores
of a mirage-like lake guarded
by a ruined black castle, out
in the deep desert. **See p.215**

▲ Qusayr Amra

The eastern desert

F or hundreds of kilometres east of Amman, the stony **Eastern Desert** plains extend unbroken to the Iraqi border – and beyond, clear to Baghdad. This is the harshest and least populated part of Jordan, with a bare handful of roads linking small, dusty towns and frontier villages. The two exceptions are **Zarqa**, an industrial city and transport hub, and **Mafraq**, amiable but remote-feeling capital of the northeast. East of Mafraq, in the black basalt desert hugging the Syrian border, sit the stark ruins of **Umm al-Jimal**, enormously romantic in the cool evening.

However, the main reason to come out here is to follow the "**Desert Castles loop**", a circuit of desert roads that runs past a string of early-Islamic inns and hunting lodges, collectively dubbed the "Desert Castles". For its mosaics and its remote atmosphere, newly restored **Qasr Hallabat** is one of the best, matched by elegant **Qasr Harraneh** and the uniquely frescoed **Qusayr Amra**.

At the circuit's farthest point, 100km east of Amman, lie the castle and twin villages of **Azraq**, Lawrence of Arabia's desert headquarters, set in a once-majestic oasis in the heart of the **eastern Badia**, which stretches from the populated central belt of the country east and north to the Syrian and Iraqi borders. Nearby the unremarkable town of **Safawi** gives access to a host of

Ideas for exploring eastern Jordan

Of all Jordan's regions, the east is most under-visited. Few tourists bother to come out here – but even if you're relying on public transport, it's easy to construct a **one-night tour**: start with a bus from Amman to Zarqa, head east to **Qasr Hallabat** (p.196), then continue to **Azraq** (p.202). Next day return to Zarqa and switch buses for Mafraq and then **Umm al-Jimal** (p.192), before returning from Mafraq to Amman or Jerash.

Renting a car (see p.39) buys you the freedom to roam at your own pace, opening up sites such as Harraneh and Amra that have no public transport access. If that doesn't appeal, many of Amman's budget hotels offer competitively priced one-day trips by taxi to Harraneh, Amra and Azraq; for more, see p.195.

To add a twist of adventure, talk to the Royal Society for the Conservation of Nature (RSCN; see p.51) about fixing up a half- or full-day excursion from Azraq – maybe an off-road tour of nearby sites such as **Aseikhim** (p.214) and **Biqyaw-iyya** (p.213), or **birdwatching at dawn** in the wetlands nature reserve (p.208). They can also arrange trips to far-flung desert locations, including **Jawa** (p.213) and **Burqu** (p.215).

desert attractions, including the holy tree of **Biqya'wiyya** and the spectacular **Qasr Burqu**, a ruined black castle on the shores of a mirage-like lake, which lies remote in the far desert, just 50km from the Iraqi border.

Transport practicalities

Public transport in the desert is predictably thin. From Amman, take a bus to either Zarqa – from where buses head to Azraq (via Hallabat) – or Mafraq, for buses to Umm al-Jimal and the desert towns further east. For information on transport options around the "**Desert Castles loop**", turn to p.195.

Zarqa and around الزرقاء

Some 20km northeast of Downtown Amman, and connected to the capital by a ribbon of low-income suburbs, industrial **ZARQA** is Jordan's second-largest city. There's little reason to spend time here except to catch an onward bus – to

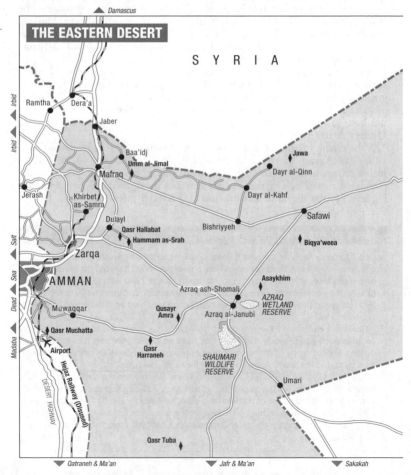

nearby **Khirbet as-Samra**, with its Roman-Byzantine ruins; **Hallabat**, at the start of the "Desert Castles" loop; or direct to **Azraq**.

Zarqa has two **bus stations**, 1km apart, within walking distance of the central clock tower. The **New Station** serves Amman – either Tabarbour or Mahatta stations – as well as Madaba and elsewhere. A shuttle bus runs from here to the **Old Station**, or you could walk left on the main road under the canopy for 500m and then aim for the clock tower. Useful bus routes from the Old Station include to Azraq, Hallabat, Khirbet as-Samra, Mafraq and Jerash.

Khirbet as-Samra   الخربة السمرا

If time is spare, you might take a couple of hours to visit isolated **KHIRBET AS-SAMRA**, about 20km northeast of Zarqa. Decked in wildflowers in spring and baked brown in summer, these hills were once crossed by caravans travelling the Roman Via Nova Traiana, and the town – then named **Hattita** – flourished for five hundred years or more. A Roman cohort was garrisoned here during the fourth century, and archeologists have uncovered eight Byzantine churches, all with mosaic floors.

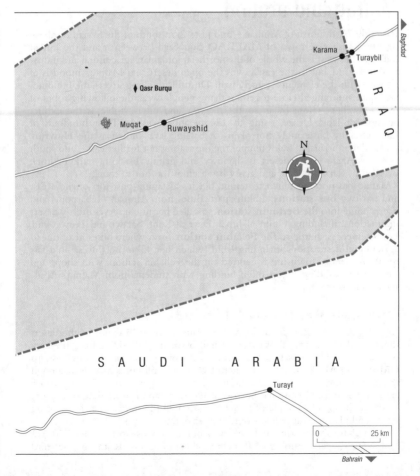

Unfortunately, Hattita is better in the telling than the seeing: all the mosaics have either been removed or covered over for safekeeping and it's hard to make sense of the site. The sense of countrified isolation is as good a reason as any to visit. (Khirbet as-Samra is best known in Jordan for its huge wastewater treatment plant, but fortunately this isn't in sight or smell of the old village.) Walking around the ruins will bring you to a large reservoir, near which is the **Church of St John**, a tiny place identifiable by its white limestone (instead of the otherwise ubiquitous black basalt) and paved floor, complete with apse. Further on are the foundations of the west wall of the original **Roman fort**, traceable around to the exposed **East Gate**, with the threshold and bases of flanking twin towers visible. The site guardian will help guide you around and show you photos from the French team (Ⓦwww.afasr.org) who excavate here; he deserves a tip.

Buses run from Zarqa, or you could **drive**: turn right 4km past Zarqa's clock tower to Hashmiyya, then right again after another 13km. You'll see the ruins after 6km.

Mafraq and around المفرق

Roughly 70km north of Amman – and just 12km south of the Syrian border – lies the ramshackle town of **MAFRAQ**. Squeezed between it and the Jordan Valley to the west is the whole of the northern Jordanian agricultural and industrial heartland, but to the east yawns the open desert, and Mafraq's mood is of a tussle with the elements scarcely won. Dust fills the long streets, the buildings are squat and ranged close together; many people wear the billowing robes of desert dwellers. Close by in southern Syria, and often visible, is the extinct volcano of Jebel Druze, rising to 1800m and surrounded for hundreds of kilometres by blisteringly hot plains of basaltic lava known as the **Hawran**. Near Mafraq irrigated fields temper the monotony, but further east – and south as far as Azraq – the desert is shadowy and grimly blackish, stark bedrock overlaid by dark boulders and glassy basalt chips too hot to touch.

Mafraq has nothing much to tempt, but it's a staging-post for journeys east and has two **bus stations**, 1.5km apart. Buses from Amman (Tabarbour) and Zarqa come into the **Bedouin station**, so called because it serves mostly desert destinations, including Umm al-Jimal, Dayr al-Kahf, Safawi and Ruwayshid. Local serveeces shuttle to the **Fellahin station**, from where buses head out to agricultural destinations including Irbid (which lies 45km northwest on a fast road) and Jerash. Town life is centred on the Fellahin station, with shops and cafés in surrounding streets often bustling with students from Mafraq's Al al-Bayt University.

Umm al-Jimal أم الجمال

In 1913, the American archeologist H.C. Butler wrote: "Far out in the desert there is a deserted city all of basalt, [rising] black and forbidding from the grey of the plain." The romance and sense of discovery accompanying a visit to **UMM AL-JIMAL** (literally "Mother of Camels") still holds true, even though the plain is now irrigated, and a modern village with good roads has grown up around the ruins. The site has been well excavated and is rewarding to explore – you could spend a couple of hours here, though the sun can be fierce: bring water, and plan to visit before noon or after 3pm.

Umm al-Jimal was occupied for seven hundred years up to about 750 AD. Following Queen Zenobia of Palmyra's rebellion against Rome in the third

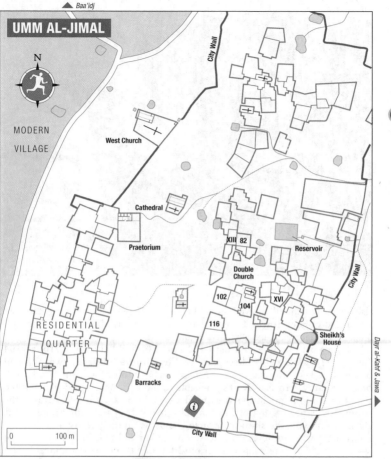

century, the village was rebuilt as a military station on the fortified frontier of the Roman Empire. It prospered as an agricultural and commercial centre; a sixth-century conversion to Christianity resulted in fifteen churches going up. However, an onslaught of plague, war, the Muslim conquest and a massive earthquake led to the town's abandonment.

Umm al-Jimal's appeal lies in its ordinariness. Although it is roughly contemporary with the grand city of Jerash, only a day's ride westward, Umm al-Jimal has no temples or impressive monumental buildings. There's not even any evidence of the town's original Roman name, which remains unknown. The archeologist who excavated the ruins, Bert de Vries, perceptively explained Umm al-Jimal as "a symbol of the real life of Rome's subjects".

The site

The bus can drop you at a point where the modern road cuts through Umm al-Jimal's ancient town walls. Start a one- or two-hour walking tour at the nearby **barracks**, dating from the fifth century. In the eastern wall the basalt

▲ Site workers at Umm al-Jimal

slab door, which still moves on its hinges, gives onto a courtyard. The late Byzantine **corner tower** is inscribed with crosses and the names of the four archangels: Gabriel, Raphael, Michael and Uriel.

Picking a path between **Houses 102 and 116**, and left around **House 104** (see map, p.193), will deliver you to the **double church**, two adjacent basilicas tucked into the houses around them, fronted by a small ablutions basin. Nearby **House XVI**'s lockable double doors would have fitted together snugly, and inside is a good example of a corbelled ceiling, the strong basalt beams supporting a much greater load than limestone could. Back behind you, the **sheikh's house** is outside on the left. Its large internal courtyard has a cantilevered staircase on the left and two in front forming a V-shape; stables were ranged at ground level, with bedrooms above. If you leave the courtyard through the gate here, you'll spot a beautiful **double-arched window** three storeys up.

From here, wandering north through the loose, clinking basalt leads to a huge **reservoir** – now fenced off – that was originally Roman. Just west of the reservoir, a scramble through **House 82** brings you into **House XIII**, with mangers and an interlocking stone ventilation screen – partially obscured by a recently built arch – dividing space for livestock within the house.

It's a 150-metre walk across to the four graceful and strikingly silhouetted arches of the **West Church**. The structure that remains is the division between the nave and a side-aisle; beautiful Byzantine crosses are carved on the arches. A little way south the **cathedral** sports a reused lintel stone mentioning Valens, Valentinian and Gratian, co-emperors in 371 AD. Close by is the **praetorium**, with a triple doorway. One of the rooms nearby has strings of barbed wire across its entrances and is often used to pen a herd of beautiful white camels belonging to the local sheikh. From here, your starting point at the Barracks is nearby.

Roman enthusiasts could drive to see a well-preserved stretch of the **Via Nova Traiana**, which survives near **BAA'IDJ**. Take the perimeter road around

Umm al-Jimal to the West Church and fork left; after 7km, a left turn at a T-junction, right at a small roundabout and straight on at a bigger roundabout will bring you after 600m to the cambered Roman road, pointing across the fields north (right) towards Bosra and south (left) towards Amman.

The "Desert Castles" loop

For most visitors, the main reason to head east is to explore Jordan's "**Desert Castles**", a group of early-Islamic buildings dotted around the desert – the best of which are now easily accessible by ordinary vehicles driving on proper roads. Most date from the **seventh century**, when the **Umayyad** dynasty was ruling from Damascus: bedouin at heart, the Umayyad caliphs seem to have needed an escape from the pressures of city life, and so built a network of hunting lodges, caravanserais and farmhouses to serve as rural retreats. Nineteenth-century archeologists came up with the term "Desert Castles" – yet few of the buildings are true castles, and many were built on what was then semi-fertile agricultural land. Archeologists have suggested replacement titles – desert complexes, country estates, farmsteads – but none exactly fits the bill.

These are some of Jordan's most atmospheric ancient buildings – most notably **Qasr Harraneh** and **Qusayr Amra**, which lie near each other on a fast road between Amman and the oasis town of **Azraq** (itself worth a stop for its nature reserve, eco-friendly lodge and links to Lawrence of Arabia; see p.202). A different road to Azraq, from the city of Zarqa, passes by the well-restored fortress of **Qasr Hallabat**, making it easy to follow a loop in either direction from Amman.

Harder-to-reach sites in the area include the ruined **Qasr Mushatta**, near Amman's airport, and **Qasr Tuba**, marooned in the roadless desert south of Harraneh.

Transport practicalities

Transport options around the "**Desert Castles loop**" – which starts and finishes in Amman, with Azraq as its furthest point – are limited, since two of the best sites (Harraneh and Amra) are inaccessible by public transport. You could cobble the route together with a combination of buses and paid hitching, but many travellers opt instead to join "tours" run by several of Amman's budget hotels, notably the *Farah*, *Cliff* and *Palace* (book at least one day ahead; contact details on p.92). For around 18–20JD per person (with a minimum of, usually, three people to make the trip viable), you get door-to-door transport to Harraneh, Amra, Azraq and back, with waiting time at each; sometimes Hallabat is included (if it isn't, try and get it added to the itinerary), but lunch is not. This is the cheapest and easiest way to see the loop in a day: you're unlikely to get a better price if you negotiate directly with a taxi-driver in Amman, who may not know the route anyway. However, if there are two or more of you, you'll save money – and gain in convenience – by **renting a car** (see p.39) and driving yourself: directions are given in each account below.

Although Qasr Burqu (p.215) and Qasr Tuba (p.201) can be grouped archeologically with the sites on the loop, they are so far off any beaten tracks that it's

There's a **map** of the area on p.190.

only possible to reach them with a local guide and a **4x4 vehicle**, best booked through an adventure tour operator with expert knowledge; the RSCN (see p.51) is a good first point of contact.

Qasr Hallabat قصر الحلابات

QASR HALLABAT (daily 8am–6pm; winter closes 4pm), perfectly situated on a small hill 30km northeast of Zarqa, is one of the most elaborate of the "Desert Castles". A Roman fort was built in black basalt on this site in the second century to guard the Azraq road, and parts of it still survive, but much of the building dates from an eighth-century Umayyad restoration in contrasting white limestone, when a mosque was added and mosaic floors laid. A Spanish archeological team has done extensive work here in recent years, clearing much rubble and bringing order to the site. It is now perhaps the most satisfying of all the Desert Castles to explore, full of desert atmosphere – and, for now, still largely unvisited.

If you're **driving**, follow Hashmi Street east from Downtown Amman direct to the Zarqa clock tower; 22km further, in Dulayl, turn right and Hallabat is 7km ahead. Coming from Azraq, Hallabat lies 53km along the road signed for Zarqa. **Hallabat** village has two separate halves – Hallabat al-Gharbi (West) and Hallabat ash-Sharqi (East). Buses from Zarqa drop off in Gharbi, near the site's Visitor Centre. Admission is currently free, but a small charge may be imposed in future.

From the Visitor Centre it's a walk of 200m up a stony path to the hilltop site, where the guardian will emerge to escort you. You come first to the beautifully rebuilt Umayyad **mosque**, many of its doorway arches sporting distinctive scalloping. Alongside, a modern door beneath a wobbly **entrance arch** – one shake and it'd be rubble – leads into the main building's spacious, stone-flagged **courtyard**, in an L-shaped layout and flanked in black and white. To left and right, tall basalt walls lead into rooms filled with reused blocks inscribed in Greek; in several places you can see remnants of the original herringbone-patterned plaster. A scramble to the corner towers – the highest points of the ruins – can help with orientation; from here, as well as panoramic views over the undulating desert hills, you can spot older blocks from the tiny original **Roman fort** which occupied one corner of the site. Opposite, a water channel runs under the stairs, carrying rainwater from the roof to cisterns under the courtyard and outside the walls. Filling the centre of the building is a large square room complete with a dazzling carpet mosaic in a diamond design; the adjacent portico also features mosaics of birds and fish.

Hammam as-Srah حمام الصرح

Roughly 3km east, in Hallabat ash-Sharqi, lies a small Umayyad bath-house, **HAMMAM AS-SRAH**, currently under restoration. Similar to, though smaller than, Qusayr Amra, its *caldarium* (hot room) is nearest the road, followed by the *tepidarium* (warm room) with the hypocaust system of underfloor heating and terracotta flues in the walls. The *apodyterium* (changing room) is furthest away, next to the original entrance, where there's some decorative cross-hatching on the walls.

If you're facing the building, there's a minor T-junction 300m to the left. At this junction turn right and continue for 2km to reach the main Zarqa–Azraq road.

From Hallabat, the main road runs east for 53km to **Azraq** (see p.202).

Qasr Mushatta   قصر المشتى

The largest of the "Desert Castles", **QASR MUSHATTA** (Arabic for "Winter Palace") lies southeast of Amman, just beyond the north runway of Queen Alia Airport – clearly visible on both takeoff and landing.

It probably dates from the 740s and is moderately well preserved, although it was never finished. The site is enclosed by a square wall 144m along each side, with collapsed towers all round and portions of intricate classical-style **carving** surviving. Similar pieces at one time covered all of the exterior, but as a sop to Kaiser Wilhelm of Germany before World War I, the Ottoman sultan Abdul Hamid II had most of them stripped off and presented to the Pergamon Museum in Berlin, where they are still on display. The whole site is littered with unfinished work, capitals and column drums; along with the carving, everything hints at a splendour of design that was never fully realized.

To get there, **drive** south out of Amman on the airport highway. Exactly 6.5km past the Madaba exit look for a small white mosque on the northbound (left-hand) side of the highway, followed 200m later (also on the northbound side) by a minor turn-off. This is the road you want. Continue south until you can make a U-turn, then return northbound and turn right down the turn-off. Keep straight, following Air Cargo signs past industrial estates and across the old Hejaz Railway tracks. After 7.4km, just before a checkpoint, you'll see the ruined palace on the left.

As you walk in, remnants of a **mosque** lie to the right, its *mihrab* set into the external wall. The palace buildings themselves are massive, built of unusual burnt brick above a stone base. The triple-arched **entrance hall** has a colonnade of beautiful swirling greenish marble columns, very striking against the reddish brick. Ahead is the huge triple-apsed **reception hall**. All around are interconnected rooms, some still with their high, barrel-vaulted ceilings in place; if you decide to explore, tread heavily to warn any resident snakes of your presence. Behind the impressive arched *iwan*s, at the back of the hall on both sides, ancient **toilets** stick out of the wall, complete with run-off drain.

Qasr Harraneh (Qasr Kharana)   قصر الحرانة

Most "Desert Castles" tours from Amman follow the loop anticlockwise onto the Azraq road, which begins from **Sahab**, a southern district of the capital. Drive south out of Downtown Amman along Prince Hassan Street (aka Madaba St) through Wihdat. In industrial Sahab, about 5km south of the major intersection Middle East Circle (*duwaar ash-sharq al-awsat*), you'll come to the flyover which carries the road from Azraq. Head left (east) on this road, beyond the factories and into the sandy-coloured desert. About 17km on, hilltop **MUWAQQAR** village is a terminus for buses from Amman's Mahatta station and also hosts a large Umayyad reservoir, dating from the early 720s AD and still in use.

Beyond Muwaqqar, it's a straight run for 38km east to **QASR HARRANEH** (often signposted wrongly in English and/or Arabic as "**Kharaneh**" or "**Kharana**").

Of all the sites in the eastern desert, Harraneh – whose name derives from the stony *harra* desert in which it sits – was probably the one which gave rise to the misnomer "Desert Castles". Standing foursquare beside the road, and visible for miles around, it looks like a fortress built for defensive purposes, with round corner towers, arrow slits in the wall and a single, defendable entrance. However, on closer examination, you'll find that Harraneh's towers are solid (and thus unmannable) and that only three-metre giants with extra-long arms could fire anything out of the arrow slits. Rather, it seems most likely that Harraneh – positioned at the meeting point of many desert tracks – was a kind of country conference centre, used by the Umayyad caliphs as a comfortable and accessible place to meet with local bedouin leaders, or even as a site where the bedouin themselves could meet on neutral ground to iron out tribal differences. It was probably built in the late seventh century; a few lines of graffiti in an upper room were written on November 24, 710.

The site

Marvellously cool and perfectly still inside, Harraneh (daily 8am–6pm; winter closes 4pm; joint ticket with Amra and Azraq JD1) is one of Jordan's most atmospheric and beautiful ancient buildings. Soak up the peace and quiet for an hour or two.

Circle left around the building to reach the sunken Visitor Centre at the back of the site. From here, you approach the main entrance facade head-on. Look up to see a distinctive band of diagonal bricks up near the top of the walls, a decorative device still in use on garden walls all over Jordan today.

As you enter the *qasr*, to left and right are long, dark rooms probably used as stables. The **courtyard** is surprisingly small, and it's here you realize how deceptive the solid exterior is: the whole building is only 35m square, but its doughty towers and soaring entrance make it seem much bigger. An arched **portico** originally ran round the courtyard, providing shade below and a corridor above – when it was in place, virtually no direct sunlight could penetrate into the interior. All the rooms round the courtyard, including those upstairs, are divided into self-contained units, each called a *bayt*, comprising a large central room with smaller rooms opening off it. This is typically Umayyad, and the same system was used in the palace at Amman, as well as at Mushatta and Tuba. Weaving in and out, you can explore your way around the deliciously musty and cool ground floor to get a sense of how the maze-like *bayt* system works. Each *bayt* most likely held a single delegation – the central, well-lit room used for meetings or socializing, the flanking, darker rooms for sleeping or storage. Harraneh had space for a total of eight delegations and their horses.

Of the two staircases, the left-hand one as you came in delivers you to the more interesting **upper western rooms**; at the top of the stairs, it's easy to see the springs of the portico arches below. The room immediately to your left upstairs is lined with stone **rosettes**. Next door, a more ornate room holds a few lines of eighth-century **graffiti**, in black painted Kufic script in the far left-hand corner above a doorway. All around are graceful blind arcades and friezes of rosettes, with the semi-domed ceiling supported on squinches.

The **northern bayts**, which are open to the sky, give onto the large **east room**, with a simple houndstooth design. From the southeast corner there's a nice view along the whole width of the *qasr* through alternately lit and dark areas. The **southern room**, with a row of little arched windows over the courtyard, has the only large window, looking out above the entrance: this may have been a watchpost. One of the small, dark rooms on the south wall has a unique **cross-vaulted ceiling**, with decorated squares and diamonds not found elsewhere. Take the stairs up again to the **roof** to watch the dustdevils spinning across the flat, stony plain.

Qusayr Amra   قصير عمرة

If you're not ready for it, you might miss the squat **QUSAYR AMRA** (daily 8am–6pm; winter closes 4pm; joint ticket with Harraneh and Azraq JD1), beside the Amman–Azraq road 15km east of Harraneh. *Qusayr* is the diminutive of *qasr*, meaning "little castle" ("Qasr Amra" is also common). A small bathhouse, Amra was built to capitalize on the waters of the Wadi Butm, named after the *butm* (wild pistachio) trees which still form a ribbon of fertility winding through the desert, now arbitrarily cleft by the highway. A short walk in the wadi-bed beyond Amra can transport you within minutes into total silence among the trees.

Amra was where the **Umayyad** caliphs came to let their hair down, far from prying eyes in Damascus. Probably built between 711 and 715 by Caliph **Walid I**, it is unmissable for the extensive **frescoes** covering its interior walls. Joyously human, vivid and detailed, they stand in stark contrast to the windswept emptiness of the desert, and feature an earthly paradise of luscious fruits and vines, naked women, cupids, musicians, hunters and the kings of conquered lands. The first Islamic edict ordering the destruction of images came from one of Walid's successors, when Amra's frescoes were just five years

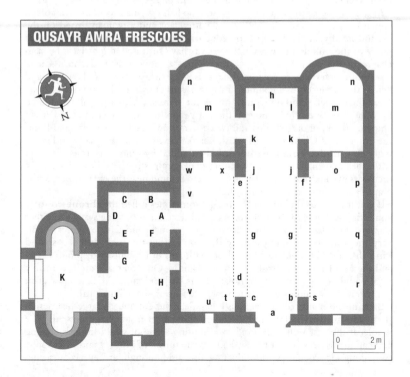

QUSAYR AMRA FRESCOES

old, but for some reason they were overlooked and have managed to survive 1300 years of fire and graffiti.

Alongside the parking area is a Visitor Centre which includes an **interpretation room**, with good information about the building and its history.

The site

As you approach the building, what you see first is the water supply system – a cistern, a deep well and the *saqiya*, or turning circle (an ox or a donkey went round and round this circle to draw water up from the well). The main door into the bath-house is opposite.

The main hall

The door opens southwards into the **main hall**, which is divided into three aisles; facing you at the back is a small suite of rooms probably reserved for the caliph. At first sight, the frescoes are disappointingly sparse, scratched with graffiti and – after the brightness of the desert sun – almost invisible. But if you wait a few minutes to let your eyes adjust, the frescoes become much easier to see, and much more rewarding to linger over.

On the sides of the arches facing you, setting the tone of the place, are a topless woman holding up a fish [**e** on the map] and a nude female dancer welcoming visitors [**f**]. Above the entrance is a woman on a bed [**a**], with figures by her side, a pensive woman reclining with a winged angel [**b**] and a female flautist, a male lute-player and a dancer [**c**], with another nude woman [**d**]. The central aisle that you're standing in mostly has real or fantasized scenes from **court life**: aside from women, there are horsemen, archers and people sitting and talking [**g**].

At the far end of the right-hand (west) aisle [**o**], a woman reclines on a golden couch beneath an awning, with a male attendant and a woman seated on the ground nearby; at the head of the couch is a **bearded man** who pops up in many of the murals and who, archeologists have surmised, might have been in charge of the bath-house. Above the figures are two peacocks and a Greek inscription referring to victory. Below is what looks like a walled city, and below that, a decorative geometric pattern runs at eye level around the room. Near the corner – and difficult to make out – are **six kings** [**p**], all conquered by Walid: the Byzantine emperor, the last Visigothic king of Spain, the Persian emperor, the king of Abyssinia and two others, now obscured (the king of India, the emperor of China or the Turkish khan). Next to them is a large and strikingly clear **nude female bather** [**q**], surrounded by onlookers, one of whom is the bearded man; he's also watching male gymnastics [**r**]. Above, wild asses, their ears pricked, are being driven into nets. Round near the entrance are some grapes and fragments showing curled toes [**s**].

If you move into the suite at the back – sometimes called the **throne room** – you'll first see leopards [**j**] and fruit trees [**k**] decorating the side walls. On either side of where the throne might have stood are male and female figures – one, very pregnant, representing fertility [**l**]. Dominating the back wall is a **seated king** [**h**], possibly Walid; two attendants with fans or fly-whisks keep him happy and there's a frieze of partridges around his head. On either side are presumably royal withdrawing rooms, with mosaic floors [**m**] and murals of fat grapes, giant pomegranates, acanthus leaves and peaches or heart-shaped fruit [**n**].

Back in the main hall the east aisle has, near the entrance, a large leaf design [**t**] beside **hunters** killing and disembowelling asses inside huge nets [**u**]. The whole of the east wall is devoted to a hunting scene of saluki hounds chasing and capturing asses [**v**]. At the far end are the muses of History and Philosophy [**w**], alongside Poetry [**x**]. Dominating this aisle, though, are everyday scenes overhead, depicting metalworkers, carpenters, blacksmiths, hod-carriers and jolly working camels.

The baths

The door in the east wall leads into the **baths**, which have a different style of decoration, probably the work of a different artist. The first room is thought to have been a changing room (*apodyterium*) or a cool room (*frigidarium*), originally floored in marble with benches on two sides. Above the door is a reclining woman, gazed on by a stubbled admirer and a cupid [**A**]. The south wall has a sequence of little figures in a diamond pattern, including a monkey [**B**] applauding a bear playing the lute [**C**]. Opposite the door is a woman with a very 1960s hairdo [**D**]; next to her are a flautist [**E**] and a female dancer [**F**]. On the ceiling overhead, blackened by smoke, is a fine sequence showing **the three ages of man**, with the penetrating gaze of the same man in his 20s, 40s and 60s. Next door is a *tepidarium*, with a plunge pool and a hypocaust system to allow warm air to circulate beneath the floor and up flues in the wall. Beside the door is a tableau of three nude women [**G**], one of them holding a child; if you follow the picture round to the right, a woman is pouring water [**H**] and is about to bathe the child [**J**].

The last room, a domed **steam room**, or *caldarium*, is next to the furnace; the holes in the wall all around supported marble wall slabs, and there are a couple of plunge pools. Above is the earliest surviving representation of the **zodiac** on a spherical surface [**K**]. Dead ahead you can easily identify Sagittarius, the centaur, with the tail of Scorpio to the left. Ophiuchus the serpent-holder is above Scorpio and below an upside-down, club-wielding Hercules. From Scorpio, follow the red band left to Gemini, the twins, and Orion. The whole map is centred on the North Star; just to the left of it is the Great Bear. Above and at right angles is the Little Bear, and twisting between the two is Draco, the snake. Just to the right, Cepheus is shrugging his shoulders, next to Andromeda with outspread arms. Cygnus the swan is just by Andromeda's left hand.

Next on the loop, 25km east of Amra, is **Azraq** (see p.202).

Qasr Tuba   قصر الطوبة

Way off any road in the depths of the desert, about 110km southeast of Amman, **QASR TUBA** is the most southerly of the "Desert Castles", and, though ruined, is the only one which still has its original atmosphere of a grand estate reached after a long and difficult journey. To get there you need a 4x4 and a reliable **guide** – either a local villager or a nature or archeology specialist from Amman or Azraq. There are three possible access **routes**. Best known is the desert track heading due south 47km from Harraneh. A more difficult alternative leads 30km west from an unmarked point on the Azraq–Jafr road (see p.205). Otherwise, from the Amman–Ma'an Desert Highway, about 14km north of Qatraneh (see p.317), a road branches east towards Tuba – but the tarmac runs out after 30km, leaving you to negotiate the last 40km or so across the stony desert. As you get close, keep an eye out for the **barrel vaults** of the buildings, visible from some way off on the south side of the Wadi al-Ghadaf.

Although remote today, Tuba was built to be a **caravanserai** on the route between Syria, Azraq and northern Arabia. It was begun around 743 AD, the same time as Mushatta, and in a similar style, with bricks built up on a stone foundation. Tuba's bricks, though, are of sun-baked mud, unique among the Desert Castles. The complex is very large and was originally planned as two enclosures, each 70m square, linked by a corridor – but only the northern half was completed. You can make out **towers** around the external wall, and around the entrance are corridors, courtyards, passageways and rooms. The arched **doorways** are particularly striking, even if all the beautifully carved stone lintels have been smashed or taken away.

Azraq الازرق

AZRAQ – Jordan's only oasis, located 100km east of Amman – has always been a crossroads for international traffic. In the past, its location at the head of the Wadi Sirhan, the main caravan route from Arabia to Syria (known as the Wadi al-Azraq before its settlement by the bedouin Sirhan tribe), meant that Azraq was both a vital trading post and a defensive strongpoint. Today, traffic passes through Azraq from five directions: highways from Syria to the north, Iraq to the east, Saudi Arabia to the south, Amman and Zarqa to the west, and the Red Sea port of Aqaba to the southwest ensure that heavy lorries thunder through the little town 24 hours a day on their way somewhere else. On the approach roads, it's not uncommon to see road-trains of twenty or thirty trucks nose-to-tail, trundling slowly through the desert together.

The reason why this little place attracts such attention is that it is – or was – the only permanent **oasis** in thirty thousand square kilometres of desert. Fed by aquifers draining millions of cubic metres of filtered rainwater into a massive shallow basin, Azraq (which means "blue" in Arabic) was surrounded by fresh-water pools and forests of palm and eucalyptus. Literally millions of migrating birds stopped off every year to recuperate in the highly improbable lushness on their long desert flights between Central Asia and Africa. Water buffalo and wild horses were common. The Romans built a fort here – **Qasr Azraq** – which

---

Winston's hiccup

Azraq is situated near the crook of the strange angle formed by Jordan's eastern border with Saudi Arabia, which zigzags here for no apparent reason. Demarcation of this border was the work of Winston Churchill, then British Colonial Secretary, who boasted of having created the new Emirate of Transjordan with a stroke of his pen one Sunday afternoon in 1921. A story grew up that, after a particularly liquid lunch that day, he had hiccuped while attempting to draw the border and – Winston being Winston – had refused to allow it to be redrawn. Thus the zigzag has been written into history as **"Winston's hiccup"**.

On closer examination, the truth is rather less engaging: Churchill in fact carefully plotted the zigzag to ensure that the massive Wadi Sirhan – holding a vital communications highway between Damascus and the Arabian interior – ended up excluded from the territory of the new emirate. Jordan's resulting "panhandle", a finger of desert territory extending east from Azraq to the Iraqi border, also had significance: with the French installed dangerously nearby in Syria, it meant that Britain was able to maintain a direct, and friendly, air corridor between the Mediterranean and India at a time when aircraft were taking an increasingly important role in military and civilian communication. The fact that the new, ruler-straight borders cut arbitrarily across tribal lands in the desert appeared not to trouble the colonial planners.

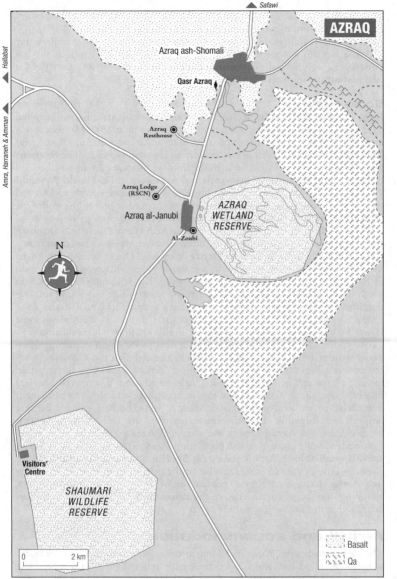

Basalt

Qa

▲ Safawi

AZRAQ

Azraq ash-Shomali

Qasr Azraq

Azraq
Resthouse

Azraq Lodge
(RSCN)

Azraq al-Janubi

Al-Zoubi

AZRAQ
WETLAND
RESERVE

N

Visitors'
Centre

SHAUMARI
WILDLIFE
RESERVE

0   2 km

▼ Jafr, Ma'an & Saudi Arabia

was continuously renovated over the succeeding centuries and chosen, in 1917, as his headquarters by Lawrence of Arabia.

However, the oasis is on its last legs. After continuous pumping from the aquifers to supply ever-growing Amman with drinking water, the springs have long since dried up. Ragged palms survive but most migrating birds head for Galilee instead. Recent work by the Royal Society for the Conservation of Nature (RSCN) to conserve and rejuvenate Azraq's **wetlands** has seen a good deal of success, but faces an uphill struggle. The underground reservoirs, exploited almost to exhaustion, are turning brackish.

It takes imagination – and an ability to block out traffic noise – to enjoy a stay in Azraq, but this is nonetheless a unique place with simple charms. It also has virtually the only tourist **accommodation** in the entire region, as well as the best **restaurant** in eastern Jordan.

Some history

Large numbers of **Paleolithic** hand axes and flint tools have been discovered around Azraq oasis, indicating a substantial settlement up to 200,000 years ago: it seems that malachite was being brought from as far away as Ain Ghazal near Amman to be worked at Azraq into delicate and beautiful earrings. The **Romans** built a fort on the site of Qasr Azraq in the third century. Qasr Azraq was also used by the **Byzantines** and the **Umayyads**, and was rebuilt in 1237 by the **Ayyubid** governor Azz ad-Din Aybak, shortly after the Ayyubid leader Salah ad-Din had expelled the main Crusader force from east of the Jordan. Still in use under the **Mamlukes** and the **Ottomans**, the *qasr* was occupied during the winter of 1917–18 by **Lawrence** and the armies of the Arab Revolt; their final attack on Damascus, which saw the collapse of Ottoman power, was launched from here.

Just after World War I, wandering **Druze**, from Jebel Druze nearby in southern Syria, occupied the castle for a while, also founding the village outside the walls in the area of two large springs of sweet water. The volcanic plains spreading south from Jebel Druze engulf the castle, and their village was – and still is – dominated by hard black-grey basalt, which is very difficult to cut and dress, giving a lumpy, unfinished look to the older parts of the village. Although some Druze became farmers, most earned their livelihood from salt production.

Barely a decade later, **Chechens** arrived at Azraq following a great emigration in 1898 from Russian persecution in their homeland in the Caucasus. They settled some 7km south of the Druze village, on flat ground near three springs feeding a large area of wetland marsh. The basalt runs out in a remarkably clear line of scarps about 4km south of the Druze village and the new settlement instead lay in an area of limestone. Most of the Chechen émigrés became farmers and fisherfolk. To differentiate between the two villages, the first became known as **Azraq Druze**, the second as **Azraq Shishan**.

Nowadays, with more a mixed population, Azraq Druze is officially **Azraq ash-Shomali** (North Azraq) and Azraq Shishan is **Azraq al-Janubi** (South Azraq) – though the old names survive in the minds of most locals. Today, the two Azraqs have a combined population of about twelve thousand, not including the large contingents of Jordanian and US air force personnel quartered at the airbase just outside town.

Arrival and accommodation

The desert roads from Zarqa and Amman meet 9km west of Azraq. All traffic is then funnelled towards a T-junction with traffic lights, from where the restaurants of Azraq al-Janubi are visible to the right, extending for about 1km southwards. To the left, some 7km along the road, lie Qasr Azraq and the village of Azraq ash-Shomali (and, 54km further on, Safawi). **Buses** from Zarqa wander through Janubi first, then turn round and head for Shomali, dropping off here and there. If you tell the driver where you want to be dropped beforehand, he'll take you to the door.

Although there are some local minibuses between the two halves of Azraq, most people just flag down any vehicle; a simple "Shomali?" or "Janubi?" to the driver suffices. A decent offer is at least JD0.50.

▲ Lounge area, Azraq Lodge

The best **place to stay** is the RSCN's lovely ⚜ *Azraq Lodge* (☎05 383 5017 or 5225, ✉tourism@rscn.org.jo; ⓦwww.rscn.org.jo; ❻), located off the main highway about 600m west of the T-junction, signposted south up a side-road. This old British army field hospital, built in the 1940s on a small rise overlooking the oasis, served for a time as a hunting lodge. After extensive renovation by the Royal Society for the Conservation of Nature – which included restoration of period features as well as some new construction – it is now an excellent hotel. The atmosphere is friendly and informal; rooms (which are all en suite, with a/c and heating) are simple but well designed; and service is faultless. Staff – all of whom are Azraq locals – can advise on activities and excursions, and arrange meals with advance notice. It's expensive (for more on which, see box, p.171), but your money helps fund the RSCN's efforts to conserve Azraq's fragile environment and support the local community. Within the *Lodge* buildings is an

Moving on from Azraq

Zarqa-bound **buses** (first around 6am, last around 5pm; JD1.50) start from Azraq ash-Shomali, cruise up and down collecting passengers, then head to Azraq al-Janubi and do the same. Stop them at any point and jump on.

No public transport serves Qusayr Amra (25km west of Azraq) or Qasr Harraneh (15km further). **Hiring a taxi** in Azraq to see these two and bring you back will cost around JD40–45 – not much less than hiring a nine-seat minibus with driver at the RSCN *Azraq Lodge* (JD50 for full day). Otherwise, you could **hitch** the whole way, or take any bus 9km west to where the Amman highway branches off and hitch from there – but fair payment to any drivers who pick you up would total not much less than the taxi fare anyhow.

At a junction 23km south of Azraq, a highway branches southeast to the **Saudi border** at Umari while the main road – used chiefly by trucks plying between Iraq and Aqaba port – stays inside Jordan, heading south into the desert to **Jafr** (after 185km) and **Ma'an** (58km further). It is long on silent desert landscapes, short on anything else. Make sure you fill your tank, check your oil and tyres and buy plenty of drinking water before you get going.

area of handicraft workshops (open to visitors by arrangement), where local women are employed in silk-screening, painting ostrich eggs and sewing textiles for sale at RSCN Nature Shops around Jordan.

Otherwise, behind the *Refa'i* restaurant at the southern end of Azraq al-Janubi is *Al-Zoubi* (☏05 383 5012; ❷), with budget en-suite rooms – all sleeping three or four – that are mostly clean. The soulless *Azraq Resthouse* aka *Tourist Resort* (☏05 383 4006; ❹) has shabby chalet-style rooms around a swimming pool; you'd be justified in wondering how a government-owned establishment gets away with illegally sinking a well to fill the pool and water the lawns. To reach it, head 2km north of the T-junction and turn west down a 1.5km-long avenue. Bargain hard at either.

Qasr Azraq   قصر الازرق

We hurried up the stony ridge in high excitement, talking of the wars and songs and passions of the early shepherd kings, with names like music, who had loved this place; and of the Roman legionaries who languished here as garrison in yet earlier times. Then the blue fort on its rock above the rustling palms, with the fresh meadows and shining springs of water, broke on our sight.

T.E. Lawrence, *The Seven Pillars of Wisdom*

Lawrence is turning in his grave at the fate of his "blue fort", **Qasr Azraq** (daily 8am–6pm; winter closes 4pm; joint ticket with Harraneh and Amra JD1). Leaving aside the 1927 earthquake, which shook some height from the walls and towers, apartment buildings now loom over the castle, the meadows have vanished and the "shining springs of water" have been diverted to keep Amman alive. Adding insult to injury, the main highway from Iraq thunders past the walls, slicing the castle away from the oasis that inspired it. Nonetheless, it remains a romantic and explorable place, with marvellous sunsets, and all the more poignant for its modest fame. A Druze family – currently in the third generation – have acted as guardians of the castle since the days of Lawrence.

As you enter the dogleg gatehouse, machicolation and an Arabic **inscription** commemorating the 1237 renovation of the castle are above your head. The massive basalt slab front door still swings on its hinges. Down at your feet, a double row of seven indentations in a threshold stone is for a gatekeeper's solitaire-type game using pebbles.

Within the courtyard, the rooms immediately to the left were patched up with palm fronds either by Lawrence's men or by later Druze occupiers. Further around, the west wall is dominated by a massive **tower**, at the base of which is

---

Azraq salt

Strangely for a freshwater oasis, Azraq has separate, extensive underground pockets of extremely salty water, which for many years allowed the village to supply much of the **table salt** used in Jordan and Iraq. However the growth of the Dead Sea salt works at Safi (which is a far bigger and more efficient operation) now means that there is no longer any profit in producing salt in Azraq. The failure of the salt business, which was once a major source of income and employment, has serious **ecological implications**. Azraq's brine is seeping into the freshwater aquifers beneath the desert and turning them brackish. Even worse, Safi's vast evaporation ponds are a major contributor to the shrinkage of the Dead Sea. It makes ecological – if not economic – sense to share Jordan's salt production between Safi and Azraq, to limit environmental damage at both sites and distribute potential profits evenly. Yet there is no sign of that happening.

▲ Main gateway, Qasr Azraq

a three-tonne basalt slab door, barely swingable to and fro: Lawrence described the whole west wall trembling as it was slammed shut. The supposed **prison** in the northwest corner features a locking hole in the door-frame rubbed smooth and shiny by centuries of curious fingers. To the north are the smoke-blackened **kitchens** and the elegant **dining hall**, and, beside them, the **stables**, supported by oddly shaped arches: a room here serves as a **museum**, displaying carved stone images of animals found nearby (which are probably Umayyad), and Roman milestones and inscribed blocks. A seven-metre **well** in the east wall was filled with water until the mid-1980s, but is now dry; the water table has dropped. Sitting skewed in the middle of the courtyard is a remarkably graceful little three-aisle **mosque**, probably built during the Ayyubid renovations. The highlight, though, is the room above the gate you entered by: this was **Lawrence's room**, accessed by stairs and in a plum position to look out over the courtyard and the palms. In *Seven Pillars* he wrote:

> In the evening when we had shut-to the gate, all guests would assemble... and coffee and stories would go round until the last meal, and after it, till sleep came. On stormy nights, we brought in brushwood and dung and lit a great fire in the middle of the floor. About it would be drawn the carpets and the saddle-sheep-skins, and in its light we would tell over our own battles, or hear the visitors' traditions. The leaping flames chased our smoke-ruffled shadows strangely about the rough stone wall behind us, distorting them over the hollows and projections of its broken face.

Azraq Wetlands Reserve   محمية الازرق المائية

Spreading east of Azraq al-Janubi village is the **Azraq Wetlands Reserve** (Ⓦ www.rscn.org.jo), a sadly depleted shadow of its former self. Before the oasis dried up, this whole area of marshes and lakes, in the midst of Azraq's *qa*, or depression, was the scene of vibrant life. Well over a hundred water buffalo roamed the area, along with wild horses and small livestock. In the winter of 1967, a staggering 240,000 ducks landed here, along with 180,000 teals, 100,000 pintails, 40,000 coots, 20,000 wigeons and 2000 mallards. Insects, molluscs and hundreds of thousands of frogs thrived; there's even a particular species of fish, the killifish, that is endemic to Azraq's pools. By 1992, though, after disastrous human intervention, there was very little left apart from some more or less deserted reed-beds and low muddy pools.

In 1998 the RSCN stepped in, and since then has launched a programme to protect the wetland area and focus efforts on conservation. A signpost opposite the petrol station in Azraq al-Janubi points the way down a side-street to the wetland reserve's **Visitor Centre** (daily 8am–6pm; winter closes 4pm). Inside, as well as a small shop, is an **interpretation room**, leading you past information boards (in English) outlining the conservation issues at play in Azraq – as well as a tank of tiny striped killifish.

Admission to the reserve costs JD7. From the Visitor Centre, the circular **Marsh Trail** (1.5km) heads off into the reed-beds. Brisk walkers could cover the circuit in ten minutes; dawdlers could find enough out there to keep them interested for hours, including ruins that are thought to be Umayyad or Roman. The water which you can see gushing into the pools between the reeds has come from Amman: it's the minuscule amount that the government is pumping back into the wetlands as a gesture towards eco-friendliness. Overlooking a waterhole near the end of the trail is a **hide** built of mud-brick, from where you can watch the birdlife – and, if you're lucky, the **water buffalo** which roam the reed-beds. Serious birders can arrange in advance with RSCN staff at the *Azraq Lodge* (see p.205) to be taken out to the hide at dawn.

Eating and drinking

Azraq's best **food** is served at the RSCN ⚥ *Azraq Lodge* (see p.205), where the restaurant is run by a local Chechen family: the meals they serve are outstanding – carefully presented home-cooked fare, including Arabic dishes of kebabs and chicken and rice, salads and fresh fruit alongside delicately flavoured Chechen

Death of an oasis

Before 1975, Azraq positively gushed with **water**, fed to the village from all points of the compass. Rain falling on Jebel Druze 80km to the north takes just a few years to filter through the basalt to Azraq's aquifers. Five springs (two in Shomali and three in Janubi) poured 34 million litres of water every day into Azraq's pools. In addition, a total of ten river beds feed into Azraq's *qa*, including the mighty Wadi Sirhan from the southeast and Wadi Rajil from the north, draining surface rainwater (separate from the underground aquifers) towards Azraq. In rainy years, the entire *qa* – fifty square kilometres in the midst of a parched and burning desert – was flooded to a depth of a metre or more with sweet water.

The abundance was too tempting to resist. In 1963, a small amount of **pumping** began from Azraq to Irbid; the oasis could replenish itself and no damage was done. But, following the 1967 war with Israel, the population of Amman in particular was swollen by hundreds of thousands of Palestinian refugees. Jordan's water infrastructure couldn't cope. In 1975, large-scale pumping to Amman began, Azraq alone supplying a quarter of the city's water. In addition, Syria dammed the Wadi Rajil, depriving the *qa* of a third of its run-off water. Jordan then tapped Azraq's aquifers deeper, this time fatally – yet still, in 1977, signed an international treaty protecting wetland habitats.

During the 1980s, Azraq gained a reputation as an attractive and fruitful place to farm: city folk began to move in and sink illegal private **wells** to irrigate their fields. Whereas in previous years such wells needed to be only 3m deep, by this time drilling ten times deeper produced no water. In 1992, after just seventeen years of abuse, the fragile wetlands dried up.

Almost two decades on, 25 million cubic metres (mcm) of Azraq water is still being pumped annually to Amman – a city which, it's been claimed, loses 55 percent of its water through leaky pipes – while as much as a further 50mcm is drawn off by an estimated 700 illegal local wells. Rainfall can only contribute under half of this amount, and at this rate the underground reservoirs have barely twenty more years' supply. Yet this shortfall is only one of Azraq's ticking time bombs. Normally, a natural balance in water pressure exists between the freshwater aquifers and neighbouring pockets of brine. However, pressure has now been dangerously lowered in the aquifers. **Seepage of salt** is already occurring, and is irreversible: once brackish, an aquifer stays brackish forever.

Almost the only lifeline is the scheme to pipe drinking water to Amman from **Diseh** (near Wadi Rum) and the proposed **Red-Dead Canal** (see p.131). The surplus they generate may mean that less water is pumped from Azraq. Time will tell whether the oasis can claw its way back from the brink.

specialities, including cheese soup, *mantaish* (a hearty dish of mutton and onions), *gelnesh* (rather like chicken and veal wontons), and more. Expect to pay JD13–15 a head. It is essential to book – for lunch or dinner – at least two days ahead.

Almost every tour bus that stops in Azraq disgorges its passengers at the *Azraq Palace Tourist Restaurant* (daily 11am–10pm), set in its own walled grounds north of the T-junction near the signpost to the Resthouse. This is truly grim, with bog-standard rice, stews and salads dished up buffet-style to a captive clientele (JD7–10 depending on choices): the decor, fake bedouin tent and caged animals are likely to appeal to only the most jaded of tour groups. Instead, aim for Azraq al-Janubi, where the main drag is lined with restaurants. Some serve truckers' fare (meat stew or roast chicken), while others – the ones with fancier decor – dish up Lebanese-style salads and kebabs to passing Saudi families. As good as any is *Al-Kahf*, or The Cave (no English sign), a sunken den made of basalt stones, with a row of neon spiders and a giant *dalleh* coffeepot outside.

Shaumari Wildlife Reserve محمية الشومري

Out in the baking desert south of Azraq, where the highest point of land for miles around is the road, raised a metre or two above the dust, nestles the **Shaumari Wildlife Reserve** (Ⓦwww.rscn.org.jo), 22 square kilometres of desert that is Jordan's leading centre for captive breeding of endangered Arabian oryx. Drive 7km south of Azraq al-Janubi and you'll see a sign for the reserve pointing right: the entrance lies 6km along this sometimes rough turn-off, marked by a grove of eucalyptus trees that is visible for miles around. No public transport runs close; if you don't have a car, the going rate for a hitch – from just about anyone in Azraq al-Janubi – is JD15 one-way.

However, at the time of writing the reserve was closed for major renovation work. Check online, or with staff at the *Azraq Lodge*, for the latest news about access. Even while the reserve is closed, it's still possible to join a **safari** (JD8pp; minimum ten people) to get close to the oryx and explore their desert habitat, which is also home to snakes, sand rats, lizards, the occasional caracal, jackal or wildcat, plus plenty of birdlife. Staff can also arrange a **night safari** (same price), a thrilling chance to get out into the desert after dark to view the nocturnal wildlife – and the astonishingly clear night skies. Either must be booked well in advance.

The Eastern Badia

Jordan tends to be defined as a desert land, yet most people – locals as well as visitors – don't ever get to know the desert, spending virtually all their time in the fertile, relatively well-watered strip of hilly territory running down the western part of the country. Although the sandy areas around Wadi Rum in the so-called Southern Badia are now well known, much less is understood about the vast stony deserts which occupy more than eighty percent of Jordanian territory, the **Eastern Badia** – covering, roughly, everything east of Amman and Mafraq, and south almost to Jafr. The Badia (pronounced "bad-ya"; from the same root as "bedouin") lacks the drama of Rum's soaring cliffs and red sand dunes, yet holds some of the most striking natural scenery in the country, from the boulder-strewn, volcanic Black Desert, or *harra*, close to the Syrian border, out to the *hamad*, or undulating limestone plateau and grasslands in the farthest corners of the country near Iraq.

Desert travel is sometimes seen as a process of combating the tedium while getting from A to B, but you'll have much more satisfaction if you abandon your itinerary and treat the desert as a destination in its own right. With suitable preparation, adventurous explorers out here will be rewarded with an extraordinary diversity of environments and some stunning natural drama.

This wedge of desert is praised by naturalists as being one of the most rewarding areas for **birdwatching** in the whole of Jordan. Recent notable **animal** sightings have included the sand cat, the Levantine viper and Tilbury's Spring-Footed Lizard, all of them rarities, and ongoing investigations have turned up 49 **plant** species new to science. In addition, there's a handful of relatively minor archeological sites that serve as a useful hook on which to hang a visit. Everything centres on the small, dusty town of **Safawi**: north lie the ruins of **Jawa**, a long-abandoned city; south is the **holy tree of Biqya'wiyya** which, legend has it, once sheltered the Prophet Muhammad; and east, barely 50km from the Iraqi border, is the astonishing, mirage-like apparition of the glittering lake and ruined black castle of **Burqu**.

Developing the Badia

Jordan's arid areas, known as the **Badia**, cover approximately 85 percent of the country, yet are home to only five percent of the population. Although its annual rainfall is less than 200mm, the Badia provides Jordan with over half its groundwater needs and almost a quarter of national GDP: today, these arid regions are seen as the country's agricultural and industrial resource base. With Jordan's ongoing population explosion, urban areas are unable to cope, and in recent years growing numbers of people have abandoned the cities and moved out to make a life in the Badia.

Traditionally, the Badia was home to the nomadic bedouin, but the growing power of urban communities in the twentieth century increasingly affected bedouin social life as well as the physical environment. Key **resources** were exploited mainly for the urban population's benefit, and services and products generated by the urban community became integrated into the lifestyle of the bedouin, reducing their sense of responsibility for the environment. Vegetation was destroyed, erosion increased, groundwater was tapped, and scarce resources were squandered. The bedouin became alienated from the central authorities.

Sheep have been a constant problem – a traditional small-scale livelihood for the bedouin that now severely threatens land resources through overgrazing by hugely expanded flocks. In one sector of the Eastern Badia, roughly 18,000 people live in an area of 11,000 square kilometres, yet they may, at certain times of year, share the land with 1.5 million sheep. And yet, perversely, the local sheep industry is almost nonexistent: Jordan imports most of its mutton from Australia, and wool is a non-starter, with most farmers shearing with hand-clippers for domestic use only. Another significant problem is **education**: a third of the Badia's children aren't enrolled in school at all. Graduates – especially women – have great difficulty finding jobs in the Badia, so the best local teachers tend to move to Amman. Badia schools give students little grounding in either the arts or vocational sciences such as agriculture or engineering; almost half the Badia's population over the age of 19 is illiterate, and just three percent are university graduates.

However, notions of the Badia and bedouin life are key to the Jordanian national character. Jordan's Higher Council for Science and Technology, with the backing of Britain's Royal Geographical Society and Durham University, has established the **Badia Research and Development Centre** (BRDC; ⓦ www.badia.gov.jo), to investigate the Badia's human and natural resources and the possibilities for sustainable development. They have identified vast potential in the Badia, ranging from mineral resources to ecotourism, traditional crafts and renewable energy, and are having some success in turning around the priorities of local farmers. Projects to introduce sustainable development in the Badia are gaining traction.

Practicalities

Transport in this most remote area of Jordan is difficult, and requires considerable forward planning. Relying on **public transport** won't get you far; there are buses from Mafraq to Safawi, with fewer heading on to Ruwayshid and beyond, but none goes anywhere near sites of interest. Even if you reach, say, Ruwayshid, your chances of being able to get out to Burqu independently – or get back from it – are virtually nil.

The way to go is in a **4x4**, well equipped with spares, communications equipment, food and plenty of drinking water, plus a local guide who knows the area. A handful of local and foreign tour operators organize **tours** – some focused on birdwatching, others on archeology – that can get you out to sites such as Jawa or Burqu. Your first point of contact should be the RSCN, either their "Wild Jordan" tourism unit in Amman (see p.51) or at the *Azraq Lodge* in Azraq. They have the expertise and local knowledge to put a special itinerary together for you,

▲ A long desert drive

and Azraq is the best base from which to explore the area. Also seek advice from the Badia Research and Development Centre (☎02 629 0111, ⓦwww.badia.gov .jo), who might be able arrange an overnight stay in Safawi with sufficient notice.

Safawi   الصفاوي

The major town of the Eastern Badia is **SAFAWI**, 75km east of Mafraq and 53km north of Azraq. It's an oil-stained, engine-roaring kind of place that's unlikely to inspire: there are no hotels and just a handful of restaurants. You may spot roadsigns to Safawi that include "H5" in brackets; this refers to a pumping station along the route of an **oil pipeline** constructed in the 1930s, which prompted the later construction of the highway alongside. Only operational for fifteen years up until the declaration of the State of Israel in 1948, the pipeline originated in Kirkuk, Iraq, with one branch running through Syria to Tripoli on the Lebanese coast, and the other through Jordan to Haifa, now in Israel. All the pumping stations along the Haifa branch were numbered with the prefix "H": H4 is just before Ruwayshid, while Safawi developed around the H5 pumping station, whose buildings are now part-occupied by the **Jordan Badia Research and Development Centre** (see box).

North of Safawi

Sandwiched between Safawi and the Syrian border are the hilly expanses of the **Hawran**, a black desert of igneous rocks spewed out in antiquity by the now-extinct volcano of Jebel Druze, just over the border. Within this strip, east of Umm al-Jimal (see p.192), are a string of rural communities and a handful of ancient sites accessible by **car**, the most impressive – Jawa – only by 4x4.

About 20km west of Safawi you'll spot to the side of the road the twin hills of **Aritayn** ("Two Lungs"); shortly after, the road swings northwest towards Mafraq around the aptly named **Jebel al-Asfar** ("Yellow Mountain"), towards the jutting scarp of Tell ar-Remah. At Bishriyyeh, a side-road branches northeast for 15km to **DAYR AL-KAHF** village, less than 5km from the Syrian border, which hosts a substantial, well-preserved Roman **fort**, dating from 306 AD.

(Coming from Umm al-Jimal, drive 7km past the site's information hut, turn left at the T-junction and then right after 22km; Dayr al-Kahf's fort comes into view 26km further.) The fort was one of many situated on the Strata Diocletiana, a frontier road designed by Emperor Diocletian to link Bosra with Azraq. The basalt walls of the overgrown fort are still standing, and some have been restored. A wander around the quiet courtyard reveals ground-floor stables and remnants of carved columns dumped in the plastered **cistern**. In the east wall one perfect arch survives; nearby rooms sport internal arches and intact corbelling. Opposite, in the west wall, is a rebuilt arched section; going through, and then looking back, reveals reused Roman columns either side of the elegant doorway. On the north side of the fort is a small **tower** overlooking a reused Roman reservoir.

The road east from Dayr al-Kahf heads on to the hamlet of **DAYR AL-QINN**, with its own crumbling Roman fort, more ruinous than its neighbour, with only a few original walls standing. Along its west wall is a line of small, internally partitioned rooms, with a hinge and a door lock still present in one surviving door-frame. At the rear of the site (north), climb up onto the highest point of the ruins to look over the large **reservoir** onto the rolling hills; the nearby white shack is the Jordanian army's frontier post, and beyond it is a square white building marking the Syrian army position. From the same spot, you can look west over one of the fort's surviving lintels to spot on the horizon the Roman tower at Ghrarba in Syria.

Jawa جاوا

About 25km east of Dayr al-Kahf – and only accessible with a 4x4 with a local guide – lie the bleak and mysterious ruins of **JAWA**, a town constructed five thousand years ago from the local basalt by an unknown people, occupied for only fifty years then abandoned. The rubbly, hard-to-decipher site stands desolate on a rocky hill; non-archeologists will probably find themselves in awe more of the spectacular surroundings of the Black Desert than of the ruins themselves. In these vast expanses of basalt, the silence and sense of ominous open space are overwhelming.

Some 2km out of Dayr al-Qinn, follow a rough track heading right off the road along the right-hand bank of the large Wadi Rajil for 5km into the desert. The substantial **walls** of Jawa will soon come into view ahead, fortifying an impressive craggy outcrop above the deep wadi, which describes a dramatic curve around the ancient city. You can park alongside a modern reservoir at the foot of Jawa's hill, and scramble up. Without specialist interpretation, it can be hard to make sense of the tumbled ruins, although the division into lower and upper districts is clear; over a thousand years after its construction, a citadel of sorts was built in the upper town during the Middle Bronze Age, presumably to serve as a caravanserai on the routes between Syria and Mesopotamia to the north and Palestine, Egypt and Arabia to the south. Scrambling around the hill, in and out of the closely packed **houses** – tiny, irregularly shaped one-room shacks – is just as impressive as stopping and listening to the silence of the surroundings, broken only by the occasional bird-call and the sound of the wind sweeping up the defile of the Wadi Rajil.

South of Safawi

On the western edge of Safawi town is the junction of the roads to Mafraq and Azraq. Almost exactly 15km along the Azraq road – but without any signs or noticeable landmarks – a side-track branches off the highway on a lovely journey towards the **holy tree of Biqya'wiyya**, well worth the tough, 35-minute ride by 4x4 across open country.

In his youth, the Prophet Muhammad is said to have travelled at the behest of a wealthy widow Khadija (who later became his wife) from his hometown of Mecca north across the desert to Syria. Accompanying Muhammad on this trading mission was Khadija's slave, Maysarah. During the journey the caravan stopped for a break near the remote home of a Christian monk named **Bahira**. While Muhammad rested under a wild pistachio tree, Bahira came up to Maysarah and asked, "Who is that man?" – to which Maysarah replied, "That is one of the tribe of Quraysh, who guard the Kaaba in Mecca." In a reply which has passed into folklore, Bahira then said, "No one but a Prophet is sitting beneath that tree." Islamic tradition holds that the particular tree beneath which Muhammad rested still lives; although there are competing claims, the prime candidate stands far out in the desert south of Safawi. The fact that dendro-chronologists have estimated the tree's age at only around 500 years detracts from the power of the legend not one jot.

As soon as you leave the Safawi–Azraq highway, the track deteriorates to reveal an old, five-metre-wide cambered pilgrims' roadway, possibly Ottoman, although known to locals as the "British Road", made of fieldstones packed together, with defined kerbstones and a central spine. This leads dead straight out across the undulating desert, visible for miles ahead without diversion. Watch for kilometre markers all along the side of this route: the first, just off the highway, is 978; after 3km of a very bumpy ride you pass a modern brick hut marked "Km 975". Around 1500m further across the stony desert is a gentle rise, on the far side of which – in a memorable flourish of natural drama – stretches a vast area of fertile rolling **grassland**, often dotted with standing water, soft on the eye and echoing with the calls of swooping birds. A little after Km 970 is another small rise, which gives onto more gentle countryside in the area known as **Biqya'wiyya**, and shortly after you'll be able to see the **holy tree** itself, which lies about 300m past Km 967 in a beautiful setting on the edge of a flowing stream feeding a modern reservoir. It's the only tree within view – indeed, just about the only tree visible on the entire journey from Safawi – in a peaceful and pleasant spot, from where stretch out vast panoramas across the open desert. Bear in mind, however, that this is a holy place, and that the local bedouin as well as pilgrims from around Jordan and elsewhere make the long journey here specifically in order to pray and spend time alone or with their families in the presence of the Prophet. Frivolity, or stripping off to go bathing in the temptingly cool water, would be most disrespectful, as would tampering in any way either with the tree itself or with the strips of cloth which pilgrims leave tied to the lower branches as a mark of respect.

Asaykhim قصر اصيخم

Some 39km south of Safawi – just past the experimental Tell Hassan renewable energy station (complete with wind pump and solar panels) – or 15km north of Azraq ash-Shomali, are the hilltop ruins of the Roman fort at **Asaykhim**, definitely worth the effort to reach for the extraordinary views and ravishing sunsets. As usual in this region, you can only get here with a 4x4 and a guide: it's a tough half-hour drive east from the Safawi–Azraq road across stones and up steep gradients, although the hilltop ruins are clearly visible from some distance away. Asaykhim was one of a string of fortified stations built along the road between Azraq and Bosra, probably in the third century AD, to protect the empire's exposed eastern frontier. It occupies a commanding position. A scramble to the summit will reveal a series of small rooms built around a **courtyard**, the walls twelve courses high in places, with a **gatehouse** and some arched ceiling supports still standing. The arch in one room on the west wall has lost the ceiling it once supported, and stands alone facing the setting sun. It's the breathtaking 360° **panorama** that makes Asaykhim memorable, far more than the ruins: locals say that you can see all the Badia from up here.

Another reason for embarking on a 4x4 trek out here is to be able to wander on foot in the natural **Safaitic art** gallery of the rugged basalt desert to the east of the hill. A surprising number of the boulders and rocks here feature some kind of prehistoric inscription or drawing, most of which are probably at least ten thousand years old: in this once-lush land, anonymous shepherds and farmers drew stylized people, camels and other animals, geometric patterns and random unknown markings on the only canvas they had available – basalt. The article "Safaitic art" by Jordanian artist Ammar Khammash, found under "Geology Tourism" at Ⓦwww.pellamuseum.org explains more.

East of Safawi

A short way east of Safawi, the highway crosses the **Wadi Rajil**, which feeds water falling on Jebel Druze in Syria south to Azraq. Soon after, you pass alongside the prominent **Jibal Ashqaf** mountains, looming on both sides above the rolling slopes of black rocks (overlaying yellowish sand) which fill the immensely long sightlines in all directions. The Ashqaf area marks a watershed, since the large **Wadi Ghsayn** which runs alongside the road further east drains water into the flat Qa Abul Ghsayn and then to Burqu and north into Syria. As you head on east, you cross the dividing line between the black stony *harra* desert and flatter limestone *hamad*, which stretches east to the Iraqi border and is much more soothing on the eye. Some 90km east of Safawi is a lazy checkpoint at **Muqat**, starting point for a journey north along the Wadi Muqat into the roadless desert towards Burqu (see below).

About 10km east of Muqat is the last town in Jordan, **RUWAYSHID**, another shabby but bustling place boasting a couple of truckers' motels and a few diners. A dual-lane highway makes short work of the 79km to the border, which is better known by the name of the Iraqi border post **Turaybil** than by the Jordanian post of **Karama**. Baghdad is about 550km further east.

Burqu قصر برقع

The *qasr* at **BURQU** (pronounced "beurkaa" with a throaty gargle: "berkoo" is wrong) can be grouped – archeologically speaking – with the "Desert Castles" of Hallabat, Azraq and others, a small Roman fort occupied and expanded during the Islamic period. However, the ruins take a poor second place to Burqu's extraordinary natural environment, both on the off-road journey to reach the site and once you arrive. The *qasr* stands on the shores of **Ghadir Burqu**, a substantial lake some 2km long which is fabulous enough by itself, hidden in the depths of the desert, but which also serves as the lifeline and congregation point for an array of animals and local and migrating birds. Proposed to become a protected nature reserve, Burqu is a wild and dramatic place, well worth the long and difficult journey. It lies at the focal point of desert tracks roughly 18km north of Muqat or 25km northwest of Ruwayshid, and is all but impossible to locate without the help of a guide with intimate local knowledge.

The **dam** 2km north of the *qasr* (which led to the lake's formation) and the jagged, broken-off tower which still rises above the ruined walls of the castle are thought to have been constructed in the third century, possibly to guard the water source for caravans travelling between Syria and Arabia. Inhabited throughout the Byzantine period – possibly as a monastery – Burqu was expanded by Emir Walid in the year 700 AD; an inscription dated 1409 might indicate occupation up to that date. The entrance into the *qasr* is on the north wall, which gives access to two **inscriptions** – one naming Walid – above the lintel of the room in the far left-hand corner of the rubble-strewn **courtyard**, next to a room with a pointed arch. In the opposite corner is a small, freestanding circular room with a cross carved into its lintel; next to it is the original **tower**, still standing to around 8m, with a tiny, easily defended door (now blocked) in one wall.

However, it's the **lake** and its flora and fauna which most impress. The journey from Muqat to Burqu crosses a large, flat *qa*, from which subterranean water rises to form the lake, full almost year-round and bordered in spring by poppies, irises and other wildflowers. Gently lapping wavelets fringe the most incongruous beach you're ever likely to stroll on.

The projected nature reserve is to be centred on this mirage-like apparition, which stands between two very different habitats. To the east is a vast expanse of *hamad*, or stony desert pavement, covered with bushes and grasses in winter. To the west sweeps the black *Harrat ash-Sham*, a moonscape of basalt rocks ranging in size from a few centimetres to a metre or more across. The rocks make the *harra* impassable even for 4x4 jeeps: hunters cannot penetrate the area, turning it into a perfect wildlife refuge. **Gazelles** roam the *harra*, in addition to hyenas, wolves, red foxes, wildcats, caracals and hares. Birders, too, will be delighted: as well as regular sightings of sandpipers, larks, wheatears and finches, Burqu boasts herons, pelicans, storks and cranes, along with buzzards, owls, vultures and even the rare Verreaux's Eagle. Rumours, as yet unsubstantiated, persist among the locals of the presence of **cheetahs**. For the latest news about access, check with staff at the *Azraq Lodge*.

Travel details

Buses and serveeces

Azraq to: Zarqa (Old station; 1hr 20min).
Mafraq (Bedouin station) to: Amman (Tabarbour station; 1hr); Safawi (1hr 15min); Umm al-Jimal (30min); Zarqa (Old station; 30min).
Mafraq (Fellahin station) to: Irbid (New Amman station; 45min); Jerash (40min).

Zarqa (New station) to: Amman (Mahatta station; 25min); Amman (Tabarbour station; 35min); Madaba (1hr); Salt (45min).
Zarqa (Old station) to: Ajloun (1hr 20min); Azraq (1hr 20min); Hallabat (40min); Irbid (New Amman station; 1hr); Jerash (45min); Khirbet as-Samra (30min); Mafraq (Bedouin station; 30min).

Useful Arabic place names

Azraq al-Janubi	الازرق الجنوبي	Hallabat ash-Sharqi	الحلابات الشرقي
Azraq ash-Shomali	الازرق الشمالي	Mafraq	المفرق
Azraq Lodge	نزل الازرق	– Bedouin station	مجمع البدو
Baa'idj	الباعج	– Fellahin station	مجمع الفلاحين
Biqya'wiyya	البقيعاوية	Muwaqqar	الموقّر
Dayr al-Kahf	دير الكهف	Ruwayshid	الرويشد
Dayr al-Qinn	دير القن	Zarqa	الزرقاء
Dulayl	الضليل	– New station	مجمع الجديد
Hallabat al-Gharbi	الحلابات الغربي	– Old station	مجمع القديم

The King's Highway

CHAPTER 5 # Highlights

* **Madaba** Amiable small town full of fine mosaics, among them a unique map of the Holy Land. See p.221

* **Mount Nebo** Awe-inspiring views from the mountain named in the Bible as the spot where Moses died. See p.231

* **Wadi Mujib** Jordan's Grand Canyon, a vast fold in the landscape now protected as a nature reserve. See p.238

* **Karak castle** Crusader stronghold, still within its original walls, perched on a crag above a busy market town. See p.242

* **Dana** Jordan's finest nature reserve, with walks, climbs and views to recharge the emptiest of batteries. See p.250

* **Feynan** Make the trek down from Dana to experience peace and quiet at this isolated, eco-friendly lodge. See p.255

▲ Hiking in the Dana Nature Reserve

5

The King's Highway

T he **KING'S HIGHWAY** – the grandiose translation of an old Hebrew term which probably only meant "main road" – is a long, meandering squiggle of a road running through some of Jordan's loveliest countryside. It has been the route of north–south trade and the scene of battles since prehistoric times. **Moses** was refused permission to travel on the King's Highway by the king of Edom, and later, the **Nabateans**, from their power base in **Petra**, used the highway to trade luxury goods between Arabia and Syria (Petra merits its own chapter, starting on p.259). When the Romans annexed the Nabatean kingdom, Emperor **Trajan** renovated the ancient road to facilitate travel and communications between his regional capital at Bosra, now in southern Syria, and Aqaba on the Red Sea coast. Early Christian pilgrims visited a number of sites on and off the road around **Madaba**, whose beautiful Byzantine mosaics still merit a pilgrimage today. The **Crusaders** used the highway as the linchpin of their Kingdom of Oultrejourdain, fortifying positions along the road at **Karak** and **Shobak** – where extensive remains of castles survive – and also at Petra and Aqaba.

However, with the development by the **Ottomans** of the faster and more direct Darb al-Hajj (Pilgrimage Route), from Damascus to Medina and Mecca through the desert further east – and the subsequent construction of both the Hejaz Railway and the modern Desert Highway along the same route – the King's Highway faded in importance. Only tarmacked along its entire length in the 1950s and 1960s, today it is a simple road, often rutted and narrow, which follows the contours of the rolling hills above the Dead Sea rift. Linking a series of springs, and also following the line of maximum hilltop rainfall, the road runs through fields and small towns: travelling on it can give you a glimpse of the reality of rural life for many Jordanians, and also open up possibilities for exploration of the untouristed countryside. One particular draw is the spectacular **Dana Nature Reserve**, set in a deep and isolated valley, with good facilities for camping and hiking.

Transport practicalities

Whether you have a day or a week, the best way to travel on the King's Highway is by **rental car**, since there is no public transport running the length of the road.

All **buses** from Amman to towns along the highway start out on the faster but duller Desert Highway and only cut west on feeder roads at the last moment. Thus, Karak-bound buses bypass Madaba, Tafileh buses bypass Karak, Shobak buses bypass Tafileh, and buses to Petra or Aqaba bypass them all. Public

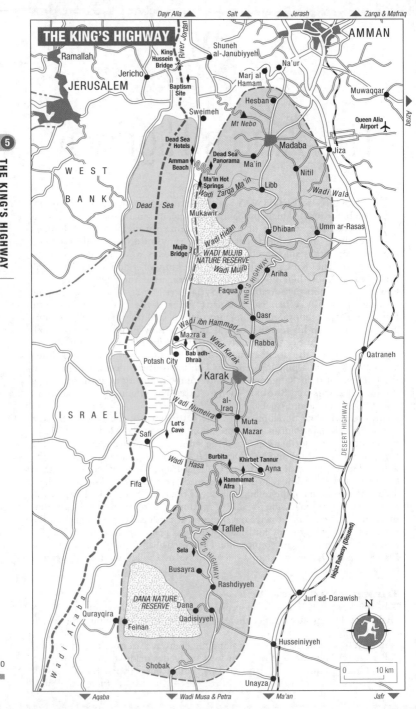

THE KING'S HIGHWAY

▲ Dayr Alla   ▲ Salt   ▲ Jerash   ▲ Zarqa & Mafraq

AMMAN

Ramallah

Jericho

JERUSALEM

King Hussein Bridge

River Jordan

Shuneh al-Janubiyyeh

Na'ur

Muwaqqar

Baptism Site

Marj al Hamam

Sweimeh

Hesban

Mt Nebo

Queen Alia Airport ✈

Azraq

WEST

BANK

Dead Sea Hotels

Amman Beach

Dead Sea Panorama

Ma'in

Madaba

Jiza

Ma'in Hot Springs

Libb

Nitil

Dead Sea

Wadi Zarqa Ma'in

Wadi Wala

Mukawir

Dhiban

Umm ar-Rasas

Wadi Hidan

Mujib Bridge

WADI MUJIB NATURE RESERVE

Wadi Mujib

Ariha

Faqua

KING'S HIGHWAY

Qasr

Wadi ibn Hammad

Mazra'a

Wadi Karak

Rabba

Potash City

Bab adh-Dhraa

Qatraneh

Karak

Wadi Numeira

al-Iraq

ISRAEL

Muta

DESERT HIGHWAY

Lot's Cave

Mazar

Safi

Burbita

Khirbet Tannur

Wadi Hasa

Ayna

Hammamat Afra

Fifa

Hejaz Railway (Disused)

Tafileh

Sela

KING'S HIGHWAY

Busayra

Rashdiyyeh

Jurf ad-Darawish

N

DANA NATURE RESERVE

Dana

Qadisiyyeh

Qurayqira

Feinan

Husseiniyyeh

Wadi Araba

Shobak

0   10 km

Unayza

▼ Aqaba   ▼ Wadi Musa & Petra   ▼ Ma'an   Jafr ▼

transport along the King's Highway is limited to a series of point-to-point local bus routes: to make any sort of distance you either have to switch buses several times in small villages or resort to **hitching**.

The best **overnight stops** are at Madaba, where there's a choice of mid-range family-run hotels, and Dana, which has guesthouses and nature camping. Karak, the most obvious midway stop on the highway, is a disappointment: it has only one decent hotel and the plainest of restaurants.

Note the warning on p.121 concerning the various **scams** and cut-price deals operated by Amman hotels keen to service the market for trips along the King's Highway to Petra. The most reliable and best-value of these private bus services is operated by the *Mariam Hotel* in Madaba (see p.224).

Madaba to Wadi Mujib

Much as it did in antiquity, the initial portion of the King's Highway south of Amman runs through small farming villages interspersed among wide plains of wheat. The edge of the plateau overlooking the Dead Sea rift is never far from the road, and countless tracks lead off westwards into the hills teetering over the lowest point on earth. The largest town, and only worthwhile place to stay, is **Madaba**, capital of its own governorate. South of Madaba, the King's Highway meanders across several valleys draining rainwater off the hills, including the dramatic canyon of **Wadi Mujib**.

Madaba مادبا

The easy-going market town of **MADABA**, 30km southwest of Amman, is best known for the dozens of fine Byzantine **mosaics** preserved in its churches and museums. An impressive sixth-century mosaic map of the Holy Land takes top billing in package tours, but the town's narrow streets, dotted with fine old Ottoman stone houses, lead to plenty more examples that are often ignored by visitors in a hurry. Excursions to the mosaics at **Mount Nebo** – the peak where Moses looked over the Promised Land – as well as numerous other natural and historical attractions (outlined on p.233), make Madaba an ideal base for two or three days of exploration. Add to this easy access to Amman, the Dead Sea and the Baptism Site of Jesus (see p.137), as well as a clutch of pleasant mid-range hotels – not to mention a location just 18km from Queen Alia International Airport – and Madaba becomes a viable, good-value alternative to basing yourself in the capital.

Some history

Madaba is first mentioned in the Old Testament as having been conquered – along with the rest of the land of **Moab** – by the Israelites, who then parcelled it out to the tribe of Reuben. The city was won back for Moab in the middle of the ninth century BC by King Mesha (as proclaimed in the famous Mesha Stele; see p.240), at which point the Israelite prophet **Isaiah** stepped in,

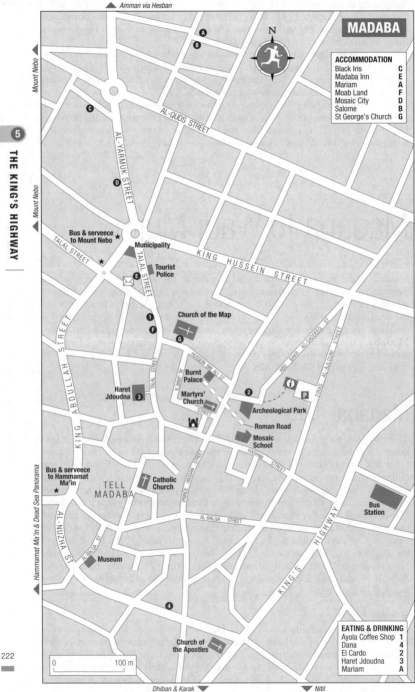

MADABA

ACCOMMODATION
Black Iris — C
Madaba Inn — E
Mariam — A
Moab Land — F
Mosaic City — D
Salome — B
St George's Church — G

Amman via Hesban

Mount Nebo

Mount Nebo

THE KING'S HIGHWAY

5

AL-QUDS STREET

AL-YARMUK STREET

Bus & serveece to Mount Nebo

Municipality

TALAL STREET

Tourist Police

KING HUSSEIN STREET

Church of the Map

Burnt Palace

Haret Jdoudna 3

Martyrs' Church

Archeological Park

Roman Road

Mosaic School

HASHMI STREET

Bus & serveece to Hammamat Ma'in

TELL MADABA

Catholic Church

KING ABDULLAH STREET

AL-NUZHA ST

Hammamat Ma'in & Dead Sea Panorama

AL-BALQA STREET

Museum

Bus Station

KING'S HIGHWAY

Amman via Airport Road

Church of the Apostles

Dhiban & Karak

Nitil

0   100 m

222

EATING & DRINKING
Ayola Coffee Shop — 1
Dana — 4
El Cardo — 2
Haret Jdoudna — 3
Mariam — A

prophesying doom: "Moab shall howl over Nebo and over Medeba: on all their heads shall be baldness and every beard cut off... everyone shall howl, weeping abundantly." After some further turmoil during the Hellenistic period, with the city passing from Greek hands to Jewish to Nabatean, the **Roman** Provincia Arabia brought order; by the third century AD, Madaba was minting its own coins.

Christianity spread rapidly and, by 451, Madaba had its own bishop. Mosaicists had been at work in and around the town since well before the 390s, but **mosaic art** really began to flourish in Madaba during the reign of the Emperor Justinian (527–65). Towards the end of that century, Bishop Sergius oversaw a golden age of artistic accomplishment: surviving mosaics from the Cathedral (576), the Church of the Apostles (578), the Church of Bishop Sergius at Umm ar-Rasas (587), Madaba's Crypt of St Elianos and Church of the Virgin (both 595) and the Moses Memorial Church on Mount Nebo (597) – as well as, conceivably, the famed mosaic map of the Holy Land – all date from his period in office. When the **Persian** armies came through in 614, closely followed by the **Muslims**, Madaba surrendered without a fight and so retained its Christian identity and population; churches were still being built and mosaics laid for another hundred years or more. A mosaic discovered at Umm ar-Rasas mentions a bishop of Madaba as late as 785.

Madaba was abandoned during the **Mamluke** period and its ruins – by then strewn over a huge artificial mound, or *tell* – lay untouched for centuries. In 1879, conflict between Christian and Muslim tribes in Karak led to ninety Catholic and Orthodox families going into voluntary exile; they arrived at Madaba's uninhabited *tell* shortly after, laid claim to the surrounding land and began to farm. The **Ottoman** authorities in Damascus rubber-stamped the fait accompli but gave the settlers permission to build new churches only on the sites of previously existing ones. It was in 1884, during clearance work for a new church, that Madaba's remarkable **mosaic map of the Holy Land** was uncovered, closely followed by many more mosaics which lay in churches and houses all over the town. Scholars and archeologists arrived from all over the world, and their investigations still regularly uncover mosaics and remnants of the past beneath the streets of the modern town centre.

These days the social and religious balance of the town is changing, in a process of urbanization that has seen tens of thousands of **Muslim** families migrating from nearby villages to occupy Madaba's suburbs and outskirts. Although **Christians** still comprise the overwhelming majority of inhabitants in the city centre (estimates put the proportion at over 95 percent), Madaba's total Christian population today is around 14,000 in a greater municipality that has ballooned above 120,000.

Arrival, information and accommodation

Buses from Amman, Dhiban and elsewhere (there are no buses from Karak) arrive at the **bus station**, situated on the King's Highway about ten minutes' walk to the east of the town centre. The **tourist office** (daily 8am–5pm; ✆05 325 3563) is in the Visitor Centre, reached from Abu Bakr as-Saddeeq Street or the car park just below it. Also check out ⓦ**www.visitmadaba.org**, the excellent website of the Madaba Tourism Association. For details of some fine opportunities for **adventure excursions** near Madaba, including canyoning, trekking and mountain-biking, see p.234.

Madaba is one of Jordan's most characterful towns, and has a pack of decent, good-value mid-range **hotels** – many of them family-run and most offering a genial, easy-going ambience that's hard to find in Amman.

Moving on from Madaba

From the **bus station** there are four bus routes running to different points in **Amman**: more or less direct to Tabarbour, Mahatta and Wihdat stations, and a long way round to Muhajireen station, via Hesban and Na'ur. The last departs around 9pm. Buses also run to **Zarqa**, from where there are connections east to Azraq. In addition, buses run from Madaba over the crest of **Mount Nebo** and down to **Shuneh al-Janubiyyeh** in the Jordan Valley; to reach the **Dead Sea**, ask the driver if he'll go a bit further and drop you off at "Amman Beach", or just take a connecting bus to Amman Beach from Shuneh.

An alternative is to book a taxi at discount rates through the *Mariam Hotel* (see listings) and share the cost between three or four passengers: at the time of writing, the *Mariam* can do a return trip from Madaba to Mount Nebo, the Dead Sea and the **Baptism Site** for JD30, including an hour at each site; to Jerash and Ajloun for JD40; to the "Desert Castles" for JD45; to the **airport** for JD12; and direct to **Aqaba** for JD68.

For full details of getting to Mount Nebo, Hesban, Hammamat Ma'in, Mukawir and Umm ar-Rasas, see the relevant accounts on the next few pages.

Along the King's Highway to Petra

For points south along the King's Highway, nearly all regular buses terminate in **Dhiban**, the last town before the dramatic gorge of Wadi Mujib. However, Charl al-Twal, the enterprising owner of Madaba's *Mariam Hotel*, has started up his own **King's Highway taxi service** between Madaba and Petra, departing from Madaba at 10am, stopping briefly at Wadi Mujib, then for an hour at Karak, arriving in Wadi Musa around 4pm. It runs each day that at least three people have **reserved in advance** for the journey (you don't have to be staying at the *Mariam*) – and only runs from north to south. His bargain fare is JD18 per person (or, if you prefer to charter your own taxi, JD54 in total).

Black Iris north of town off Yarmouk St ☎ 05 324 1959, ⊛ www.blackirishotel.com. Clean, spacious and characterful family-run hotel, quiet and well run, with en-suite twins and doubles. A pleasant, welcoming choice. ❸

Madaba Inn Yarmouk St ☎ 05 325 9003, ⊛ www.madabainn.com. The highest-rated (and so most expensive) hotel in town, in an unbeatable location right in the centre – but not necessarily top choice: feels more like a business hotel than somewhere to relax. Rooms are neat and airy, though rather plain. ❻

🏃 **Mariam** Aisha Umm al-Mumeneen St ☎ 05 325 1529, ⊛ www.mariamhotel.com. Best hotel in Madaba (and one of the best in the country), family-run and located on a residential street ten minutes' walk north of the centre. It is rated as two stars, though easily deserves three – and, frankly, puts some four-star hotels to shame in terms of facilities, service and ambience. The rooms – spacious and bright, with en-suite bathrooms – are spotless and comfortable, while breakfast and other meals on request are served in the rooftop restaurant or on the poolside terrace. The welcoming and knowledgeable owner, Charl

al-Twal, is a mine of information on the history of Madaba (which features his own family prominently) and on travelling around Jordan. Ask about the bargain rates for local and long-distance taxis. Often full: book well in advance, especially in high season. ❸

Moab Land opposite St George's Church main gate ☎ 05 325 1318. Decent choice, run by a friendly, helpful family. Roomy en-suite twins and doubles have a nice attention to detail, some with balconies overlooking the street, and there's a great roof terrace for breakfasts with a view over the whole town. The only potential drawback is some noise from the busy street in front. ❸

🏃 **Mosaic City** off Yarmouk St ☎ 05 325 1313, ⊛ www.mosaiccityhotel.com. Another fine choice in a good location just north of the town centre – a new building, with a range of high-quality rooms that represent excellent value. Also family-run, with a warm welcome and good facilities. ❹

Salome Aisha Umm al-Mumeneen St ☎ 05 324 8606, ⊛ www.salomehotel.com. Decent small hotel that stands directly beside the *Mariam* (and so often serves as overflow). Again the rooms are airy and spacious, though they don't have quite the character of its neighbour. ❸

St George's Church ☎ 05 324 4984. In an annexe beside the Greek Orthodox "Church of the Map" is accommodation intended for pilgrims and those committed to financially and spiritually benefiting the church and its affiliated school. The spick-and-span rooms – all of them en suite – are ranged around an upper-level gallery of a brilliant white internal courtyard more reminiscent of Tangier than Madaba. There is no charge, but you're expected to make a proportionate donation.

The Town

Although most visitors rush into Madaba to view the **mosaic map** and rush out again, the town is crammed with other mosaics, many of them more complete than the map and most more aesthetically pleasing. Within the central maze of streets is a large area of excavated mosaics dubbed the **Archeological Park**, while a small **museum** and the grand mosaic floor of the **Church of the Apostles** both lie a short stroll to the south. It's also worth taking time to explore the ancient *tell* rising above the old quarter: excavations are ongoing, but strolling these residential streets brings you past churches, old Ottoman-era houses and a fascinating slice of ordinary Madaba community life.

As well as mosaics, Madaba is known for its **carpets**. If you're in the market for such items, you'll find that prices are more reasonable, and quality often better, than in Amman. Many places in the town still weave carpets on traditional upright handlooms (although these days all the actual weaving is done by Egyptian employees). For other local crafts, **Haret Jdoudna**, a complex of small shops with a restaurant set round an attractive courtyard off Talal Street, merits a wander.

▲ In the souk, Madaba

The Church of the Map

Madaba's prime attraction is a remarkable Byzantine **mosaic map** of the Holy Land, housed in the nineteenth-century **St George's Church** (Mon–Thurs & Sat 8.30am–6pm, Fri & Sun 10.30am–6pm; winter closes 5pm; JD1; Ⓦwww.christusrex.org/www1/ofm/mad). Although hyped a little excessively – and thus suffering from over a thousand visitors a day in the high season – the map is well worth seeing, notwithstanding the cramped space inside the church. To one side of the church entrance is an interpretation room, where you could eavesdrop on tour guides briefing their groups on the history and layout of the map.

Although there is no evidence of a date of composition, or the identity of the artist, the map was laid in the second half of the sixth century, in a Byzantine church that stood on the same site as the modern one but was possibly much larger; two of the original columns survive outside in the churchyard. The **map** is oriented to the east, its front edge being the Mediterranean coast, with north lying to the left.

Its **size** and **style** both mark it out as special. What survives today are fragments of the original, which comprised over two million stones, measured an enormous 15.6m long by 6m wide and depicted virtually the entire Levant, from Lebanon in the north to the Nile Delta in the south, and from the Mediterranean coast to the open desert.

Other, simpler, mosaic renderings of cities and towns – and even mosaic maps – have been uncovered around the region, but the Madaba map is unique in depicting the larger towns and cities with an **oblique perspective**, as if from a vantage point high above to the west: what you see of Jerusalem, Karak, Gaza and Nablus is the outside of the western city wall and the inside of the eastern one, with buildings inside shown accurately in 3D-style, as if the mosaicist intended to produce a city plan.

Indeed, the whole, novel purpose of laying a map on the floor of the church may have been – in addition to glorifying God's works in the lands of the Bible – to better direct pilgrims to sites of biblical significance. Although there are some inaccuracies, the mapmaker has reproduced settlements and geographical features very precisely and, even by today's standards, the work is mostly cartographically correct.

Jerusalem

What you come to first, as you walk up the aisle of the church, is **Jerusalem**, the "centre of the world" and the map's largest city, oval-shaped and labelled in red ΗΑΓΙΑ ΠΟΛΙΣ ΙΕΡΟΥΣΑ[ΛΗΜ] (The Holy City of Jerusalem). The six

---

The Miracle of the Blue Hand

St George's Church is the focus of Madaba's **Greek Orthodox** community, and services are held there every week, with carpets laid over the precious mosaic to protect it. One Sunday morning in 1976, worshippers passed in front of one of the church's many icons as normal, praying and touching it. Later in the service, someone chanced to look at the icon again – a picture of the Virgin and Child, which had been in full public view for years – and noticed that it had suddenly "grown" a third, **blue hand**, unseen by the full congregation an hour or so before. No one had an explanation, and it was declared to be a miracle, the Virgin showing Madaba a helping hand. The celebrated icon, still with its blue hand, is now on public display behind glass in the crypt.

Byzantine gates of the city are shown in their exact locations and all survive to this day, including – at the northern edge of the city, marked by a tall column – the **Damascus Gate** (in Arabic, *Bab al-Amud*, or Gate of the Column). The long, colonnaded *cardo maximus* runs from here due south to the **Zion Gate**. In the western wall of the city, the only breach is for the **Jaffa Gate**, from which the *decumanus* (today's David St) runs east to join the *cardo*, with a dogleg hooking south behind the Citadel. Of Jerusalem's many churches, the biggest is the Church of the Holy Sepulchre, a centrally located complex of buildings topped with a red roof and the Dome of the Resurrection. At the southern end of the *cardo* is the New Church of the Mother of God, with a double yellow doorway; this was consecrated on November 20, 542, which helps in dating the Madaba map. Outside the walls to the southeast, a large patch of damage obscures everything up to the Dead Sea, but the four letters ΓΗΘC (GETHS) indicate the garden of **Gethsemane**.

The rest of Palestine

North of Jerusalem, a badly charred section conceals **Nablus**, identified as ΝΕΑΠΟΛΙC (Neapolis). From here, if you look between the pews against the left-hand wall of the church, you'll find an isolated fragment of mosaic showing a patch of modern-day Lebanon, giving an idea of the full extent of the original map. To the east of Nablus lies **Jericho** (IEPIXω), shown face on, surrounded by palm trees. Nearby, a small watchtower guards a crossing for rope-drawn ferries across the River Jordan – one fish swims downriver to a salty death in the Dead Sea, while another tries frantically to swim against the current. On the east bank, a gazelle flees from a lion (obliterated in antiquity). Just below is an enclosed spring marked "Ainon, where now is Sapsafas" (ΑΙΝωΝ ΕΝΘΑ ΝΥΝ Ο CΑΠCΑΦΑC), the location of the **Baptism Site** of Jesus.

West of Jerusalem are crowded more place names and biblical references, including, outside the southwestern corner of the city, the "field of blood" (ΑΚΕΛ ΔΑΜΑ), bought with Judas Iscariot's thirty pieces of silver (Matthew 27). The nearest major town is the unwalled Lod (ΛωΔ); just below, in large red letters, is marked the allocation of land to the tribe of Dan ([ΚΛΗ]ΡΟC ΔΑΝ). Below, and to the left of the patch of damage, is a tiny red-domed building, with the Mediterranean Sea beyond; this was one of the possible locations for **Jonah**'s being thrown up onto dry land out of the belly of the whale – ΤΟ ΤΥ ΑΓΙΥ ΙωΝΑ (The [sanctuary] of St Jonah).

To the south of Jerusalem, on the edge of the surviving mosaic, lies **Bethlehem** (ΒΗΘΛΕΕΜ), shown surprisingly small compared to less important towns. Due south is the land of Judah (ΙΟΥΔΑ). Hard up against the pillar of the church is the sacred tree of Abraham (Genesis 18), identified as Η ΔΡΥC ΜΑΜ[ΒΡΗ] (the oak of Mambre) near **Hebron**.

The Dead Sea, Transjordan and the Nile

Central to the map is the long, sausage-shaped **Dead Sea**, with shipping indicating trade links in antiquity. Of the two boats, the left one is being rowed with a cargo of what seems to be salt. The right one has an open sail and a yellowish cargo, which might be wheat. The detail of both crews, though, has been obliterated by iconoclasts. On the northeastern shore of the sea are the hot springs of Callirhoë (ΘΕΡΜΑ ΚΑΛΛΙΡΟΗC) at the outflow of the Wadi Zarqa Ma'in, showing pools and flowing water. To the east, all that remains of Trans-jordan is a stretch of mountainous land reaching out as far as **Karak** ([ΧΑΡ]ΑΧΜωΒ[Α] or Kharakh-Moba, the fortress of Moab), fortified and isolated on its hilltop. On the southeastern tip of the sea, near Zoora (ΖΟΟΡΑ), is **Lot's Cave** (ΤΟ ΤΥ ΑΓΙΥ Λ[ωΤ]), a church commemorating the site where Lot was drunkenly seduced by his two daughters. The four letters **EPHM** are the beginning of the Greek word for "desert".

The final section of the map is the most difficult to relate to reality. Against the right-hand wall of the church curl the arms of the **Nile** delta; however, instead of flowing from south to north, the Nile is depicted as flowing from east to west. In order to squeeze the river onto his strictly rectangular map, and also to keep faith with the notion of all the Rivers of Paradise – the Nile being one of them – flowing from the east (Genesis 2), the mosaicist used artistic licence to twist things around. The major city of the region is **Gaza** ([Γ]ΑΖΑ), on the westernmost edge of the surviving map, intricately depicted with walls, towers, streets and buildings.

The Archeological Park

A short stroll round the back of St George's Church will bring you to Hussein bin Ali Street and the **Burnt Palace**. A sixth-century patrician mansion, the palace was destroyed by fire early in the seventh century; its large floor mosaics include an image of the Roman city-goddess Tyche and several hunting scenes. Also within this area is a swathe of second-century **Roman road** and the **Martyrs' Church**, which has fine floor mosaics.

Barely 100m southeast is the impressive **Archeological Park** (daily 8am–6pm; JD2 joint ticket with Church of the Apostles and Madaba Museum). It houses some of the most striking mosaic images in the country and is well worth an hour. Left of the ticket office hangs a Hellenistic-period mosaic, the oldest discovered in Jordan, taken from Herod's palace at Mukawir. Walking right past more mosaics brings you to an open plaza; follow the catwalk over a stretch of diagonally paved Roman road (some 2m below the present road surface) to reach the well-worn mosaic floor of the ruined Church of the Prophet Elias, dated to 607/8, and, below it, the tiny Crypt of Elianos, from 595/6.

Cross over the Roman road again to the fine **Hippolytus Hall** mosaic, housed beneath a protective hangar. Dating from the early sixth century, probably from the reign of Justinian, the mosaic lay in what must have been a breathtakingly lavish private house. Less than a century later, though, the house was demolished and the mosaics buried to make way for the construction of the adjacent Church of the Virgin. Closest to the doorway is a diamond grid showing birds and plants. Next to this, and damaged by the foundations of an ancient wall, is a panel depicting the myth of Phaedra and Hippolytus; an almond-eyed Phaedra, sick with love for her stepson Hippolytus, is supported by two handmaidens and awaits news of him with a falconer in attendance (the image of Hippolytus himself has been lost). Above is a riotous scene. To the right, a bare-breasted Aphrodite, sitting on a throne next to Adonis, is spanking a winged cupid with a sandal; all around, the Three Graces and a servant girl have their hands full dealing with several more mischievous cupids, one of which is upsetting a basket of petals. Outside the acanthus-leaf border of the main mosaic – itself decorated with hunting scenes of leopards, lions and bears – are three women, personifications of (from the left) Rome, Gregoria and Madaba, seated next to a couple of hideous sea monsters.

The stepped catwalk leads you on to overlook the circular nave of the **Church of the Virgin**. Just discernible around the edge of the main mosaic are images of flowers dating from the construction of the church, in the late sixth century. Most of what is now visible dates from a geometric redesign completed in 767, during the Muslim Abbasid period. Swirls, knots and endlessly twisting patterns

The mosaics of Jordan

Hundreds of floor-laid **mosaics** in stone have survived in Jordan, from a first-century BC example at Herod's palace at Mukawir (now on display in Madaba) through to pieces from the eighth century AD, when Christian mosaicists were still at work under the Muslim caliphate. Specific styles were used for places of worship and for civilian buildings, whether public baths, private mansions or the palaces and hunting lodges of the Umayyads. During the reign of the Byzantine Emperor Justinian, for example, a retro taste for classical motifs was popular: many secular buildings were decorated with scenes taken from **Greek and Roman mythology**. Churches, of course, couldn't be decorated with the same pagan designs, but in addition to dedicatory inscriptions recording names of bishops and benefactors, and **Christian symbols** such as the lamb and the fish, **Classical-style personifications** of the sea, the earth and the seasons appeared on church floors throughout Jordan. These church mosaics served to dazzle and awe visitors to the house of God and, in an age of almost universal illiteracy, to teach the events of the Bible pictorially; the many representations of buildings and great cities may also have served as a rudimentary atlas.

Mosaic artists worked from **pattern-books** compiled in regional cultural centres, above all Constantinople. One result of this common artistic heritage is the predominance of **pastoral** scenes – which, in provincial backwaters such as Transjordan, also represented the reality of daily agricultural life for many people. The regularly recurring watery vignettes of ducks, boats and fish were rooted in a classical taste for representations of life on the **Nile**, and **hunting** scenes, often featuring lions, leopards and other extraordinary creatures, grew out of the Roman practice of capturing wild beasts for amphitheatre sports. In addition, Transjordanian mosaicists portrayed in detail an encyclopedia of **flora and fauna**, drawn from local experience, the tales of travellers (elephants, crocodiles and octopus), and the realms of imagination (sea monsters and phoenixes).

However, the controversy in the eighth and ninth centuries concerning the **depiction of people** which raged across Byzantium and Transjordan – then already in the control of the Muslim armies – led to many mosaics being disfigured. What was under attack, from **iconoclasts** both Byzantine and Umayyad, was, at heart, polytheism. For centuries, Christians in the East had been venerating religious images in paint, stone and mosaic in a way that more ascetic elements in the Byzantine hierarchy considered too close for comfort to antique paganism. In 726 Emperor **Leo III** banned the use of icons in worship. In Transjordan, under Umayyad control, a parallel movement within Islam had just as much practical impact. The Prophet Muhammad is reported to have taught that God is the only creator; interpreting this to imply that human "creation" of images of living creatures was blasphemous, the Umayyad caliph **Yazid II** (719–24) issued a directive to destroy all depictions of people – and, by extension, animals – throughout the Muslim empire. Transjordan's mosaicists had no choice but to obliterate with blank stones all images of people and animals in existing mosaics. Sometimes they did this with care, but it seems they were often in a panic: many of Jordan's mosaics now feature surreal clouds of haze hanging over what were once portraits. Some mosaics survived unscathed by having been buried in earlier years; others, laid after the order was given, avoided the issue by remaining studiously abstract. After 120 years of bitter controversy, the Christian ban was rescinded, but the Muslim injunction remained and still applies today.

Madaba is keeping its mosaic tradition alive: alongside the Archeological Park in the town centre stands the **Madaba Institute for Mosaic Art and Restoration**, or MIMAR (☏ 05 324 0723), where students learn how to restore ancient mosaics as well as create their own designs. Call ahead for a tour of their workshops.

encircle a central medallion, with an inscription urging the congregation to "purify mind, flesh and works" before looking on Mary.

The catwalk delivers you to a small colonnaded courtyard next to the hangar, hung with more mosaics, some from nearby Ma'in. There are depictions of Hesban and Gadaron (Salt), but the most interesting piece is over in the far corner. A mosaic picture of an ox has been lovingly obliterated with a tree (all that remains are hooves and a tail); similar care was taken in disfiguring many of the mosaic images in and around Madaba, implying that much iconoclasm was effected by local artists working under orders, rather than by religious zealots charging through the town destroying whatever they saw.

Church of the Apostles

At the corner of Nuzha Street and the King's Highway lies the **Church of the Apostles** (daily 8am–6pm; JD2 joint ticket with Archeological Park and Madaba Museum), housed beneath a large and graceful new arched building.

The church itself was a huge 24m by 15m basilica with a couple of side-chapels, built in 568, the high point of the Madaba school of mosaic art. The centrepiece of the mosaic is a personification of the sea, a spectacular portrait of a composed, regal woman emerging from the waves, surrounded by jumping fish, sharks, sea monsters and even an octopus. She holds a rudder up beside her face and is making a curious, undefinable hand gesture. The main body of the mosaic features pairs of long-tailed parrots; the acanthus-leaf border is filled with animals (a crouching cat, a wolf, a hen with her chicks) and boys at play. In the corners are distinctive, chubby human faces.

Madaba Museum

Just off Nuzha Street, southwest of the town centre, the small **Madaba Museum** (daily 8am–6pm; JD2 joint ticket with Archeological Park and Church of the Apostles) is worth a quick look. Nestled in a residential courtyard, the museum buildings were formerly houses themselves and feature mosaics uncovered by the residents during modern renovation work. Down some steps is a partly damaged mosaic featuring a naked satyr prancing in a Bacchic procession (although Bacchus himself is missing). Through an arch and to the right is the **al-Masri house**, with a mosaic showing a man's head and pairs of animals between fruit trees. Outside, steps lead down to the museum rooms, with pottery and coins discovered at local sites, but the most appealing exhibit is at the very back – the tiny chapel of the **Twal house**, laid with an exquisite mosaic floor featuring a lamb nibbling at a tree. Climb the steps back up to a quiet courtyard at the top, where there's a mosaic pavement from Hesban and open views across the roofs and fields.

Eating and drinking

The best **restaurant** in town – in fact, one of the best in the country – is ✳ *Haret Jdoudna* (daily 11am–midnight; ☎05 324 8650, ⓦwww.haretjdoudna.com & ⓦwww.romero-jordan.com), about 100m south of the Church of the Map. The restaurant (whose name means "Courtyard of our Forefathers") comprises two old houses beside each other, one with an elegant cross-vaulted interior dating from 1905, the other with its original colourful floor-tiles imported from Haifa in 1923; perhaps the most pleasant place to eat is in the quiet courtyard between the two. A mere JD10–12 will buy you a meal of superb Arabic food in a tasteful, atmospheric setting; cold *mezze* highlights are the *jibneh bil zaatar* (goat's cheese in thyme), the vegetarian *warag aynab* and excellent *muhammara*, while the hot *mezze* include stuffed mushrooms and *sambousek* (pastry filled with meat or cheese). As well as kebabs, there's a choice of chicken- or hummus-based *fatteh*. This is a popular out-of-town choice for gourmet Ammanis, and bookings are essential for Thursdays and Fridays.

Otherwise, the rooftop restaurant at the *Mariam* hotel is a fine choice for keenly priced home-cooked specialities including soups, kebabs and roast chicken. For simpler fare, there are strings of cheap diners along Nuzha Street near the museum and also Yarmouk Street. The *Ayola* coffee shop, opposite the Church of the Map, has bedouin-style decor and an English menu, but nonetheless draws some locals for its snacks and drinks. Two large restaurants that are geared mainly towards tour groups are the *Dana*, just up from the Church of the Apostles (☎05 324 5749) and *El Cardo*, opposite the Archeological Park (☎05 325 1006). Both do buffets of Arabic staples when there's a group in, and offer à la carte choices for around JD10 per head.

Mount Nebo   جبل نيبو

About 10km northwest of Madaba, a series of peaks referred to collectively as **MOUNT NEBO** (in Arabic, Siyagha) comprise one of the holiest sites in Jordan, with a unique resonance for Jews, Christians and Muslims alike. Having led the Israelites for forty years through the wilderness, **Moses** finally saw, from this dizzy vantage point, the Promised Land that God had forbidden him to enter; after he died on the mountain, his successor Joshua went on to lead the Israelites across the river into Canaan. In Christian and Jewish tradition, Moses was buried somewhere on or in Mount Nebo, but Muslims (who regard Moses as a prophet) hold that his body was carried across the river and placed in a tomb now lying off the modern Jericho–Jerusalem highway. The lack of earthly remains on Nebo, though, doesn't temper the drama accompanying a visit: the mountain, and the church on its summit, feel so remote – and the view is so awe-inspiring – that the holiness of the place is almost tangible. Besides, the marvellous **mosaics** on display in the church would be reason enough in themselves to visit.

The Moses Memorial Church

The focus of a visit is the **Moses Memorial Church** (daily 8am–6pm; winter closes 4pm; JD1). The first structure on this site may have dated from classical times, but by 394 AD it had been converted into a triapsidal church floored with mosaics. The church was expanded during the sixth century and later, until it became the focus for a large and flourishing monastic community; the monastery is known to have been still thriving in 1217, but by 1564 it had been abandoned. In 1933, the ruined site was purchased by Franciscans, who began excavating and restoring the church and the surrounding area. Today, Siyagha (originally Aramaic for "monastery") remains both a monastic refuge and the headquarters of the energetic Franciscan Archeological Institute (Ⓦwww .custodia.org/fai).

Extensive renovation work was completed in 2009: at the time of writing, it wasn't clear exactly what the layout of the redesigned complex would be. As you walk through to the church entrance, you'll come to a cliff-edge platform beneath a huge, stylized cross in the form of a serpent – inspired by Jesus' words

There's a **map** of the King's Highway on p.220.

in John 3: "As Moses lifted up the serpent in the wilderness, so must the Son of Man be lifted up". From here, a panoramic view of the Land of Milk and Honey takes in the northern shore of the Dead Sea, the dark stripe of the River Jordan in its valley, Jericho on the opposite bank and, haze permitting, the towers on the Mount of Olives in Jerusalem amid the hills opposite.

Within the church, to the left is the **Old Baptistry**, which boasts the most entertaining of all the mosaics in and around Madaba. Completed in August 531, it was rediscovered in 1976, when the mosaic which had been laid over it in 597 (now hung on the wall) was removed for cleaning. The huge central panel features four beautiful and intricately designed tableaux. At the top, a tethered zebu is protected by a shepherd fighting off a huge lion, and a soldier lancing a lioness. Two mounted hunters with dogs are spearing a bear and a wild boar. Below, things are more peaceful, as a shepherd sits under a tree watching his goat and fat-tailed sheep nibble at the leaves. Closest to the catwalk, a dark-skinned Persian has an ostrich on a leash, while a boy next to him is looking after a zebra and an extraordinary creature that is either a spotted camel or a creatively imagined giraffe.

The main hall of the church is divided by columns into a nave and aisles and (at any rate, before the renovation works) was adorned with mosaic panels including some from the **Church of St George** at Mukhayyat (see below), showing peacocks, a lion and other animals. One, featuring doves and a deer around a date palm, dates from 536 and has, on one side, the name *Saola* in Greek and, on the other, either the same name in old Aramaic script, or – some historians claim – the word *bislameh* ("with peace") in Arabic; were the latter to be correct, this would be the earliest example of Arabic script found in Jordan, predating Islam by a full century. However, due to the similar formation of letters in the two languages, it's impossible to be certain.

In another part of the church, what was formerly a funerary chapel became the **New Baptistry** in 597, also hosting several mosaics, while the apse of the **Theotokos (Virgin Mary) Chapel**, which was added to the main building in the seventh century, features a stylized representation of the Temple of Jerusalem and a perfect and endearingly bright-eyed gazelle, complete with a little bell around its neck.

Practicalities

Buses and **serveeces** from central Madaba go as far as the village of **FAYSALI-YYEH**, 2km short of Mount Nebo. To get to the church, you'll either have to walk it, offer the bus driver a bit extra to take you on, or wait instead at Madaba bus station for one of the less frequent buses to Shuneh al-Janubiyyeh in the Jordan Valley, which run past the gates of Mount Nebo. Getting a **taxi** to take you from Madaba to Mount Nebo, wait, and bring you back shouldn't cost more than JD12–15, a little more if you include other sites.

Beyond the church gates, the road plunges off the back of Mount Nebo in a series of switchbacks down to a point on the Amman–Dead Sea road, 1200m below. From Madaba, chartering a taxi for the return journey to the **Baptism Site** (see p.137) will cost around JD25–30.

Near Mount Nebo

About 1km back along the road towards Madaba from Mount Nebo, a clutch of restaurants marks a road leading steeply down the hillside to **AYOUN MUSA**, the Springs of Moses, one of the reputed locations for Moses striking the rock and water gushing forth (the Ain Musa spring above Petra is another). The spring itself, marred by a modern pumping station, is overlooked by lush foliage and is set in beautiful countryside – the vineyards nearby produce some of Jordan's best wine – but aside from a couple of tiny ruined churches about ten minutes' walk beyond the spring, you'll find little of specific interest. All the mosaics discovered in the churches down here were long ago removed to Mount Nebo. Plans to build a cable car linking Ayoun Musa to Mount Nebo seem to have come to nothing.

Back on the main road, about 1km further brings you to the village of Faysali-yyeh, and a turn to **MUKHAYYAT**, site of the biblical town of Nebo and home to five ruined churches and yet another outstanding mosaic. At the first fork, the older road (left) will bring you, after about 2km, to a small car park at the foot of a small but steep hill; on the summit sits the **Church of Saints Lot and Procopius**. A modern building protects the large, almost perfectly preserved floor mosaic, featuring bunches of grapes, tableaux of vine-harvesting and musically accompanied grape-treading, along with rabbit-chasing and lion-hunting. The most entertaining pieces are between the column stumps: nearest the door are a fisherman and a man rowing a boat either side of a church, and two peculiar fish-tailed monsters, while opposite lie vignettes of geese and ducks in a pond full of fish and lily pads.

Visible on the hilltop beyond Saints Lot and Procopius, the ruined sixth-century **Church of St George** occupies the highest peak on the mountain. Its mosaics are on display at Mount Nebo, but the view remains breathtaking. There are three more churches dotted around the valley nearby (the guardian can tell you where), but none has mosaics *in situ*.

Around Madaba

Even aside from Mount Nebo, the countryside around Madaba is packed with natural and historical attractions, ranging from the World Heritage Site of **Umm ar-Rasas** and the biblical ruins of **Hesban** to the luxury spa resort of **Ma'in Hot Springs**, ranged around a series of thermal waterfalls tumbling within an isolated canyon. Near the hot springs stands the excellent museum and restaurant at the remote **Dead Sea Panorama** complex, while on a King's Highway journey southwards, you might take the time to head into the hills to explore King Herod's ruined mountain-top palace at **Mukawir**.

Hesban   حسبان

Beside the modern village of **HESBAN**, 9km north of Madaba and about 22km southwest of Amman (signposted from Na'ur, off the Dead Sea highway), rises a huge *tell* – rarely visited, despite interesting ruins and good signage.

Remains testify to occupation from the **Paleolithic** Age onwards. In the thirteenth century BC, with the name **Heshbon**, this was "the city of Sihon, king of the Amorites" (Numbers 21). As the **Israelites** approached, they "sent messengers unto Sihon" seeking permission to pass through his territory "by the king's highway, until we be past thy borders". Sihon refused, and was defeated in battle by the Israelites, who then took up residence in Heshbon. After they departed to Canaan, the city was fortified by the **Ammonites**, abandoned, and then re-fortified in the second-century BC **Hellenistic** period. The **Roman** historian Josephus named Hesbus, or Esbus, as one of the cities strengthened by Herod the Great; by the second century AD it was flourishing, due to its position at the junction of the Via Nova Traiana and a transverse

Adventure excursions around Madaba and Ma'in

Thanks to the folded landscape of canyons, gorges, valleys and hills around Madaba, Mukawir and the Ma'in hot springs, there are some great opportunities for adventure trips and excursions. Although many of the Jordanian specialists listed on p.50 will be able to help, check first with **Terhaal** (⊕05 325 1005, ⓦwww.terhaal.com), an excellent professional adventure activity firm based in Madaba, with intimate knowledge of these mountains and countryside. As an added enticement, several of Terhaal's full-day trips include a meal hosted by a local family – a unique opportunity to sample rural village life and authentic home cooking.

Among Terhaal's wide range of trips, detailed on its website, are relatively short, easy **gorge-walking** excursions down Wadi Waleh or Wadi Karak, as well as long, difficult **canyoning** adventures in Wadi Manshala, Wadi Mukheiris and others. One popular route leads down the Wadi Zarqa Ma'in, from the *Six Senses* hotel to the Dead Sea shore at ancient Callirhoë (see p.135). Most of these are full-day trips, involving anything from six to twelve hours of walking, canyoning, swimming through deep pools and, sometimes, abseiling down waterfalls. Expect to pay JD50–70 per person for the more straightforward trips; two or three times that for the tougher adventures. Bear in mind that the terrain is often difficult: within the sweltering, breezeless gorges temperatures can soar and **dehydration** can strike even the most experienced of walkers. You need to be at least moderately fit and carry lots of water. The *Six Senses* hotel also leads shorter hikes, up onto the cliffs around the Zarqa Ma'in valley; contact them for details. These walks and others are described in more detail in *Jordan: Walks, Treks, Caves, Climbs & Canyons* by Tony Howard (see p.404).

The hills around Madaba are also perfect for **mountain-biking** and Terhaal offers several trips, including a full-day route from Madaba to Mukawir, as well as easy rides down to the Dead Sea and a half-day exploring dolmen fields. These run as scheduled trips (see website for dates; JD25–50 per person) and also on request.

Another option is to talk to the "Wild Jordan" team at the Royal Society for the Conservation of Nature (RSCN; see p.51) about trekking from the *Six Senses* hotel over the hills into the neighbouring **Mujib Nature Reserve** (see p.241) for a day of sightseeing, hiking, swimming and birdwatching.

Roman road connecting to Jericho and Jerusalem. From the fourth century, the city was an important **Christian** ecclesiastical centre, and remained a bishopric until after the **Umayyad** takeover. During the **Abbasid** period, after the eighth century, it became a pilgrims' rest-stop, and regained some significance as a regional capital under the **Mamlukes** in the fourteenth century. Hesban was repopulated in the 1870s by the local **Ajarmeh** bedouin, and remains a quiet agricultural village.

Buses run from Madaba and from Amman's Muhajireen station (via Na'ur); be sure to specify you want Hesban, since most Madaba–Amman buses follow a different road. The site guardian is happy to show visitors around.

Archeologists (see ⓦwww.madabaplains.org) recently uncovered a network of Iron Age **caves** which riddle the *tell*, leading to speculation concerning their possible connection to Moses and the Israelites; one particularly significant find was an unbroken pottery cup dating from 1200 BC – precisely the right period. On the summit are the fallen columns of a Byzantine **church** (its mosaic floor is now in the Madaba museum), as well as a Mamluke **mosque**, and **baths** with furnace and plunge pools. Panoramic views extend west to Jericho and Jerusalem, north into Gilead, east to the desert highlands, and south to Dhiban and even Karak, bringing home the strategic value of the site.

Ma'in hot springs حمامات ماعين

About 30km southwest of Madaba, at the end of one of Jordan's steepest, most tortuous roads, **MA'IN HOT SPRINGS** (Hammamat Ma'in in Arabic) make for a great side-trip off the King's Highway. Continuously dousing the precipitous desert cliffs of the **Wadi Zarqa Ma'in** with steaming water – varying between a cosy 40°C and a scalding 60°C – the springs (and the whole valley, which lies more than 250m below sea level) have long been popular with weekend day-trippers. The waters have been channelled to form **hot waterfalls**, there are hot spa pools, natural and artificial saunas, full spa facilities at the adjacent luxury hotel – but it's still not too hard to escape the melee and find a quiet, steamy niche in the rock all to yourself. If you're feeling energetic, **hiking** some or all of the way down the deep gorge to the Dead Sea is an exhilarating counterpoint to lying around in hot water all day. Bear in mind that Fridays, especially in spring and autumn, see the valley packed with day-trippers from Amman and Madaba.

At the time of writing there was no **public transport** serving the hot springs: the only option was to take a **taxi** from Madaba for around JD20 return (less if you book through the *Mariam Hotel*; see p.224). You may find the situation has changed when you visit; ask your hotel reception for the latest.

The approach road through Ma'in

The road from Madaba passes first through fields and the small farming community of **MA'IN**; the village, perched on its *tell*, is mentioned in the Bible, and excavations in its Byzantine- and Umayyad-period churches revealed many mosaics, now on display in the Madaba Archeological Park. Beyond Ma'in, the terrain dries out, and the road begins to heave and twist around the contours of land above the Dead Sea. Thin tracks off to the left give options for picnic spots on slopes perched high above cultivated sections of the Wadi Zarqa Ma'in; to the right, the views over the desert hills down to the fairy-tale Dead Sea, luminous blue in a valley of brown, are incredible. The road keeps coiling and recoiling in steep switchbacks until you come to a well-marked **T-junction**. Turning right here will bring you past the **Dead Sea Panorama** museum and restaurant (see p.134), and on down to the Dead Sea shore, while turning left leads steeply down over the cliff-edge of the Wadi Zarqa Ma'in gorge and on down, via a series of switchbacks, to the hot springs on the valley floor.

Two small archeological sites can be visited near Ma'in village with your own transport. About 1km before Ma'in village, if you fork left at an avenue of trees, after about 5km you'll come to **MAGHEIRAT**. Lines of Neolithic standing stones crisscross the road here; up on the hilltop to the right is a largely unexcavated **stone circle** in a double ring. Back at Ma'in village, if you turn left and head south through orchards into open country – increasingly covered with white dust from a nearby quarry – you'll see, on the left in an unguarded field, a Neolithic **standing stone** known as *Hajar al-Mansub*, carved (in antiquity) on its reverse side as an enormous phallus. Theories abound as to its purpose and context.

A mountain circuit

Likely to be completed by the time you read this will be a new, sealed road linking the Ma'in hot springs with Mukawir (see p.236), making it possible to follow a long, scenic and often very steep **circuit** of roads to and from Madaba – south along the King's Highway, up to Mukawir, down to the hot springs, up again (to the Dead Sea Panorama, for example) and back to Madaba.

The hot springs and spa complex

The road down off the clifftop leads to the **main gate** into the valley (daily 6am–5pm), where non-hotel guests pay JD10 for access to the public pools, spa areas and waterfalls (there are also pools and waterfalls which are accessible only to guests of the hotel).

The **hot waterfalls** tumble down off the cliffs to one side of the valley, steam rising from a series of pools below, where you can sit and enjoy a shoulder-pounding from the water. The two waterfalls nearest the hotel are public and open to all, as are nearby pools and seating areas, though you may find that some zones are reserved for "families" (which means solo men do not have access).

Sitting in mid-valley is the five-star *Evason Ma'in Hot Springs* **hotel** (☏05 324 5500, Ⓦ www.sixsenses.com; ❾), which includes a *Six Senses Spa*. Opened in 2009, this is a super-luxury resort: rooms in the hotel are superbly presented – spacious and well designed in a chic Asian-influenced style, with stone floors and dark wood. Every room has a balcony. The hotel has its own secluded **spa** zone slightly down the valley, away from the public areas, where you can indulge in a wide variety of spa treatments and massages. The only **restaurants** are within the hotel, although alongside the public pools and seating areas you'll find places doing snacks, sandwiches and *shawerma*. The hotel charges non-guests JD30 to access its private spa and other facilities – but may turn you away if they're busy.

Dead Sea Panorama   مجمع بانوراما البحر الميت

From the T-junction of roads before you descend to enter the gorge of the Wadi Zarqa Ma'in, it's a short drive to the well-signed **Dead Sea Panorama**, which includes the excellent Dead Sea Museum, viewpoints and a fine restaurant. The complex is covered in detail on p.134. The same road continues past the Panorama, descending in a series of hairpin turns down to the Dead Sea shoreline road.

Mukawir   مكاور

The King's Highway heads south from Madaba through quiet, picturesque farmland for 13km to **Libb**, where a well-signed road branches right for a long, slow 20km across the windblown hilltops to the small village of **MUKAWIR** (pronounced "m-KAA-whirr"), views yawning away in all directions. The main reason for visiting is to make the short hike up to the isolated conical hill beyond the village, which is topped with the ruins of the **palace of Machaerus**, where Salome danced for King Herod, and where John the Baptist was beheaded.

During the first century BC, the hill was a stronghold of the Jewish Hasmonean revolt against the Seleucids, and was fortified to be a buffer against Nabatean power further south. In the last decades of that century, **Herod the Great**, king of Judea, constructed a walled citadel at Machaerus and developed road access to the site from the Dead Sea port at Callirhoë, 8km west, although trade on the King's Highway – just 22km east – remained under the control of the Nabateans. According to the Roman historian Josephus, it was at Machaerus that **Salome** danced her famously seductive dance for the head of **John the Baptist** (see box, opposite).

In 66 AD, during a Jewish revolt against **Roman** rule, the rebels seized Machaerus and held it for seven years, eventually surrendering when faced by Roman forces preparing to assault the fortress (in an almost identical situation at Masada, west of the Dead Sea, a Jewish resistance force committed mass

Salome's dance

In an act forbidden under Jewish law, Herod Antipas, son of Herod the Great, married his brother's wife (named Herodias). When he was publicly accused of adultery by a local holy man named **John the Baptist**, Herod had the troublemaker arrested and imprisoned at Machaerus. Some time later, at a birthday celebration in the Machaerus palace, Herod was so impressed by the dancing of Salome, Herodias' daughter, that he promised her anything she wanted. Salome, prompted by her mother (who wanted rid of the holy man), requested John's head on a platter – and Herod obliged.

Christian tradition holds that John was buried where he died, in a well-signposted **cave** near the hill, but Islam, according to which John (or **Yahya** in Arabic) is a prophet, keeps two shrines holy, one for his body (the same cave) and another in Damascus for his severed head, which was supposedly taken to that city and buried where the Great Mosque now stands.

suicide rather than submit). The Romans immediately moved into Machaerus, razed the buildings, massacred the local civilian population and departed. The hill has remained quiet since.

Today, a visit is more likely to entice for the truly awe-inspiring views and the beautiful, rolling countryside, carpeted with wildflowers in spring, than for the archeology. Kestrels wheel against the Dead Sea haze above a handful of gleaming modern columns which sprout from the part-excavated rubble on the hilltop. Of the palace ruins, a few rooms are discernible, as are the remains of the Roman **assault ramp** on the far slopes of the hill and the line of an **aqueduct** across the saddle. A **mosaic** – the oldest discovered in Jordan – once lay in the baths complex, but has been removed to Madaba for display.

Occasional **buses** run from Madaba to Mukawir village. You may be able to persuade the driver to take you the extra 2km to the car park opposite the hill; if not, it's a pleasant walk. From the car park, a steep but easy fifteen-minute climb across the saddle and up some steps brings you to the hilltop ruins, known gloomily to the locals as Qal'at al-Meshneqeh ("Citadel of the Gallows").

Bani Hamida centre   بني حميدة

The Mukawir area is the homeland of the **Bani Hamida** tribe, now well known in Jordan following the success of a highly publicized project to revive traditional weaving skills among the women of the tribe, providing them and their families with an additional source of income and vocational training possibilities. On the outskirts of Mukawir village is the **Bani Hamida centre** (hours variable, but normally Sun–Thurs 8am–2pm), sister outlet to the shop in Amman (see p.119), where you can buy beautiful rugs, wall-hangings and other knick-knacks. As you'd expect for high-quality handmade goods, nothing is cheap – but you're free to watch the women weaving and there's absolutely no pressure to buy; however, if you fancy splashing out, you can be certain that what you're getting is the genuine article.

Umm ar-Rasas   أم الرصاص

A small farming village on a backroad midway between the King's Highway and the Desert Highway, **UMM AR-RASAS** was the site of the Roman garrison town of Kastron Mefaa, which developed during the Byzantine and Umayyad periods into a relatively important city: large **mosaic** floors from some of its many churches survive and are on display. Nearby is a striking Stylite

tower. Although archeologically significant, the site is a minor attraction – worth a detour if you have your own transport.

A Visitor Centre stands alongside the (fenced) ruins: follow trails which lead through the ancient city – past buildings and arches – to a modern shelter protecting the mosaics. Well-designed catwalks lead you over the intricate mosaic floor of the **Church of St Stephen**, dated to 785, over 150 years after Muslim rule was established in Jordan. The apse has a dazzling kaleidoscopic diamond pattern swirling out from behind the altar, and the broad nave is framed by mosaic panels showing cities of the day: closest to the door is Jerusalem, with seven Palestinian cities below, including Nablus, Asqalan and, at the bottom, Gaza. On the far side are seven Transjordanian cities, headed by Kastron Mefaa itself, with Philadelphia (Amman), Madaba, Hesban, Ma'in, Rabba and Karak below. The central section is filled with scenes of fishermen, seashells, jellyfish and all kinds of intricate detail of animals, fruit and trees, although in antiquity iconoclasts blocked out virtually all representations of people. Alongside is an older mosaic belonging to the **Church of Bishop Sergius**, dated to 587. Its main feature is a rectangular panel in front of the altar featuring pomegranate trees and very wise-looking rams; on the other side of the catwalk, hard up against the exterior wall, a beautifully executed personification of one of the seasons survived the iconoclasts by having had a pulpit built over it at some point.

Attractive though they are, Umm ar-Rasas's mosaics are only half the story; don't leave without standing awhile at the foot of the village's peculiar square **tower**, 1km away from the ruins and represented on the church floor by Kastron Mefaa's own mosaicists as an identifying feature of their city. Windblown and mysterious, the fifteen-metre tower (known in Arabic as *Burj Sam'an*) is solid, without internal stairs, yet at the top is a room with windows in four directions. Rough crosses are carved on the three sides facing away from the city, but details of intricate carving survive on the topmost corbels. This would seem to have been the Stylite tower of a Christian holy man; the fifth-century ascetic **Simon Stylites** spent 38 years atop a pillar near Aleppo, and a cult of pilgrimage grew up around him and later imitators who isolated themselves from worldly distractions in order to concentrate on their prayers. At the foot of the tower once stood a church; nearby are cisterns and a building which may have been a hostel for pilgrims. Today, almost wrenched apart by earthquakes, the tower is home only to pigeons and kestrels, and stands sheathed in supportive scaffolding. Restoration may be complete when you visit.

Practicalities

The only **buses** to Umm ar-Rasas run a few times daily from Madaba, on back roads via **NITIL** – this route is also driveable (reckon on 32km or so), though complicated: you may have to ask directions from locals here and there. The easier driving route is to turn east off the King's Highway in Dhiban (see below): this road leads after 16km to Umm ar-Rasas, and after another 14km to a marked junction on the Desert Highway.

Wadi Mujib and around

One of Jordan's most spectacular natural features lies midway between Madaba and Karak – the immense **Wadi Mujib**, dubbed, with a canny eye on the tourist dollar, "Jordan's Grand Canyon". The name, however, is well earned, as the King's Highway delivers you to stunning viewpoints on either rim over a

There's a **map** of the King's Highway on p.220.

vast gash in the barren landscape, cutting through 1200m of altitude from the desert plateau in the east down to the Dead Sea in the west. It is every bit as awe-inspiring as its Arizonan cousin and has the added selling-point of the memorable road journey winding down to the valley floor and up the other side. A large chunk of the surrounding territory now forms part of the protected **Mujib Nature Reserve**, offering the chance for wilderness hiking and canyoning as good as any you'll find in the Middle East.

South to Dhiban ذيبان

South of Madaba, the first of a series of large wadis slicing west–east across southern Jordan is the lush **Wadi Wala**, a little beyond Libb – pleasantly dotted with vineyards and shaded by groves of pine and eucalyptus. From the valley floor, you can drive west on a riverside road for some 15km into the quiet and beautiful **Wadi Hidan**. This road terminates in a dead end, but Hidan itself goes on to meet the Mujib River just before the Dead Sea; with a guide, it's possible to follow the river on foot for about 6km between basaltic cliffs up to the edge of an eighty-metre waterfall (which marks the start of an area off-limits to walkers), although you must then climb up the cliffside and make your way back to the road.

Back on the highway, when you reach the top of the southern slope of Wadi Wala, a stretch of the Roman Via Nova Traiana is visible on the valley floor behind. Some 10km further (33km south of Madaba), **DHIBAN** is the last town before the Mujib canyon. A signposted turn here heads east for 16km to Umm ar-Rasas (see p.237) and, after another 14km, the Desert Highway.

Apart from irregular student buses, there is no public transport through Wadi Mujib (although see p.121 for details of private tours from Amman, and p.224

▲ The King's Highway winding down into Wadi Mujib

The Mesha stele

These days a largely unregarded village, in the past **Dhiban** was an important city, capital of Moab and mentioned many times in the Old Testament. In around 850 BC, a man named **Mesha**, described as a "shepherd king", liberated Moab from Israelite aggression, built a palace in Dhiban and set about refortifying the King's Highway against future attack.

Almost three thousand years later, in 1868, a German missionary travelling in the wild country between Salt and Karak was shown by Dhibani bedouin a large basalt stone inscribed with strange characters. Unaware of its significance, he nonetheless informed the German consul of his discovery, who then made quiet arrangements to obtain the stele on behalf of the Berlin Museum. However, a French diplomat in Jerusalem who heard of the discovery was less subtle; he travelled to Dhiban, took an imprint of the stele's text and there and then offered the locals a large sum of money. Suddenly finding themselves at the centre of an international furore over a seemingly very desirable lump of rock, the bedouin refused his offer and sent him packing; they then did the obvious thing and devised a way to make more money. By heating the stone over a fire, then pouring cold water on it, they successfully managed to shatter it, and thus sell off each valuable fragment to the covetous foreigners one by one. Meanwhile, scholars in Europe were studying and translating the imprint of the text, which turned out to be Mesha's own record of his achievements, significant as the longest inscription in the Moabite language and one of the longest and most detailed original inscriptions from the biblical period yet discovered. The mostly reconstructed stele now sits in the Louvre in Paris; having become something of a symbol of national pride, copies of it are displayed in museums all over Jordan.

from Madaba): all **southbound buses terminate at Dhiban**. However, Dhibanis are well aware of foreigners' desire to travel through Mujib, and have a nice little earner going offering their pick-ups as taxis. Asking around at the shops on Dhiban's central roundabout for a ride through the canyon will quickly bear fruit; the going rate for a full car to **Ariha**, the first village on the southern rim, is around JD10. From Ariha, local buses continue south along the King's Highway to Karak.

Through the Wadi Mujib   وادي الموجب

Some 2km south of Dhiban, the vast canyon of the **Wadi Mujib** opens up spectacularly in front, over 500m deep and 4km broad at the top. Just over the lip of the gorge is a small rest stop and viewing platform. The dramatic canyon is an obvious natural focal point, and in biblical times, Arnon, as it was named, was the heartland of Moab, although with shifts in regional power it frequently marked a border between tribal jurisdictions; today, it divides the governorates of Madaba and Karak. The sheer scale of the place is what takes your breath away, with vultures, eagles and kestrels wheeling silently on rising thermals all around, and the valley floor to the right losing itself in the mistiness of the Dead Sea. The broad, flat plain of the wadi bed, now dammed, is noticeably hotter and creaks with frog calls.

After snaking up Mujib's southern slope, the King's Highway emerges onto the flat Moabite plateau, fields of wheat stretching off in all directions. The first village on the southern rim, about 3km from the gorge, is **ARIHA**, and from here the highway ploughs a straight furrow south through small farming communities to two towns nurturing minor remnants of a more glorious past. **QASR**, 12km south of Ariha, boasts a Nabatean temple east of the town, while

RABBA, 5km on – once an important Roman and Byzantine settlement – hosts the remains of a Roman temple west of the road behind the modern town. Midway between Qasr and Rabba, a side-turning gives access to hikes along the spectacular Wadi ibn Hammad (see box, p.242).

Mujib Nature Reserve محمية الموجب الطبيعية

Much of the area between the King's Highway and the Dead Sea shore as far north as Ma'in, and including the lower 18km of the Mujib River, forms the **MUJIB NATURE RESERVE** (for more, see p.135; Ⓦ www.rscn.org.jo). This swathe of diverse terrain extends from the hills alongside the King's Highway, at 900m above sea level, all the way down to the Dead Sea shore at 400m below sea level, and includes seven permanently flowing wadis within its 212 square kilometres. The biodiversity of this apparently barren area is startling: during ecological surveys of the reserve, four plant species never before recorded in Jordan were discovered, along with the rare Syrian wolf, Egyptian mongoose, Blanford's fox, caracal, striped hyena, two species of viper, the venomous desert cobra, and large numbers of raptors. Nubian ibex roam the mountains on Mujib's southern plateau. This is one of the most dramatic areas of natural beauty in Jordan – well worth the time and effort to experience.

The reserve's only base at the King's Highway end of the valley is a small office in **FAQUA** village (Ⓣ 03 231 3059), northwest of Qasr, but this is not geared up for enquiries. For all bookings and information, contact the RSCN's Wild Jordan tourism unit in Amman (see p.51), or call down to the main **visitor centre** at the western end of the valley, down by the Mujib Bridge on the Dead Sea road (see p.135). Everything must be booked in advance, and all routes are closed during Ramadan.

Most of the reserve's **hiking trails** begin from the lower end of the reserve by the Dead Sea shore, outlined on p.135. An exception is the rugged **Mujib trail** (15km; 7hr; JD40pp, minimum five people; Nov–March only), a difficult route that begins from Faqua and descends rapidly into the reserve proper, ending at the Raddas mountain ranger station. With advance planning it's possible to follow a request permission for a difficult full-day route from Faqua all the way to the Dead Sea (April–Oct only), following the Mujib River with deviations at obstacles and passing through wild and varied scenery. This links up with the Malaqi Trail (see p.135) at the confluence of the Wadi Hidan for the final stretch down through the stunning Mujib Siq. All routes require an RSCN guide.

See p.234 for details of similar routes outside the reserve, around Wadi Zarqa Ma'in and Mukawir. The box on p.242 outlines some routes further south around Karak, including the beautiful **Wadi ibn Hammad**.

Karak to Shobak

The southern stretches of the King's Highway pass through an increasingly arid landscape dotted with lushly watered settlements. **Karak**, southern Jordan's most important town, still lies largely within its Crusader-era walls and boasts one of the best-preserved castles in the Middle East. The deep canyon of **Wadi**

Hasa to the south, overlooked by an extinct volcano, runs a close second to Mujib for natural drama. From **Tafileh** a little beyond, the highway rises into the Shara mountains, well over 1500m above sea level (and considerably more above the deep Dead Sea rift to the west); up here are both the magnificent **Dana Nature Reserve** and another Crusader castle at **Shobak**. A little way south, the dry, jagged mountains conceal ancient Petra (see p.259).

Karak الكرك

A busy town atop an isolated hill still encircled by Crusader walls, **KARAK** is the unofficial capital of southern Jordan. Roughly midway between Amman and Petra, it's also a natural place to break a journey along the King's Highway. The huge and well-preserved Crusader **castle** which occupies the southern tip of the hill is one of the finest in the Middle East, second only to Syria's Krak des Chevaliers for explorability.

As well as the King's Highway passing north–south at Karak, major roads lead east to Qatraneh on the Desert Highway (see p.317) and west down to Mazra'a and Safi on the Dead Sea road, where the ancient site of **Lot's Cave** (see p.137) makes a good day-trip. Whether by bus or in your own car, the road heading west from Karak down to the Dead Sea (26km) is one of Jordan's great **scenic drives**, especially in the afternoon, when low sunlight makes the walls of the steep Wadi Karak glow.

Some history

The hill on which Karak stands – with sheer cliffs on three sides and clear command over the Wadi Karak leading down to the Dead Sea – features both in the Old Testament and on Madaba's Byzantine mosaic map as a natural defensive stronghold. The **Crusaders** began building a fortress on a rocky spur atop the hill in 1142.

Adventure excursions around Karak

As well as trails around Madaba (see p.234) and others within the Mujib reserve (see p.241), there are several attractive **canyons** near Karak that are worth exploring. Many of the specialist guides listed on p.50 know some routes, as do **Terhaal** (T 05 325 1005, W www.terhaal.com), an adventure company based in Madaba.

The full-day gorge-walk down the stunning **Wadi ibn Hammad**, 34km north of Karak, starts from a pool fed by a hot spring, accessed down a tortuous side-road midway between Qasr and Rabba. The canyon – briefly subterranean initially – extends for 12km down to the Dead Sea, 500m below, passing through beautiful mixed terrain, rich with palms, ferns and, in springtime, a breathtaking array of wildflowers. The only obstacle is a five-metre waterfall, located about 2km east of the Dead Sea road; the path around it leads right, up the cliffs, before descending to follow the lower river bed out to the Dead Sea road, where you can pick up buses between Mazra'a and Karak.

Wadi Numeira, south of the village of Al-Iraq, 34km south of Karak, is equally enjoyable. If you start from the end of the tarmac road in Al-Iraq, it's a hike of 18km (8hr), but you can cover the first 5km of dirt track by 4x4, leaving 13km to do on foot (6hr). The route, which passes through a green canyon between barren mountains, climaxes in a narrow 100m gorge, bringing you out onto the Dead Sea road between Mazra'a and Safi. You may need a rope for a 5m drop at one point.

These walks and others in the area are described in more detail in *Jordan: Walks, Treks, Caves, Climbs & Canyons* by Tony Howard (see p.404).

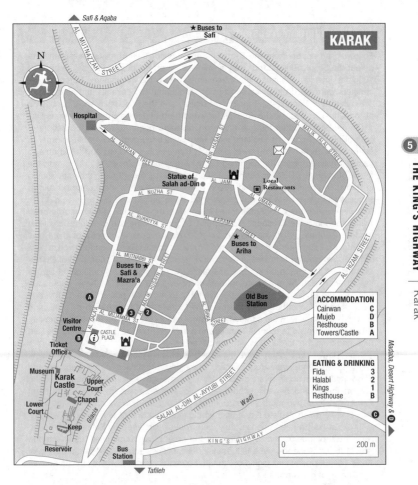

KARAK

Safi & Aqaba

★ Buses to Safi

Hospital

Statue of Salah ad-Din

Local Restaurants

Buses to Ariha ★

Buses to Safi & Mazra'a ★

Old Bus Station

Visitor Centre

Ticket Office

Museum

Karak Castle

Upper Court

Chapel

Lower Court

Glacis

Keep

Reservoir

Bus Station

Tafileh

Madaba, Desert Highway & D

ACCOMMODATION	
Cairwan	C
Mujeb	D
Resthouse	B
Towers/Castle	A

EATING & DRINKING	
Fida	3
Halabi	2
Kings	1
Resthouse	B

0   200 m

KING'S HIGHWAY

The castle's construction was initiated by the knights of the successful First Crusade, but its eventual downfall is inextricably linked with the personalities of those who came later, specifically **Reynald of Chatillon**. A ruthless warrior who arrived in the Holy Land in 1147 on the Second Crusade, Reynald was both vicious and unscrupulous, and it was specifically to avenge his treachery that the Muslim commander, **Salah ad-Din**, launched a campaign to expel the foreign invaders. In 1177, Reynald married Lady Stephanie, widow of the Lord of Oultrejourdain. Safely ensconced in Karak, he began a reign characterized by wanton cruelty: one of his more notorious pleasures involved encasing the heads of his prisoners in wooden boxes so that, when he flung them off the castle walls, he could be sure that they hadn't lost consciousness by the time they hit the rocks below. In 1180, he robbed a Mecca-bound caravan on the King's Highway in violation of a truce; Salah ad-Din was forced to swallow his anger until a suitable time for revenge could be found.

In 1183, the wedding of Reynald's heir was celebrated within the walls of Karak castle at the very moment that Salah ad-Din and his army, having already

The Crusaders in Transjordan

Following an appeal from the Byzantine emperor for foreign military assistance to defeat the Seljuk Turks, it took only a few years from the pope's first call to arms of 1095 for invading Christian European armies to seize **Jerusalem**. European-run statelets were set up in quick succession throughout the Levant – the Kingdom of Jerusalem, the Counties of Tripoli and Edessa, and the Principality of Antioch. One of the Christian lords, **Baldwin**, was crowned King of Jerusalem on Christmas Day 1100, and it was under his rule that the Crusaders began to realize the benefit of controlling the Transjordanian land route from Syria into Egypt and Arabia, in order to stand between the Muslim power bases in Damascus and Cairo and to be able to harass Muslims making the pilgrimage to the Arabian holy places. In 1107, simply the threat of attack by Baldwin's army persuaded a Seljuk force to flee their stronghold in **Petra**, and persistent harrying over a decade or more in the area around **Ajloun** successfully played havoc with established trade patterns in the region. In 1115, Baldwin crossed the Wadi Araba from Hebron with the intention of fully incorporating Transjordan into the Crusader realms, and began construction of a large castle at modern **Shobak**, which he named *Le Krak de Montreal* ("Fortress of the Royal Mountain"). Establishment of a string of Crusader possessions soon followed, at Aila (Aqaba), Wu'ayra and Habees at Petra, and Tafileh. However, the Lordship of Oultre-jourdain, as it came to be known, was far from impregnable, and infiltration across the River Jordan by a Muslim raiding party in 1139 seems to have persuaded Paganus the Butler, by then the effective ruler, to move his power base northwards from Shobak. Construction of the massive fortress at **Karak** began in 1142, and twenty years later, with the addition of another citadel at Ahamant (possibly Amman), Crusader-controlled territory in Transjordan extended from the River Zarqa to the Red Sea, and from the Jordan Valley to the desert.

Such power was short-lived, however. Between 1169 and 1174, the Karak headquarters underwent four sieges, managing to survive partly because the opposing Muslim armies were divided. By 1174, though, Salah ad-Din had united the Muslim forces and began methodically to oust the Crusaders from Transjordan. Karak withstood two more sieges during 1183, but the tide was turning: the Latin armies were much depleted, and their young king, Baldwin IV, was dying of leprosy. In 1187, at **Hattin** near Tiberias, they were roundly defeated by Salah ad-Din, who soon after took Jerusalem. Wu'ayra and the great prize, Karak itself, capitulated in late 1188, and Shobak – the last Transjordanian possession – fell in the spring of 1189. The Europeans struggled on, but just a century later the entire Holy Land was once again under Arab rule.

invaded the town, were poised just beyond the north moat ready to attack. Lady Stephanie sent plates of food from the banquet to the Muslim army beyond the walls; in response, while his men were trying to bridge the moat and catapulting rocks against the walls, Salah ad-Din enquired which tower the newly-weds were occupying. In an expression of his impeccable chivalry, he then ordered his army to direct their fire elsewhere.

Karak withstood that siege, but at the **Battle of Hattin** in 1187, the Crusaders, stymied by the strategic ineptitude of Reynald and others, were defeated. The victorious Salah ad-Din characteristically spared the king and the Crusader lords – all apart from Reynald, whom he personally decapitated. The besieged Crusader garrison at Karak held out for months; they sold their wives and children in exchange for food, and resorted to eating horses and dogs, but surrender was inevitable. Karak capitulated in November 1188.

Ayyubid and **Mamluke** occupiers of the castle rebuilt and strengthened its defences. Under the **Ottomans**, anarchy was the rule rather than the exception. During a rebellion in 1879, Karaki Christians abandoned their town, moving north to settle among the ruins of ancient Madaba. In 1894, troops finally imposed order but Karak's ruling families – among them, the Majali clan – remained restless. In 1908 they rallied a local force and stormed Karak's government buildings, forcing the Ottoman garrison to seek refuge in the castle. After eight days, troops arrived from Damascus, publicly executed the rebel leaders and declared the Majalis outlaws. Even today Karak retains a reputation for political activism, yet – a little ironically, considering the family history – the Majalis are now at the heart of the Jordanian establishment, boasting government officials and even a prime minister or two among their number.

Arrival and accommodation

The King's Highway makes a poorly signposted zigzag around Karak; if you're **driving** it's easy to get confused. At a T-junction 12km south of Rabba, just by the *Mujeb Hotel*, turning left leads 34km west to Qatraneh on the Desert Highway (see p.317), while turning right brings you 4km through hilly suburbs to another T-junction at the foot of Karak castle. From here, turn left for the King's Highway to Tafileh, turn right to spiral up the hill into Karak. As you drive up, the only road through the walls into Karak town centre is a poorly marked turning on the left at the crest of the hill, just before an archway. If you miss it and start going down the back of the hill, make a U-turn: this road continues all the way down to the Dead Sea.

Buses from Amman (via the Desert Highway), Ma'an, Tafileh, Aqaba and elsewhere arrive at the bus station, at the foot of the hill by the King's Highway junction outside town. The only viable way to get to the castle from here is by taxi.

Karak stands halfway between Amman and Petra, and appears to make sense as an overnight stop, but in truth you'd do much better to press on to Dana: with one exception Karak's **hotels** are a disappointment.

Cairwan facing the town across a valley ☎03 239 6022 or 079 525 0216, Ⓔ moaweyahf@hotmail.com. Best of Karak's few hotels, a clean, well-cared-for guesthouse converted from a family home: interiors are cosy, with armchairs, sofas, polished brass and an old gramophone, while guest rooms (all en suite) are decent and comfortable. They also have a spacious apartment, holding two double rooms, two bathrooms (with a jacuzzi), a lounge and a kitchenette (JD40–50, depending on the season). It's fairly simple – don't expect boutique chic – but cosy and pleasant. Air conditioning costs extra. ❸–❹

Mujeb 4km east of Karak, at the junction of the King's Highway from Rabba and the Desert Highway link from Qatraneh ☎03 238 6090. A very tired hotel that makes a living from serving lunches to passing tour groups: the dining room is pleasant and the welcome is warm, but stay overnight and you're paying for dirty rooms, greasy carpets, threadbare sheets, broken fittings and a musty air of neglect. No public transport into town. ❸–❹

Resthouse about 50m north of the castle ☎03 235 1148. Long-standing tourist hotel and restaurant beside the castle that is well past its best. The rooms (all en suite) tread the thin line between retro character and merely being old. They are overpriced because of the handy location, and all have memorable views over the valley below. Not to be confused with the nearby *Guest House* or *Best House*. ❹

Towers/Castle about 100m north of the castle ☎03 235 4289. Adequate budget hotel near the castle. Cheaper rooms share a bathroom, while slightly more expensive en-suite ones on upper floors boast good valley views. Nonetheless, pretty basic. ❷–❸

There's a **map** of the King's Highway on p.220.

Buses for **Amman**'s Wihdat station and Ma'an (via the Desert Highway), **Tafileh** (via the King's Highway) and **Aqaba** (via the Dead Sea/Wadi Araba road) only operate between 7am and about noon. You might be lucky and find a bus after that time, but don't rely on it. To get to **Dana**, take a bus to Tafileh and another to Qadisiyyeh, or opt for a taxi (about JD30). Buses north along the King's Highway, terminating in **Ariha** on the rim of Wadi Mujib, leave from a side-street in the middle of town; to get to **Madaba** from Ariha, you'll have to hitch through the canyon to **Dhiban** (see p.239) and catch another bus there northwards. Buses to **Mazra'a** and **Safi** on the Dead Sea shore leave from a different street corner in town and go past Bab adh-Dhraa; those for Safi also go past the turn-off for Lot's Cave.

From Karak to Petra
One bus may leave Karak around 3pm for **Wadi Musa/Petra** (JD5), but only via the Desert Highway. Otherwise catch a bus to **Ma'an** and change there for a minibus or serveece to Wadi Musa. If you want to follow the King's Highway to Petra, the slow way of getting there involves a minibus to **Tafileh**, another to **Qadisiyyeh**, hitching to **Shobak** and a minibus or serveece into Wadi Musa: it's likely to take all day. Otherwise, the quicker option by **taxi** (2hr 30min) costs JD50–60 for a full car (about double what it would be via the Desert Highway): ask your hotel or staff at the castle visitor centre to hunt down a driver, or just stop one on the street and ask.

The Town

Everything you need in Karak is within a few minutes' stroll of the castle, at the highest point of town. Just in front of the castle is the **Castle Plaza** area, a tasteful complex of restored Ottoman buildings around a newly paved plaza beneath the castle walls, including the old al-Hammidi mosque and a **Visitor Centre** (Sat–Thurs 8am–5pm, Fri 10am–4pm).

In sharp contrast is Karak's humdrum town centre. Venturing down any of the narrow streets that lead north from the castle – most of them lined with grand but grimy Ottoman-era balconied stone buildings – will bring you nose-to-nose with Karak's bustling everyday shops and markets. The focus of town is an equestrian statue of Salah ad-Din, occupying a traffic junction about 400m north of the castle, around which spreads Karak's souk.

Karak castle   قلعة الكرك

Occupying a rocky spur on the southern edge of the town centre, **Karak castle** is first, and most impressively, visible on the approach from the east, its restored walls and glacis looming above the ravine below. **Admission** (Sat–Thurs 8am–5pm, Fri 10am–4pm; JD1) is across a wooden footbridge spanning the moat from behind the Castle Plaza complex. The castle has seven separate levels, some buried deep inside the hill, and the best way to explore is to take a **torch** and simply let your inquisitiveness run free: it's quite possible to spend two or three atmospheric hours poking into dark rooms and gloomy vaulted passageways.

A good place to start is by heading up the slope once you enter, then doubling back on yourself into a long, vaulted passageway along the inside of the huge north wall built by the Crusaders. Down here, close to the original entrance of the castle in the northeastern corner, are a **barracks** and, on the right, the **kitchens**, complete with olive press and, further within, a huge oven. You emerge along the **east wall**, close to the ruined **chapel**. Over the battlements the restored glacis heralds a dizzy drop, and facing you is the partly complete

Mamluke **keep**, the best-protected part of the castle. It's not difficult to climb to the highest point, from where there are scarily vertiginous views in all directions. In a sunken area between the chapel and the keep lie the remains of a Mamluke **palace**, while at the bottom of some steps just behind the chapel's apse is a beautifully carved stone panel. Of the two rooms opposite the panel, the one on the right features some reused Nabatean blocks set into the wall; next door, Reynald's extensive and suitably dank **dungeons** lead off into the hill. Back at the carved panel, a passageway to the left eventually brings you out, after passing another barracks, near the entrance. If you head down from here to the lower western side of the castle, you'll come across the **museum**, offering fascinating background to the history of the castle and the local area. Equally interesting is a restored Mamluke **gallery** nearby, running virtually the length of the west wall at the lowest level of the castle.

Eating and drinking

Karak's **restaurants** are pretty uninspiring. Opposite the castle are the touristy *Kings* and *Fida*, with mediocre kebab and chicken dishes, slightly bettered by the buffets served up at the *Resthouse* beside the castle. Just round the corner from the *Fida*, the Syrian-run *Halabi* is the height of friendliness and, although the simple fare is nothing to write home about, the cosy interior is an atmospheric place to sit and eat. The town centre has a host of ordinary Arabic eateries – but you'd do better to take a taxi 3km out of town to the lively, student-oriented suburb Al-Marj, where you'll find a clutch of good hummus and falafel restaurants, terrace cafés for smoking *argileh* and a hint of nightlife.

South of Karak

The King's Highway floats along the wheat-sown plateau south of Karak for 10km to **MUTA**, best known today as the home of one of Jordan's leading universities, but also the scene, in 629 AD, of the first major battle between the Byzantine Empire and the nascent Muslim army on its first surge out of Arabia. On this occasion, the Muslims were routed, and its generals, including the Prophet Muhammad's adopted son Zaid bin Haritha and his deputy Jaafar bin Abi Talib, were killed. Some 3km south of Muta on the King's Highway, in the town of **MAZAR**, a large, royally funded mosque has been constructed over the shrines of Zaid and Jaafar.

South of Mazar, the landscape becomes increasingly wild. The major natural feature here is the immense **Wadi Hasa**, replete with hot springs at Hammamat Afra and an ancient Nabatean temple atop Jebel Tannur. Further south, past the attractive regional capital of **Tafileh**, the hills rise further, to the RSCN nature reserve at **Dana** and on to **Shobak**, site of a ruined Crusader castle.

Khirbet Tannur   الخربة التنور

A little way out of Mazar, two roads, old and new, descend past the cultivated fields of Ayna village into the vast **Wadi Hasa**, a natural boundary which marked the transition from Moab into the land of Edom. Dominating the

247

There's a **map** of the King's Highway on p.220.

wadi is a huge and elementally scary **black mountain** – actually an extinct volcano – which clashes so startlingly with the white limestone all around that it seems to be under a permanent, ominous cloud. The Nabateans clearly felt something similar, since they built, on the conical hill of Jebel Tannur directly opposite, a large temple complex, **Khirbet Tannur**, ruined today but still visitable.

As you rise out of the wadi bed, a broken concrete sign on the right side of the highway, 24km from Mazar, marks the track leading to Khirbet Tannur. This is passable for a little way by car, but eventually you'll have to get out and make the tough climb across a saddle and up the steep slope to the atmospheric ruins. The temple area dates from the second century AD. Unfortunately, excavations in the 1930s carted off virtually everything of any interest, and all the carving and statuary that used to adorn the site now gathers dust in museums in Amman and Cincinnati. Yet, however hard it is to imagine the complete structures which once stood here, the windswept isolation of this rugged summit resurrects the presence of the Nabatean gods more potently even than Petra's quietest cranny.

You arrive on the summit more or less where the Nabatean worshippers would have arrived: in front is a humped threshold, originally part of the entrance **gateway** to a paved courtyard. It's easy to make out the wall foundations of three **rooms** to the right, and although only random chunks of decorative carving survive, many of the courtyard's **flagstones** are still in place. Ahead is a raised platform on which stood the small **temple**, its entrance originally crowned with a large carved image of the goddess Atargatis bedecked with vines and fruit (now on display in Amman). Within the holy of holies stood images both of Atargatis and the god Zeus-Hadad.

Hammamat Afra   حمامات عفراء

Barely 2km from the Khirbet Tannur turning, the King's Highway is carried over Wadi Laban, a tributary of Wadi Hasa, on a small bridge; no buses follow the small turning off to the right side, but private transport can take you further along this narrow and winding side-road deep into the valley to reach a set of hot springs. Bear in mind that these are popular weekend getaways for local families: head out here on a Friday and you're unlikely to be alone.

A turn-off after 7km leads down to **Hammamat Burbita**, in a broad and sunny part of the valley, with the river fringed by reed-beds and some cultivation – but the only access to the thermal springs here is within a rather grim, graffitied concrete complex. You'd do better to head back up and continue along the road.

After 5km of narrow switchbacks, high above the valley floor, you reach a gate across the road giving access to **HAMMAMAT AFRA** (open 24hr; JD5). There are some leisure facilities here, but this is not a tourist spa: the atmosphere is unequivocally Jordanian. The **hot pools** (four outdoor ones for men, one indoors for women) are set down in a gorge between high, narrow cliffs that cut out most of the direct sunshine, and are generally well maintained. The water is a striking rust-red colour from the high iron content, and genuinely hot: the last pool on the left – popularly known as the *megla*, or frying pan – is a broiling 52°C. The walls all along the narrow valley drip water, with mineral reds and mossy greens daubing the white limestone. Splashing barefoot up or down the warm river here is as much pleasure as flopping around in the pools with everybody else. A couple of kiosks sell snacks and cold drinks, but most people set up barbecues on the various terraces around the site. Simple **chalets** (❷) offer basic overnight accommodation.

Tafileh الطفيلة

South of Wadi Hasa, the King's Highway begins to climb into the Shara mountains, eventually reaching a small plateau where a road branches east (left) to the Desert Highway (if you're heading north along the King's Highway, the signposting at this junction is confusing and it's easy to lose the way). It was near here that, in January 1918, the only fully fledged battle of the Arab Revolt took place, Faysal and Lawrence's armies sweeping away an Ottoman force only to be halted in their tracks by heavy snow.

Some 25km south of the turn-off for Hammamat Afra, the picturesque town of **TAFILEH** comes into view, spread along gently curving terraces, with orchards of fruit and olives blanketing the hillside below. Although a governorate capital and a sizeable town, Tafileh has no specific attractions to make for (the signposted "castle" in the middle of town comprises a single, inaccessible tower, most likely Mamluke), and you'll probably find yourself stopping only to switch buses. However, note that buses stop running by about midday: if you arrive in the afternoon you'll find no buses to Dana, Petra or Amman – and so your only option will be to negotiate with the local taxi-drivers.

About 4km south of Tafileh is a turn-off westwards, signed for Aqaba and Fifa. This is the last surfaced road connecting the King's Highway and Wadi Araba until you reach Aqaba. It offers truly spectacular views out over the desert as it coils down to **Fifa** (see p.137), just south of the Dead Sea.

Sela السلع

In the rugged hills south of Tafileh looms the remote mountain fastness of **SELA**, which offers a taxing but memorable hike up to a summit with magnificent views. The village of **Ain al-Baydha**, about 10km south of Tafileh, marks a turn-off heading steeply down the cliffside to the picturesque hamlet of **As-Sil**, with old stone cottages – not unlike Dana (see p.250) – clustering higgledy-piggledy on an outcrop. The giant sandstone mountain of Sela looms opposite the hamlet, on the other side of a deep ravine; As-Sil is just about accessible by ordinary car, but to go on you'll have to resort to 4x4 or your own leg-muscles. A **guide** is essential, since this is barren and inhospitable terrain. Either start out early in the day, and ask around for help in Ain al-Baydha village, or consult the RSCN staff at Dana in advance.

A biblical account in II Kings narrates the story of the seventh-century BC King Amaziah of Judah, who attacked Edom, defeated a ten-thousand-strong army and seized "Selah", while II Chronicles says that, during the same campaign, Amaziah threw ten thousand captive Edomites off the "rock". Some archeologists have related present-day Sela with these events (the Hebrew word for "rock" is *sela*), but others have suggested that these events took place at the similarly remote, inaccessible mountain Umm al-Biyara at Petra – partly since the Greek word *petra* also means "rock". Neither case has been conclusively proved, and even the discovery of a worn **inscription** in Babylonian cuneiform, carved in a smoothed rectangle in the cliff-face on the side of the mountain of Sela (and just about visible to the naked eye from As-Sil), hasn't provided any further insight. The one-hour hike up to the summit from As-Sil heads down into the valley, then up via a Nabatean-style rock-cut stairway; once at the top, aside from exploring the various cisterns and chambers, you're rewarded with outstanding **views** over the rocky domes and towers of this folded landscape.

At the end of the road leading down through Ain al-Baydha into As-Sil is an open car park on a terrace viewpoint, alongside a restored complex of stone cottages converted into a café and restaurant. Locals drive out here from Tafileh and the nearby villages for open-air sunset parties – especially on a Thursday and Friday – to play music, smoke *argileh* and generally hang out. Join them if you fancy.

Dana Nature Reserve محمية ضانا الطبيعية

In **Qadisiyyeh**, a small town (population 18,000) located 27km south of Tafileh and 24km north of Shobak, a steep road winds down off the King's Highway to **Dana**. This hamlet (population 40) lies at the eastern edge of Jordan's flagship **DANA NATURE RESERVE** (Ⓦ www.rscn.org.jo), which encompasses 320 square kilometres of terrain around the breathtaking Wadi Dana, stretching as far as Wadi Araba in the west. The village has been the scene of an extraordinary – and successful – social experiment conducted by the RSCN to rejuvenate a dying community by protecting the natural environment. Clinging to the edge of the cliff below the King's Highway, Dana is the starting point for a series of walks and hikes through one of Jordan's loveliest protected areas. Whether you stay for an hour or a week, you won't want to leave.

The reserve's terrain drops from 1500m above sea level at Dana to below sea level west of Feynan, and its **geology** switches from limestone to sandstone to granite, ecosystems varying from lush, well-watered mountain slopes and open oak and juniper woodlands to scrubland and arid sandy desert. The list of **flora** and resident **fauna** is dizzying: a brief roundup includes various kinds of eagles, falcons, kestrels and vultures, cuckoos, owls, the Sinai rosefinch and Tristram's serin; wildcats, caracals, hyenas, jackals, badgers, foxes, wolves, hares, bats, hedgehogs, porcupine and ibex; snakes, chameleons and lizards galore; freshwater crabs; and, so far, three plants new to science out of more than seven hundred plant species recorded.

Arrival

By the most direct **driving** route, Dana lies 202km south of Amman (7th Circle). Head due south on the Desert Highway to Husseiniyya, then turn west (27km) to the large Rashdiyyeh cement factory, from where Qadisiyyeh is 3km to the left (south). The turn-off down the cliffside into Dana is marked with a small brown sign at the top end of Qadisiyyeh village.

As you approach from the north you'll see several signs to the Dana Nature Reserve pointing off into the countryside: though they don't say so, these are indicating an access route into the northern fringe of the reserve around the Rummana campsite. If you want Dana village, stay on the road until you reach the cement factory, then go 3km further to the turn-off in Qadisiyyeh.

Dana also lies 53km north of Petra (Wadi Musa). Follow the main road through Shobak town, then pick up signs to Tafileh: ignore roads to the right signed Amman (they join the Desert Highway at Unayza). Keep going straight into Qadisiyyeh, then drive all the way up the long main street to find the turn-off (left) to Dana at the top of the village.

The only **bus** into Dana shuttles regularly to and from Qadisiyyeh on the King's Highway above the village. Qadisiyyeh has regular bus links from Tafileh – as well as one or two from Amman (Wihdat station) – but the section of the King's Highway to the south, between Qadisiyyeh and Shobak, has very little public transport. Hitching is one option, or bargain hard for a **taxi**: a full car to Dana from Shobak or Tafileh should cost about JD15–20, or from Wadi Musa about JD30–35.

The story of Dana

Dana is unique, not only in Jordan but in the whole Middle East – a positive, visionary programme combining scientific research, social reconstruction and **sustainable tourism**. For most of the twentieth century Dana was a simple farming community thriving on a temperate climate, three abundant springs and good grazing; indeed, some inhabitants had previously left Tafileh specifically for a better life in the village. But as Jordan developed new technologies and the general standard of living rose, a growing number of villagers felt isolated in their mountain hamlet of Ottoman stone cottages. Some moved out in the late 1960s to establish a new village, **Qadisiyyeh**, on the main Tafileh–Shobak road, and the attractions of electricity and plumbing rapidly emptied primitive Dana. The construction of the huge Rashdiyyeh cement factory close by in the early 1980s was the last straw: with well-paid jobs for the taking, most locals saw the daily trek up from Dana to the factory as pointless, and almost everyone moved to Qadisiyyeh.

Dana lay semi-abandoned for a decade or more, its handful of impoverished farmers forced to compete in the local markets with bigger farms using more advanced methods of production. This was what a group of twelve women from Amman discovered in the early 1990s as they travelled across the country to catalogue the remnants of traditional Jordanian culture. Realizing the deprivation faced by some of the poorest people in the country, these **"Friends of Dana"** embarked on a project to renovate and revitalize the fabric of the village under the auspices of the **Royal Society for the Conservation of Nature**. Electricity, telephones and a water supply were extended to the village and 65 cottages renovated. People started to drift back to Dana. The RSCN quickly realized the potential of the secluded Wadi Dana for scientific research; in a project funded partly by the World Bank and the UN, they turned the area into a protected **nature reserve**, built a small research station next to the village and, in 1994, launched a detailed ecological survey.

Continued grazing by thousands of domesticated goats, sheep and camels couldn't be reconciled with the need for environmental protection and so was banned; studies were undertaken into creating sustainable opportunities for villagers to gain a livelihood from the reserve. The ingenious solution came in redirecting the village's traditional crops to a new market. Dana's farmers produced their olives, figs, grapes, other fruits and nuts as before, but instead they sold everything to the RSCN, who employed the villagers to process these crops into novelty products such as organically produced jams and olive-oil soap for direct sale to relatively wealthy, environmentally aware consumers, both Jordanian and foreign. Medicinal herbs were introduced as a cash crop to aid the economic recovery, and the last Dana resident familiar with traditional pottery-making was encouraged to teach her craft to a younger generation. Dana soon hit the headlines, and in 1996 the RSCN launched **low-impact tourism** to the reserve, with the traditional-style *Guesthouse* going up next to the research buildings. Local villagers – some of whom were already employed as research scientists – were taken on as managers and guides. "Green tourism" awards followed, and, with Dana becoming better known as a tourist destination, locals opened a couple of small, budget hotels within the village. A campsite was established in the hills at Rummana, and in 2005 the RSCN opened a new "wilderness lodge" at the lower, western end of the reserve at Feynan – both of them built and staffed by local people. In only one generation, moribund Dana has been given a new lease of life.

On the way down into Dana, a **viewpoint** gives a tremendous panorama of Wadi Dana and the roofs of the old stone cottages below. Further down, as you clatter down the steep cobbled street into the village centre, you come to a **fork**: go straight on to the small hotels in the village, turn left to the RSCN *Guesthouse*.

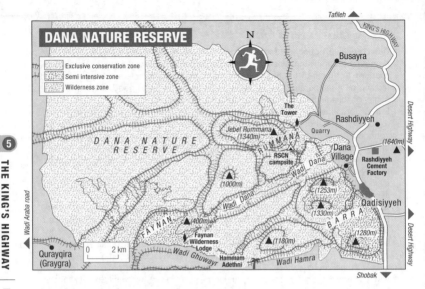

DANA NATURE RESERVE

Exclusive conservation zone
Semi intensive zone
Wilderness zone

N

Tafileh ▲

KING'S HIGHWAY

Busayra

Desert Highway ▶

The Tower

Rashdiyyeh ●

Jebel Rummana (1340m) ▲
Quarry
(1640m) ▶

D A N A   N A T U R E
R E S E R V E

RSCN campsite ▲

Dana Village

Rashdiyyeh Cement Factory

(1000m) ▲

Wadi Dana

(1253m) ▲

(1330m) ▲

Qadisiyyeh

Wadi Araba road ◀

F A Y A N

(400m) ▲

B A R R A

Desert Highway ▶

(1280m) ▲

Faynan Wilderness Lodge

(1180m) ▲

Qurayqira (Graygra)

0   2 km

Wadi Ghuwayr
Hammam Adethni

Wadi Hamra

Shobak ▼

Accommodation and eating

Dana's **accommodation** – whether in a building or under canvas – isn't cheap but, considering what's been achieved in the village, the wonderful atmosphere and the great walking on offer, is worth the extra and more. The lack of shops or restaurants means that, for **eating**, you must either take all meals at your hotel or campsite, or bring in supplies for picnics and self-catering; a mix of the two is in many ways the best solution.

RSCN Dana Guesthouse   بيت الضيافة

For its cosy atmosphere, simple comforts and an incredible silence, a night at the small RSCN-run ⚑ **Guesthouse** (☎03 227 0497, ⊜tourism@rscn.org.jo; ❻–❼) is likely to be one of your most memorable in Jordan. Stay here a few days and let the atmosphere seep into your bones: there's nowhere else like it in the country. It's worth every penny.

The building and its furniture were designed by architect Ammar Khammash (ⓦwww.khammash.com) in a skilful and attractive blend of traditional Jordanian styles and a chic minimalism in stone and iron. By the time you read this, a planned extension may already be open; the original building, though, holds just nine rooms. All of them, and the main terrace, overlook the full length of the still Wadi Dana: at night, lights twinkling on the Dead Sea and the call of nightjars echoing eerily up the valley make for an unforgettably

> **Prices** at Jordan's RSCN-run nature reserves are high. The RSCN makes no apologies for this: it says that the reason it exists is to protect Jordan's natural environment, and that it has built lodges and developed tourism as a tool for generating funds to help conservation and support rural communities. You may or may not agree with their pricing policy – but this kind of responsible tourism is virtually unknown in the Middle East, and the RSCN are pioneers. For now, until tourism schemes emerge that are truly community-owned, paying extra to visit the RSCN reserves is a good way to ensure that your money goes to benefit rural people and habitats.

serene experience. Queen Noor, wife of the late King Hussein, famously called the views "ten-star", and it's hard to argue with her.

The **rooms** – doubles, triples and one quad – are kept spotlessly clean by the cheerful and amenable staff, and all bar one have a private balcony perched over the valley. You can pay more to have the only room with an en-suite bathroom (all the rest share bathrooms), but should always **book weeks in advance**, either direct or with the RSCN's "Wild Jordan" tourism unit in Amman (see p.51).

Room rates include a good breakfast. With advance notice, staff can prepare lunches and dinners (JD6–15), as well as hikers' lunchboxes: if you're staying the night, make sure to book dinner.

Alongside the *Guesthouse* is a **nature shop** (daily 8am–4pm) selling local products such as herbs, fruit and jewellery, as well as textiles, gifts and other handmade items from RSCN projects around the country. Beside it is a kids' **learning zone**, where displays give a sense of Dana's natural context.

Other hotels in Dana village

A couple of small hotels in Dana village offer a budget option. The ⚑ **Dana Hotel** (☎03 227 0537 or 079 559 7307, ✉suleimanjarad@yahoo.com, ⓦwww .danavillage.piczo.com; ➊), in the village centre on the left, is part of the "Sons of Dana and Qadisiyyeh Tourism Co-operative": profits go to support local low-income families (notably putting students through university). The hotel occupies one of the old stone cottages, sympathetically renovated. It's a great, atmospheric little place, with simple rooms ranged around a quiet stone-flagged courtyard, plus more rooms in an annexe across the street. There's a choice of en-suite or shared bathrooms, plus the option of sleeping in the tent on the roof. Breakfast is included; other meals cost JD5.

Further on, at the back of the village, rises the **Dana Tower Hotel** (☎03 227 0226 or 079 568 8853, ✉dana_tower2@hotmail.com; ➊). Occupying four of the old cottages, this is a slightly less sympathetic restoration: if you like backpacker graffiti on the walls, flags of the world, the aroma of joss sticks and

▲ Dana Hotel, Dana village

trinkets dotted about, this place is for you. The owners have dissociated themselves both from the RSCN and the village co-operative, so despite its hippyish appearance, this is a purely profit-making business. Rooms are decent and clean, and include breakfast (other meals are JD5). Transport to or from Qadisiyyeh and Petra is discounted.

RSCN Rummana campsite   مخيم الرمانة

The great Dana outdoors is best experienced by **camping**, but in order for the RSCN to control numbers within the reserve you're not allowed to pitch your own tent. Instead, aim for the 🏕 **Rummana campsite** (March–Oct; ⓔ tourism@rscn.org.jo; ④–⑤), in the hills to the north of Wadi Dana. To stay, you must **book in advance** through the Dana *Guesthouse*, letting them know when and how you intend to arrive, whether you want meals cooked, and so on. There are twenty tents, all of them solid and roomy and capable of sleeping four or more: rates are about JD24pp for double or triple, plus JD12pp above that. Prices include a mattress, pillows, blankets, a towel and access to a proper, clean toilet block with cold showers. Staff can prepare **meals** on request (JD6–15).

To get to Rummana from Dana, the walk is an easy couple of hours around the head of the valley, or you can request a free transfer from the *Guesthouse*. Driving **south** down the King's Highway, the Rummana turning is before Dana: turn right 22km south of Tafileh, just before the main road cuts through a small wood, at a blue sign for "Ain Lahda" and a small brown sign for the campsite. Driving **north** from Dana village, at the top of the access road turn left (up the hill) on the main Qadisiyyeh–Tafileh road, and follow this for about 5km; just beyond where the road cuts straight through the middle of a small wood, turn left at the same brown sign for the campsite. This brings you down below the level of the main road onto a wide, bumpy gravel road used by trucks; carry on, past a huge quarry on the left, and then down a signposted left turn. About 1km further you'll come to the "**Tower**" – a small building with an office and a lookout terrace – where you must park. This marks the entrance to the reserve.

From copper to leather

In antiquity, **Feynan** was a major industrial area for smelting **copper**. As early as five thousand years ago, simple wind-fired kilns were being used to extract copper for ornaments and tools. Mining and smelting techniques progressed through the Bronze and Iron Ages, reaching a peak under the Romans, when Feynan hosted the largest copper mines in the empire. Wealth-generation continued into the Byzantine era – from when many of the extant ruins at Feynan date – and archeological investigations to discover more about the site remain ongoing.

Today, too, Feynan is thriving: the local Azazmeh bedouin are participating in an RSCN scheme that is altering the rural economy to place greater emphasis on environmental protection. For years, their goats have been overgrazing reserve land and decimating the local flora, but rather than banning them – which would merely foment ill-will and shift the problem elsewhere – the RSCN is attempting instead to invest in them, fattening the goats in large pens outside reserve land and training local women to produce new craft items from goat leather; both projects mean that the goats sell for higher prices at market and that their owners can additionally raise the value of each animal by selling the hide. You can ask to visit the leather workshops at Feynan to see more. Crafts made from Feynan goat leather are on sale at RSCN nature shops around Jordan.

Check in at the Tower, and staff will radio ahead to summon the shuttle bus (actually a small truck), which will take you down the hill to the campsite, which is located in an idyllic spot at the foot of Jebel Rummana. The shuttle to and from the Tower (and, on request, back to the Dana *Guesthouse*) is free.

RSCN Feynan Lodge نزل فينان البيئى

Down at the lower, western end of the reserve at Feynan stands the RSCN's 🕏 **Feynan Lodge** (Sept–June; ℮ tourism@rscn.org.jo; ❼). To stay, you must **book in advance** through the Dana *Guesthouse*, letting them know when and how you intend to arrive, whether you want meals cooked, and so on.

Feynan is a desert area, quite unlike Dana – down here it's hot, dry and dusty, and the solar-powered, environmentally friendly lodge (designed, again, by Ammar Khammash) is both a base for active exploration of the surrounding area and an isolated retreat for those seeking solitude. It has electricity, but all 26 rooms – designed in an attractive, spartan style (with en-suite bathrooms) and laid out on two levels around an internal courtyard – are lit only by candles set into mirrored niches. The walls are thick, and windows are either small or shielded from full sun, making the interior cool and pleasant in even the hottest weather. There's an attractive communal sitting and eating area, with a traditional oven for staff to prepare **meals** on request (JD6–15), including vegetarian dishes from local ingredients. The atmosphere of the place is bewitchingly calm, peaceful and contemplative – especially at night, under clear skies amid flickering candlelight.

There is no access to the lodge by paved road: the only way to get here is on foot from Dana (a five-hour walk) or with a 4x4 from the nearest villages to the west, **Qurayqira** (pronounced "graygra") or its neighbour **Rashaydeh**: for more info, see p.356. From a turn-off (signposted Feynan) on the Wadi Araba road about 135km north of Aqaba or 40km south of Fifa, a road runs for 17km to Qurayqira and another 5km on to Rashaydeh, where the tarmac ends. From either village, you can ask around for a 4x4 ride on the 10km of desert track to the lodge itself, or arrange a lift in advance through the RSCN.

Walks in and around the Dana reserve

Once you arrive in Dana, it's worth stopping in at the RSCN-run **Guesthouse** – whether you're staying there or not – both for the views from their terrace (binoculars are available if you'd like to do a spot of birdwatching) and to get some firsthand **information** about the reserve's wildlife from the experts. They have leaflets detailing a number of walks and activities, and can provide a trained **nature guide** for any of the walks at a fixed rate: JD15 for 1–2hr, JD25 for 3–4hr, JD35 for 5–6hr, or JD85 for full-day trails (including down to Feynan). Many of the walks require you to take a guide, but there's a handful of routes on which you can strike out alone: the website ⓦ www.rscn.org.jo lists them all. All these walks and others in the area are described in *Jordan: Walks, Treks, Caves, Climbs & Canyons* by Tony Howard: p.404 has details of this and also of some excellent field guides to local flora and fauna.

Admission to the reserve for any of the walks costs JD7, but this fee is waived if you stay overnight at RSCN accommodation in Dana, Rummana or Feynan. Otherwise, if you stay at one of the budget hotels in Dana village, or if you arrive for the day and choose to tackle a self-guided trail without hiring an RSCN nature guide, then you must pay.

Walks from Dana village

The most obvious walking route in the reserve is the magnificent **Wadi Dana Trail** (14km; 5–6hr) from the village along the downward-sloping floor of the

The Dana–Petra trek

One of the Middle East's most impressive long-distance treks – recently dubbed "Jordan's Inca Trail" – links Dana village and Feynan with **Petra** (45km; 3–5 days; guide compulsory). The general direction heads far off any beaten tracks, from Dana to Feynan, across open country towards Shobak, and then to "Little Petra" in order to arrive at Petra via a back route over the mountains. It's a challenging, but extraordinarily rewarding, walk.

However, it is not waymarked – and, in fact, there is no single accepted path. Many of the specialist independent guides listed on p.50 can lead you from Dana to Petra, but they won't necessarily all go the same way (and some paths are more beautiful than others). Some propose two nights camping out between Feynan and Little Petra; others say three. A handful of tour operators in the UK and elsewhere offer the route as part of a Jordan package, but if you'd like to tackle it independently, talk to RSCN staff at the Dana Guesthouse (or at the "Wild Jordan" centre in Amman), for an idea of the logistics – and then compare with some of the independent specialists: particularly recommendable for the Dana–Petra route is Yamaan Safady. One key point is to determine what facilities are on offer at each overnight stop: some guides will carry everything with them, others will bring in trail support so that tea and meals are ready when you arrive.

The walk itself is epic, covering a range of terrain from highland forests to wild, rolling hills and scorching deserts, dropping down to the floor of the Wadi Araba, then climbing again into the sandstone mountains. There's little point trying to compress it into words: if you're a wilderness fan, this one's for you.

wadi, an easy walk passing from the lush green gardens of Dana through increasingly wild and desolate terrain to Feynan. This can be done alone or with a guide – as can the easy **Village Tour** (2km; 2hr), a stroll around Dana to enjoy the views and visit the workshops where local women make silver jewellery and prepare dried fruit.

All other trails can be done only with a guide. The **White Dome Trail** (8km; 3hr; March–Oct only) is a beautiful walk that follows a contour around the head of the valley, passing first through the spring-fed terraced gardens of Dana and then beneath the massive escarpment up to Rummana.

Another highly explorable area is Al-Barra, a fifteen-minute drive south of the village, where lush woodlands give way to networks of canyons and gorges cutting into the mountainous landscape. This is the starting point for the superb **Feathers Canyon Trail** (3km; 3hr) to Shaq ar-Reesh ("Canyon of the Feathers"), a Nabatean mountain retreat. The walk begins in flower-filled meadows and quiet terraces, but involves a bit of scrambling and climbing through a narrow gorge to reach the spectacular summit, dotted with cisterns and water-channels. Al-Barra is also the start and finish for the **Nawatef Trail** (2km; 2hr), heading out to the springs and ruins at Nawatef and back on a different route. The beautiful but difficult **Wadi Dathneh Trail** (16km; 8hr) also starts from Al-Barra, passing between the red cliffs of Wadi Hamra before reaching the verdant oasis of Hammam Adethni and following flowing water all the way down to Feynan.

Walks from Rummana campsite

All walks from Rummana operate only when the campsite is open (roughly March–Oct). Highly recommended is the **White Dome Trail** (8km; 3hr; guide compulsory) to Dana, outlined above, or the alternative **Dana Village Trail** (5km; 4hr; guide compulsory), following a rougher track.

All other trails can be walked without a guide. The easy **Campsite Trail** (2km; 1hr) leads on a circular route around the Rummana area, offering stunning views and birdwatching lookouts. The moderate **Rummana Trail** (2.5km; 2hr) follows a trail through the juniper trees up to the summit of Jebel Rummana ("Pomegranate Mountain") for the views down into Wadi Araba: it's also easy to spot raptors up here, and if you head up at dawn you may see ibex. Across from the campsite is the **Cave Trail** (1km; 1.5hr), a short, rough walk leading to a set of caves above Shaq al-Kalb ("Dog Canyon"), residence of hyenas, wildcats and wolves.

A short walk from the campsite is a **bird hide** overlooking a small pool – ideal for early morning observation of birds and ibex – and should you fancy stretching your legs instead of sitting on the shuttle bus, the walk back up to the Tower from the campsite takes about an hour.

Walks from Feynan Lodge

All walks from Feynan operate only when the lodge is open (Sept–June) and all require a guide. The **Feynan Copper Mine Trail** (3km; 2hr) is a circular walk around the area's antiquities, including Bronze and Iron Age copper mines, remains of Byzantine churches, a Roman tower and more. An alternative is the easy **Wadi Ghwair Trail** (8km; 3–4hr) which follows the gravel bed of the Wadi Feynan to the confluence with the Ghwair canyon. It's also possible to tackle the **Feynan Trail** (14km; 6hr) – the long hike from Feynan all the way up the valley floor, passing from stony desert up to the forested highlands of Dana.

Feynan also hosts some eco-friendly **mountain-bike** trails of 2km, 4km and 8km, circling around the lodge and the nearby archeological ruins. Bike rental costs JD10/JD20 per person for a half/full day – and if you'd like a guide to accompany you, there's an extra fee of JD23/JD85.

Shobak castle قلعة الشوبك

Perched dramatically like a ship on the crest of a hill, **Shobak castle** was the first to be built by the Crusaders in Transjordan (see p.244 for some Crusader history). In a more ruinous state than Karak castle, and much rebuilt by Mamlukes and Ottomans, it's nonetheless well worth an exploratory detour.

As they are today, the **walls** and **towers** are Mamluke, and all the towers which stand have beautifully carved external calligraphic inscriptions dating from rebuilding work in the 1290s. As you enter, down and to the left is a small **chapel**, at the back of which are pools and channels of unknown usage. Below the chapel runs a long, dank and pitch-dark **secret passage**, which brings you out in the middle of the castle if you head right, and outside the walls if you head left. Back alongside the chapel is the original **gatehouse**, to the left side of which are two round wells which presage an even scarier secret passage – a dark and foul opening with, according to legend, 375 broken and slippery steps leading down into the heart of the hill. Even archeologists only got to number 150 or so before giving up, but this was the castle's main water supply: somehow the Crusaders knew that by digging down so far they'd eventually hit water. A prudent "No Entry" sign now bars entry: tourists who have ignored this and started down this staircase anyway (including a potholing expert who tried it in 2008) have ended up seriously injuring themselves, describing how the stairs crumbled away under their feet. The gatehouse gives onto a street, at the end of which is a building with three **arched entrances**, one topped by a calligraphic panel; up until the 1950s the castle was still inhabited, and this building was the

There's a **map** of the King's Highway on p.220.

old village school. If you head through to the back and turn right, a long vaulted corridor leads you out to the north side of the castle, and a maze of abandoned **Ottoman cottages**, beneath which is an exposed **Ayyubid palace** complex, with a large reception hall and baths. Further round towards the entrance stand the beautiful arches of a **church**, beneath which is a small room filled with catapult balls and chunks of carved masonry.

Practicalities

The castle lies 3km west of **SHOBAK** town, which is 24km south of Qadisi-yyeh and 27km north of Wadi Musa. Buses and some serveeces run to Shobak direct from Amman's Wihdat station (mornings only) and from Wadi Musa (all day), but there is virtually no public transport from Qadisiyyeh. **No buses** run up to the castle, so without your own transport you'll need to persuade a taxi-driver to take you or face a stiff climb. A small, simple **campsite** is signposted from the castle and the village.

Set in acres of lush orchards, Shobak is Jordan's leading producer of apples, but this quiet farming village has also been trying for years to reap some benefit from the tourists heading south to Petra. Aside from some good local **restaurants** on the main drag, its numerous **groceries** beat those in Wadi Musa on both price and quality: if you intend to picnic in Petra, you'd do well to stock up here in advance.

Travel details

Buses and serveeces

Dana to: Qadisiyyeh (10min).
Karak to: Amman (Wihdat station; 2hr); Aqaba (3hr); Ariha (40min); Ma'an (2hr); Mazra'a (30min); Safi (40min); Tafileh (1hr).
Madaba to: Amman (Tabarbour, Muhajireen, Mahatta or Wihdat stations; 30min); Dhiban (40min); Faysaliyyeh (Mount Nebo; 15min); Hesban (10min); Ma'in village (15min); Mukawir (1hr); Shuneh al-Janubiyyeh (1hr); Umm ar-Rasas (50min).
Qadisiyyeh to: Dana (5min); Tafileh (40min).
Shobak to: Amman (Wihdat station; 2hr 45min); Ma'an (30min); Wadi Musa/Petra (30min).
Tafileh to: Amman (Wihdat station; 2hr 30min); Aqaba (2hr 30min); Karak (1hr); Ma'an (1hr); Qadisiyyeh (40min).

Useful Arabic place names

Ain al-Baydha	العين البيضاء	Nitil	نتل
Ariha	اريحا	Qadisiyyeh	القادسية
Dana	ضانا	Qasr	القصر
Faqua	فقوع	Qurayqira	القريقرة
Faysaliyyeh	الفيصلية	Rabba	الربة
Feynan	فينان	Shobak	الشوبك
al-Iraq	العراق (جنب المؤتة)	Siyagha	صياغة
Khirbet al-Mukhayyat	الخربة المخيط	Wadi Hasa	وادي الحسا
Ma'in	ماعين	Wadi ibn Hammad	وادي ابن حماد
Mazar	المزار	Wadi Numeira	وادي النميرة
Muta	مؤتة		

Petra

CHAPTER 6 # Highlights

* **Petra By Night** Magical late-night guided walks into Petra for traditional music and storytelling by candlelight. See p.279

* **The Siq** Dramatic entrance to the ancient city, through a high, narrow gorge. See p.284

* **The Treasury** Jordan's flagship monument, a towering facade dominating the entrance to Petra. See p.285

* **High Place of Sacrifice** Mountain-top altar with stunning views over Petra. See p.289

* **The East Cliff** A line of impressive royal tombs carved out of a cliff overlooking the city centre. See p.292

* **The Monastery** A long climb is rewarded with a close-up viewing of Petra's most imposing facade. See p.303

* **Jebel Haroun** One of Jordan's holiest sites, with a shrine to Moses' brother Aaron perched on a high summit. See p.307

▲ The Monastery Petra

6

Petra البتراء

Petra is incredible. Tucked away in a remote valley basin in the heart of southern Jordan's Shara mountains and shielded from the outside world behind an impenetrable barrier of rock, this fabled ancient city of ornate classical facades is wreathed in a sense of mystery and drama. Since a Western adventurer stumbled on the site in 1812, it has fired imaginations, its grandeur and dramatic setting pushing it – like the Pyramids or the Taj Mahal – into the realms of legend. Today, it's almost as if time has literally drawn a veil over the once-great city, which grew wealthy enough on the caravan trade to challenge the might of Rome: two millennia of wind and rain have blurred the sharp edges of the facades and rubbed away at the soft sandstone to expose vivid bands of colour beneath, putting the whole scene into soft focus.

Where Petra sits, in a valley basin between two lines of jagged peaks, there's only one route in and out, and that passes through the modern town of **Wadi Musa**, on the eastern side of the mountains. In the last few decades this town has grown to serve the lucrative tourist trade to Petra, and has all the hotels, restaurants and services you'd expect: there's nowhere to stay within the ancient city itself, and virtually nowhere to eat either. The single entrance gate into Petra is in Wadi Musa, but once you've crossed the barrier you're immediately thrown into the rocky landscape of the desert. There is no urban development of any kind within Petra, and the local culture is all rural. Spending a few days here is a constant to-and-fro – down-at-heel Wadi Musa providing all the necessities of life, and majestic Petra all the historical and natural drama.

Some history

In prehistory, the Petra region saw some of the first experiments in farming. The hunter-gatherers of the **Paleolithic Age** gave way, over nine thousand years

Weather conditions

Petra is situated in the mountains, at around 1100m above sea level. In **spring** (March–May) and **autumn** (Sept–Oct) it is pleasantly warm, with highs around 25–30°C and virtually no chance of rain. In **summer** (late May to early Sept) it can be blisteringly hot during the day, perhaps above 40°C. However, with the altitude and the desert conditions, nights year-round are cool. In **winter** (Nov–Feb), Petra can be cold, often not getting above 10–15°C during the day and dropping below freezing at night: rain is to be expected, and snow is not uncommon.

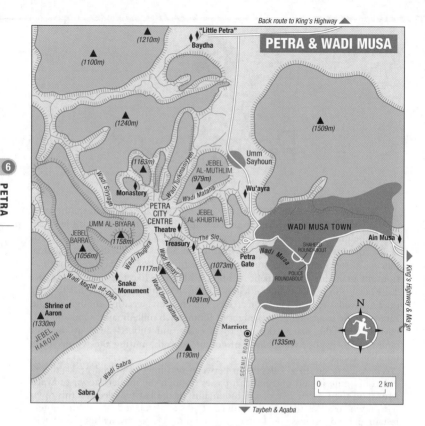

"Little Petra"
Baydha
(1210m)
(1100m)
(1240m)
(1509m)
Umm
Sayhoun
(1163m)
JEBEL
AL-MUTHLIM
(979m)
Wu'ayra
Wadi Mataha
Monastery
PETRA
CITY
CENTRE
JEBEL
AL-KHUBTHA
WADI MUSA TOWN
UMM AL-BIYARA
Theatre
The Siq
Ain Musa
JEBEL
BARRA
(1158m)
Treasury
SHAHEED
ROUNDABOUT
(1056m)
Petra
Gate
(1073m)
POLICE
ROUNDABOUT
(1117m)
Snake
Monument
(1091m)
N
Shrine of
Aaron
(1330m)
Marriott
JEBEL
HAROUN
(1335m)
(1190m)
0   2 km
Sabra

King's Highway & Ma'an

▼ Taybeh & Aqaba

ago, to settled communities living in walled farming villages such as at **Baydha**, just north of Petra. Nomadic tribes passed through the Petra basin in the millennia following, but the spur to its development came with attempts at contact between the two great ancient powers of **Mesopotamia** and **Egypt**. The desert plateaux of Mesopotamia, to the east of the King's Highway, were sealed off by high mountains from the routes both across the Naqab (Negev) to Gaza and across the Sinai to Egypt; somehow a caravan route across the barrier had to be found if contact was to be made. Petra, where abundant springs tumble down into the Wadi Araba through a natural fault in the mountains, was prime choice, marking the spot on the north–south King's Highway where an east–west passage could connect the two empires.

The first significant mention of Petra is in the Old Testament, as the **Israelites** approached **Edom** after their forty years in the desert. Local legend – running against the geographical evidence – maintains that it was in the hills just above Petra that God ordered Moses to produce water for the Israelites by speaking to a rock. Moses instead struck the rock, and the spring that gushed is today named **Ain Musa** (Spring of Moses), its outflow housed beneath a small domed building at the eastern entrance to the town of Wadi Musa. **King Reqem** of Edom (Reqem was the Semitic name for Petra, and he was probably just a local chieftain) refused permission to the Israelites to pass through his territory, but before they departed, Moses' brother Aaron

(Haroun in Arabic) died, and was buried supposedly on top of **Jebel Haroun** overlooking Petra. A white shrine atop the mountain is still a site of pilgrimage for Jews, Christians and Muslims alike.

Just after 1000 BC, the Israelite **King David** moved to take control of Petra and the whole of Edom – by now rich on the proceeds of copper production as well as trade. His son **Solomon** consolidated the Israelite grip on trade and technology, and for fifty years diverted Petra's profits into his own coffers. However, after his death, the Israelite kingdom collapsed and feuding erupted. Some Edomites withdrew to a settlement on top of the impregnable **Umm al-Biyara** mountain overlooking central Petra and to a village at **Tawilan** above Ain Musa. Fluctuations in regional power soon after led to Petra passing from Edomite hands to **Assyrian** to **Babylonian** to **Persian**: such instability left the way open for a new people to stamp their authority on the land and stake a claim to its future.

The Nabateans

The first mention of the **Nabateans** was in 647 BC, when they were listed as one of the enemies of Ashurbanipal, last king of Assyria; at that stage, they were still a tribe of bedouin nomads inhabiting northern and northwestern Arabia. When the Babylonians depopulated much of Palestine during the sixth century BC, many Edomites came down from Petra to claim the empty land to the west. In turn, the Nabateans migrated out of the arid Arabian desert to the lusher and more temperate mountains of Edom, and, specifically, to the well-watered and easily defended prize of Petra. Whereas the Edomites had occupied the hills above Petra, the Nabateans quickly saw the potential for developing the central bowl of the valley floor. The migrants arrived slowly, though, and for several centuries it seems that most stuck to their bedouin lifestyle, building little other than a temple and refuge atop **Umm al-Biyara**. However, displaying the adaptability that was to become their trademark, the Nabateans soon gave up the traditional occupation of raiding the plentiful caravans that passed to and fro in favour of charging the merchants for safe passage and a place to do business. It was probably around this time that the first organized, permanent trading emporium was established at Petra, and Edom became known as **Arabia Petrea**.

The Roman author Diodorus Siculus reports that the Greek **Seleucid** ruler of Syria, **Antigonus**, attacked Petra in 312 BC, both to limit Nabatean power and to undermine Ptolemaic authority. His troops sneaked in under cover of darkness, and found that all the Nabatean men were away. The Greeks slaughtered a few women and children and hurriedly made off with as much booty as they could carry – silver, myrrh and frankincense. However, someone managed to raise the alarm, since within an hour, the Nabateans were in pursuit. They rapidly caught up with the complacent army, massacred all but fifty, recovered the valuables and returned home. In true merchant style, though, the Nabateans instinctively recognized that war would do no good to their flourishing business, and so sent a mollifying letter of explanation to Antigonus. The general pretended to accept, but was secretly fuming; he let some time pass before sending another army against Petra. The small garrison they encountered, however, easily repelled the attackers. Comfortably ensconced in their unassailable headquarters, the Nabateans acted the wealthy tycoon: unruffled by the skirmish, they reached into their deep pockets to buy peace from the humiliated Greeks.

Over the following two centuries, the battling between Seleucid Syria and Ptolemaic Egypt for control of Alexander's empire enabled the Nabateans to fill the power vacuum in Transjordan and extend their kingdom far beyond Petra. By 80 BC they were in control of Damascus. Petra grew ever more wealthy on its profits from **trade**, standing at the pivots between Egypt, Arabia and Syria, and between East Asia and the Mediterranean. Traditional commodities such as **copper**, **iron** and Dead Sea **bitumen**, used for embalming in Egypt, were losing ground to **spices** from the southern Arabian coast – myrrh, balsam and frankincense, the last of which was central to religious ritual all over the Hellenistic world. Pepper, ginger, sugar and cotton arrived from **India** for onward distribution. **Chinese** documents even talk of imports of silk, glass, gold, silver, henna and frankincense from a place known as Li-Kan, taken to be a corruption of "Reqem". Nabatean power seemed limitless, and even when **Pompey** sent troops against Petra in 62 BC, the Nabateans were able to buy peace from the Roman Empire for the price of three hundred talents of silver. Petran prosperity grew and grew.

Petra's golden age

The first centuries BC and AD saw Petra at its zenith, with a settled population of perhaps as many as 30,000. The Roman author **Strabo** describes it as a wealthy, cosmopolitan city, full of fine buildings and villas, gardens and watercourses, with Romans and other foreigners thronging the streets, and a democratic king. "The Nabateans," reported Strabo, "are so acquisitive that they give honours to those who increase their possessions, and publicly fine those who lose them." However, the writing was on the wall. The discovery of the monsoon winds had begun to cause a shift in trade patterns: overland routes from Arabia were being abandoned in favour of transport by **sea**. In addition, Rome was sponsoring the diversion of inland trade away from the upstart Petra,

Burckhardt made up a story that he had vowed to sacrifice a goat at the shrine of the Prophet Aaron atop Jebel Haroun near the ruins: an unimpeachably honourable motive for pressing on.

As he and his guide approached Wadi Musa (then known by its old name of **Elji**), they were stopped by the Liyathneh tribe, camped near Ain Musa, who tried to persuade them to sacrifice their goat there and then, with the white shrine in plain view on the distant summit. But Sheikh Ibrahim insisted on going on, much to the irritation of his guide. They went down the steep hill, on into the Siq, and arrived at the Treasury. Burckhardt somehow managed to make detailed notes and a sketch of the facade, and they continued throughout the city in this way, Burckhardt writing and sketching in secret, his guide becoming ever more suspicious. They reached the foot of Jebel Haroun as dusk was falling, and Burckhardt finally submitted to his guide's insistence that they make the sacrifice and turn back.

Burckhardt's adventures continued: he arrived in Cairo to prepare for his great African expedition, but quickly got tangled in bureaucracy. In the meantime he travelled deep into Nubia, crossed the Red Sea to Jeddah (and was probably the first Christian ever to enter Mecca, where his Quranic learning deeply impressed the city's religious judge), and explored Sinai, but back in Egypt in 1817, he contracted dysentery and died in eleven days, with his journey to the Niger not even begun. All Burckhardt's journals were published after his death, *Travels in Nubia* and *Travels in Arabia* overshadowed by the news of his rediscovery of Petra, published in 1822 in **Travels in Syria and the Holy Land**. His **grave**, bearing his pseudonym Sheikh Ibrahim, is visitable in a Muslim cemetery in Cairo. Its existence shows that, far from being simply a game or ploy, Burckhardt's alter ego took on a genuine life of its own.

---

instead directing it into Egypt and via the Wadi Sirhan into Syria, presaging the rise of **Palmyra**. Pressure on Nabatea to come to heel was inexorable. The last Nabatean king, **Rabbel II**, tried moving his capital from Petra north to Bosra, but eventually had to strike a deal with Rome. On his death in 106 AD the entire Nabatean kingdom passed peacefully into Roman hands.

The Roman, Byzantine and Crusader eras

Under the **Romans**, Petra became a principal centre of the new Provincia Arabia, and seems to have undergone something of a cultural renaissance, with the theatre and Colonnaded Street both being renovated. The city was important enough to be visited by Emperor **Hadrian** in 130 AD, and possibly also by Emperor **Severus** in 199. However, the tide of history was turning, and by 300 Petra was in serious decline, with houses and temples falling derelict through lack of maintenance. Palmyra, an oasis entrepôt in the eastern Syrian desert, was on the ascendant, and sea trade into Egypt was well established; Petra was stuck between the two, and there was no reason to keep it alive. Roman patronage began to drift away from the city, and entrepreneurs and merchants followed.

Petra's decline was drawn out. **Christianity** was adopted as the official religion of the empire in 324, but for many decades after that the proud Nabateans mingled elements of the new faith with remnants of their own pagan heritage. The massive earthquake of 363, according to the contemporary bishop of Jerusalem, levelled half of Petra, although the city limped on for another couple of centuries. In 447, the **Urn Tomb** was converted into a huge church, and both the lavishly decorated **Petra Church** and plainer **Ridge Church** were built within the following century or so. Nonetheless, by the time of the seventh-century Islamic invasion, Petra was more or less deserted, and the earth-quake of 749 probably forced the final stragglers to depart the crumbling city.

On their push through Transjordan in the early twelfth century, the **Crusaders** built small forts within Petra at **Al–Habees** and **Wu'ayra**, though these were tiny outposts of their headquarters at nearby Shobak and were abandoned less than a century later. In 1276, the **Mamluke** sultan Baybars – on his way from Cairo to suppress a revolt in Karak – entered Petra from the southwest and proceeded through the deserted city "amidst most marvellous caves, the facades sculptured into the very rock face". He emerged from the Siq on June 6, 1276, and, as far as records show, was the last person, other than the local bedouin, to see Petra for over five hundred years.

The modern era

On August 22, 1812, a Swiss explorer, Jean Louis **Burckhardt** (see box, p.264), entered the Siq in heavy Arab disguise in the company of a local guide. His short visit, and the notes and sketches he managed to make, brought the fable of Petra to the attention of the world once again. In May 1818, two commanders of the British Royal Navy, Charles Irby and James Mangles, spent some days sightseeing in the ancient city, but it was the visits of **Léon de Laborde** in 1826 and the British artist **David Roberts** in 1839 that first brought plentiful images of Petra to the West. Laborde's engravings were often fanciful and cloyingly romanticized, but Roberts's drawings were relatively accurate. As well as helping to shape the legend of Petra in Western minds – **Burgon's** oft-quoted line about the "rose-red city" (see p.288) appeared within a few years – they also launched tourism to the place. The second half of the nineteenth century saw a steady trickle of earnest visitors, even though Petra was still a destination way off any beaten tracks, reached only with extreme hardship by horse or camel from Jerusalem. Serious archeological investigation began at the turn of the century, with specialists cataloguing all Petra's monuments in 1898 and producing the first accurate maps in 1925.

By this time, the Thomas Cook Travel Company had set up a camp in Petra for European tourists, offering the choice of tent or cave accommodation; until a regular bus service from Amman began in 1980, facilities around the site remained minimal. Wadi Musa town was a backwater, despite the designation of Petra as a national park. In the early 1980s, after protracted but fruitless negotia-tions, the government ordered the **Bdul** tribe (see p.293), who had been resident in Petra's caves for as long as anyone could remember, to move out to **Umm Sayhoun**, a purpose-built settlement of small breezeblock houses 4km away. The prospect of electricity, running water, health care and better education for the kids proved irresistible, and, in dribs and drabs, the Bdul departed. Devel-opment of the site and archeological exploration then took off: Petra was added to UNESCO's list of World Heritage Sites in 1985, and four years later a group of concerned local establishment figures set up the **Petra National Trust** (PNT; ⓦ www.petranationaltrust.org), a not-for-profit NGO campaigning on issues of the environment, antiquities and the region's cultural heritage.

Today a buffer zone of over 900 square kilometres of land, from Shobak to well south of Rajif, is formally protected, while a core 264 square kilometres around the site itself is defined as the strictly regulated **Petra Archeological Park** (ⓦ www.petrapark.com). Recent years have seen a host of new projects, ranging from ongoing digs at several locations to major engineering works repaving the Siq, installing upgraded tourist facilities around the site and beauti-fying Wadi Musa town.

Wadi Musa وادي موسى

WADI MUSA is an anomaly, a dusty southern Jordanian town given an unfamiliar twist with lots of signs in English, a huge number of hotels and a noticeable diminution in the usual hospitality towards foreigners. In sharp contrast to the rest of Jordan, where decency and respect are the unswerving norm, Wadi Musa shows a distressing tendency towards rip-offs, wheedling and outright hassle. Businesses and individuals all too often overcharge and under-deliver. It's a badly run, seedy little place.

If you stay for a while you may pick up on the town's rather sad air of powerlessness. This is epitomized by the local farmers and small-business people who are well aware that their hands are tied (either by decision-makers who don't always put local interests first or by regional instability that can decimate the town's income for months on end), and exemplified by the substandard hotels serviced by bored, lonely guest workers from Egypt and northern Jordan, who see little of the whirlwinds of cash that blow into town with every tour bus.

Arrival

All main roads to Petra meet just above **Ain Musa**, a spring in the hills to the east of Wadi Musa town which is marked by a small triple-domed building sheltering a rock – traditionally, the rock struck in anger by Moses – from beneath which the spring emerges. From here, the whole of Wadi Musa town is strung out for 4km along a main road which heads downhill all the way, offering spectacular views out over the craggy mountains and eventually termi-nating at the ticket gate into Petra.

Partway down is an intersection known as the **Police Roundabout** (Wadi Musa's police station is alongside it), from where a turn-off heads left through residential districts towards the neighbouring village of Taybeh and eventually out of town, passing big hotels such as the *Marriott* on the way.

The centre of Wadi Musa, just below the police intersection, is marked by the small **Shaheed Roundabout**, although there are no signs naming it (it's often dubbed the Central, or Midtown, Roundabout instead). Clustered near here are most of Wadi Musa's shops, banks, mosques, cafés and hotels, as well as the bus station.

At the bottom of the hill from the town centre is a strip known as the **Tourist Street**, with hotels, cafés and restaurants on one side and the valley bed on the other. It ends at the landmark *Mövenpick* hotel, with the Petra Visitor Centre and ticket gate just beyond.

Petra is approximately:
- 250km south of Amman (3hr)
- 120km north of Aqaba (1hr 45min)
- 100km north of Wadi Rum (1hr 30min)
- 50km south of Dana (1hr)

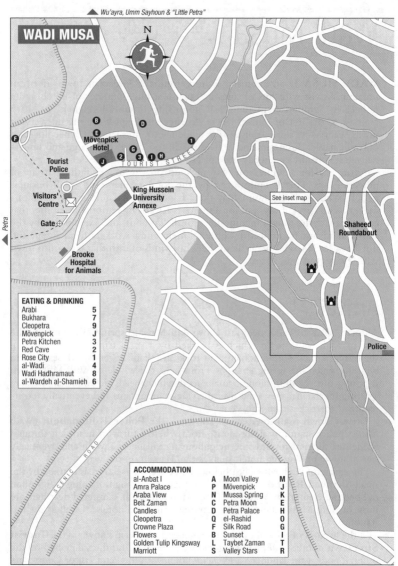

▲ Wu'ayra, Umm Sayhoun & "Little Petra"

WADI MUSA

N

Petra ◄

Mövenpick Hotel

Tourist Police

Visitors' Centre

Gate ⊕

TOURIST STREET

King Hussein University Annexe

Brooke Hospital for Animals

See inset map

Shaheed Roundabout

Police

EATING & DRINKING

Arabi	5
Bukhara	7
Cleopetra	9
Mövenpick	J
Petra Kitchen	3
Red Cave	2
Rose City	1
al-Wadi	4
Wadi Hadhramaut	8
al-Wardeh al-Shamieh	6

SCENIC ROAD

ACCOMMODATION

al-Anbat I	A	Moon Valley	M
Amra Palace	P	Mövenpick	J
Araba View	N	Mussa Spring	K
Beit Zaman	C	Petra Moon	E
Candles	D	Petra Palace	H
Cleopetra	Q	el-Rashid	O
Crowne Plaza	F	Silk Road	G
Flowers	B	Sunset	I
Golden Tulip Kingsway	L	Taybet Zaman	T
Marriott	S	Valley Stars	R

▼ Taybeh, S & T

By car

From Amman, the most direct route to Petra is 235km, safely driveable in around two and a half hours (without stops). Head south from 7th or 8th Circle on the **Desert Highway** past the airport: after 180km you'll come to the **Unayza** junction, which has a signposted turn-off west to Petra. From here, a smooth, upgraded road takes you quickly and easily on to Wadi Musa through Shobak; partway along it joins the King's Highway. Follow it straight all the way and it delivers you to Ain Musa.

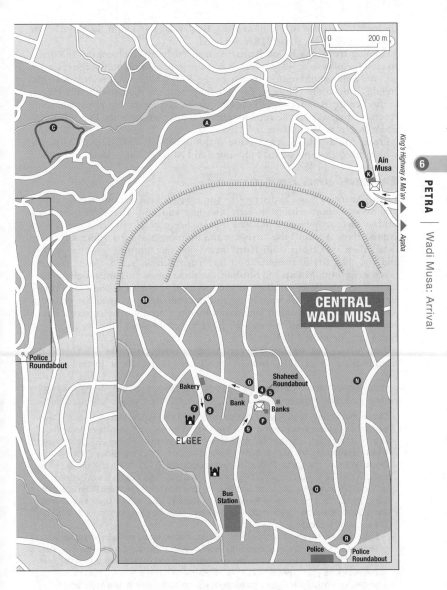

If you fancy a slower, more scenic approach, opt for a beautiful **backroad**. About 16km south of Shobak town, you'll see a right turn signposted to Hisha and Beidha. This narrow, twisting road leads through the trees up to the crest of a ridge, where you suddenly get expansive views out over Petra's valley and the jagged peaks beyond. Carry on down (the straight line of a road visible on the valley floor points directly at a cleft in the mountains – this is "Little Petra"; see p.311). Take the signposted left turn just before you reach Little Petra (10km from the King's Highway), and you enter Wadi Musa the back way, passing

269

through rolling desert terrain and the Bdul village at Umm Sayhoun before ending up, 8km on, at the *Mövenpick* hotel.

Coming **from Aqaba or Rum**, the main highway climbs out of the desert to crest the plateau at Ras an-Naqab. A left turn here, at the top of the hill, takes you onto the southernmost stretch of the King's Highway, leading across the rolling fields to the village of **Taybeh**; from here, the road, unofficially known as the **Scenic Road**, clings to the cliffside, passing several big hotels and some spectacular views over the Petra mountains until it arrives at the Police Roundabout in central Wadi Musa.

From Ma'an, the quickest route is the signposted road through **Udhruh**, which meets the Shobak road just above Ain Musa: 33km in total.

By bus and serveece

From Amman buses and serveeces run from Wihdat station (via the Desert Highway) – most reliably in early morning and mid-afternoon, though on Fridays there may be nothing after midday. See p.121 for more details. **From Aqaba** three or four buses arrive in the morning and early afternoon (more details on p.353), **from Wadi Rum** there is just one morning bus a day (p.324), and you might find one afternoon bus **from Karak** (p.246). More frequent buses arrive from **Ma'an** and **Shobak**, but these towns are hardly high on most visitors' agenda. Buses on all routes are restricted – or nonexistent – on Fridays. Bear in mind that if you want to get to Petra from Amman, Aqaba or just about any other town in southern Jordan, and there are no direct buses, take a bus to Ma'an instead: frequent connections leave Ma'an for Wadi Musa, or it's easy to find a taxi for around JD10.

Wadi Musa's **bus station** is in the centre of town, down the hill behind the main mosque about 300m south of the Shaheed Roundabout. Instead of being

Moving on from Wadi Musa

Two or three buses **to Amman**'s Wihdat station (via the Desert Highway) – plus a few serveeces – depart between 6 and 8am, with another couple of bus departures around 11am–1pm. The last bus to Amman is a coach run by the JETT company, which leaves from the Visitor Centre daily at 4.30pm (JD7; buy tickets from Jeff's Bookshop near the Visitor Centre; driver's mobile ☏077 731 0850) and drops off at the JETT office in Abdali (see p.86). Two or three buses **to Aqaba** leave between 6 and 8am, plus another one at around 3–4pm. One bus leaves **to Wadi Rum** at about 6am. There might be a bus **to Karak** (via the Desert Highway) at about noon. Fares for all these are in the order of JD4–6. Journey times are given in "Travel details" at the end of this chapter.

These few routes are all very popular, and you should **book seats in advance**. Ask your hotel manager the day before to reserve you a place on a bus for the next morning. All buses start from the **bus station**, but if you've reserved a seat the bus should come to your hotel's door. If you're not ready when it arrives, it won't wait.

Buses leave hourly until mid-afternoon for **Ma'an**, which has fairly frequent connections to Amman, Aqaba and Karak. There are also regular buses to **Shobak**, which has no connections to anywhere but is a good place to start a hitch up the King's Highway to Qadisiyyeh and beyond.

If you know you must travel on a Friday – when there are far fewer buses – check schedules in advance with your hotel.

Chartering a **taxi** to Rum costs about JD40, to Aqaba JD40, to Karak JD50–55, to Amman on the Desert Highway JD75, or to Amman along the King's Highway JD100 or more.

> **Information**
>
> For useful **information** about Petra and the services on offer in Wadi Musa, go to the official website ⓦwww.petrapark.com – and then compare with the unofficial site ⓦwww.jordanjubilee.com. For details of the Petra Visitor Centre and the practicalities of booking guides, turn to p.278.

dropped here, you could ask the bus driver to let you out at the hotel of your choice along the way. In a **serveece** you're more likely to find that the driver "recommends" a particular hotel by taking you to the door: he does this to earn a commission from the hotel, who will correspondingly charge you more for your room. Be aware that hotels which encourage this kind of deception are unlikely to be the best in town. See p.121 for details of similar scams employed by some Wadi Musa serveece drivers.

Alternative methods of arrival include a morning coach run daily by the JETT company from their Abdali office in Amman (details on p.121); note that this drops off only at the Visitor Centre down by the gate, not at the bus station. There is also a private bus arriving daily **from Madaba via the King's Highway** operated by the *Mariam Hotel* – full details on p.224.

Town transport

The only means of transport within Wadi Musa is **taxi**. The standard tourist rate for a ride through town – from the Petra ticket gate to Ain Musa or anywhere in between – is JD2, but to reach that figure you'll have to bargain hard each time. There are always plenty of taxis sharking around the streets; to book one, call ☏03 215 6777 or ask at your hotel reception.

The **walk** along the main road between the town centre and the Petra gate is 2km – easy going down, miserable going up, especially after a full day of walking in Petra. Some hotels offer **free transport** to and from the gate in the morning and the evening; check details in advance.

Accommodation

Wadi Musa has **accommodation** to suit all budgets. There are dozens of hotels, but many are drab mid-range places without much style or comfort; our recommendations pick out the best. Low-budget travellers have several recommendable places, but the few luxury hotels are acceptable, if rarely outstanding. Service is almost universally poor.

Hotel prices here are more open to **bargaining** than anywhere else in Jordan, especially in the low seasons (June–Aug & Nov–Feb). **En-suite bathrooms** are offered as standard in virtually all hotels above budget level. Another feature of Wadi Musa is that all hotels have **rates** for "room only", "bed and breakfast" and "half-board" (breakfast and dinner, though meals in some of the smaller places can be skimpy): make sure you confirm what you want when you check in.

Campsites

The best **campsite** in the Petra area is the ⚜ *Ammarin Camp* (☏079 975 5551, ⓦwww.bedouincamp.net; ❸), a bedouin-style permanent encampment run by the Ammareen tribe, and located in a beautiful, quiet spot out near "Little Petra" (see p.311): from the Little Petra access road, you turn off at the signpost and drive for 1km on a marked dirt-track to reach the campsite, which is tucked away out of site behind a crag. A **taxi** here from Wadi Musa would cost about JD8–10.

The site has a series of long, low bedouin goat-hair tents divided up into sections and given concrete floors: you sleep on reasonably comfortable beds with mattresses, and there is a block with proper, flushing toilets plus hot and cold running water. The big plus is that you are completely away from the hustle and bustle of Wadi Musa, nestling in amongst the mountains under a starry sky – and that your money is going straight to the Ammareen community co-operative. The experience is wonderful – and being able to escape from Wadi Musa for a night or two is a great relief. The rate given above (➌) covers **bed and breakfast**. Other meals are available, but if you're watching the pennies try and self-cater: dinner – though delicious, and comprising a range of hot and cold dishes served around the campfire – is charged at a hefty JD35 per person. You can also pitch your own tent here (JD15pp) or park a motor-home (JD20).

As you drive between Petra and Little Petra, you'll see off to the side of the road a couple more "luxury camps", most prominently the *King Aretas Camp*. These are run by tour company entrepreneurs, and are neither luxurious nor attractive – yet have the gall to charge JD80–100 per person half-board. Avoid.

Inexpensive hotels

The main thing to look out for in a **budget hotel** in Wadi Musa is **heating**: summer nights are pleasantly cool (several of the better hotels offer cut-price rates for sleeping on a mattress on the roof), but all during winter and even as late as April, mornings and evenings can be chilly. **Location** is also an issue: you have to weigh up whether you'd rather pay more to be closer to the Petra gate, or would prefer to be up in the town centre near cafés and shops.

If you're travelling on a budget, be aware that Wadi Musa is unique: unlike anywhere else in Jordan there are people involved in the lower echelons of the tourism industry here who unashamedly target backpackers for money or sex (or both). If you keep your ear to the ground, and monitor the online travel forums, you'll come across stories of pushy staff at particular hotels, rip-off taxi-drivers, restaurant owners playing the gigolo, and worse. If we haven't reviewed a particular hotel here, there's probably a good reason why you should avoid it. Common petty deceptions include paying taxi-drivers to bring tourists to the door (and then charging the tourists extra to make up) and/or setting a loss-leading room rate of, say, 3JD per person before extracting profit on meals, transport, internet, beers and so on: one particularly lucrative line is in touting cheap desert tours of Wadi Rum (for more on this, see p.326). As far as harassment goes, a favoured ploy is to offer to show visitors some amazing remote viewpoint, or invite guests to an evening meal at a special desert campsite. Women on their own in Wadi Musa should never accept such an offer.

All the hotels listed below are marked on the **map** on p.268.

Araba View ☎03 215 6107. Rock-bottom basic rooms, with Wadi Musa's best views from the rear balcony. Lack of heating lets it down. Go for the en-suite rooms on the upper floor. ➊

Cleopetra ☎03 215 7090 or 077 658 2384, Ⓔcleopetra_h@hotmail.com. One of the best budget hotels in Wadi Musa, run by the affable, knowledgeable and traveller-savvy Mosleh Farajat. Rooms are clean, comfortable and good value; by the time you read this, the plans for expansion may also be complete, which means bigger, better rooms and more facilities. Rates include a good breakfast, free transport to and from the Petra gate and free drinks. An excellent choice. ➊–➋

Moon Valley ☎03 215 7131, Ⓔhotelmoonvalley @yahoo.com. A decent choice located a short walk down the hill from Wadi Musa town centre. Rooms are comfortable and reasonable value, and service is relatively forthcoming. ➌

The Valentine Inn is a busy backpacker hotel in the middle of Wadi Musa. If you google it, you'll find mixed reviews. However, please note that Rough Guides do not recommend the Valentine Inn as a place to stay.

Mussa Spring ☏03 215 6310, ✉musaspring_hotel@yahoo.co.uk, ⊛www.geocities.com/mussaspring. Long-standing backpackers' favourite, situated right up beside Ain Musa, with friendly, efficient staff and a sociable atmosphere. Rooms are basic but clean: there are singles, doubles and dorms, both en suite and with shared bathrooms. Rates include free transport to and from the gate. ❶–❷

el-Rashid ☏03 215 6800, ✉rashid@joinnet.com.jo. Decent option overlooking the central roundabout, with clean, cosy and quiet rooms, relatively amenable service and a good reputation. ❸–❹
Sunset ☏03 215 6579, ⊛www.petrasunset.com. The only budget hotel on the tourist street close to the gate – and it's a surprisingly good option. Rooms are all en suite; some are a bit too poky for comfort, but most are perfectly adequate, if characterless. ❷

Mid-range hotels

There's a large number of **mid-range** hotels in Wadi Musa, almost all of them existing for tour-group business (and few of them with rooms or service standards as good as they should be). Rates for individuals are frequently much higher but you can limit the damage by reserving well ahead; if you arrive without a reservation, it pays to shop around. Hotels close to the gate charge considerably more than those back in town.

All the hotels listed below are marked on the **map** on p.268.

Al-Anbat I ☏03 215 6265, ⊛www.alanbat.com. Great value, with friendly service and a cosy atmosphere. These rooms – in the main building and the four-floor rear extension – are some of the largest in Wadi Musa: airy and spacious, with high ceilings, decent furniture and balconies offering exceptional sunset views from this elevated location high above Wadi Musa town. Free transport to and from the gate, a place to pitch a tent (or park a caravan) and good meals add to the appeal. There are more, cheaper rooms at the *Al-Anbat II* annexe down in the town centre. ❹
Amra Palace ☏03 215 7070, ⊛www.amrapalace.com. Decent three-star hotel on a quiet backstreet in the town centre – big, too, with 72 rooms – that has attractive pine decor, a nice little palm-shaded garden and a covered swimming pool. It's used chiefly by whistle-stop tour groups, which means both service and ambience aren't what they should be, but the quality of rooms can make up for that. ❺–❻
Candles ☏03 215 5333, ✉candles@nets.com.jo. An uninspired three-star, which only just scrapes a recommendation here – partly for its location, a short walk from the Petra gate, and partly for its upper-floor rooms, particularly the corner room 101 and the junior suite 311, both of which offer space and views that make up for the small and disappointing bathrooms. Bargain them down. ❺

Flowers ☏03 215 6771, ✉flowershotel@hotmail.com. Comfortable but cramped two-star rooms are slightly overpriced, but only because of the hotel's great location, a short walk from the Petra gate. With on-the-ball management and a returning clientele of small-group hiking tour companies, it's popular and often full. ❹
Petra Moon ☏03 215 6220, ⊛www.petramoonhotel.com. Well-kept little two-star hotel a short walk from the Petra gate, with clean, comfortable en-suite doubles (some offering fine views) and spot-on service from easy-going manager Samir Nawafleh, who offers Rough Guide readers a ten percent discount on request. ❹
Silk Road ☏03 215 7222, ⊛www.petrasilkroad.com. Characterful, pleasant upper-three-star on the tourist street down by the Petra gate, frequently used by tour groups and excellent value for money. Renovated throughout in 2008, including with new beds and mattresses. A reliable hotel with a reputation to uphold. ❻
Valley Stars Inn ☏03 215 5733, ⊛www.valleystarsinn.com. The closest Petra gets to a boutique hotel, located slightly above the town centre: just eight rooms, spacious, clean and quiet, with stone-tiled floors and stylish interiors. A great choice for individual travellers seeking to escape the demands of Petra's mass-market tourism. ❹–❺

Luxury hotels

At the **luxury** end of the scale, global chains – Marriott, Crowne Plaza, Mövenpick – compete with homegrown five-star hotels such as the award-winning *Taybet Zaman* and *Beit Zaman*. But, in general, Petra is surprisingly poorly served: at such a famous location you might expect world-class design, top-level facilities and impeccable service, but none of the hotels on offer truly matches up in all areas. All the hotels listed below are marked on the **map** on p.268.

Beit Zaman ☏ 03 215 7401, ✉ front .office@beitzaman.com, ⓦ www.jordan tourismresorts.com & ⓦ www.beitzaman.com. Eye-popping five-star hotel that occupies the old Nawafleh quarter of Wadi Musa, spreading back up the hillside within the town. The old stone cottages of this traditional village-within-a-village have been converted into luxury rooms – 129 of them, covering an area of 43,000 square metres. (Unless you phone reception for a golf-cart, be prepared to do a bit of walking.) The hugely spacious rooms – some with balcony – have been tastefully appointed, with traditional fabrics and rugs set against rough sandstone blocks, part-exposed, part-plastered in white. The hotel includes a fine-dining restaurant and Wadi Musa's largest swimming pool. ❾

Crowne Plaza ☏ 03 215 6266, ⓦ www.cprpetra .com. A decent, reliable five-star hotel, located very close to the gate (a short stroll from the Visitor Centre); this is a favourite with individuals and upscale tour groups alike. The design of the hotel is a bit old-fashioned (it was built in the 1980s), and rooms are comfortable but bland. It's worth visiting to sit out on their poolside, perched in front of the rocky ravines – especially at night when floodlights illuminate the mountains. Its *Guesthouse* annexe, right beside the gate, is less pricey, but is usually given over exclusively to tour groups. ❾

Golden Tulip Kings' Way ☏ 03 215 6799, ⓦ www.goldentulipkingsway.com. Pleasant, if generic, four-star choice up at Ain Musa, with comfortable (though rather cramped) rooms and attentive service. This place makes for an especially good choice in summer, when it can be noticeably cooler and more pleasant up here than in the town. However, no free rides are offered down to the gate. ❽–❾

Marriott ☏ 03 215 6407, ⓦ www.marriott.com /mpqmc. An excellent five-star choice, located 4.5km out of town high up on the Scenic Road, with spectacular views over the mountains. Public areas are comfortable but not excessively grand, and there's a good swimming pool with a panoramic view across the valley. Rooms are good, with big windows, well-appointed bathrooms and large beds. Service is outstanding – perhaps the best in Wadi Musa. ❾

Mövenpick ☏ 03 215 7111, ⓦ www .movenpick-petra.com. Petra's top choice, superbly designed in traditional Damascene style right down to the last exquisite detail. The stunning four-storey courtyard atrium, with its mosaic-tiled fountain and palm trees, vies for gasps with the adjacent bar, its hand-painted walls inlaid with turquoise and gold leaf, and featuring hand-carved wooden screens and embroidered fabrics. The guest rooms are immaculate, service is calm and efficient, and the location – metres from the Petra gate – ideal. Don't miss the roof garden at sunset. Its sister property, the similarly grand *Mövenpick Nabatean Castle*, located 6.5km out on the Scenic Road, is often used only for tour groups and sometimes has restricted opening: check with the main hotel. ❾

Petra Palace ☏ 03 215 6723, ⓦ www .petrapalace.com.jo. A fine local four-star hotel on the main tourist street near the Petra gate – extended first in 2007 and then in stages there-after, eventually reaching 170 rooms in total. The exterior and lobby are lavish; some rooms in the older wing are merely competent, but the newer rooms are bigger and better appointed, some with poolside access. A very popular choice with tour groups from around the world: as an individual, bargain hard to bring the rate down. ❼–❽

Taybet Zaman ☏ 03 215 0111, ✉ reservation @taybetzaman.com, ⓦ www.jordantourismresorts .com & ⓦ www.taybetzaman.com. Award-winning luxury hotel built on the old Ottoman quarter of Taybeh village, 11km from Wadi Musa. Each old cottage is now a self-contained single or double "room", tastefully furnished and fitted out to inter-national five-star standard; there are restaurants, bars, a pool, Turkish bath, shops and two heliports tucked away in different corners of the "village", which is separated off from the rest of workaday Taybeh by a high perimeter wall. The only thing lacking, of course, is any kind of original atmos-phere: this place is now firmly on the tourist map and is often heaving with groups, at which times service standards suffer badly. ❾

PETRA | Wadi Musa: Accommodation

6

The Town

There's not much to do in **Wadi Musa**. Attempts to create an artisans' quarter in **Elgee**, a cluster of restored stone cottages behind the town centre (and also the original name for the Wadi Musa settlement), have come to nothing: it's pleasant to stroll here, away from the bustle, but there's nothing to see or buy.

The best shopping is down on the Tourist Street near the gate, where you'll find a string of **craft and souvenir shops**, selling postcards and trinkets as well as rugs and antiques. Several are the retail outlets for local women's cooperatives, selling handmade crafts, while the Sand Castle shop is notable for its high-quality antiques, including pieces in copper, brass, silver and wood from Syria, Yemen and elsewhere, as well as handwoven carpets. Nearby on the same street is the **Made In Jordan** gallery and gift shop, run by the Petra Moon tour company. Here, the crafts come from charitable suppliers such as the Royal Society for the Conservation of Nature, the Jordan River Foundation, the Noor al-Hussein Foundation and the Royal Marine Conservation Society (JREDS) – all of which employ chiefly rural women (in JREDS' case, the wives and daughters of Aqaba fishermen) to produce traditional crafts and handmade items of the highest quality. Also on show are pieces made by individual artisans from Wadi Musa and around Jordan.

The same building hosts the **Petra Kitchen**, an idea (also by Petra Moon) to give added perspective to a Petra visit. This is not a true restaurant; rather, it is a way for a small number of visitors at a time to get hands-on experience of local culture by working with a team of Wadi Musa women to prepare ingredients, cook an evening meal and then eat together. Under guidance you chop, mix and assemble a range of salads, soup, hot and cold *mezze* (starters), a main course such as *mansaf* or *maqlouba*, and bedouin coffee and tea – the idea being that you learn new culinary techniques, handle unfamiliar products and break the social ice at the same time. The ingredients all come from Wadi Musa or the nearby Dana Nature Reserve; the tableware comes from the women's ceramics workshop at Iraq al-Amir near Amman (see p.149); and the aprons, tablecloths and napkins were all hand-embroidered by women working with the Jordan River Foundation. To take part in the courses, which run when demand is

Petra tour companies and guides

Down on the "Tourist Street" near the Petra ticket gate are a handful of experienced and well-respected tour companies who – as well as covering trips around Jordan – can put together short adventure-style excursions on the fly. Ideas include a sunset horseride at Baydha, a half or full day's hiking, horseriding or mountain-biking in the hills above Wadi Musa, a two-day camel trek to Sabra, including full support, and so on. Talk first to **Petra Moon** (☏03 215 6665, ⓦwww.petramoon.com) and **La Beduina** (☏03 215 7099, ⓦwww.labeduinatours.com), then compare with **Zaman Tours** (☏03 215 7723, ⓦwww.zamantours.com) and **Jordan Tours & Travel** (☏03 215 4666, ⓦwww.jordantours-travel.com).

Smaller operations, run by recommended individual guides in Wadi Musa and focused mainly on hiking and low-key wilderness exploration, include **Jordan Beauty Tours** (☏079 558 1644, ⓦwww.jordanbeauty.com) and **Jordan Inspiration Tours** (☏077 609 7581, ⓦwww.jitours.com).

To get well off the beaten track, contact the **Ammareen tribe** through their campsite at "Little Petra" (☏079 975 5551, ⓦwww.bedouincamp.net; see also p.271): the website is very detailed, and includes outlines of guided treks on foot and by camel through areas of southern Jordan little known to outsiders.

sufficient (generally every evening in high season) you must **book in advance** with the Petra Moon tour company (☎03 215 6665, ⊛www.petramoon.com). They can also extend the concept to run as a five-day **culinary course**, including exploratory trips to local markets and different menus each night.

Eating and drinking

For **eating in Wadi Musa**, most travellers either stick with whatever's on offer in their hotel or end up chewing pizza at one of the distinctly ordinary restaurants on the Tourist Street down by the Petra gate. There are some better places up in town. As usual, though, the only places for **drinking alcohol** are in the big hotels or a couple of specifically designated bars. All places listed here are marked on the map on p.000.

🏃 **Arabi** one of Wadi Musa's best local restaurants, located just up from the main roundabout. It's always busy, and does a wide range of basic dishes – falafel, hummus, *fuul*, salads, kebabs and more, served with fresh flat bread. The place is clean, staff are friendly and prices are low: a meal shouldn't cost you more than JD4–5.

Bukhara a sociable restaurant in the town centre, with streetside tables offering views of the mountains. The speciality is grilled meat: mouthwateringly aromatic smoke from the barbecuing kebabs regularly wafts over the street. A locals' favourite.

Cleopetra restaurant not to be confused with the *Cleopetra* hotel, this is an OK diner, empty during the day but often crowded with *shawerma*-munching locals at night. Avoid the rather tasteless buffet meals, however.

Mövenpick hotel ☎03 215 7111. The hotel's *Al-Saraya* restaurant (daily 6.30–10.30pm) has a lavish buffet, from fresh vegetables wok-fried as you watch, through gourmet breads, kebabs, fresh fish and an array of salads to proper Black Forest gateau, everything top quality. It's not cheap (about JD20–25), but the quality and variety are excellent. When there is enough business – that is, when they have a tour group who aren't inside Petra – they also do a buffet lunch here (noon–3.30pm). Alongside, but several notches up the scale, *Al-Iwan* (daily 7–11.30pm) offers seriously sophisticated à la carte dining for JD50 and up. In addition, the hotel bakery shop (daily 9am–7pm) sells delicious croissants and fresh-baked loaves. If

---

Eating inside Petra

There are only limited facilities for **eating** once you get **inside Petra** – and prices are higher than usual (understandable, considering everything has to be trucked in). Along the path near the theatre are stalls offering tea and snacks, while around the Qasr al-Bint you'll find some **tent cafés** offering adequate – sometimes pretty good – buffet lunches for about JD10 or so.

The only proper **restaurant** inside Petra is the *Basin* (daily 11.30am–4pm, depending on weather conditions; ☎03 215 6266), located beneath shady tree cover opposite the Qasr al-Bint. It is run by the *Crowne Plaza* hotel, with whom it's not a bad idea to book in advance: busy times can see tour groups occupying every table. Buffet lunch, including a full range of salad dishes, falafel, barbecue/kebabs and dessert, costs JD15.50. To be honest it's barely worth it: unless you're a dedicated carnivore, go for the salads-only option, at half the price. They have cold beer in cans and on draught (JD5–7).

Your best option is to carry supplies with you for the day. All hotels can provide a **lunchbox** on request – from a budget hotel, reckon on JD3–5 for bread, cheese, fruit, yoghurt and a drink. Groceries and minimarkets in the centre of Wadi Musa can provide simple **picnic fare**, but nothing so energy-sustaining as nuts or dried fruit. The Sanabel bakery, just below the Shaheed Roundabout, is open from before dawn. Bear in mind that in the summer you'll need to be drinking four or five litres of **water** a day, possibly more; unless you can carry it all, you should budget on shelling out JD1–2 at the tent cafés for water or a soft drink to keep yourself hydrated along the way.

all this is beyond you, settle for Swiss ice cream in the stunning atrium.

Petra Kitchen not a true restaurant, but still one of Petra's best dining experiences. See "The Town" account above.

Red Cave a good choice on the Tourist St near the gate. The interior is large and cool, and the food is excellent, including – among many staple dishes – a bedouin *gallaya* (rice with lamb or chicken in a spicy tomato/onion sauce). Reckon on a meal for around JD6.

Rose City Restaurant close to the gate, a basic, inexpensive diner with an all-day buffet and a handful of à la carte staples.

al-Wadi passable food, with pleasant terrace tables set out in the evening overlooking the town-centre roundabout. However poor service can let it down – and some of the staff imagine themselves to be God's gift to women.

Wadi Hadhramaut wonderful little restaurant in the town centre, with no English sign (it's diagonally opposite *Bukhara*), named after a desert area of eastern Yemen. Though the chefs are Egyptian, and the clientele Jordanian, the signature dish is a Yemeni *mandi* – a delicious concoction of tender chicken, vegetables, spices, nuts and *labneh* yoghurt laid over a bed of rice.

al-Wardeh al-Shamieh a reliable choice (also signed as *Shami Flower*) in the town centre serving simple, good-quality Arabic food. Don't expect to pay the same price as the locals, however: an ordinary nosh here of hummus, falafel and tea is likely to cost as much as JD5.

Listings

Hammams steam the dust out of your pores in a *hammam* – either five-star versions in the big hotels (notably the *Marriott*) or simpler establishments in Wadi Musa town centre such as the pleasant but rather frenetic Salome (☎03 215 7342).

Library with half a dozen books, the elegant, wood-panelled Burckhardt Library (daily 10am–10pm, roughly), on the mezzanine floor of the *Mövenpick Hotel*, barely counts as a place of study, but it's nonetheless a cool, peaceful spot for some quiet downtime and is just about the only place in Wadi Musa where nobody's trying to sell you something.

Medical facilities the well-equipped Queen Rania Hospital – with 24hr emergency room – is about 5km out of town on the Scenic Road towards Taybeh. Pharmacies in Wadi Musa town centre have qualified English-speaking staff.

Police in emergency, dial ☎191. Police patrol most parts of the Petra ruins in daylight hours. Headquarters (☎03 215 6551) is off the Police Roundabout in Wadi Musa, while English-speaking tourist police are available 24hr in their main office (☎03 215 6441) opposite the Visitor Centre.

Post offices Wadi Musa's post offices (all daily 8am–5pm, Fri close noon) lie at Ain Musa; beside Shaheed Roundabout; and 50m from the gate.

Petra البتراء

After you've finished coping with the practicalities of bed and board in Wadi Musa, **PETRA** comes as an assault on the senses. As you leave the entrance gate behind, the sense of exposure to the elements is thrilling; the natural drama of the location, the sensuous colouring of the sandstone, the stillness, heat and clarity of light – along with a lingering, under-the-skin quality of supernatural power that seems to seep out of the rock – make it an unforgettable adventure.

Whether you're in a group or alone, you'd do well to branch off the main routes every now and again. These days Petra sees somewhere around three thousand visitors a day in peak season. The place is physically large enough to absorb that many (although archeologists and environmentalists are both lobbying for controls on numbers), but the central path that runs past the major sights can get busy between about 10am and 4pm. Taking a ten- or fifteen-minute detour to explore either side of the path or wander along a side-valley is a good idea, since not only does it get you out of the hubbub, but it's also liable to yield previously unseen views and fascinating little carved niches or facades. All over Petra, the Nabateans carved for themselves paths and signposts, shrines and houses in what seem to us remote and desolate crags.

Practicalities

The **Petra Visitor Centre** (daily 6am–10pm; ℡03 215 6020, ⓦwww .petrapark.com), 50m from the gate, is the main office for information, with efficient, helpful staff. Core hours are 7am–6pm (4pm in winter): beforehand only the ticket window is open, and afterwards there are only security guards on duty. Inside is also a **shop** for books, maps and souvenirs (same times).

See the box below for details of proposed changes to the practicalities of visiting Petra: by the time you visit, information given in this section may be obsolete.

Tickets

All **tickets** are sold from a window beside the Visitor Centre main door. Admission costs a hefty JD21 for one day, JD26 for two days, or JD31 for three or four days; this refers to blocks of consecutive days, with no chopping and changing allowed. Children under 15 go free. Tickets are dated, stamped and non-transferable (you have to sign multi-day passes and carry ID), and they're checked at the gate as well as at varying points within Petra; even if you hike several kilometres out of the way to avoid the gate (some foolhardy folk endanger their lives doing just that), there's no guarantee a police officer won't pop up on some remote crag and ask to see your ticket. Note that "Little Petra", Baydha and Wu'ayra currently fall outside the (undefined) ticketed area, and so have free entry.

Round the corner from the Visitor Centre is the **Petra gate**, the single public entrance into the site (open for admission daily 6am–5pm, winter closes 4pm; return permitted until dusk). Following increasing concern over the damage done by tourism, it is forbidden for visitors to stay in Petra after sunset, and you may be asked to start on the long walk out well in advance. In any case it's potentially dangerous to do some of the longer descents (such as from the Monastery or the High Place) in low light.

A new vision

At the time of writing, plans are in place to completely reorganize the whole way that visitors experience Petra. Instead of one ticket granting admission to the entire site, there is to be separate ticketing for each of seven marked trails: you choose in advance which trails you wish to follow and purchase tickets for those routes at the Visitor Centre (which, itself, is to be completely rebuilt). There is to be waymarking of trails within Petra for the first time, along with information boards in English and Arabic at major sites. The Turkmaniyya road, behind the *Basin* restaurant, will be consolidated – enabling visitors to be driven out of the site, rather than facing the long walk back to the gate. Eco-toilets are to be installed at key points, as will more refreshment kiosks and rest areas. The horse-handlers will be in uniform and their carriages are to be redesigned for comfort and safety.

By the time you visit, much of this may already be in place – and the intention is to have introduced most or all of the changes by 2011. Time will tell how they impact on a visit.

There's enough to explore in Petra that you could easily spend days or weeks in the place. Shelling out for a one-day ticket will have you running around like crazy to get value for money; if your pockets are deep enough, paying for four days buys time to pace yourself and explore to your heart's content.

Major **highlights**, which count as unmissable, are the **Siq**, the **Treasury**, the **High Place of Sacrifice**, the **Monastery**, a walk up the **Colonnaded Street**, and the **Royal Tombs**. With a break for lunch, and a little time for personal exploration, seeing all this would occupy a pretty exhausting ten-hour day.

If you have even one extra day, your options widen considerably. Choosing an entry or exit route other than the Siq for one trip – via **Madras**, **Wadi Muthlim/Mataha** or **Wadi Turkmaniyyeh** – can give you a feel for outlying landscapes. Depending on your taste for archeology or nature, you could then devote more time to exploring the city centre slopes and the East Cliff, or choose one or two of the many hikes and climbs. You should also budget some downtime to take in the extraordinary late-afternoon **views** from the Qasr al-Bint up the Colonnaded Street towards the fiery East Cliff.

With "Little Petra" (Siq al-Barid) being free-entry, you should wait to take your half-day excursion to Wu'ayra, Little Petra and, possibly, Baydha until the morning after your Petra ticket has expired.

Petra By Night

In times gone by, a visit to Petra wasn't complete without spending a night in the ruins, wandering the rocky paths by moonlight and sleeping in a tomb cave. This is now banned – which has led an informal group of Wadi Musa tour operators to come up with a new approach to Petra that aims to recapture some of that romantic spirit of adventure – and largely succeeds. "**Petra By Night**" is an after-dark guided excursion into the ancient city that adds an entirely new dimension to your experience of the place; the **candlelit walk**, leaving the lights of Wadi Musa behind to enter the pitch-dark valley in silence (talking and mobile phones are banned), is magical. Nothing can match the atmosphere of walking through the Siq at night, with only the light of candles placed every few metres to guide the way. The climax comes as you reach the Treasury plaza, where candles throw flickering shadows onto the great facade as a **bedouin musician** plays on a pipe. The magic lingers while tea is served and you listen to a **story** told by a local guide.

The trip leaves every Monday, Wednesday and Thursday at **8.30pm** from the Visitor Centre (arrive 15min early to register), and delivers you back to the Visitor Centre around 10.30pm. Tickets cost JD12 – and you must **book in advance**, either through your hotel or directly with a local tour company: Petra Moon (see p.275 for contact details) is the most reliable.

"Petra By Night" has become so popular that it's not uncommon to have 150 or 200 people doing the walk. The best advice in these circumstances is to linger at the very back of the crowd: that way, you avoid most of the chatter on the way down and will be walking through the Siq more or less alone in the moonlight. The bedouin piper keeps playing until everyone has arrived at the Treasury, so you won't miss anything. Then there's nothing to stop you heading back early, before the crowd, for another lonesome walk in silence through the Siq, beneath moon and stars.

Guides

The Visitor Centre is where you can hire a professional, accredited **guide**, at fixed prices (current rates are posted on the wall): JD20 for a simple two-and-a-half-hour tour of the major sights, or JD50 for a four-hour tour around the main central areas plus either the Monastery or the High Place of Sacrifice.

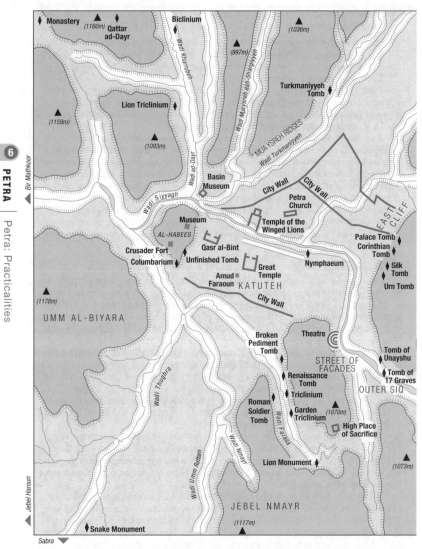

Although you can walk unguided to and from most of the main sights while staying this side of foolhardiness, there are still plenty of places in Petra where you shouldn't venture without a guide. We've mentioned this in the accounts below where relevant. Aside from the dangers of twisted ankles (or worse) scrambling around rocky cliffs, once you leave the main routes it's easy to lose the path. A specialist guide for a day-trip to the summit of Jebel Haroun, or one of the other outlying attractions, will cost upwards of JD100.

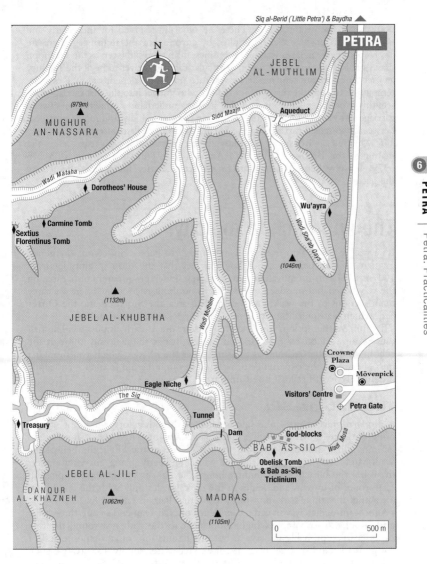

6

Horses

The Visitor Centre is also where you can book and pay for a **horse** to take you down to the Siq entrance, although at JD7 for a walk of 800m, it's not much of a thrill. Of this sum, JD5 goes to the owner of the horse (who is, almost without exception, not the person holding the reins) and JD2 goes to the Petra authorities. The only income gained by the handler is in tips.

It's forbidden to ride horses through the Siq, but a **horse and carriage** seating two can be taken all the way through the Siq to the Treasury for JD20 return – also bookable at the Visitor Centre. These are officially reserved for the elderly and infirm, but in practice can be booked by anyone. For the return leg, there are always plenty of carriages waiting for business from tired sightseers as the afternoon draws on, but if you arrange with a particular carriage-driver to be at the Treasury at a set time for your return ride, he will turn up: his fee depends on it. Resist the temptation to copy the many weary visitors who just get into the first carriage they see; this a breach of honour, and also leads to underhand competition between carriage-drivers to muscle in on each other's business. Ugly arguments over cash between two stalled carriages in the Siq are a feature of Petra afternoons.

If you see a **horse** or **donkey** being mistreated, you can refer the matter to the **Brooke Hospital for Animals** (Sat–Thurs 8am–3pm; ☎03 215 6379, ⓦwww.thebrooke.org), an English-run charity located to the left of the gate.

The approach to the city

It's a walk of over 3km from the gate through to Petra's city centre, the gentle gradient of five percent concealing the fact that the drop in altitude (from 1027m to 861m) is equivalent to a 45-storey skyscraper – barely noticeable on the way down, but murder for tired thighs on the way back up. There are three main sections to the walk: the **Bab as-Siq** area, the **Siq** itself and the **Outer Siq**, which leads into the city centre past the Roman-style **theatre**.

If you have the option, you'd do well to start out as early as possible. The first tour groups set off by 8.30 or 9am, which brings them noisily through the echoing Siq to the Treasury as the sun strikes the facade (which you shouldn't miss). However, the experience of walking through the Siq in silence and alone is definitely worth at least one 6am start.

The Bab as-Siq

A modern gravel path – one side for horses, the other for pedestrians – leads from the gate down through a lunar landscape of white rocky domes and looming cliffs known as the **Bab as-Siq** ("Gate of the Siq"); the bed of the Wadi Musa, carrying water during the winter and early spring, curves alongside. In all but the bleached-out midday hours, the light is soft enough to pick up earth tones of browns and beiges in the rock, but it's only with the last rays of the sunset that there's any hint of the pink that Petra is famous for.

Almost immediately, you can see evidence of Nabatean endeavour: three huge **god-blocks**, 6 to 8 metres high, loom next to the path just round the first corner, carved probably to serve as both representations of and repositories for the gods to stand sentinel over the city's vital water supply. Twenty-five such god-blocks exist in Petra, deemed by the locals to have been the work of *jinn*, or genies, and so also termed **jinn-blocks**; another name is **sahrij**, or water-tanks (ie tanks holding divine energy next to flowing water). The middle one has shaft graves cut into it, implying that it may also have served as some kind of funerary monument. Opposite the god-blocks are some caves, one of which has an obelisk carved in relief, representing the soul of a dead person. Such carved shrines abound in every corner of Petra's mountains, and, for those with time to explore, the small side-valleys off this section of the Bab as-Siq are filled with tombs, water channels, niches and shrines: behind the blocks, the area of domes known as **Ramleh** is cut through by parallel wadis (one of which is Wadi Muthlim; see p.285), and is equally explorable.

Nabatean religion

As much as they created a blend of Arab culture with Mediterranean, the Nabateans also blended inherited elements of the ancient **religions** of Egypt, Syria, Canaan, Assyria and Babylon with elements of the Greek and Roman pantheons, to create specifically Petran forms of worship.

Central to their religion was **rock**. Jehovah, the god of the Israelites was said to inhabit a blank rock called Bet-El ("House of God") – and this insistence on non-figurative representation was shared by many Levantine and Arabian peoples. It was passed on to the Nabateans, in contrast to the Egyptians' and Assyrians' lavish portrayals of gods and goddesses. Concepts such as "the Lord is my rock" also appear many times in the Old Testament, implying an extension of the "House of God" idea so that the rock actually represents the deity itself. Nabatean deities were thus often represented simply by squared-off rocks, termed "**god-blocks**". In addition, a later development gave the rock a third aspect: that of the altar, the contact point between the divine and the material.

At the head of the Nabatean pantheon was **Dushara**, "He of the Shara" (the mountains around Petra), later identified with the Greek god Zeus and the Syrian Hadad. The fact that his name is so closely tied to the locality indicates that he may originally have been an Edomite, rather than a Nabatean, god. To the Nabateans, Dushara was the sun, the Creator, and he was often represented by an obelisk – the visual materialization of a beam of light striking the earth. With the mingling of Semitic and Mediterranean ideas, Dushara also came to be associated with Dionysus, god of wine, and so began to assume human form, bedecked with vines and grapes (as at the Nabatean temple on Jebel Tannur).

At Dushara's side were **Atargatis**, the goddess of fertility, of grain, fruit and fish; **Allat** (which means simply "The Goddess"), who represented the moon; **Manat**, the goddess of luck and fate, suggested to have been the patron deity of Petra and possibly the goddess worshipped at the Treasury; and **al-Uzza** ("The Mighty One"), assimilated with the Egyptian goddess Isis and the Roman goddesses Diana, deity of water and fertility, and Venus, embodied by the evening star and representing spiritual and erotic love. Allat, al-Uzza and Manat are all mentioned by name in the Quran, implying that their cult was still active and popular in Mecca as late as the seventh century, the time of the Prophet Muhammad.

The Nabateans also had many smaller gods, including **al-Kutbay**, god of writing; **She'a-al-Qawm**, the patron deity of caravans; **Qos**, originally an Edomite god; and **Baal-Shamin**, a Phoenician god especially popular in northern Nabatea, who had a temple somewhere near the modern mosque in the centre of Wadi Musa town.

The Obelisk Tomb and Bab as-Siq Triclinium

The first major Nabatean monuments are a few metres further on, and – being on an exposed corner – badly eroded. Although apparently the upper and lower halves of a single monument, the **Obelisk Tomb** and **Bab as-Siq Triclinium** may be separate entities, carved at different times. Above, four huge obelisks guard the entrance to a cave in the rock; such freestanding obelisks are like the god-blocks, representing a god and storing divine energy in a material form. Between the four is an eroded figure in a niche; the cave behind holds graves. Below, the *triclinium*, or dining room, is a single chamber with stone benches on three walls, for holding banquets in honour of the dead. On the opposite side of the path, 5m off the ground, is a bilingual **inscription** in Nabatean and Greek, recording that one Abdmank chose this spot to build a tomb for himself and his children, although it's not certain that this refers to the monuments opposite.

Just past the Obelisk Tomb is a path leading to the hidden Petran suburb of **Madras**, tucked into the hills to the left (south), from where it's possible to cross the hilltops over the Jebel al-Jilf plateau, avoiding the Siq, to the top of the high, narrow Danqur al-Khazneh valley leading down to the Treasury; the views are stunning, and the sense of isolation is worth the scramble if you've already seen the Siq. However, the route is far from clear, relying on worn Nabatean rock-cut stairs, and you'll need a guide.

The dam and tunnel

Back on the path, the curving northern bank of the wadi is liberally pockmarked with caves and niches, round to the point where the path is taken over the wadi bed by a bridge and the Wadi Musa itself is blocked by a **dam**; this is almost exactly the same configuration as was built by the Nabateans in about 50 AD, and for the same reasons: to divert the floodwaters of the Wadi Musa away from the Siq so that the principal entry into the city could remain clear year round. It's here, at the mouth of the Siq, that all horseriders must dismount and that entrance tickets will be checked. On the opposite bank of the wadi are four obelisks, one mentioning a man who lived in Reqem (Petra) but died in Jerash.

To the right, the Nabatean-carved, eight-metre-high **tunnel** – guarded by another, solitary god-block – enabled the floodwaters to feed into the **Wadi Muthlim** leading north around the gigantic Jebel al-Khubtha; today, this is an alternative way into Petra (see box, p.285).

The Siq

From the crowded, horse-smelly bridge, the path drops sharply down over the lip of the dam into Petra's most dramatic and awe-inspiring natural feature – the **Siq** gorge, principal entrance into the city, yet invisible until you're almost upon it. Overhead, the path was originally framed by an ornamental **arch**, which collapsed in 1896 although its abutments survive, decorated by the smoothed-out remnants of niches flanked by pilasters. All the way along the left-hand wall is a Nabatean rock-cut **water channel**, and on the right-hand wall further along are the remains of terracotta pipes for water, both probably dating from the same time as the reorganization of the city water supply that prompted the building of the dam. At various points, you'll come across worn patches of the Roman/Nabatean road which originally paved the Siq along its entire length, in between stretches of newly consolidated pathway.

The Siq was formed when tectonic forces split the mountain in two. The waters of the Wadi Musa subsequently found their way into the fault, laying a bed of gravel and eroding the sharp corners into curves as smooth as eggshell, helped by the cool winds that blow in your face all the way down. The path along the wadi bed twists and turns between high, bizarrely eroded sandstone cliffs for 1200m, sometimes widening to form broad, sunlit open spaces in the echoing heart of the mountain, dotted with a tree or two and cut through by the cries of birds; in other places, the looming 150-metre-high walls close in to little more than a couple of metres apart, blocking out sound, warmth and even daylight. All the way down, high, narrow wadis feed in from either side, most of them blocked by modern dams (often set back to show the remains of the original Nabatean dams) to limit both flood danger and unauthorized exploration: once you're in the Siq, the only way is onward or backward. Dotted along the walls at many points are small **votive niches**, some Greek-style with pediments, others with mini god-blocks. After about 350m, a small **shrine** has been carved on the downhill side of a freestanding outcrop of rock, with two god-blocks, the larger of which is carved with eyes and a nose. A little further

The Wadi Muthlim route

Although you should definitely follow the Siq into Petra at least once (and probably more than once, at different times of day), if you've allocated several days to a visit, the beautiful **Wadi Muthlim** is a good alternative entry route through stunning scenery, but taking no less than two hours to deliver you to the Nymphaeum in the city centre. Due to the very real danger of flash floods, you shouldn't attempt it at all during the rainy season – roughly November to March – and even as late as May, there may be difficult-to-avoid standing pools of water harbouring water snakes: wading would be a big mistake.

Before beginning the walk, you can take a small detour from the dam to the **Eagle Niche**, set in the rocks 400m to the northwest. Cross the wadi over the roof of the tunnel and head left up the second side-valley; it's a short scramble over the smooth, hot rock up to a set of small niches carved in the right-hand wall, one of which features a strikingly carved eagle with wings outspread.

Back at the tunnel, Wadi Muthlim – full of oleanders, but with high walls cutting out all sound bar the occasional birdsong – is easily passable up to the remains of another Nabatean dam; beyond here, the path gets steadily narrower until you reach a point where a massive boulder all but blocks the way. It's possible to squeeze past, and the path continues to narrow until, with the wadi floor no wider than your foot, you reach a T-junction; arrows on the solid walls all around will point you left. This cross-wadi is the **Sidd Maajn**, equally narrow, but beautifully eroded by flowing water. As you proceed, seemingly moving through the heart of the mountain, you'll notice the Nabateans were here before you: there are dozens of carved niches, some featuring pediments, other curving horns. It's around here that the way might be blocked by rockpools. Eventually, you'll emerge into the open **Wadi Mataha** (see p.310), about 600m northeast of Dorotheos' House, and the best part of 2km northeast of the Nymphaeum.

on, on the left-hand wall at a sharp right-hand bend, is a merchant in Egyptian-style dress leading two large **camels**; the water channel originally ran behind all five sets of legs, and it's just possible to trace the worn outline of the camels' humps in the rock wall.

When you think the gorge can't possibly go on any longer, there comes a dark, narrow defile, framing at its end a strip of extraordinary classical architecture. With your eye softened to the natural flows of eroded rock in the Siq, the clean lines of columns and pediments come as a revelation. As you step out into the daylight, there is no more dramatic or breathtaking vision in the whole of Jordan than the facade of the Treasury.

The Treasury

Perfectly positioned opposite the main route into Petra, the **Treasury** was designed to impress, and, two thousand years on, the effect is undiminished. What strikes you first is how well preserved it is; carved deep into the rockface and concealed in a high-walled ellipse of a valley (known as Wadi al-Jarra, "Urn Valley"), it has been protected from wind and rain from day one. The detailing of the capitals and pediments on the forty-by-thirty-metre facade is still crisp. The best times to view the Treasury are when the sun strikes it directly, between about 9 and 11am, and late in the afternoon, around 5 or 6pm, when the whole facade is suffused with a reflected reddish-pink glow from the walls all around.

The name "Treasury" is not Nabatean, and derives from the local name for such a seemingly inexplicable construction – **Khaznet al-Faraoun** ("Treasury of the Pharaoh"). Unaware of classical history, and unable to fathom why anyone should carve such a monument, the bedouin of Wadi Musa tagged it as the work of the pharaoh, lord of black magic. In pursuit of the Israelites after the Exodus (the legend goes), the pharaoh was slowed down by having to carry all his treasure, so he created the Treasury and deposited his riches in the urn at the very top of the facade, out of human reach. For centuries after Petra's abandonment, bedouin marksmen tried to shatter the urn, and so release the treasure, but to no avail: their only success was in blasting chunks off the solid urn.

▲ The Treasury, Petra

To the left of the facade, a set of stairs comes down into the valley from the Danqur al-Khazneh area. Off to the right, a wall blocks the narrow north end of the Wadi al-Jarra; if you climb over the wall, then double back to scramble up the rocks, you'll reach a small, jutting plateau, with a perfect view from above of the Treasury and the whole bustling plaza in front of it.

The Treasury facade

The **carvings** on the Treasury facade, though much damaged by iconoclasts, are still discernible and show to what extent Nabatean culture was an amalgam of elements from the Hellenistic and Middle Eastern worlds.

The Treasury is normally dated to the first century BC, possibly to the reign of King Aretas III Philhellene ("the Greek-lover"), who brought architects to Petra from the centres of Hellenistic culture throughout the Mediterranean. Atop the broken pediments, framing the upper storey, are two large eagles, symbols of the Nabateans' chief male deity, Dushara. In a central position on the rounded *tholos* below the urn is what's been identified as a representation of Isis, an Egyptian goddess equated with the Nabatean goddess al-Uzza; in the recesses behind are two Winged Victories, although the remaining four figures, all of whom seem to be holding axes aloft, haven't been identified. Two lions, also symbolizing al-Uzza, adorn the entablature between the two storeys. At ground level, the mounted riders are Castor and Pollux, sons of Zeus. The parallel marks up the side of the facade, which occur in a couple of other places in Petra, may well have been footholds for the sculptors and masons.

One column is obviously new, a brick-and-plaster replacement for the original, which fell in antiquity. This neatly demonstrates one of the most extraordinary features of **Nabatean architecture**. A normal building that lost a main support like this would have come crashing down soon after; these Nabatean columns, though, support nothing. Like most of Petra's monuments, the entire Treasury "building" was sculpted *in situ*, gouged out of the unshaped rock in a kind of reverse architecture.

At the base of the facade, recent **excavations** into the four metres of gravel that overlie the original Nabatean surface revealed that the Treasury was carved above a line of older facades, also probably tombs, which are now viewable through a grille set into the ground.

Inside the Treasury doorway – unlike the scene in *Indiana Jones and the Last Crusade*, when Indy finds stone lions and Crusader seals set into the floor – there's only a blank **square chamber**, with smaller rooms opening off it, the entrance portico flanked by rooms featuring unusual round windows above their doors. Access to the interior is barred, but you can poke your nose in. The function of the Treasury is unknown, but a significant clue is the recessed **basin** on its threshold with a channel leading outside, clearly for libations or ritual washing. None of Petra's tomb-monuments has this feature, but the High Place of Sacrifice does, suggesting that the Treasury may have been a place of worship, possibly a tomb-temple.

The Outer Siq

From the Wadi al-Jarra, the path – known here as the **Outer Siq** – broadens and is lined with tombs in varying states of erosion. Steps lead up to a large cavern on the right, lined with benches inside and rather smelly. Opposite is a line of tombs at different heights, showing how the wadi floor rose during Nabatean occupation of Petra; most are badly eroded. One has the crow-step

Petra colours

One of the most breathtaking aspects of Petra – for many people surpassing even the architecture – is its **colourful sandstone**, famously celebrated in a particular tourist's memoirs almost 150 years ago. As the artist **Edward Lear** strolled up the Colonnaded Street on a visit in 1858, coolly noting "the tint of the stone… brilliant and gay beyond my anticipation", his manservant and cook, Giorgio Kokali, burst out in delight, "Oh master, we have come into a world of chocolate, ham, curry powder and salmon!" **Agatha Christie** preferred to see the rocks as "blood-red", and a character in her *Appointment with Death*, set in Petra, comes out with a line describing the place as "very much the colour of raw beef".

Unfortunately for posterity, however, the most famous lines on Petra's colours are less engaging. In 1845, **John William Burgon**, later to become Dean of Chichester, wrote in his poem *Petra*:

It seems no work of Man's creative hand,
By labour wrought as wavering fancy planned;
But from the rock as if by magic grown,
Eternal, silent, beautiful, alone!
Not virgin-white like that old Doric shrine,
Where erst Athena held her rites divine;
Not saintly-grey, like many a minster fane,
That crowns the hill and consecrates the plain;
But rose-red as if the blush of dawn
That first beheld them were not yet withdrawn;
The hues of youth upon a brow of woe,
Which Man deemed old two thousand years ago,

Match me such a marvel save in Eastern clime,
A rose-red city half as old as Time.

No advertising copywriter could have dreamt up a better final line, and Burgon's words have hung over Petra ever since: you'll be sick of reading **"rose-red city"** on every map, poster and booklet by the time you leave. Tellingly, Burgon had never been to Petra when he wrote it; he finally went sixteen years later, and at least then had the humility to write, if only in a letter to his sister, "there is nothing rosy about Petra".

Over the centuries, wind has rubbed away at the soft sandstone of Petra's cliffs to reveal an extraordinary array of colours streaking through the stone. The most colourful facades in Petra are the **Silk Tomb** and the **Carmine Tomb**, both on the East Cliff and bedecked in bands of rainbow colours, while the cafés on the path below are set in caves no less breathtaking. Elsewhere, the lower walls of the **Wadi Farasa** are streaked with colour, and the **Siq** cliffs are striped with everything from scarlet to yellow to purple to brown, to complement the green foliage on the trees, the pink of the oleander flowers, and the deep blue sky. The one place in Petra that's truly "rose-red" is the **Treasury**, lit in the afternoons by low reflected sunlight off the pinkish walls.

ornamental design that originated in Assyria and was adapted by the Nabateans to reappear in dozens of Petra's facades: a band of rising and falling zigzags running horizontally across the top of the facade. As the path broadens, in the corner of the right-hand cliff – pointed to by the terracotta pipe that has emerged from the Siq – the **Tomb of 17 Graves** is being restored behind scaffolding. If you look up and to the left of it, you'll spot one of the clearest examples of Nabatean facade-building; the **Tomb of Unayshu** (see p.292) presents a sharp profile of a clean classical facade facing left, carved from a rough outcrop of rock behind that looks barely capable of supporting it.

The path then opens out to the left to expose the **Street of Facades**, an agglomeration of dozens of facades carved side by side out of the rock on at least four different levels. Most are simple, cornice-free designs, probably some of the earliest carving in Petra. It's around here that you'll come across the first of Petra's many **cafés**, all of which offer water, shade and soft drinks.

The theatre

A few metres ahead sits Petra's massive **theatre**. Obviously classical in design and inspiration, it's nonetheless been dated to the first century AD, before the Romans annexed Nabatea but at a time when links between the two powers must have been strong. Though the Romans refurbished the building after they took over in 106, the basic design was still **Hellenistic**, with seats coming right down to the orchestra's floor level. As many as 8500 people could be accommodated, more even than in the vast theatre at Amman. Aside from the stage backdrop and the ends of the banks of seating, the entire edifice was carved out of the mountainside; one whole street of facades was wiped out to form the back wall of the auditorium, leaving some of their interiors behind as incongruous gaps. Much renovation work has been done here in recent years, in particular to build up the stage area, with its niches in front and elaborate *scaenae frons* behind (tumbled in the earthquake of 363), the high back wall of which would have sealed off the theatre from the street outside.

The path continues past **cafés** on both sides down to a point at which the Wadi Musa turns sharp left (west) into the **city centre** (see p.295). Way up to the right, a row of some of Petra's grandest monuments has been etched into the **East Cliff** (see p.292), while straight ahead the valley opens up towards Baydha, with the **Wadi Mataha** (see p.310) coming in from the northeast.

The account of the main path through Petra continues on p.295.

The High Place of Sacrifice route

A little before you reach the theatre, a set of steps leading south up a rocky slope to one side of a deep valley gives access to the **High Place of Sacrifice**, a diversion off the main path, but an unmissable part of a visit. Even if you have only one day in Petra, this is still worth the climb, about thirty or forty minutes with safe steps at all tricky points – there's no scrambling or mountaineering involved. You can return the same way, but steps also lead down off the back of the mountain into **Wadi Farasa**, forming a long but interesting loop that delivers you (after about two and a half hours) to the Qasr al-Bint. The breathtaking **views** and some of Petra's most extraordinary **rock-colouring** make the hike worthwhile, quite apart from the wealth of Nabatean architecture at every turn and the dramatic High Place itself. The path is well travelled, and you're unlikely to find yourself alone for more than a few minutes at a time.

The route up from the Outer Siq

The steps up are clearly marked, guarded by several god-blocks, and wind their way into the deep cleft of the beautiful Wadi al-Mahfur; at several points, the Nabatean engineers took their chisels to what were otherwise impassable outcrops and sliced deep-cut corridors through the rock to house the stairs. The sign that you're reaching the top, apart from one or two impromptu cafés beneath bamboo shelters, is the appearance on your left of two very prominent **obelisks**, both over 6m high. As in the Bab as-Siq and elsewhere, these probably represent the chief male and female Nabatean deities, Dushara and al-Uzza, although far more extraordinary is to realize that they are solid: instead of being placed there, this entire side of the mountain-top was instead levelled to leave them sticking up. The ridge on which they stand is still marked on modern maps with the bedouin name of Zibb Attuf, the Phallus of Mercy (often adapted to Amud Attuf, the Column of Mercy), implying that the notion of these obelisks representing beneficial fertility was somehow passed down unchanged from the Nabateans to the modern age. Opposite stand very ruined walls, the last remnants of what could have been a **Crusader fort** or a Nabatean structure. Broken steps lead beside it up to the summit.

The High Place of Sacrifice

As you emerge onto the hand-levelled platform atop the ridge, the sense of exposure after the climb is suddenly liberating. The **High Place of Sacrifice** (*al-Madhbah* in Arabic) is one of the highest easily accessible points in Petra, perched on cliffs that drop an almost sheer 170m to the Wadi Musa below. It's just one of dozens of High Places perched on ridges and mountain-tops around Petra, all of which are of similar design and function. A platform about 15m long and 6m wide served as the venue for the religious ceremonies, oriented towards an **altar**, set up on four steps, with a basin to one side and a socket into which may have slotted a stone representation of the god. Within the courtyard is a small dais, on which probably stood a table of (bloodless) offerings.

What exactly took place up here – probably in honour of Dushara – can only be guessed at, but there were almost certainly libations, smoking of frankincense and animal sacrifice. What is less sure is whether **human sacrifice** took place, although boys and girls were known to have been sacrificed to al-Uzza elsewhere: the second-century philosopher Porphyrius reports that a boy's throat was cut annually at the Nabatean town of Dunat, 300km from Petra. At Hegra, a Nabatean city in the Arabian interior, an inscription states explicitly: "Abd-Wadd, priest of Wadd, and his son Salim... have consecrated the young man Salim to be immolated to Dhu Gabat. Their double happiness!" If such sacrifices took place in Petra, the High Place would surely have seen at least some of them. It's also been suggested that Nabatean religion incorporated **ritual exposure of the dead**, as practised among the Zoroastrians of Persia; if so, the High Place would also have been an obvious choice as an exposure platform. You can survey the vastness of Petra's mountain terrain from here, and the tomb of Aaron atop **Jebel Haroun** is in clear sight in the distance.

The ridge extends a short distance north of the High Place, nosing out directly above the theatre, with the tombs of the Outer Siq minuscule below. From here, it's easy to see that the city of Petra lay in a broad valley, about a kilometre wide and hemmed in to east and west by mountain barriers; north the valley extends to Baydha, south to Sabra. It looks tempting to scramble down the front of the ridge, but there is no easily manageable path this way; it would be dangerous to try it.

The route down via Wadi Farasa

It's easy to go back the way you came, but the route down the western cliff of the Attuf ridge via **Wadi Farasa** ("Butterfly Valley") is far preferable. The route leads directly straight ahead (south) as you scramble down from the High Place past the ruined Crusader walls, keeping the bamboo café on your right. After 50m you'll come to stairs winding downward to your right along the valley wall; the way is often narrow and steep but always clear. Note that it's also possible to descend via **Wadi Nmayr**, parallel to Wadi Farasa, but this is a very difficult, concealed path and should only be attempted with a knowledgeable guide.

The Lion Monument and Garden Triclinium

Part of the way down into the Wadi Farasa you'll come to the **Lion Monument** carved into a wall. This may have been a drinking fountain, since a pipe seems to have fed water to emerge from the lion's mouth. The creature itself, as on the Treasury facade, represented al-Uzza, and the monument was probably intended both to refresh devotees on their way up and prepare them for the ceremonies about to be held at the High Place. The precipitous stairs beyond, which give views of the monuments below, bring you down to the **Garden Triclinium**, a simple monument overlooked by a huge tree in a beautiful, hidden setting, which got its name from the carpet of green that sprouts in springtime in front of the portico. Two freestanding columns are framed by two engaged ones; within is a small square shrine. Stairs to the right of the facade lead to a huge cistern on the roof, serving the Roman Soldier Tomb below.

The Roman Soldier Tomb and around

A beautiful set of rock-cut stairs to the left of the Garden Triclinium brings you down to the complex of the **Roman Soldier Tomb**. Although not immediately apparent, the two facades facing each other across the wadi formed part of a unified area, with an elaborate colonnaded courtyard and garden between them, long vanished. The tomb itself is on your left, a classical facade with three framed niches holding figures probably representing those buried within; the interior chamber has a number of recesses for the dead. Opposite the tomb, with an eroded but undecorated facade, is a startlingly colourful **triclinium**, unique in Petra for having a carved interior. The walls have been decorated with fluted columns and bays, all worn to show streaks of mauves, blues, pinks, crimsons and silver. Why this *triclinium* was decorated so carefully, and who was buried in the tomb opposite, isn't known; even the name is only a supposition from the middle of the tomb's three figures, a headless man wearing a cuirass.

Stairs lead down over the lip of a retaining wall to the wadi floor, and it is around here that the colouring in the rock is at its most gorgeous. Plenty of tombs crowd the lower reaches of the wadi; one of the most interesting is the **Renaissance Tomb**, topped by an urn and with an unusual arch above its doorway also carrying three urns. Nearby is the **Broken Pediment Tomb**, above the level of the path, displaying an early forerunner of the kind of broken pediment found on Petra's grandest monuments, the Treasury and the Monastery.

Zantur, Katuteh and Amud Faraoun

As you emerge from the wadi into the open, you should bear in mind that you're still the best part of half an hour from reaching the main routes again. From here onwards, though, there's not a scrap of shade and you're quite often walking in stifling breezeless dips between hills. In addition, the path isn't immediately clear. You should bear a little right, initially keeping out of the wadi bed, and aim for the left flank of the smooth rounded hill dead ahead. This hill is **Zantur**, Petra's rubbish dump, and it crunches underfoot with fragments of pottery: as well as coarse, crudely decorated modern shards, there are countless chips of beautiful original Nabatean ware – very thin, smooth pottery that's been skilfully painted. As long as you don't start digging, you can take whatever you like.

Within metres are the remains of the house of a wealthy Nabatean merchant at **Katuteh**, suddenly abandoned for some reason (possibly, archeologists theorize, as a result of having the city's garbage dumped in the back garden). Swiss teams are currently excavating the villa.

The path eventually curls around to the western flank of the hill and **Amud Faraoun**, called Zibb Faraoun ("Pharaoh's Phallus") by the bedouin. This standing column, which must have formed part of the portico of a building – part-visible buried in the rubbly hill behind – now serves as a useful landmark and resting spot. Paths converge here from all sides; to the **southwest** is the main route into Wadi Thughra towards Umm al-Biyara, Jebel Haroun and Sabra; to the **west** is a path accessing a route up al-Habees; to the **northwest** are the Qasr al-Bint (see p.301) and the tent cafés; and to the **northeast** a path runs behind the markets area of the city centre (see p.300), parallel to the Colonnaded Street.

The East Cliff

About 250m beyond the theatre, just before the Wadi Musa makes its sharp left turn, solid, modern steps lead to the **East Cliff**, looming up to the right above the city centre. This whole elbow of Jebel al-Khubtha is ranged with some of Petra's most impressive facades, collectively known as the **Royal Tombs**. If you have anything more than half a day in the city, you should fit them in; the climb is easy and the views are marvellous. From down below, in the direct, reddish light of late afternoon, the entire cliff seems to glow with an inner translucence, and is one of the sights of Petra. However, it's probably best to aim to be up here in the morning shadows, with the sun lighting up the valley and the mountains opposite.

From **right to left**, the first tomb on the cliff – separate from the big ones, and missable if you're short of time – is the **Tomb of Unayshu**, viewed in profile from the Outer Siq and easiest to get to by scrambling up the rocks opposite the High Place staircase. This is part of a complete Nabatean tomb complex, and features a once-porticoed courtyard in front, with a *triclinium* to one side.

The Urn Tomb

Heading north from Unayshu above the main path, past another well-preserved tomb facade, you join the modern steps leading from below up to the soaring facade of the **Urn Tomb**, with its very large colonnaded forecourt partially supported on several storeys of arched vaults. The Bdul know the tomb as Al-Mahkamah, "**the Court**", dubbing the vaults As-Sijin, "**the Jail**". Whether it was later used in this way or not, the whole structure would seem originally to have been the tomb of somebody extremely important, quite probably one of the Nabatean kings – but who exactly isn't known. Set into the facade high above the forecourt between the engaged columns are spaces for three bodies; this is a unique configuration in Petra, since such *loculi* are

The bedouin named for changing

From time immemorial, the caves and dens of Petra have been occupied by one of Jordan's poorest and most downtrodden tribes, the **Bdul**. Surrounded by tribes living traditional tent-based lifestyles (the **Saidiyeen** to the south and west, the **Ammareen** to the north, and the **Liyathneh** to the east), the Bdul remain a community apart, looked down upon for their poverty, small numbers (only about three hundred families) and cave-centred lifestyle.

Most bedouin tribes can trace their lineage back to a single founding father (whether real or fictitious), but mystery surrounds the origin of the Bdul. Some Bdul, naturally enough, claim descent from the Nabateans, but this may just be wishful thinking. Most claim that the name Bdul derives from the Arabic word *badal*, meaning to swap or change, and was given to the tribe after the survivors of a massacre at the hands of Moses and the Israelites had agreed to convert to Judaism; at some point in the centuries following, the tribe converted again, this time to Islam. Much more plausible is the possibility that the Bdul earned their name from being a nomadic tribe that decided to settle in the ruins of Petra, changing their habits to suit a more stable existence.

The Bdul were slow to benefit from the growth in tourism in Petra, largely because of cut-throat competition with the more cosmopolitan and better-educated Liyathneh of Wadi Musa. When the *Resthouse* opened in the 1950s, Liyathneh were hired as construction workers, hotel staff, book- and postcard-sellers and even to provide horses for rides into Petra; their near-monopoly on tourist facilities in Wadi Musa has persisted to this day. Adding insult to injury, a USAID report dating from the establishment of Petra as a National Park in 1968 acknowledged that the Bdul held traditional rights over park lands, but nonetheless recommended that they be **resettled** elsewhere. This sparked a fifteen-year battle to oust the Bdul from Petra, which saw the tribe's traditional lifestyle of agriculture and goatherding decimated, income instead dribbling in from the refreshment cafés within Petra and the few individuals offering crafts and antiquities – real and fake – to tourists. In the mid-1980s, tempted by material comforts in the new, purpose-built village of Umm Sayhoun, many Bdul families finally left the caves of Petra for the breezeblock houses on the ridge. Some still herd a few goats, others cultivate small plots, but most Bdul are refocusing their energies on making an income providing services to tourists. You'll meet Bdul adults and kids in all corners of Petra, running the tent cafés or offering tea and trinkets in the hills, and often happy to chat (in surprisingly fluent English). The "bedouin named for changing", as archeologist Kenneth Russell dubbed them, are embracing change yet again.

For excellent background on the Bdul by anthropologist Rami Sajdi, go to ⓦwww.acacialand.com – and also see Ruth Caswell's pages about the tribes of Wadi Musa at ⓦwww.jordanjubilee.com. The best modern account of Bdul life in Petra is **Married to a Bedouin** (ⓦwww.marriedtoabedouin.com; see also p.400), a book by New Zealander Marguerite van Geldermalsen, who came to Petra on holiday in 1978, fell in love with a local souvenir-seller and stayed to marry him and raise a family. Marguerite still lives in Petra, running a souvenir stall in the site and occasionally leading tours. She welcomes visitors (by appointment) – see her website for details.

normally inside the monument, and they seem to have been placed here as an indication of the importance of their occupants. The central one – possibly that of the king himself – is still partially sealed by a stone which formerly depicted the bust of a man wearing a toga. The urn which gave the tomb its name is at the very top.

Due, no doubt, to its dominating position in the city's landscape, the tomb was later converted into a major church, possibly Petra's **cathedral**; the large

▲ The Urn Tomb, Petra

interior room features, near the left-hand corner of the back wall, a Greek inscription in red paint recording the dedication of the church by Bishop Jason in 447 AD. Probably at the same time, two central recesses of the original four were combined to make a kind of apse, and myriad holes were drilled in the floor to support all the relevant ecclesiastical furniture: chancel screens, a pulpit, maybe a table, and so on. The **view** from the forecourt, which takes in the full sweep of the valley (and even the urn atop the Monastery), is one of Petra's best.

The Silk Tomb, Corinthian Tomb and Palace Tomb

Working your way around the cliff, you'll come to the **Silk Tomb**, unremarkable but for its brilliant colouring. The facade of the nearby **Corinthian Tomb** is something like a hybrid and ramshackle Treasury. It has the Treasury's style on the upper level – a *tholos* flanked by a broken pediment – but below, it's a mess, the symmetry thrown out by extra doors on the left. It has also suffered badly at the hands of the wind. However, such an exposed position on the corner of the cliff – directly in line with the Colonnaded Street – points to the fact that, like the Urn Tomb, this may well have been the tomb of another Nabatean king, visible from everywhere in the city.

Adjacent is an even more ramshackle jumble, the very broad **Palace Tomb**, boasting one of Petra's largest facades. There are at least five different storeys, the top portions of which were built of masonry because the cliff turned out to be too low, and so subsequently collapsed. The unevenly spaced line of engaged columns on the second row clashes nastily with the orthodox lower level. Protected by the cliff, the extreme right-hand edge of the facade still has some sharply carved detail surviving.

The Sextius Florentinus Tomb, Carmine Tomb and the Khubtha High Places

From the Palace Tomb, tracks lead west towards the city centre, and northeast hugging the cliff round to the peaceful **Sextius Florentinus Tomb**, positioned facing north where a finger of the cliff reaches the ground. Sextius Florentinus was a Roman governor of the Province of Arabia who died about 130 AD, and must have chosen to be buried in Petra rather than in the provincial capital of Bosra. The facade of his tomb, with a graceful semicircular pediment, is one of the most pleasing in the city. A few metres north, behind a tree, is the spectacular **Carmine Tomb**, girt with breathtaking bands of colour, but, by virtue of its position, hardly ever noticed. Wadi Zarnug al-Khubtha, which divides the two, holds a path which gives reasonably easy, if steep, access to little-visited High Places and a few scattered ruins perched atop the massive **Jebel al-Khubtha**, the main barrier standing between Petra and Wadi Musa town. The views from on top are tremendous – especially of the theatre – but you'd have to be keen (and sure-footed) to try it.

The path beyond Sextius Florentinus along the Wadi Mataha is described on p.310.

The city centre

As you round the corner of the path leading from the theatre, the **city centre** of Petra, focused along the Cardo Maximus, or **Colonnaded Street**, stretches out ahead, framed by the barrier range of mountains – and the flat-topped giant Umm al-Biyara – behind. Although there are excavations continuing on the flat, rounded hills to either side, the overall impression is of rocky desolation; however, in Petra's prime, the landscape in all directions was covered with buildings – houses big and small, temples, marketplaces – all of them long since collapsed. Many archeologists theorize that much of Petra is in fact still hidden beneath the dusty soil, and that all the facades and what few buildings have so far been exposed are the tip of the iceberg.

Until you reach the **Temenos** at the far end of the Colonnaded Street, the only monument actually on the street is the **Nymphaeum**, although both the **northern** (right-hand) and **southern** (left-hand) slopes hold plenty of interest. Petra's main museum, the **Basin Museum**, lies just beyond the Temenos. Looming over the city centre from the west is a pinnacle of rock known as **Al-Habees**, separate from the huge mountains behind and featuring, partway up, another small museum and – on the summit – a crumbling Crusader fort and some of the best views in all of Petra.

The Nymphaeum

One of the few trees in the city centre – a huge, lush pistachio – stands proudly over the ruined **Nymphaeum**, these days more popular as a shady hangout for the bedouin police than anything else. Virtually nothing remains of the ancient superstructure, and even the retaining wall is modern. However, its location is key, at the confluence of the Wadi Musa, flowing from east to west, and the Wadi Mataha, bringing the water diverted by the dam at the Siq entrance into the city from the northeast. It may also have been the terminus for the terracotta pipes and channels bringing water through the Siq itself. The sight and sound

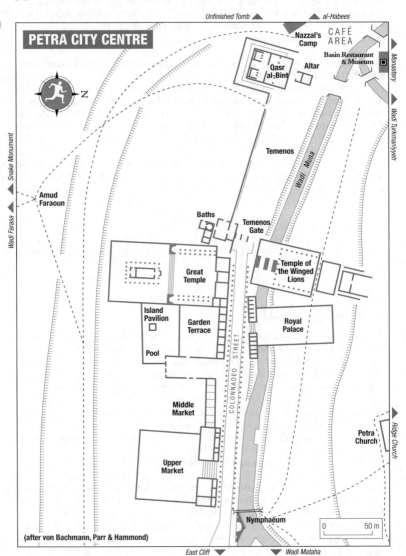

PETRA CITY CENTRE

Unfinished Tomb ▲

al-Habees ▲

Nazzal's Camp

CAFÉ AREA

Qasr al-Bint

Altar

Basin Restaurant & Museum

Monastery ▶

N

Wadi Turkmaniyyeh ▶

Temenos

Wadi Musa

Snake Monument ▶

Amud Faraoun

Baths

Temenos Gate

Wadi Farasa ▶

Great Temple

Temple of the Winged Lions

Island Pavilion

Garden Terrace

Royal Palace

Pool

COLONNADED STREET

Middle Market

Petra Church

Ridge Church ▶

Upper Market

Nymphaeum

0   50 m

(after von Bachmann, Parr & Hammond)

East Cliff ▼

Wadi Mataha ▼

of water splashing freely from such a monument must have been wonderful in such a parched city centre.

The Nymphaeum is where you'll end up if you've walked the Wadi Muthlim route from the dam (see p.285); it's equally possible to walk the route in reverse, although the initial stretch will be down in the wadi bed, and less appealing than following the East Cliff around to join Wadi Mataha further north (see p.310). You should allow a minimum of two and a half tough hours – preferably three – from the Nymphaeum to circumambulate Jebel Khubtha and get back to the gate.

The northern slopes

The **northern slopes** – formally dubbed Jebel Qabr Jumayan – that rise to the right as you look along the Colonnaded Street from the Nymphaeum, host the stunning **Petra Church** mosaics and a clutch of smaller Byzantine sites on the hills above, as well as one of the city's longest-standing excavations, the **Temple of the Winged Lions**.

The Petra Church

Above and behind the Nymphaeum stands a modern shelter protecting the Byzantine **Petra Church**, as it's been unimaginatively dubbed. This is a large tripartite basilica, roughly 26m by 15m, with three apses to the east and three entrances to the west, accessed from a stone-paved atrium. It was built in the late fifth century, and remodelled about fifty years later. Around 600 it was burned, and remained derelict until earthquakes shook it down shortly afterwards. Surviving in both aisles of the church, though, are superbly detailed **floor mosaics** depicting the bounty of creation, dated stylistically to the early sixth century. Much of the stone used to build the church was pilfered from the ruined Nabatean and Roman monuments all around, and now lies tumbled down the slopes in front.

The spectacular **south–aisle mosaics** are in three rows, the central line of personifications of the seasons flanked by rows of animals, birds and fish. From door to altar, the middle line features fishermen and hunters interspersed with Ocean (with one foot on a fish), a delightfully clear-faced Spring, and Summer with her breast bared and holding a fish. The **north–aisle mosaics** depict people and indigenous and exotic animals and birds, including a camel-like giraffe, a hyena, boar, bear and leopard. Archeologists also found thousands of gilded glass tesserae, indicating that lavish **wall mosaics** once adorned the

▲ Byzantine mosaic, Petra Church

church, and they managed to reconstruct – from more than a hundred pieces – a huge marble tub with panthers for handles (which is now in the Basin Museum). At the rear (west) of the atrium is a superbly well-preserved fifth-century **Baptistry**, with a cruciform font surrounded by four limestone columns. The presence of such a large church so richly decorated – and the discovery of the Petra scrolls – merely highlights how little is known about Byzantine Petra, and how much awaits discovery.

From in front of the Petra Church, great **views** extend over the valley. To the left is the East Cliff; ahead is the Great Temple; and to the right you can clearly see the unusual Unfinished Tomb (see p.302), carved into the base of Al-Habees.

The Blue Church and Ridge Church

On a ridge just above the Petra Church is the **Blue Church**, so named for its bluish granite columns. Not a great deal is known about this building, and work is ongoing. A short climb to the top of the hill that peaks behind the Petra Church will bring you to the austere **Ridge Church**, a much smaller building (some 18m by 13m) perched on a ridge at the northwestern edge of Byzantine-era Petra, overlooking the Wadi Turkmaniyyeh behind and the whole of the city centre in front. Dated to roughly the same time as the Petra Church, much of the church's interior paving survives, but there's no decoration. What's most interesting about the place is that archeologists found almost no remnants of the building's superstructure nearby, although they did find a hoard of water-washed stones in the church courtyard brought up from the wadi below. From this confusing evidence, they came up with an elaborate theory for the church's destruction. At a time of increasing political instability, they postulate, the

Petrans deliberately dismantled the church – which lay hard up against the city wall – in order to use its stones as missiles against invaders approaching from below. When the church had been razed, they collected more stones from the wadi to hoard against future attacks, but these were forgotten as, possibly, the city was overrun from a different direction. Any truth in this tale has yet to be confirmed.

The Temple of the Winged Lions

Overlooking the Temenos Gate west of the Petra Church is the **Temple of the Winged Lions**, the principal building of the northern slope. It was named for unusual column capitals featuring winged lions (one of which is in the Basin Museum), but would – so the excavator suggests – have been more appropriately named the Temple of al-Uzza, for it seems to have been dedicated to her. Dated approximately to the early first century AD, the building was approached via a bridge across the Wadi Musa, parts of which you can still see on the banks. Worshippers would have proceeded across ascending terraces, an open colonnaded courtyard and a portico into the temple itself, featuring close-packed columns and an altar platform. The floors were paved in contrasting black, brown and white marble, and the walls decorated with painted plaster; archeologists uncovered both a painter's workshop – with paints and pigments still in their ceramic pots – and a marble-cutter's workshop adjoining the temple.

One of the most spectacular discoveries, also now on display in the Basin Museum, was a small rectangular stone **idol**, complete with a stylized face and

The Petra scrolls

A hugely significant archeological find was made by accident in a storage room at the northeast corner of the Petra Church on December 4, 1993: archeologists stumbled on a cache of 152 **papyrus scrolls**, tumbled higgledy-piggledy from the shelves that presumably once carried them, which had lain buried beneath 4m of rubble. Analysis of the scrolls is still incomplete, but they have given tantalizing glimpses of life in Byzantine Petra, a period that is rarely accounted for.

The whole archive seems to have belonged to one Theodore, born in 514, who at the age of 24 married a young woman from a family already connected with his own by marriage in a previous generation. Theodore became archdeacon of the "Most Holy Church of NN in the metropolis" – presumably the Petra Church. Most of the documents date from a sixty-year period, roughly 528 to 588, and comprise property contracts, out-of-court settlements and tax receipts, providing a wealth of detail about everyday life. Transfers from one family to another of vineyards, arable land, orchards, living quarters and stables within a fifty-kilometre radius of Petra were all dutifully recorded. One man's will specifies that after his mother's death, all her assets were to be donated to the "House of Aron", the Byzantine monastery atop Jebel Haroun. Farmers, tailors, doctors, slaves and soldiers are all mentioned by name, including one Abu Karib ibn Jabala, known to have been a military commander of the Arab tribes. However, Petra was decisively Christian at this time, and monks and priests feature prominently, not least a Bishop Theodore, who may have been the same Theodore who took part in a synod at Jerusalem in 536. Another reference is to a priest "of her, our All-Holy, Praised Lady, the Glorious God-Bearing and Eternally Virgin Mary", indicating that there may be a church to Mary yet to be uncovered in Petra. Only once the content of the scrolls has been fully published can investigation proceed any further, but this is just another sign that archeologists have only just begun to scratch Petra's surface.

a hole between the eyes (possibly for a set of horns, the symbol of the goddess Isis, to be inserted); the inscription along the base reads "Goddess of Hayyan son of Nybat". Adjacent to the temple to the east is a large unexcavated area of rubble deemed to have been a **royal palace**, also with a bridge over the wadi, but no work has as yet been done on it.

The southern slopes

From the Nymphaeum all the way along the paved Colonnaded Street westwards, columns on your left (south) stand in front of what have been dubbed Petra's **markets**. Alongside the **Great Temple** further along is the **Garden Terrace**, once a fertile, leafy area flowing with water. Ranged along street level in front of the markets, to either side of the grand staircases, were small shops, which may have been refitted in the Byzantine period; some have been renovated, but work to excavate the market floors and outbuildings remains ongoing.

The Garden Terrace

Although there's not a great deal of above-ground evidence, the area alongside the Great Temple has been identified as an area of ornamental gardens, dubbed the **Garden Terrace**. This was laid out in Petra's "golden age" – the late first century BC – as a place of refuge in the city centre, tucked in amongst the grand temples and busy shops all around. In front, nearest the street, was a flat area that comprised the gardens themselves. Behind, occupying the whole southern area of the terrace, was a large **pool**, 43m long by 23m wide (and about two and a half metres deep), surrounded by a colonnade. Occupying an **island** in the centre of the pool was a small, rectangular pavilion. The beauty of such a site can only be imagined.

The Great Temple

Alongside the Garden Terrace at the western end of the street, and accessed by a set of steps leading up from the street, is the late first-century BC **Great Temple**, or Southern Temple, an extremely grand affair, one of the largest complexes in the city at seven thousand square metres. Excavation work by US teams remains ongoing.

Worshippers originally climbed a staircase from street level through a now tumbled monumental gateway onto the hexagonally paved **lower temenos**, featuring triple colonnades to east and west culminating in semicircular benched alcoves. The **temple** itself stands some 25m above street level, fronted by four enormous columns which were originally stuccoed in red and white. Within the *cella* stands a renovated Nabatean theatre, or **theatron**, about 7m in diameter, which would have seated at least three hundred people, and might have been a council chamber. The whole building is extremely complex, set on different levels, with internal and external corridors flanking it on east and west. In addition, tumbled columns and chunks of architectural elements (many of them beautifully carved) all point to the fact that this was one of Petra's most important monuments. As yet, though, not even the deity who was worshipped here is known.

Scramble to the highest point of the walls for **views** west to the arches of the Crusader fort atop Al-Habees, north across the wadi to the Temple of the Winged Lions, behind which lie the valley tombs of Wadi Muaysreh ash-Shargi-yyeh, and northeast to the Petra Church, with Umm Sayhoun behind it and Mughur an-Nassara to one side.

The Temenos

In most Roman cities, the main east–west and north–south streets ploughed straight furrows from city gate to city gate. However, as at Bosra, the heterodox Nabateans blocked off Petra's main street at one end and turned the area beyond – hard up against the mountain cliffs – into a **Temenos**, or sacred temple precinct. Framing the western end of the Colonnaded Street stand the partially reconstructed remains of the **Temenos Gate**, marking the end of the commercial sector of Petra and the entrance to the main area of worship. Sockets in the threshold indicate that great doors once closed off all three entrances of the gate; the floral frieze which survives on the easternmost facade of the gate was originally framed by freestanding columns which stood just in front and to either side.

As you pass through the gate, the impression remains of having left the city behind; the courtyard – occupied at the far end by, on one side, camels and, on the other, the bulk of a temple – is huge, paved and open, and at times of religious celebration would have been thronged with people. Low walls enclosed the Temenos on both sides, although the northern one has been eroded away by the waters of the Wadi Musa. Just inside the Temenos Gate to the south are three domed rooms tentatively identified as **baths**, only partially excavated. All along the south wall is a double row of stone benches, some 73m in length, leading almost up to the main feature of the Temenos, the Qasr al-Bint, the only freestanding monument as yet uncovered in the whole of Petra. Just visible from the Temenos, over the hill to the south, is the tip of the Amud Faraoun (see p.292).

The Qasr al-Bint

The **Qasr al-Bint al-Faraoun** ("Palace of Pharaoh's Daughter") is nothing of the sort. Its name derives from another far-fetched bedouin tale of the pharaoh, who, it's said, after stashing his riches in the Treasury, and still desperate to let nothing slow him down in his pursuit of the Israelites, stashed his daughter away here for safekeeping. Interestingly enough though, an inscription naming Suudat, daughter of the Nabatean king Malchus II (40–70 AD), and probably from the base of a statue, was found on the steps; according to historian Iain Browning, this indicates that some link between the *qasr* and the daughter of a powerful man may not be so fanciful after all.

The building is a huge, square Nabatean temple, dating from the late first century BC, oriented to the north and facing a huge, freestanding altar, some 13m by 12m and at least 3m high. The **altar**, clad in marble, showed a blank wall to the north, and was originally approached by steps from in front of the temple. From here looking back, the four gigantic columns of the temple portico, standing at the head of a broad staircase wider than the building and topped by an architrave and pediment, would have made a deeply impressive sight. The huge arch that survives today was probably only a relieving arch for a lower, horizontal lintel of the doorway into the *cella*, which spanned the width of the building and was lit by windows high up in each wall. Behind, the holy of holies was divided into three separate chambers, or *adyta*. The central one is slightly raised, and has engaged columns along the walls and another relieving arch overhead; this is where the god-block or cult statue would have stood. The temple's dedication is unknown, but Dushara is the most obvious candidate.

Tent cafés and **camel drivers** crowd the courtyard in front of the Qasr al-Bint, and this is the main rest area for gathering strength before you continue to explore or start the long walk back to the gate (which takes a full hour uphill by the most direct route through the Siq). In front of the *qasr*, a bridge crosses the Wadi Musa to the *Basin Restaurant* and museum; from the other bank, the **Wadi Turkmaniyyeh** dirt road (see p.309) wends its way out of the city to Umm Sayhoun.

The Basin Museum

Shaded by a prominent grove of trees opposite the Qasr al-Bint is the *Basin Restaurant* (see p.276) and adjacent **Basin Museum** (daily 8am–3.30pm; free). The latter is definitely worth a quick look if only to give yourself a break from all the imposing architecture. It holds excellent informative noticeboards on Petra's history and geography (including a fascinating digression into the frankincense trade), as well as information about the Nabateans. Plenty of finds are on display from all periods of occupation at Petra, stretching right back to Neolithic times, among which Nabatean coins, pottery and some beautiful and delicate jewellery are the most engaging. Specific pieces that stand out are the idol from the Temple of the Winged Lions, statues of Aphrodite and Dionysus, and the massive panther-handled marble tub from the Petra Church.

Al-Habees

The modern building next to the Qasr al-Bint – now used by the Department of Antiquities – is known as **Nazzal's Camp**, and was formerly Petra's sole hotel (of eleven rooms), built by the Nazzal family in 1943 on the site of Thomas Cook's old three-bed campsite established nine years before. Early Cook's tourists were offered the option of sleeping instead in one of the caves cut into **Al-Habees** looming overhead. These caves are used now as storage areas and offices for the police, but one has been converted into a small **museum** (daily except Tues 8am–3.30pm, sometimes closed Fri; free), accessed up stairs in front of Nazzal's Camp and well worth a look. The chamber is crammed full of marvellous statuary, including busts of various Roman gods, an eagle with outspread wings perched on a thunderbolt (symbol of Zeus), and a headless statue of Hercules recovered from the theatre.

From the museum it's possible to follow the path around the mountain on the initial stretches of a processional way to the summit. A little way around is an open area overlooking the beautiful Wadi Siyyagh, with plenty of rock-cut caves – whether they're tombs or houses isn't certain – as well as a small **High Place**, in perfect isolation above a prominent crow-step facade and sunken courtyard in the so-called **Convent Group** of monuments. Beyond, though, the Nabatean stairway is worn and dangerous, and the best way up to the summit is now via a staircase on the southern flank of the mountain, for which you must return to Nazzal's Camp.

The Unfinished Tomb and Columbarium

Overlooking the rubbly hill directly behind Nazzal's Camp is one of Petra's most interesting monuments, the **Unfinished Tomb**. This is a part-complete facade, and shows how Nabatean craftsmen worked from the top down, scooping out the interior as they went. Beside it is the **Columbarium**, a strange monument covered inside and out with hundreds of tiny square niches that had an unknown function: the name literally means "dovecote", implying that each niche held a bird, but no dove could roost here and the niches seem too small to hold funerary urns, as has also been suggested.

The Al-Habees Crusader fort

To reach the **Crusader fort** on the top of Al-Habees, you should continue south up the rubbly hill from the Columbarium, and follow a sign pointing right, even though it appears to point at the blank rubbly cliffside. As you get nearer, you'll spot the modern, restored stairs which take you up to the summit; it's an easy fifteen-minute climb, although there is one wooden footbridge without railings on the way. A gate with a rock-cut bench marks the approach to the fort, after which you'll have to scramble over loose stones up to a gatehouse. From here, you must find your own way the last little bit to the top; steps rise at one point over the barrel vault of a small room. The layout of the ruined fort itself – only occupied for a few decades in the twelfth century – is jumbled and confusing, but the 360-degree views are quite stunning.

Wadi Siyyagh

Just to the north of Al-Habees, **Wadi Siyyagh** – which takes the waters of the Wadi Musa down to Wadi Araba – was formerly one of the most gorgeous and quiet short walks you could take in Petra. This was once an exclusive residential neighbourhood of the city, enclosed between high walls, and there are plenty of houses and tombs, a Nabatean quarry and a well to explore. However, the wadi is now a short cut for local people driving their pick-ups, and a cave near the eastern end is home to a **generator** that keeps the *Basin Restaurant* and the Department of Antiquities offices operational; the roar of the thing echoes for a good half-hour down the wadi, the first 150m of which are now also covered with litter.

Persevere with the walk, though, and after half an hour or so you'll reach the well-tended "Roman Gardens" (not Roman at all), now maintained by local people. Beyond, you'll find pools and waterfalls en route to Bir Mathkoor (see p.356) in the desert of Wadi Araba, 16km from Petra, but route-finding is not always obvious in this harsh terrain and some scrambling on steep cliffs is necessary; you should be fully confident in your skills, or hire a guide for the journey.

The Monastery

Petra's most awe-inspiring monument is also one of the most taxing to reach. The **Monastery** (*ad-Dayr* in Arabic) boasts a massive facade almost fifty metres square, carved from a chunk of mountain nearly an hour's climb northwest of the city centre, 220m above the elevation of the Qasr al-Bint. Daunting though this sounds, there are well-trodden steps the whole way, as well as plenty of places to rest; a tranquil holy spring two-thirds of the way up is almost worth the climb by itself. Even if you've had your fill of facades, the stupendous views from the mountain-top over the entire Petra basin and the Wadi Araba make the trip essential.

Whether you want to **ride a donkey** to the summit or not (prices are *very* negotiable), you'll most likely have to beat off the hordes of kids riding alongside offering them as "Air-condition taxi, mister?" Bear in mind that the archeological authorities would prefer that you walked: all those little hooves are seriously degrading the Nabatean-carved sandstone steps on the route up. Either way, by far the best time to attempt the climb is in the **afternoon**; not only is the way up mostly in shadow by then, but the sun has moved around enough to hit the facade on the summit full-on.

▲ Local entrepreneur, Petra

The route up to the Monastery

The route passes in front of the *Basin* restaurant and museum, and leads dead ahead into the soft sandy bed of the Wadi ad-Dayr. The steps begin after a short distance, and soon after there's a diversion pointed left to the **Lion Triclinium**, a small classical shrine in a peaceful bushy wadi, named for the worn lions that flank its entrance. A small round window above the door and the doorway itself have been eroded together to form a strange keyhole shape. The frieze above has Medusas at either end; to the left of the facade is a small god-block set into a niche.

The processional way up to the Monastery is broken after another patch of steps by a sharp left turn where the Wadi Kharrubeh joins from in front; a little way along this wadi – off the main path – you'll find on the right-hand side a small **biclinium**, a ceremonial dining room with two stepped benches facing each other. Back on the path, after a step-free patch, the climb recommences. Some twenty or thirty minutes from the *Basin*, where the steps turn sharply left, you can branch right off the main path into a narrow wadi; double-back to the left, follow a track up and then right onto a broad, cool, protected ledge overlooking a deep ravine below. This is the **Qattar ad-Dayr**, an enchanted mossy grotto enclosed by high walls, completely silent but for the cries of wheeling birds and the continual dripping of water; it's a perfect spot for a picnic. Here, the one place in Petra where water flows year-round, the Nabateans built a *triclinium* and cisterns, and made dozens of carvings, including a two-armed cross.

As the steps drag on, the views begin to open up, and you get a sense of the vastness of the mountains and valleys all around. With tired legs, it's about another twenty minutes to a small sign pointing right to the **Hermitage**, a sheer-sided pinnacle of rock featuring a less-than-gripping set of caves carved with crosses. Another ten minutes, after a squeeze between two boulders and a short descent, and you emerge onto a wide, flat plateau, where you should turn right for the Monastery.

The Monastery

The **Monastery** facade is so big that it seems like an optical illusion – the doorway alone is taller than a house. A local entrepreneur has thoughtfully set up a café in a cave opposite: sink down at one of the shaded tables in front to take in the full vastness of the view. At first glance, the facade looks much like the Treasury's, but it's much less ornate; indeed, there's virtually no decoration at all. The name "Monastery" is again a misnomer, probably suggested by some crosses scratched inside; this was almost certainly a **temple**, possibly dedicated to the Nabatean king **Obodas I**, who reigned in the first century BC and was posthumously deified. Inside is a single chamber, with the same configuration of double staircases leading up to a cultic niche as in the Qasr al-Bint and the Temple of the Winged Lions. The flat plaza in front of the monument isn't natural: it was levelled deliberately, probably to contain the huge crowds that gathered here for religious ceremonies. You can pick out traces of a wall and colonnade in the ground to the south of the plaza, near where you entered. The opposite side (the left flank of the monument as you face it) has a scramble-path which can take you up to the **urn** on the top of the facade, which is no less than 10m high. Leaping around on the urn is a test of mettle for the local goat-footed kids, and some even shimmy to the very top; follow them with your life in your hands.

There are dozens more monuments and carvings to explore around the Monastery, not least of which is a cave and stone circle directly behind the refreshments cave. At any point, once you climb off ground level, the views are breathtaking. The cliff to the north (left) of the facade is punctuated for well over 100m with Nabatean caves, tombs and cisterns; some 200m or so north of the Monastery, you'll stumble onto a dramatically isolated **High Place**, with godlike **views** over the peaks down to the far-distant Wadi Araba, over 1000m below.

The only route back into Petra from the Monastery is the way you came up. Like all these descents, it's too rocky and isolated even to think about attempting it after sunset.

Further afield

There are plenty of sights of interest to explore beyond Petra's central valley. Although they're more difficult to reach, and generally have less striking architecture once you arrive, just the experience of hiking through Petra's incredible landscape is thrilling enough: all of these walks involve getting well off the popular tour-group tracks, and it's quite possible the only people you meet will be local families. Few visitors to Petra venture beyond the city-centre sights, the High Place and the Monastery, but if you do you'll be greeted by a panorama of barren peaks and wild canyons. All but experienced trekkers should take a guide to enter this wilderness.

Sights within striking distance are ranged along Petra's main valley to either side of the city, so we've divided the treks into two sections, namely **southwest** and **northeast** of Petra's city centre. **Siq al-Barid** (known as "**Little Petra**") and **Baydha**, some 9km north of Petra, are treated separately: they're accessible on long walks across country, but with the distance involved you're more likely to want to get to them on a half-day taxi excursion.

Southwest of Petra

Walking routes to the southwest of Petra begin from the Amud Faraoun. A path from there drops down to follow the main **Wadi Thughra** along the base of the cliffs, from which all the following sights can be reached. **Umm al-Biyara** is the flat-topped mountain overlooking the whole of Petra; a tough climb up steps delivers you to Nabatean ruins and the remains of a seventh-century BC Edomite settlement, and to vertiginous panoramas few people other than mountaineers ever get to experience. The **Snake Monument**, a single block carved as a huge snake, is over 2km southwest of Petra but on the flat. From there, a path branches out to the steps leading up the holy mountain **Jebel Haroun**, on the summit of which is the little white shrine visible from just about everywhere in Petra and Wadi Musa, the tomb of Moses' brother Aaron. Beyond the Snake Monument, **Sabra** is a southern suburb of Petra, mostly unexcavated and featuring a semi-ruined amphitheatre, a full day's hike on the flat through gorgeous open countryside.

Umm al-Biyara

Petra's hardest climb (other than off-route scrambling) is up **Umm al-Biyara**, likely to take a full hour from base to summit and requiring something of a head for heights: a couple of exposed scrambles might give you the flutters. You definitely need a guide, and should only make the climb in the afternoon when the east face of the mountain is in shadow.

As you head southwest from the Amud Faraoun, Wadi Umm Rattam comes in from the left after 350m; keep straight and, a little beyond, branch right (west) on a path directly towards a gully on the western edge of the massif, itself dotted all the way along with facades at different levels. The initial stages of the Nabatean **processional way** have collapsed, but a little to the south you'll find some modern steps, which lead you round to join the Nabatean path again higher up, part original, part restored. A little further is a sweeping hairpin ramp, deeply gouged out of the rockface to form a high corridor. Beyond here, the way is often eroded and, though there are some cairns to mark it, the drops are precipitous. You emerge at the south edge of the **summit plateau**, a scrubby slope that rises another 30m to the highest point on the northwest. The **Edomite settlement** is dead ahead, with many high dry-stone walls and corridors excavated; from the evidence of lamps, jars and looms, it seems that this community was a quiet, peaceful one, but it must have been important enough to receive a letter from Qaush-Gabr, king of Edom around 670 BC: his seal was discovered in the ruins. *Biyara* means "cisterns", and there are plenty up here, probably Nabatean. All along the eastern rim are ruins of Nabatean buildings commanding spectacular bird's-eye views over the Petra basin, 275 sheer metres below; the mountain vistas to the west, from the highest point of the plateau, are no less stunning. There are only two ways down: the fast way, and the way you came up.

The Snake Monument

The path to the Snake Monument is the same as for Umm al-Biyara in the initial stretches, except instead of branching off the Wadi Thughra you should keep going ahead through the undulating countryside. This was (and is) the main road into Petra from the south. After around thirty minutes or so you'll see a very prominent, top-heavy **god-block** atop an area of caves and tombs which has been dubbed the "Southern Graves"; these caves are still inhabited by Bdul families, so you shouldn't be exploring too inquisitively without being invited in. Poised above and to the left of the god-block, not immediately apparent, is the **Snake Monument**, a worn block carved with a large, coiled serpent overlooking the tombs and houses below. If you head another five minutes or so along the valley, you'll come to a flat area with trees that's been fenced around and cultivated; it's here that paths divide – south to Sabra, southeast towards the foot of Jebel Haroun.

Jebel Haroun

Jebel Haroun – Aaron's Mountain – is the holiest site in Petra and one of the holiest in Jordan, venerated by Muslims as the resting place of Prophet Haroun, as well as by Christians and Jews. There persists some local resistance to tourists casually climbing the mountain simply for the views, or to gawk: you should bear in mind that this is a place of pilgrimage. The trip there and back takes at least **six hours** from Petra city centre, involving a climb of almost 500m (a donkey can take you for all but the last twenty minutes), and you shouldn't attempt it without a guide, six to eight litres of water, some food, respectable clothing and a sense of humility. Don't bother if you're expecting an impressive shrine (it's small and unremarkable) or outstanding views (they're equally good from the Monastery and Umm al-Biyara). If you choose to visit, you should consider bringing a sum of money with you to leave as a donation.

Rosalyn Maqsood, in her excellent book on Petra (see p.403), explained the power of Jebel Haroun well:

Believers in the "numinous universe" accept that certain localities can be impregnated with the life-giving force of some saint or hero – transforming the sites into powerhouses of spiritual blessing. Traces of their essential virtue would cling to their mortal leavings even though their spirits had passed to another and better world. Holiness was seen as a kind of invisible substance, which clung to whatever it touched. So the virtues (the Latin word *virtu* means "power") of saints would remain and be continually renewed and built up by the constant stream of prayer and devotion emanating from the pilgrims who found their way there. These places are visited to gain healing, or fertility, or protection against dangers psychic and physical, or to gain whatever is the desire of the heart. Jebel Haroun is such a place… There is nothing there, really, and no one to watch you – so why should you remove your shoes, or leave an offering? Only you can answer this.

From the cultivated area near the Snake Monument, a path leads down into the Wadi Magtal ad-Dikh. A little beyond a cemetery on the right-hand side, and past a rock ledge called **Settuh Haroun** (Aaron's Terrace) at the foot of the mountain, where pilgrims unable to climb make an offering (Burckhardt slaughtered his goat here), there is a reasonably clear path up the mountain. Check in the tent at the bottom of the mountain whether the guardian will be around to open the shrine at the top; if not, you should collect the keys from him before heading up.

A plateau just below the summit was the location of a **Byzantine monastery** dedicated to Aaron; excavations are ongoing under a Finnish team. The small domed **shrine of Haroun** on the peak was renovated by the Mamluke sultan Qalawun in 1459, replacing earlier buildings which had stood on the same site. Up until then, the caretakers had been Greek Christians, and it was in the late sixth century that the Prophet Muhammad, on a journey from Mecca to Damascus, passed through Petra and climbed Jebel Haroun with his uncle. The Christian guardian of the shrine, a monk named Bahira, prophesied that the boy – then aged 10 – would change the world. Today, pilgrims bedeck the shrine with rags, twined threads and shells, the Muslim equivalent of lighting a candle to the saint.

Sabra

At the zenith of its economic power, Petra must have been processing goods from dozens, possibly hundreds, of caravans, and it was obviously not desirable to have hordes of foreign merchants – not to mention camels, random travellers and all the hangers-on associated with the caravan trade – pouring into the city centre. The Nabateans therefore built for themselves "suburbs" on all the main routes into the city, where business could be done, camels fed and watered, and goods stored well away from the sensitive corridors of power. **Bir Mathkoor** (see p.356) in Wadi Araba was the western suburb dealing with trade to and from Gaza; **Siq al-Barid** (see p.311), the northern, for trade with Palestine and Syria; **al-Khan** (the area near the modern ticket gate) may have been the eastern, receiving goods from the Arabian interior; and the southern suburb – with goods arriving from the Red Sea and Hejaz – was **Sabra**. Little has been excavated here, and the walk from Petra (9km) could take two and a half hours or more, much more appealing as a day-long round-trip hike in open country than a ruin hunt.

There are two routes down to Sabra from Petra, both on the flat the whole way. The first, and more open, goes from the cultivated area near the Snake

---

A two-day hike to Jebel Haroun and Sabra

A fascinating walking route from Petra involves a technically not too challenging seven-hour trek (20km) over Jebel Haroun to the solitude of the Roman theatre in Wadi Sabra, beyond which is a palm-fringed spring, followed on the second day by a direct route back to Petra (9km).

Though the Sabra valley is obvious when looking south from the summit of Jebel Haroun (the route up the mountain is given on p.307), the best way into it is not. After you've returned down the zigzag path from the summit, note the small paths which lead southeast across the upper edge of the valley to a ridge on its far side. Follow this ridge down to reach **Wadi Sabra**, and continue down to find the **theatre** partially concealed by oleanders. The "Waters of Sabra" spring lies just beyond. There are rough spots for wilderness camping nearby. On the second day, the route back to Petra takes a direct line northeast up Wadi Sabra, following the main (right) fork of the watercourse where the valley splits. Finding your route only becomes tricky after emerging from the valley, 4km before Wadi Musa: your objective is clear but the way to it is not, and you're faced either with a scramble up the long hillside to the Scenic Road hotels, or devious route-finding along the lower slopes to arrive near the Petra gate. This is not a trek for the inexperienced, but anyone familiar with mountain terrain should be able to hike it with confidence.

Monument, around the humped Ras Slayman hill and through the Ragbat al-Btahi pass between peaks before dropping to the sandy wadi floor; shortly after, **Wadi Sabra** joins from the left. As an alternative, you could head southwest from Amud Faraoun, then after 350m turn left (southeast) along Wadi Umm Rattam, which crosses to hug the eastern side of the valley below Jebel Nmayr; after a little less than an hour, aim right (southwest) to follow Wadi Sabra, which is eventually joined by the first path. A little ahead are the ruins of Sabra, set in beautifully green, rolling countryside well watered by a spring, **Ain Sabra**. On the left is a large rock-cut **theatre** with, above the auditorium, a large cistern that was used to provide a head of pressure for flooding the place so that the Nabateans could apparently indulge in mock sea battles. Ruinous evidence of the size of Nabatean Sabra is everywhere around – houses, monumental buildings, niches and several temples.

Continuing south from Sabra through the awesome **canyons** of lower Sabra and Tibn to the villages of Taybeh or Rajif is a more serious prospect and takes a further day or two. It's wild and magnificent country, only suitable for experienced trekkers or those with a knowledgeable guide. Routes are described in detail in Tony Howard's book on trekking in Jordan (see p.404).

Northeast of Petra

There are two main walking routes northeast from Petra, following the two wadis that join the Wadi Musa in the city centre. On the western side of the valley is the quiet **Wadi Turkmaniyyeh** – also often called **Wadi Abu Ullaygeh** – along the bank of which runs the only driveable track into and out of Petra (forbidden to the general public without written permission from the Wadi Musa tourist police). On the eastern side of the valley, the rocky **Wadi Mataha** hugs the east face of Jebel al-Khubtha, giving access to strenuous walking routes out to Wadi Musa town which avoid the Siq. Set in the heart of the lunar-looking domes behind the *Crowne Plaza* hotel is the ruined Crusader fort of **Wu'ayra**.

The Wadi Turkmaniyyeh route

Joining the Wadi Musa between the Qasr al-Bint and the *Basin Restaurant*, **Wadi Turkmaniyyeh** is a very pleasant walking route to take out of Petra to the north, a small sandy valley with the hundred-metre-high jagged cliffs on your left contorted into weird shapes. There are two groups of tombs along the way: if you enter the **Wadi Muaysreh ash-Shargiyyeh**, which joins Wadi Turkmaniyyeh on the left barely five minutes from the restaurant, after about 350m you'll come to a dense gathering of facades; and five minutes further northeast along Wadi Turkmaniyyeh you'll see, ranged up on the **Muaysreh Ridges** to your left, plenty more, with niches, double-height courtyards and a tiny High Place dotted among them. Either of these areas would repay scrambled exploration, well away from the crowds; and both Wadi Muaysreh ash-Shargiyyeh and its neighbour Muaysreh al-Gharbiyyeh provide walks (7km; 2hr 30min) linking Petra with Baydha and Siq al-Barid, both of them emerging from Petra's valley onto a cultivated plateau 4km southwest of Siq al-Barid (which is concealed behind a small hill).

About 1km along Wadi Turkmaniyyeh from the *Basin* restaurant you'll see the facade of the **Turkmaniyyeh Tomb** on the left, with the entire bottom half broken away. Between the two pilasters is the longest inscription in Petra in Nabatean, a dialect of Aramaic, dedicating the tomb and the surrounding property to Dushara. All the gardens, cisterns and walls mentioned in the inscription must have been swept away by the floodwaters of the wadi, as, indeed, the facade almost has been.

From here, the road begins 1500m of tight switchbacks as it climbs the ridge to the police post on the outskirts of **Umm Sayhoun**, the breezeblock village constructed for the Bdul in the 1980s. Buses shuttle regularly from the village into Wadi Musa, about 4km away; they follow the road to the right, curling around the head of the valley and south past Wu'ayra to the *Mövenpick* hotel.

The Wadi Mataha route

From the Sextius Florentinus Tomb (see p.295), a path hugs the Jebel al-Khubtha northeast along the broad **Wadi Mataha**. After 300m or so, you'll spot a complex of rock-cut dwellings known as **Dorotheos' House** set into the cliff on your right, so called because the name "Dorotheos" occurs twice in Greek inscriptions within a large *triclinium* here. Opposite, on the western side of the wadi, are **Mughur an-Nassara** (the "Caves of the Christians") a still-populated rocky crag dotted with dozens of tombs and rock-cut houses, many of which are carved with crosses (thus the name). The whole outcrop is worth exploring and commands an excellent view of Petra from the north. About 600m northeast from Dorotheos' House is the point at which the narrow **Sidd Maajn** joins the larger Wadi Mataha from the east.

There are two routes back to civilization from here, neither of them particularly easy, and both susceptible to flash-flooding in the winter and spring. First – and less complicated – is to follow the Wadi Muthlim route (see p.285) in reverse; this brings you to the dam at the mouth of the Siq. The other route takes you into the heart of the mass of rocky domes west of Wu'ayra, where it's easy to get lost; from the Wadi Mataha, you should be certain you have at least two hours of good daylight left, or you may find dusk falling with you stranded in a hundred-metre-high blind gorge and nobody in earshot. From the Sidd Maajn junction, continue north only another 100m or so along Wadi Mataha, and scale the dark rusty rocks to your right. This ridge gives you a view down into the Sidd Maajn from above, and along the parallel wadis leading south away from you into the mountain. As you walk left (east), you'll spot – like an enchanted bridge – a Nabatean **aqueduct**, gracefully spanning a wadi below. You need to aim for the wadi which leads south-southeast into the domes from a point directly at the foot of the aqueduct; make a wrong move at this point, and you'll have trouble later on extricating yourself. This is **Wadi Sha'ab Qays** and, like all of the wadis hereabouts, is long, straight and perfectly still; tracks and fresh goat droppings are good signs that you're going roughly in the right direction. You'll have to scrape past woody oleanders rooted in the sandy bed, but the going is easy enough until you reach a gigantic boulder (featuring an endearing little niche) all but blocking the way. There's just enough room to squeeze through on the right. Much further along, you'll come across a Nabatean water channel, which you can follow all the way out of the domes and towards the *Crowne Plaza* hotel.

Wu'ayra

On the edge of the domes, only about 200m east of Wadi Sha'ab Qays but utterly inaccessible from it, stands the Crusader fort of **Wu'ayra**. The ruins themselves are only of passing interest, but the location of the place is fairy-tale stuff, balanced on a razor-edge pinnacle of rock with sheer ravines on all sides and a single bridge giving access.

After King Baldwin led the Crusaders into Transjordan in 1115, founding their headquarters at Shobak, his forces rapidly set about consolidating their defences; Wu'ayra (called by them Li Vaux Moise, or "Moses' Valley") was one outpost constructed the following year, al-Habees another, with forts also going up at Aqaba and Tafileh. Wu'ayra was only briefly in Frankish hands, though: after some tussling over possession, Salah ad-Din seized control for good only seventy years later.

The fort is only accessible off the road towards Umm Sayhoun about 1km north of the *Mövenpick* hotel, the spot handily marked out by a gaping rectangular tomb to the left of the road. Aim for a gap in the rocks about 10m left of the tomb, and you'll find the straightforward path down to where the **bridge** spans the chasm. The **gatehouse** on the other side, with benches and a graffitied niche, gives into the castle **interior**, rough, rocky and ruined.

"Little Petra" (Siq al-Barid) and Baydha

Petra's northern suburb of **Siq al-Barid** is often touted to tourists as "**Little Petra**" – which, with its short, high gorge and familiar carved facades, isn't far wrong; however, although it sees its share of tour buses, the place retains an atmosphere and a stillness that have largely disappeared from the central areas of Petra. Adding in its location in gorgeous countryside and its proximity to **Baydha** (a rather less inspiring Neolithic village), it's well worth half a day of your time. Most travellers choose to visit by taxi, combining the two places with a quick peek at Wu'ayra (see above) on the way; the going rate for a full car from Wadi Musa there and back, with a wait included, is about JD15.

"Little Petra" (Siq al-Barid)

The route follows the road north from the *Mövenpick* hotel, past the Wu'ayra fort. Just beyond here, where the road curves left, you can park on the shoulder for one of Petra's best **views**, a breathtaking sweep over the central valley of the ancient city, with many of the monuments in view, dwarfed by the mountains.

Further on, past Umm Sayhoun, the road heads on across rolling, cultivated uplands that are breathtakingly beautiful after Petra's barren rockscapes. About 8km from the *Mövenpick*, a T-junction signs Shobak to the right (this is the back-route to the King's Highway; see p.269). The entrance to the **Siq al-Barid**, or "**Little Petra**", itself is about 800m to the left. You are now beyond Bdul territory in the lands of the Ammareen tribe; a signpost points off the Little Petra access road to the Ammareen campsite (see p.271). In front is a parking area, where kids hawk trinkets and guides offer their (unnecessary) services.

This whole area was a thriving community in Nabatean times, and there's evidence in almost every cranny of Nabatean occupation. Just before you reach the Siq entrance, there's a particularly striking **facade** on the right, with a strange, narrow passage for an interior.

As you enter, you'll realize why this was dubbed Siq al-Barid (the "Cold Siq"): almost no sun can reach inside to warm the place. It's only about 350m long, with alternating narrow and open sections, and differs from most areas of Petra firstly in the density of carved houses, temples and *triclinia* – there are very few blank areas – and secondly in the endearingly quaint **rock-cut stairs** which lead off on all sides, turning it into a multistorey alleyway that must once have hummed with life. Feel free to explore on all sides; there are a few highlights, but every corner has something worth seeing. In the first open area is what was probably a **temple**, fronted by a portico, below which is a very explorable little rock-cut house. The second open area has four large **triclinia**, which could well have been used to wine and dine merchants and traders on their stopover in Petra. A little further on the left, stairs climb up to the **Painted House**, a *biclinium* featuring one of the very few Nabatean painted interiors to have survived the centuries: on the ceiling at the back is a winged cupid with a bow and arrow; just above is a bird, to the left of which is a Pan figure playing a flute. The third open area culminates in rock-cut stairs which lead through a narrow gap out onto a wide flat ledge; the path drops down into the wadi (Petra is to the left), but you can scramble up to the right for some excellent views.

Baydha

If you emerge from the Siq al-Barid and head right on a track that hugs the cliff all the way round, after fifteen minutes or so you'll come to the Neolithic ruins of **Baydha**, which date from around nine thousand years ago, when the first experiments in settled agriculture were happening. There are two main levels of occupation: the first, from about 7000 BC, involved building a wall around what was formerly a temporary camping ground. The round stone houses inside were partly sunk into the ground and supported on a framework of vertical wooden posts (now rotted away). The occupants seemed to have farmed goats and possibly other animals, as well as cultivating a wide variety of cereals and nuts: querns, tools and stones for grinding and flints are dotted all over the site. After a fire sometime around 6650 BC, the village was rebuilt with "corridor houses", characterized by long, straight walls and large communal areas in addition to smaller rooms. Sometime around 6500 BC, and for a reason as yet unknown, Baydha was abandoned. Although the Nabateans later farmed the site, no one lived here permanently again.

Travel details

Buses and serveeces

Wadi Musa to: Amman (Wihdat station; 3hr); Aqaba (1hr 45min); Karak (2hr); Ma'an (40min); Shobak (30min); Taybeh (20min); Umm Sayhoun (15min); Wadi Rum (1hr 30min).

Useful Arabic place names

Ain Musa	عين موسى	Taybeh	الطيبة
Bir Mathkoor	بئر مذكور	Umm Sayhoun	ام صيحون
Petra	البتراء	Wadi Musa	وادي موسى

Petra unpackaged

Of all Jordan's tourist destinations Petra is the most celebrated – and the most packaged. A modern gateway marks entry to the site; you follow a path neatly laid with gravel and defined with kerbstones; you pass standardized souvenir kiosks; you explore on pre-defined trails. Yet less than twenty years ago you could roam at will – there were no trails and no kiosks – and twenty years before that you could spend the night in the ancient city. Tourism has forced the pace of change, but there are still many unusual perspectives to discover.

Petra by night ▲

Petra by night

One of the most powerful – and, oddly, easiest – ways of capturing some of the old magic of exploring Petra is to book for the locally run "Petra By Night" walking excursion. Turn to p.278 for a full account of the practicalities, timings and prices. If you play your cards right, hang back at the end of the group, and take your time on the walk in, you can find yourself pretty much alone for most of the evening, walking quietly through the Siq under starlight and allowing some of the majesty of Petra's **natural setting** to come through in a way that is often lost in the dust, the heat and the bustle of a daytime visit.

The Qasr al-Bint, as it was when newly built ▲

The Qasr al-Bint today ▼

Petra as it was

Although Petra is visually stunning even if you know nothing of the site's history, a little knowledge of who built these monuments (and why) can add hugely to your experience of the site – and also allows your imagination to recreate some of what Petra must have felt like in its heyday. As the images on this page show – one of the **Qasr al-Bint** temple as it is today, the other an authentic, accurate rendering of what the same building would originally have looked like, as created by archeological designer and artist Chrysanthos Kanellopoulos (see p.297) – what today appear to us to be heaps of dusty ruins at one time formed a graceful, elegant city. Grand temples and busy shops lined the main streets. Fountains played alongside lush gardens. A cosmopolitan mix of merchants and townspeople relaxed in cool, shady spots out of the sun. Learning about Petra's past enriches any stroll through its present.

Shooting the breeze, Petra ▼

Petra through the back door

Almost everybody who visits Petra stays in a hotel in the adjacent town of Wadi Musa, walks in and out through the main gateway, follows the main path for most of the day and sees Petra's major monuments – the Treasury, the Theatre, the Monastery, and so on – in the same order. This works very well if you have limited time, but if you have more than one day there is much to be said for tackling some **new approaches**.

There's no need to stay in Wadi Musa: you may find small, locally run guesthouses opening soon in the neighbouring village of Umm Sayhoun, run by the Bdul tribe (see p.293), or you could opt to stay with the **Ammarin tribe**, who operate an excellent camp (see p.271) near Little Petra. Staying with the Ammarin takes you completely out of Petra's usual run of packaged experiences, and also gains you access to Ammarin guides, who are able to lead you on their own paths through the hills and into the ancient city the back way – so that you walk through the site against the tide. The celebrated **Dana–Petra trek** (see p.256) often includes this route.

In future years look out for a new nature reserve, due to be established by Jordan's Royal Society for the Conservation of Nature (RSCN) in the hills of Jabal Mas'uda, south of Petra. As well as new walking trails and lodge-style accommodation, this will offer more unusual approaches – perhaps riding into Petra on horseback, or trekking for several days to reach the city as merchants might have done millennia ago.

▲ Byzantine mosaic, Petra Church

▼ View of the Monastery, Petra

The Monastery, Petra ▲

The Theatre, Petra ▲

Married to a Bedouin ▼

Married to a Bedouin

Marguerite van Geldermalsen, author of Married to a Bedouin *(www .marriedtoabedouin.com) — the story of how she came to Petra as a tourist and ended up staying — reflects on the changes she has witnessed.*

"I started writing *Married to a Bedouin* when I realized how much our way of life had changed.

When Mohammad and I were married in Petra in 1978, about seventy families lived in the ancient site; some in tents of woven goat-hair and others, like us, in 2000-year-old caves. They herded goats, planted winter crops and sold trinkets and old coins to the tourists. I learned to live like them — carting water from the spring, baking bread on an open fire and using kerosene for our lamps.

In 1985 we were moved to the overlooking hillside of Umm Sayhoon, partly to protect the archeological site but also to improve our quality of life with running water and electricity. Our children attended the village school and we became commuters — going into Petra to tend our souvenir and coffee shops, then riding home on camels and donkeys to turn on our televisions, put laundry into our washing machines and, eventually, hook up to the internet.

Mohammad and I had been married 24 years when he died. Soon after, I left Jordan. I felt my reason for living there had gone.

Now I understand that I left to write my story; I needed the distance to see clearly. Although Mohammad is no longer in Petra, through him I have become woven into the fabric of the place. In 2007 I returned — and settled straight back in."

The southern desert and Aqaba

CHAPTER 7 **Highlights**

❋ **Desert driving** Three long desert drives capture the spirit and look of the Jordanian landscape: the Desert Highway from Amman, the Wadi Araba road, and, least travelled of all, the Ma'an–Azraq road through Jafr. See p.317

❋ **Ras an-Naqab** Legendary panoramic views out over the sandy Hisma desert from the edge of Jordan's highland plateau. See p.320

❋ **Wadi Rum** Rugged and majestic: simply one of the world's most alluring desert destinations. Think towering cliffs, red dunes and sleeping under the stars. See p.321

❋ **Aqaba** Diving, snorkelling and year-round sunbathing at Jordan's only beach resort, on the Red Sea. See p.336

▲ Wadi Rum

The southern desert and Aqaba

T he huge eastern deserts of Jordan are mostly stony plains of limestone
or basalt, but much of the **southern desert** to the south and southeast
of Petra is sand, presaging the dunes and vast emptinesses of the
Arabian interior. The principal town of the south, Ma'an, is eminently
missable, but you shouldn't leave Jordan without having spent at least some
time in the extraordinary desert moonscape of **Wadi Rum**, haunt of
Lawrence of Arabia and starting point for camel treks into the red sands. At
the southern tip of the country, squeezed onto Jordan's only stretch of
coastline, the peaceful town of **Aqaba** is a pleasant counterpoint to the
breathtaking marine flora and fauna which thrive in the warm Red Sea
waters just offshore.

Two of the three north–south highways connecting Amman with Aqaba are
desert roads, and only really of interest as access routes to and from southern
Jordan, so we've included them in this chapter. The easternmost of the three,
the so-called **Desert Highway**, follows the line of the old Hejaz Railway and
serves as a demarcation boundary between well-watered hills to the west and
the open desert. The westernmost of the three is the **Wadi Araba road**, which
hugs the line of the Israeli border south of the Dead Sea. The middle route of
the three – the King's Highway – is covered in detail in Chapter 5.

Transport is straightforward. Plenty of buses run along the Desert
Highway to Ma'an and Aqaba, and you can get connections from both of
them to all other destinations in the region. Aqaba is also a major entry point
to Jordan, with an international airport, a land crossing with Israel and a ferry
port serving Egypt.

Destinations in the south are often less appealing than the journeys to get to
them, and the freedom a **rental car** gives really comes into its own when you're
travelling in the desert here. Being able to stop and walk even 100m away from
the highway, to get a firsthand experience of the wide open vistas rather than
seeing them skim past a dirty window, is a fine way to get a taste of this incredible natural environment.

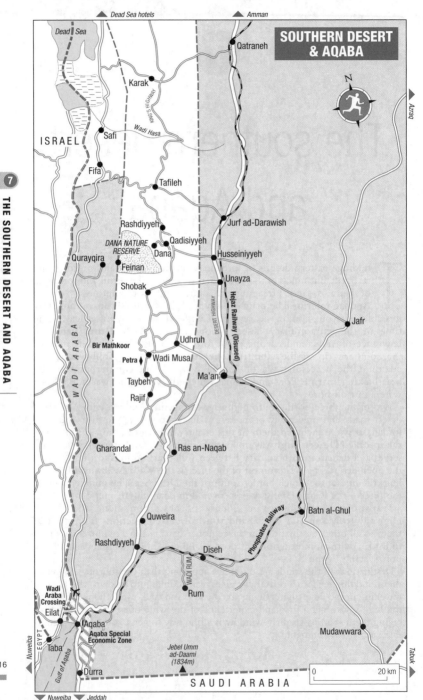

SOUTHERN DESERT & AQABA

N

Dead Sea hotels

Amman

Azraq

Dead Sea

Qatraneh

Karak

ISRAEL

Safi

Wadi Hasa

Fifa

Tafileh

Jurf ad-Darawish

Rashdiyyeh

Qadisiyyeh

DANA NATURE RESERVE

Dana

Husseiniyyeh

Qurayqira

Feinan

Unayza

Shobak

Jafr

Bir Mathkoor

Udhruh

Petra

Wadi Musa

Ma'an

Taybeh

Rajif

Gharandal

Ras an-Naqab

Quweira

Batn al-Ghul

Rashdiyyeh

Diseh

Phosphates Railway

WADI RUM

Rum

WADI ARABA

Wadi Araba Crossing

Eilat

EGYPT

Aqaba

Aqaba Special Economic Zone

Mudawwara

Jebel Umm ad-Daami (1834m)

Taba

Gulf of Aqaba

Durra

Nuweiba

SAUDI ARABIA

Tabuk

0   20 km

DESERT HIGHWAY

Hejaz Railway (Disused)

Nuweiba   Jeddah

The Desert Highway

The fastest but least romantic of the three routes linking Amman and the south of Jordan, the **Desert Highway** can whisk you from the capital to Petra and beyond in a fraction of the time the same journey would take on the slow King's Highway – but with a fraction of the interest. For the most part, the journey south is framed by bleached-out desert hills rolling off into the distance, the monotony broken only by feeder roads branching west at regular intervals to towns on the King's Highway – in north-to-south order, Dhiban, Karak, Tafileh, Dana and Shobak (all described in Chapter 5) and Wadi Musa/Petra (Chapter 6). The Desert Highway is the route followed by tankers and heavy lorries running between Aqaba's port and the industrial zones around Amman and Zarqa; it may be a dual-lane highway but traffic can be dense in parts. This is also the principal road into and out of Saudi Arabia, and all summer long features a tide of big, well-suspensioned minivans packed with holidaying Saudi or Gulf families heading north to resorts in Syria or Lebanon. Most people prefer doing these huge cross-desert drives in the cool of the night, so you'll find services on the highway open until the small hours but often shut in the heat of the afternoon.

This route is older than it appears, as the road was built mostly along the line of the **Hejaz Railway** (see p.110), which itself shadowed earlier Ottoman **pilgrimage** routes through the desert from Damascus to Mecca. During the sixteenth century, the Ottoman authorities built forts roughly a day's journey (about 30km) apart all down the length of the route, to guard local water sources and to serve as accommodation for the pilgrims; some of these "hajj forts" survive today, but almost all are ruined and/or inaccessible, the preserve of kestrels and archeologists.

Qatraneh القطرانة

From Amman's 7th and 8th Circles, the Desert Highway (doubling up in its initial stretches as the Airport Road) heads more or less due south. After exits for the Dead Sea, then Madaba and then the airport itself – at which point the glitzy billboard ads lining the highway abruptly halt – traffic swishes on south past the busy town of **JIZA** (with its Mamluke fort, now a bedouin police station) and the infamous desert prison at **Suwaqa**. Just before Suwaqa, some 74km south of 7th Circle, is a small blue sign for Qasr Tuba pointing east into the desert; the ruins repay the effort needed to reach them (see p.201), but you need a 4x4 and a knowledgeable guide for the 54-kilometre desert journey.

Many bus drivers take a break at **QATRANEH**, 90km south of Amman. This dusty town has made a living out of introducing roadside culture to Jordan, and a handful of generally decrepit and overpriced snack bars line the highway, exploiting nod-and-wink understandings with bus operators to fleece hungry passengers. If you have your own transport, make instead for the excellent *Baalbaki Tourist Complex*, 9km north of Qatraneh (☎079 550 1793), also known as *Qasr al-Janoob* (*"South Castle"*). Kept clean and very well equipped, it boasts spotless public toilets (ask for the "Western toilets", which are usually kept locked), a basic canteen-style restaurant, a small supermarket, authentic crafts from Bani Hamida and other charitable foundations (priced no higher than in Amman) and a bookshop of sorts. Out back, alongside a simple garden shaded by olive trees, are a few plain but comfortable **motel rooms** (❸), all en suite.

Within Qatraneh, the small two-storey hajj **fort** (signed as Qatraneh Castle), built under the sixteenth-century Ottoman sultan Suleiman the Magnificent, is situated by a wadi 300m west of the road and is in well-preserved condition. The guardian will let you in (he deserves a tip), and a wander round the empty, restored interior makes for an atmospheric interlude.

Just beyond Qatraneh is the turn-off west to Karak. Continuing south on the Desert Highway, you'll pass the *Sultani Tourism Complex* (℡079 556 1245), 23km south of Qatraneh, another popular rest area, complete with restaurant and souvenir shops, but there's little more to distract you. Around **Hasa**, 50km south of Qatraneh, are some phosphate mines; other major signposted turn-offs include at **Jurf ad-Darawish** (69km south of Qatraneh) west to Tafileh; at **Husseiniyyeh** (83km) west to Dana and east to Jafr; and at **Unayza** (92km) west to Shobak and Petra.

Ma'an معان

MA'AN, 214km south of Amman, is the capital of the southern desert, a dyed-in-the-wool bedouin town at the meeting point of highways from Amman, Iraq, Aqaba and Saudi Arabia, as well as countless smaller desert roads and tracks. A frontier staging-post from its earliest days, Ma'an only began to assert itself after the **Hejaz Railway** came through in 1904, transforming an isolated desert encampment into a thriving settlement. Even after the establishment of Transjordan, Ma'an lay in a poorly demarcated frontier zone, with closer links to the Hejaz region of northwestern Arabia than to Amman. These days farmers come in to do business in the markets, and the Hussein bin Talal University brings a little student colour to the streets, but for the most part Ma'an is an ordinary, hard-working city. It is bypassed by the Desert Highway, and there's little reason to visit other than to grab a bite or to change buses. The bus station lies on the edge of the **old quarter**, where Hejazi-style mud-brick houses cluster around palm-laden wadis, and shady gardens – sealed off from the outside world behind crumbling walls – make for a pleasantly cool retreat in such a hot, dry city. A short stroll from the bus station is the signposted **Ma'an Castle** – not a castle at all, but a sixteenth-century hajj fort. It has been in continuous use since then, and was the town prison as late as the 1980s. It is currently used by the Ministry of Culture and Department of Antiquities, but is usually open – you're free to wander around the courtyard and peek into the old rooms. Behind, on the banks of a wadi, is the **King Abdullah Gardens**, featuring shady spots to relax under the palms, a kids' playground and a small café.

The King Abdullah I Palace and Museum

Ma'an's sole touristic draw is the **King Abdullah I Palace and Museum** (Sun–Thurs 8am–4pm; free), a grandiose title for a modest, late-Ottoman stone building near the old train station, which was where Abdullah stopped in 1920 on his intended push northwards from the Hejaz to Damascus. After he left in February 1921, it was used briefly as a hotel before lapsing into disuse, prior to renovation in the mid-1990s. The interior has now been converted into a small museum, mostly comprising photos of Abdullah conducting international diplomacy as the Emir of Transjordan in the 1930s and 1940s. Captions are in Arabic only, but the guardian can talk you through the highlights. Adorning one wall is the first-ever Jordanian flag, flown for the first time in 1918, before the country existed. Glass cases hold household items from Abdullah's stay, and the crumbling walls still show remnants of the original frescoed decoration dating from the time of Sultan Abdel Hamid II. There haven't been any passenger trains in Ma'an for decades, and the **railway** – just beyond the museum building – is now used solely for transporting phosphates from desert mines to Aqaba port.

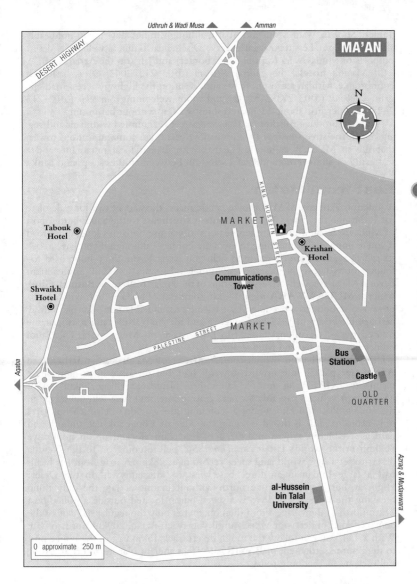

Udhruh & Wadi Musa ▲   ▲ Amman

DESERT HIGHWAY

MA'AN

N

Tabouk Hotel ◉

Shwaikh Hotel ◉

KING HUSSEIN STREET

M A R K E T

Krishan Hotel ◉

Communications Tower ◉

PALESTINE STREET

M A R K E T

Bus Station

Castle

O L D
Q U A R T E R

Aqaba ◀

Azraq & Mudawwara ▶

al-Hussein bin Talal University

0   approximate   250 m

To reach the museum, head 2km east of town on the road towards Mudawwara and Azraq, then follow the signed turn-off right for 1km. There's no public transport, but a taxi will take you there and back for a few JDs.

Practicalities

Ma'an is the hub of **public transport** in the south, and if you can't find a bus running directly from one southern town to another you can almost always find a connection from Ma'an instead. The **bus station** is 500m southeast of the town centre, and has reasonably regular services to and from Amman, Karak,

Tafileh, Shobak, Wadi Musa and Aqaba, although things slow down noticeably after about 2pm. Less regular buses serve Diseh, near Rum, as well as the desert outposts of Mudawwara (on the Saudi border) and Jafr (on the Azraq road).

Of Ma'an's **hotels**, the central *Krishan* (℡03 213 2043; ❶) is basic but comfortable, with an atmospheric veranda. Out on the highway access road, the grimy *Tabouk* (℡03 213 2452; ❶) and more welcoming *Shwaikh* (℡03 213 2428; ❶) offer just-about-adequate rooms with or without bathroom.

The main produce **market** on Palestine Street is crammed with fruit and veg, and it's in the streets nearby (in the shadow of a huge communications tower) that life in Ma'an is at its most active, with decent local restaurants and a scattering of **shawerma** and falafel stands in between clothes shops and banks.

East from Ma'an

A junction 7km east of Ma'an town centre marks the start of two long, desolate roads through the desert. The main route is **southeast** to the Saudi border post of Mudawwara, and there are few reasons to venture onto this long, quiet road if you're not actually intending to cross the border – although if you have a 4x4, it's worth searching out a guide to help you navigate the three-hour, hard-to-follow route across the desert west from Mudawwara to Rum. Some 80km beyond Ma'an is a well-preserved station of the Hejaz Railway at **Batn al-Ghul**, while at **MUDAWWARA** itself, 113km southeast of Ma'an – also with a well-preserved station, now occupied by a friendly extended family – an old railway carriage blown up in 1917 by Lawrence and the Arab armies still rests near the disused tracks. Occasional buses run from Ma'an to Mudawwara. The Saudi border lies 15km beyond Mudawwara.

The other road from the junction 7km east of Ma'an leads **northeast** to **Azraq** (see p.202) and onwards towards Iraq, but the only buses along here terminate at **JAFR**, an amiable but rather dilapidated village 58km out of Ma'an. Few vehicles pass this way, and getting stuck out here without a ride in the endless Plains of Flint under a scorching sun wouldn't be much fun. Jafr's only claim to fame is that it is set on the edge of a huge salt flat, smooth and hard as a tabletop, where in 1997 a British team clocked up an impressive 869kph in the world's fastest car, *ThrustSSC*, before going on to the Nevada desert to set a new world land speed record of 1228kph. A road from Jafr heads past a large Jordanian air force base west to Husseiniyyeh on the Desert Highway, but if you continue north without exiting at Jafr, the only thing breaking the long desert drive is a speed bump located outside a police post 71km north of the village. From then on, there's only the regular *tha-dum* of the concrete road under your wheels until you reach Azraq, 209km north of Jafr. With a 4x4, you can follow the rough desert track 15km east of the police post to the remote settlement of **BAYIR**, site of an ancient Nabatean fort and well, still used by the bedouin today.

South from Ma'an: Ras an-Naqab

The principal route from Ma'an to Petra (33km) runs from the centre of town across the Desert Highway and through **Udhruh**. Continuing south from Ma'an on the Desert Highway itself you'll pass another couple of exits marked for Petra (both of which meet the road from Udhruh just above Ain Musa), and then the *Al-Anbat Tourist Complex*, another rest stop. Just past here is the final turn-off for Petra, some 33km southwest of Ma'an; this is the start of the so-called "**Scenic Road**" which runs into Wadi Musa through Taybeh (see p.270).

A few hundred metres further, the Desert Highway reaches the edge of the highland plateau at **RAS AN-NAQAB**, from where the most stupendous panoramic views over the sandy deserts of the **Hisma** region suddenly open up in front of you. Pull off, if you can, to savour them.

Once you've negotiated the route down from Ras an-Naqab, the highway scoots across the sandy floor of the desert, with the sheer mountains of Rum clearly visible off to the left of the road for much of the way. Some 41km from Ras an-Naqab and a little beyond the village of **QUWEIRA**, a clearly marked left turn at Rashdiyyeh points the way to Wadi Rum.

Wadi Rum   وادي رم

One of the most spectacular natural environments in the Middle East, the desert scenery of **WADI RUM** (rhymes with "dumb", not "doom") is a major highlight of a visit to Jordan. The wadi itself is one of a sequence of parallel faults forming valleys in the sandy desert south of the Shara mountains. They are oriented almost perfectly north–south, shaped and characterized by giant granite, basalt and sandstone **mountains** rising up to 800m sheer from the desert floor. The rocky landscape has been weathered over the millennia into bulbous domes and weird ridges and textures that look like nothing so much as molten candle-wax, but it's the sheer bulk of these mountains that awes – some with vertical, smooth flanks, others scarred and distorted, seemingly dripping and melting under the burning sun. The intervening level corridors of soft red sand only add to the image of the mountains as monumental islands in a dry sea. Split through by networks of **canyons** and ravines, spanned by naturally formed **rock bridges** and watered by hidden **springs**, the mountains offer opportunities galore for scrambling and rock-climbing, where you could walk for hours or days without seeing another soul.

However you choose to do it – and the best way is to **book in advance** for a one- or two-day tour with one of the specialist local guides listed on p.327 – you should clear at least one night in your schedule to **sleep in the desert** here. The sunsets are extraordinary; evening coolness after the heat of the day is blissful; the clarity of the desert air helps produce a starry sky of stunning beauty; and the tranquillity of the pitch-dark desert night is simply magical. It's an unforgettable experience.

Bear in mind, too, the **extremes of temperature**: although it may be killingly hot during the day, nights even in summer can be chilly and, in winter, a dusting of frost isn't uncommon.

Some history

Although an arid, open desert, the Rum area is far from depopulated. Wadi Rum and its surrounds have abundant fresh water, and, aside from the tents of semi-nomadic bedouin scattered in the desert, there are a handful of modern villages in the area, including **Rum** itself in the heart of its eponymous wadi. There's also extensive evidence of past cultures, with plenty of **rock-carved drawings** and ancient **Thamudic inscriptions** still visible (the Thamud were a tribe, cousins of the Nabateans, who lived as nomads in the deserts of northern Arabia), as well as a single, semi-ruined **Nabatean temple**.

T.E. Lawrence ("of Arabia") waxed lyrical about the Rum area, describing it as "vast, echoing and godlike", and, appropriately enough, much of the epic *Lawrence of Arabia* was filmed here in the early 1960s, prompting tourists to visit in dribs and drabs during the years after.

However, until the late 1980s, Rum village was still comprised mostly of bedouin tents at the end of a rough road, with a single radio-phone serving the lone Desert Patrol fort. In 1984, a British climbing team led by Tony Howard requested permission from the Ministry of Tourism to explore the possibilities for serious **mountaineering** in and around Wadi Rum. With assistance from the bedouin and the backing of the ministry, an excellent book resulted, which brought the area into the forefront of mainstream tourism for the first time.

Since then, the local Zalabieh and Zuwaydeh bedouin – sub-clans of the great Howeitat tribe that is pre-eminent in the area – have established

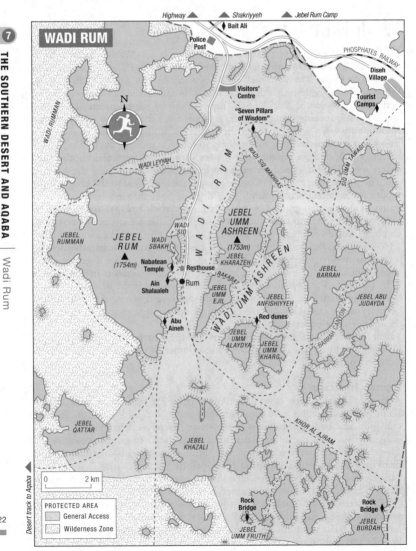

Desert track to Aqaba

Although the landscapes in and around Rum look similar, three clearly defined tribal areas intersect here. The Protected Area of Wadi Rum itself, in and around Rum village, is the territory of the **Zalabia**. The area around Disi village, east and northeast of Wadi Rum (including the easternmost part of the Protected Area) is **Zuwaydeh** land. North and west of Wadi Rum, around the village of Shakriyyeh, live the **Swalhiyeen** tribe.

As you approach the Visitor Centre, the jeeps parked outside the walls belong to the Zuwaydeh: they are permitted to follow routes only in the outlying "Operator 2" zone. Beyond the Visitor Centre, through the gateway, are cars belonging to the Zalabia; they stick to "Operator 1" routes in the central heartland of Wadi Rum. The *Bait Ali* complex (see p.327) is in Swalhiyeen territory, and has guides for camel, horse and 4x4 trips in this less-explored area.

There's much jockeying for position among the tribes, with the Protected Area administrators bending over backwards to upset nobody (and thereby pleasing nobody either). Although the legendary landscapes of Wadi Rum itself fall within Zalabia territory, there is nothing to stop you exploring further afield.

THE SOUTHERN DESERT AND AQABA | Wadi Rum

7

co-operatives to organize tourism. With the proceeds of their cooperative, the Zalabieh of Rum village built breezeblock houses and a school, and bought buses to link the village with Aqaba and Wadi Musa. The mid-1990s saw a tourist boom that has shown few signs of abating: during the peak months of March, April, September and October, the deserts around Rum can be thronged with visitors, a strange mix of budget backpackers, well-heeled groups bussed in on whirlwind tours, and serious professional climbers. Rum is now a **Protected Area** under the control of ASEZA, the municipal authority of Aqaba, and controls have been put in place to limit environmental degradation while allowing sustainable tourism to continue. Bureaucratic disputes aside, you'll quickly find that, however you manage it, escaping into the desert is infinitely more rewarding than hanging around the Visitor Centre amid the tour-group hubbub.

Arrival

There's only one **road** into Wadi Rum, signposted east off the Desert Highway at the village of Rashdiyyeh, which lies 41km south of Ras an-Naqab and 42km north of Aqaba. This road, shadowed by a freight-only railway track, skirts the mountains and a couple of hamlets for some 17km to a fork in the road marked by a police post: the village of **DISI** (also spelled **DISEH**) and other hamlets lie to the left, while the road ahead bends right into the long avenue of Wadi Rum itself, passing after 4km the **Visitor Centre** on the way towards **RUM** village, where the tarmac ends.

By bus and taxi

With most visitors booked on all-inclusive bus tours, there's very little **public transport** in or out of Wadi Rum. It's impossible to make a day-trip without

Wadi Rum is approximately:
- 300km south of Amman (3hr 30min)
- 100km south of Petra (1hr 30min)
- 60km north of Aqaba (1hr)

Moving on from Rum

Buses out of Rum are few and far between. There is one bus to Aqaba (JD2), departing around 7am – another may go at about 8.30am if there's sufficient demand – and there is one bus to Wadi Musa/Petra (JD5) at about 8.30am. That's it. These timings are not reliable, and you should check details with your guide or at the Visitor Centre in advance and on the morning itself. If you miss these, or if you want to reach any other point, it's fairly easy to hitch a ride out to the highway junction at Rashdi-yyeh (expect to pay for this, up to JD7–8 if you're the only passenger), from where buses pass reasonably frequently, south (left) to Aqaba and north (right) to Ma'an and Amman. An alternative is to arrange a **taxi** through your guide or at the Visitor Centre. For a full car (three or four passengers) expect to pay about JD20 to central Aqaba, about JD25 to Aqaba's ferry terminal or the border crossing into Israel, about JD40 to Petra/Wadi Musa, about JD80 to Amman.

your own transport. Bus service on Fridays is likely to be curtailed or non-existent.

From Aqaba, there are buses to Rum at around 1 and 3pm (JD2), with an additional bus sometimes departing around 11am. These aside, you could take just about any bus heading north from Aqaba (towards Ma'an, Amman, Wadi Musa or Quweira, for example) and ask to be let out at the Rashdiyyeh junction, from where hitching is easy: the standard price for a carload of people from the junction into Rum is about JD7–8.

From Petra (Wadi Musa), a bus departs for Rum at about 6am (JD5; see also p.000). If you miss this, take a bus towards Aqaba (or, alternatively, one to Ma'an and change there for Aqaba), and ask to be dropped at the Rashdiyyeh junction, from where you can hitch.

Chartering a **taxi** is a viable way of getting to Rum. Split between three or four passengers, fares are reasonably good value: from central Aqaba about JD20, from Aqaba's ferry terminal or the Israeli border crossing about JD25, from Petra/Wadi Musa about JD40, from Amman about JD80.

The Visitor Centre

At the entrance to Wadi Rum stands the **Visitor Centre** (daily 7am–10pm; T03 209 0600 or 077 742 0472, Wwww.wadirum.jo), at the northern edge of the Protected Area alongside the outcrop of Tell Hassan. This is where all buses and cars must stop, and where the **admission fee** to Rum must be paid – at the time of writing this was JD2 per person, but is likely to rise to JD7 or so. Around 35 percent of it goes to the local bedouin cooperatives (either Rum,

The Seven Pillars?

Although the free handout map, and almost all tourist literature, names the soaring pinnacles of rock directly opposite the Visitor Centre as the "**Seven Pillars of Wisdom**", this is a fabrication, made up in the last few years by some marketing executive to cash in on the legend of Lawrence. (Five of the pinnacles are in plain view; the other two are round the side.) Lawrence never mentioned this mountain, and took the title of his most famous work from the Book of Proverbs (9:1): "Wisdom has built a house; she has hewn out her seven pillars". The local bedouin referred to this mountain as **Jebel al-Mazmar** long before outsiders had ever heard of Rum. It seems tragic that even they are now calling it the "Seven Pillars".

Disi or Swalhiyeen, depending on which trip you choose to take), with the remainder going to the Wadi Rum development administration.

The Visitor Centre is not unattractive, a sweep of low, modern buildings set around a large gravel courtyard; for many visitors, bussed in on whistle-stop tours, this will be their sole experience of the Rum deserts, and it has been designed with their needs in mind. There are a few small shops – including a **nature shop** (daily 8am–5pm), selling locally produced crafts and jewellery items – and the pleasant, welcoming *Rum Gate* **restaurant** (daily 8am–4pm; ⓣ03 201 5995, ⓦwww.captains-jo.com), which serves simple salads and a few daily specials, mainly to lunching tour groups – tables on the rear terrace give spectacular views over the open desert.

Further round is an **Interpretation Hall**, housing fascinating displays on bedouin culture, local wildlife and protection of the desert environment, alongside a projection room showing a short **film** introducing Rum. You can also climb the two short towers across the courtyard, for eagle-eye **views** over the magnificent landscape.

Organizing a desert excursion

Aside from **walking** solo, the only way for independent travellers to get out into the desert and see the sights is by paying for an off-the-peg **driving tour**, or by prearranging an itinerary with a local **guide**, who will drive you around and, if you choose, also host you **overnight** at a desert campsite. (If you've rented a 4x4 yourself, you shouldn't head off alone. It's very easy to get confused and lost in the open desert, to say nothing of ending up bogged in soft sand.)

Of the 5,500 people who live in the Rum area, including Disi and outlying villages, roughly forty percent make their living from tourism. However, if you take the 2,000 people who live in and around Rum village itself, that figure rises to around 95 percent. Almost everybody has given up keeping goats, and now survives by providing **guide and driving services** to visitors.

This means that the bedouin of Rum are, on the whole, skilled, business-minded professionals: they know how to showcase the desert – and their own culture – to best effect. However, it pays to be aware that there are strict rules in place surrounding guide services.

Choosing a guide

The most rewarding, cost-effective and – in short – best way to see Wadi Rum independently is to **choose a guide in advance** and **book directly** with them.

It pays to do a bit of **advance planning**. Work out how much time you have available, and roughly what you'd like to see or do. Then compare our listing below with the guide recommendations at trustworthy websites such as ⓦwww.jordanjubilee.com and ⓦwww.nomadstravel.co.uk (and possibly ⓦwww.wadirum.info, though that site is under development) – along with your own research – to select a handful of guides that seem suitable. Email them directly to get a quote for what they can offer at what price.

Once you've made your choice, make a firm **written confirmation** as far in advance as possible – especially in the busy peak seasons of April and October – and at the very least two days before your arrival. Your guide is then permitted to meet you at the Visitor Centre (or elsewhere; some will meet you at the Rashdiyyeh highway junction on request), and escort you into the desert for your agreed programme. Guides are not permitted to pick up tourists at the Visitor Centre without a booking.

Cut-price tours of Wadi Rum: a warning

Numerous scammers – notably at cheap hotels in Wadi Musa and, to a lesser extent, in Aqaba, Amman and Dana – offer cut-price tours of Wadi Rum that may leave you disappointed. Here's why.

• **Wadi Rum or Disi?** Unlicensed operators are not permitted to bring tourists into the Wadi Rum Protected Area, which is patrolled by rangers. This means that anyone offering cut-price tours of Wadi Rum – such as a budget hotel in Aqaba or Petra – will not be taking you into Wadi Rum*: they will, instead, drive you around the deserts of Disi nearby, and host you at one of the Disi tourist camps. There's nothing wrong with Disi – it's beautiful – but it's not what you're paying for. Yet these scammers will swear blind that you're being taken to the real Wadi Rum – even to the extent of lying to you about which camp you're in (we've had reports of tourists being dumped at one of the Disi camps by a driver who told them it was *Bait Ali*).

Just so you know: camps within the Wadi Rum Protected Area are small, placed in isolation from one another far out in the desert, accessible only by 4x4 and sleep ten or fifteen people maximum in bedouin-style goat-hair tents. Camps at Disi are larger, sometimes cheek-by-jowl with one another, accessible by tour buses driving on dirt tracks, often set around circular performance areas with amplified music and electric floodlights, and sleep anywhere from 50 to 250 people, often in army-style canvas tents pitched in rows.

• **Commission?** If you pay, say, JD25 to a hotel in Petra for a tour of Wadi Rum, it's likely that at least JD10 of that will go straight into the pocket of the hotelier. That leaves JD15 for the man who's actually going to drive you around – which means you get a very short tour. For comparison, the going rate for a decent tour of Wadi Rum booked directly with a reputable guide, including overnight camping, all transport, meals and facilities, is roughly JD40–60 per person. Pay significantly less than that, and you can be sure you'll be short-changed.

• **Guide or driver?** At cut-price rates you are unlikely to be hosted by a guide – that is, someone who lives in Wadi Rum, speaks English and can explain the area and its sights to you. Instead you're likely to get someone who can drive the car, but little else – probably friendly enough, but possibly not even Jordanian.

Being taken around the desert in a 4x4 is never cheap – why should it be? – and that's even more true for somewhere as extraordinary (and fragile) as Wadi Rum. Out here, you really do get what you pay for.

The Cleopatra hotel in Wadi Musa is an exception – to our knowledge, this is the only Petra hotel offering tours that genuinely do enter Wadi Rum.

Programmes vary enormously, but an average **cost** for a basic overnight stay – a full day in a 4x4 visiting various desert sites and a night at a campsite in the deep desert, including all meals, transport, bedding and other facilities – is around JD40–60 per person, depending on the size of the group and the excursions requested.

An alternative option is to bring in a licensed Jordanian tour operator, who can sort everything out for you – though you will pay a premium for their services. Many are excellent: some work with particular guides; others, including Petra Moon (see p.275), maintain their own campsite within the Protected Area. Beware the plethora of unlicensed operators – including budget hotels in Petra and elsewhere – who will try to convince you that their "special" cut-price tour is a great way to see Wadi Rum on the cheap: it is not. See the box above for some reasons why.

You're the boss. If you'd prefer to see the desert from the back of a **camel** – or even a **horse** – rather than in a 4x4, say so: most guides can oblige, or will pass you onto a specialist. And if you want to be **alone**, say so: the easy-to-overlook downside of 4x4 excursions, and, to a lesser extent, camel treks is that neither allows you to soak up the silence and isolation of the desert at your own walking pace. It's perfectly possible to hire a guide to drive your gear out to a campsite in the desert while you take your time and walk there, or you could arrange for a **one-way ride** by 4x4 or camel out to a particular spot from where you then walk back.

Some recommended guides

Aodeh Abdullah ☏079 561 7902, ⓦwww .aodeh.de. Good-value budget tours by jeep and camel, plus overnight desert camping.

Atallah Sweilhin ☏079 580 2108, ⓔrumhorses@yahoo.co.uk. Acknowledged specialist in horse-riding trips around the Rum area, based at a stables near the village.

Attayak Ali ☏079 589 9723, ⓦwww .bedouinroads.com. Highly respected guide, offering top-quality jeep tours as well as excellent hiking and trekking programmes. Often booked solid.

Attayak Aouda ☏079 583 4736, ⓦwww .rumguides.com. Lively, engaging guide, handling innovative jeep and camel trips as well as great adventure activities including rock-climbing. Book early.

Difallah Ateeg ☏077 730 9239, ⓦwww .thebedouinguide.com. Experienced specialist in trekking and jeep trips, short and long.

Mohammed Hammad ☏077 735 9856, ⓦwww.bedouinguides.com. Dedicated mountain specialist, managing scrambling and rock-climbing trips of all kinds.

Mohammed Hussein ☏077 747 2074, ⓦwww .wadirumadventures.com. Budget-priced guide, offering basic jeep and camel tours to get a taste of the desert environment.

Mohammed Sabah ☏077 731 4688, ⓦwww .wadirumsunset.com. Specializing in low-cost jeep and camel trips and basic overnight desert camping.

Mzied Atieq ☏077 730 4501, ⓦwww .mzied.com. A wonderful host, charming and knowledgeable, with many years of experience. Offers a wide range of options for hiking, trekking, camel treks and jeep trips, as well as overnight stays at his excellent campsite in the deep desert.

Sabbah Ali ☏079 681 9447, ⓦwww .desert-experience.org. Experienced guide offering jeep and camel trips as well as specialist trekking and scrambling in the mountains.

Sabbah Eid ☏077 789 1243, ⓔsabbah _azlapih@yahoo.com. Specialist in hiking, trekking and especially rock-climbing.

Salem & Saleem Lafi ☏079 648 2801, ⓦwww .jordantracks.com. Brothers who run the only fully accredited travel agency in Rum, authorized to make hotel bookings and tourist arrangements all round Jordan. Offers a range of jeep and hiking trips within Rum, including some climbing and scrambling, plus horseriding.

Salem & Suleiman Mutlak ☏077 742 4837, ⓦwww.wadirum.org. A good choice of well-managed tours, reaching some unusual spots in the deep desert, plus excellent overnight camping.

Zedane al-Zalabieh ☏079 550 6417, ⓦwww .drschef.de/zedane. Last but not least – recommended budget-priced jeep trips and overnight desert camping.

Bait Ali

A great alternative base is **Bait Ali** (☏079 554 8133 or 077 754 8133, ⓦwww .baitali.com), a desert compound located in the Shakriyyeh area, just outside Rum. It is signposted off the main road, 15km east of the Rashdiyyeh junction and about 2km west of the police post marking the fork to Disi. The signpost leads you north across the railway and onto a desert track – passable with care in an ordinary car – to the site itself.

It stands hidden behind a rocky outcrop, with views across the desert plains. Tahseen Shinaco and his English wife Susan own and run the place; they – and their staff – are the height of hospitality. The public lounge areas, decorated in traditional style, are sheltered and cool, and include a dining and entertainment area. There is also a **swimming pool** (guests JD5, non-guests JD10); the water comes from aquifers beneath Disi.

Wadi Rum from above

Hot-air ballooning can offer a romantic way to experience the grandeur of Wadi Rum. You take off – generally at dawn, although there are some afternoon flights, depending on demand and weather conditions – from near the *Bait Ali* camp for a serene float over the mountains: an hour's flight costs JD130 per person (minimum three people). Other aerial adventures include sightseeing in a **weight-shift ultralight** aircraft – an open-air powered glider, operated in tandem with a qualified pilot (JD30 for 15min; JD80 for 45min). These and more are run by Jordan's **Royal Aero Sports Club** (☏03 205 8050, ⓦwww.royalaeroclub.com), based at Aqaba airport. Book everything far in advance.

Accommodation includes compact little adobe chalets (❹), nicely made and decorated, with bamboo ceilings, tiled floors and proper beds – everything decent, spotlessly clean and comfortable. Some have bathrooms en suite; others share facilities. There are also small army-style tents (❸) – check a few, since some beds are better than others.

The main attraction – aside from the warmth of the welcome – is that *Bait Ali* is located within the territory of the Swalhiyeen tribe, who are quite separate from the Zalabia of Rum and the Zuwaydeh of Disi, and so are able to offer unique trips by camel, horse or 4x4, at their own rates, into landscapes that most visitors don't get to experience. Added draws include **adventure activities** such as dune-buggies and land-sailing – and this is also the base for hot-air ballooning trips (see box above).

Climbing in Wadi Rum

If you're intending to do technical rock-climbing, then you should contact one of Rum's handful of UK-trained **mountain guides**, all of whom have full equipment and plenty of experience. A few other locals also guide rock climbs; like many Rum bedouin they are naturally competent climbers, and have learnt rope techniques by climbing with experienced visitors. However, Jordan has no system of qualification for mountain guides: staff at the Visitor Centre can put you in touch with someone suitable, but you should establish his experience before agreeing terms. There is an informative leaflet on environmental and safety guidelines, *Climbing and Trekking in Wadi Rum Protected Area*, available free at the Visitor Centre. For more information, see ⓦwww.nomadstravel.co.uk, ⓦwww.wadirum.net and ⓦwadiram.userhome.ch.

Arriving without a booking

If you turn up at the Visitor Centre **without a booking**, check the notice-boards by the ticket office which describe a dozen routes in and around Rum by 4x4 (and some others by camel), with prices for each. Simply choose which route you'd like to do, pay the fee and you're then assigned the next **driver** (or camel boy) in line. This can be a perfectly satisfactory way to see the desert: most drivers (there are dozens) are friendly and professional. However be aware that these guys are not guides: they may not speak English, may only know a few sites of interest and may not be driving the most comfortable 4x4 in the world.

These turn-up-and-go excursions from the Visitor Centre are divided into areas: "**Operator 1**" routes cover ground within the heartland of Wadi Rum; "**Operator 2**" routes are in more outlying (but not necessarily any less beautiful) areas to the north and east around Disi. At the time of writing a basic two-hour tour **by 4x4** taking in the Nabatean temple at Rum village, Abu Aina spring and the Khazali inscriptions (Operator 1) – or alternatively the scenic drive through Siq Umm Tawagi (Operator 2) – costs JD35 for a full car, seating between four and six people. Several different tours, on various routes, last three, four or five hours, up to an eight-hour tour covering all major sites as far south as the rock bridges at Umm Fruth and Burdah, plus a sunset viewpoint, for JD80 for the car. **By camel** a short ride of one or two hours costs JD10–15 per person, up to JD30 for a full day.

Independent accommodation and eating

Facilities for **independent travellers** are not great: the whole system of tourism at Rum is geared up either for large tour groups or for individuals who have booked in advance with a specific guide; in the latter case, all your meals and accommodation will be part of the agreed programme and so taken care of by your guide. In addition, since no public transport leaves Rum during the afternoon it's impossible to turn up on spec, do a tour in the desert and then depart.

However, once you've paid your admission fee at the Visitor Centre, you can cadge a lift down the road into Rum village, 7km south. Here, the first building you come to, on the right-hand side, is the **Resthouse** (☏03 201 8867), which formerly served the function of information centre, meeting point, restaurant, café, campsite and social centre. These days, with most tourists remaining back at the Visitor Centre, it's quieter than it was, but is still a good place for a meal (JD10–15) or a quiet drink; alcohol is served. Across the road are a couple of local eateries. The *Resthouse* also offers basic **accommodation** (❶) – either doss down on a mattress on the roof (with blankets), pitch your own tent on the sand behind the building, or use one of the tents already there (which allows access to showers).

It's also possible to turn up at one of the big **tourist camps** outside the Protected Area – which all focus on tour-group business – and negotiate a bed for the night (❸–❹ inc. half-board). Most are ranged side-by-side around the base of Jebel Umm Bdoun near Disi village; it's fairly easy to hitch a ride out there. Top choice is *Captain's Camp* (☏079 551 0432, ⓦ www.captains-jo.com), which sleeps a total of 140 people in comfortable little half-tented suites with proper beds and bed linen; groups often get bussed in and out for dinner or a quick glass of tea under the (imported) palm trees, but it remains fairly congenial. *Hillawi Camp* (☏079 675 5600) is vast, sleeping up to 400 people in army-style tents pitched in rows – when a big group is in this can feel almost like a small town in the desert, with electric lights strung across the mountainside above the camp, cauldrons of food cooking and dancers entertaining the crowds. Its neighbours – *Moon Valley (Wadi Qamar)*, *Oasis Desert*, *Desert Palm* and more – are in the same mould, while *Jabal Rum Camp* (☏079 557 3144), on the plains behind Shakriyyeh, sleeps 260 people in army-style tents, also with music and dancing nightly. There are no guides or transport available at any of these, though if you ask you'll be shunted along to someone who can help.

Sights and walks close to Rum

Although the Visitor Centre is geared up to a set pattern of routes, don't feel restricted to touring named sites: if you have a couple of hours to spare, there's nothing to stop you walking out across the sands in whichever direction you fancy.

Crossing to the east side of Wadi Rum from the Visitor Centre transfers you from tour-group hubbub into stillness and solitude. Following the cliffs of the massif south for a few minutes will give you a more intimate flavour of the desert environment than a bouncing 4x4 ride ever could. Another way to lose the bustle is to drive (in an ordinary rental car) past Disi to the unvisited villages of Twayseh and Mensheer. The desert out here is just as explorable – and the views just as awesome – as in and around Wadi Rum itself.

Below we've outlined a handful of the more popular and accessible sights around Rum, and also given a few pointers for **hikers** to get off the beaten track. If you intend to stay in Rum for some time, or if you're at all serious about trekking (guided or independent) or climbing, get hold of the excellent **books** by Tony Howard and Di Taylor (see p.403): *Treks and Climbs in Wadi Rum Jordan* has detailed, technical route descriptions, *Walks & Scrambles in Wadi Rum* is a booklet of short, easy-to-accomplish excursions, and some of the routes from both also feature in *Jordan: Walks, Treks, Caves, Climbs & Canyons*.

An insider's view

Ruth Caswell, author of ⊛ www.jordanjubilee.com, has been visiting and writing about Wadi Rum for twenty years. Here she sheds some light on the background of a generation of bedouin who now make their living as tourist guides.

Two cousins I know, Muhammad and Mahmoud [names have been changed], who are guides at Rum, are both from the Zilabia tribe, a branch of the great Aneizat tribal confederation. Both of them were born in the mid-1970s, in the desert, in the family tent. When they were children they attended the army school in Wadi Rum, usually walking up to 10km in the mornings and then returning to the family camps in the afternoon (school finishes at about 2pm). Sometimes they rode a donkey, sharing it with their friends. After school and during school holidays they looked after their family's animals, often moving tens of kilometres across the desert in search of grazing. They learned to hunt for meat in the mountains, and to gather the medicinal herbs they found there. Both families had a number of goats, but they were (and still are) too valuable to be killed for meat except for special occasions.

The usual transport was by camel. Muhammad's father bought one of the first jeeps to be seen in Wadi Rum when Muhammad was 12 years old; they quickly realized that the jeep was more expensive to run than the camel was, so its use was strictly rationed. It certainly wasn't to be used for things like taking the children to school. Muhammad's family used to spend the winters sheltered in the Barra canyon; during the spring they made their way slowly across the desert, spending the high summers on a plateau across the border in Saudi Arabia. Then back again during the autumn. Mahmoud's father preferred to travel from east to west, from the Mudawwara mud flats to the Abu Aina spring in Wadi Rum.

It is not surprising that these men and their brothers and sisters know the desert and the mountains intimately, nor that they are good walkers.

Another trait that they nearly all share is complete independence whenever possible. Because they were not brought up to be able to call a doctor, a vet or a mechanic, they all know a fair bit about treating an injury or an illness, caring for a sick or injured animal or repairing a car. They are confident in their own abilities in almost any situation. Most of the bedouin guides in Wadi Rum have the same or similar backgrounds. The few exceptions are from the families that preferred to remain near to the fort in Wadi Rum that was built by the Desert Patrol and a sure source of water, rather than moving with the seasons. These people might know the deep desert less well than the others, but nonetheless all the Rum guides are still bedouin to the core.

▲ Desert cairn, Wadi Rum

Any of the routes in and around Rum can be strung together to form a two-, three- or four-day adventure, with intervening nights spent camping in the desert. There are also plenty of opportunities for journeys further afield, including the **desert track to Aqaba** (50–70km), covered in a day by 4x4, two or three by camel. It's possible to reach Mudawwara by camel in about four days, Petra or Ma'an in five or six.

Jebel Rum   جبل رم

From the Visitor Centre, follow the road south along the west side of Wadi Rum for 7km to reach the *Resthouse* on the edge of Rum village. Jebel Rum rises to the right, Jebel Umm Ashreen to the left. Walking alongside the telephone poles that lead away behind the *Resthouse*, within five minutes you'll come to a small

It barely needs saying, but here goes: it would be **suicidally reckless** to tackle any of the mountain routes in and around Wadi Rum without a local guide. Walking on the desert floor is fine, but even then, if you choose to do a long-distance walk alone, you should register your intended route at the Visitor Centre and let staff know when you are planning to return. For multi-day walks, and all types of scrambling or climbing, it is essential to have a **knowledgeable local guide** with you, whether you're on your first or fiftieth visit: this is exceptionally harsh terrain and apparently safe rock can be treacherous.

Nabatean temple dating from the first or second centuries AD tucked up against the daunting cliffs of **Jebel Rum**, with Nabatean inscriptions on the walls and columns overlaid by later Thamudic graffiti.

From the temple, a modern cylindrical water tank is in plain view a little way south; a path leads from the tank up the hillside and around the cliffs above the mouth of a little valley, past springs lush with mint. On the south side of the little valley, at the head of a Nabatean rock-cut aqueduct, is **Ain Shalaaleh**, a beautiful, tranquil spot cool with water and shaded by ferns and trees, evocatively described by Lawrence in Chapter 63 of *Seven Pillars of Wisdom*. Nabatean (and modern) inscriptions are all around and there are stunning views out across Wadi Rum. Taking your time, you could devote a relaxing half-day to visiting these two places alone.

Most camel- and car-drivers, though, can't be bothered with climbing the slope to reach the spring, and instead lead visitors who have negotiated for a trip to "**Lawrence's Spring**" south along the valley floor to the rather mundane spring at **Abu Aineh**, which is marked by a tent pitched alongside a square concrete pumping block near a scree slope. Both are valid destinations, but the confusion has now become written into history, with the official map marking Abu Aineh as "Lawrence's Spring". Insist on Ain Shalaaleh, if that's where you want to go.

From Ain Shalaaleh, it's not hard to work your way east around an outcrop and south over a pass onto a path above the desert floor. About 500m further on, another pass to the right will deliver you to the bedouin tent and spring at Abu Aineh – also easily reachable on a simple one-hour valley-floor walk 3km south from the *Resthouse*.

A much longer and more serious undertaking is to **circumnavigate Jebel Rum** – from the *Resthouse* to just beyond Abu Aineh, then north, passing to the east of Jebel Rumman and across a saddle into Wadi Leyyah – but this could take nine hours or more and is only for the fit. A much easier prospect is walking northwest from the *Resthouse* along the small, well-watered **Wadi Sbakh**, between the cliffs of Jebel Rum and the outcrop of **Jebel Mayeen**; you'll eventually have to make a short scramble over a saddle into the tiny, narrow **Wadi Sid**, often dotted with pools, from where a scramble leads down to the road a little north of Rum village, making a pleasant three-hour round-trip.

Jebel Umm Ashreen   جبل أم عشرين

The west face of **Jebel Umm Ashreen** – the "Mother of Twenty", named (depending on whom you talk to) for twenty bedouin killed on the mountain, or twenty hikers swept away in a flash flood, or a crafty woman who killed nineteen suitors before marrying the twentieth – is pierced by a number of explorable ravines and canyons. Northeast of the *Resthouse*, between the highest peak of the Umm Ashreen massif and Jebel Kharazeh, is **Makhman Canyon**, explorable for about a kilometre along its length.

Directly east of the *Resthouse* is an enormous ravine splitting Jebel Kharazeh from Jebel Umm Ejil. Just beside it, a complex maze of canyons is negotiable all the way through the mountain. Once up and over a concealed gully alongside the ravine – the only way into the mountain – you emerge on a hidden plateau dotted with wind-eroded towers and framed by looming molten cliffs. Diagonally left is **Kharazeh Canyon**, and you can work your way along it for some distance before the cliffs close in. The main route follows **Rakabat Canyon** southeast from the plateau, but path-finding is complex in this closed-in, rocky gorge, requiring plenty of scrambling up and down through interlinking ravines. You eventually emerge beneath the magnificent orange dunes of **Wadi Umm Ashreen**, from where you could walk south around the massif back to Rum village. To do the full trip (10km; at least half a day), you need confidence on easy rock, a good head for heights and experience of route-finding; if in any doubt, take a local guide.

You could also head east across the valley from the Visitor Centre into **Wadi Siq Makhras**, which narrows as it cuts southeast through the Umm Ashreen massif, eventually delivering incredible views over the vast and silent Wadi Umm Ashreen. The walk from here south around the massif to the *Resthouse* (12km) can be shortened by navigating Rakabat Canyon from east to west. Other routes of 10–12km from the eastern opening of Wadi Siq Makhras involve heading northeast through Siq Umm Tawagi (see below) to get picked up in Disi village, or southeast to camp overnight in Barrah Canyon. If you don't fancy such long hikes, you can arrange in advance to be picked up at any identifiable intermediate spot by camels or 4x4 for the return journey.

Longer trips from Rum

For those with more time to spend in the area, there are literally dozens of possible jaunts, whether you're into climbing and scrambling or would prefer to

Arabian oryx in Rum

Wadi Rum is the setting for an ongoing experiment in wildlife reintroduction. The **Arabian oryx** (*Oryx leucoryx*) – a white antelope with long, straight horns that formerly roamed the deserts of the Middle East – has been extinct in the wild in Jordan for many decades. A captive breeding programme in the 1970s and 80s at Shaumari (see p.210) was successful, but after the first Gulf War 1.7 million sheep and goats, brought into Jordan by refugees from Iraq, decimated the rangelands through overgrazing, rendering the planned oryx release impossible. Oryx have remained in captivity at Shaumari ever since. Other regional projects have fared little better: Oman's oryx reintroduction recently failed due to excessive poaching, and schemes in Dubai, Abu Dhabi, Syria and elsewhere have had varying degrees of success – always (bar one release area in Saudi Arabia) with the oryx remaining behind fences.

In 2009, after meticulous planning over several years, twenty oryx were brought to Wadi Rum from Abu Dhabi for acclimatization in a large, fenced zone behind Jebel Rum, away from tourist routes, before release into the open desert. Forty more oryx are due to follow, in two phases. By all accounts, the local bedouin are thrilled to see the animals back in the area – oryx have a uniquely poetic resonance in bedouin culture – and have vowed to protect them, not least because they also recognize that oryx-spotting safaris could become a major money-spinner. Time will tell how the project beds in: for up-to-date information, ask at the Visitor Centre.

investigate inscriptions. The following gives an idea of what to expect from the more impressive sites, but again Tony Howard's books cannot be recommended highly enough for their clear and detailed route descriptions. These sites are far enough away from Rum that you'll need to rent transport: by 4x4 a three- or four-hour excursion could whisk you round most of them and still leave time for the sunset; a stately tour by camel would take days.

South of Rum

About 8km south of Rum, on the desert track to Aqaba, rises **Jebel Qattar** ("Mountain of Dripping"), origin of several freshwater springs. A short walk up the hillside brings you to the largest spring, Ain Qattar, which was converted by the Nabateans into a well. Stone steps in an area of lush greenery descend into a hidden, underground pool of cold, sweet water, drinkable if a little mossy. South and west of Qattar, just off the Aqaba track in the beautiful hiking area around **al-Maghrar** are a handful of "sunset sites", popular spots for late-afternoon 4x4 excursions (though the places that give the best sunset views change according to the seasons).

The titanic chunk of mountain opposite Qattar is **Jebel Khazali**. It's suppos-edly named for a criminal, Khazal, who was pursued up to the summit and, with nowhere to run, leapt off, whereupon he miraculously floated to earth and landed unharmed. The mountain's north face is split by a mammoth canyon, entered by a ledge on the right, the inner walls of which are covered at different heights with stylized **Thamudic rock drawings** of people, horses and pairs of feet. It's possible to scramble your way up through the cool, narrowing ravine, dodging the pools of stagnant water, for about 200m until you meet unscaleable rock.

The area east and south of Khazali is full of small domes and outcrops, with a cat's cradle of wadis and hidden valleys running through and between the peaks. To the south, a small, easily climbed **rock bridge** rises from the desert floor at **Jebel Umm Fruth**, but for most trekkers the highlight of the area is the impressive rock bridge perched way off the desert floor on the north ridge of **Jebel Burdah**. Best photographed from the east, the bridge is best scaled from the west; it's an easy but serious climb, especially if you're not that good with heights. Non-climbers should only attempt it in the company of a guide – preferably one who has a rope to protect the last few metres of climbing before the bridge, which is dangerous and exposed. The sense of achievement at reaching the bridge, though, is marvellous, and the views are stupendous.

A guided ascent of Jebel Rum requires climbing competence, but an ascent of Jordan's highest mountain, **Jebel Umm ad-Daami** (1830m), some 40km south of Rum on the Saudi border, can be achieved by anyone – it's often harder to find a driver who knows the way than it is to reach the summit. Once you've driven there, the scramble up the north ridge is straightforward, and the summit provides superb views over both countries. You can overnight in the desert, perhaps at a bedouin camp among the beautiful **Domes of Abu Khsheibah**, midway back to Rum.

East and north of Rum

East of Wadi Umm Ashreen is an area of soft sand, with some scrambleable **red dunes** rising to 20m or more against the north face of Jebel Umm Alaydа. Very close by, some of the best Thamudic carvings can be seen on **Jebel Anfishiyyeh**, including a herd of camels – some ridden by hunters, others suckling their calves – and some strange circle-and-line symbols. A little southeast, **Jebel Umm Kharg** has on its eastern side a small Nabatean

Lawrence of Arabia

Very few of the events concerning T.E. Lawrence and the Arab Revolt can be pinned down with any accuracy. The Arab protagonists left no record of their actions and motivations, and the single account of the Revolt is Lawrence's own, his famous **Seven Pillars of Wisdom**, written after the war, lost, rewritten from memory and published in 1926. By then, though, the image of Lawrence as a true British hero was firmly in place; he was almost universally seen as a soldier of integrity and a brilliant strategist, honest and courageous, who acted with genuine altruism in leading the Arabs to victory and was betrayed by his own officers. The image is a beguiling one, and stood the test of dozens of biographies. Even one of his closest friends describing him as "an infernal liar" didn't crack the facade.

But with the gradual declassifying of British war secrets – and dozens more biographies – elements of a different truth have slowly been taking hold. Lawrence was undoubtedly close to **British Intelligence**; indeed, even in his early 20s, Lawrence's work on an archeological dig in northern Syria may have been a front, enabling him to photograph engineering work on the nearby Berlin–Baghdad railway. His supposed altruism during the **Arab Revolt** seems to have been firmly rooted in a loyalty to his own country and a hatred of the French. During the Revolt, Lawrence was well aware of the Sykes–Picot Agreement that was to carve up the Levant, and seems to have wanted to establish Arab self-rule mostly to stop the French gaining any control. Although his own conscious betrayal of the Arabs racked him with guilt, he justified himself on the grounds that it was more important to defeat Germany and the Ottomans. Details have also emerged of Lawrence's dishonesty and self-glorification: biographers who have compared Seven Pillars to documentary evidence have regularly come up against inconsistencies and outright lies perpetrated by Lawrence, often for his own self-aggrandizement.

Lawrence is much less highly regarded in Jordan, where he is often seen as an imperialist who sought to play up his role in what was essentially an Arab military victory, achieved and led by Faysal. Although he pretended to have Arab interests at heart, in fact – as was shown by the events after the Revolt – his loyalty to British interests never wavered.

Nonetheless, as the years pass and the biographies pile up, the myth persists of Lawrence the square-jawed, blue-eyed buccaneering English bedouin as portrayed by Peter O'Toole in David Lean's 1962 film epic Lawrence of Arabia. But in 1919, Lawrence's friend Colonel Richard Meinertzhagen recorded a conversation that they'd had about the text of Seven Pillars: "He confesses that he has overdone it, and is now terrified lest he is found out and deflated. He told me that ever since childhood he had wanted to be a hero. And now he is terrified at his brazen imagination. He hates himself and is having a great struggle with his conscience." This seems as appropriate an epitaph as any to a life still shrouded in mystery.

structure, named – wrongly – "Lawrence's House", which commands spectacular panoramic views out over the desert.

Further east lie Jebel Barrah and Jebel Abu Judayda, divided by the sandy, easily negotiable and very atmospheric **Barrah Canyon**, which winds between the cliffs for some 5km; this is an often-used overnight camping stop, the journey best done with camels. North of Barrah, between a group of three peaks, the hidden valley of **Siq Umm Tawagi** features plenty of Thamudic rock drawings as well as a totally fake recent carving of two faces which the tour guides will claim are Lawrence and Emir Abdullah – tragically, this canyon is now being dubbed "Lawrence's Siq" as a result. Umm Tawagi is a good second-day route from Barrah to a pick-up point in Disi village, about 15km north. From Barrah, it's also possible to round the Umm Ashreen massif and return to Rum.

The wild landscape north of Disi and Shakriyyeh is just as impressive and half as well known. Three easily accessible sites stand out to give a taste of the area. In the foothills just east of Disi, at the base of **Jebel Amud** amidst dozens of Thamudic inscriptions, is a large slab of rock covered in lines and interconnected circles which, it has been theorized, is an ancient map – although what it refers to isn't known. About 6km north of Shakriyyeh are some amazing Thamudic drawings at **Abu al-Hawl**; the name means "father of terror" and suits well the extraordinary experience of coming across two-metre-high figures with stubby outstretched limbs carved into a remote desert cliff. About the same distance again north is a breathtaking rock arch at **Jebel Kharaz**. You could either take a half-day drive out to these two spots, or treat them as stop-offs on a long desert journey northwest to Petra or northeast to Ma'an. Also in this area is "**The Palace**", a castle-like compound which some guides claim featured in the film *Lawrence of Arabia*. It was in fact built for the French TV game show *The Desert Forges*, which ran for one series in 2001 before being pulled.

Aqaba العقبة

Jordan's beach resort of **AQABA** (say it "acka-buh") glories in an idyllic, sunny setting on the shores of the Red Sea, at the southernmost tip of the country. From a standing start, in the last decade or so it has transformed itself into a world-class leisure destination. Hotels at all grades are springing up in the town as well as on the adjacent beaches and luxury waterfront developments; invest-

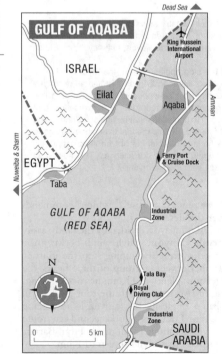

ment is pouring in to improve the city's infrastructure and facilities; and charter flights direct into Aqaba's international airport are allowing holidaymakers to bypass Amman and the north of the country altogether. Some of the best diving and snorkelling in the world is centred on the unspoiled **coral reefs** which hug the coast just south of the town – an engaging counterpoint to the nearby desert attractions of Petra and Wadi Rum.

The main driver of growth has been the **Aqaba Special Economic Zone** (ASEZ; Ⓦ www.aqabazone.com), which covers the city and its surrounds. Set up in 2000 with tax breaks for business and lowered customs duties, it has been wildly successful. Aqaba is booming.

And yet, despite the recent appearance of package tourists flip-flopping through the town centre in shorts or bikinis, Aqaba's proximity to – and historical links with – Saudi Arabia make this

Developing Aqaba

With tax breaks stimulating international investment into Aqaba, the range of **development projects** in and around the city is dizzying. In recent years, the entire city centre has been revamped, with new street furniture, public art and extensive replanting of palm trees (after the palm groves that used to line Aqaba's shore had all been uprooted by previous, less visionary city authorities). New **shopping malls** have gone up, large numbers of **hotels** have opened or are due to open, extensive **residential suburbs** are being built to cater for the city's ballooning population and plans have been unveiled to move the entire **port**, from its current position on the edge of the city centre 20km south to the area beside the Saudi border, thereby opening up a fresh area of waterfront for leisure development. **Tala Bay** (ⓦwww .talabay.jo), a wedge of luxury apartments, hotels and restaurants around a marina and sandy beach 15km south of Aqaba city centre, is already open – with a golf course on the way – as is (after 2010) the **Saraya** development west of the city centre (ⓦwww.sarayaaqaba.com), taking in villas, apartments, hotels, water parks and beach facilities. Under development behind **Saraya**, and due for completion in phases up to 2016, is **Ayla Oasis** (ⓦwww.aylaoasis.com), where a narrow section of seafront is being opened up to feed into a large lagoon extending inland against the Israeli border; expect more luxury residences and a string of four- and five-star hotels, as well as perhaps an access channel to serve the projected Red Sea–Dead Sea canal (see p.131). Add in plans to revamp some admittedly shabby, run-down parts of the city centre, and Aqaba, already rejuvenated in the last decade, looks set to be transformed.

actually one of the more socially **conservative** urban centres in Jordan. Historically neither a trading port nor a commercial hub, Aqaba was only ever significant as a stopping-off point for pilgrims travelling to and from Mecca. If you've come expecting a pacy, cosmopolitan mini-Beirut, or mini-Dubai, you'll be disappointed. The contradictions between deep-set tradition, big business and mass tourism look set to give small-town Aqaba a lively spin in the years ahead.

The town is starting to experience a year-round **high season**. Jordan's standard peaks (March–May & Sept–Nov) are supplemented by European tourists seeking Aqaba's pleasantly warm sunshine in the winter months (Dec–Feb). Summer (June–Aug) is the main Saudi and Gulf holiday season, and also when Eastern European holidaymakers come to sizzle on the beaches. The hajj pilgrimage – in November until 2011, then October from 2012 – is an added complication, with thousands of Egyptian and North African pilgrims stopping off in Aqaba on their way home. And the town can be booked solid on holiday weekends, as Ammanis and others head for a short break by the seaside.

Another factor to reckon with is the extreme **heat and humidity**. During the four mild months around Christmas, a few days in Aqaba can pleasantly warm the chill of Amman from your bones (not for nothing does King Abdullah keep a winter residence here), but for the rest of the year, daytime temperatures damply soar. The four months of summer can be stifling, with July and August's fifty-degree days and thirty-degree nights too much to bear.

Some history

For years Aqaba was overshadowed by its huge Israeli neighbour Eilat, which was founded in 1949 on what used to be arid desert and is clearly visible sprawling around the opposite shore of the Gulf of Aqaba. However, Aqaba's location is much more naturally favoured than Eilat's: a series of freshwater springs barely a metre or two below Aqaba's beaches has ensured almost continuous habitation

▲ Courtyard of the Mamluke fort, Aqaba

of the shore at least since Nabatean times, although the town in or near Aqaba's position has changed names many times. In biblical times it was called Elot. Through the Roman and Islamic periods this was adapted variously into Aela, Ailana or Aila. The Arabic word aqaba means "alley", and is a shortening of "Aqabat Aila", a title referring to the narrow Wadi Yitm pass that was the only route into the town through the mountains to the north.

One of the earliest references to the area comes in the Old Testament (I Kings). King Solomon built a large port at Ezion Geber "beside Elot on the shore of the Red Sea" both for trade and also to house his new navy. During the 1930s, excavations at **Tell al-Khaleifeh**, a little west of Aqaba, seemed to indicate occupation around the time of Solomon, but archeologists – hampered by construction of the modern Jordanian–Israeli border fence – later pinpointed occupation to have begun during the eighth century BC, much later than Solomon. Ongoing investigation is suspended while the *tell* lies in a militarily restricted zone, but nonetheless the real Ezion Geber must have been close by.

The **Nabateans** controlled a series of ports from Aqaba all down the eastern Gulf coast. Aqaba's fresh water also ensured that the town became a caravan stop for merchants arriving from Arabia, with routes leading north to Petra and Syria, northwest to the Mediterranean coast at Gaza and west across the Sinai desert into Egypt. A highway constructed by the Roman Emperor **Trajan** in 111–14 AD led to Aqaba from his provincial capital at Bosra (Syria).

Recent excavations beneath the beach have revealed the world's **oldest purpose-built church**, dated to around 300 AD; during the **Byzantine** period Aqaba was the seat of a bishopric. It was the first prize to fall to the **Muslims** on their military advance northwards in 630, and flourished throughout the early Islamic period, hosting a theological seminary. By the tenth century, Aqaba was an important stop on the pilgrimage route to Mecca.

On their push into Transjordan after 1115, the **Crusaders** – led by Baldwin of Jerusalem – seized the town and built a castle, although no trace of it survives.

In response, the Muslim resistance fortified a small offshore island, known to the Crusaders as the Île de Graye (today dubbed Pharaoh's Island), and within a century Salah ad-Din had retaken Aqaba on a campaign which eventually led to Jerusalem.

A small **Mamluke** fort on the shore was rebuilt in the early sixteenth century just before the **Ottoman** seizure of power, and it survives today. For three hundred years, Aqaba became again an important caravan stop, but the opening of the Suez Canal in 1869 dealt a death blow. For the first time, seaborne trade around the region, and between Europe and Asia, became an economically viable alternative to the camel caravans; equally, for Turkish and Syrian Muslims, making the pilgrimage to the Holy Places by sea through Suez was infinitely preferable to the arduous journey through the desert via Aqaba. The town's fortunes rapidly declined, and during the 1917 **Arab Revolt**, the forces of Faysal and Lawrence were able to surprise the small Ottoman garrison by approaching through the desert from the north: with all defensive artillery directed towards the sea, Aqaba fell with barely a skirmish. Ironically, when David Lean arrived in 1962 to stage the same incident for *Lawrence of Arabia*, he thought Aqaba looked wrong – and so departed to film the sequence in southern Spain instead.

Modern Aqaba

The sleepy fishing village was only dragged into modernity following a 1965 readjustment of the international border: Saudi Arabia got a patch of interior desert in exchange for Jordan's gaining an extra few kilometres of coastline and coral reef south of Aqaba. This made room for construction of full-size **port** facilities, and since then Aqaba has seen a resurgence in overland trade, although the camel caravans of antiquity have been replaced by a continuous stream of juggernauts: Aqaba port is the sole outlet for Jordan's principal export, phosphates, as well as the transit point for goods trucked to and from Iraq. With the recent shift in priorities away from industry towards **beach tourism**, the dowdy, endearingly run-down Aqaba of old is being unceremoniously shouldered aside – and its long-standing **fishing** industry has been reduced to just a hundred individuals.

Arrival

The **highway** entering Aqaba from the north coils along the line of the Wadi Yitm, still today, as in antiquity, the only negotiable route through the craggy mountains that seal Aqaba off. Bypass routes to the port ensure that heavy trucks are diverted away from the city. As you approach the outskirts, you might have to stop for a brief luggage inspection at a customs post marking the boundary of the Special Economic Zone (see p.65 for more). The highway heads on into the centre of town, connecting with the **Corniche**, or coast road; this hugs the shore right (west) to a hotel zone, and left (east) past the city centre to the South Coast, location of more hotels and beaches, plus the port and ferry terminal.

Aqaba is approximately:
- 330km south of Amman (3hr 45min)
- 280km south of Dead Sea hotels (3hr 30min)
- 120km south of Petra (1hr 30min)
- 60km south of Wadi Rum (1hr)

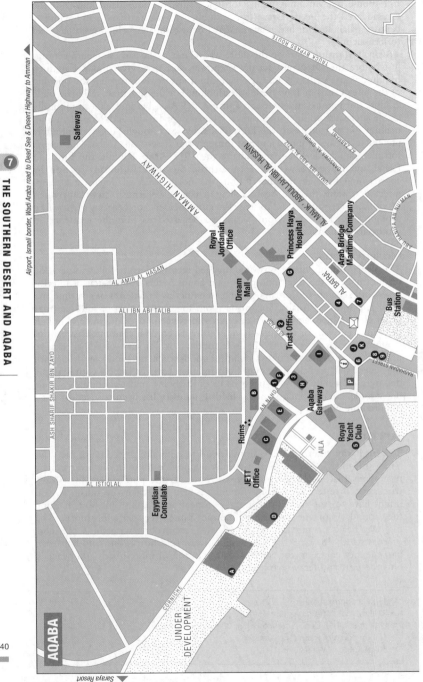

AQABA

Airport, Israeli border, Wadi Araba road to Dead Sea & Desert Highway to Amman

Saraya Resort

Safeway

AMMAN HIGHWAY

ASH SHARIF SHAKIR IBN ZAYD

AL AMIR AL HASAN

ALI IBN ABI TALIB

AL ISTIQLAL

Egyptian
Consulate

JETT
Office

Ruins

CORNICHE

UNDER
DEVELOPMENT

AILA

Royal
Yacht
Club 5

Aqaba
Gateway

AN NAHDA

YA'RUB ST

Trust Office

Dream
Mall

Royal
Jordanian
Office

Princess Haya
Hospital

AL MALIK ABDULLAH IBN AL HUSAYN

HUTAYM IBN ABD AL QAYS

QAHTAN AL SHIBI

AT ZABAYR

Arab Bridge
Maritime Company

AL BATRA

TRUCK BYPASS ROUTE

Bus
Station

BAGHDADI STREET

ABU HANIFA AN NU'MAN

A
B
C
D
E
F
G
H
1
2
3
4
5
6
7
8
9
J
K
P
i

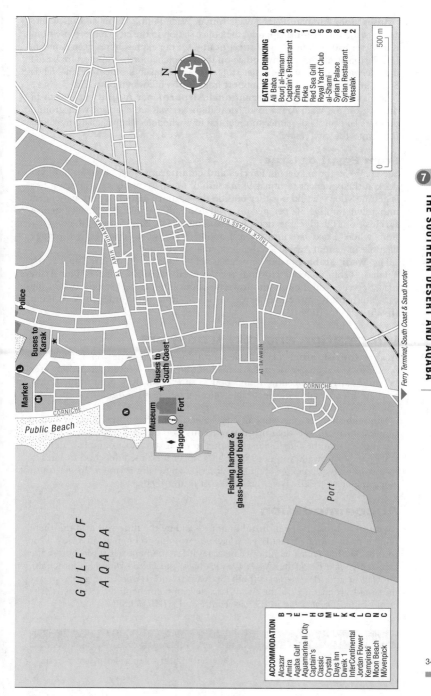

▶ Ferry Terminal, South Coast & Saudi border

EATING & DRINKING
Ali Baba	6
Bourj al-Hamam	A
Captain's Restaurant	3
China	7
Floka	1
Red Sea Grill	C
Royal Yacht Club	5
al-Shami	9
Syrian Palace	8
Syrian Restaurant	4
Wesalak	2

ACCOMMODATION
Alcazar	B
Amira	J
Aqaba Gulf	E
Aquamarina II City	I
Captain's	H
Classic	G
Crystal	M
Days Inn	F
Dweik 1	K
InterContinental	A
Jordan Flower	L
Kempinski	D
Moon Beach	N
Mövenpick	C

GULF OF AQABA

Public Beach

Police

Buses to Karak

Market

CORNICHE

Buses to South Coast

Museum

Fort

Flagpole

Fishing harbour & glass-bottomed boats

Port

CORNICHE

AT TA'AWUN

AL AMIR MUHAMMAD

TRUCK BYPASS ROUTE

N

0   500 m

Buses from Amman, Petra (Wadi Musa), Wadi Rum, Ma'an and elsewhere arrive at the **bus station**, opposite the police station in the city centre; those from Karak (via Safi) terminate on a street nearby. Of the express buses from Amman, **JETT** stop at their company's office on the Corniche north of the centre beside the *Mövenpick* hotel, while **Trust** stop at their company's office on An-Nahda Street in the centre. Onward transport from Aqaba is covered on p.353.

Aqaba's **King Hussein International Airport** (code AQJ) is 9km north of the city, off the Wadi Araba road. Most flight arrivals are charters, with ground transfers laid on. Taxis gather to meet the few scheduled flights, charging about JD12 into the city centre.

From Egypt or Israel

See pp.35–36 for full details. **Ferries and catamarans** from Nuweiba in Egypt dock at the passenger terminal, 9km south of town. Arrival is straightforward, as is getting your visa. Taxis gather outside the terminal gates to whisk passengers into town for JD1.50 per person or JD6 for the whole car. Smaller **cruise ferries** from Taba Heights dock at the marina in Tala Bay, 15km south of Aqaba, from where a taxi fare into town is about JD10 (some dock beside the huge flagpole in central Aqaba – walking distance from hotels).

The **Wadi Araba border** between Israel and Jordan (known in Israel as the Yitzhak Rabin or Arava crossing) is 5km north of Aqaba, off the Wadi Araba road. Serveeces do the run into town for about JD3 per person or JD12 for the car. Alternatively, you could take a taxi direct from this border to Wadi Rum (JD25) or Petra (JD40).

Information and city transport

Aqaba's **tourist office** (daily 8am–8pm, Nov–March closes 6pm; ☏03 203 5360, ⓦ www.aqaba.jo) occupies a small hut under the trees in the parking area behind Aqaba's main central roundabout, a short walk from most of the hotels. Staff are friendly and knowledgeable, offering free maps and information about goings-on around town.

Although there is a network of city buses, most serve outlying suburbs. The simplest way to **get around town** is on foot: walking the length of the Corniche (from the *InterContinental* hotel to the fort) takes around half an hour. If it's too hot to walk, you need only lift a finger for a meterless **taxi** to screech to a stop for you; reckon on JD1–2 for ride anywhere in town. To get south along the coast to Tala Bay, a taxi will cost nearer JD10.

Accommodation

Aqaba has a broad range of **hotel** options – and by the time you read this there will be many more. At Tala Bay a *Mövenpick* was due to open as this book went to press, with a *Hilton* to follow. The Saraya development has seven hotels: the "six-star" *Nikki Beach*, the *Qala'a*, *Qasr al-Aqaba* and *Dar al-Masyaf* (all Jumeirah), *Al-Manara* and *Bab al-Bahar* (both Starwood) and *Westin*. Five more, as yet unnamed, are planned in the Ayla Oasis development behind Saraya, as well as a mid-range *Domina Inn* in the city centre and a *JW Marriott*.

Aqaba visas

See p.65 for details of the **free visas** issued on arrival at Aqaba's airport, land borders and ferry port.

All this will ease Aqaba's room shortage, but you should nonetheless always **book in advance**, no matter what your budget. When choosing a room, factor in the stifling **heat**: the romance of a sea view – along with a beautiful panorama **westwards** across the bay towards Eilat – brings with it exposure to the scorching force of the sun. For the sake of a cool night's sleep, you might do better to choose a room facing east to the mountains or north over the city, and then keep the windows and the drapes closed all day.

Budget hotels

Aqaba has a fair choice of **budget** accommodation, but many places are geared up more for long-stay Egyptian guest workers than Western tourists: below are the best of the bunch. You also need to bear in mind the excessive heat and humidity: a working ceiling fan is a minimum requirement, but if you're paying ❷ prices and above you should be getting decent air conditioning. Either way, avoid rooms with west-facing windows, which get the full force of the afternoon sun. All these hotels are marked on the map on p.340.

Amira town centre ☎03 201 8840. Twelve simple rooms are no-frills and sensibly priced – a bit grimy, but otherwise comfortable and spacious. ❷

Bedouin Garden Village South Coast, 12km south of town ☎079 540 1640, ⓦwww.bedouin-hotels .com. About as bedouin as a bikini, but nonetheless a decent, attractive option for budget accommodation, with an easy-going, hippyish atmosphere. There's a mix of "chalets" plus clean toilets and showers and a pleasant, shaded tent area for lounging. They do inexpensive meals (fish barbecues are an evening favourite), and snorkelling excursions. You can also pitch a tent here (JD10). Located 100m from the beach, above the road. ❸

Bedouin Moon Village South Coast, 12km south of town ☎079 538 1979, ⓦwww.bedouinmoonvillage .com. Located alongside *Bedouin Garden Village* and in much the same style, with similar facilities and atmosphere. Another option – *Mermaid Village* – is going up nearby, too. ❸

Dweik 1 Town centre ☎03 201 2984. Another adequate town-centre option, slightly shabby but decent and welcoming. ❶

Jordan Flower Town centre ☎03 201 4378. Marginally the best of the three budget hotels that stand beside each other on this street (the others are *Petra* and *Jerusalem*), with some en-suite rooms that aren't bad at all – big and relatively comfortable. ❶

Mid-range hotels

Many **mid-range** hoteliers have gone to town on their lobby decor, but do less well when it comes to the rooms: a four-star reception desk can prelude two-star facilities. Furthermore, as much as JD15–20 can separate rooms with a sea view from those facing the mountains – if you're prepared to negotiate, you could nab yourself a bargain. All these hotels (bar the *Coral Bay*) are marked on the map on p.340.

Alcazar town centre ☎03 201 4131, ⓦwww.alcazarhotel.com. A friendly, welcoming two-star hotel, well located in the centre, with stone-floored rooms that are airy and pleasant, set around a four-storey atrium open to the sky. Further attractions include the Seastar diving centre, one of the biggest pools in town and free transport and access to the Club Murjan beach complex on the South Coast. A characterful choice. ❸–❹

Aquamarina II City town centre ☎03 201 5165, ⓦwww.aquamarina-group.com. Long-standing though rather uninspired tourist hotel in the heart of the city centre, offering spacious, comfortable

rooms that are a better bet than at the other properties in this Aqaba-only hotel group. ❼

Captain's town centre ☎03 206 0710, ⓦwww.captains-jo.com. Excellent upper-three-star hotel (nearer four-star) in the centre of town, with sleek well-kept rooms offering a touch of designer style – gadgets, good fabrics, tile floors, chic bathrooms with bowl basins and multi-jet showers, and so on. Rooms are a touch on the compact side, but still very comfortable. Service is quick and professional. ❼

Classic town centre ☎03 205 0070. Surprisingly good, modest boutique-style hotel slightly away from the tourist strip (opposite the Haya hospital).

Rooms are spacious and well kept, and rates are keen: a bargain. ❹

Coral Bay At the Royal Diving Club, 17km south of town ☎03 201 5555, Ⓦ www.coralbay.jo. Well-designed three-star hotel, with 69 rooms – most with a sea view – on a beautiful, quiet stretch of beach well away from the town bustle. Rooms are pleasant and have some character, though poor service lets it down badly and the rack rate is wildly overpriced – bargain hard. ❼

Crystal Town centre ☎03 202 2001, ⓔ crystalhotelaqaba@yahoo.com. Remarkably good three-star hotel in the centre, overlooking shopping streets and near the souk. A showy,

upmarket lobby preludes a range of large, comfortable rooms, well kept and rather stylish. ❺–❻

Days Inn Town centre ☎03 203 1901, Ⓦ www .daysinn.com. Occupying an odd building (begun as a shopping mall, then converted partway up into a hotel), this is a handsome, competitively priced holiday hotel with a rooftop mini-pool that sizzles in summer. All but a handful of the 110 rooms have balconies, and those that don't are huge corner rooms. Also several connected family suites. ❻

Moon Beach Corniche ☎03 201 3316. Pleasant, comfortable small hotel well located near the fort – the rooms are generic though decent enough, and there's a good breakfast on offer. ❸–❹

Luxury hotels

Aqaba has seen a boom in both the number and quality of **luxury** four- and five-star hotels in the last few years – and the trend is set to continue. See "Accommodation" above for some of the world-class hotels that are likely to open before this book is next revised, substantially boosting top-end room availability in and around the city. Hotels in town are marked on the map on p.340.

Aqaba Gulf Corniche ☎03 201 6636, Ⓦ www .aqabagulf.com. Landmark city-centre hotel which gets most of its custom from tour groups and business travellers. Rooms are functional and pleasant enough, though interiors are unremarkable. A major drawback is that it has no private beach and does not offer beach access elsewhere. ❽

InterContinental Corniche ☎03 209 2222, Ⓦ www.interconti.com. Outstanding five-star hotel on its own slice of beach, gazing south over the water. Rooms are large and very well appointed, and the hotel's facilities range from top-notch restaurants to a spa and fitness centre. Super-stylish. ❾

Kempinski Corniche ☎03 209 0888, Ⓦ www .kempinski-aqaba.com. Another fine holiday hotel on its own sandy beach, offering chic, state-of-the-art interiors. Every one of the 201 rooms and suites has a sea view, thanks to the building's curved design. ❾

Marina Plaza Tala Bay, 15km south of town ☎03 209 2900, Ⓦ www.marinaplaza.org. Four-star holiday hotel in the Tala Bay development, set back from the beach (though with beach access) and

arrayed around a large pool area. Its 267 rooms are bright, spacious and modern, there's a spa, regular transport into town and excursions laid on. ❾

Mövenpick Corniche ☎03 203 4020, Ⓦ www .movenpick.com. Lavish hotel complex, variously dubbed by the locals "the fairy palace" for its twinkling lights and "the prison" for the curiously designed set of bars that slides across every window. Inside, it's airy, spacious and beautifully designed, with the pool placed up on a bridge over the road that connects the hotel proper (on the north side of the road) with the condominium section on the beach to the south. Rooms are very well appointed, with everything you'd expect. ❾

Radisson SAS Tala Bay, 15km south of town ☎03 201 4448, Ⓦ www.radissonsas.com. Exceptional resort hotel in the Tala Bay marina development, looking out over a west-facing beach to the Sinai mountains opposite. The hotel is huge, offering more than 330 rooms of differing grades, characterized by contemporary styling and five-star service. Several restaurants, cafés and pool areas – including swim-up bars and infinity pools – as well as diving, snorkelling, fishing, sailing and excursions persuade you never to step outside. ❾

The Town

Aqaba town centre is a dense network of streets and alleys clustered around the junction of the Corniche and the main highway from the north. Here you'll find the bulk of the town's smaller hotels, dozens of cafés and restaurants, the main produce market, access to the public beach and all of Aqaba's promenading, street-based nightlife. Aside from shopping, sights within the town are limited to a **Mamluke fort** and small **museum** south of the centre, and the open excavations of Islamic-period **Aila** to the north. All are worth checking out, although try and do so early in the morning, before the sun has had a chance to turn up the heat. Otherwise, of course, Aqaba is perfect for relaxing by the pool, beach-bumming and tackling some **diving and snorkelling**; see p.348 for details.

Aqaba Gateway: the "Jordan Experience"

Alongside the main traffic circle on the Corniche rises the **Aqaba Gateway**, fronted with a *McDonalds*. This odd complex was conceived by Hollywood director Irvin "Shorty" Yeaworth (famous for 1958's *The Blob*) to be a mini-theme park, hosting costumed characters parading amidst a traditional-style souk of spices and jewellery. It was only part-completed when, in 2004, Yeaworth was killed in a traffic accident near Tafileh. Subsequently, the building works were rushed through and the retail units filled as quickly as possible – with the result that it has become just another mall, packed with fast-food outlets, albeit with a replica Arab dhow moored on a lagoon in the middle.

Yeaworth's *pièce de résistance* (which survives him) is the multimedia **Jordan Experience** (daily hourly 11am–7pm; JD6). A guide leads you on a short tour through a darkened "siq", with spotlit displays and recorded voices telling stories of Jordan's past and present. Another door opens, and you are led into **the world's largest motion-base cinema**, something akin to IMAX, with a large screen and wraparound sound. The movie itself (which lasts about twenty minutes) comprises footage of Jordan filmed from the air: as the camera angle shifts, so does the floor of the cinema, tilting from side to side and forward and back to match the pictures. It's kitsch, but entertaining.

The public beach and flagpole

Aqaba's free-entry **public beach** – comprising the few hundred metres from the Aqaba Gateway roundabout south to the fort (see below) – is a great place to soak up some local atmosphere. Steps lead down from the Corniche road, past patches of cultivated garden beneath the palm trees, to the beachfront promenade, where families stroll and kids sell chewing gum and knick-knacks. Loosely partitioned cafés have been rigged up on the beach all down this stretch, with radios blaring, women sitting in the shallows fully clothed, hubbly-bubbly smoke wafting over everything, and square-eyed families glued to TVs balanced table-on-table within a metre of the lapping waves. Jetties extending out into the water are lined with café tables. It's a great spot to catch a flavour of what Aqaba used to be like, before the developers moved in. Needless to say, though, this is not the place either for a relaxing spot of sun worship or for women to take a dip wearing anything less than an overcoat.

At the southern end of the public beach, and directly alongside the fort (see below), Aqaba's most identifiable landmark – a giant **flagpole** – soars above what is known as Great Arab Revolt Plaza. This open space on the waterfront, a focus for the evening *passeggiata*, commemorates the successful attack on

Beaches, watersports and excursions

If you're staying at a hotel that does not have its own **beach**, ask at reception whether any deals are in place to allow guests beach access. Otherwise, all the five-star beach hotels can accommodate non-guests – though for a hefty **fee** (roughly JD15–25) and you may be turned away at busy times. Elsewhere, the best and cleanest beaches, where foreign women will get no hassle whatsoever, are south of town at Club Murjan and the **Royal Diving Club** (about JD10–15). Both have a proper restaurant, and both operate private shuttle buses to and from the town centre (see "Dive centres", p.351).

All the big hotels, beach clubs and dive centres (listed on p.351) offer a range of **watersports**. Prices and options vary, but expect speedboat trips, waterskiing, banana/inner-tube rides, jetskiing, canoeing, windsurfing, parasailing and more. Many of the hotels work with the local **Sindbad** company (☏03 205 0077 or 079 555 6076, ⓦwww.sindbadjo.com), so you could check prices and offers with them directly.

A number of operators (including Sindbad) run **cruises** into the Gulf of Aqaba – sample prices include JD25–30pp for an eat-aboard cruise, including a modest lunch or dinner on the yacht, or a ninety-minute sunset cruise at JD15pp. Many can also rent out sailing yachts and motor yachts for private excursions or fishing trips.

Pharaoh's Island

One of the most popular day-voyages is to **Pharaoh's Island**, a rocky islet in Egyptian waters about 17km southwest of Aqaba (and 250m off the Egyptian coast). In the twelfth century, to counter a castle at Aqaba built by the Crusaders (now lost), Salah ad-Din's Muslim resistance fortified this barren islet, dubbed by the Crusaders the Île de Graye. The castle's towers and passageways have been restored, but the main reason for coming is to **dive or snorkel** in the maze of reefs off the northeastern tip of the island. The only way to get there is on an organized tour, which run daily when there's sufficient demand. Just about any hotel or dive centre can take a booking; expect to pay JD40–50pp, which includes everything, including lunch on board. Departure is around 10am, and you're back in Aqaba by 5pm. Book at least one day ahead, and leave your passport: the operator has to organize a temporary Egyptian visa. It's not possible to cross from the island to the Egyptian mainland.

Glass-bottomed boats

Otherwise you could opt for a quick trip in a **glass-bottomed boat**, which has a viewing window to see below the surface. Dozens chug around the public beaches sharking for customers, though many are rather dilapidated: plans are in train to clean them up and organize the business. A trip in one of these simple craft should cost around JD10–15 per hour for a full boat. (Note that some disreputable boat captains will dive down and snap off bits of coral to hand to their oohing-and-aahing clients. This is not only illegal but also kills the reef. If it happens, refuse to pay for the trip and report the incident to the tourist office.) A more upmarket alternative is to go with a glass-bottomed boat tour through a big hotel (or Sindbad again): a comfortable three-hour trip, including snorkelling kit and refreshments on board, costs about JD25pp.

▲ A day out at the beach, Aqaba

Aqaba in 1917 by Arab armies under Faysal and Lawrence, which ousted an Ottoman garrison and opened the way for final victory with the capture of Damascus the following year. At 132m, this is one of the tallest freestanding flagpoles in the world. It flies not the Jordanian flag, but the flag of the Great Arab Revolt, also adopted for a time by the short-lived Kingdom of the Hejaz (which fell to Saudi forces in 1925). It can be seen from all four countries around the gulf: Egypt, Israel, Jordan and Saudi Arabia.

Aqaba fort and museum

At the base of the flagpole stands Aqaba's atmospheric Mamluke **fort** (daily 8am–7pm, winter closes 4pm; JD1). The impressive entrance is flanked by semicircular **towers**, each bearing a calligraphic invocation to Allah; the arch that currently spans the gap between them is much narrower than the original, the line of which can still be traced. Overhead is a panel bearing the Hashemite coat of arms, installed following the victory in 1917. The fort was built in 1320; inside the gloomy cross-vaulted entranceway, a long **inscription** runs around the walls, celebrating renovations by the penultimate Mamluke sultan Qansawh al-Ghawni ("slayer of the unbelievers and the polytheists, reviver of justice in the universe") in either 1504–05 or 1514–15. A roundel commemorates further rebuilding work in 996 AH (1587 AD), by which time the Ottomans were in power.

Through a dark passageway lies a domed area, beyond which opens the large **courtyard**, dominated by a huge eucalyptus. This fort was the main focus of Aqaba's caravan trade for centuries, and rooms all around the walls – some of which have been restored – testify to its more hospitable function as caravan-serai for much of its later life. The ruined section to the right as you enter the courtyard was destroyed mostly by shells fired from British gunboats during the Arab Revolt. Opposite the entrance is a concrete-and-plaster mosque; steps to the left of it can bring you up onto the highest point of the walls for a dreamy view through the palm trees and over the blue gulf waters.

Beside the fort is Aqaba's little **museum** (same hours and ticket). The collection includes coins and pottery from Egypt (including a fine lustre-ware bowl from tenth-century Fatimid Cairo), Iraq, Ethiopia and some exquisite tenth- and eleventh-century Chinese ceramics. Among Islamic-era frescoes and three exquisite Nabatean bronze figurines, found at Wadi Rum, you'll spot the first milestone of the Roman Via Nova Traiana, inscribed "from the borders of Syria to the Red Sea" and discovered on the beach. The museum occupies part of the **House of Sheikh Hussein bin Ali**. Hussein – the current king's great-great-grandfather – spent six months here during 1924, in an attempt to overturn the 1923 Anglo-Jordanian Treaty, which had separated Transjordan from the Hejaz and Palestine (and had excluded him from power). A room contains mementoes of the visit: huge *mansaf* platters, coffee grinders, camel saddles and copperware.

Across from the fort is Souk Ayyadi, a small shop run by the non-profit Jordan Micro Credit Company (Ⓦwww.tamweelcom.org), selling an excellent range of crafts, textiles, ceramics and jewellery from charitable projects all over Jordan.

Aila

The ruins of the Islamic-period town of **Aila** (daily 8am–sunset; free) lie in an unromantic location, alongside the Corniche road sandwiched between the Royal Yacht Club and the *Mövenpick* hotel. It's nonetheless an interesting site, well described on good information boards.

You enter through a gateway which is also more or less where the original **Syrian Gate** would have met the road from the northeast. To the right, the foundations of towers projecting out of the city wall can be followed down to the **Egyptian Gate**, the history of which reflects the history of the whole city. In the early Islamic period, the gate was about 3m wide, flanked by the two semicircular towers still apparent and featuring a round arch overhead. A stump in front is the remnant of a central column, built some time in the eighth century to narrow the arch. A century or two followed during which Aila was at its zenith; however, debris dumped outside the walls caused the ground level to rise, at which point the towers were used as storerooms. Rebuilding work resulted in the current smaller, pointed arch over the gate, but Aila's days were numbered, and eventually the gate was sealed, serving only as a drain.

From the Egyptian Gate you can walk along a street – well below current beach level – past simple shops and houses. Some 50m along, at the centre of the city, is the **Pavilion Building**, converted in the ninth or tenth century into a two-storey residence, with rooms set around a courtyard. The road from the Egyptian Gate would have continued straight across to the **Hejaz Gate**, now in the grounds of the yacht club opposite. Another road led from the Pavilion Building right to the **Sea Gate** and left to the Syrian Gate. Towards the Corniche lies what was a relatively large **mosque**, with a *mihrab* and double row of columns.

Some 200m northwest, in an open area behind the JETT bus station, excavations have uncovered the earlier **Roman** and **Byzantine** city, including rooms, a city wall and remains of a **church**, dated to 290 or 300 AD. Though older buildings, in Syria and elsewhere, are known to have been converted into churches in the 260s, this is the oldest-known structure in the world to have been designed and built as a church. It was abandoned after an earthquake in 363 and sand has preserved the mud-brick walls to a height of almost 5m.

Diving and snorkelling at Aqaba

Some of the world's best **diving and snorkelling** is packed along the 27km of coastline between Aqaba and the Saudi border, and the town has several dive centres. If you've never been snorkelling before, Aqaba is an easier, and more instantly attractive, place to start than nearby Eilat (Israel) or Sharm el-Sheikh

Coral conservation

Coral reefs are formed of millions of individual creatures called **polyps**, which come together to create a single, compound organism. The various species of polyp produce hard external skeletons, which remain intact after the polyp dies; sand and other detritus fills up holes and cracks, and the reef is built up little by little, with new corals growing on the surface of the stony mass. Some coral colonies are several centuries old. To avoid damaging the reefs:

- **never stand on the coral** – any kind of pressure can damage or kill the outermost polyps. If you opt for a boat dive, make certain that the captain ties up to one of the mooring buoys already in place all round Aqaba, and doesn't just drop anchor onto the reef. If he claims that his selected site has no buoy, then insist that you be taken instead to a site that does have one.

- **don't enter the sea from the beach** – the reef begins directly from the shallows. Instead, use jetties or boat entries.

- **never break the coral** – snapping off a particularly colourful bit of coral not only kills that section of the reef, it's also pointless: after a few days out of water, all coral turns grey.

- **avoid kicking up sand** – clouds of grit settling on the reef can smother the outermost polyps.

- **don't litter, feed the fish** or **buy marine souvenirs**, such as corals, shells or starfish.

(Egypt), with the reef shelving gently directly from the beach, cutting out the need for boat entries. Diving beginners can go down accompanied by an instructor in complete safety; there are more than a dozen dive sites along the coast to choose from.

The major advantage of diving in Jordan rather than Egypt's Sinai coast or the handful of sites off Eilat is the almost untouched condition of the **coral**. Fish abound in greater densities elsewhere in the Red Sea (although you're still likely to come face-to-face with more marine life than you could shake a stick at), but Aqaba was a relatively slow and careful starter in dive tourism, and so has managed to avoid severe deterioration of the reefs. Compared to the Sinai's two million annual dives, and Eilat's three-quarters of a million, Aqaba sees only about twenty thousand dives a year. Work by local environmental NGOs – principally the **Royal Marine Conservation Society** (Ⓦ www.jreds.org) – is raising awareness of conservation issues. Almost 9km of Aqaba's south coast is protected as the **Aqaba Marine Park** (Ⓦ www.aqabamarinepark.jo), which extends 350m offshore and 50m inland.

Wherever you choose to dive or snorkel, wide fields of near-perfect soft corals stretch off into the startlingly clear blue water, huge heads of stony corals growing literally as big as a house. Fish life is also thrillingly diverse, with endless species of small and large multicoloured swimmers goggling back at you from all sides. Butterflyfish, angelfish, parrotfish and groupers are all common, as are shoals of damselfish, jewelfish and even moray eels. Experienced divers should not miss the chance to go down at **night**. All the dive centres listed below offer one-off dives, boat dives, PADI courses and more.

Dive sites

Aqaba's South Coast hosts more than a dozen **dive sites**, although, confusingly, different dive centres use different names, and sometimes divide one site into two or more areas (Dive Aqaba, for instance, list more than thirty sites, including several technical dives in deep water). Always consult with a dive centre in advance about the latest conditions; the account below – which runs from north to south – is not meant to be exhaustive.

Just south of the Marine Science Station's fenced-off area is the **King Abdullah Reef**, which extends for several hundred metres offshore and is good for snorkelling as well as diving; close by is the steeply sloping **Black Rock**, with a wide variety of massive hard corals and the added attraction of occasional

▲ The public beach, Aqaba

turtle sightings. Some 4km north of the Royal Diving Club and barely 50m from the shore lies the **wreck of the Cedar Pride**, a Lebanese cargo ship sunk here in 1986 as an artificial reef. Lying in 30m of water, it's now covered in soft corals. Very close by is the gently undulating **Japanese Gardens**, colourful and good for snorkellers.

A little further south are the unmissable **Gorgonion I** and **II**, the reef gently inclining down to 30m or so with spectacular fish life and perfectly preserved coral growth of all kinds stretching off to all sides. The **Canyon** has a shallow slope leading off for several hundred metres to a drop-off plunging over 45m, the whole slope split from the shallows outwards by a steep-sided ravine; its neighbour, the **New Canyon**, hosts an old field tank, sunk here to create a barrier to encourage reef growth. **Blue Coral**, named for a bluish lacework coral found here, is a little south.

Just north of a fenced-off nature reserve, **Moon Valley** offers an undulating reef framed by sandy beds, and is also the entry point for the **Long Swim**, taking divers or experienced snorkellers 700m south beyond the reserve fence to the Royal Diving Club jetty, past patches of dense coral interspersed with sandy valleys. From the jetty itself, the **Aquarium** (to the north) and the **Garden** (to the south) are both superb for divers and novice snorkellers alike.

Independent dive centres

Above and Below town centre, Al-Saada St opposite *Captain*'s restaurant ☎03 201 3735 or 078 807 4828, ⊛www.aboveandbelow.info. Friendly, long-established Jordanian–British dive centre (formerly Seastar) and accredited tour company, which uses the *Alcazar* hotel's private beach complex Club Murjan on the South Coast reefs.

Aqaba Adventure Divers 12km south of town, at the beach ☎079 584 3724, ⊛www.aqaba-divers .com. Small, flexible team offering a range of dives, often with one-on-one personal service.

Barracuda Diving Club 15km south of town, by Tala Bay ☎03 206 0501, ⊛www.goaqabadive .com. A professional approach and long-standing local experience.

Dive Aqaba town centre, Al-Saada Street opposite *Captain*'s restaurant ☎079 660 0701, ⊛www.diveaqaba.com. Outstanding service and expertise from a knowledgeable Jordanian– British team.

Jordan Frogman town centre, Gold Street ☎079 569 4980, ⊛www.jordanfrogman.com. Easy-going, family-run operation attached to a marine services company.

Royal Diving Club 17km south of town ☎03 201 7035, ⊛www.rdc.jo. Located on the reefs, offering beach access (JD15) for snorkelling directly from their jetty, as well as free transport.

Eating and drinking

Aqaba shakes a leg when the sun goes down, and many **restaurants and cafés** have terrace tables (or balconies) for alfresco dining. The obvious thing to plump for when you're by the sea is **fish** – but note that only a few bottom-end restaurants serve the local catch: the big hotel restaurants import all their fish and seafood frozen from Yemen and the Gulf. Most Arabic restaurants around town serve the signature Lebanese dish *sayyadieh* – fish (most often spiced red mullet) on buttery rice with pine nuts. You'll also spot lots of familiar Western-style fast-food outlets around town, from burgers to pizza to fried chicken.

If you're heading to Rum or Petra for a few days, stock up on picnic supplies beforehand, since even basic food in both places is priced at a premium. Check out Aqaba's early-morning fruit and veg **market**, the good Humam **super-market** on Al-Batra Street or the big Safeway north of the centre.

There's not much local demand for **bars**: independent places tend to come and go, while those that survive, such as the *Rover's Return* in the Aqaba Gateway mall, can be rather bereft of atmosphere. A better bet is to aim for one of the big hotels, all of which have decent pubs – *Abu Nawwas* in the *Mövenpick* is one of the best.

Cafés and juice bars

The compact area around An-Nahda and As-Saada streets, extending onto the main Hammamet al-Tunisieh Street (with illuminated fountains along its central strip), is a great place to stroll after dark – here you'll find lots of **cafés**, families and friends walking together, people hanging out. Near the *Crystal Hotel* are **juice bars** offering anything from plain orange juice to sensational mango-guava-strawberry-banana concoctions. Dozens of tea- and **coffee houses** all over town come into their own in the evening, laying out chairs and setting up a TV for locals to while away the twilight hours with coffee and a hubbly-bubbly. Cafés down on the public beaches give much the same service, with added sea views. After dark, parlours on the strip in front of the *Jordan Flower Hotel* do a roaring trade in cups of super-sweet, strangely elastic local **ice cream**.

Restaurants

All these **restaurants** are marked on the map on p.340.

Ali Baba town centre. Landmark restaurant on the central roundabout, with a full complement of *mezze* and Arabic main courses, as well as a good fish selection. It's OK, but you rarely see any locals eating here. As this book went to press new owners were reportedly taking over, so things may be different when you visit.

Bourj al-Hamam At *InterContinental* hotel, Corniche ☎ 03 209 2222. Aqaba's best upmarket Lebanese restaurant by miles, serving exquisite speciality dishes on the open sea-view terrace. Everything, from the fresh-baked flat bread to the salads, grills and hot and cold *mezze*, is top quality, service is warm and the setting lovely. An expensive treat.

Captain's Restaurant town centre, An-Nahda St ☎ 03 206 0710. Large, bustling restaurant on the main drag with a good reputation – and so often full. The fish is good, and you can also get dishes like pasta and all the normal Arabic staples at moderate prices.

China town centre, Al-Batra St. Climb to the top of the stairs for a surprisingly good Chinese, with a range of excellent soups and all the usual meat, chicken and veg dishes, plus sweet-and-sour fish. Good value.

Floka town centre, An-Nahda St ☎ 03 203 0860. A rather good fish restaurant in the heart of the hotel district. Their *sayyadieh* is excellent, and a range of other, more familiar European dishes are well prepared and courteously served. Expect a bill in the order of JD10–15.

Mohandes town centre, Hammamet al-Tunisieh St. A locals' restaurant serving some of the best Arabic fast food in town – crispy falafel, tasty hummus and *fuul*, eggs, salads, *shawerma* and so on. JD5 will fill you up.

Red Sea Grill At *Mövenpick* hotel, Corniche ☎ 03 203 4020. Of the hotel's range of fine-dining restaurants, this is the stand-out choice – a romantic, open-air spot down on the beach, serving up excellent fish and seafood in a pleasant, candle-lit ambience. Evenings only.

Royal Yacht Club town centre, off the main Corniche roundabout ☎ 03 202 2404, ⓦ www.romero-jordan.com. Calm, classy restaurant, run by *Romero* of Amman (a high recommendation) and with efficient, friendly service. A top-quality Italian menu is padded out – a little incongruously – with Lebanese *mezze* and Japanese sushi, but ignore all that and concentrate on the main attractions: pasta, authentic pizza and fish mains, with an excellent wine list to accompany. Also has a terrace overlooking the marina. Expect a bill above JD20 a head.

al-Shami town centre, Raghadan St. This narrow street behind the main market area is shoulder-to-shoulder Arabic restaurants, serving simple fare at inexpensive prices. Despite its touristy appearance, this is one of the best, with good food and an upstairs terrace (with a/c).

Syrian Palace town centre, Raghadan St. Beside the *Al-Shami*, another great choice for low-budget local dishes.

Syrian Restaurant town centre, Al-Batra St. Ordinary locals' cafeteria serving plain but excellent food.

Wesalak town centre, As-Saada St. You're spoiled for choice for terrace cafés in Aqaba, but this is one of the nicest – a funky, modern, outgoing espresso bar-cum-meeting place with the most comfortable armchairs in town: install yourself on the pavement terrace, and let the evening drift by. As well as a full range of coffees and soft drinks, they do excellent ice cream and smoothies, hubbly-bubbly water-pipes and a range of low-priced sandwiches, light bites and simple grills and kebabs.

Moving on from Aqaba

Transport connections out of Aqaba include a selection of buses around southern Jordan and to **Amman**, ferry services to nearby **Egypt** and an easily accessible overland crossing point into **Israel**.

Domestic destinations

From the bus station in the middle of town minibuses head to **Amman**'s Wihdat station via the Desert Highway (5hr; about JD6). Quicker serveeces follow the same route (4hr; about JD7.50). JETT (☎03 201 5222, ⬤www.jett.com.jo) runs large air-conditioned coaches (first 7am; last 7.30pm) from their office beside the *Mövenpick* hotel to three points in Amman: Wihdat station (3 daily; JD6.50), Tabarbour station (3 daily; JD7) or their office in the Abdali district (6–8 daily; JD7). Trust International Transport (☎03 203 2200) runs air-conditioned coaches from their Aqaba office on An-Nahda Street to their Amman office near the Safeway supermarket by 7th Circle (4–6 daily: first 7.30am, last 7pm; JD7.50). It's worth calling ahead to confirm schedules and book a seat.

There are three or four buses a day to **Petra/Wadi Musa** (around 8–9.30am and 1–3pm, although timings depend on demand). Others run via Rajif to **Taybeh** village, a short bus ride from Wadi Musa. More regular buses serve **Ma'an**, from where you can catch another bus (or taxi) to Wadi Musa. Buses depart Aqaba for **Wadi Rum** at around 1 and 3pm, with an additional bus

---

Tours to Wadi Rum

Tours to **Wadi Rum** are advertised at one-man-band tour companies and budget hotels all over Aqaba – if you express interest, they'll dig out a photo album of their adventures, plus glowing testimonials from happy customers. If all you want is to be driven out to a campsite somewhere in the desert near Wadi Rum (see p.326 for more on this), have dinner and be brought back to Aqaba in the morning – often, it seems, in the company of "guides" who may not be Jordanian and/or speak little or no English – then these jaunts (at JD20–25pp) are great value. But for more serious trips, cheap excursions won't do. Talk instead to experts such as **Above and Below** (☎03 201 3735, ⬤www.aboveandbelow.info). Try also Peace Way (☎03 202 2665, ⬤www .jordantrips.com) and Captains (☎03 206 0710, ⬤www.captains-jo.com), though be aware that you might get fobbed off with a trip around Disi, rather than Wadi Rum. Another possibility – with both good and bad feedback – is Quteish & Sons, trading as Wadi Rum Desert Service (☎03 201 3882, ⬤wadirumdesertservice.tripod.com). All the adventure operators listed on p.50 can set up a trip from Aqaba to Wadi Rum on request.

sometimes departing around 11am; see p.324 for other options. Buses to **Karak** depart from a street 100m south of the bus station. All these routes are restricted – or non-existent – on Fridays. Trust International Transport (see above) runs two coaches daily direct to **Irbid** (6hr; JD11.50); book the day before.

A **taxi** from Aqaba to Wadi Rum costs about JD20, to Petra about JD40, to the Dead Sea upwards of JD70.

Royal Jordanian (☎06 510 0000, ⓦwww.rj.com) has two **flights** a day from Aqaba to Amman's Queen Alia airport (JD48). Buy tickets online, at the airport or at RJ's city office near Dream Mall. By the time you read this, Royal Falcon (☎06 556 1652, ⓦwww.royalfalcon.com.jo) may also be flying to Amman.

To Israel

The **Wadi Araba** border crossing into Israel (Sun–Thurs 6.30am–8pm, Fri & Sat 8am–8pm) – also known as the "Southern Crossing" – is signposted off the Wadi Araba highway about 5km north of Aqaba. Taxis (marked "Southern Pass Service") run from Aqaba bus station to the border for JD3 per person, or JD12 for the whole car. There's a JD5 **departure tax** and most nationalities are issued with free Israeli visas on arrival. A taxi into Eilat is about NIS40 – or walk from the border about 500m to the Kibbutz Elot bus stop on the main road, from where you can flag down a bus for the last couple of kilometres into town. Note that during the Jewish *shabbat* – effectively from Friday 2pm until Saturday dusk – all Israeli public transport and many services shut down. Egged buses (ⓦwww.egged.com) depart Eilat frequently for Tel Aviv and Jerusalem (both 5hr; NIS70).

To Egypt

There are two **ferry** services from Aqaba to Egypt. Arab Bridge Maritime (☎03 209 2000, ⓦwww.abmaritime.com.jo) runs boats to **Nuweiba**, 70km southwest of Aqaba – though their timetable is notoriously unreliable (it can change from month to month) and you should expect lengthy delays: six hours or more is not uncommon. Check details in person at their city-centre office (see map p.340). At the time of writing a **catamaran** departs daily at 1pm (1hr; economy JD50; first class JD64) and a slow **ferry** departs daily at midnight (JD46; 3hr). Aqaba's passenger terminal lies 9km south of town, reached by serveece (JD1.50pp) or taxi (JD6). There's a departure tax of JD5. Although it's possible to get an **Egyptian visa** on the boat, getting one ahead of time will save endless bureaucratic chaos; the consulate in Aqaba (see opposite) offers straightforward on-the-spot service. At **Nuweiba port**, taxi-drivers do the run into town (8km) for about LE20. Alternatively beside the port is Nuweiba's main bus station, with buses five times a day to Cairo (via Taba; 8hr; LE55) and three times a day south to Dahab (1hr; LE11) and Sharm (3hr; LE20), interspersed with very negotiable serveeces. Check with Arab Bridge for details of extra boats in peak season (during summer, at the end of Ramadan, and around the hajj and Eid al-Adha).

Sindbad (☎03 205 0077 or 079 555 6076, ⓦwww.sindbadjo.com) runs a ferry to the marina at **Taba Heights**, 70km north of Nuweiba. It's designed as the return leg of a cruise for people staying in Taba's luxury hotels, but qualifies as hassle-free passenger transport. Boats depart from the marina at Tala Bay, 15km south of Aqaba (taxi about JD10), daily at around 6.30 and 7.30pm – plus there's a boat most days at about 1–2pm from a jetty at the giant flagpole in central Aqaba. The one-way fare is about JD50, which includes taxes and marina fees; journey time is half an hour. It is essential to book at least one day in advance, and advisable to also hold an Egyptian visa before you travel. Taba

Heights has several luxury hotels (cheapest is *El Wekala;* Ⓦwww.threecorners .com; ➏), or you could flag down transport heading north into Taba or south to Nuweiba.

It's cheaper and often easier to go **overland** through the Israeli resort of Eilat (total journey time about 2–3hr), but avoid crossing during the Jewish *shabbat* (between about 2pm Friday and 8pm Saturday), when it's difficult to find transport in Israel. Once you're inside Israel (see above for details), a combination of walking and city buses will get you to the Egyptian border (*hagvul hamitzri* in Hebrew), 6km south of Eilat, but it's easier to take a taxi (around NIS80–100). The Eilat–Taba border is open 24 hours a day – there's an Israeli departure tax of NIS90 and an Egyptian entry tax of US$8 – but you can only get a Sinai visa here (free), valid solely for the coast between Taba and Sharm el-Sheikh: if you want to travel on to Cairo, you must hold a full Egyptian visa in advance. From Taba's bus station, buses run to destinations including Sharm (2 daily; 4hr; LE27) and Cairo (4 daily; 7hr; LE55). Serveeces charge much more. Note that the passport stamps you pick up overlanding through Israel will disqualify you from subsequently entering Syria and many other Middle Eastern countries.

Listings

Airport information ☎03 201 4474.
Books the Yamani and Redwan bookshops opposite the post office have excellent ranges of English-language books and international newspapers.
Car rental all the big global firms are repre-sented in Aqaba – walk from one to the other on and around An-Nahda St to compare prices, or opt for local agencies: the Above and Below tour company (☎03 201 3735, Ⓦwww .aboveandbelow.info) can offer competitive rates with Save Rent-a-Car.
Consulate Egyptian Consulate, Istiqlal St ☎03 201 6171 – 15min walk north of Corniche. Visa applica-tions Sun–Thurs 9am–3pm; collection is on-the-spot or after a short wait; one photo is needed (or they'll

photocopy your passport photo instead). Three-month tourist visas cost JD12 (single entry) or JD15 (multiple entry). "Sinai-only" visas, valid only for travel along the east Sinai coast as far as Sharm el-Sheikh (including St Catherine's), are issued free.
Hospital Princess Haya hospital (☎03 201 4111) has a 24hr emergency room and recompression chamber, as well as staff trained to deal with diving accidents.
Police in emergency, dial ☎191. Headquarters of the tourist police are at the Wadi Araba border (☎03 201 9717). The main police directorate (☎03 201 2411) is in the outskirts, with a town-centre office opposite the bus station.
Post office town centre (daily 7.30am–7pm, Fri closes 1pm).

The Wadi Araba road: Aqaba–Dead Sea

The road running due **north from Aqaba** along the floor of the vast **Wadi Araba** is much overlooked as a fast route back to the Dead Sea and Amman, but if you have your own transport this is much preferable to the tedious Desert Highway via Ma'an. However, it's a long drive: 280km from Aqaba to the Dead Sea hotels, passing through only a few villages on the way. The only public transport that lets you hop on or off are minibuses between Aqaba and Tafileh or Karak.

There are few sights other than the scenery. In the southern parts, expect sandy desert, isolated acacia trees and rolling dunes, backed by giant mountains. Local bedouin tend to allow their camels to graze freely beside the road. At some points, the border fence with Israel is beside the road: traffic on the mirror-image Israeli highway on the other side is clearly visible, as are the irrigated fields cultivated by a string of desert kibbutzes.

At **GHARANDAL**, 70km north of Aqaba, the Chinese company who built this road left behind a pagoda as a memento. Some 40km further, there's the welcome sight of the *Beir Mathkoor Café* (☏03 206 3650), a **refreshment stop** and petrol station open all hours. Shortly after, a sign points off the road to **BIR MATHKOOR**, which was the westernmost caravan suburb of Petra, tucked away in the mountains to the east of the road (you can spot the white shrine atop Jebel Haroun from here). The Nabatean ruins, however, are likely to inspire only the most enthusiastic of archeologists.

About 130km north of Aqaba, a turn to Fidan and **QURAYQIRA** is also signposted for the RSCN's *Wilderness Lodge* at **FEYNAN**, located at the western end of the **Dana Nature Reserve**. See p.255 for details of spending a night here. The turn-off is passable in an ordinary car for 17km to Qurayqira village itself (pronounced "graygra") and for another 5km to Rashaydeh village – but there the road runs out. You'll need a 4x4 – or a lift from a local – for the extra 10km across the desert to the lodge.

Beyond the Qurayqira turning, another gently rising 35km of highway brings you to the edge of a scarp with the whole of the Dead Sea plain stretching in front. The small agricultural settlement of **FIFA** is at the bottom of the slope, with a signed turn-off climbing east into the mountains to Tafileh (see p.249).

The stretch from Fifa northwards past **SAFI** is covered on p.137 as the **Dead Sea road**, which leads eventually to Amman.

Travel details

Buses and serveeces

Aqaba to: Amman (JETT office, Abdali; 6–8 daily; 4hr); Amman (Tabarbour station; 4hr); Amman (Trust office, 7th Circle; 4–6 daily; 4hr); Amman (Wihdat station; 4hr); Irbid (6hr); Karak (3hr); Ma'an (1hr 30min); Quweira (45min); Wadi Musa (1hr 45min); Wadi Rum (1hr).

Ma'an to: Amman (Wihdat station; 2hr 30min); Aqaba (1hr 30min); Disi (1hr 20min); Karak (2hr); Wadi Musa (40min).

Wadi Rum to: Aqaba (1hr); Wadi Musa (1hr 40min).

Domestic flights

Aqaba to: Amman (1–2 daily; 45min).

Useful Arabic place names

Disi	الديسة	Ras an-Naqab	راس النقب
Durra	الدرة	Rashdiyyeh	الراشدية
Jafr	الجفر	Rum	رم
Mudawwara	المدوّرة	Wadi Araba	وادي عربة
Quweira	القويرة		

Contexts

Contexts

History

The **history of Jordan** is a history of occupation. Never the seat of an empire, the country – known in the past as "Transjordan" (ie the land across the Jordan river) – has been tramped by foreign armies and merchants since the pharaohs. Until independence in the mid-twentieth century, the indigenous people, chiefly bedouin tribes, tended to live under the nominal – and often ineffectual – rule of governors sent from Transjordan's more powerful neighbours.

Only relatively small parts of the country – the well-watered northern highlands and Jordan Valley – have ever been able to support large populations. Since prehistoric times, huge tracts of land to the south and east have received very little rainfall and have no rivers; only tiny populations of nomadic or semi-nomadic bedouin have been able to live there. Thus the history of Jordan revolves largely around events in the fertile north and west. The history of the desert survives only in the culture and oral traditions of the bedouin themselves.

The Stone Age: up to 3200 BC

During the **Paleolithic** period (c.500,000–17,000 BC), Jordan's climate was a good deal wetter than it is today, and what is now desert was then semi-fertile savannah. The local population of hunter-gatherer hominids, as well as foraging for wild plants, preyed upon the area's native big game, which included lions, elephants, bears and gazelle. Flint and stone handaxes from this time have been found all over the country, most significantly in enormous quantities at the **Azraq oasis** in the eastern desert.

Some time around 17,000 BC, at the beginning of the **Epipaleolithic** period, major changes took place in Transjordan. The previously nomadic hunter-gatherers began to make seasonal camps, broadened their diet to include small mammals and – most importantly – learnt how to domesticate goats and cultivate some wild grains. These new proto-farmers, who used complex tools such as sickles and pestles and mortars, have left evidence of their building work all over Jordan: small, circular enclosures and huts solidly built with subterranean foundations.

From about 8500 BC onwards, during the **Neolithic** period, three profound shifts altered the pattern of life. First, responding to the introduction of new food sources from agriculture and animal husbandry, people began to opt for the certainties of community life, establishing permanent villages such as at **Baydha**, near Petra. The large Neolithic settlement at **Ain Ghazal**, northeast of Amman, was made up of many rectangular, multi-roomed houses, some with plastered floors. From the discovery here and across the region of skulls covered with plaster, their eye sockets stuffed with bitumen, it seems that one aspect of village life was veneration – or even worship – of the dead. The oldest statues in the world, dating from around 6000 BC, were uncovered at Ain Ghazal: one-metre-high androgynous figures with huge, painted eyes, now on display in Amman.

A second shift resulted from changing weather patterns: as temperatures rose, the eastern savannah dried out and became virtually uninhabitable. Desertification marked a clear distinction between Transjordan's arid east and fertile west, forcing most people to congregate in the western areas that, today, still hold the greater population.

But the most important innovation of Neolithic times was the discovery of how to make **pottery**. Around 5000 BC, potters arrived in Transjordan from the more advanced civilizations of Mesopotamia (in modern Iraq). By 4000 BC or so, during the **Chalcolithic** period, copper had been smelted for the first time for use in fashioning hooks, axes and arrowheads, and the new metal began to be used in conjunction with pottery and flint-working to considerably improve the quality of life. People slowly began to turn away from subsistence hunting towards planned cultivation: olives, lentils, dates, barley and wheat were all common, as was sheep- and goat-breeding. The area's principal copper deposits were at **Faynan** in Wadi Araba, but the largest Chalcolithic village discovered in Jordan is at **Teleilat Ghassul** in the Jordan Valley, where mud-brick houses with roofs of wood, mud and reeds were constructed around large courtyards. Here, pots were decorated and of good quality, and woven baskets were sturdy. From the evidence of the village's mysterious murals of masked figures, stars and geometric motifs, it seems that Ghassulian women decorated themselves with necklaces of shells and stones, while men took pride in tattoos.

The Bronze Age: 3200–1200 BC

Towns from the **Early Bronze Age** (c.3200–1950 BC), although still relying on copper ("Bronze Age" is a misnomer from the early days of archeology), often included strong defensive fortifications, probably to keep the marauding nomadic tribes of the open countryside away. The new technology of water management led to collection and some storage of supply against drier times. New customs of burial also developed, sometimes involving the digging of deep shaft tombs: at **Bab adh-Dhraa** on the Dead Sea, archeologists have uncovered over twenty thousand such shafts, perhaps containing up to a quarter of a million corpses in total. Other burial customs – possibly brought from Syria or Anatolia – involved the construction of **dolmens** (two or more stone slabs standing side by side, capped by another slab), which can be found throughout the Jordanian countryside.

Elsewhere in the region at this time, the extraordinary innovation of **writing** was leading to the development of highly sophisticated civilizations. To the south, Egypt was unified into one kingdom, while to the north and east, Anatolia and Mesopotamia saw the rise of equally complex urbanized cultures. Occupying the area midway between the three, the simpler people of the Levant, who wouldn't start to use writing for another millennium or so, fell into the role of merchant middlemen. The first significant commerce began to flow between the great powers.

Around 2300 BC, many of the fortified towns in Transjordan were destroyed, although there is some controversy as to whether this was due to conquest by a new people, the Amorites, or simply an earthquake. A decrease in rainfall levels coupled with a general rise in temperature almost certainly played its part, too.

The **Middle Bronze Age** (c.1950–1550 BC) saw trade between Egypt, Arabia and the city-states of Syria and Palestine continuing to flow through Transjordan, generating wealth and facilitating the spread of ideas and culture. It was during this period that artisans mixed copper with tin for the first time; the resulting metal, **bronze**, allowed much harder and more durable tools and weapons to be made than before. Transjordanian towns such as Amman, Irbid and Pella (as well as Jericho, on the western bank of the river) built massive, banked earth ramparts, implying a need for security – as borne out by the eighteenth-century BC conquests of the Hyksos who overran much of the

Levant. Probably nomadic herders from Central Asia, the Hyksos interrupted the steady indigenous cultural growth of Transjordan, replacing it with new, foreign elements. As well as importing a more graceful and technically accomplished style of pottery, they also introduced both horses and chariots to the Middle East.

Following the expulsion of the Hyksos around 1550 BC by the Egyptian Seventeenth Dynasty, Transjordan – and the rest of the Levant – saw an expansion of Egyptian influence during the **Late Bronze Age** (c.1550–1200 BC), especially under Pharaoh Tuthmosis III. Despite conflict further north, occupied Transjordan remained relatively peaceful and prosperous, and the presence of pottery from Mycenaean Greece and Cyprus indicates strong trade links.

By 1200 BC, however, the peace and prosperity of the eastern Mediterranean had been shattered, probably by the arrival of unknown invaders collectively termed **"Peoples of the Sea"**, one group of whom, the Philistines, settled around Gaza (giving rise to the name Palestine). The principal cities of Greece and Cyprus fell to these foreigners, the Hittite Empire in Anatolia collapsed, wealthy city-states in Syria were razed and the Egyptian occupiers of Transjordan retreated to face the onslaught at home. In addition, events surrounding a group of tribes known as the Israelites – about which ample, if contradictory, records survive – began to alter the power balance in Transjordan and Palestine.

Biblical accounts of the Bronze Age

Genesis records that **Abram**, a native of the city of Ur – most likely in modern Iraq – travelled at some time probably well before 2000 BC with his wife and extended family to Canaan (Palestine). After some years, the land – already home to existing tribes of Canaanites and others – was unable to support so many people, and bickering ensued between Abram's tribe and that of his nephew **Lot**. Abram offered a separation: Lot would be given the choice of taking his tribe and flocks either east or west of the River Jordan, and whichever direction he chose, Abram and his tribe would go the other way. Lot chose to go east and pitched his tents at the southeastern corner of the Dead Sea. Abram went west and eventually settled near Hebron, meanwhile having a vision of God granting him in perpetuity the land that Lot had spurned.

After the adaptation of Abram's name to **Abraham** following another vision, Lot's home city of Sodom – and others nearby – were destroyed. The only survivors were Lot and his two daughters, who lived for a time in a cave in the desert. Fearful that their tribe would die out since no man had escaped with them other than their father, the elder of Lot's two daughters hatched a plan to get their father so drunk he wouldn't be able to tell who they were, whereupon they would seduce him and thus preserve the family. Everything worked to plan and both daughters gave birth to sons; the elder named her child **Moab**, and the younger **Ben-Ammi**, or "father of Ammon".

Meanwhile Abraham had had two sons, the first – **Ishmael** – by his Egyptian mistress Hagar, and the second – **Isaac** – by his wife Sarah. On Sarah's insistence, Hagar and Ishmael were banished to the desert, and the biblical record concentrates on Isaac's two sons, Esau and Jacob. (The Quran, though, concentrates on Ishmael, who had twelve children and died at the age of 137; Muslims and especially Arabs view him as their forebear. The hajj pilgrimage centres on commemoration of Hagar and Ishmael's banishment.) Jacob persuaded Esau to sell his inheritance and, by dint of trickery, also gained the blessing of his father to rule over his brother. The two then separated, Jacob fleeing to an uncle's house and after a series of visions changing his name to **Israel** (which means "he who wrestled with God"). Esau married into Ishmael's family and settled in the southern part of Transjordan, known as **Edom**. Its southern neighbour **Midian** (modern Hejaz), and its northern neighbours **Moab** and **Ammon**, as well as Edom itself, were all established kingdoms by soon after 2000 BC.

The Bible makes no further mention of Transjordan until the **Exodus**, which occurred several centuries after Esau. The most accepted chronology places it during the reign of Pharaoh Merneptah (c.1236–1217 BC), but it may have been over two centuries earlier. The Book of Numbers records that, after expulsion from Egypt and several generations of wandering in the Sinai, the Israelites, an extended group of twelve related tribes descended from Abraham's grandson, Israel, arrived in the southern Palestinian desert near Aqaba, on a journey towards the lands west of the Jordan that had been granted by God to the tribal patriarch Abraham. The Israelite sheikh Moses and his brother Aaron had a vision from God instructing them to speak to a rock to produce water for their tribes; Moses, though, struck the rock, and for this transgression both he and his brother were denied future entry to the Promised Land.

After Aaron's death on **Mount Hor** (possibly Jebel Haroun near Petra), the Israelites apparently followed the route of the present Desert Highway northwards. A little way north of modern Qatraneh, the Israelites defeated the **Amorites** in battle and destroyed their cities, including Hesban, Dhiban and Madaba. They proceeded north to Dera'a (just over the modern Syrian border), defeated King Og and returned to make camp in "the plain of Moab" opposite Jericho, probably near modern Shuneh al-Janubiyyeh. Alarmed at the presence of such powerful newcomers on his borders, the king of Moab made a military pact with the kings of Midian, but after a seer prophesied only victory for the Israelites, the combined Moabite–Midianite forces lost heart, and were attacked and routed. Three Israelite tribes occupied Transjordan from Dhiban as far north as Gilead (the hills around modern Jerash) and the Golan Heights. Moses then had several visions and, sometime probably around 1200 BC, at the age of 120, died on **Mount Nebo** near Madaba. Soon afterwards, his successor Joshua led the Israelite tribes across the Jordan into the Promised Land.

The Iron Age: 1200–332 BC

With the bulk of the Israelite forces safely on the other side of the Jordan, the years after 1200 BC saw a consolidation and development of the Transjordanian kingdoms of Ammon, Moab and Edom, all three of which lay on the lucrative Arabian–Syrian trade route for gold, spices and other precious goods.

By about 1000 BC the Israelites were strong enough to declare a united Kingdom of Israel; under **King David**, they seized control of virtually the entire Levant and won several victories in Transjordan. Edom managed to regain some independence following David's death in 960 BC, but it wasn't until David's son **Solomon** died some thirty years later that the Israelite empire fell. The last vestiges of Israelite control in Transjordan were erased during the mid-ninth century BC, partly by the efforts of Mesha, apparently king of Moab, who recorded his victories on the "**Mesha Stele**" (see p.240), a basalt stone set up in the Moabite capital, Dhiban. To the north, Ammon, centred on modern Amman, prospered, while to the south, Edom had developed skill in mining and smelting copper and had major settlements near Busayrah, Petra and Aqaba, although much of the Edomite population may have been nomadic or semi-nomadic.

By the mid-eighth century BC **Assyrian** forces had captured Damascus and parts of Israel. It was only by paying tribute that Ammon, Moab and Edom managed to retain their independence and continue to exploit the north–south flow of trade.

Barely a century later, in 612 BC, the Assyrians were themselves defeated by an alliance of Medes (from modern Iran) and **Babylonians** (from Iraq); the latter then took control in the Levant, limiting the independence of the Transjordanian kingdoms and, in 587 BC, destroying Jerusalem and deporting thousands of Jews. Chaotic Babylonian rule was then overrun by the **Persian Empire**, the largest yet seen in the region. The Persians released the Jews from captivity in Babylon and permitted them to rebuild their temple at Jerusalem. The indignant Ammonites and Moabites took this to be a declaration of sovereignty and attacked, only to be repulsed by the direct intervention of the Persian leadership.

Two centuries of relatively stable Persian rule were brought to a swift end by the military adventures of the Greek general known as **Alexander the Great**. In 333 BC, at the age of 21, he defeated the Persian army in southeastern Turkey and proceeded to conquer the entire Levant and Egypt before heading east. At his death in Babylon in 323 BC, Alexander controlled an empire stretching from Greece to India.

The Greeks and the Nabateans: 332–64 BC

Alexander's conquest of the Persian capital Persepolis in 332 BC confirmed **Hellenistic** control over the formerly Persian lands of the Levant, and ushered in a period of dominance over Transjordan by Alexander's successors that lasted for three centuries. On Alexander's death, his generals **Seleucus** and **Ptolemy** divided the eastern part of his empire between them: Palestine, Transjordan and southern Syria went to Ptolemy, while Seleucus took northern Syria and Mesopotamia. Bitter struggles for the upper hand ensued, with much of Transjordan caught in the crossfire. After more than a century of fighting, the Seleucids finally wrested Transjordan away from the Ptolemies in 198 BC. Meanwhile, many new and rebuilt Transjordanian cities had been flourishing, including Philadelphia (Amman), Gerasa (Jerash), Pella and Gadara (Umm Qais) – though virtually the only Hellenistic monument to survive today is a lone palace in the countryside west of Amman, **Qasr al-Abd**.

Long before these events, and possibly as early as the sixth century BC, a nomadic tribe of Arabs had wandered out of the deserts to the south and taken up residence in and around Edom. Slowly these **Nabateans** had abandoned their nomadic ways and founded a number of settlements in southern Transjordan, northern Arabia and the Naqab (Negev) desert of modern Israel, probably using their position to plunder the caravans heading out of Arabia loaded with luxury goods. The Roman historian Diodorus Siculus, writing much later, describes "Arabs who are called Nabatei" occupying Petra around 312 BC (for more on Petra's history, see p.261). The Nabateans – who had switched from plundering caravans to providing them with safe passage – managed to remain largely independent throughout the Seleucid–Ptolemaic power battles.

With the Seleucid victory of 198 BC, trade again prospered in Transjordan and the Nabateans expanded their realm, absorbing many Hellenistic influences which worked their way into the art and architecture of Petra. By 150 BC – co-existing alongside Seleucid rule in western Transjordan – the independent **Kingdom of Nabatea** extended along a strip of eastern Transjordan as far north as the Hawran, and south into the Hejaz. The Nabateans were accumulating vast profits from trade across the Middle East in everything from Indian silks and spices to Dead Sea bitumen and, most importantly, a monopoly over trade in frankincense and myrrh. Both were central in religious ceremonies throughout the West and both were produced only in southern Arabia; transport overland from the Arabian coast terminated at the sole taxation and international distribution centre at Petra.

Meanwhile riots were breaking out in Judea against Hellenistic rule. In three successive years – 167 to 165 BC – Jewish rebels defeated the Greek army four times. The Jewish leader **Judas Maccabeus** then invaded northern Transjordan. Less than a century later, Judas's successor occupied the whole of Transjordan as far south as Wadi Hasa, with the Nabatean kingdom – by now extended to Damascus but still confined only to a slice of the country east of the King's Highway – remaining independent. With nothing appearing likely to put a stop to the growth of Nabatean wealth and influence, and faced by an increasingly unstable political situation, the generals of **Rome** decided that the time had come to impose some law and order.

Rome and the Nabateans: 64 BC–324 AD

In 64 BC, the Roman general **Pompey** took Damascus and ordered Nabatean forces to pull back from the city. After proceeding to annex most of the region, Pompey sent a force to Petra to subdue the Nabateans, but the Nabatean king was able easily to repulse the attack and dip into his treasury to pay the Romans off.

Pompey turned his attention elsewhere. The group of Hellenized northern Transjordanian cities that included Gerasa, Gadara, Philadelphia and Pella had been badly damaged under the Jewish occupation; Pompey restored their infrastructure and granted them some local autonomy. With shared cultural and economic ties, these cities – in a region of Transjordan known as the **Decapolis** ("Ten Cities"; see p.156) – agreed to pay taxes to the Romans and so retained independence.

In 44 BC, Julius Caesar was assassinated in Rome. The **Parthians** – based in Mesopotamia and Persia – took the chance to attack, and the Nabateans sided with them; following Rome's reassertion of its power, the Nabatean king was forced to dip into his treasury again to placate the generals. The local Roman placeman, Herod the Great, twice attacked the Nabateans to ensure consistent payments. By the time of Herod's death in 4 BC, Rome was in control of the region, with Transjordan divided into three spheres of influence: to the north, the Decapolis remained independent; Palestinian Jewish puppet-kings ruled central Transjordan (although Philadelphia remained part of the Decapolis); and the south comprised the rump Kingdom of Nabatea, still nominally independent, though coming under increasing pressure to submit to Rome.

Herod the Great's successor, Herod Antipas, married a daughter of the Nabatean king Aretas IV, but soon afterwards divorced her, and married his brother's wife instead. Unable to ignore such an insult, Aretas sent an army against Herod and won, but showed magnanimity in withdrawing peacefully. A local holy man, John the Baptist, condemned Herod's incestuous marriage, was imprisoned at the royal palace at **Machaerus** and, at the behest of Herod's stepdaughter Salome, beheaded.

Jewish uprisings in Palestine during the mid-first century AD gave a chance for the Nabateans to weigh in militarily and so restore amicable relations with Rome. The Nabatean king was personally present at the Roman capture of Jerusalem in 70 AD. Many Palestinian Jewish rebels sought refuge at Machaerus, but the Roman army razed the palace in 72 AD and slaughtered everyone inside.

By this stage it was clear to the Nabateans that their days of independence were numbered. A new trading centre far to the north, **Palmyra** – positioned on Roman-sponsored routes that were growing in popularity – was chipping away at Petra's business, and the Nabatean king Rabbel II, seeing Roman dominance all around, almost certainly made a deal permitting the Romans to annex the Nabatean lands peacefully. In 106, on Rabbel's death, the whole of Transjordan – with the exception of the Decapolis – was incorporated into the

▲ Roman chariot-racing at Jerash

new Roman **Province of Arabia**, under the Emperor **Trajan**, with a new capital at Bosra, in Syria.

From Trajan to Constantine: 106–324 AD

Roman city planners, engineers and construction workers moved into Transjordan. Large forts were built near Karak, Petra and in the north to house the massed legions; Petra itself, along with Philadelphia, Gerasa, Gadara and other cities, was renovated and Romanized; and, by 114 AD, a new fortified road – the **Via Nova Traiana** – was in place, running from Bosra right the way through Transjordan to the Red Sea at Aila (Aqaba). Trajan's successor, Hadrian, paid the province a visit in 130, staying in **Gerasa**, by this time one of the most splendid of Rome's provincial cities. During the second and third centuries, Transjordan gained new sophistication under the Romans, and prosperity rose to an unprecedented level. In 199, the Emperor Septimius Severus toured the province with his Syrian wife; although many overland trade routes from Arabia had been diverted to Palmyra and seaborne trade along the Red Sea was flourishing, Petra was still important enough to merit a visit. It was around this time that **Azraq**, at the head of a major route to and from the Arabian peninsula, was fortified for the first time.

Nonetheless, the desert fringes of the empire remained open to infiltration, and in 260, Persian **Sassanians** invaded from the north. Six years later, the Roman military commander, based in Palmyra, was murdered, precipitating a rebellion throughout Syria led by a local queen, Zenobia. The situation was perilous enough to force the Emperor **Diocletian** (284–305) to take drastic measures. Retaining overall command from his base in Turkey, Diocletian split the empire into eastern and western administrations under separate emperors, and then proceeded to strengthen the infrastructure of the eastern fringes, building forts and new roads, among them the **Strata Diocletiana** linking Azraq with Damascus. Meanwhile, with Palmyra's predominance annulled through its association with rebellion, trade through Transjordan once again began to flourish, and the Red Sea port of Aila took on a new importance.

A new force was also beginning to make itself felt. The influence of **Christianity** went much deeper than the extent of its practice (by a mere fourteen percent or so of the empire's population) might show. The Emperor **Constantine** had already converted by 324 when he made Christianity the official religion of the eastern empire. Six years later, he confirmed the eclipse of Rome by founding a new Christian imperial capital – Constantinople (modern Istanbul).

The Byzantine period: 324–636

The **Byzantine** period – so named because Constantinople had been built over the ancient Greek colony of Byzantium – saw long-lived Roman institutions coexisting with the new Christian faith, which flourished within a broadly Greek culture. Transjordan experienced a steady growth of population coupled with energetic construction projects and important artistic development.

Constantine's mother, Helena, started a trend of **pilgrimage** by journeying to Jerusalem in 326. It was around this time that the first church on Mount Nebo was built to commemorate Moses' death, and the area around Nebo and Madaba became the focus for pilgrimage in Transjordan. Following the final divorce between Rome and Constantinople in 395, many churches were built, often on the foundations of Roman temples and often decorated with ornate **mosaics**. Madaba, in particular, was a flourishing centre for mosaicists, especially during the reign of **Justinian** (527–65). Church building and mosaic art in Transjordan (see p.229) entered a golden age.

Twin disasters were to bring both artistic development and, indirectly, the empire itself to an end. The first was **plague**, which struck Transjordan during Justinian's reign and wiped out much of the population. A far more sustained threat came from the Persian **Sassanians**, who, in the sixth century, launched a series of raids against the Euphrates frontier, breaking through to sack Antioch in 540. There followed over eighty years of titanic, but inconclusive, struggle in Syria between Byzantium and Persia – Transjordan remaining quiet throughout – which was only ended by the Emperor **Heraclius'** recapture of Syria in 628.

During the struggles (and unknown to either combatant), far to the south an Arab holy man named **Muhammad** had been gathering around himself a large band of followers following a series of divine visions. Initial sorties northwards had won over a few desert tribes but the **Muslims**, as they styled themselves, lost their first battle with Byzantium, near Karak in 629. Muhammad himself died in Mecca in 632, but his armies, led by Abu Bakr, the first caliph ("successor"), and fired by the zeal of a new religion, pushed northwards again, seizing Damascus from Heraclius in 635. On the banks of the River Yarmouk the following year, they defeated a Byzantine army exhausted from decades of war.

The early caliphs of Islam: 636–1250

After the Yarmouk victory, it took the Muslim armies barely ten years to dismantle Byzantine control over the Levant, although the Byzantine Empire itself limped on for another eight hundred years. By 656, the whole of Persia and the Middle East was ruled from the Muslim capital at Medina. That year, the third caliph, Othman, was murdered. When his successor, Ali, dismissed many of Othman's appointees – including Muawiya, governor of Syria – civil war broke out among the Muslims, brought to an end only by negotiations held probably at Udhruh near Petra in 659. Ali was subsequently assassinated, and Muawiya, a member of the **Umayyad** clan, was acclaimed caliph in 661. This marked a schism in Islam, which persists today, between the **Sunnis** – the orthodox majority who accept the Umayyad succession – and the minority **Shi'ites**, who believe the succession should have passed instead to Ali, a relative of Muhammad's, and his descendants.

The Umayyads: 661–750

Muawiya's first decision was to relocate the Muslim capital away from Arabia to the vibrant metropolis of Damascus. At one stroke, Transjordan was transformed: not only was it on the direct pilgrimage route between the imperial capital and the holy sites in Mecca and Medina, but it also suddenly lay at the heart of a rapidly expanding empire, which, at its fullest extent, reached from India virtually to the Pyrenees. The Umayyad caliphs began a vigorous campaign of monument-building throughout the Levant, which included both the Dome of the Rock in Jerusalem and the Great Mosque of Damascus. At heart, however, they were desert people, and their most enduring legacy to Transjordan is a series of buildings in the eastern desert, now known as the "Desert Castles": some, such as **Qasr Harraneh**, were places where the caliphs could meet with the bedouin tribes of the area, while others – **Qusayr Amra**, **Qasr Mushatta** – were lavish country mansions or hunting lodges. Motivated less by adherence to Islamic orthodoxy than by older Arab notions of honour, loyalty and rule by negotiation, the Umayyads had a lively aesthetic sense, valuing intellectual curiosity, poetry and wine in roughly equal quantities. Christianity was widely tolerated, and churches were still being built in Transjordan up to the middle of the eighth century.

Abbasids and Fatimids: 750–1097

Followers of stricter interpretations of Islam eventually gained the upper hand, possibly aided by a devastating earthquake which struck the region in 749. A year later, Damascus fell to a new dynasty, the **Abbasids**, who shifted the Muslim capital eastwards to Baghdad, a symbolic move embodying a rejection of the liberal Umayyad spirit in preference for more strait-laced Mesopotamian methods. Transjordan – instantly reduced to a provincial backwater – fell into obscurity.

During the ninth century, internal dissent whittled away at the power of the Abbasid caliphate, and by 969 a rival, Shi'ite-derived caliphate had been proclaimed in Cairo by the Tunisian **Fatimid** dynasty, who took control of Palestine, Transjordan and southern Syria soon after, destroying many churches and harassing Christian pilgrims. In 1037, Seljuk Turks took power in Baghdad and within fifty years had defeated both the Fatimids and the Byzantines to regain Transjordan for orthodox Islam.

These tides of Muslim conquest and reconquest sweeping the Holy Land, coupled with the anti-Christian feeling aroused by the Fatimids and a Byzantine request for military aid against the Seljuks, didn't go unnoticed in the West. In 1095 Pope Urban II, speaking in France, launched an appeal for a European force to intervene in the chaos in the Middle East, to restore Christian rule in Palestine and, above all, to liberate Jerusalem. This holy war was termed a **crusade**.

Crusaders and Ayyubids: 1097–1250

In 1097, a 100,000-strong Christian army – comprising seasoned troops and peasant rabble alike – arrived at Constantinople. Two years later, they seized Jerusalem, slaughtering every man, woman and child in the city. Within forty years, there was a strip of Crusader-held territory running from southern Turkey to the Red Sea, part of it incorporating the Lordship of Oultrejourdain (Transjordan) with its two castle strongholds at **Karak** and **Shobak** (see also p.244). In 1144, local Muslim forces started to eat into Crusader realms in northern Syria, inspiring a wave of strong Muslim resistance to the invaders, led after 1176 by a Kurdish officer named **Salah ad-Din al-Ayyubi** (or Saladin). Having already disposed of the Fatimids in Cairo (and by doing so uniting the Muslim world), Salah ad-Din routed the Crusaders on the battlefield in 1187 and retook Jerusalem, coastal Palestine and Transjordan. After his death in 1193, his dynasty, the **Ayyubids**, ruled the Muslim forces from their power base in Cairo. Waves of Crusaders nonetheless continued to arrive from Europe over the next decades, and rule of Levantine coastal areas shifted to and fro.

Mamlukes and Ottomans: 1250–1915

The Ayyubids came to rely for their military strength upon a band of highly disciplined and trained slave-troops, known as "the owned ones". Most of these **Mamlukes** were Turks or Caucasians from southern Russia who had been bought at market. Once trained, they were given property, goods and women; their lack of local tribal allegiance guaranteed loyalty to their master. In 1250, however, the worm turned: with the Ayyubid sultan on his deathbed, the Mamlukes seized power for themselves.

They soon faced a challenge. In 1258, a **Mongol** army under Genghis Khan's grandson Hulagu destroyed Baghdad and swept westward through Transjordan to Galilee, where they were halted by a Mamluke army. The victorious general, **Baybars**, claimed the title of sultan and proceeded to eject the last remaining Crusaders from the Levant.

During the fourteenth century, the Mamluke unification of Syria and Egypt provided some peace for the embattled Transjordanian population, who continued to facilitate north–south commerce and provide shelter to Muslim pilgrims. Another Mongol invasion in 1400 under Tamerlane overran much of Syria; Mamluke finances – which relied on the Red Sea shipping trade – were further undermined by the Portuguese discovery of a new sea route around Africa to India.

Meanwhile, in northwestern Turkey a new dynasty had been gathering power, and, in 1453, these **Ottomans** seized Constantinople, erasing what was left of the Byzantine Empire. The Ottoman leader **Selim the Grim** occupied Damascus, Transjordan and Jerusalem in quick succession, eventually suspending the last Mamluke sultan from the gallows in Cairo.

Ottoman expansion continued apace (halted only at the gates of Vienna in 1683) but although imperial architects lavished care and attention on Damascus and Jerusalem, Transjordan apart from inns built along the pilgrimage route between Damascus and Mecca, was allowed to fall into decline, its people left largely to themselves. European merchants based in ports and cities all around the region quietly siphoned wealth away from the imperial coffers, and the Ottoman Empire crumbled.

In 1798, **Napoleon Bonaparte** invaded Egypt, but lost power less than a decade later. In the 1830s, the new Egyptian ruler Ibrahim Pasha embarked on a military adventure through Transjordan and the Levant which looked poised to overthrow Ottoman rule altogether but for the intervention of the British, who preferred the presence of a feeble and ineffective sultan to that of an enthusiastic and powerful young general. Trade on the Red Sea was revivified by the opening of the Suez Canal in 1869, but the canal itself, which represented the fastest sea route from Europe to India, remained under sole control of the British, who were by now firmly installed in Egypt and nurturing imperialist designs on Palestine.

In the 1870s, Russian persecution of Muslims in the Caucasus region east of the Black Sea led to waves of refugees arriving in Turkey. The Ottoman authorities dumped them onto ships bound for Levantine ports. These **Circassian** and **Chechen** farmers settled throughout the region, working their way inland to Transjordan and colonizing the long-abandoned ruins at Amman, Jerash and elsewhere. In a separate but contemporary development, Russian persecution of **Jews** in modern Poland and Lithuania also created refugees who settled in the Levant, this time in Palestine. Jewish activists soon codified a philosophy of organized Jewish settlement of Palestine – **Zionism**.

The decline of the Ottoman Empire: 1900–15

By the turn of the century, there was a spate of railway building around the Levant. The French were establishing a network in Syria; the German Berlin–Baghdad railway had reached Aleppo; and in Palestine, the British had long been operating a line from Jaffa to Jerusalem. To counter this European influence, and in a bid to bolster his religious authority, the sultan announced the construction of an Ottoman-sponsored **Hejaz Railway** (see p.110), to run from Damascus south through Transjordan, terminating at the holy city of Mecca. As well as transporting Muslim pilgrims, the sultan also had an eye on facilitating the rapid mobilization of Ottoman troops should the Arab nationalism that was beginning to stir in the Hejaz come to a head. Transjordanian labour was vital in the construction of the line – as were the thick forests around Ajloun and Shobak, felled indiscriminately for fuel. By 1908, the track had reached Medina, 400km short of Mecca. A coup in Constantinople the following year led to seizure of power by secular Turkish nationalists, and the railway got no further.

On the outbreak of **World War I**, the puppet sultan sided with the Germans, bringing the Ottoman Empire into conflict with both Britain – eagerly eyeing the newly discovered oilfields in Iraq and Persia – and France. Turkification was proceeding apace, with a ban on the use of Arabic in schools and offices, arrests of Arab nationalist leaders in Damascus and Beirut, and, in 1915, the first of the twentieth century's genocides, when over a million Armenians were killed. Observing from Cairo, the British conspired on the best way to foment ill-will towards Turkish authority into full-scale rebellion. Negotiations with opposition leaders in Cairo and Damascus to involve Arab forces in a revolt against the Turks broke down, but contact with **Sharif Hussein**, the ruler of Mecca and self-styled "King of the Arabs", was more fruitful. Its consequences, and the events surrounding the end of World War I, have directly caused almost a century of war in the Middle East.

British promises and the Arab Revolt: 1915–18

When the Ottoman Empire entered World War I, the sultan had declared a *jihad* (an Islamically sanctioned struggle) against the Western powers. Alarmed at the possible repercussions of this in Muslim areas under their control, the British were keen to enlist for their side the support of Sharif Hussein, an authoritative religious dignitary and direct descendant of the Prophet Muhammad. In 1915, ten letters, known as the **McMahon Correspondence**, passed between Sir Henry McMahon, British High Commissioner in Egypt, and Hussein, in which Britain pledged to support Arab claims for independence if Hussein sparked a revolt against Turkish authority. Hussein's initial claims were for an independent Arab state stretching from Aleppo to the Yemeni coast, but McMahon countered this by stating that Arab claims were excluded from three areas: the districts of Basra and Baghdad in Iraq (which the British wanted for themselves), the Turkish Hatay region around modern Antakya, and – most significantly – "portions of Syria lying to the west of the districts of Damascus, Homs, Hama and Aleppo". Sharif Hussein took this clause to refer to Lebanon, and accepted the terms. Confident of British backing, he proclaimed Arab independence on June 16, 1916, and declared war on the Turks.

Meanwhile, the British had other ideas. Following negotiation with France and Russia, the secret **Sykes–Picot Agreement** of May 1916 carved up the Middle East into areas of colonial dominance, riding roughshod over the promises made to Sharif Hussein about Arab independence. Under the agreement, France was handed power in southeastern Turkey, Lebanon, Syria and northern Iraq, Britain in a belt of land stretching from Haifa to Baghdad and the Gulf, with most of Palestine to be administered by an international body. The colonial powers told nobody of their plans (Sharif Hussein only learnt of them more than a year later).

Also in 1917, in a letter addressed to a leader of Britain's Jewish community, which came to be known as the **Balfour Declaration**, the British Foreign

Secretary Arthur Balfour wrote that "His Majesty's Government view with favour the establishment in Palestine of a national home for the Jewish people." Hussein had agreed to Arab claims being excluded from the "portion of Syria lying to the west of Damascus", and, in an attempt to cover their backs, British ministers later claimed – extraordinarily – that this clause referred to Palestine. The Balfour Declaration thus completed an astonishing triangle of mutually incompatible promises and agreements made by the British government between 1915 and 1917. Their consequences are still being suffered today.

The Arab Revolt: 1917–18

Meanwhile, still assuming wholehearted British support, Sharif Hussein – aided by two of his sons, **Abdullah** and **Faysal** – had launched the **Great Arab Revolt**. A ragtag army of thirty thousand tribesmen quickly seized Mecca and Jeddah from Ottoman forces, and, in January 1917, local notables, as well as Britain, France and Italy, recognized Sharif Hussein as "King of the Hejaz", leader of the first independent Arab state. In its initial stages, the British lent their support to the Arab Revolt principally in the form of Second Lieutenant **T.E. Lawrence**, later mythologized as "Lawrence of Arabia" (see p.335). Leaving Abdullah to pin down a forlorn Turkish garrison in Medina, Faysal – with Lawrence – led an army northwards to the port of Aqaba, a strategic prize through which the Arabs would be able to receive weaponry and material support from the British Army in Egypt. Ottoman defences in the town, protected on two sides by arid mountains, focused all their attention on attack from the sea. Holed up to the south, Lawrence instead planned a looping overland route through the desert, and with a small force emerged from the mountains to launch a surprise attack on the town from the north. The plan worked, and Aqaba fell on July 6, 1917.

Faysal's Arab forces then came under the command of the British general **Allenby**, who was leading several divisions from Egypt towards Jerusalem. The Arabs and the British worked their way northwards, the Arabs using the old castle at Azraq as a base during the winter of 1917–18. After Jerusalem fell to the British, the Arab armies skirmished up the Hejaz Railway line, taking Ma'an, Karak and Amman. The final assault was launched from Azraq, and on October 1, 1918, Faysal and Lawrence entered Damascus, ending Ottoman rule in the Levant.

The establishment of the emirate: 1918–23

By now, the French (working to the Sykes–Picot Agreement) had designs on Syria and Lebanon, while the British and the Zionist Jews (working to the Balfour Declaration) had designs on Palestine. When, in 1920, elected Arab delegates to the government in Damascus declared the Levant independent under King Faysal, and Iraq independent under King Abdullah (who was still in the Hejaz), both Britain and France came out in sharp denunciation. Within six weeks, administrative control – termed a "**mandate**" – over the Middle East was awarded by an international conference to the colonial powers, forming borders within the Levant for the first time and splitting Palestine and Iraq (awarded to Britain) away from Syria and Lebanon (handed to France). The French forcibly ejected Faysal from Damascus and the British suppressed open rebellion in Iraq. In Mecca, the stunned Sharif Hussein realized the extent of the betrayal. "I listened to the faithless Englishmen," he muttered to a group of confidants. "I let myself be tempted and won over by them."

The position of Transjordan remained unclear for some time. Britain informed a meeting of sheikhs at Salt that it favoured self-government for Transjordan, but then did little to foster it. Arab discontent was growing at British and French duplicity: Abdullah raised an army in Mecca, intending to liberate Damascus from the French. He arrived in Ma'an on November 21, 1920, to a rousing reception of Transjordanian sheikhs and Arab nationalists.

From Ma'an, Abdullah's path lay through British-held Transjordan, still neither part of the Palestine Mandate nor fully autonomous. He proceeded north without hindrance, arriving in the village of Amman on March 2, 1921, to cheering crowds of mounted tribesmen. Confronted by a fait accompli, but obligated to prevent attack on the French from British territory, the new British Colonial Secretary **Winston Churchill** (accompanied by his special adviser T. E. Lawrence) proposed a separate British mandate to be established in Transjordan; in exchange for Abdullah's abdication of the throne of Iraq in favour of Faysal, Britain would offer Abdullah the temporary title of Emir (Prince) of Transjordan, until "some accommodation" could be made with the French in Damascus. With the knowledge that he was being brought to heel, Abdullah attempted to secure the unification of Palestine with Transjordan, but was told that Britain had other plans for Palestine which took account of Jewish national aspirations. Well aware that Transjordan was the best he and the Arabs were likely to get for the moment, Abdullah accepted.

The territory that Abdullah took control of in April 1921 was undeveloped and anarchic. The borders drawn by Churchill were more or less arbitrary, frequently cutting across tribal areas and grazing grounds. The three existing Transjordanian governments – centred in Irbid, Salt and Karak – had virtually no authority and were overlaid by a patchwork of unstable local sheikhdoms. The population numbered about 230,000, of which over 200,000 were Muslim Arabs, the remainder Christian Arabs and Muslim Circassians. Over half were **fellaheen**, or landowning tribal village-dwellers (there were only four towns holding more than ten thousand people); a quarter were semi-nomadic bedouin concentrated in the north and west, and the rest were fully nomadic, relying on their livestock and on raiding the *fellaheen*, pilgrimage caravans and each other for survival. Amman held around 2400 people. Political loyalties were rooted in tribalism, and although the population at large tended towards common aims – desire for an Arab ruler, hatred of the French for their destruction of the Kingdom of Syria, distrust of the British for their double-dealing – they lacked a collective voice. When Abdullah arrived, apart from a brief challenge in Salt, he was accepted without question as a unifying leader.

For their part, the British wrote Transjordan out of the Palestine Mandate. On May 15, 1923, under an **Anglo-Jordanian Treaty**, the British formally recognized Abdullah as head of the new **Emirate of Transjordan**, describing it as a national state being prepared for full independence under the supervision of the British High Commissioner in Jerusalem.

Consolidation of the emirate: 1923–28

In Mecca, Abdullah's father Sharif Hussein was furious at being supplanted. In January 1924, he departed for Aqaba, where he ignored his son's, and British, authority and started to rule in his own right. It rapidly became apparent, though, that his dream of becoming 'king of the Arabs' was in tatters – much as was the Arab heartland itself. Syria was controlled by the French, who had carved Lebanon from it; Iraq was ruled by one son, Faysal, Transjordan by another, Abdullah; Palestine was under the thumb of the British; and late in

1924 the Hejaz was invaded by a fundamentalist central Arabian tribe led by **Abd al-Aziz al-Saud**, who shortly afterwards established the Kingdom of Saudi Arabia. As a crowning ignominy, the British exiled Hussein to Cyprus, where he spent his last days.

Meanwhile, Abdullah set about consolidating power in his newly chosen capital of **Amman** (favoured over the fractious Salt). The 1920s and 1930s saw the forging of a cohesive political unity from among the disparate tribes, with one of Abdullah's earliest acts being the creation of a centralized security force, named the **Arab Legion**.

Throughout this period, the British guaranteed funding for central government, in exchange for British advisers maintaining close contact with Abdullah. A pragmatist, as visionary as he was realistic, Abdullah knew that the British still called the shots, and that without Britain – specifically, without military assistance and money – the emirate could never survive. By compromising where necessary, Abdullah maintained progress towards his ultimate goal of independence, though his concessions to the British tarnished his reputation among Arab nationalists. To assuage growing discontent, Abdullah promulgated the **first Transjordanian constitution** in 1928. A year later, representative elections to a legislative council placed Transjordanians in real power for the first time.

With his domestic affairs stable, Abdullah was able to turn his attention further afield – specifically to the increasingly fraught situation in Palestine.

Abdullah I and Palestine: 1920–39

Palestine had always had a small native Jewish community, resident for the most part in the towns, Arabic-speaking and culturally Palestinian. Since the 1880s, however, Jews from central and eastern Europe had been arriving, many of them tough-minded nationalistic **Zionists**, for whom the area was not simply a holy land to be shared among religious communities but the rightful national homeland of the Jews of the world. As it became obvious that the Balfour Declaration was to become official mandate policy in Palestine, a **militant Arab reaction** to Zionism developed, denouncing Britain's perceived right to hand the country over to the Jews. In Amman, Abdullah quickly grasped the political reality – principally that Britain was in a position to dictate its will and that at least some degree of Jewish immigration to Palestine was inevitable. He put forward the proposal that if the Jews were prepared to accept the extension of his own rule over Palestine, they would be left free to govern themselves with all civil rights guaranteed; this would not only secure the Jewish position in Palestine with minimum cost to the existing local population, but it would also enable Jews to settle in Transjordan, where they could contribute much-needed money and skills to the country's development.

Amid the increasingly hot-headed politics of the time, such a vision was doomed to failure. The Jews wanted more in Palestine than mere political autonomy under a Muslim king, and rejected his proposals. Mainstream Arab opinion viewed Abdullah's plan as overly concessionary, and from this time on, doubts were laid in Palestinian minds as to Abdullah's motives. Reservations were fuelled by the leader of the Palestinians, **Hajj Amin al-Husseini**, Mufti of Jerusalem. A strict hardliner who refused to compromise an inch with the Jews, Hajj Amin led calls for a complete ban on Jewish immigration and land purchase, ahead of a declaration of Palestinian independence; he was aided by a silent alliance with the British, who had no desire to see Abdullah extending influence over a land he wasn't supposed to be ruling. Amman became the focus for the Palestinian opposition to Hajj Amin, which believed that the only way of saving Palestine for the Arabs was to cultivate British goodwill and offer limited concessions to the already entrenched Zionist settlers.

Anti-Zionist feeling among Palestinian Arabs exploded into violence in the 1920s and 1930s, put down with increasing harshness by the British. With the coming to power of the Nazis in Germany in 1933, Jewish immigration to Palestine increased dramatically, as did Arab attacks on both Jewish and British targets. From 1933 onwards, Abdullah began to appoint Palestinians to positions of power in Amman, but in such a charged atmosphere, his pragmatism in backing both Arab dialogue with the Jews and Arab concessions to the British merely fanned Palestinian distrust of his motives. In 1937, a **Royal Commission** arrived from London to assess the political situation. The Palestinian leadership boycotted the commission's proceedings; under threat of arrest, Hajj Amin fled to Lebanon.

The build-up to World War II: 1937–39

With war in Europe looking increasingly likely, Britain attempted to secure its position in the Middle East, an area commanding vital land and water routes and, most important, harbouring oil. The Royal Commission report of 1937 recommended **partitioning** Palestine between Arabs and Jews, but this was rejected by the all-or-nothing Palestinian leadership. In May 1939, with war imminent, the British suddenly offered a dramatic U-turn. On the table was **full independence** for Palestine after ten years, with severe limitations in the meantime on land transfers to Jews and with Jewish immigration permitted only subject to Arab approval. The Jews immediately rejected the proposal. In Amman, Abdullah hailed it as the best the Palestinian Arabs could ever hope to get, but Hajj Amin denounced the deal as a British ploy. The rejectionists won the day.

Seeing reason dissipating before him, Abdullah wrote: "The pillars of Zionism in Palestine are three: the Balfour promise; the European nations that have decided to expel the Jews from their lands; and the extremists among the Arabs who do not accept any solution. So behold Palestine, breathing its last."

Independence and the loss of Palestine: 1939–52

World War II had little impact in Transjordan, other than to delay advances towards independence. However, Abdullah's Arab Legion served loyally alongside the British elsewhere in the Middle East, helping to retake Baghdad from the Axis powers in 1941 (which paved the way for the British victory at El-Alamein the following year), and helping to eject the Vichy French from Syria and Lebanon. Abdullah deserved reward. What he hoped for – as he had done for decades – was the throne of a new Greater Syria. However, neither the Syrians nor the Lebanese would accept anything less than independence now the French had been removed from power; and the king of Saudi Arabia, already faced by a strong monarchy in Iraq, had no desire to see another in Transjordan (Britain and the United States were both aware by now of the vast oil reserves in Saudi Arabia, and were willing to bend over backwards to avoid upsetting King Saud). Syria and Lebanon were granted independence, but Transjordan remained under British mandate until the 1946 **Treaty of London**, which granted the emirate independence. In May, the Transjordanian cabinet switched Abdullah's title from emir to king, and officially changed the name of the country to the **Hashemite Kingdom of Jordan** (see box, p.376 for an explanation of the term "Hashemite").

Glubb Pasha

The name of **General Sir John Bagot Glubb** is generally better known in Jordan than T.E. Lawrence: there are still old-timers in Amman who remember him with some affection as an upstanding soldier and asset to the young emirate – though many other Jordanians associate his name with the colonialist treachery of the British.

Glubb was instrumental in establishing the Arab Legion, as the British-officered Transjordanian army was known. From 1918, he served first in British-controlled Iraq, famously halting incursions of bedouin fighters from the desert by establishing a loyal bedouin force. In 1930 he was posted to Transjordan, which was suffering from similar tribal raids. Glubb set up the bedouin **"Desert Patrol"**, which, after subduing the raids, went on to evolve into an elite army unit, serving in World War II and the 1948 war with Israel. In 1939, Glubb took over supreme command of the Arab Legion and became known as **"Pasha"**, an honorific title awarded to senior Jordanian officers. However, with the rise of Arab nationalism and the accession to the throne of the young King Hussein in 1953, Glubb began to appear increasingly outdated, and, worse, a tool of British imperialism. Dismissed in 1956, he went on to write dozens of well-respected books on Jordan and Arab history, including his autobiography *A Soldier with the Arabs*. He died in England in 1986.

Meanwhile, the situation in Palestine had been worsening, with a flood of post-Holocaust Jewish immigration and a simultaneous campaign of terror by underground Jewish groups aimed at the British. In 1947, Britain announced that it would unilaterally pull out of its Palestine mandate. That November, the UN approved a plan to partition Palestine into a Jewish and an Arab state, with Jerusalem administered internationally. The Jews were unhappy, having been denied Jerusalem, and mainstream Arab opinion was outraged at the whole idea of conceding any kind of Jewish state in Palestine. On May 15, 1948, the last British troops departed from Haifa. Jewish forces immediately declared an independent **State of Israel**. Disorganized Arab armies, led by Jordan's Arab Legion, simultaneously entered the region intent on taking the land allotted to the Jews by the UN. By the time fighting ended in July, Jordan had occupied a swathe of the interior of Palestine, as well as the eastern districts – and Holy Places – of Jerusalem. The entire Galilee region and the valuable fertile coastal strip, including the towns of Haifa, Jaffa, Lydda and Ramle, had been lost to Israel. Hundreds of thousands of Palestinians fled, or were forcibly ejected, from towns and villages throughout the country, most seeking refuge in the Jordanian-held sector, known as the **West Bank**. In four years, the kingdom's population jumped from 435,000 to 1.5 million, of whom two-thirds were Palestinian (including more than half a million refugees living in temporary camps).

After the hostilities, Abdullah convened a meeting in Jericho of Palestinian notables to proclaim the absorption of the Jordanian-occupied West Bank into Jordan proper. In April 1950, Jordan formally annexed the West Bank under the guise of "**uniting the two banks**".

Meanwhile the newly formed **Arab League** ruled that Arab countries should not grant citizenship to Palestinian refugees, lest the disowned and displaced should then lose their claim to their homeland. To this day, Palestinians who sought refuge in Lebanon, Syria and Egypt remain stateless and without rights. Jordan was the only Arab country to go against this policy; it formally resettled its Palestinian refugees, granting them full Jordanian citizenship and civil rights. Abdullah's policy enabled Palestinians in Jordan to rebuild their lives, but it ran entirely against mainstream Arab thinking that refused to accept the fact of

Israel's existence. Citizenship notwithstanding, most Palestinians – in Jordan and elsewhere – felt betrayed by Abdullah's policies from as far back as the 1920s, and particularly by his perceived eagerness to absorb Arab Palestine under the Hashemite banner. On July 20, 1951, as Abdullah was entering the al-Aqsa mosque in Jerusalem for Friday prayers, a young Palestinian stepped up and shot him dead. A bullet intended for Abdullah's 15-year-old grandson, Hussein, ricocheted off a medal on the boy's chest.

On Abdullah's assassination, the throne passed to Abdullah's 40-year-old son **Talal**, who was in Switzerland receiving medical treatment. Talal returned to Amman, but his increasingly erratic behaviour made it clear that he was unfit to rule. In 1952, he abdicated in favour of his eldest son, Hussein.

King Hussein's early years: 1952–67

Born in 1935, **King Hussein** was educated in Britain, at Harrow School and Sandhurst military academy. He succeeded to the throne before his seventeenth birthday, and was crowned king in May 1953. The Cold War was well established, and the new king found himself caught between a powerful Egyptian–Syrian–Saudi bloc on the one hand, closely allied with the Soviets, and on the other, the controlling British presence at the heart of his government pushing him towards the pro-Western Baghdad Pact (a British-designed defensive treaty against Soviet aggression, subscribed to by Iraq, Turkey, Iran and Pakistan). In addition, the 1948 war had utterly changed the character of Jordan, and had thrown a cosmopolitan, well-educated and urbanized Palestinian population into the midst of an outnumbered Transjordanian population with an entirely different, rural and bedouin-based culture. Most of the Palestinians yearned to return to their lost homeland, and were unwilling to follow the conciliatory and pro-Western Hashemite line; many favoured instead the **pan-Arabism** espoused by the charismatic Egyptian leader, **Nasser**.

Crisis loomed for Hussein in 1955 and 1956. In nine months, five prime ministers came and went. Jordan's declaration of Cold War neutrality angered the British, which in turn led to violent street protests in Amman. Hussein dismissed the British commander-in-chief of the Jordanian army, **Glubb Pasha**, and replaced him with a Jordanian, but anti-Western feeling continued to run high, especially after the British–French–Israeli invasion of Egypt during the **Suez Crisis** of 1956. Jordan's pro-Soviet prime minister **Suleiman Nabulsi** ended the 1948 Anglo-Jordanian treaty, replacing the British subsidy to Jordan with contributions from Saudi Arabia, Syria and Egypt (the last two soon defaulted). British troops left Jordan for good in July 1957.

To make up the financial shortfall, Hussein requested aid from the US and soon afterwards took control of army appointments and suppressed political parties and trade unions. The US declared its determination to preserve Jordan's independence, and when Syria allied itself with the USSR in September 1957, US forces sent a large airlift of arms to Amman.

Throughout the 1950s Egypt and Syria, both then revolutionary republics, kept up a bombardment of anti-Hashemite propaganda, with Nasser's **Radio Cairo** particularly vocal in denigrating both the Jordanian government and King Hussein. On February 1, 1958, Egypt and Syria announced – to wild celebrations on the streets of Jordan as everywhere in the Arab world – their merger in a **United Arab Republic** (UAR); as a counter-move, two weeks later, the Hashemite monarchies of Jordan and Iraq announced their own merger in an **Arab Federation**. The latter body survived barely five months, with the entire Iraqi royal family being slaughtered in a military coup in July. Meanwhile there was open Muslim insurrection in Lebanon, supported by the new UAR against the Christian-led and staunchly pro-American Lebanese government. Anti-Western feeling in the Middle East was at a peak, and the only obstacles most observers saw standing in the way of pan-Arab unity were the Lebanese Christians and Jordan's Hashemite monarchy. Few gave the latter much chance of survival.

The American response to the crisis was to bomb Lebanon. Meanwhile, the US administration had received a request for help from Jordan, which had run out of oil. However, with the revolutionary forces in Syria and Iraq sealing off their borders, and the Saudi king in thrall to Nasser's popularity, the only remaining direction by which the US could deliver oil to Jordan was over **Israeli airspace**. Amazingly, Hussein applied to Israel for permission, which was granted, and the airlift commenced, to a barrage of scorn from all Arab sides. Soon after, Britain flew troops into Amman to bolster the regime; they too arrived over Israel and the insults rang out again. Nonetheless, in Jordan, democracy had been sacrificed for stability, and Hussein's **security services** kept a tight lid on the simmering discontent. Palestinian bombs exploded in Amman, and, in 1960, the prime minister was assassinated, but repeated attempts on the king's life were foiled.

Opposition to Hussein died down, not least because US aid – and substantial remittances from Jordanians working in the Gulf – were fostering tangible **economic development**: Jordan's potash and phosphate industries were taking off, modern highways were being built, unemployment was down as construction teams expanded East and West Bank cities, and tourism to Jordanian Jerusalem, Bethlehem, Hebron and the West Bank, as well as East Bank sites, was bringing in much-needed hard currency. Ties with the Saudi Arabian monarchy were also strengthening in the face of communism and Arab nationalism. Perhaps most important of all, Hussein reluctantly approved the creation of a political body to represent the Palestinians, the **Palestine Liberation Organization (PLO)**, founded in 1964. Its charter, in a specific rebuff to Jordanian claims on the West Bank, stated that it was to be the "only legitimate spokesman" for the Palestinian people.

The Six-Day War and Black September: 1967–74

During 1966, relations with Syria deteriorated and Jordan suspended support for the PLO, accusing its secretary of pro-communist activity. Syria and the

PLO both appealed to the Jordanian people to revolt against King Hussein. Clashes followed and PLO-laid bombs exploded in Amman. At the same time, skirmishes with Israeli troops led Jordan to introduce conscription. The prospect of war with Israel seemed inevitable. In May 1967 Hussein flew to Cairo to throw in his lot with Egypt and Syria.

On June 5, Israel launched a pre-emptive strike against its Arab neighbours. By the end of the **Six-Day War**, Jordanian losses were devastating: Israel was occupying East Jerusalem and the entire West Bank. Israel had seized the Jawlan (Golan Heights) from Syria and the Gaza Strip and Sinai Peninsula from Egypt. In the eyes of the entire Arab world, this was a catastrophe: Egypt and Syria had lost relatively small areas of strategic importance, but Jordan had lost fully half its inhabited territory, a third of its population, its prime agricultural land and – most ignominious – control over the Muslim and Christian holy sites in Jerusalem. Up to a quarter of a million refugees crossed to the East Bank, putting the government, economy and social services under intolerable pressures.

The crushing defeat gave Palestinians in Jordan cause to believe that King Hussein and the other Arab leaders were unable or unwilling (or both) to liberate their homeland. King Hussein rapidly included equal representation from the East and West Banks in the National Assembly, but this was never going to satisfy Palestinian demands. The rift grew between the government and the Palestinian guerrilla organizations in Jordan – principally Fatah, led by **Yasser Arafat**, chairman of the umbrella PLO. After 1967, these groupings – funded by the Gulf states and receiving arms and training from Syria – took control in Jordan's refugee camps, backed also by widespread grassroots support from Jordan's majority Palestinian population. A **fedayeen** ("martyrs") movement developed within the camps, which took on the appearance of a state-within-a-state, intent on liberating Palestine by their own independent efforts. The *fedayeen* took for granted their ability to overrule King Hussein in his own country, and launched military operations against Israel. The ensuing reprisals, however, caused extensive damage to the border areas – now Jordan's only remaining agricultural land – and seriously undermined any possibilities for a peace settlement with Israel, on which the country's long-term future depended.

Black September and its aftermath: 1970–74

Fedayeen opposition to the Hashemite monarchy, rooted in revolutionary socialism, remained implacable. Street battles flared in 1968, and in June 1970, the Jordanian army mobilized in Amman to assert authority over the guerrilla movements. There was an attempt on the king's life. In September, *fedayeen* **hijacked** three international aircraft to an airfield near Mafraq, ostensibly demanding the release of imprisoned comrades, but equally intent on embarrassing King Hussein in the eyes of the world and forcing the issue of the Palestinian revolution in Jordan. Once emptied of passengers and crew, all three aircraft were spectacularly blown up; the *fedayeen* then took over Irbid proclaiming a "people's government", and the country exploded into violence. By the end of "**Black September**", full civil war was raging, with thousands dead and injured. Conflict continued for months but by April 1971, the Jordanian army had pushed the *fedayeen* out of Amman. Three months later, after a violent offensive on Palestinian positions around Jerash and Ajloun, forces loyal to the king were back in control. The *fedayeen* fled to Lebanon to continue their fight (within four years, civil war had broken out in Lebanon as well). Palestinian commandos made three unsuccessful attempts to hijack

Jordanian aircraft, and, in September 1971, members of the Black September faction of Fatah assassinated another Jordanian prime minister.

In March 1972 King Hussein made an attempt to regain Palestinian political credibility by announcing plans for a **federation** of Jordan and Palestine, but criticism of the plan was almost universal, from Israel, from the exiled Palestinian organizations and from Egypt. A military coup was only just averted. Jordan's isolation in the Arab world was almost complete. Nonetheless, Hussein attended a **reconciliation summit** with presidents Sadat of Egypt and Assad of Syria, which resulted in a general amnesty for all political prisoners in Jordan, including Fatah activists. Jordanian security services and intelligence organizations were beefed up to deter dissident activity; political parties remained banned and the country had no elected parliament. Jordan stayed out of the 1973 Egyptian–Syrian **October War** (or Yom Kippur War) against Israel, but garnered little kudos for doing so.

The Rabat summit and Camp David: 1974–80

Throughout 1974, King Hussein attempted to preserve his claim over the West Bank, flying in the face of the increasing power and prestige of the PLO (Yasser Arafat had that year been invited to address the UN General Assembly). In October 1974, at the **Arab Summit Conference** in Rabat, Morocco, twenty Arab heads of state passed a resolution recognizing the PLO as the "sole legitimate representative of the Palestinian people". King Hussein reluctantly agreed to this, effectively ceding Jordan's claims both to represent the Palestinians and to reincorporate the West Bank into the Hashemite realm.

In 1974, Egypt and Syria signed disengagement agreements with Israel; in 1975 and 1976, King Hussein held secret talks with Israel over the West Bank, which later collapsed due to Israel's proposal to retain control over thirty percent of the territory. The new realities were thrown into turmoil by Egyptian President Sadat's peace initiative in visiting Jerusalem in 1977; Hussein tried to stand as an arbiter between Egypt and the rejectionist Arab states (led by Syria), while still demanding Israel's complete withdrawal from East Jerusalem, the West Bank and Gaza. Jordan joined the rest of the Arab world in scorning the US-sponsored Egypt–Israel **Camp David accords** of 1978, and, as a reward, was promised $1.25 billion annually by wealthy **Iraq**. Throughout the 1970s, economic relations with Iraq had been improving, with Iraq funding the expansion of Aqaba port and construction of major highways. When Iraq invaded Iran in September 1980, launching the bloody **Iran–Iraq War**, Jordan benefited greatly from the passage of goods through Aqaba bound for Iraq.

The Palestinians and the first intifada: 1980–89

Since Black September, the PLO's bid for authority over Palestinians on the East Bank had – bizarrely – reinforced the stand of both Transjordanian and Israeli hardliners. The former had never viewed the Palestinians as true Jordanians anyway. The latter saw the Hashemite monarchy as the sole obstacle to annexation of the West Bank by Israel; under the slogan "**Jordan is Palestine**", they pressed for a Palestinian revolution east of the Jordan, offering to help it along by expelling Palestinians from the West Bank. Needless to say, this rapidly dampened Palestinian opposition to King Hussein in Jordan.

In 1982, the PLO was ejected from its Beirut headquarters by the **Israeli invasion of Lebanon**, and sent into further exile in Tunis; humiliated, Arafat looked to King Hussein for some way to challenge Israeli hegemony. Hussein reconvened Jordan's National Assembly, comprising representatives from both banks of the Jordan, for the first time since 1967, as a forum for discussion of moderate Palestinian opinion away from the extremist intransigence of the Syrian position. Israel even permitted West Bank deputies to travel to Amman. In March 1984, the first **elections** in Jordan for seventeen years (and the first in which women could vote) took place, although political parties were still banned and the eight seats up for grabs were East Bank only.

Less than a year later, in opposition to a widely denounced peace plan put forward by US President Reagan (who refused to talk to the PLO), Hussein and Arafat agreed to allow Jordan to start direct negotiations with Israel under UN auspices, on the basis of Hussein's formula of "**land for peace**" – that is, the return of lands occupied by Israel in 1967 in exchange for a comprehensive Arab-Israeli peace. Hardline Syria, though, forced Hussein to drop the initiative, partly by assassinating Jordanian diplomats and partly by uniting the Abu Nidal Palestinian guerrilla organization with Arafat's main PLO rival, George Habash, to attack the accord. At the end of 1985, Hussein and Syria's President Assad issued a joint statement rejecting any direct peace negotiations with Israel; Hussein's motivation for this was also to put pressure on Arafat to accept **UN Resolution 242**, without which the PLO could gain no international credibility. "242" had been a thorn in the side of the Arabs since 1967, since it called ambiguously for Israel to withdraw from "occupied territories" (which could be taken to mean whatever anyone wanted) and referred to the Palestinians as "refugees", thus implying a denial of the existence of a Palestinian nation and the right of Palestinians to self-determination, and accepting the right of Israel to exist. Hamstrung by extremist attitudes embedded within the PLO, Arafat couldn't stop the PLO Executive Committee reiterating its opposition to 242 in December 1985.

Although rumours of secret talks between Hussein and the Israeli Prime Minister Shimon Peres persisted through the mid-1980s, publicly Jordan continued to reject Israeli proposals for peace talks which excluded PLO participation. In November 1987, King Hussein managed to convene in Amman the first full meeting of the Arab League for eight years and, acting in the interests of Arab unity, was able to draw Egypt back into the fold after its expulsion for making peace with Israel.

The first intifada and Jordan's West Bank pull-out: 1987–89

In December 1987, an incident in the Gaza Strip sparked a widespread violent Palestinian uprising against Israeli occupation of the West Bank and Gaza, termed the **intifada**, or "shaking-off". Israel was unable to suppress the uprising, and, alarmed at the possibility of demonstrations turning violent, the Jordanian security services enforced their own clampdown on any shows of solidarity. The intensity of the revolt, as well as the Israeli response to it and the news that emerged of horrendous living conditions among Palestinians under Israeli occupation, alerted world opinion to the necessity of a comprehensive settlement in the Middle East. The US Secretary of State, George Shultz, came up with a plan, but since it refused participation by the PLO and also neglected to address the Palestinian right to self-determination, it was rejected by every Arab state.

In a momentous decision on July 31, 1988, with the *intifada* in full swing, King Hussein announced the **severing** of all legal and administrative links between Jordan and the West Bank. By doing so, he effectively ended Hashemite claims to Arab Palestine which had been playing beneath the surface of political machinations in the region since 1917. The 850,000 Palestinians on the West Bank welcomed the clean break. Israel, however, immediately began restricting the activities of West Bank Palestinian institutions. Anti-Hashemite opinion cynically suggested that Hussein wanted to demonstrate the inability of the PLO to run public services and conduct international diplomacy without the backing of Jordan.

Shortly afterwards, on November 15, the PLO unilaterally proclaimed an independent **State of Palestine**, endorsing UN Resolution 242 and thus implicitly recognizing the right of Israel to exist (within its pre-1967 frontiers). Jordan and sixty other countries recognized the new state. The following month, Yasser Arafat renounced violence on behalf of the PLO in front of the UN General Assembly.

Democracy and the first Gulf War: 1989–91

In Jordan, the pull-out from the West Bank caused the value of the dinar to fall dramatically, and the austerity measures that followed resulted in **price rises** of up to fifty percent on basic goods and services. In April 1989, anti-government **riots** broke out in depressed southern towns such as Karak and Ma'an. The prime minister and the entire cabinet resigned, forcing a **general election** that gave a surprising boost to the Islamist and leftist opposition. 1990 was a year of desperate crisis for Jordan. The dinar had lost two-thirds of its value in two years and unemployment was running at twenty percent. Fraud and embezzlement had been uncovered at the country's second-largest bank, and the scandal had spread to the national airline and some 37 other companies. In addition, a huge influx of Jews into Israel from the former Soviet Union was resulting in ever more settlements going up on the West Bank and a consequent flood of Palestinians crossing the river into Jordan. With the West Bank Palestinians under almost continuous curfew, the *intifada* seemed to have fizzled out.

The first Gulf War: 1990–91

As the 1980–88 Iran–Iraq war juddered to a halt, it became clear that Iraq was in no position to repay its loans from the Gulf states. President Saddam Hussein campaigned to have the loans cancelled, but **Kuwait** stood out by refusing to accede. This quarrel was complicated by a long-standing border dispute between the two countries – and by the fact that the disputed area was rich in oil. King Hussein of Jordan pressed for a resolution to the crisis by Arab mediation, but before steps could be taken, Iraq suddenly **invaded** Kuwait on August 2, 1990. Saddam Hussein quickly proclaimed the annexation of Kuwait to Iraq.

The UN Security Council imposed **economic sanctions** on Iraq four days later, precipitating a further crisis in Jordan. Thousands of Jordanian refugees returned destitute from Iraq and Kuwait, ending substantial foreign remittances to the kingdom and placing a huge burden on the country's social services. Petroleum prices rose sharply, as Jordan's supply of free Iraqi oil (in return for loans) dried up; fully a quarter of Jordan's export trade had been to Iraq, and this was terminated; and business at Aqaba port was cut overnight, as the road to Iraq was closed to trade.

It was clear that Saddam Hussein's actions flouted international law. King Hussein attempted to get the Arab League to mediate in the crisis, but he was countered by Saudi Arabia, Egypt and Syria leading calls for international action. In August, King Hussein started a round of peacemaking, giving a televised address to the US Congress urging withdrawal of the multinational force in Saudi Arabia. In November, he warned the World Climate Conference of the potentially disastrous environmental effects of war – borne out by Iraq's later ignition of Kuwaiti oil installations. The following month, he proposed a peace plan linking the Iraq–Kuwait dispute with the Arab–Israeli conflict, and advocating dialogue amongst Arab leaders.

His efforts proved fruitless: on January 16, 1991, the **Gulf War** began, sparking widespread anti-Western and anti-Israel demonstrations throughout Jordan. Petrol rationing was introduced in Jordan, which only bolstered pro-Iraqi sentiment. Popular opinion held that the US-led coalition was pursuing double standards, condemning Iraqi aggression against Kuwait yet condoning Israeli aggression in the occupied territories; that the Gulf States were greedy, unwilling to share their new-found oil wealth with other Arabs; and that the West, by weighing in against Iraq, was supporting the oil-rich states against the poorer Arab states. In the region, King Hussein was highly regarded for being the only leader to articulate this opinion fully, although he was lambasted for it in the West.

After hostilities ceased in March, the US Congress cancelled an aid programme to Jordan in punishment for the king's stance. Kuwait regarded its sizeable Jordanian and Palestinian community as collaborators with the Iraqis, and expelled them all – about 300,000 people – to Jordan, a further burden on the country's social infrastructure.

Peace and crises: 1991–99

In 1991, a new **National Charter** improved openness within government, eased bureaucracy and lifted the ban on political parties, which had been in effect since 1963. Martial law, which had been in force since 1967, was repealed. Jordan's first one-person one-vote, multi-party **elections** of November 1993 saw a 68 percent turnout, with the majority of candidates being independent centrists loyally backing the king, although the Islamic Action Front (the political arm of the Muslim Brotherhood) gained strong support.

New moves in the Middle East **peace process** were initiated by the US in Madrid in October 1991, Jordan participating in a joint delegation with the Palestinians. The peace talks soon hit deadlock, but, unknown even to King Hussein, Israel's new left-wing government and the PLO were engaged in secret talks in Oslo. In September 1993, they emerged with a **Declaration of Principles** on Palestinian self-rule in the occupied territories. Soon after, Jordan and the PLO signed agreements on economic and security cooperation, closely bonding the ongoing Israeli–Palestinian and Israeli–Jordanian peace talks together into a single framework.

On July 25, 1994, in Washington, King Hussein and Israeli Prime Minister Yitzhak Rabin formally ended the state of war that had existed between their two countries since 1948. A full **peace treaty** followed in October, opposed both by Syria and by Islamists within Jordan. A clause in the treaty acknowledging King Hussein as the custodian of the Holy Places in Jerusalem initially brought complaints from the PLO that it undermined Palestinian claims to the city, later mollified.

In August 1996, under intense pressure from the International Monetary Fund to institute austerity measures, the government ended **subsidies** on grain which were producing a ballooning economic deficit. The result was an immediate doubling of bread prices, and discontent, especially strong in the poorer towns of the south, flared into open **rioting**. King Hussein suspended parliament and sent troops and tanks into Karak and elsewhere to suppress the disturbances, but the austerities remained. The election in 1996 of an extreme right-wing government in Israel, headed by **Binyamin Netanyahu**, brought the ongoing Middle East peace process to a grinding halt.

For many Jordanians, 1997 was a year of shattered confidence, as the country was exposed to a series of domestic and regional crises. Early in the year, a Jordanian soldier opened fire on Israeli schoolgirls visiting Baqoura in northern Jordan, killing seven. King Hussein attempted to mend ties with Israel by personally visiting the bereaved families, a gesture which inspired much admiration in Israel and much contempt in the Arab world (no bereaved Arab families have ever been consoled by an Israeli leader, the argument ran). Anti-Israel feeling surged in Jordan. In July, nine major political parties announced their intention to boycott the November parliamentary election, as a sign of their opposition to normalizing relations with Israel. Diplomatic relations with Israel were almost terminated in September, after a botched assassination attempt in Amman by Mossad, the Israeli intelligence service, on an official at the Jordanian bureau of the Palestinian Islamist group Hamas. Days before the Jordanian elections in November, Human Rights Watch issued a damning report on the state of human rights in Jordan. The elections themselves were held to be a whitewash, with extremely low voter turnout and 62 out of 80 seats won by pro-government or independent centrist candidates. Only 19 out of 524 candidates were women, none of whom was elected (the king later appointed three women to the Senate). A report from Jordan University showed unemployment in the country standing at a crippling 22–27 percent, double the official estimate.

The death of King Hussein

Throughout the 1990s, concern had been bubbling under Jordanian politics about the **health** of King Hussein. In August 1992, one of his kidneys was removed during an operation for cancer; spring 1996 saw an operation for an enlarged prostate, and during 1998 he underwent chemotherapy for lymph cancer. All these procedures were done in the US, his youngest brother, **Prince Hassan**, being sworn in as regent on each occasion. In October 1998, Hussein witnessed the **Wye River Accords**, guaranteeing Israeli withdrawal from more West Bank land in return for security safeguards from the Palestinians. (Two months later Israel suspended the agreement in the face of deepening domestic tension, and the Netanyahu government collapsed.) The king's appearance at Wye River, to free the negotiations from deadlock despite obvious physical frailty, inspired respect but also doubts about his ability to continue his public duties.

In January 1999, after six months of treatment in the US, Hussein flew back to Jordan. It was clear his health was failing. In a controversially abrupt letter, he publicly removed Hassan from the **succession** after 34 years as Crown Prince, and placed in his stead his own eldest son, Abdullah. Within hours, Hussein had suffered a relapse. After unsuccessful treatment in the US, he returned again to Amman where he died three days later, on February 7, 1999, at the age of 63, having been in power for 46 years – one of the longest-serving executive heads of state in the world. His funeral drew worldwide media attention, with more than **fifty heads of state** in attendance. Even at a time of tragedy, such a turnout, demonstrating the international community's high regard for Jordan and its king, was a significant fillip to national confidence.

Jordan under Abdullah II

On the death of Hussein, a swearing-in ceremony confirmed the succession to **King Abdullah II**, who was crowned in July 1999. Abdullah was born in 1962 to Hussein's second wife, an Englishwoman, formerly Toni Gardiner, who took the name Princess Muna al-Hussein when she converted to Islam. Abdullah was educated at Oxford and Sandhurst; when he acceded, it was said at first that he spoke better English than Arabic. His prominent role in the Jordanian military ensured wholehearted support among East Bankers, while the fact that his wife, **Queen Rania**, is a scion of a notable Palestinian family from Tulkarem on the West Bank safeguarded his reputation among Jordanians of Palestinian origin.

Faced with continuing turmoil in Israel and Palestine, Abdullah has played only a minor role in suing for regional peace. In September 2000, the notorious right-wing Israeli general **Ariel Sharon** sparked outrage by touring Jerusalem's Haram ash-Sharif, the third-holiest site in Islam. Within weeks Sharon had won the Israeli elections, his bullish presence as prime minister effectively halting progress in international peace negotiations. The **second intifada** which followed, incomparably bloodier than its forebear of the late 1980s, has continued past the death in November 2004 of Yasser Arafat and the January 2006 stroke which incapacitated Ariel Sharon. Throughout, it has been widely supported by the Jordanian people, aided by such vocal bodies as Jordan's **Anti-Normalization Committee**, an informal grouping which agitates against any contacts – political, social or cultural – with Israel or Israelis.

When a coalition of forces led by the US invaded Iraq in March 2003, launching the **Second Gulf War**, Jordan limited its involvement, refusing to open its airspace to coalition aircraft and staying out of the ground war. One poll stated that just nine percent of Jordanians supported military action. One consequence of the war is that Jordan has absorbed a million or more refugees from Iraq. Such vast numbers have put considerable strain on the country's health care, housing and education systems. Coordinated **suicide bomb attacks** on three hotels in Amman in November 2005 that killed sixty people – for which Abu Musab al-Zarqawi, the Jordanian leader of 'Al-Qaeda in Iraq', claimed responsibility – had the unintended effect of turning many ordinary Jordanians against Al-Qaeda. US forces killed Zarqawi in an airstrike inside Iraq in June 2006, reportedly on a tip-off from Jordanian intelligence.

Economic reform is where Abdullah has made most impact. Jordan became the first country (other than Israel) to negotiate a **free trade agreement** with the US, and now has several Qualifying Industrial Zones (QIZs), where goods are manufactured or processed jointly by Jordan and Israel for distribution to the US duty- and quota-free. In 2001, the low-tax Aqaba Special Economic Zone (ASEZ) was launched to attract investment to Jordan's Red Sea coast, significant foreign investment flowing soon thereafter. **Privatization** of state concerns, such as Jordan Telecom and the airline Royal Jordanian, have proceeded apace. Jordan joined the World Trade Organization and has hosted several full meetings of the World Economic Forum. A new programme of socioeconomic reform was instituted in late 2007. Although the ending of state subsidies on petrol and consumer goods a few months later caused prices to jump, the beneficial impacts of reform are being felt and – as regards the economy, at least – many Jordanians are cautiously optimistic.

Prospects

For many people living in the Middle East, the "9/11" attacks on New York and Washington in September 2001 reinforced the urgency of establishing peace and prosperity in their region, and the general need for **dialogue** between the West and the Muslim world. In Jordan, as in virtually all Arab states, there is a discrepancy between the motivations and preoccupations of government and those of the general population. The vast majority of Jordanians have no problem with their government's policy of maintaining warm relations with the West, as long as this is based on mutual respect and a fair crack at social and economic development. However many people instead face unemployment and poverty, and feel that their beliefs and concerns are being slighted while injustice persists both at home and across the region. This alienates them not only from decision-makers in their own country but also from the source, as many see it, of their and their neighbours' cultural and political oppression – the West and, specifically, the US. Radicalization often follows.

The principal challenge for King Abdullah, as for many Arab leaders, is to foster the rise of a practical, responsive **body politic** that is able, in Jordan's case, to incorporate strands of liberal democracy, homegrown tribalism and Islam, and give each an outlet for expression. Of equal importance is the development of a tolerant, participatory **civil society** to limit polarization and extremism. On both fronts, Jordan is generally held to be leaps and bounds ahead of most states in the region, but it is held back by the lack of progress on the key issue that casts a shadow over the whole region: a just and comprehensive resolution of the Israeli–Palestinian problem. It is increasingly obvious that while conflict persists in Israel and/or Palestine, there can only ever be limited and ultimately unsatisfying social, economic or political development in Jordan.

It can fairly be said that both King Abdullah I and King Hussein recognized this fact and devoted their careers, and their lives, to addressing it. By promoting economic reform – and thereby raising the standard of living for ordinary Jordanians – King Abdullah II has demonstrated his key role in promoting regional stability and creating a framework for sustainable development at home.

Flora and fauna

Jordan has a great variety of wildlife, not least because it lies at the crossroads of the Mediterranean, Arabia and Africa. The deserts contain a rich flora and fauna especially adapted to the harsh environment, and there's even life in the Dead Sea – you just need a microscope to see the species of bacteria which are known to occur.

Mosaics, rock art and frescoes paint a picture of Jordan's wildlife at a time when its significance was as a source of food (and, later, sport). Ancient rock art in the eastern deserts depicts gazelles, ibex and ostriches, and stone corrals remain as evidence of systematic trapping by previous generations of bedouin. Eighth-century frescoes at Qusayr Amra suggest that hunting game, such as the onager (a wild ass from Persia), was a great attraction for visitors from Damascus. These images also afford a glimpse of some larger animals which have subsequently become extinct due to excessive hunting and habitat destruction. It's hard to imagine today that leopards, Asiatic lions, cheetah, Syrian bears and crocodiles once roamed Jordan's deserts, forests and rivers. It's also hard to appreciate how quickly the thousands of gazelles present until the mid-1940s were reduced to near-extinction following the arrival of automatic weapons and motor vehicles; ostrich, Houbara bustard, oryx and onagers all went the same way.

For many years, Jordan's Royal Society for the Conservation of Nature (**RSCN**) has pursued a plan to **re-establish populations** of some of the country's extinct mammals in the wild. Projects involving oryx, Nubian ibex and roe deer have all been marked by success, even though most of these animals' former ranges have been overgrazed by goats and sheep.

Major habitats

Jordan's varied topography, climate and geology interact to produce a patchwork of often tightly packed **habitats**: you can travel from pine forest to desert in an hour's drive. Broadly speaking, the country can be divided into four major regions: the rift valley, rift margins, highlands and interior deserts. Each of these contains a range of habitats which vary north to south, west to east and from low to high altitudes. In addition, there are habitats specific to the desert oases, rivers and coast.

The **rift valley** comprises – from north to south – the Jordan Valley, the Dead Sea, Southern Ghor, Wadi Araba and the Gulf of Aqaba (before continuing on to the Red Sea and the East African Rift Valley). The whole valley is warm to hot, the only appreciable rain falling in the north, which is exposed to rainfall from Mediterranean weather systems and thus lushly vegetated.

The **highlands** constitute a spine of hills running north–south down the length of the country, dissected by major wadi systems flowing westwards. Terrain in the north, up to 1250m above sea level, comprises the country's richest agricultural land. Further south and east, a reduction in altitude and rainfall produces an undulating, steppe terrain (now mostly arable). The Shara mountains in the south, behind Petra, reach 1700m; their steppe habitat is unique in Jordan. Towards Aqaba, dissected granite mountains add further variation to this upland range.

Between the highlands and the rift valley, a deeply incised, west-facing escarpment contains some of the most dramatic of Jordan's scenery, including Petra and Dana. As you descend, habitats within this **rift margin** change with the drop in rainfall.

The interior **deserts**, covering eighty percent of Jordan's area, are typically flat, with geological variations controlling a complex pattern of fascinating habitats. Flint and limestone deserts predominate, with sand deserts rarer. Of considerable interest is the basalt desert, a vast expanse of boulders harbouring a unique fauna adapted to live in this harsh habitat. The Rum desert is far from flat, with Jordan's highest mountains (reaching above 1800m) among its towering peaks; the valleys between contain the country's finest sand dunes, largely stabilized with broom and other scrub. Much of the eastern desert's sporadic rainfall drains into mud flats or *qa*s which, for brief, irregular periods, support huge quantities of life from invertebrates to the birds that feed on them.

Water is a valuable resource, and **rivers** are in short supply. Much of the flow of the Jordan River is now diverted for agriculture: a mere trickle remains. Many of its tributaries are now dammed, and as a result, the future for riverine wildlife in Jordan looks uncertain. Azraq was a textbook **oasis** until water extraction put an end to the natural flow of its springs. Other oases are small, such as those along the base of the rift margins and at Aqaba. Jordan's few kilometres of arid, sparsely vegetated **coastline** are fringed by coral reef, before the seabed plunges to depths of over 500m.

Mammals

A little detective work is needed to spot Jordan's mammalian wildlife, as many of the larger animals survive only in the remotest corners and the smaller animals are typically nocturnal. Discarded quills offer the only clue that nocturnal **porcupines** have been through; the **Palestinian mole rat** gives itself away by leaving telltale molehills. The pine forests around Dibbeen are home to **Persian squirrels**, closely related to Europe's red squirrel; even if you don't see one, you can look for the chewed pine cones they leave behind.

Excepting a chance sighting of **Nubian ibex** at Dana or Mujib, or a **Dorcas gazelle** in Wadi Araba, the largest wild mammal you are likely to see in Jordan is a **red fox**, not to be confused with the ubiquitous feral dogs. Jordan's few **wolves**, **jackals** and **striped hyenas** keep well away from humans. Felines are represented by the wildcat and the **caracal**, both quite rare. Next largest is probably the **Cape hare**, which has evolved to become more rabbit-sized in the warm Arabian climate. But by far the most abundant are the varieties of **mice**, **gerbils**, **jerboas** and **jirds** – hamster-like rodents that make their home in desert burrows. A few **rock hyrax** – a burrowing rodent that's a close relative of the elephant, though just the size of a cat – remain in Dana and Rum. You may glimpse a **mongoose** scurrying along the banks of the River Zarqa.

The one-humped **dromedary**, the camel found in Arabia, has a history inextricably associated with that of the bedouin, and it has been a beast of burden as well as a source of milk and meat for many thousands of years. All Jordan's camels are domesticated, any vestiges of wild stock having vanished long ago.

Birds

Jordan has a lot to offer the birdwatcher: there are many resident bird species, some native to the Middle East, while others have European and even African affinities. Some species migrate vast distances to breed in Jordan, others winter here from points further north. Add to these the through-migration of literally millions of birds in spring and autumn – either dropping in for a rest or just flying over – and it is not difficult to imagine how well over four hundred species have been identified in a relatively small country, with additional species being added each year.

Although some locals do **hunt** under licence from the RSCN, it is a relief that Jordanian culture differs from that of much of the Mediterranean, where birds are slaughtered in their millions using nets, bird-lime and guns. Traditional Arab hunting with falcons (or even bringing falcons into the country) is also illegal, and it is regrettable that visiting hunters and falconers continue to have an impact by trapping migratory birds of prey in the eastern deserts.

Native bird species

Jordan has eight endemic Near East species – **sooty falcon**, **sand partridge**, **Tristram's grackle**, **Hume's tawny owl**, **Arabian babbler**, **hooded wheatear**, **Arabian warbler** and **Syrian serin**; their breeding ranges include Jordan's southern rift valley, rift margins and Rum desert. Of these, the starling-like grackle, with its orange wing flash and evocative whistling call, is the most likely to be seen.

Jordan's **deserts** are home to many characteristic birds. These include the many larks and wheatears, each of which is superbly adapted to its chosen habitat, such as **Temminck's horned lark** in the flat, eastern deserts, **hoopoe lark** in sandier areas and **white-crowned black wheatear** in the rockiest mountains. Although Jordan's national bird, the **Sinai rosefinch**, is only the size of a small sparrow, the male's vivid pink plumage evokes Jordan's rose-red city of Petra and the red cliffs and desert sands of Wadi Rum. Sunbirds are the Old World equivalent of the hummingbird, and in Jordan the male **Palestine sunbirds** flash iridescent purple and blue as they hover – for example, by the borage flowers in the Dana campsite. The basalt desert is also home to a unique population of **mourning wheatears**, whose virtually all-black colouring better matches its surroundings.

Migrant and breeding bird species

Jordan's position at the crossroads between Europe, Asia and Africa results in a cosmopolitan bird community. Species such as **black-eared wheatear**, **woodchat shrike**, **hoopoe** and **black-headed bunting** have affinities with southeastern Europe. Jordan is on the southern extreme of several species' ranges, such as **blue** and **great tits**. The **Cyprus warbler** and **Cyprus wheatear** also have restricted breeding ranges, and occur in Jordan on migration. The African influence is less obvious, though many migrant species retreat to Africa in winter. Isolated pairs of the **Verreaux's eagle**, more at home feeding on hyraxes in east and southern Africa, are also found in Jordan.

The country also hosts several species that are globally or regionally threatened, including **griffon vulture** and **lesser kestrel** (which breed in Jordan) and **imperial eagle**, **Levant sparrowhawk** and **corncrake** (which are found in Jordan on migration or in winter).

Spring migration sees millions of birds returning from wintering in Africa to their breeding grounds in eastern Europe and western Russia, via the rift valley. Migrant **warblers**, **pipits** and **wagtails**, for instance, use every available scrap of cover in which to shelter and refuel, whether on a traffic island in Aqaba, a sewage works, a clump of bushes in the open desert or in the meagre shade underneath a parked car. From late February through to May, vast numbers of **raptors**, including eagles, buzzards, kites, hawks and falcons, use traditional routes over Jordan's rift margins, typically seeking out a remote hillside to roost overnight before continuing. The head of the Gulf of Aqaba is a migration bottleneck, and north from here they peel off to get to their specific destinations. In contrast, the migration front is much broader in autumn, when birds are not averse to stopping off to eat or drink.

In wet winters, the inflow of the River Jordan into the Dead Sea gives rise to a layer of fresh water which persists for some time above the salt water before mixing; in these circumstances, it's possible to witness the rather incongruous sight of **ducks** swimming on the Dead Sea. **Herons** often gather at places like the Mujib delta to feed on the fish that die when they reach the saline water.

Insects

Insects are particularly obvious in the hotter seasons. **Butterflies** are colourful and easy to spot, though, as with birds, where you are will dictate whether you see European or Arabian species. Representatives of the swallowtails, blues, coppers, whites, marbled whites, fritillaries, painted ladies and tortoiseshells all occur, some migrating in spectacular fashion in their hundreds of millions. One of the rarest and most beautiful of the migrant butterflies is the large orange, black and white **plain tiger**, which is commoner in some springtimes than others.

It is easy to see all shapes and sizes of beetles in Jordan – around 1700 species have been identified in the country. The long-legged, black **pitted beetle** is one of the most obvious, as are **scarab beetles** and **dung beetles**. Large black **millipedes** are a feature of Jordan's ruins, such as Jerash.

Jordan has three species of **scorpion** (pale-yellow and black in colour), all of which can inflict sufficiently painful stings to warrant a visit to hospital. Unless you are particularly lucky (or unlucky), you're unlikely even to see one, unless you make a habit of turning over stones. Solifugids, or **camel spiders**, are formidable hunters, but are not venomous despite having a strong bite.

Grasshoppers, moths, dragonflies, solitary wasps, cicadas, locusts and praying and ground mantises are other obvious insects, with the list practically endless. Bluebottle-like flies are a pest, especially in the hot Jordan Valley summer. Mosquitoes tend to be more of an irritation than a pest or health hazard.

Reptiles, amphibians and freshwater fish

No desert would be complete without **lizards**. Around fifty species have been identified in Jordan, the largest of which is the **desert monitor**, reaching 130cm in length. There are nocturnal **geckos** with their sticky toe-pads, hammer-headed **agamas**, smooth-skinned **skinks** and long-tongued **chameleons**. In Wadi Araba, you may glimpse the 65cm **spiny-tailed** (or **Dhab**) **lizard** – with its chunky, scaly tail – before it flees down its burrow. At Petra the dazzlingly turquoise male **Sinai agama** is one of the most eye-catching.

Snakes are much talked about and feared, but rarely seen. There are 24 species, including five that are venomous, particularly the **Palestine viper** and the **horned viper**.

Where there is water, **marsh frogs** occur in an extraordinary variety of colours and patterns, though it's easier to hear their croaking than it is to find them. There are a small number of freshwater **fish** in the River Jordan and its tributaries. On the mud flats of Azraq, millions of dormant eggs hatch when the area floods, giving rise to vast populations of the small **killifish**, which provide a valuable food source to migrating birds.

Red Sea life

The clear, warm waters of the **Gulf of Aqaba** host a fringing **coral reef**, the most northerly in the world, which is particularly rich in coral and fish species. The shallow reef flat lies closest to the shore, but this soon gives way at the reef crest to the steeply shelving reef slope. Elsewhere, in sandy bays and at the head of the gulf, sea-grass beds host colonies of **garden-eels**. Looking like blades of tall grass at first glance, these long sinuous creatures soon disappear into their burrows when approached.

Some one thousand species of fish occur off Aqaba, including the slimline **angel-** and **butterfly fishes**, coral-eating **parrot fishes**, predatory **groupers**, parasite-picking **cleaner wrasse**, shoals of red **jewelfish**, luminescent "**flash-light fish**", and the oddly shaped **box fishes**. Of the venomous fish, the **lionfish** is one of the most beautiful in the reef with its feather-like fins, whereas the **stonefish** is as ugly as they come, dull, bulky and covered in wart-like protrusions. Seeing a **turtle**, **shark** or **porpoise** off Aqaba requires a calm sea and a lot of luck; diving affords a better chance than watching from the shore or in a glass-bottomed boat.

Flora

For a country that is eighty percent semi-desert, Jordan's **plant** list is outstanding. Visit the higher ground in March or April, especially after a wet winter, and you will witness swathe after swathe of green, red and blue blanketing the hillsides.

On the downside, the desert landscape has changed dramatically following human introduction of sheep and goats, which has accelerated wind and rain erosion and desertification, putting tremendous pressure on the native wildlife. **Overgrazing** of the fragile semi-desert flora is ubiquitous, with the effects visible at Shaumari; compare the thick bushes inside the enclosures with the pitiful remnants outside. Many of Jordan's trees are grazed – the evergreen oaks, for example – and have responded by growing small, tough leaves at grazing height. Other trees are much hacked for firewood. Unusually heavy snow in the highlands can even snap mature trees under its weight.

Shrubs and herbaceous plants

Cyclamen are one of the earliest blooms, making their first appearance in late winter, followed by poppies, anemones and crocuses in March. Most of Jordan's 22 species of **orchid** flower in April in the highland forests of the northwest. April is also the optimum time to see the **black iris**, Jordan's national flower. One of at least four irises that are endemic to this region, it isn't actually jet-black, rather a very dark purple. The upland hillsides are often carpeted with low spiky bushes and aromatic herbs such as thyme and sage-brush (*Artemesia*). In summer, **thistles**, which grow in profusion and in great varieties, take on a new beauty as the six rainless months of fierce heat turn almost everything into a desiccated, buff-brown relic. However, some flowers do bloom at this time, for example the **sea-onion**, which carpets the flatter ground inside Petra and flowers in July; in autumn, **crocuses** add the only touch of colour when everything else is parched.

In early spring, if the ground warms up after winter rains, the **deserts** can become flushed with grasses and flowers, though this isn't on a dramatic scale and is often short-lived: if the sheep and goats don't eat the new arrivals, they soon succumb to the heat. White **broom** bushes line the wadis; a parasitic broomrape, the **cistanche**, is a spike of yellow in the semi-desert. **Desert melons**, found in the eastern desert, are poisonous and avoided by animals, and wild **capers** grow in the Jordan Valley.

Trees

Trees are largely restricted to the highlands, especially the Mediterranean regions of the northwest. Several species of evergreen and deciduous **oaks**, **Aleppo pines**, **carob** and **strawberry trees** can still be found in Jordan, along with fast-growing, introduced **eucalyptus**, **cypress** and **casuarinas**. **Almond** trees bloom early and **figs** grow wild near water sources in the hills. Ancient, gnarled **junipers** are characteristic of the Petra and Dana mountains. Natural **forest** remains only in parts of the northern highlands (mainly pines) and in the inaccessible mountain landscape around Dana and Petra (oak and juniper). Forests were undoubtedly more extensive in the past, and the operation of the Hejaz Railway is often cited as a major destroyer of woodlands, which were cut down to fuel the trains.

On lower ground, **acacias** give Wadi Araba a distinctly African look, while palms are found by freshwater springs such as Aqaba and Azraq. Wadi Butm, at Qusayr Amra, gets its name from the Arabic word for the ancient **Atlantic pistachio** trees that line the wadi. Although not nut-producing, they provide vital shelter for much resident and migrant wildlife. Similarly rare is the **funeral cypress**, of which a small number of reportedly native trees remain near Dana.

By Ian J. Andrews

Islam

It's almost impossible to make any sense out of the Middle East – or Jordan – without knowing something of **Islam**. Well over ninety percent of Jordan's population are Muslim, and the practice and philosophy of Islam permeate most aspects of daily life. What follows is the briefest of backgrounds.

Islam was the third of the great monotheistic religions to originate in the Middle East, and places itself firmly in the tradition begun by Judaism and Christianity. Abraham is seen as the first Muslim, and Islam itself is defined as a reaffirmation, correction and consummation of the earlier faiths.

Islam was propagated in the seventh century AD by a merchant named **Muhammad** from the city of Mecca, in the Hejaz region of what is now Saudi Arabia. Muhammad is seen as the last of a series of prophets sent by God to earth; among earlier prophets were Abraham, Noah, Moses, Solomon, Job, John the Baptist and Jesus, whose messages, for whatever reason, had been lost or corrupted over the centuries. Muhammad was sent to revive and refine the words of past prophets.

The basic principles of Islam are that there is one God (in Arabic, Allah), and he must be worshipped; and that Muhammad is his final prophet. The main sources of the religion are the Quran (or Koran) – the revelation Muhammad received during his lifetime – and Muhammad's own actions.

The Quran

Muslims regard the **Quran** (literally, "recitation") to be the word of God, as revealed by the angel Jibril (Gabriel) to Muhammad from about 610 AD, when Muhammad was about 40, until his death in 632. There is a noticeable difference in the style of the Quran between the early portions – which have the ring of soothsaying about them, arising from Muhammad's early role as mystic – and the later portions, which go into detail about the conduct of Muslim life, as befits Muhammad's status as the leader of a large group of followers.

The principal emphasis of the Quran is on the **indivisibility of God**. Human duty is to demonstrate gratitude to God by obedience and worship – *islam* itself means "submission" – for he will judge the world on the Day of Resurrection. Islamic concepts of heaven, as reward, and hell, as punishment, are close to

---

The Amman Message

In 2004, King Abdullah published the **Amman Message**, a communiqué drawn up with Muslim authorities from around the world to declare – as its summary states – "what Islam is and what it is not, and what actions represent it and what actions do not. Its goal [is] to clarify to the modern world the true nature of Islam and the nature of true Islam." The message specifically rejects extremism as being a deviation from Islamic belief and the accompanying press release talks of Abdullah's "determination to ward off Muslim image-tarnishing, marginalization and isolation".

A subsequent convention of two hundred Muslim scholars from over fifty countries issued a three-point declaration confirming the Amman Message. This recognized diversity of opinion within Islam, prohibited the practice (common among extremists) of declaring other Muslims as apostates and clarified who (and who may not) issue religious edicts, or fatwas. For the full text, and background information, go to Ⓦwww.ammanmessage.com.

Christian ideas, although the way they are described in the Quran is very physical, even earthy. God sent the prophets to humankind in order to provide the guidance necessary to attain eternal reward.

The Quran is divided into 114 chapters, or **suras**. The first *sura* is a prayer which Muslims recite frequently: "Praise be to God, Lord of the Worlds, the Compassionate, the Merciful, King of the Day of Judgement. We worship you and seek your aid. Guide us on the straight path, the path of those on whom you have bestowed your Grace, not the path of those who incur your anger nor of those who go astray." After this, the *suras* are in approximate order of length, starting with the longest and ending with the shortest; many are patched together from passages revealed to Muhammad at different periods of his life.

According to traditional Islamic belief, the Quran is the word of God which has existed forever. It is unique, and is the miracle which Muhammad presented to the world to prove his prophethood. However, not everything the Quran reveals is comprehensible; the book itself declares that it contains "clear" verses and "obscure" verses. On occasions, it appears to contradict itself. As a result, an elaborate literature of **interpretation** of the Quran developed. Early specialists put forward the idea that some revelations were made for a particular place or time and were cancelled out by later revelations.

The Hadith

The Quran provided a basic framework for the practices and beliefs necessary for Muslims, but it didn't go into much specific detail: of 6616 verses, only eighty concern issues of conduct. For precise guidance, Muslims also look to the example and habitual practice *sunna* of the Prophet Muhammad himself, as well as his words and actions. These were remembered by those who had known him, and transmitted in the form of reports, **hadith**, handed down within the Muslim community – *hadith* is generally translated into English as "**traditions**".

Although Muhammad himself didn't claim any infallibility outside revealing the Quran, Muslims around him seem to have collected these *hadith* from a very early time. Scholars soon began categorizing them by subject. It was obvious, though, that many of the reports of what the Prophet said or did weren't authentic; tales wove their way into his legend, and some of those who transmitted reports of his doings undoubtedly invented or exaggerated them. Scholars therefore developed a science of *hadith* criticism, requiring both specific content of what the Prophet is supposed to have said or done, and, more importantly, a traceable chain of transmission back to the Companion of the Prophet who had originally seen or heard it. Biographical dictionaries – to ascertain just how reliable a transmitter was – rapidly became a distinctive feature of Arabic literature. Two particularly refined collections of *hadith* from the late ninth century are generally held to have an authority second only to that of the Quran.

The pillars of Islam

Drawn both from the Quran and the *hadith*, there are five basic religious duties every Muslim must perform.

Statement of faith

Firstly, and most simply, is the **statement of faith** (*shahada*): "I testify that there is no god but God, and that Muhammad is the Messenger of God." If you say this with sincerity, you become a Muslim.

The Islamic Calendar

The **Islamic calendar** is dated from sunset on July 15, 622 AD, the start of the *hijra* (migration) of the Prophet Muhammad from Mecca to the nearby city of Medina; the Western (Gregorian) year 2010 AD mostly coincides with the Islamic year 1431 (AH 1431). Whereas the Western calendar is solar, the Islamic one (like the Jewish) is lunar, and thus one Muslim year contains slightly over 354 days. The effect of this is that Muslim religious festivals move in a slow cycle backwards through the seasons, each one arriving about eleven days earlier, according to the Western calendar, than it did the previous year. To convert from an Islamic year number to a Western one, divide it by 1.031, then add 621 or 622 (depending on which month you're in). An easier option is to consult an online calendar, such as the one at ⓦ www.islamicfinder.org.

The names of the Islamic **months** are: Muharram, Safar, Rabia Awwal, Rabia Thaani, Jumada Awwal, Jumada Thaani, Rajab, Shaaban, Ramadan, Shawwal, Dhul Qida and Dhul Hijja. All have either 29 or 30 days, with the new month declared only when the crescent moon has been sighted.

Prayer

A Muslim must perform formal **prayer** (*salat*) five times a day. Since the day begins at sunset, the five times are sunset (*maghrib*), evening (*isha*), dawn (*fajr*), midday (*duhr*) and afternoon (*asr*), the exact times set in advance by the religious authorities. Before performing the *salat*, a Muslim must be in a state of **ritual purity**, achieved by rinsing out the mouth, sniffing water into the nostrils, washing the face, head, ears, back of the neck, feet, and lastly the hands and forearms. All mosques, big or small, have ablutions fountains adjacent for worshippers to cleanse themselves.

The faithful are summoned to prayer by the **muezzin**; in previous centuries, he would climb the minaret of the mosque and call by shouting, but almost everywhere in Jordan this has now been overtaken either by a taped call to prayer or by amplification. Nonetheless, the sound of the *adhan* (call to prayer) has a captivating beauty all its own, especially down in the echoing valleys of Amman when dozens of mosques are calling simultaneously, repeating in long, melodious strings: "God is most great! (*Allahu akbar!*) I testify that there is no god but God. (*Ashhadu an la ilaha illallah.*) I testify that Muhammad is the Messenger of God. (*Ashhadu anna Muhammadan rasulullah.*) Come to prayer! (*Hayya alas-salah!*) Come to salvation! (*Hayya alal-falah!*) God is most great! (*Allahu akbar!*)" The dawn call has another phrase added: "Prayer is better than sleep."

Once worshippers have assembled in the mosque, another call to prayer is given. Prayers are led by an **imam**, and are performed in a **ritualized cycle** facing towards Mecca without shoes on: standing with hands slightly raised, bowing, prostrating, sitting on one's haunches, and prostrating again. During the cycle, worshippers recite verses of the Quran, particularly the opening *sura*. Repetition of the cycles is completed by everyone turning and wishing peace on each other.

One way in which Islam differs from Christianity and Judaism is that it has **no priests**. The *imam* who leads the prayers has no special qualification to do so, other than enough knowledge of the Quran to enable him to recite, or perhaps some standing in the local community. Anyone may lead prayers, and there is no claim to special religious knowledge or holiness marking out an *imam* from any other Muslim.

The midday prayer on Fridays is a special congregational prayer, and Muslims are expected to attend a large mosque of assembly, where a religious or political **sermon** is also given (and generally broadcast on loudspeakers). The sermon must include a mention of the legitimate ruler – in fact, this is one of the traditional ways for a population to bestow legitimacy on a ruler. If the mosque is controlled by the government, the sermon is often used to endorse government policy; if it is independent, the Friday sermon can be used as a means to incite rebellion among the faithful. This is part of the reason why many political demonstrations in the Muslim world begin from the mosque after the midday prayer on a Friday.

Although it's preferable for men to pray together in the mosque, it's not obligatory, and you'll see many men throughout Jordan instead laying down a small **prayer mat** in their shops, or by the side of the road, to mark out a space for them to pray alone. Women almost always pray at home. Non-Muslims are permitted to enter mosques in Jordan, but only at the discretion of the officials of that particular mosque; however, you must always be dressed suitably modestly. If you're not praying, you don't have to go through any ritual ablutions.

A very common sight in Jordan is to see men holding strings of "worry beads", passing them rhythmically through their fingers in an almost unconscious action as they walk or sit quietly. The beads – *tasbih* or *subhah* – are **prayer beads**, and they always come in strings of 33 or 99, representing the 99 revealed names of God. As one passes through the fingers, the prayer is *subhanallah* ("Glory to God"); the next one is *al-hamdulillah* ("Thanks be to God"), the next *Allahu akbar* ("God is most great"), these three being repeated in a mantra until the cycle of 99 has been completed.

Alms

All Muslims who are able to do so should pay one-fortieth of their own wealth for purposes laid down in the Quran: for the poor, for those whose hearts need to be reconciled, for the freeing of slaves, those who are burdened with debts, for travellers, for the cause of God, and so on. This payment of **alms** is called *zakat*, literally "purification", and is primarily regarded as an act of worship: the recipients are less important than the giving, which is always done anonymously.

Fasting in the month of Ramadan

Ramadan is the ninth month of the Muslim year, and was the time at which Muhammad received his first revelation; it's a holy month, during which all Muslims must **fast** from dawn to sunset each day. All forms of consumption are forbidden during daylight hours, including eating, drinking and smoking, and any form of sexual contact. However, this is only the outward show of what is required: one *hadith* says, "There are many who fast all day and pray all night, but they gain nothing but hunger and sleeplessness." Ramadan is a time of spiritual cleansing.

As the Muslim calendar is lunar, Ramadan doesn't fall in a specific season each year: summer Ramadans in the Middle East, when the days are fourteen or fifteen hours long and the heat draining, can be particularly taxing, but Ramadan is an intense month at any time of year. Families get up together before dawn for a quick breakfast (many people then go back to bed for another few hours' sleep). During the day, shops, offices and public services all operate limited hours. As the afternoon draws on, people hurry home to be with their families for *iftar*, the fast-breaking meal, eaten at sunset. After dark, a hectic round of socializing over large meals often brings distant relatives together for the only time in the year. Ramadan is quieter in Jordan than, say, Egypt (where Ramadan nights involve huge, festive street parties), but nonetheless a special mood of excitement grips people all over the country. The month ends with a three-day festival, **Eid al-Fitr**, also a time for family get-togethers.

Pilgrimage

Mecca was a sacred place long before the time of Muhammad, its central feature the **Kaaba**, a fifteen-metre-high stone cube inset with a smaller, holy black stone. Islam incorporated both the Kaaba and a set of rituals involved with pagan worship at Mecca into its own set of rituals around the hajj, or **pilgrimage**, which takes place in the twelfth month, Dhul Hijja. (A lesser pilgrimage, known as the *umrah*, can be undertaken at any time of year.) Every Muslim who has the means must make the pilgrimage to Mecca at least once in his lifetime. These days, over two million descend each year on Mecca for the hajj from all over the world, the whole operation coordinated by the Saudi Ministry of Hajj.

The Kaaba, now in the central precinct of the vast Grand Mosque at Mecca, is held to have been built by Abraham and his son Ishmael on the ruins of a shrine built by Adam, the first human. Male pilgrims wear only two lengths of plain, unsewn cotton cloth (symbolizing the equality of all before God); women veil their hair but must leave their faces uncovered, to express confidence and an atmosphere of purity. Everybody circumambulates the Kaaba seven times, emulating the angels who circle the throne of God, and kisses the black stone if they can. They go to the Well of Zamzam, discovered by Ishmael, and run between two small hills, commemorating the frantic running in search of water by Hagar – Abraham's concubine and Ishmael's mother – after Abraham had left them both in the desert. One day is spent on the arid Plain of Arafat, listening to sermons, praying and standing on the Mount of Mercy. All the pilgrims go to Mina, a suburb of Mecca, and hurl stones at three pillars, symbolically stoning the Devil. The hajj ends with the four-day festival of **Eid al-Adha**, celebrated throughout the Islamic world, when all who are able slaughter a sheep to commemorate Abraham's sacrifice – he was about to kill his son but God stopped him and provided a ram instead (Jews and Christians hold that the victim was to have been Isaac, but Muslims believe it was Ishmael).

There are often parties and celebrations to welcome home those who have returned from the hajj, and in Jordan you'll sometimes see murals painted by pilgrims on the outside walls of their houses, depicting the mosque at Mecca (with the Islamic symbol of the crescent often prominent), the Kaaba and other details of what they saw and experienced on their journey.

The bedouin today

This article, by Dr Géraldine Chatelard, Research Fellow at the French Institute for the Near East (IFPO) in Jordan, is an edited version of her introduction to *Bédouins Aujourd'hui en Jordanie*, an outstanding book of photos by Nabil Boutros that was published by Amman's French Cultural Centre (@www .lecentre-jo.org) in 2008. The English translation is by Isabelle Ruben.

For centuries the **bedouin** have been in transition between a nomadic life in the arid margins and a settled, urban life. Transition and mobility are difficult notions for sedentary people to grasp, for they defy categorization. The sedentary outlook through which the world is normally perceived is so dominant that the bedouin themselves sometimes have doubts about what makes them distinctive: is it their nomadic lifestyle, their skill as herders in an arid environment, their tribal organization, or their values and morality? These questions are a reflection of the diversity of bedouin society, which is neither isolated nor separated but, rather, is dynamic and eager to harness the benefits of the modern world while preserving its values of solidarity, pride and honour.

Many of today's bedouin have transformed their spatial mobility into **social mobility**, a process which, in Jordan, began in the 1930s. First was recruitment into the armed forces and the government, then came widespread schooling. Bedouin families developed agriculture, mostly abandoning camel husbandry in favour of sheep and goats. They took advantage of modern technology – motor vehicles (particularly the water tankers that made them less dependent on natural constraints) and now mobile phones. The nomads who formerly moved seasonally across several hundred kilometres became transhumant herders living in tents for only part of the year, or sometimes not leaving their villages at all and entrusting their herds to shepherds. At the same time, a new generation has been settling in the towns, completing higher education and taking up professional careers while still maintaining strong links with their original villages and tribes – a process which has ensured the preservation of bedouin values and identity in an urban setting.

Use of space

The **bedouin tent** (known as *beit ash-sha'ar*, meaning "house of hair") is a mobile shelter with internal spaces that can be rearranged using movable partitions: transitions from exterior to interior, sunlight to shade, heat to cool are adjustable according to need. There is always a clear division between the public and private sides of the tent, usually in the form of a partition – decorated on the public side, backed by furniture (a chest, mattresses, bed coverings) on the private side.

Domestic tents are erected and maintained by the **women** of the family, or under their supervision. They make the tent from goat hair and sheep's wool, weaving strips on a horizontal loom which they then sew together. They also repair the tent regularly. In remote areas of Wadi Araba or the Hisma, single or widowed men who live alone will often choose a rock shelter or cave: a tent has little meaning without a female presence.

The symbolic function of the tent, over and above its practical aspect, is that of a space where guests can enjoy the **hospitality** and protection of the master of the house, expressed by the preparation and ritualized serving of Arabic coffee around the central hearth of the public side. This tradition is anchored in bedouin values: even when the tent has completely lost its domestic function and is erected alongside a house, it still represents the continuation of those values and thus of bedouin identity.

The domestic tent is adapted to the social norms that regulate relations between men and women and which allow **family honour** to be preserved. However, there are no areas that are reserved exclusively for either sex. Movement between the tent's public and private spaces depends on whether only close family, or outsiders, are present. The basic rule is that the women leave the reception area when guests are present who are not close family members. However, the matriarch of the family will always make it her duty to receive visitors in the reception area if her husband is absent. In any case, the women can listen to conversation from the private side of the tent and take a peek through the weave of the partition – a common practice when marriage negotiations are being discussed between men.

Associations with the tent remain strong, even in **houses** (which most bedouin own), where the reception area – clearly separated from family space – is large and and has a fireplace to serve as a hearth as well as thick curtains recalling the tent's partitions. The house's interior is often extended outside, with a tent erected nearby.

Today, the poorest bedouin live on the outskirts of towns, or in the most arid and rocky zones overlooking the Dead Sea, the Jordan Valley and the Wadi Araba. These last real nomads can be recognized by their tents of sewn sack-cloth, which is cheaper than woven goat hair.

Figures of authority

Photographs of **figures of authority** are often on display in reception tents and salons, cars and offices. Their prominence is a way of demonstrating to whom the owner acknowledges authority – and, equally, from whom the owner's authority originates. Respect and authority are intimately linked values, above all with regard to the respect universally shown to Islam.

Respect for authority is one of the fundamentals of bedouin society, and of Arab society in general. The head of the family is required to make decisions concerning his wife and children, yet bedouin families are only moderately patriarchal: wives, particularly as they get older, take active part in family decisions. Bedouin men recognize the importance of **female responsibility** in a traditional lifestyle and many encourage their daughters in academic study and professional careers. Nevertheless, the father of the family always retains the right of absolute veto on personal choices. Grandfather's photo on display reminds everyone of the respect due to him, but also shows that his son – now the head of the family – is authorized to exercise domestic authority in his place.

At a higher social level, heads of families recognize the authority of a man to whom they are all related. This individual – generally given the title "**sheikh**" – has to represent his kinship group amongst other groups (for example, when there are conflicts to resolve) or to outside institutions. He is a mediator, and his authority does not replace that of the father of the family, who remains master of his own decisions. Adherence by family heads to collective action is not a foregone conclusion.

Codes of honour

A sense of **honour** is an essential masculine quality for the bedouin, to the extent that if a man loses his honour, he also loses his right to participate fully in bedouin society. This explains the efforts that every man makes to maintain and increase his honour, and that of his tribe. The welcome of guests has resisted changes in lifestyle: a man of honour must be **generous** – excessively so if he can afford it.

He must also be generous with his time – listening to the complaints of members of the tribe and others and helping them get a job or a place at university, assisting with administrative dealings, mediating between individuals or families in conflict. Every bedouin man must respond to a request for assistance even if he does not have the means to do so. This is why bedouin are sometimes more apt to "say" than to "do", which upsets only those who don't understand their code of honour.

The behaviour of **women** is also an essential part of family and tribal honour: virtue, high morals and respect for the rules of separation between men and women are obligatory. Following these rules does not imply meekness or lack of character. Many strong female personalities in bedouin society enjoy broad respect because they follow the code of honour unfailingly.

Transmissions

Visit a bedouin village and you might have the impression that **children** have free rein, with very few constraints placed on them. In fact, they are living an education in which they learn limits for themselves and make the direct experience of pain and danger – though within a framework: if the parents are absent, another member of the community is almost certainly nearby and can exercise authority. It is a tough education with no pampering, where from their earliest years children become accustomed to the realities that will be their adult lives, including familiarity with livestock and the responsibilities of pastoral and domestic work.

Children used to be educated by spending time with adults. Nowadays, traditional methods of transference of knowledge and behaviour compete with widespread **schooling**. Not many bedouin families choose a transhumant life for their children when they can send them to school instead. Even the poorest families time their seasonal movements to match the school calendar. It is not unusual to meet young women or men at university whose illiterate parents still live in a tent.

Yet schooling creates a distancing from **traditional knowledge**. Tribal history and the immensely rich oral literature of the bedouin that has been transmitted for generations have lost out to new media. Knowledge of animal husbandry, of herbal remedies for both humans and animals, of weaving techniques, of effective management of water resources are not being passed on. While people in wealthy, urbanized countries are rediscovering the importance of traditional knowledge, entire swathes of bedouin culture and tradition are disappearing largely unregarded. The staged bedouin encounters offered by tour operators in the theme park that Wadi Rum has become are a pale reflection of genuine bedouin culture.

There is no need to mourn the loss of a difficult way of life (which most of those still living it aspire to leave). But one can reflect, with the bedouin themselves, on ways of validating and preserving their knowledge and culture.

By Dr Géraldine Chatelard

Books

I t can be difficult to find **books** focused on Jordan. Millions of words have been written about Palestine, Israel, Lebanon, Egypt and Syria, but Jordan is all too often relegated to patchy later chapters or mentions in passing. If you fancy going direct to English-language **publishers** specializing in the Middle East, start with Al-Saqi (@www.saqibooks.com), Garnet/Ithaca (@www.ithacapress .co.uk), Interlink (@www.interlinkbooks.com), Stacey International (@www .stacey-international.co.uk) and I.B.Tauris (@www.ibtauris.com). The selection of recommendations below is a personal one, and necessarily omits much.

Literature

Diana Abu-Jaber *Arabian Jazz*. Feisty, funny and touching first novel from Abu-Jaber, a Jordanian-American, about the life and daughters of a Jordanian widower transplanted to a poor community in upstate New York.

Inea Bushnaq (ed) *Arab Folktales*. Delightful collection of translated tales, including a section of bedouin stories entitled "Tales Told In Houses Made of Hair".

Mahmoud Darwish *Memory for Forgetfulness: August, Beirut, 1982*. Startling prose-poems, written as the Israeli army was laying siege to the city. Darwish (1942–2008) was the Arab world's best-loved modern poet; this, though, is perhaps the easiest way into his extraordinarily visceral and moving style.

Fadia Faqir *My Name is Salma*. Affecting novel from this accomplished Jordanian-British writer, focusing on a young Middle Eastern asylum-seeker in England who is running from her vengeful family after giving birth out of wedlock. Themes of alienation and cultural displacement – alongside a fine evocation of an outsider's view of British society – are woven skilfully through a narrative that shifts seamlessly between the present and the past.

Fadia Faqir *Pillars of Salt*. Exceptionally skilful and lyrical novel set in the cities and countryside of mandate-period Jordan, which manages to champion both the rights of women and the traditional values of bedouin culture. Two women, one from the city, the other from a bedouin tribe, end up in a mental hospital after abuse at the hands of their male relatives; the fluid and compelling story traces the elements of their resistance to domination.

Marguerite van Gelder-malsen *Married to a Bedouin*. Wonderful insight into bedouin life by this remarkable New Zealander, who visited Petra on holiday in 1978, fell in love with a local souvenir-seller, and stayed to marry him and raise a family. Her fascinating tales of learning how to adjust to bedouin society and how she built the life she wanted are told with humour and compassion.

Ghassan Kanafani *Men in the Sun*. Perhaps the best-known modern Arabic short story, about three men journeying across the desert from Amman to Kuwait. Kanafani was a Palestinian activist (and was assassinated at the age of 36), but his stories, far from being political diatribes, are tender, lyrical and superbly plotted.

T.E. Lawrence *The Seven Pillars of Wisdom*. Doorstop classic, valuable for being the only firsthand account of the Arab Revolt of 1917–18, which swept across Jordanian territory. Otherwise, it's really rather dull, with Lawrence's day-by-day recounting of battles, discussions, fights and intrigues quickly wearing thin.

Abd al-Rahman Munif *Story of a City: A Childhood in Amman.* Rambling tales of life in Amman in the 1940s, recalling the city passing from a period of bucolic innocence through World War II and the tragic loss of Palestine. A gentle memoir, padded out with digressions and family tales.

Ibrahim Nasrallah *Prairies of Fever.* Intense postmodern novel by a leading Jordanian journalist. The protagonist, a young teacher hired to work in a remote part of the Arabian

peninsula, is pronounced dead on page one; from then on, his struggle to keep a grip on his life shifts from past to future, from reality to halluci-nation, from human to animal.

Queen Noor *Leap of Faith: Memoirs of an Unexpected Life.* A readable and inspiring account of Noor's extraor-dinary life, from her American upbringing to her long-lasting marriage with the late King Hussein.

Adaia and Abraham Shumsky *A Bridge across the Jordan.* Engaging tale based on personal memoirs of the friendship that developed between a Jewish master carpenter from Jerusalem and Emir Abdullah of Transjordan, when the former was invited to Amman in 1937 to work at the Royal Palace.

History and society

Alan George *Jordan: Living in the Crossfire.* Remarkable book that combines acute political analysis with reportage-style interviews with Jordanians from a range of social backgrounds to produce a candid picture of life in contemporary Jordan.

Albert Hourani *A History of the Arab Peoples.* Hourani's wonderfully articulate and highly erudite prose draws threads through centuries of history, yet remains easily readable.

Terry Jones and Alan Ereira *Crusades.* If you don't know anything about the Crusades, start here. Funny, sharp and only two hundred pages long, it covers everybody and every-thing, with at least one interesting digression on every page.

Amin Maalouf *The Crusades through Arab Eyes.* Fascinating take on all the noble stories of valiant crusading normally touted in the West. Drawing on the extensive chronicles

kept by Arab historians at the time, Maalouf paints a picture of a civilized Arab society suddenly having to face the violent onslaught of a bunch of European barbarians. Superbly readable.

Ghazi bin Muhammad *The Tribes of Jordan.* Knowledgeable account of the nature of tribal society at the turn of the twenty-first century by a former royal adviser for Tribal Affairs, giving valuable insight into the bedouin foundation of Jordanian society.

Philip Robins *A History of Jordan.* An excellent history, incisive and intelligent, which brings the story through to the first years of King Abdullah II's reign.

Kamal Salibi *The Modern History of Jordan.* An outstanding account of the founding and development of the country from the Arab Revolt to the early 1990s, by this leading Lebanese historian.

Islam

Karen Armstrong *The Battle for God.* Sympathetic investigation of fundamentalism in Judaism, Christianity and Islam, explaining the roots, motivations and mindset of religious extremism. Armstrong's other works, all similarly brilliant, include *A History of God*, *A History of Jerusalem* and *Islam: A Short History*.

John L. Esposito *Islam: The Straight Path.* The best-written and most intelligent handbook to what Islam means, where it came from and where it seems to be going.

Maxime Rodinson *Muhammad.* Superbly researched secular account of the life and works of the Prophet, exploding many myths and giving Islam the kind of intelligible, human face it lacks in much Western writing. Unputdownable.

Coffee-table books

Raouf Sa'd Abujaber & Felicity Cobbing *Beyond the River: Ottoman Transjordan in Original Photographs.* An absorbing collection of archive images, including the first-ever photos of Petra (dated 1852), interspersed with knowledgeable accounts of Victorian exploration.

James Nicholson *The Hejaz Railway.* Lavish tome devoted to the history of the famous Damascus–Medina railway built by the Ottomans a century ago. Filled with fascinating photographs, detailed maps and blow-by-blow accounts of the railway's operation and eventual demise.

Michele Piccirillo *The Mosaics of Jordan.* Eminently learned explication of every mosaic to have been uncovered in Jordan (as of the early 1990s), with large, clear photographs and massive historical detail. A lavish volume, with a JD100 price tag to match.

Jane Taylor *Petra and the Lost Kingdom of the Nabataeans.* An infectiously enthusiastic evocation of the history of Petra and wider Nabatean society, liberally scattered throughout with the author's beautiful photographs. Don't be put off by its coffee-table format: this is a work as appealing intellectually as visually, penetrating the myths surrounding the Nabateans with clarity and providing unparalleled perspective for a visit to their capital.

Jane Taylor *Jordan: Images from the Air.* Beautiful, large-format book of aerial photographs of Jordan, taken in all seasons and at numerous destinations. The images are stunning, given added force by the authoritative accompanying text.

Travel

Michael Asher *The Last of the Bedu.* Engrossing tales of epic desert travel, seeking to illuminate the myths surrounding bedouin culture across the whole Middle East from Syria to Oman to Sudan. A disappointingly skimpy look at the Bdul and Howeitat of Jordan doesn't detract from the author's uniquely insightful empathy with his subject.

Gertrude Bell *The Desert and the Sown.* Hard-to-read account of a 1905 journey from Jerusalem to Antioch. Although concentrating on the more populated and engaging lands in Syria, the book contains some interesting vignettes from Transjordan.

John Lewis Burckhardt *Travels in Syria and the Holy Land.* Reprint of the original 1822 tome, describing a massive jaunt around the Levant by a pioneer traveller and explorer, who, partway through his journey, stumbled upon Petra. His style is surprisingly and refreshingly upbeat, bringing the wildness of Transjordan in this period very much to life.

Annie Caulfield *Kingdom of the Film-Stars.* A light, chatty read, as the author takes in the sights of Jordan against the background of her falling in love with a Jordanian man.

Jonathan Raban *Arabia.* Engaging and deeply insightful tales of the Gulf States, Yemen, Egypt and Jordan in 1978 at the height of oil wealth, and before the Lebanese civil war and attempts at peace with Israel had had much impact on the Arab world. Much more than mere travelogue, the book is perceptive, fluently written and sympathetic, as relevant today as when it first appeared.

Kathryn Tidrick *Heart Beguiling Araby.* Entertaining analysis of the enduring fascination of the English for Arabia over the centuries, focused on a detailed trawl through the life and works of Burton, Palgrave, Blunt and Doughty, plus sections on the early explorers and on Lawrence and twentieth-century Arabists.

Specialist guides

Ian J. Andrews *The Birds of the Hashemite Kingdom of Jordan.* The best ornithological field guide from a longtime leader of birdwatching tours to Jordan. Privately published by the author (⊛www.andrewsi. freeserve.co.uk) and also available in Jordan.

Tony Howard *Treks and Climbs in Wadi Rum, Jordan.* Written by a professional climber with years of experience in Rum, and containing detailed rock-face plans and precise descriptions of equipment-assisted ascents, this is an invaluable full-length guide for dedicated pros.

G. Lankester Harding *The Antiquities of Jordan.* Written in 1959 by the then British director of the Department of Antiquities. The histories of the different sites are engagingly well written, and photographs often show that ancient sites have crumbled faster in the last few decades than in the previous few centuries.

Jarir Maani *Field Guide to Jordan.* Superb full-colour pocket-sized field guide to Jordan's natural environment, with detailed notes – and outstanding photographs – of every flower, bird, animal and insect listed. Also with useful sections on history, geology and archeology. Available widely in Jordan and at ⊛www.fieldguidetojordan.com.

Rosalyn Maqsood *Petra: A Travellers' Guide.* Vivid and entertaining guide to Petra, featuring detailed walking tours and a comprehensive history, with much careful detail devoted to the religious and spiritual culture of the place.

Sue Rollin and Jane Streetly *Blue Guide: Jordan.* Exhaustive survey of Jordan's archeological sites.

Isabelle Ruben *Field Guide to the Plants and Animals of Petra.* Full-colour field guide to the mammals, birds, reptiles and insects to be seen at Petra, with detailed notes on each and informative text on the medicinal uses of plants, herbs and flowers. Available at ⓦwww.petranationaltrust.org.

🏃 **Di Taylor and Tony Howard** *Jordan: Walks, Treks, Caves, Climbs and Canyons.* Published in the US as *Walking in Jordan.* Outstanding selection of more than a hundred walking routes across the country, updated in a 2008 edition. Taylor and Howard have been climbing and

trekking in Jordan since 1984, making this an invaluable companion if you're planning to head off the beaten track and explore independently.

Jane Taylor *Petra.* Accomplished, well-written work on the history and individual sites of Petra, with some engaging tales and magnificent photos. Jane Taylor is a longtime resident of Jordan and writes with grace and authority.

Cuisine

🏃 **Cecil Hourani** *Jordan – The Land and the Table.* Slim volume that is unique for examining the centrality of food to the different elements within Jordanian society, including (unusually) the Armenians, Chechens and Circassians. Fascinating recipes for rarely seen dishes are interspersed with insightful accounts of culture and agriculture.

Tess Mallos *The Complete Middle East Cookbook.* Top-quality collection of recipes from Greece to

Afghanistan that is perhaps the only cookbook in the world to enthuse over Jordanian cuisine. All your favourite *mezze* are here, plus a recipe for *mensaf.*

Claudia Roden *A New Book of Middle Eastern Food.* Food as cultural history; perhaps the most absorbing cookbook ever written and invaluable for getting a handle on the importance of food to Arab and Middle Eastern societies.

Language

Language

Arabic

M any people in Jordan are fluent in English, and many more have a working knowledge. However, plain communication isn't necessarily the only consideration. Jordanian culture is deeply rooted in the verbal complexities of the **Arabic** language, and being able to exchange pleasantries in Arabic, or offer the appropriate response to an Arabic greeting, will endear you to people more than anything else. The most halting "*assalaamu alaykoom*" is likely to provoke beams of joy and cries of "You speak Arabic better than I do!"

Arabic is phenomenally hard for an English-speaker to learn. There are virtually no familiar points of contact between the two languages: the script is written in cursive from right to left; there's a host of often guttural sounds which take much vocal contortion to master; and the grammar, founded on utterly different principles from English, is proclaimed as one of the most pedantic in the world.

Briefly, the three forms of Arabic are:

• **Classical** – the language of the Quran, with many words and forms which are now obsolete.

• **Modern Standard** (*fuss-ha*) – the written language of books and newspapers, and the Arabic spoken in news broadcasts and on formal occasions. Identical throughout the Arab world and understandable from Morocco to Oman. Although most people can read *fuss-ha*, nobody uses it in everyday life and few ordinary people can speak it.

• **Colloquial** (*aamayya*) – umbrella term for the many dialects of spoken Arabic. In Jordan, as in all other Arabic-speaking countries, the colloquial language has no proper written form. Pronunciation varies from district to district and, furthermore, the vocabulary and verb forms of Jordanian Arabic can be markedly different from the related Palestinian, Syrian and Iraqi dialects. Further afield, the Arabic spoken in Morocco is a foreign language to Jordanians, who find it more or less incomprehensible. Egyptian Arabic is a lingua franca, understandable throughout the Arab world because of the prevalence of movies and TV soap operas emanating from Cairo.

Very few decent Jordanian Arabic **phrasebooks** exist; your best bet is the excellent **teach-yourself course** *Colloquial Arabic (Levantine)* by Leslie McLoughlin. The clearest introduction to writing and **reading Arabic script** is *The Arabic Alphabet* by Nicholas Awde and Putros Samano, a slim volume that is invaluable for getting a handle on how the language works.

Pronunciation

Throughout this book, Arabic has been transliterated using a common-sense what-you-see-is-what-you-say system. However, Arabic vowel-sounds in particular often cannot be rendered accurately in English letters, and stress patterns are a minefield – the only way to pick them up is to mimic a native speaker. The following are four of the most difficult common sounds:

kh represents the throaty rasp at the end of the Scottish "loch".

gh is the same sound as *kh*, but voiced: it sounds like the gargled French "r".

q represents a very guttural *k* sound made far back in the throat; it approximates to the sound you might make when imitating the glugging of a wine bottle being emptied. In some Palestinian accents this becomes an unsounded glottal stop (*baqlawa* becomes *ba'lawa*), while in bedouin areas many people change it into a straightforward hard *g* sound (*baqlawa* becomes *baglawa*).

aa is especially tricky: constrict your throat muscles tightly like you're about to retch, open your mouth wide and make a strangulated "aaah" sound. Ridiculous as it feels, this is about as close as an English-speaker can get, and won't make Jordanians laugh. To keep things simple, the sound hasn't always been transliterated (it stands at the beginning of "Amman", for instance).

In this book, *ay* has been written where the Arabic rhymes roughly with "say", except where common usage dictates otherwise. Arabic *f* and *s* are always soft ('Muslim' not 'Muzlim'; 'Islam' not 'Izlam'), and *r* is heavily trilled. Generally pronounce an *h* sound: *ahlan* (welcome) features a clear and definite exhalation of breath, as does *mneeh* (happy). Where two consonants fall together, pronounce them both: *hamam* means "pigeon" but *hammam* means "bathroom". The subtleties between the two different kinds of *s*, *t*, *d*, *h* and *th* are too rarefied to get into here.

Useful words and phrases

Where the form of a word or phrase differs depending on whether the speaker is male or female, we've shown this with (m) and (f): to say "I'm sorry", a man says "*mitaasef*", a woman "*mitaasfeh*". Where the form differs depending on who you're speaking to, we've shown the two separated by a slash, with the form for addressing a man first, thus: "*allah yaafeek/yaafeeki* (to a woman)". Note also that all words and phrases ending -*ak* are for addressing a man; if you're addressing a woman, substitute -*ik*.

Greetings are often said in long strings, barely waiting for a response, while pumping your interlocutor's hand, and – if you're the same sex – looking him/her in the eyes. Old friends might also indulge in a complex ritual of double and triple kisses on both cheeks, but as a foreigner you won't be roped into this.

Greetings		
assalaamu alaykoom	peace be upon you (all-purpose greeting in any situation, formal or informal)	
sabahl-khayr	good morning (literally, "morning of abundance")	
masa il-khayr	good afternoon/ evening	
shoo akhbarak?	what's your news?	
keefak?	how are you?	
keef halak? (also keef il-hal?)	how's your status?	
keef sahtak?	how's your health?	
keef shughulak?	how's your work?	
keef al-awlad?	how are the kids?	
keef hal ahlak?	how's the family?	
al-afyeh	wellbeing/good health	
gawak	your strength (only in rural dialects)	
shlawnak?	what's your colour? (ie "how are you?")	

marhaba	hello (said by one already settled to someone arriving from outside)
ahlan	welcome (generally formal)
salaam	hi
tisbah (tisbahi to a woman) ala-khayr	good night
ma assalaameh	goodbye (literally, "go with peace")

Responses to greetings

wa alaykoom assalaam	and upon you be peace (the response to assalaamu alaykoom)
ahlan feek or beek (ahlan feeki or beeki to a woman)	it's you who are welcome (the response to ahlan)
marhabtayn or ahlayn	two hellos/welcomes [back to you]; responses to marhaba
al-hamdulillah	thank God (all-purpose response to any of the variations on "how are you?"; covers a range of moods from "everything's great!" to "can't complain" or even "not so good really")
hala	no translation; simply an acknowledgment of having been greeted
mneeh (m)/ mneeha (f)	I'm well
(kulshee) kwayyis (m) /kwayyseh (f)	(everything's) good
(kulshee) tamam	(everything's) perfect
tayyib (m)/taybeh (f)	I'm doing fine
maashi il-hal	I'm OK
allah yaafeek/ yaafeeki (to a woman)	May God give you health
sabahn-noor	morning of light (response to sabahil-khayr)

masa en-noor	afternoon/evening of light (response to masa il-khayr)
wa inta/inti (to a woman) min ahlo	the response to tisbah/ tisbahi ala-khayr
allah ysalmak	God keep you safe (the response to ma assalaameh)

Basic terms

naam	yes
leh	no
maashi	OK
shukran	thank you
afwan	you're welcome
minfadlak	please
afwan; or lao samaht (samahti to a woman)	excuse me; both terms are used to attract someone's attention; afwan is also a casual apology (eg if you bump into someone)
mitaasef (m) /mitaasfeh (f)	I'm sorry
insha'allah	hopefully, God willing
aysh ismak?	what's your name?
ismi...	my name is...
btihki ingleezee?	do you speak English?
ana biritanee/irlandee	I'm British/Irish
amerkanee	American
canadee	Canadian
ostraalee	Australian
noozeelandee	New Zealand
(if you're a woman, add -yyeh to the above)	
mabahki/mabafham arabee	I don't speak/ understand Arabic
ana bafham shwayyet arabee	I understand a little Arabic
ana mish fahem (m) /fahmeh (f)	I don't understand
shoo manato bil ingleezee?	what's the meaning of that in English?
mumkin, tooktoobliyaha lao samaht?	could you write it for me, please?

maalesh	never mind/forget it/it's OK/don't worry
mafee mushkelah	no problem
mittel ma biddak	as you like
ana khamseh wa-ashreen senneh	I'm 25 years old
ana (mish) mitjowez (m)/mitjowzeh (f)	I'm (not) married
rah nitjowez essenneh al-jay	we're getting married next year
mabrook!	congratulations!
allah ybarrak feek (feeki to a woman)	God bless you; the response to *mabrook*, but also used widely to acknowledge someone's kindness to you
maandi awlad	I have no children
aandi walad/ waladayn /thalaath awlad	I have 1/2/3 children
yalla	let's go
ma dakhalak	it's none of your business
eem eedak!	get your hands off me!
utruknee le-halee!	leave me alone!
rooh	go away
mabaaraf	I don't know
mabagdar (aamalo)	I can't (do that)
shwayy-shwayy	slowly
bsooraa	quickly
hela	immediately
khalas	enough/finished/stop it
mish mumkin	it's impossible
ana taaban (m) /taabaneh (f)	I'm tired
ana mareed (m) /mareedeh (f)	I'm unwell
khuthni ala al-doktoor	get me to a doctor

Directions and travel

shmal/ymeen /dooghri	left/right/straight on
gareeb/baeed	near/far
hawn/hunak	here/there

wayn...	where is...
funduq Petra?	the Hotel Petra?
al-mujemma al-bussat?	the bus station?
al-mahattat al-sikkat al-hadeed?	the train station?
agrab mawqaf lal-servees?	the nearest serveece stop?
maktab al-bareed?	the post office?
makhfar al-shurtah?	the police station?
al-bank?	the bank?
imta bitrik awwal /akher bus lal Amman?	when does the first /last bus leave for Amman?
hadal-bus birooh ala Jerash?	does this bus go to Jerash?

Banks, shops and hotels

masari	money or cash
maftooh/msekker	open/closed
imta rah yiftah?	when will it be open?
biddi asruf...	I want to change...
dollarat	dollars
masari ingleeziyyeh	British pounds
shikaat siyahiyyeh	traveller's cheques
kam dinaar rah aakhoud?	how many JDs will I get?
fee comishon?	is there a commission?
andak Jordan Times?	do you have the Jordan Times?
biddi...	I want...
ishi thaani	something else
ahsan min hada	better than this
arkhas/zay hada	cheaper/like this
kbir/zgheer	a big/small one
akbar/azghar	a bigger/smaller one
gadaysh hada?	how much is it?
mabiddi hada	I don't want this
ktir ghali	it's too expensive
andak ghurfeh fadiyyeh?	do you have a room free?
le-shakhs wahad	for one person
le-shakhsayn	for two people
le-thalaath ashkhas	for three people
bagdar ashouf al-ghurfeh?	can I see the room?
fee...	is there...
balconeh?	a balcony?

takht mizwej?	a double bed?
my sukhneh?	hot water?
hammam bil-ghurfeh?	an en-suite bathroom?
marwaha?	a fan?
hada mish nutheef, ferjeenee wahad thaani	it's not clean, show me another one
fee hammam hawn?	is there a toilet here?
gadaysh al-layleh?	how much for one night?

Numbers

Note that, unlike words, numbers are written from left to right.

sifr	·	zero
wahad	١	one
ithnayn	٢	two
thalaatheh	٣	three
arbaa	٤	four
khamseh	٥	five
sitteh	٦	six
sabaa	٧	seven
thamanyeh	٨	eight
tisaa	٩	nine
ashra	١·	ten
hidash	١١	eleven
ithnash	١٢	twelve
thalaatash	١٣	thirteen
arbatash	١٤	fourteen
khamstash	١٥	fifteen
sittash	١٦	sixteen
sabatash	١٧	seventeen
thamantash	١٨	eighteen
tisatash	١٩	nineteen
ashreen	٢·	twenty
wahad wa-ashreen	٢١	twenty-one
thalatheen	٣·	thirty
arbaeen	٤·	forty
khamseen	٥·	fifty
sitteen	٦·	sixty
sabaeen	٧·	seventy
thamaneen	٨·	eighty
tisaeen	٩·	ninety
miyyeh	١··	a hundred
miyyeh wa-wahad	١·١	a hundred and one

miyyeh wa-sitteh wa-ashreen	١٢٦	126
meetayn	٢··	two hundred
thalaath miyyeh	٣··	three hundred
elf	١···	one thousand
elfayn	٢···	two thousand
arbaat alaaf wa-khamesmiyyeh wa-arbaa wa-tisaeen	٤٥٩٤	4594
milyon		million
rube		one quarter
nuss		one half

Telling the time

gadaysh se'aa?	what time is it?
se'aa ashra	it's ten o'clock
ashra wa-khamseh	10.05
ashra wa-ashra	10.10
ashra wa-rube	10.15
ashra wa-toolt	10.20
ashra wa-nuss illa-khamseh	10.25
ashra wa-nuss	10.30
ashra wa-nuss wa-khamseh	10.35
hidash illa-toolt	10.40
hidash illa-rube	10.45
hidash illa-ashra	10.50
hidash illa-khamseh	10.55

Days and months

yom	day
layl	night
isbooa	week
shahr	month
senneh	year
imbaarih	yesterday
al-yom	today
bukra	tomorrow
essubbeh	this morning
baad edduhr	this afternoon
al-messa	this evening
al-layleh	tonight
bukra bil-layl	tomorrow night
essebt	Saturday
al-ahad	Sunday
al-ithnayn	Monday

al-thalaatha	Tuesday	ayyar	May
al-arbaa	Wednesday	huzayran	June
al-khamees	Thursday	tamooz	July
al-juma	Friday	aab	August
kanoon thaani	January	aylool	September
shbaat	February	tishreen awwal	October
athaar	March	tishreen thaani	November
nisaan	April	kanoon awwal	December

Food and drink glossary

L

LANGUAGE | A food and drink glossary

Basic stomach-fillers

khubez	flat, round bread
falafel	spiced chickpea mixture, deep-fried; stuffed into *khubez* with salad to make a *sandweesh* (sandwich)
shwarma	shreds of lamb or chicken in *khubez*
fuul	spiced fava beans, mashed with lemon juice, olive oil and chopped chillis; side dishes include raw onion (*basal*), fresh mint and/or pickled vegetables
fuul masri	blander Egyptian-style *fuul*; without chilli but served with a dollop of *tahini* instead
hummus	dip of chickpeas mashed with *tahini*, lemon juice, garlic and olive oil
manaqeesh zaatar	small round of dough sprinkled with olive oil and *zaatar* (a mixture of dried thyme, marjoram, salt and sesame seeds), and baked until crispy
batatas	potatoes; by extension, French fries

tahini	sesame-seed paste
rooz	rice

Restaurant appetizers (*mezze*)

shorba(t addas)	(lentil) soup
s'laata	salad; chopped tomato and cucumber
tabbouleh	parsley and tomato salad with cracked wheat
fattoush	Lebanese salad with chopped parsley and squares of crispy fried bread
baba ghanouj	dip made from roasted mashed aubergine
moutabbel	*baba ghanouj* with added *tahini*
labneh	thick-set yoghurt, similar to sour cream
shanklish	crumbly goat's cheese with tomato
warag aynab	stuffed vine leaves
kibbeh	ovals of spiced minced meat and cracked wheat
sujuk	fried spicy mini-sausages
mahshi	"stuffed"; by extension, a selection of stuffed vegetables such as peppers and aubergines
makdoos	pickled aubergine

The main course

mensaf	boiled lamb or mutton on rice with a tangy yoghurt-based sauce, pine nuts and spices
musakhan	chicken steamed with onions, sumac (a lemon-flavoured berry) and pine nuts, served on flat bread
magloobeh	literally "upside-down": chicken on steamed rice with grilled vegetables
(nuss) farooj	(half-)chicken; usually spit-roasted
kebab	pieces of lamb or chicken char-grilled on a skewer with onions and tomatoes
kebab halaby	spiced minced meat char-grilled
shish tawook	chicken kebab
fatteh	spiced meat or chicken baked with rice, hummus, pine nuts, yoghurt or bread
mulukhayyeh	lamb or chicken stewed with spinach-like greens
fasooliyeh	bean stew, often in meat broth
mujeddrah	rice and lentils with onions
Daoud Pasha	meatballs stewed with onions and tomatoes
lahmeh	meat
djaj	chicken-meat
kharouf	mutton or lamb
khanzir	pork
kibdeh	liver
kelaawy	kidney
samak	fish
khoodar	vegetables
zayt	oil
meleh	salt
filfil	pepper

Arabic sweets (halawiyyat)

k'naffy	shredded-wheat squares filled with goat's cheese, smothered in hot honey syrup
baglawa	layered flaky pastry with nuts
gatayyif	pancakes filled with nuts and drenched in syrup
ftayer	triangles of flaky pastry with different fillings
hareeseh	syrupy almond and semolina cake
muhallabiyyeh	rose-scented almond cream pudding
Umm Ali	corn cake soaked in milk, sugar, raisins, coconut and cinnamon, served hot
maamoul	rose-scented biscuits with dates or nuts
barazik	thin sesame biscuits
awameh	syrup-coated deep-fried balls of dough
asabya zaynab	syrupy figs
mushabbak	crunchy honey-coated pastries
karabeedj halaby	sugar-coated curlies
rooz b'laban	rice pudding with yoghurt
halwa	dense, flaky sweet made from sesame

Drinks (mashroobat)

my	water
gahweh	coffee
shy	tea
naana/yansoon	mint/fennel (tea)
zaatar/helbeh	thyme/fenugreek (tea)
marrameeya	sage (tea)
babbohnidj	camomile (tea)
sahleb	thick, sweet, milky winter drink
haleeb	milk
tamarhindi	tamarind drink

kharroub	carob drink
soos	liquorice-root drink
luz	sweet almond-milk
aseer/koktayl	juice/juice cocktail

Fruits (*fawakeh*)

mooz	banana
boordan	orange
tfah	apple
njas	pear
grayfroot	grapefruit
jezer	carrot
manga	mango
jowaffah	guava
dourrag	peach
limoon	lemon (also drink)
aynab	grapes
karaz	cherries
rummaan	pomegranate
mishmish	apricot
teen	fig

battikh	watermelon
shimmam	melon
balah	crunchy unripe dates
tamar	soft ripe dates

Nuts, seeds and simple provisions

foustoug	peanuts
foustoug halaby	pistachios
boondoog	hazelnuts
luz	almonds
kashoo	cashews
bizr	dry-roasted seeds
zbeeb	raisins
bayd	eggs
zaytoon	olives
jibneh	cheese
laban	yoghurt
zabadi	high-fat yoghurt with cream
zibdeh	butter
asal	honey
marrabeh	jam

Glossary

The first list below is a glossary of Arabic terms in common usage in Jordan. Common alternative spellings, as well as singulars and plurals, are given where appropriate in brackets. Afterwards is a list of English terms used in the guide to describe features of architecture.

Arabic terms

abu Literally "Father of" – used as a familiar term of respect in conjunction with the name of the man's eldest son, as in "Abu Muhammad".

ain (*ayn, ein*) Spring.

argileh (*arjileh, narjileh, nargileh*) Floor-standing water-pipe designed to let the smoke from the tobacco – which is kept smouldering by small coals – cool before being inhaled through a chamber of water. The sound of the smoke bubbling through the water gives the pipe its common name in Jordan of "hubbly-bubbly".

bab Gate or door.

badia Jordan's desert areas.

bahr Sea.

balad Nation or city.

baladi Countryfied, rural.

Balqa (Balka, Balga) The fertile hill-country around Salt, west of Amman.

bani (*beni*) Tribe.

bayt (*beit, bait*; pl. *byoot*) House.

bedouin (also *bedu*) Generally refers to nomadic or semi-nomadic people who live in desert areas within a tribal social structure. Some Jordanian bedouin tribes, however, have long been settled in towns and cities and, although taking pride in their bedouin culture and ancestry, are indistinguishable in dress and lifestyle from urbanized Jordanians.

bir (*beer*) Well.

birkeh (*birka, birket*) Reservoir, pool, lake.

burj Tower.

daraj Flight of steps.

darb Path or way – "Darb al-Hajj" is the ancient pilgrimage route from Damascus to Mecca, following the present Desert Highway.

dayr (*deir*) Literally monastery or convent; by extension, a catch-all term for any ancient ruin of unknown usage.

diwan Formal architectural space, not necessarily within a house, intended for tribal discussions.

duwaar Circle (ie traffic intersection).

fellaheen (*fellahin*; sing. *fellah*) Settled peasant farmers.

ghor "Sunken land", ie the Jordan Valley.

hajj (*haj, hadj*; f. *hajjeh*) The holy Muslim pilgrimage to Mecca and Medina; by extension, a title of respect, either for one who has literally made the pilgrimage, or – more commonly – simply for one who is of advancing years and thus deserving of honourable treatment.

hamad Stony desert pavement.

hammam (pl. *hammamat*) Turkish steambath; bathroom or toilet; or a natural hot spring.

harra Rocky desert.

Hawran (Hauran) The basalt desert plains around Mafraq.

imam Prayer leader of a mosque, cleric.

iwan (*liwan*) Arched reception area at one end of a courtyard in traditional Arab architecture.

jamia "Place of assembly", ie a large, congregational mosque.

Jawlan Arabic equivalent for the Hebrew Golan.

jebel (*jabal*; pl. *jibal*) Hill or mountain.

jellabiyyeh Ankle-length outer robe worn by men.

jissr Bridge.

keffiyeh (*quffiyeh*, *kafiya*, etc) Patterned headscarf worn by men.

khirbet Ruin.

k'neeseh Church.

manara Minaret, the tower attached to a mosque, from which the call to prayer sounds.

masjid "Place of prostration", ie a small, everyday mosque.

maydan (*midan*) Public square, or traffic intersection.

mihrab Niche in the wall of a mosque indicating the direction of Mecca, and thus direction of prayer.

minbar Pulpit in a mosque, from which the Friday sermon is given.

muezzin (*mueththin*) The one who gives the call to prayer.

mujemma "Assembly point", used to describe an open-air bus or service station.

nahr River.

qa Topographical depression, pan.

qal'a (*kalaa*) Fortress, citadel.

qasr (*kasr*; pl. *qusoor*) Palace, mansion; by extension, castle, fortress or a catch-all term for any ancient ruin of unknown usage.

qibla The direction in which Mecca lies, and therefore the direction in which Muslims pray.

qubba Dome; by extension any domed building.

Quran (Koran) The holy book of Islam.

qusayr (*kuseir*) Diminutive of *qasr*.

Ramadan Holy month in the Muslim calendar.

riwaq Colonnade.

sahra General term for desert; can also refer to sandy desert in particular.

sharia Street or way.

shari'a Set of laws based on Quranic precepts.

shebab Literally "youth", but used most commonly where English uses "guys", as a casual term of greeting to peers.

sheikh (*shaykh*) Tribal leader; consequently, mayor of a town or village.

souk (*suq*, *souq*) Market or bazaar.

tariq Way, path or road.

tell (*tal*, *tall*) Hill; by extension, an artificial mound concealing ancient remains, resulting from the continuous collapse and rebuilding of settlements, one on top of another.

umm (*um*, *oum*) "Mother of" – used as a term of respect in conjunction with the name of the woman's eldest son, as in "Umm Muhammad".

wadi Valley or watercourse (also refers to dry or seasonal riverbeds).

waha Oasis.

Architectural terms

apse Semicircular recess behind the altar of a church.

architrave Lintel resting on columns or piers, forming the lowest part of an entablature.

atrium Open inner courtyard of a Roman villa; also the court in front of a Byzantine church.

basilica Rectangular, apsed building; the earliest style of church.

biclinium Room with two benches, often a banqueting hall.

cardo Colonnaded main street of a Roman city; usually running north–south.

cella Inner sanctum of a classical temple.

corbel Projection from the face of a wall supporting a horizontal beam.

Corinthian Order of Classical architecture, identifiable by acanthus-leaf decoration on column capitals.

cornice The upper part of an entablature; also a moulding running along the top of a wall.

decumanus Main street of a Roman city; usually running east–west.

engaged column Column attached to or partly set into a wall.

entablature Element of Roman architecture positioned between the columns and the pediment; consists of architrave, frieze and cornice.

frieze Part of an entablature between the architrave and cornice, often decorated with figures.

glacis Slope below the walls of a castle, designed to be difficult to scale.

hypocaust Roman heating system allowing hot air to circulate beneath a floor raised on small pillars.

Ionic Order of Classical architecture, identifiable by fluted columns with scrolled capitals.

loculus Niche designed to hold a single body in a communal or family cave-tomb.

machicolation A projecting parapet of a castle or fort often above a doorway with holes below through which to pour boiling oil, etc.

narthex In a church, an area spanning the width of the building at the end furthest from the altar.

nave Central part of church, normally flanked by aisles.

nymphaeum A Roman public fountain dedicated to water nymphs and decorated with statues.

orchestra In a classical theatre, the semicircular area in front of the stage.

pediment The shallow triangular gable over a door, window, etc.

propylaeum Monumental entrance gateway to a temple precinct.

scaenae frons The wall at the back of a stage in a classical theatre.

squinch Small arch which spans the right angle formed by two walls, thus supporting a ceiling dome.

temenos Sacred enclosure of a temple.

tetrapylon Monumental four-sided structure supported on arches, usually at an important intersection of streets.

tholos Round section of building surrounded by columns.

triclinium Roman dining hall, most often with three benches.

Travel store

Visit us online
www.roughguides.com
Information on over 25,000 destinations around the world

- **Read** Rough Guides' trusted travel info
- **Access** exclusive articles from Rough Guides authors
- **Update** yourself on new books, maps, CDs and other products
- **Enter** our competitions and win travel prizes
- **Share** ideas, journals, photos & travel advice with other users
- **Earn** points every time you contribute to the Rough Guide community and get rewards

BROADEN YOUR HORIZONS

Small print and
Index

A Rough Guide to Rough Guides

Published in 1982, the first Rough Guide – to Greece – was a student scheme that became a publishing phenomenon. Mark Ellingham, a recent graduate in English from Bristol University, had been travelling in Greece the previous summer and couldn't find the right guidebook. With a small group of friends he wrote his own guide, combining a highly contemporary, journalistic style with a thoroughly practical approach to travellers' needs.

The immediate success of the book spawned a series that rapidly covered dozens of destinations. And, in addition to impecunious backpackers, Rough Guides soon acquired a much broader and older readership that relished the guides' wit and inquisitiveness as much as their enthusiastic, critical approach and value-for-money ethos.

These days, Rough Guides include recommendations from shoestring to luxury and cover more than 200 destinations around the globe, including almost every country in the Americas and Europe, more than half of Africa and most of Asia and Australasia. Our ever-growing team of authors and photographers is spread all over the world, particularly in Europe, the USA and Australia.

In the early 1990s, Rough Guides branched out of travel, with the publication of Rough Guides to World Music, Classical Music and the Internet. All three have become benchmark titles in their fields, spearheading the publication of a wide range of books under the Rough Guide name.

Including the travel series, Rough Guides now number more than 350 titles, covering: phrasebooks, waterproof maps, music guides from Opera to Heavy Metal, reference works as diverse as Conspiracy Theories and Shakespeare, and popular culture books from iPods to Poker. Rough Guides also produce a series of more than 120 World Music CDs in partnership with World Music Network.

Visit www.roughguides.com to see our latest publications.

Rough Guide travel images are available for commercial licensing at www.roughguidespictures.com

Rough Guide credits

Text editor: Helena Smith
Layout: Pradeep Thapliyal, Anita Singh
Cartography: Deshpal Dabas
Picture editor: Nicole Newman
Production: Rebecca Short
Proofreader: Karen Parker
Cover design: Chloë Roberts
Photographer: Jean-Christophe Godet
Editorial: Ruth Blackmore, Andy Turner, Keith
Drew, Edward Aves, Alice Park, Lucy White,
Jo Kirby, James Smart, Natasha Foges, Róisín
Cameron, Emma Traynor, Emma Gibbs, Kathryn
Lane, Christina Valhouli, Monica Woods, Mani
Ramaswamy, Harry Wilson, Lucy Cowie, Helen
Ochyra, Amanda Howard, Lara Kavanagh, Alison
Roberts, Joe Staines, Peter Buckley, Matthew
Milton, Tracy Hopkins, Ruth Tidball; **Delhi**
Madhavi Singh, Karen D'Souza, Lubna Shaheen
Design & Pictures: **London** Scott Stickland, Dan
May, Diana Jarvis, Mark Thomas, Chloë Roberts,
Sarah Cummins, Emily Taylor; **Delhi** Umesh
Aggarwal, Ajay Verma, Jessica Subramanian,
Ankur Guha, Sachin Tanwar, Anita Singh, Nikhil
Agarwal, Sachin Gupta
Production: Vicky Baldwin

Cartography: **London** Maxine Repath, Ed
Wright, Katie Lloyd-Jones; **Delhi** Rajesh
Chhibber, Ashutosh Bharti, Rajesh Mishra,
Animesh Pathak, Jasbir Sandhu, Karobi Gogoi,
Alakananda Bhattacharya, Swati Handoo
Online: **London** George Atwell, Faye Hellon,
Jeanette Angell, Fergus Day, Justine Bright, Clare
Bryson, Aine Fearon, Adrian Low, Ezgi Celebi,
Amber Bloomfield; **Delhi** Amit Verma, Rahul Kumar,
Narender Kumar, Ravi Yadav, Debojit Borah,
Rakesh Kumar, Ganesh Sharma, Shisir Basumatari
Marketing & Publicity: **London** Liz Statham,
Niki Hanmer, Louise Maher, Jess Carter, Vanessa
Godden, Vivienne Watton, Anna Paynton, Rachel
Sprackett, Libby Jellie, Laura Vipond, Vanessa
McDonald; **New York** Katy Ball, Judi Powers,
Nancy Lambert; **Delhi** Ragini Govind
Manager India: Punita Singh
Reference Director: Andrew Lockett
Operations Manager: Helen Phillips
PA to Publishing Director: Nicola Henderson
Publishing Director: Martin Dunford
Commercial Manager: Gino Magnotta
Managing Director: John Duhigg

Publishing information

This fourth edition published September 2009 by
Rough Guides Ltd,
80 Strand, London WC2R 0RL
14 Local Shopping Centre, Panchsheel Park,
New Delhi 110017, India
Distributed by the Penguin Group
Penguin Books Ltd,
80 Strand, London WC2R 0RL
Penguin Group (USA)
375 Hudson Street, NY 10014, USA
Penguin Group (Australia)
250 Camberwell Road, Camberwell,
Victoria 3124, Australia
Penguin Group (Canada)
195 Harry Walker Parkway N, Newmarket, ON,
L3Y 7B3 Canada
Penguin Group (NZ)
67 Apollo Drive, Mairangi Bay, Auckland 1310,
New Zealand
Cover concept by Peter Dyer.

Typeset in Bembo and Helvetica to an original
design by Henry Iles.

Printed in Singapore

432pp includes index

A catalogue record for this book is available from
the British Library

ISBN: 978-1-84836-066-2

1   3   5   7   9   8   6   4   2

Help us update

We've gone to a lot of effort to ensure that the
fourth edition of **The Rough Guide to Jordan**
is accurate and up-to-date. However, things
change – places get "discovered", opening hours
are notoriously fickle, restaurants and rooms raise
prices or lower standards. If you feel we've got it
wrong or left something out, we'd like to know,
and if you can remember the address, the price,
the hours, the phone number, so much the better.

Please send your comments with the subject
line "**Rough Guide Jordan Update**" to ©mail
@roughguides.com. We'll credit all contributions
and send a copy of the next edition (or any other
Rough Guide if you prefer) for the very best
emails.

Have your questions answered and tell others
about your trip at
Ⓦcommunity.roughguides.com

Acknowledgements

Matthew Teller would like to thank all those individuals throughout Jordan who have been so willing to help, guide or offer support with such warmth and generosity. In particular: HE Maha Khatib, Minister of Tourism, Amman, and her staff and colleagues; HE Khalid Irani, Minister of Environment, Amman; Nayef Al-Fayez, Fayez Al-Khouri, Saed Al-Zawaideh and colleagues, Jordan Tourism Board, Amman; David Symes and colleagues, JTB London; Mamdouh Bisharat; Nadim Sawalha, Amin Matalqa and all the cast and crew of *Captain Abu Raed*; Mona Hawa and colleagues, ASEZA; Khaled Burgan at GAM; Dr Faris Nimry at the Jordan Museum; Mohammed Hallak of Reliable Rent-a-Car, Amman; Nancy Lloyd at bmi; Ziad Fostuq, Lucie Aslou and colleagues at IHG Jordan, and Jade Adnett, Suzanne Seyghal and Kim Tomlins at IHG EMEA; Bruno Huber and colleagues at Mövenpick; Maher Bers and colleagues at Kempinski Amman, and Ursula von Platen for Kempinski in London; Chris Johnson, Abdullah Abu Rumman and colleagues at RSCN/Wild Jordan, and everyone at the reserves around the country; Lianne Romahi at Fairtrade Jordan; Mahmoud Bdour; Charl Al-Twal; Daniel Adamson, Mahmoud Twaissi, Ramez Habash, friends and colleagues at the Abraham Path Initiative and Al-Ayoun Trail; Stellan Lind of RACE, Jerash; Deeb Hussein at Pella, and Peter Fischer at Tell Abu Kharaz; Gill Balchin; William Sawalha; Wendy Botham at Petra Moon; all at Wadi Rum; Abed Humood & Rakan Mehyar at Terhaal; Thaer Darwish at Sindbad; Capt Yousef Mou'men at Royal Aero Sports Club; Mona Deeb and colleagues at Nabad Art Gallery; Geraldine Chatelard; Ali Bader; Omar Zumot; Harun Dursun; Marguerite van Geldermalsen; Emad Omar; Ola Mubaslat; Omar Hajawi; Yamaan Safady; and many, many more too numerous to name.

At **Rough Guides**, grateful thanks are due to Helena Smith for her skilful editing, Monica Woods for calm and patient guidance, Nicole Newman for picture research, Pradeep Thapliyal for typesetting and Deshpal Dabas for maps.

Thanks are also due to Ian Andrews, Anna Hohler, Michelle Woodward and Karinne Keithley. I am fortunate to have had the friendship, insight and support of Jane Taylor through this and previous editions. Tony Howard and Di Taylor's boundless energy is an inspiration. Ruth Caswell's infectious enthusiasm remains a delight. Thanks, too, to Madian al-Jazerah, Richard and Janet Adams and family, and Bill and Mona. Above all, to Neville and Sheila Teller – and Han.

This edition is dedicated to Ishaq bin Maher bin Nabil al-Loha.

Readers' letters

Many thanks to all those readers who took the time to get in touch with comments on the last edition, new discoveries in Jordan or just an account of their travels. Apologies if we've misspelt or misunderstood anyone's name. Thanks to:

Geoffrey Archer, Elisabeth Banks, Jaap de Boer, Simon Bopp, Jane Craft, Joanna Dench, Krystyna Deuss, Mathias E. Frey, Oihana Garcia, Simon Gregory, Carrie Heffern, David Heyes, Nigel Hissey and Derek Collins, Paul Horne, Jenny Johns, Jeff King, Kristina Kinney, Justine Kirby, Petra Kopp, Paul MacInnes, Michael Malenfant, Scott McRae, Margery Nzerem, Kai and Laurence Opperman, Maaike Van Adrichem, Daphne Wong.

SMALL PRINT

Photo credits

All photos © Rough Guides except the following:

Introduction
Black iris © Jtb Photo/photolibrary
Bedouin guards, Petra © Naftali Hilger/
photolibrary

Things not to miss
05 Bedouin pouring tea, Bedouin camp, Wadi
Rum © Eitan Simanor/photolibrary
06 Muslim military fort of Ajloun © Nico Tondini/
photolibrary
07 Trekking, Wadi Rum © Norbert Eisele-Hein/
photolibrary

09 Tourists on camels in Petra © Christian Kober/
photolibrary
10 The Baptism Site © Matthew Teller

Petra unpackaged colour section
The Qasr al-Bint today © Jtb Photo/photolibrary
The Qasr al-Bint, as it was © Chrysanthos
Kanellopoulos
Married to a Bedouin book cover © Courtesy
Little Brown Books

SMALL PRINT

Index

Map entries are in colour.

Map symbols

maps are listed in the full index using coloured text

▪▪▪▪	Undisputed international boundary	▣	Restaurant/bar
▬▬··	Other border	⊥	Gardens
▬▬▬	Chapter division boundary	⚠	Campsite
═══	Main road	@	Internet access
═══	Minor road	(i)	Tourist office
-----	Tunnel/underpass	⊠	Gate
:::::	Dirt road	⏝	Bridge
▥▥▥▥	Steps	★	Bus/serveece stop
▥▥▥▥	Cliffs	✈	Airport
▬▬▬	Railway	P	Parking
-----	Path	E	Embassy
▬▬▬	Wall	⊞	Hospital
─────	River	⊠	Post office
— ·—	Ferry route	⛫	Mosque
—∕—	Waterway and dam	▮	Building
⋏⋏	Mountain range	╪	Church
▲	Peak	◯	Stadium
⇒	Swamp	▦	Park
⍊	Oasis	⌑	Salt pan
♦	Point of interest	▦	Beach
◉	Accommodation	◩	Economic zone